Chemical Dependency Counseling

SECOND EDITION

*This book is dedicated to
Robert, Nyshie, and Shane,
some of the absolute best people in the world.*

Chemical Dependency Counseling

A Practical Guide

SECOND EDITION

Robert R. Perkinson

Sage Publications
International Educational and Professional Publisher
Thousand Oaks ▪ London ▪ New Delhi

For information:

Sage Publications, Inc.
2455 Teller Road
Thousand Oaks, California 91320
E-mail: order@sagepub.com

Sage Publications Ltd.
6 Bonhill Street
London EC2A 4PU
United Kingdom

Sage Publications India Pvt. Ltd.
M-32 Market
Greater Kailash I
New Delhi 110 048 India

Printed in the United States of America

Library of Congress Cataloging-in-Publication Data

Perkinson, Robert R.
    Chemical dependency counseling : a practical guide / by Robert R. Perkinson.— 2nd ed.
       p. cm.
    Includes bibliographical references and index.
    ISBN 0-7619-2388-8 (alk. paper)
    1. Substance abuse—Patients—Counseling of. 2. Dual diagnosis—Patients—Counseling of. I. Title.
    RC564 .P47 2001
    362.29'186—dc21

                                  2001004081

03 04 05 10 9 8 7 6 5 4 3 2

Acquiring Editor:	Nancy Hale
Editorial Assistant:	Vonessa Vondera
Production Editor:	Claudia A. Hoffman
Copy Editor:	D. J. Peck
Typesetter/Designer:	Tina Hill
Indexer:	Molly Hall
Cover Designer:	Michelle Lee

Contents

Appendix Contents

Preface

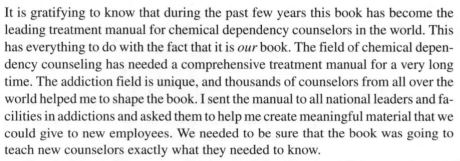

It is gratifying to know that during the past few years this book has become the leading treatment manual for chemical dependency counselors in the world. This has everything to do with the fact that it is *our* book. The field of chemical dependency counseling has needed a comprehensive treatment manual for a very long time. The addiction field is unique, and thousands of counselors from all over the world helped me to shape the book. I sent the manual to all national leaders and facilities in addictions and asked them to help me create meaningful material that we could give to new employees. We needed to be sure that the book was going to teach new counselors exactly what they needed to know.

Chemical dependency counselors have a difficult but incredibly rewarding job. When you first meet your patients, you want to know that you have all of the tools necessary to give them the best treatment they could get anywhere in the world. You can find comfort in the fact that the best in the business helped me to create this manual. Because this is our book, it is vitally important that you help me. If you see anything in the text that is not right, then please contact me on the Web at www.robertperkinson.com and let me know.

New medications keep changing the field, and this will get better in the future as we understand more about the neurophysiology of addiction. New drugs such as naltrexone, acamprosate, SSRIs (selective serotonin reuptake inhibitors), LAAM (levo-alpha-acetylmethadol), and buprenorphine have proven to benefit patients. Some cut relapse rates in half, and they can be a substantial adjunctive treatment. Counselors need to keep up on new medications and use them whenever possible to maximize recovery.

I have included gambling as a special problem in this edition. Gambling is a chronic relapsing brain disease like chemical dependency, and counselors will see more of this disease in the future. It is the only addiction that is growing at a rapid rate, and about half of gamblers have a problem with substance abuse. The drug for gamblers is the chemical "high" that the brain produces when gambling. Gamblers definitely go into the same numb zone that all addicts do when using. The brain becomes hijacked by the chemicals that are created in the brain from being in action (e.g., planning the bet, making the bet, waiting for the bet to come in). Once the gambling has stopped, the pathological gambler goes into a state of dysphoria that can be relieved only by gambling. Many professionals do not believe that gambling is an addiction, but those of us who work with addicts know that it is the same thing, with the same symptoms of tolerance and withdrawal seen in substance abusers.

As you read this book, you will find that it suggests a spiritual journey. This is one of the things that our colleges in medicine, education, and mental health do not understand. They are taught that it is unethical to tell your patients about your own spirituality, whereas chemical dependency counselors do that all of the time. The program of Alcoholics Anonymous tells us that no human power could have relieved our alcoholism but that God could and would if He were sought. An addict can recover without a Higher Power, but nothing sets an addict back on his or her feet like a connection with a Higher Power. If you ask the American Society of Addiction Medicine (ASAM) physicians what was the most important element in their recovery, they will say that it was Alcoholics Anonymous, a program of spiritual principles.

Alcoholics Anonymous is a fellowship of men and women with a common purpose. On May 11, 1935, Bill Wilson met with Bob Smith, and the basic premise of Alcoholics Anonymous was born. The two men were supposed to get together for 15 minutes, but they talked for more than 6 hours. Wilson had recently had his spiritual awakening, but it was not enough to keep him sober. He needed another alcoholic to talk with. Smith, or "Dr. Bob," did not want another person trying to get him sober, but Wilson said that he was not there to keep Dr. Bob sober but there to keep himself sober. So the meeting took place, and the common bond of one drug addict talking to another became the core of recovery. That is what worked then, and it is what works now.

The most important thing that any counselor can give to his or her patients is time. Take the time to listen. Listen, listen, listen until you begin to understand. I have never met a patient I did not like so long as I took the time to listen enough to get into his or her world. If you know where the patient is, then you can guide him or her out of the darkness. If you only know where you are, then the patient will be lost. Your presence is more healing than any technique you will ever use. Your presence tells the patient that he or she is important and that you care for him or her. Once the patient begins to help others in recovery, the patient restores his or her sense of self-worth and is well on the way to recovery.

This book is not meant to be everything that a counselor needs to know to pass his or her state or national certification examination. It is not every little fact or a theory book, and it does not cover all of the programs that can help a substance abuser. Other treatments such as rational recovery, smart recovery, harm reduction, and psychotherapy can be effective, but they rarely are used in leading treatment centers. Many leading hospitals, colleges, and universities have different methods of treatment, and they all work.

This book is the traditional treatment outlined by ASAM in the second edition of *Principles of Addiction Medicine* (Graham, Schultz, & Wilford, 1998). This is the treatment used by all of the leading treatment centers in the world. When new counselors get their first jobs, this is the work that they will be doing. It combines a Twelve Step program with cognitive behavioral therapy and a motivational enhancement approach. Counselors help patients to journey toward truth, motivating them to change old maladaptive thoughts and behaviors with new adaptive thoughts and behaviors. This book details the state-of-the-art tools necessary to provide quality treatment meeting the highest standards of accrediting bodies. The program works through Steps One to Five of Alcoholics Anonymous, and it is designed for all levels of care. Outpatient professionals will work through fewer steps; the more, the better. Some programs will work through Step One, and some will work through Steps One to Five. The policies and procedures outlined in this manual have been accredited with commendation by the Joint Commission on Accreditation of Healthcare Organizations (JCAHO) for more than a decade.

The Chemical Dependence Treatment Planner (Perkinson & Jongsma, 1998a, 1998b), along with *The Addiction Treatment Planner* (2001), is a companion volume to this manual. Using the treatment planner or, better yet, the planner's *TheraScribe* computer program, counselors can easily write effective treatment plans based on this material. This makes the paperwork avalanche more manageable, and counselors can spend more time with their patients.

The counselor must be aware that treatment never can be static. It must be fluid, ever changing to fit the particular situation and patient. You must negotiate with your patient and not tell him or her what to do. No two patients can be treated in the same way. The counselor must learn to use his or her own unique skills. There is no one like you. About 25% of Americans die of substance abuse, and that means you are desperately needed. Thank you for who you are and for what you are doing. I believe that you will find the field of chemical dependency counseling exciting, challenging, and a great deal of fun.

— Robert R. Perkinson

Acknowledgments

■

This manual was shaped by many professionals trying to develop a text that we could be proud of and use daily. The work of training new staff members is exhausting for everyone in the field, and it became necessary to have a standard text that everyone coming on board could read and understand. It had to be a practical book, simple and easy to use, and not bogged down by theory or extraneous material. The following professionals played a role in text development, sharing their training and expertise, and going over the manual in fine detail. I thank each of them from the bottom of my heart.

Nancy Waite-O'Brien, Ph.D., Clinical Director, Betty Ford Center at Eisenhower

Daniel Anderson, Ph.D., President Emeritus, Hazelden

Linda Kaplan, Executive Director, National Association of Alcoholism and Drug Abuse Counselors

Michael Ford, President, National Association of Addiction Treatment Programs

Richard Weedman, President, Healthcare Network Inc.

Eleanor Sargent, Project for Addiction Counselor Training, National Association of Alcohol and Drug Abuse Counselors

Bob Carr, Ph.D., Director, Substance Abuse Program, Veterans Administration Regional Hospital, Sioux Falls, SD

Terry O'Brien, Member of Board of Directors, Hazelden

Carol Davis, Counselor, Betty Ford Center at Eisenhower

Carol Regier, Executive Director, Keystone Treatment Center

Chris O'Sullivan, Ph.D., Assistant Professor, University of South Dakota

Bob Bogue, Clinical Supervisor, Keystone Treatment Center

Jim Nageotte, Sage Publications

Julie Braaten, Accreditation Coordinator, Keystone Treatment Center

All of the staff, past and present, of Keystone Treatment Center

CHAPTER
ONE | # The First Hours

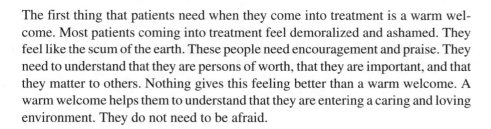

The first thing that patients need when they come into treatment is a warm welcome. Most patients coming into treatment feel demoralized and ashamed. They feel like the scum of the earth. These people need encouragement and praise. They need to understand that they are persons of worth, that they are important, and that they matter to others. Nothing gives this feeling better than a warm welcome. A warm welcome helps them to understand that they are entering a caring and loving environment. They do not need to be afraid.

How to Greet Patients

You need to convey to patients that you understand how they feel and that you will do everything in your power to help them. When greeting a new patient, it is as if you are welcoming a long-lost brother or sister back into your family. This person is not different from you; this person is you. Treat the person the same way in which you would want to be treated yourself. The more the patient senses your goodwill and unconditional positive regard, the less alienated and frightened the patient will feel.

When you speak to your new patients, reach out and touch them. This physical touch says a lot about you and a lot about the patients. Patients often think that no one wants to touch them again. You prove that this thinking is inaccurate.

Use your own judgment in deciding when and where to touch. Be sensitive. Some people can be hugged, but others cannot. Some patients can be touched on the arm. If you feel as though you can only shake a patient's hand, then do this. Make it a warm handshake. As you do these things, you are developing your therapeutic alliance, and you are giving the patient the most important thing that he or she needs—love.

The initial words you choose are important. Patients remember your words. Patients come back after years and describe their first few hours in treatment. They remember the exact things that people said. They seal them inside their hearts. You want them to remember the good things.

Examples

Introduce yourself and say something like the following:

> "Welcome to [name of treatment center]. You've made a good choice. I'm proud of you. This is a victory not only for you but for all of the people you will help recover."

> "This is a new start. Good going." (Give the thumbs-up sign.)

> "Good job. We are going to take good care of you."

> "I know this was a difficult decision for you, but you won't be sorry. This is the beginning of your new life."

> "We are happy to have you. Try everything in your power to stay in treatment. It gets better every day."

Notice how each of these statements welcomes the patient and enhances his or her self-esteem. Welcome. You are a good person. You made a good choice. We are going to take good care of you.

Ask whether the patient wants anything. How can you help? Nothing shows that you care better than to offer to get the patient something small—juice, food, milk, or coffee. This shows that you care and that the patient is worth caring for. You are giving the patient new ideas. Treatment is not going to hurt. You are willing to respond to the patient's needs. "This treatment thing might be okay," the patient begins to think. "I just might be able to do this."

How to Handle Family Members

If the patient came into treatment with family members, then make sure to tour the facility with the family as a whole. This helps the patient to make the transition between the family at home and the new family in treatment. When you have all the information that you need from the family members, they should be encouraged to leave the treatment setting. To have them linger unnecessarily can be detrimental to the patient's transition. The patient needs to focus on himself or herself and to orient to treatment. Family members who cling are rare, but they do exist. These people need to be separated from the patient and given reassurance that the patient is in a safe place. Someone in the family program might be willing to talk to the family members for a while to encourage them and answer any questions they might have. Remember that you are bonding with the patient and his or her family members. You want them all to see you as someone they trust.

Beginning the Therapeutic Alliance

From the first contact, your patients are learning some important things about you. You are friendly. You are on their side. You are not going to beat anybody up or shame or blame them. You answer any questions. You are honest and hold nothing back. You provide the information, and they make the decisions. They see you as a concerned professional. They begin to have hope that you can help them. The therapeutic alliance is built from an initial foundation of love and trust.

You give patients the idea that you are going through treatment with them. They do not have to feel alone. Neither of you can do this alone. Both you and your patients are needed in cooperation with each other. Patients know things that you do not know. They have knowledge that you do not have. They know themselves better than anybody, and they need to learn how to share themselves with you. Likewise, you know things that they do not know. You know the tools of recovery. You have to share these tools and help the patients to use them. This is a cooperative effort. It is as if you are on a wonderful journey together.

The Importance of Trust

Your patients must develop trust in you. To establish this trust, you must be consistent. You must prove to the patients, time and time again, that you are going to be actively involved in their individual growth. When you say that you are going to do something, you do it. When you make a promise, you keep it. You never try to get something from the patients without using the truth. You never manipulate, even to get something good. The first time your patients catch you in a lie—even a small one—your alliance will be weakened.

Patients must learn that the clinical staff works as a team. What patients tell you—even in confidence—they tell the whole team. Patients occasionally will test this. They will tell you that they have something to share but that they can share it only with you. They want you to keep it secret. This is a trap that many beginning counselors fall into. The truth is that all facts are friendly, and all accurate information is vital to treatment. You must explain to the patients that if they feel too uncomfortable in sharing certain information with the clinical team, then they should keep it secret for now. Maybe they can share this sensitive information in their Fifth Step. No matter what the patients decide to do, you are going to share everything they tell you with the clinical staff. You trust the team, and you encourage the patients to do the same. Most patients will share the information when they see how much you trust each other.

Patients must understand that you are committed to their recovery but that you cannot recover for them. You cannot do the work by yourself. You must work together cooperatively. You can only teach the tools of recovery. The patients have to use the tools to establish abstinence.

Dealing With Early Denial

The first few hours of treatment are not a time for harsh confrontation. It is a time for love, support, and encouragement. The great healer in any treatment is love, and love necessitates action in truth. All patients come into treatment in some form of denial. They have been dishonest with themselves and others. They are lying, and they will lie to you. Your job is to reveal the lies as gently as possible, reflecting truth. You do not want to hurt the patients or incur their wrath, but you must be dedicated to the truth. This program demands rigorous honesty.

Patients lie to themselves in many ways. They do not want to see the whole truth because the truth makes them feel anxious. They keep this anxiety under control by deceiving themselves. They distort reality just enough to feel reasonably comfortable. They defend themselves against the truth with unconscious lies called defense mechanisms. "As long as we could stop using for a while, we thought we were all right. We looked at the stopping, not the using" (Narcotics Anonymous, 1988, p. 3).

Patients minimize reality by thinking that the illness is not so bad. Then they rationalize by thinking that they have a good reason to use drugs. Then they deny by stubbornly refusing to see the problems at all. Treatment is an endless search for truth.

Those who do not recover are people who cannot or will not completely give themselves to this simple program, usually men and women who are constitutionally incapable of being honest with themselves. There are such unfortunates. They are not at fault. They seem to have been born that way. They are naturally incapable of grasping and developing a manner of living which demands rigorous honesty. (Alcoholics Anonymous, 1976, p. 58)

Your job as a chemical dependency counselor is to love the patients in truth knowing that the truth will set them free from the slavery to the lies.

Example of an Initial Contact

Approach the patient. Reach out and take the patient's hand. "Hi, Ralph." Use the patient's first name. "I'm _____ [your name]. I'm going to be your counselor. How are you doing so far?"

The patient looks at the floor and then at the wall. You know the importance of silence and wait.

The patient finally looks up. "I'm okay, I guess."

"The first 3 days are going to be the hardest. After that, it's going to be all downhill. This is the beginning of recovery. Is there anything I can do for you right now to make you feel more comfortable?"

"I don't think so," Ralph says, looking relieved.

Lean forward and touch the patient's arm. "If you feel uncomfortable, I want you to tell me or the nurse, okay? We want you to feel calm and tranquil through withdrawal. How you feel is important to us." The therapeutic alliance is being established.

The patient might never have experienced unconditional positive regard before. It might seem strange to the patient. To many patients, it is unbelievable. They come into treatment with preconceived ideas about how treatment is going to go. Many think that they are going to be shamed, blamed, or punished. When they are greeted with love and affection, it comes as a great surprise. Your words of support and concern are as soothing as a warm bath.

All chemically dependent patients, at some level, want to punish themselves. They feel guilty about what they have done, and they are waiting for the executioner. They expect to be treated poorly. When you treat them with respect, they ask themselves why people are treating them so nice. *Could it be that they are worth it?*

Tell your patients that they are important. The staff cares about how they feel and what they want. You are here to help. You want to help. You are going to respond to the patients' needs. It might be tough for a while, but things are going to get better.

How to Check for Organic Brain Dysfunction

■

Patients need to be checked for medical problems, particularly organic brain syndrome, as quickly as possible. Some patients coming into treatment are organically compromised and need immediate medical treatment to prevent further damage. Patients may be intoxicated, may be in withdrawal, or may have a serious vitamin deficiency called Wernicke's encephalopathy.

You should be familiar with how to check a patient for these cognitive problems. The Cognitive Capacity Screening Examination (Appendix 1) is an excellent way of screening for organic brain problems (Jacobs, Bernhard, Delgado, & Strain, 1977). The Mini-Mental State Examination is a similar assessment test (Folstein, Folstein, & McHugh, 1975). Either of these tests is a brief 10-minute assessment of how the brain is functioning. The test is simple and comes up with a score. If the patient falls below the cutoff score, then inform medical professionals of the possible organic problems. If you notice anything unusual about how the patient moves, acts, or speaks, then tell a physician or nurse. Always count on your medical staff or the patient's family physician. They are more skilled at these examinations than you are.

The Initial Assessment

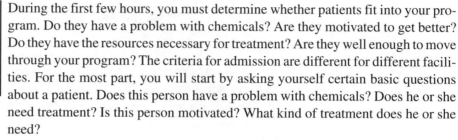

During the first few hours, you must determine whether patients fit into your program. Do they have a problem with chemicals? Are they motivated to get better? Do they have the resources necessary for treatment? Are they well enough to move through your program? The criteria for admission are different for different facilities. For the most part, you will start by asking yourself certain basic questions about a patient. Does this person have a problem with chemicals? Does he or she need treatment? Is this person motivated? What kind of treatment does he or she need?

Two quick screening tests for alcoholism have been developed: the Short Michigan Alcoholism Screening Test (SMAST [Appendix 2]) (Selzer, Winokur, & van Rooijen, 1975) and the CAGE Questionnaire (Appendix 3) (Ewing, 1984). The SMAST is a 13-question version of the original Michigan Alcoholism Screening Test (MAST). The SMAST has been shown to be as effective as the MAST. It has greater than 90% sensitivity to detect alcoholism. It can be administered to the patient or to the spouse.

The Substance Abuse Subtle Screening Inventory (SASSI) was developed to screen patients when they were defensive and in denial. The SASSI measures defensiveness and the subtle attributes that are common in chemically dependent persons. It is a difficult test to fake, unlike the MAST or the CAGE Questionnaire. The SASSI gives the patients the opportunity to answer honestly about their problems with chemicals, but it also measures the patients' possible abuse using questions that do not pertain to chemicals (Creager, 1989; Miller, 1985). Patients can complete the SASSI in 10 to 15 minutes, and it takes only 1 or 2 minutes to score. It accurately identifies 98% of patients who need residential treatment, 90% of nonusers, and 87% of early-stage abusers (Miller, 1985).

The Addiction Severity Index (ASI) is a widely used structured interview that is designed to provide important information about what might contribute to a patient's alcohol or drug problem. The instrument assesses seven dimensions that typically are of concern in chemical dependency: medical status, employment/support status, drug/alcohol use, legal status, family history, family/social relationships, and psychiatric status. The ASI is designed to be administered by a trained technician and takes about 1 hour (McLellan, Luborsky, & Woody, 1980).

The Recovery Attitude and Treatment Evaluator (RAATE) is a measure of patient readiness. It assesses patient resistance and impediments to treatment. The instrument is a structured interview that measures five scales: degree of resistance to treatment, degree of resistance to continuing care, acuity of biomedical problems, acuity of psychiatric problems, and extent of social/family/environmental systems that do not support recovery (Mee-Lee, 1985, 1988).

As the counselor, you need to constantly ask yourself about patients' stage of motivation and introduce appropriate motivating strategies to move the patients up a level. The manual will give you thousands of ways of doing this. No two patients are alike, so you must be creative in helping the patients to see the inaccuracies in their thinking and move toward the truth. The *precontemplation* stage is where the individuals are not intending to take action with regard to their substance abuse problem in the foreseeable future. *Contemplation* is where the individuals intend to take action within the next 6 months. *Preparation* is where the persons intend to take action within the next month. *Action* is where the persons have made overt attempts to modify their lifestyles. *Maintenance* is where the individuals are working a recovery plan and attempting to prevent relapse. If you can move the patients up to the next stage, then you can be sure that treatment is working (Prochaska & DiClemente, 1983; Prochaska, DiClemente, & Norcross, 1992; Prochaska, Norcross, & DiClemente, 1994).

Patients at different stages of motivation will need different motivating strategies. In the precontemplation stage, patients underestimate the benefits of change and overestimate its cost. They are not aware that they are making these mistakes in judgment and believe that they are right. Environmental events can trigger persons to move up to the contemplation stage. An arrest, a spouse threatening to leave, or an intervention each can increase motivation to change.

Patients in the preparation stage have a plan of action to cut down or quit their addictive behavior. These patients are ready for input from their doctors, counselors, or self-help books and should be recruited and motivated for action. Action is where the patients are changing their behavior to cut down or quit the addiction. These are patients who have entered early recovery and are actively involved in treatment.

In the maintenance stage, patients are still changing their behavior to be better and are working to prevent relapse. People who relapse are not well prepared for the prolonged effort needed to stay clean and sober. All patients need to be followed in aftercare because they need encouragement and support to stay in recovery. Addicts typically do not have the skills needed to work a program in early recovery. This takes a time commitment and discipline.

As the counselor, you constantly try to raise your patients' awareness about the causes, consequences, and possible treatments for a particular problem. Interventions that can increase awareness include observation, confrontation, interpretation, feedback, and education. You constantly point out the need to reevaluate the environment and how behavior change can be beneficial to everyone. Encourage the patients to reevaluate their self-images and how they are negatively affected by the addictive behavior. Encourage the patients to learn the new skills of honesty, helping others, and seeking relationships with a Higher Power (Prochaska & DiClemente, 1983; Prochaska et al., 1992, 1994).

Laboratory tests can be used to corroborate suspicions about excessive alcohol use that have been generated by the history and physical. None of the tests alone or in combination can diagnose alcoholism, but they add to the certainty of the diagnosis and warn patients of physical complications. High serum levels of liver enzymes can represent alcohol-induced hepatic injury. Gamma-glutamyl transferase (GGT) is elevated in two thirds of alcoholics. Aspartate aminotransferase (AST) and alanine aminotransferase (ALT) are elevated in about one half of alcoholics. Alteration of fat metabolism causes elevated serum triglycerides in about one fourth of alcoholics. Alkaline phosphatase is elevated in about one sixth of alcoholics. Total bilirubin is elevated in about one seventh of alcoholics. Mean corpuscular volume (MCV) is elevated in about one fourth of alcoholics. Uric acid is elevated in about one tenth of alcoholics (Brostoff, 1994; DuPont, 1994; Wallach, 1992).

American Society of Addiction Medicine Patient Placement Criteria | All patients need to be assessed constantly in the following six dimensions:

1. Acute intoxication and/or withdrawal complications
2. Biomedical conditions and complications
3. Emotional/Behavioral conditions and complications
4. Treatment acceptance/resistance
5. Relapse/Continued use potential
6. Recovery/Living environment

These are the areas of assessment that have been developed by the American Society of Addiction Medicine (ASAM) in the second edition of its handbook, *Patient Placement Criteria for the Treatment of Substance-Related Disorders* (Mee-Lee, Gartner, Miller, Shulman, & Wilford, 1998). All counselors need to have a copy of this document and use these criteria in deciding which level of care patients need. (A copy of the criteria can be obtained from the American Society of Addiction Medicine, 4601 North Park Avenue, Upper Arcade, Suite 101, Chevy Chase, MD 20815.) The manual details specific criteria for admission, continued stay, and discharge for all levels of treatment (adult and adolescent).

For brevity, the present book concentrates on the criteria for admission and discharge of outpatient and inpatient treatment. These are the criteria that you, as the counselor, will use most often. The criteria are as objective and measurable as possible, but some clinical interpretation is involved. Psychoactive disorders are no different from any other medical evaluation. Assessment and treatment are a mix of objectively measured criteria and professional judgment. The six dimensions that need to be assessed are as follows:

1. Acute intoxication and/or withdrawal complications
   a. What risk is associated with the patient's current level of intoxication?
   b. Is there significant risk of severe withdrawal symptoms based on the patient's previous withdrawal history and amount, frequency, and recency of discontinuation of chemical use?
   c. Is the patient currently in withdrawal? To measure withdrawal, use the Clinical Institute Withdrawal Assessment of Alcohol (Appendix 5) or Benzodiazepine Scale (Mee-Lee et al., 1998) or the Narcotic Withdrawal Scale (Appendix 6) (Fultz & Senay, 1975).
   d. Does the patient have the supports necessary to assist in ambulatory detoxification (or "detox") if medically safe?
2. Biomedical conditions or complications
   a. Are there current physical illnesses, other than withdrawal, that may need to be addressed or that may complicate treatment?
   b. Are there chronic conditions that may affect treatment?
3. Emotional and behavioral complications
   a. Are there current psychiatric illnesses or psychological, emotional, or behavioral problems that need treatment or may complicate treatment?
   b. Are there chronic psychiatric problems that affect treatment?

4. Treatment acceptance or resistance
    a. Is the patient objecting to treatment?
    b. Does the patient feel coerced into coming to treatment?
    c. Does the patient appear to be complying with treatment only to avoid a negative consequence, or does he or she appear to be self-motivated?
5. Relapse potential
    a. Is the patient in immediate danger of continued use?
    b. Does the patient have any recognition of, understanding of, or skills with which he or she can cope with his or her addiction problems to prevent continued use?
    c. What problems will potentially continue to distress the patient if he or she is not successfully engaged in treatment at this time?
    d. How aware is the patient of relapse triggers, ways of coping with cravings, and skills at controlling impulses to continue use?
6. Recovery/Living environment
    a. Are there any dangerous family members, significant others, living situations, or school/working situations that pose a threat to treatment success?
    b. Does the patient have supportive friendships, financial resources, or educational vocational resources that can increase the likelihood of treatment success?
    c. Are there legal, vocational, social service agency, or criminal justice mandates that may enhance the patient's motivation for treatment?

Patients must be able to understand treatment. They must be intellectually capable of absorbing the material. They must be physically and emotionally stable enough to go through the treatment process. They cannot be actively harmful to themselves or to others. They cannot be overtly psychotic. They cannot have such a serious medical or psychiatric problem that they cannot learn.

Diagnostic and Statistical Manual *Criteria for Diagnosis*

To make a diagnosis, use the criteria listed in the current edition of the *Diagnostic and Statistical Manual of Mental Disorders (DSM)* published by the American Psychiatric Association. (A copy of the *DSM* can be obtained from the American Psychiatric Association, 1400 K Street, N.W., Washington, DC 20005.) A new edition comes out every few years, so there will be changes in the criteria from time to time. The 1994 criteria (American Psychiatric Association, 1994) are listed in Appendix 4.

Diagnosis: Drug Abuse

A. A maladaptive pattern of psychoactive substance use leads to clinically significant impairment or distress indicated by one or more of the following, occurring within a 12-month period:

1. Recurrent substance use resulting in a failure to fulfill major role obligations at work, school, or home (e.g., repeated absences or poor work performance related to substance use; substance-related absences, suspensions, or expulsions from school; neglect of children or household)

2. Recurrent use in situations where use is physically hazardous (e.g., driving an automobile or operating a machine when impaired by substance use)
3. Recurrent substance-related legal problems
4. Continued substance use despite having persistent or recurrent social or interpersonal problems caused or exacerbated by the effects of the substance (e.g., arguments with spouse about consequences of intoxication, physical fights)

B. The symptoms never met the criteria for psychoactive substance dependence for this class of substance.

Questions for You to
Ask the Patient

1. What are your drinking and drug habits?
2. Was there ever a period in your life when you drank or used drugs too much?
3. Have drugs or alcohol ever caused problems for you?
4. Has anyone ever objected to your drinking or drug use?

If you are unable to diagnose abuse, then check with the family. The patient may be in denial, and you might get more of the truth from someone else. A family member, particularly a spouse or a parent, might give you a more accurate clinical picture of the problems.

If you diagnose abuse, then move on to the dependency questions.

Diagnosis:
Chemical Dependency

A maladaptive pattern of substance use leads to clinically significant impairment or distress, as manifested by three or more of the following, occurring at any time during the same 12-month period:

1. Tolerance, as defined by either of the following:
   a. A need for markedly increased amounts of the substance to achieve intoxication or desired effect
   b. Markedly diminished effect with continued use of the same amount of the substance
2. Withdrawal, as manifested by either of the following:
   a. The characteristic withdrawal syndrome for the substance
   b. The same (or a closely related) substance taken to relieve or avoid withdrawal symptoms
3. The substance is often taken in larger amounts or over a longer period of time than was intended.
4. There is a persistent desire or one or more unsuccessful efforts to cut down on or control substance use.
5. A great deal of time is spent in activities necessary to obtain the substance (e.g., visiting multiple doctors, driving long distances), to use the substance (e.g., chain smoking), or to recover from its effects.
6. Important social, occupational, and/or recreational activities are given up or reduced because of substance use.
7. The substance use is continued despite knowledge of having a persistent or recurrent psychological or physical problem that is likely to have caused or been exacerbated by the use of the substance (e.g., current cocaine use

despite recognition of cocaine-induced depression, continued drinking despite recognition that an ulcer was made worse by alcohol consumption).

Specify if:

With physiological dependence: Evidence of tolerance or withdrawal
Without physiological dependence: No evidence of tolerance or withdrawal

Explain to the patient that the diagnosis is your best professional judgment. It is important that the patient makes up his or her own mind. The patient needs to collect the evidence for himself or herself and to get accurate in his or her thinking. Does the patient have a problem or not? This is a good time to explain about denial and how it keeps patients from seeing the truth.

How to Determine the Level of Care Needed

Once you know that the patient has a significant problem, you must decide the level of care the patient needs. There are four levels of care generally offered across the United States:

Level 0.5: *Early intervention.* Early intervention is an organized service delivered in a wide variety of settings. Early intervention is designed to explore and address problems or risk factors that are related to substance use and to assist patients in recognizing the harmful consequences of inappropriate substance use. Patients who need early intervention do not meet the diagnostic criteria of either chemical abuse or chemical dependency, but they have significant problems with substances. The rest of the treatment levels include patients who meet the criteria for psychoactive substance abuse or dependency.

Level I: *Outpatient treatment.* Outpatient treatment takes place in a nonresidential facility or in an office run by addiction professionals. Patients come in for individual or group therapy sessions, usually fewer than 9 hours per week.

Level II: *Intensive outpatient/partial hospitalization.*
   Level II.1: *Intensive outpatient treatment.* This is a structured day or evening program of 9 or more hours of programming per week. The program has the capacity to refer patients for their medical, psychological, or pharmacological needs.
   Level II.5: *Partial hospitalization.* Partial hospitalization generally includes 20 or more hours of intense programming per week. This program has ready access to psychiatric, medical, and laboratory services.

Level III: *Residential/inpatient services.*
   Level III.1: *Clinically managed, low-intensity residential services.* This is a halfway house.
   Level III.3: *Clinically managed, medium-intensity residential services.* This is an extended care program oriented around long-term management.

Level III.5: *Clinically managed, high-intensity residential services*. This is a therapeutic community designed to maintain recovery.

Level III.7: *Medically monitored intensive inpatient treatment*. This is a residential facility that provides a 24-hour structured treatment. This program is monitored by a physician and is able to manage the psychiatric, physical, and pharmacological needs of its patients.

Level IV: *Medically managed intensive inpatient treatment*. This is a 24-hour program that has the resources of a hospital. Physicians provide daily medical management.

Criteria for Outpatient Treatment (adults)

An adult patient qualifies for outpatient treatment if he or she meets the diagnostic criteria for psychoactive substance use disorder as defined by the current *DSM* and if the patient meets all six of the following criteria:

1. The patient is not acutely intoxicated and is at minimal risk for suffering severe withdrawal symptoms.
2. All medical conditions are stable and do not require inpatient management.
3. All of the following conditions exist:
   a. The individual's anxiety, guilt, and/or depression, if present, appear to be related to substance-related problems rather than to a coexisting psychiatric/emotional/behavioral condition. If the patient has psychiatric/emotional/behavioral problems other than those caused by substance use, then the problems are being treated by an appropriate mental health professional.
   b. Mental status does not preclude the patient from comprehending and understanding the program or from participating in the treatment process.
   c. The patient is not at risk for harming himself or herself or others.
4. Both of the following conditions exist:
   a. The patient expresses a willingness to cooperate with the program and to attend all scheduled activities.
   b. The patient may admit that he or she has a problem with alcohol or drugs, but the patient requires monitoring and motivating strategies. The patient does not need a more structured program.
5. The patient can remain abstinent only with support and can do so between appointments.
6. One of the following conditions exists:
   a. The environment is sufficiently supportive to make outpatient treatment feasible. Family or significant others are supportive of recovery.
   b. The patient does not have the ideal support system in his or her current environment, but the patient is willing to obtain such support.
   c. Family or significant others are supportive, but they need professional interventions to improve chances of success.

Criteria for Inpatient Treatment (adults)

An adult patient needs inpatient treatment if he or she meets the *DSM* diagnostic criteria for substance use disorder and meets at least two of the following criteria:

1. The patient presents a risk of severe withdrawal or has had past failures at entering treatment after detox.

2. The patient has medical conditions that present imminent danger of damaging health if use resumes or concurrent medical illness needs medical monitoring.

3. One of the following conditions exists:

   a. Emotional/behavioral problems interfere with abstinence and stability to the degree that there is a need for a structured 24-hour environment.

   b. There is a moderate risk of behaviors endangering self or others. There are current suicidal/homicidal thoughts with no action plan and a history of suicidal gestures or homicidal threats.

   c. The patient is manifesting stress behaviors related to losses or anticipated losses that significantly impair daily living. A 24-hour facility is necessary to address the addiction.

   d. There is a history or presence of violent or disruptive behavior during intoxication with imminent danger to self or others.

   e. Concomitant personality disorders are of such severity that the accompanying dysfunctional behaviors require continuous boundary-setting interventions.

4. Despite consequences, the patient does not accept the severity of the problem and needs intensive motivating strategies available in a 24-hour structured setting.

5. One of the following conditions exists:

   a. Despite active participation at a less intensive level of care or in a self-help fellowship, the patient is experiencing an acute crisis with an intensification of addiction symptoms. Without 24-hour supervision, the patient will continue to use.

   b. The patient cannot control his or her use so long as alcohol or drugs are present in the environment.

   c. The treatments necessary for the patient require this level of care.

6. One of the following conditions exists:

   a. The patient lives in an environment where treatment is unlikely to succeed (e.g., chaotic, rife with interpersonal conflict that undermines the patient's efforts to change, nonexistent family, other environmental conditions, significant others living with the patient who manifest current substance use and are likely to undermine the patient's recovery).

   b. Treatment accessibility prevents participation in a less intensive level of care.

   c. There is a danger of physical, sexual, or emotional abuse in the current environment.

   d. The patient is engaged in an occupation where continued use constitutes a substantial imminent risk to personal or public safety.

Criteria for Outpatient Treatment (adolescents)   An adolescent patient qualifies for outpatient treatment if he or she meets *DSM* criteria for substance use disorder and the following dimensions:

1. The patient is not intoxicated and presents no risk of withdrawal.

2. The patient has no biomedical conditions that would interfere with outpatient treatment.

3. The patient's problem behaviors, moods, feelings, and attitudes are related to addiction rather than to a mental disorder, or the patient is being treated by an appropriate mental health professional. The patient's mental status is stable. The patient is not at risk for harming himself or herself or others.

4. The patient is willing to cooperate and attend all scheduled outpatient activities. The patient is responsive to parents, school authorities, and staff.

5. The patient is willing to consider maintaining abstinence and recovery goals.

6. A sufficiently supportive recovery environment exists to make outpatient treatment feasible:

   a. Parents or significant others are supportive of treatment, and the program is accessible.

   b. The patient currently does not have a supportive recovery environment but is willing to obtain such support.

   c. The family or significant others are supportive but require professional intervention to improve chances of success.

Criteria for Inpatient Treatment (adolescents) To qualify for inpatient treatment, the adolescent must meet the *DSM* criteria for substance use disorder, all of the dimensions for outpatient treatment, plus at least two of the following dimensions:

1. The risk of withdrawal is present.

2. Continued use places the patient at imminent risk of serious damage to health, or a biomedical condition requires medical management.

3. History reflects cognitive development of at least 11 years of age and significant impairment in social, interpersonal, occupational, or educational functioning, as evidenced by one of the following:

   a. There is a current inability to maintain behavioral stability for more than a 48-hour period.

   b. There is a mild to moderate risk to self or others. There are current suicidal/homicidal thoughts with no active plan and a history of suicidal/homicidal gestures.

   c. Behaviors are sufficiently chronic and/or disruptive to require separation from the current environment.

4. The patient is having difficulty in acknowledging an alcohol or drug problem and is not able to follow through with treatment in a less intense environment.

5. The patient is experiencing an intensification of addiction symptoms despite interventions in a less intense level of care; the patient has been unable to control use so long as alcohol or drugs are present in his or her environment; or the patient, if abstinent, is in crisis and appears to be in imminent danger of using alcohol or drugs.

6. One of the following conditions exists:

   a. The environment is not conducive to successful treatment at a less intense level of care.

   b. The parents or legal guardians are unable to provide consistent participation necessary to support treatment in a less intense level of care.

c. Accessibility to treatment precludes participation in a less intense level of care.

d. There is a danger of physical, sexual, or emotional abuse in the patient's current environment.

How to Share the Diagnosis With the Patient

You need to discuss your findings with the patient and, if possible, with the patient's family. If you are in recovery yourself, this is not a good time to share much of your story. This might frighten the patient and make him or her wonder about your own state of health. The patient needs a stable and well-adjusted counselor. You can tell the patient that you are recovering, but do not get into war stories about your drinking and/or using days.

As you share the diagnosis with the patient, make sure to take the time to encourage and reinforce him or her for having the courage to come into treatment. Check out how the patient feels. It is not good to be suffering, and this patient has been in misery for a long time. It was scary to come into treatment, but the patient made it. You are proud of the patient. Most persons who complete their first inpatient treatment ultimately achieve a stable recovery. They might have to come into treatment again, or even again and again, but the first treatment is a major turning point. Patients learn things in the first treatment that they never forget. They learn that there is a disease called *chemical dependency,* that there is treatment for it, that treatment does not hurt, and that people can live happy, sober lifestyles.

Example of How to Share the Diagnosis

After the initial assessments are over, have a talk with the patient about the diagnosis.

"Ralph, I have gone over the assessments carefully with the staff. You have been diagnosed as having alcohol dependence and cannabis dependence. Do you have any questions?"

"I don't think the pot has ever been a problem for me," the patient says with a concerned look on his face. The patient apparently wants to hold on to his use of marijuana. He wants to give up the alcohol that has caused him a lot of problems, but he wants to keep the option open on using cannabis.

You understand and immediately intervene. "That's a common belief. You think that because alcohol has given you most of the problems, it is the only problem. We have found that all mood-altering chemicals are a problem. You cannot just quit the booze and smoke a little dope. Studies show that if you were to quit drinking and just use pot, the pot ultimately would lead you back to drinking. This is called cross-tolerance. Both drugs—alcohol and cannabis—do essentially the same thing. They are downers. They are a way of treating feelings inappropriately. What we learn in treatment is how to use our feelings appropriately."

Assigning a Treatment Buddy

Once you have made your initial assessment and believe that you have the beginnings of a therapeutic alliance, introduce the patient to a treatment buddy. Check the patient list and come up with a patient of the same sex who is doing well in the program. This person usually will be a few weeks ahead of your new patient in the program. Try to match personalities a bit so that the two people will have a good chance of hitting it off. Get the cooperation from the buddy first and then introduce the two. Tell the patient that the buddy will give him or her a tour of the treatment setting and will introduce the new patient around. Tell the buddy to share his or her experiences, strengths, and hopes with the patient. Do not leave the patient alone. The worst thing for someone just coming into treatment is to be left alone where the illness can work unencumbered. Patients who isolate themselves have a much higher chance of leaving treatment against medical advice (AMA).

Tell the treatment buddy to stick with the patient until the patient adjusts to treatment. This will take a varying amount of time depending on the patient. If the patient is resisting, then you will have to be more aggressive and keep him or her with the buddy for a longer period of time. You might have to trade off buddies, particularly if this is a difficult patient. This Twelfth Step work is good for all parties concerned—the patient and the buddies. There is nothing like working with someone in early recovery to solidify one's own program.

The Intoxicated Patient

The intoxicated patient can be difficult for everyone to deal with. Substance intoxication is the organic brain syndrome that is produced by the ingestion of high doses of all classes of psychoactive substances except nicotine. Central nervous system depressants—opiates, inhalants, alcohol, barbiturates, benzodiazepines, and so on—create intoxicated states characterized by slurred speech, lack of coordination, and an unsteady gait. Central nervous system stimulants—cocaine, amphetamines, and so on—create signs including agitation, talkativeness, vigilance, and grandiosity. Cannabis produces euphoria and an altered time sense. Hallucinogens produce hallucinations, usually of a visual nature. Inhalants produce a light-headed feeling and confusion (Schuckit, 1984).

How to Determine the Level of Intoxication

Any patients who have taken enough of a drug to compromise their vital signs are experiencing toxic reactions. This is a drug overdose where the patients have taken so much of a drug that their bodies cannot function properly.

Patients who demonstrate a drug-related syndrome (with relatively stable vital signs) and who show signs of withdrawal are in *substance withdrawal*. Withdrawal is evidenced by physical and psychological symptoms that develop when a physically addicting drug is stopped too quickly. The cells have undergone neuroadaptation and are responding to the lack of drugs in the patient's system. Withdrawal is a constellation of symptoms that give the patient the opposite feeling of being intoxicated on his or her drug of choice. Alcoholics feel nervous, and amphetamine addicts feel depressed.

Patients with stable vital signs and no symptoms of withdrawal who have drug-induced confusion are experiencing an organic brain syndrome. Organic brain syndrome is characterized by confusion, disorientation, and decreased intellectual functioning (Schuckit, 1984).

The Patient's Reaction to Intoxication

Patients in these acute organic brain syndrome states can seem to be relatively normal or extremely bizarre. They can be actively psychotic, relaxed and comfortable, or in a panic. They can experience intense flashbacks. High doses of amphetamines, cocaine, or phencyclidine (PCP) may produce organic delirium. Delirium is characterized by disorganized thinking and reduced ability to maintain attention. The patient will not be able to follow a conversation. The disorganized thinking will be manifested by rambling, irrelevant, or incoherent speech. This delirium usually is brief (less than 6 hours) after amphetamine or cocaine use, but it can last for up to a week after PCP use (Schuckit, 1984; Spitzer, 1987).

Acute use of amphetamines, cocaine, or PCP may result in a delusional state. Delusions are false beliefs that are intractable to logic. The patient may feel that someone or some group is out to get him or her. The patient may think that he or she has strange or unusual powers. These delusions usually are brief, lasting from several hours to several days, but in some patients they can last for up to a year, even in the absence of further drug use. Hallucinogen use can result in the development of delusions (Vardy & Kay, 1983). Brief psychotic states also have been reported following cannabis use (Hollister, 1986).

During acute intoxication and withdrawal, it is not unusual to see patients complaining of hallucinations. These hallucinations usually are visual or tactile and rarely are auditory. Lights may seem too bright, or sounds may seem too loud and startling. This is a transient psychotic state. The patients may see trailing of objects (e.g., when the patients move a hand, they see a brief image extend behind the solid object like a jet contrail). The walls or floor might seem to move, or the patients might see bugs or other things that are not there. The patients may feel something unusual on or under their skin. These hallucinations usually are brief, but the patients will need to be reassured and supported. The patients' brains are chemically correcting. These negative experiences can be used to give the patients evidence that they need to stop abusing chemicals.

What to Do With an Intoxicated Patient

Never argue with intoxicated patients. This will get you nowhere. They probably are not going to remember the conversation anyway. Briefly introduce yourself, let the medical staff examine these patients, and let the patients sleep it off. Intoxicated patients and patients in withdrawal will mainly be the responsibility of the medical staff. These staff members will be watching the patients carefully and monitoring their vital signs.

There is an old idea that has been floating around the field for years that patients should hurt in withdrawal. The theory goes that this will help patients to learn that they have a problem. To do this would be a medically unsound practice. It is inappropriate to subject patients to severe withdrawal symptoms just to teach them a lesson. Some of them would die. Patients should be medicated to a point where they stay in mild withdrawal. This hurts enough.

Intoxicated patients who want to talk will have to be reassured and educated. They are not bad people. They are sick. If they want to talk a lot, then let some of the other patients do the talking. Join in if you must. The patients will definitely need to trade off. This is very tiring work, but it is beneficial for them to see the intoxicated patients so messed up. It reinforces for the other patients that they never want to go through this again.

Patients need to be educated about withdrawal. What can they expect? The main thing that patients need to hear is that things are going to get better. With every hour that passes, things are going to improve. The staff is not going to let the patients feel too uncomfortable. Things are going to feel uncomfortable sometimes, but the staff is not going to allow the pain to reach intolerable levels.

Many of the patients' thoughts and feelings now are chemically induced. The patients need to understand that they are going to have some wide mood swings in acute withdrawal. Most patients will be feeling depressed, agitated, irritable, and crabby at various times. They need to have their fears and concerns put to rest. Let them talk. Answer their questions. Listen. These patients need a lot of attention.

Example of a Conversation With an Intoxicated Patient

As you walk into the patient's room, there is a heavy sweet smell of booze in the air. "Hi, Barbara, how are you doing?"

"Not good," the patient says. There is a pained look on her face.

"It will get better," you might respond, reaching out and squeezing the patient's arm. "I promise you that. You're going to get free of this thing."

"I hope so."

"It's going to happen," you might say. "Either you will hook into this program or you will die. It's as simple as that."

"I don't want to do that."

"I know you don't," you say. "No one wants to feel miserable. Looks like you've been feeling pretty bad."

"Yeah."

"Well, that's all over now. The nurse will keep you as comfortable as possible, and when you're ready, we'll start to work."

"Okay."

Stay and chat for the next 20 minutes or so. It should be all casual and comforting—no heavy stuff. All questions need to be answered. Then you should close the session. "There will be a lot of people looking in on you for the next few days, Barbara. Don't stay in here by yourself. There's an old AA saying that what we cannot do alone, we can do together." Then stand up and put your hand on the patient's shoulder. "Hang in there. I'll be in to see you often. If you need to talk, my office is right down the hall."

Detoxification

Except for the hallucinogens, PCP, and the inhalants, prolonged drug or alcohol use is accompanied by the development of drug tolerance and physical dependence. In the case of withdrawal from the central nervous depressants (alcohol, barbiturates, and benzodiazepines), tremulousness, sweating, anxiety, and irritability may give way to life-threatening seizures and delirium. Opioid withdrawal is not life threatening, although the patient feels uncomfortable (Group for the Advancement of Psychiatry Committee on Alcoholism and the Addictions, 1991). Withdrawal from central nervous system stimulants may be accompanied by a "crash" characterized by depression, fatigue, increased need for sleep, and increased appetite (Gawin & Ellinwood, 1988; Kasser, Geller, Howell, & Wartenberg, 1998).

You must be able to determine where patients are in withdrawal. This is best accomplished by using the Clinical Institute Withdrawal Assessment of Alcohol Scale (Appendix 5). This scale can be modified to rate withdrawal from the benzodiazepines. To score withdrawal from narcotics, use the Narcotic Withdrawal Scale (Appendix 6) (Fultz & Senay, 1975). Patients who are in moderate to severe withdrawal need to be assessed every hour until the symptoms are under control (Adinoff, Bone, & Linnolila, 1988).

Detoxification is the gradual safe elimination of the drug from the body. Some drugs, such as alcohol, are detoxified quickly, usually within a few days, but the benzodiazepines may take weeks or months (Burant, 1990; Schuckit, 1984). Many patients are suffering from polysubstance withdrawal, and this can complicate the clinical picture. The drugs most likely to cause serious physical problems are the depressants. These patients can deteriorate rapidly.

How Patients React in Detoxification

Most any physical or mental symptom can present itself in withdrawal. No heavy confrontation is necessary. These patients are sick and irritable. They are sleeping poorly. They have powerful cravings. This is where many patients walk out of treatment. They feel as though they cannot stand the symptoms anymore. These patients need medication, reassurance, and support. You must be gentle. Keep telling them over and over that it will get better. If they stay clean and sober, then they never will have to go though this misery again.

In withdrawal, patients are restless and have strong cravings. This physiological and psychological need for the substance is the primary motivating force behind drug addiction. The patients' bodies are driving them to return to their drugs of choice. The cells are screaming for relief. The patients have been in withdrawal hundreds of times before, but they always have treated it by getting intoxicated again. Now they are going to stick it out, striving for recovery. All of these patients think about leaving treatment, but when they get to feeling a little better, they reach the greatest chance of actually going out the door. You must be on top of this by constantly assessing where the patients are both physically and psychologically.

Detoxification should be managed in a room that is reduced of excessive stimulation. The area needs to be quiet and without bright lights. Familiar people, pictures, a clock, and clothes are helpful. Soft conversation that reassures patients and keeps them oriented is best. The staff should display a positive attitude of mutual respect. Reassuring touches, such as taking a pulse and putting a hand on a shoulder, are helpful (Baum & Iber, 1980).

Once the acute withdrawal syndrome has passed, patients remain in a protracted abstinence syndrome for weeks or even years. Relapse is higher during this period of physiological adjustment. The protracted abstinence syndrome varies depending on the drug of dependency. Typically, it is a symptom constellation opposite of that which the patient was using the drug to produce (e.g., the patient using stimulants to increase energy will experience lethargy) (Geller, 1990).

The AMA Threat

■

Patients in an inpatient or outpatient setting can present an AMA threat (they can leave treatment against medical advice). They usually isolate themselves first from the treatment peers and staff. Addictive thinkers must lie to themselves and believe that the lies are the truth for the illness to work. The addiction cannot exist in the light of the truth. The disease has a much better chance of working in isolation. That is why patients must not be left alone in early treatment until they have stabilized.

The illness cooks a stew of inaccurate information—minimization ("My use is not that bad"), rationalization ("I have a good reason to use"), projection ("It's not my problem, it's their problem"), and denial (a stubborn refusal to see the truth). All of these defenses are used to distort reality.

You may first get wind of an AMA threat as you assess a patient, or you may learn of it from another patient or from a staff member. The patient shares that he or she is thinking about leaving treatment. You must intervene when you see this problem developing. As the patient tells more and more lies to himself or herself, the patient becomes convinced that the lies are the truth. The patient keeps collecting information that proves that the illness is right.

For the most part, patients' reasons will be inaccurate. They are distortions of reality. Patients might not be aware that the real reason why they are leaving treatment is to use their drugs of choice. Patients delude themselves. They are craving, but many of them do not know it. They believe the inaccurate thinking.

Example of an AMA Intervention

The intervention desperately needed here is the truth. Every time the patient brings up a reason for leaving treatment, you challenge him or her with the truth. Be gentle. The truth is on your side, and a big part of the patient wants to know the facts. Do not talk to the illness side of the patient. Talk to the side that wants to get well.

Patient: I can quit on my own.

Counselor: You've tried that before, and you have always failed.

Patient: This time I can do it.

Counselor: Your alcoholism is worse now than it's ever been. It's not better, it's worse.

Patient: I will go to meetings.

Counselor: You may do that for a while, but it is my opinion that you won't be able to make it out there.

Patient: I think I can.

Counselor: You have had that thought a hundred times before. Give the disease some credit. It's stronger than you are. Alcoholics Anonymous says that no human power can remove our alcoholism. You will never lick this thing on your own.

Patient: I'll go to church.

Counselor: You need treatment.

Patient: I've got some marital problems that I need to work out. I can't do that in here.

Counselor: The best thing you can do for your marriage is to stay in here and get into a stable recovery. Why don't we call your wife and see if she wants you to leave?

Patient: I don't fit in here.

Counselor: What can you do to improve that situation? Maybe you can help someone else.

Patient: I'm not like these people. Their problems are much worse than mine.

Counselor: Didn't you get two DWIs?

Patient: Yes.

Counselor: But you're not like these people?

Patient: No.

Counselor: You have a lot of skills. You can do this.

This conversation can go on for quite some time. The longer you expose the lies that the patient is telling himself or herself, the better the chance of keeping the patient in treatment. If you have to, see whether the patient will agree to stay in treatment for 1 more day or even 1 more hour. The longer the patient stays, the more opportunity you have to turn him or her around.

How to Use the AMA Team

The AMA team is a group of three or more of the treatment peers who have been selected by the staff to help other patients who are at risk of leaving treatment early. Have them share their experiences, strengths, and hopes with the patient. Often, this group will be more effective than you are. It is easier for a patient to trust people who are in treatment. In an outpatient setting, if you do not have an AMA group, then maybe one of the patients further along in the program will agree to encourage the patient to stay.

If there are any consequences that a patient will face if he or she leaves treatment, this is the time to bring these things out. The patient may have been court ordered into treatment. The patient's employment may be in jeopardy. A spouse or parent may have given the patient an ultimatum—get treatment or else. Use every angle you can so long as it is based in the truth.

The patient must be confronted with the truth until he or she hears it. There is a healthy side of the patient—the side that is sick of this problem and wants to recover. The truth is a very powerful tool. It is even more powerful when delivered in an atmosphere of loving support.

Some counselors believe that they have to hammer away at a patient's denial aggressively until they literally "break through it," but it cannot be like a war where each person tries to attack the other. The aggressive technique is not recommended. The therapeutic alliance is too important to wound. The therapeutic alliance must be built on mutual acceptance, trust, and unconditional positive regard. It is impossible to trust someone who is verbally beating on you. Raising your voice in anger rarely is beneficial to patients. This behavior harms your relationship and makes your job even harder than it already is. You will get angry with patients. That is normal; everyone does. But do not act abusively. Treat patients the same way in which you would want to be treated.

How to Use the In-House Intervention

If all else fails, then you might have to arrange an in-house intervention. Here you gather the patient's family and concerned others together and have them tell the patient why they want him or her to stay in treatment.

Have each of the participants write a letter stating how the patient's chemical dependency has adversely affected the participant. The participants need to give specific examples of how they were hurt when the patient was intoxicated or hung over. They share how they are feeling now and ask for what they want. They write down exactly what they are going to do if the patient does not agree to stay in treatment. A spouse could state that she has been humiliated in front of friends. If the patient does not stay in treatment, then she will divorce him. An employer could say that he is weary of the patient calling in sick. If the patient does not stay in treatment, then he will be fired. The kids could say that they have been embarrassed by the patient and want out of the home. A parent could talk about the lies and mistrust in the home and say that they are going to withdraw their financial support.

In an intervention, the family members are going to need a lot of encouragement. You need to help them with their letters and practice the intervention without the patient present. Once the group is gathered, bring the patient in and have each member share his or her letter. If the patient is still unwilling to stay in treatment, then you can open the group up for discussion. Again, every time the patient gives the family a good reason for leaving, you and the family will tell the patient the truth.

How to Respond to Patients Who Leave AMA

Do everything in your power to keep your patients in treatment, but if they decide to leave early, then wish them well and invite them to come back if they have further problems. Many patients will leave for a time and then return. Whatever happens, remember that when the patients were in treatment you told them the truth. Patients leaving treatment are no reflection on you or your skills. You did not lose. You planted the seed of the truth that will grow later.

Programs that are more genuinely loving will keep more patients than will programs that are confrontive. The key balance is to confront the patients in an atmosphere of support. A loving environment is attractive, and everyone wants more. You will know that you have struck the right balance when many of your patients are reluctant to leave treatment at the end of their stays. They have felt so accepted, loved, and supported that they do not want to leave an environment in which they have made major growth.

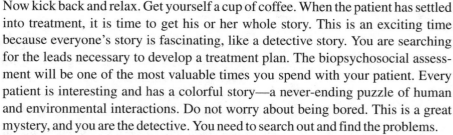

CHAPTER
TWO | The Biopsychosocial Interview

Now kick back and relax. Get yourself a cup of coffee. When the patient has settled into treatment, it is time to get his or her whole story. This is an exciting time because everyone's story is fascinating, like a detective story. You are searching for the leads necessary to develop a treatment plan. The biopsychosocial assessment will be one of the most valuable times you spend with your patient. Every patient is interesting and has a colorful story—a never-ending puzzle of human and environmental interactions. Do not worry about being bored. This is a great mystery, and you are the detective. You need to search out and find the problems.

The purpose of the biopsychosocial is to find out exactly what the problems are and where they came from. Then you need to decide what you are going to do about them. All diseases have biological, psychological, and social factors that contribute to dysfunction. These ingredients mingle together, leaving the patient in a state of "dis-ease." The patient does not feel easy; he or she feels dis-easy. There are no major psychiatric diseases that do not have biopsychosocial components. All chemical dependency affects the cells (biology); the emotions, attitudes, and behavior (psychology); and the relationships (sociology).

To do your biopsychosocial, you will need the Biopsychosocial Assessment form (Appendix 32) and a quiet place where you will not be disturbed. The interview will take at least 1 hour, maybe 2 hours, or maybe more. Many beginning counselors get bogged down in this interview because they become overwhelmed with information or they try to begin treating the problems too early. This interview is not for treatment. It is for assessment. The best way of keeping out of these traps is to let the patient do most of the talking. You ask the questions and let the patient tell his or her story while you write it down. Ask for more information only if you are confused or uncertain about what the patient is describing. You must understand the story and how the patient feels.

It will take you a while to become a skilled interviewer. It takes keen insight to see the problems clearly as they develop. You will get better at this as you become more experienced.

How to Conduct the Interview

■

Begin the biopsychosocial by telling the patient what you are going to do. "The purpose of this interview is to see exactly what the problems are, where they come from, and what we are going to do in treatment. From this information, we will develop the treatment plan. You need to keep things real accurate here. Don't make things bigger than they were or smaller than they were. Just tell me exactly what happened. Any questions? Let's begin."

Now relax and begin your interview. Do not be in a hurry. This is fascinating and fun. Ask the following questions and write the answers down in the blanks provided on the biopsychosocial form.

Date:

Patient name:

Age:

Sex:

Marital status:

Children:

Residence:

Others in residence:

Length of residence:

Education: (mark highest grade completed)

Occupation:

Characteristics of the informant: Mark down whether or not you trust the information that the patient is giving you. Is the patient reliable? If so, then write "reliable informant." If you do not trust the information for some reason, then write why you mistrust it. You might want to write "questionable informant."

Chief complaint: This is the chief problem that brought the patient to treatment. Use the patient's own words. If someone else gives you the chief complaint, then list that person as the informant. "What was the chief problem that brought you to treatment?"

History of the present problem: This is everything that pertains to the chief complaint. One good approach with histories is to say something like this: "As they are growing up, kids have a real accurate idea when things are right with them and when things are wrong. Go back into your childhood and tell me where you think things began to go wrong for you. From that point, tell me the whole story including what is bringing you into treatment now."

Let the patient tell his or her story, and for the most part, you just copy it down. Use as many direct quotes as you can. Guide the patient only when you need to do so. You want the story to flow in a rough chronological order. Most patients will do this naturally, but everyone jumps around a little. Stop the patient if he or she is going too fast or if you do not understand something. Do not let the patient ramble and get caught up in irrelevant details. Look for the problem areas.

The history of the present problem must contain the following information:

- *Age of onset:*
- *Duration of use:*

- *Patterns of use:* How does the patient drink? Is this patient a binge drinker or a daily drinker? Does the patient drink all day or only after work? How often does the patient drink?
- *Consequences of use:* These are physical, psychological, and/or social problems caused or exacerbated by drinking.
- *Previous treatment:* Who did the patient see? What was the treatment? What were the results?
- *Blackouts:*
- *Tolerance:*
- *Withdrawal symptoms:*

Past history: A history of the patient's life, from infancy to the present, is the next phase of the interview. The categories include the following:

- *Place of birth:*
- *Date of birth:*
- *Developmental milestones:* "Did you have any problems when you were born? Problems walking, talking, toilet training, reading, or writing? Did anyone ever say that you were a slow learner?" Cover developmental problems and intellectual problems here. Determine as best you can whether the patient can understand the material presented in your program. Most AA material is written at a sixth-grade level. Patients who read two grade levels below this are going to need special assistance.
- *Raised with:* This includes primary caregivers, brothers, and/or sisters and what it is like to live with them.
- *Ethnic/cultural influences:* "What's your ethnic heritage? Are you French? Dutch? German?" A black inner-city teenager is going to be a lot different from a midwestern farmer. You need to know something about the culture. How does the culture relate to things such as time orientation, family, sharing, cooperation, and taught customs that guide relationships? (For further information on cultural differences, read the book *Counseling the Culturally Different* [Sue & Sue, 1999].)
- *Home of origin:* "When you were growing up, how did it feel in the house where you were raised?"
- *Grade school:* "What kind of a kid were you in grade school? How did you get along with the other kids and the teachers?"
- *High school:* "What kind of a student were you in high school?"
- *College:* "What were you like in college?"
- *Military history:* "Were you ever in the armed services? For how long? What was your highest rank? Did you get an honorable discharge?"
- *Occupational history:* "Briefly tell me about your work history. What kind of work have you done?" Include the longest job held and any consequences of drug or alcohol use.
- *Employment satisfaction:* "How long have you been at your current job? Are you happily employed?"
- *Financial history:* "How is your current financial situation?"
- *Gambling:* "Have you ever had a problem with gambling?"

- *Sexual orientation:* "How old were you when you first had sex? Have you ever had a homosexual contact?"
- *Sexual abuse:* "Have you ever been sexually abused?"
- *Physical abuse:* "Have you ever been physically abused?"
- *Current sexual history:* "Are you having any current sexual problems?"
- *Relationship history:* Briefly describe this patient's relationship and friendship patterns. Does the patient have any close friends? Is the patient in a romantic relationship now? How is that going? Include consequences of chemical use. Some helpful questions include the following. "Do you have close friends? Have you ever been in love? How many times? Tell me a little bit about each relationship."
- *Social support for treatment:* "Does your family support you coming into treatment? What about your friends?" Thoroughly assess the patient's recovery environment. How supportive are family and friends going to be about recovery?
- *Spiritual orientation:* "Do you believe in God or a Higher Power or anything like that? Do you engage in any kind of religious activity, go to church, or anything like that?"
- *Legal:* "Are you having any current problems with the law? Have you ever been arrested?"
- *Strengths:* "What are some of your strengths or some of your good qualities?"
- *Weaknesses:* "What are some of your weaknesses or some of your qualities that aren't so good?"
- *Leisure:* "What do you do for play, entertainment, or fun? What has been the effect of your chemical use?"
- *Depression:* "Have you ever felt depressed or down most of the day, almost every day, for more than 2 weeks?" If the patient has signs of depression, this needs to be flagged for the medical staff.
- *Mania:* "Have you ever felt so high or full of energy that you got into trouble or people thought that you were acting strangely?" Mania is a distinct period of abnormally elevated, expansive, or irritable mood. This mood must be sustained for at least 2 full days.
- *Anxiety disorders:* "Have you ever been anxious for a long time? Have you ever had a panic attack?"
- *Eating disorders:* "Have you ever had any problems with appetite or eating, gorging, purging, starving yourself, or anything like that?"

Medical history:

- *Illnesses:* "Have you ever had any physical illnesses, even the small ones, measles, mumps, or chicken pox?"
- *Hospitalizations:* "Have you ever been in a hospital overnight?" Write down the reason for each hospitalization.
- *Allergies:* "Do you have any allergies?"
- *Medications at present:* "Are you taking any medication?"

Family history:

- *Father:* "How old is your father? Is he in good, fair, or poor health? Any health problems? What's he like? How did he act when you were growing up?"
- *Mother:* "How old is your mother? Is she in good, fair, or poor health? What was she like when you were growing up?"
- *Other relatives with significant psychopathology:* "Did anyone else in your family have any problems with drugs or alcohol or any other kind of mental disorder?"

Mental status: This is where you formally test the patient's mental condition.

- *Description of the patient:* Describe the patient's general appearance. How would you be able to pick the patient out of a crowd? Note the patient's age, skin color, sex, weight, hair color, eye color, scars, glasses, mustache, and so on.
- *Dress:* How is the patient dressed? Describe what the patient is wearing and how he or she is dressed. Is the patient overly neat, sloppy, casual, seductive, or formal?
- *Sensorium:* Is the patient fully conscious and able to use his or her senses normally, or does something seem to be clouding the patient's sensorium. Is the patient alert, lethargic, or drowsy? Intoxicated patients will not have a clear sensorium.
- *Orientation:* The patient is oriented to person, place, and time if the patient knows his or her name and location and today's date.
- *Attitude toward the examiner:* What is the patient's attitude toward you—cooperative, friendly, pleasant, hostile, suspicious, or defensive?
- *Motor behavior:* Describe how the patient is moving. Anything unusual? Does the patient move normally, restlessly, continuously, or slowly? Does the patient have a tremor or tic?
- *Speech:* How does the patient talk? Any speech or language problems? Does the patient talk normally, or is he or she overly talkative or minimally responsive? Do you detect a speech disorder?
- *Affect:* How is the patient feeling during the interview—appropriate, blunted, restricted, labile, or dramatic over production?
- *Range of affect:* What is the patient's capacity to feel the whole range of feelings? Affect ranges from elation to depression. During the interview, you should see the patient cover a wide range of affect. Does the patient's range of feelings seem normal, constricted, blunted, or flat?
- *Mood:* What is the feeling that clouds the patient's whole life? The patient might be calm, cheerful, anxious, depressed, elated, irritable, pessimistic, angry, neutral, or any other sustained feeling.
- *Thought processes:* Does the patient have a normal stream of thought? Is the patient able to come up with clear ideas, form these ideas into speech, and move the speech into normal conversation? If the patient is hard to follow, then write down why. Describe what the patient is doing that makes

the conversation difficult. Are the patient's thought processes logical and coherent, blocked, circumstantial, tangential, incoherent, distracted, evasive, or persevered?

- *Abstract thinking:* Ask the patient, "What does this saying mean to you? People who live in glass houses shouldn't throw stones." An abstract answer might be, "Don't talk about people because you might have problems yourself." A concrete answer might be, "They might break the glass." Ask the patient, "How are an egg and a seed alike?" An abstract answer might be, "Things grow from both." A concrete answer might be, "They are both round." Using such questions, determine the patient's ability to abstract. Is it normal, or is it impaired?

- *Suicidal ideation:* "Have you ever thought about hurting yourself or anything like that?" Describe all suicidal thoughts, acts, plans, and attempts.

- *Homicidal ideation:* "Have you ever thought about hurting someone else?" Describe all thoughts, acts, plans, and attempts.

- *Disorders of perception:* Disorders in how the patient perceives can be assessed by asking questions such as the following. "Have you ever seemed to hear things that other people couldn't seem to hear, like whispering voices or anything like that? Have you ever seemed to see things that other people couldn't seem to see, like a vision? Have you ever smelled a strange smell that seemed out of place? Have you ever tasted a strange taste that seemed out of place? Have you ever felt anything unusual on or under your skin?"

- *Delusions:* "Have you ever felt that anyone was paying special attention to you or anything like that? Have you ever felt that someone was out to hurt you or give you a hard time? Have you ever felt like you had any strange or unusual powers? Have you ever felt like one of the organs in your body wasn't operating properly?" A delusion is a false belief that is fixed.

- *Obsessions:* "Have you ever been bothered by thoughts that didn't make any sense, and they kept coming back even when you tried not to think about them? Have you ever had awful thoughts like hurting someone or being contaminated by germs or anything like that?" Obsessions are persistent ideas, thoughts, impulses, or images that are experienced, at least at first, as intrusive and senseless.

- *Compulsions:* "Was there anything that you had to do over and over again and you couldn't stop doing it, like washing your hands over and over again or checking something several times to make sure you had done it right?" Compulsions are repetitive, purposeful, and intentional behaviors that are performed in response to an obsession, according to certain rules, or in a stereotyped fashion.

- *Intelligence:* Estimate the patient's level of intellectual functioning—above average, average, low average, borderline, or retarded.

- *Concentration:* Describe the patient's ability to concentrate during the interview—normal, mild, moderate, or severe impairment.

- *Memory:*

    a. *Immediate memory:* Tell the patient, "Listen carefully. I'm going to say some numbers. You say them right after me: 5-8-9-3-1." After the patient has completed this task, tell him or her, "Now I'm going to say some more numbers. This time I want you to say them backward: 4-3-9." Patients should be able to repeat five digits forward and three digits backward.

    b. *Recent memory:* Tell the patient, "I'm going to give you three objects that I want you to remember: A red ball, an open window, and a police car. Now you remember those, and I'll ask you what they are in a few minutes." Patients should be able to remember all three objects after 5 minutes.

    c. *Remote memory:* The patient should be able to tell you what he or she had for dinner last night or for breakfast this morning. The patient should know the names of the last five presidents of the United States. The patient should know his or her own past history.

- *Impulse control:* Estimate the ability of the patient to control his or her impulses.

- *Judgment:* Estimate the patient's ability to make good judgments. If you cannot estimate from the interview, then ask the patient a question. "If you were at the movies and were the first person to see smoke and fire, what would you do?" The patient should give a good answer that protects both himself or herself and the other people present.

- *Insight:* Does the patient know that he or she has a problem with chemicals? Does the person understand something about the nature of the illness?

- *Motivation for treatment:* Is the patient committed to treatment? Estimate the level of treatment acceptance or resistance.

Summary and Impression

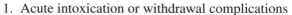

Begin with the patient's childhood and summarize all that you have heard and observed. Include all of the problems you have seen and give your impression of where the patient stands on each of the following dimensions:

1. Acute intoxication or withdrawal complications
2. Biomedical conditions or complications
3. Emotional/behavioral complications
4. Treatment acceptance or resistance
5. Relapse potential
6. Recovery environment

Diagnosis

Diagnose the problem using the *Diagnostic and Statistical Manual of Mental Disorders* (American Psychiatric Association, 1994).

Disposition and Treatment Plan

■

List and describe all of the problems that need treatment and how you plan to treat each problem.

A Sample Biopsychosocial Interview

■

Now let's go through an actual interview so that you can see how it works. We describe how you should be thinking as we go through the interview.

The patient comes into the office. She is tall and thin and is dressed in white jeans and a white sweatshirt. She smiles as she sits down. She makes good eye contact and relaxes. Her face is pretty. She does not appear to be in any acute distress.

Counselor: Give me your full name, all three names please, and spell them all.

Patient: Patty P-A-T-T-Y Jean J-E-A-N Robbins R-O-B-B-I-N-S.

Counselor: How old are you?

Patient: Twenty-eight. [*The patient seems to relax even more. She sits farther back in the chair and crosses her legs.*]

Counselor: Are you married?

Patient: No.

Counselor: Have you ever been?

Patient: No.

Counselor: Do you have any kids?

Patient: No.

Counselor: What's your current hometown?

Patient: Watertown, South Dakota.

Counselor: Who lives with you?

Patient: No one.

Counselor: How long have you lived there?

Patient: About 5 years.

Counselor: How much education do you have?

Patient: High school.

Counselor: Are you currently employed?

Patient: Yes.

Counselor: What do you do?

Patient: I am a beautician for The Cut Above.

Counselor: What was the chief problem that brought you to treatment?

Patient: I knew I couldn't go on drinking the way I was.

Counselor: When kids are growing up, they have a real accurate idea of when things are right with them and wrong with them. Go back into your childhood as early as you feel is important and tell me, where do you think things began to go wrong with you in your life? And from that point, tell me the whole story including what brings you to treatment now.

Patient: I think that as a child, I don't remember an awful lot about my childhood. I don't remember a lot of good things. I didn't have a bad childhood. I have never been abused physically or sexually or anything like that. I always felt left out, abandoned, lost, alone a lot. [*This is where the problems start. The patient grew up feeling left out, abandoned, lost, and alone.*]

Patient: I think I knew that I was loved, but I wasn't shown it very much. Going to a Lutheran school was hard on me. I never felt like I was like the other kids. [*The patient continues to feel isolated in school.*]

Patient: One year I was a class officer, and that made me feel real good. I wasn't sports-minded. I didn't feel that anyone was working with me with what I could do. My father died when I was a baby. My mother didn't listen to me. I would ask her a question, and she would just look at me. I could never get any answers. I remember asking her about how boys and girls were different. She just said, "Don't you know?" I remember, I never got any information about my period. I didn't get it until I was pretty old anyway, about 17, and by then I had to find out some things from my friends. I read a book about how to take care of myself. [*The patient is angry at her mother and harbors some resentments. This may or may not have influenced her drinking. It certainly increased her feelings of isolation and loneliness, and it influenced her ability to establish and maintain close interpersonal relationships.*]

Patient: I hear from other members of my family that my father was strict. I didn't hear good things about him, but I didn't hear bad things either. He didn't like drinking, and my mom would hide her alcohol from him. [*The patient seems to long for her father. It's in the sadness of her voice. Her mother might have had a drinking problem. It sounds as though it caused some family conflict.*]

Patient: I think my mom talked to me about this. She may have had a problem. She hid her wine bottle down in the basement. Going through school was hard because I didn't fit in with the group. I remember making up stories and trying to buy the clothes they wore to fit in, but I never did. They all caught on about what I was trying to do. It didn't work. I couldn't afford a lot of things. When I was older, I was real glad to get out of the house. I didn't date much, but when I did, I immediately fell in love. I felt like, great, somebody likes me. When they would go out with others, I was devastated. I kept grasping at them to come back. [*These relationships sound addictive. This is a problem. Listen to the powerful feeling statements she makes: "When they would go out with others, I was devastated. I kept grasping at them to come back." The patient begins to use relationships to fill the empty void within herself. She is trying to replace her dead father and her distant mother with a relationship with a man.*]

Patient: One day my girlfriend and I were eating lunch, and these guys came up to us. They asked if we wanted to go out for a ride and have a few drinks with them. They were pretty cute, you know, so we decided to go. There was this one, he said his name was Mark, he was older, and we got along really well. I was impressed by him. I could tell he liked me really a lot, more so than anyone else I had ever dated. I ended up going with him for quite a while. About a year later, I found out he was married. His name wasn't Mark, it was Andy. He had a wife and a kid. I finally called him up and told him that I knew the truth but that I loved him anyway. This was a very passionate man. He loved me. He showed me he loved me. I don't care what you say, he was able to love two people at the same time. [*The patient falls victim to another addictive relationship. This time it is with a man who is addictive himself. The intense sexual excitement that this man offers fools her into thinking that he really loves her.*]

Patient: We continued that relationship for a long time. There was a lot of pain in that relationship. I just broke up with him about 2 years ago.

Counselor: When did you start dating him?

Patient: When I was about 21. I went with him for 4 years, and 2 of those years he was married, 2 he wasn't. [*This is addictive, but is it also passive and dependent? She does not look passive. She makes good eye contact and seems to feel comfortable. We must let the story unfold to get the answer.*]

Counselor: How old were you when you first had a drink?

Patient: It was in my early teens, at a party.

Counselor: Did you drink much in high school?

Patient: No, only very occasionally.

Counselor: Okay, go on with your story. You're going out with Andy, and Andy's married.

Patient: We kept seeing each other. He kept promising that he was going to get a divorce. He didn't want to lose me. It kept going on for years and years. I would get angry at him when I found out that he was seeing somebody else other than me and his wife. I would blow up, and then I'd finally settle down, and we would continue to see each other. Every time I would get frustrated with him, I would seek someone else out. [*Again, the quick addictive fix.*]

Patient: I would find someone else who was interested in me. I had several affairs. Andy would get very angry if he found out that I was dating someone, but I felt he didn't have the right to get angry. He was married. [*There is an honesty problem here. The patient was lying to both men.*]

Patient: I went out with this guy once. He was everything I had ever dreamed of. He was tall and dark with a hairy chest. He was beautiful. I went out with him for quite a while. He really liked me, but I kept seeing Andy. The relationship with this guy, the new guy, Rob, began to get abusive. The relationship with Andy was abusive too. They'd both hit me, slap me, sometimes. They both tried to choke me. A couple of times, they raped me out of anger. Andrew wasn't ever a violent person, but then all of a sudden he got violent. He put me down a lot. He put me down all the time.

Counselor: Did he make important choices for you? [*The counselor probes the dependency problem.*]

Patient: No, I never did that.

Counselor: Is it hard for you to make decisions without some sort of reassurance from someone else?

Patient: No, I don't have any problem there, but I am attracted to men with power. They can tell me anything, and I'll believe it. I don't know what it is about powerful men, but I'm real attracted to that. Andy finally got a divorce, and I lived with him. He's a banker and very wealthy. I thought, things are going to be a lot better now. He was still controlling and manipulative, but I thought everything was going to improve. I always knew that sooner or later, I was going to be abandoned. [*Here we see the fuel for the addictive relationship. The patient chronically fears abandonment, like the abandonment that she felt as a child. This leaves her feeling anxious and vulnerable. She will do anything to keep her man, but at the same time, she fears that she will lose him.*]

Patient: He was very demanding, but I could get what I wanted by being very diplomatic. It took me a long time to learn how to do that. He always wanted me to do all kinds of things. I kept the house and the grounds immaculate. I worked and kept house and did the yard and worked at my job. [*The patient is not assertive. She has learned how to lie and manipulate to get what she wants.*]

Patient: All this time, I was drinking a lot. I was hiding my drinking. I would hide my beer cans. Sometimes he would come home, and I'd be drunk.

Counselor: How much were you drinking then?

Patient: At least a six-pack.

Counselor: Did you ever have a blackout?

Patient: Oh, yeah, I had plenty.

Counselor: Did you ever have a real bad hangover?

Patient: Yes.

Counselor: Hands ever get shaky?

Patient: No, but I would be sick. I would feel terrible—headache, upset stomach.

Counselor: What happened then?

Patient: I came home one night and caught him with another woman. He denied what was going on, but I knew. I could tell from her reaction that she didn't know about me. I talked to her, and in time we both got together with him again. I swear to God, he has the ability to love two women at the same time. I can tell he loves me.

Counselor: Healthy relationships are based on trust.

Patient: I know that. This woman and I were never mad at each other. We both knew that he was so intense that he could love us both.

Counselor: It's never loving to lie.

Patient: I like that. That makes sense. I finally broke up with him. I didn't know anyone. It was real hard, but I did it. He was furious. That was the last time he raped me. He was out of his mind.

Counselor: You don't rape somebody that you love either.

Patient: It was finally over. I fell in love with a new guy, Dave. I fell in love so fast. He was a dream come true. We had long talks about things. This guy didn't work out because I realized that I was doing all of the giving again. I'm starting to realize my pattern. I do all the giving, and I love men with power. It took me a long time to realize that. He would go to my house and watch TV and eat all my food. He never took me anywhere. I said, "Are you getting tired of me or what?" I realized that there was something I wasn't getting here. I had such feelings for David. I can't remember ever feeling like that. He was such a heartthrob.

Counselor: It's easy to get love and lust confused. [*The counselor continues to teach the patient and to show her how she has been confused about relationships. Notice that these interventions are very brief. This is not the time for therapy. It is the time for assessment.*]

Patient: That relationship ended, and I started going out with another guy. He was an alcoholic in recovery, so I cut down on my drinking some. I only saw him once a week. It was nice. One night Andy just walked in on us. It was really crazy. He just came right in as if he owned the place. I had my own place then. I was finally making the break with him, and he couldn't believe it. Dave handled it real well. Andy finally left. You know, I like a man with power. I have this thing about a man with power. I don't know what it is.

Counselor: Well, you've felt pretty powerless in your life. Someone with power would make you feel safe.

Patient: Yeah, a strong man makes me feel safe. Anyway, my drinking kept on increasing, and my relationships kept going to hell, and here I am.

Counselor: Anything in particular bring you into treatment now?

Patient: I went out and got drunk again, and I woke up with such a hangover. I said to myself, I've got to do something about this, now. I made the call right then.

This concluded the history of the present problem. Then the counselor moved right into the past history.

Counselor: Where were you born?

Patient: Livingston, South Dakota.

Counselor: When is your birthday?

Patient: June 28, 1963.

Counselor: Did you have any trouble when you were born?

Patient: No.

Counselor: Any trouble walking, talking, toilet training, reading, or writing?

Patient: No.

Counselor: You were raised with whom?

Patient: My mother and two younger sisters.

Counselor: What is your ethnic heritage? Irish? German? Do you know?

Patient: I'm Irish.

Counselor: Your home of origin, growing up with your mother and sisters. How did it feel in that house?

Patient: I felt alone. I didn't like it.

Counselor: What kind of a kid were you in grade school?

Patient: I was timid, not very outgoing.

Counselor: What kind of a kid were you in high school?

Patient: I was scared, scared to relate.

Counselor: You seem to have made real progress with that timid thing. You don't seem timid anymore.

Patient: Yeah, I really have. I don't think I'm timid anymore.

Counselor: Great. Were you ever in the armed services?

Patient: No.

Counselor: Ever go to college.

Patient: No.

Counselor: Give me a brief occupational history. What kind of work have you done?

Patient: I worked as a secretary for 5 years. I've been at my current job for about 5 years.

Counselor: Are you happily employed?

Patient: Yeah, I like my job.

Counselor: How is your current financial situation?

Patient: Good. I'm not rich, but I get along okay.

Counselor: Do you have any sexual problems?

Patient: No.

Counselor: Have you ever had a homosexual contact?

Patient: No.

Counselor: Are you currently involved with a guy?

Patient: Yes.

Counselor: How long has that been going on?

Patient: About 3 months.

Counselor: And how is that going?

Patient: Great.

Counselor: Do your friends and family support your coming into treatment?

Patient: Yes.

Counselor: Do you feel like there is any kind of a Higher Power or God or anything?

Patient: I believe in God.

Counselor: Do you attend church?

Patient: I go to the Lutheran church.

Counselor: Are you having any problems with the law?

Patient: No.

Counselor: Have you ever had any problems with the law in the past.

Patient: No.

Counselor: What are some of your strengths or some of your good qualities?

Patient: I'm caring. I get along with people real well. I think I'm intelligent.

Counselor: What are some of your weaknesses?

Patient: A drinking problem.

Counselor: What do you enjoy doing for fun?

Patient: I enjoy biking. I hike and jog.

Counselor: Have you ever had a period of time where you felt down or depressed most of the day most every day?

Patient: No.

Counselor: Have you ever felt real anxious?

Patient: No.

Counselor: Ever felt so high or filled with energy that you got into trouble or people thought you were acting strangely?

Patient: No.

Counselor: Ever had any eating problems—gorging, purging, starving yourself, anything like that?

Patient: No.

Counselor: Are you intensely afraid of anything?

Patient: No.

Counselor: Ever had any illnesses, even the small ones, measles, mumps, or chicken pox?

Patient: Measles, mumps, and chicken pox.

Counselor: Ever been in a hospital overnight?

Patient: No.

Counselor: Do you have any allergies?

Patient: No.

Counselor: Are you taking any kind of medication here?

Patient: They have me on a Valium come-down schedule.

Counselor: For what?

Patient: I have been taking Valium for about 5 years. I'm withdrawing from that. [*Current problems are supposed to be covered in the history of the present problem. The counselor did not know about the Valium until now. This happens often. The counselor now has to flip back to the history of the present problem and add this part.*]

Counselor: How much of the Valium were you using?

Patient: I was using it every day for sleep.

Counselor: Did you find yourself using more?

Patient: Yes, I had to increase what I took so it would work.

Counselor: Twice as much?

Patient: More.

Counselor: Did you ever stop using?

Patient: No.

Counselor: How much would you take every night?

Patient: I got up to about 30 mg. [*Once this information was gathered, the counselor resumed the patient's past history.*]

Counselor: Okay, how old was your father when he died.

Patient: In his 20s.

Counselor: How old is your mother?

Patient: Fifty-three.

Counselor: Is she in good, fair, or poor health?

Patient: She's in good health.

Counselor: What kind of a person is your mom?

Patient: She's quiet and demanding.

Counselor: Has anyone else in your family had any problems with alcohol, drugs, or any other kind of mental disorder?

Patient: I think my mother had a drinking problem.

This concludes the past history. Now you would complete the mental status, which we will not bore you with here, and you are ready to dictate the biopsychosocial. The patient has said a lot, and it was important for her to share these things, but you need to tell the story in an abbreviated form. Keep in the main parts of her story but exclude all of the details. At the end of the biopsychosocial, come up with a problem list and a preliminary treatment plan.

To view Patty's biopsychosocial as it was completed, see Appendix 7.

CHAPTER
THREE | # The Treatment Plan

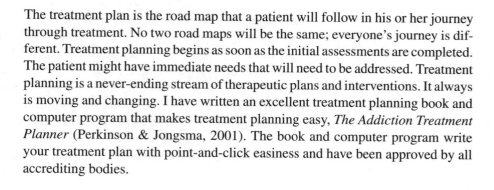

The treatment plan is the road map that a patient will follow in his or her journey through treatment. No two road maps will be the same; everyone's journey is different. Treatment planning begins as soon as the initial assessments are completed. The patient might have immediate needs that will need to be addressed. Treatment planning is a never-ending stream of therapeutic plans and interventions. It always is moving and changing. I have written an excellent treatment planning book and computer program that makes treatment planning easy, *The Addiction Treatment Planner* (Perkinson & Jongsma, 2001). The book and computer program write your treatment plan with point-and-click easiness and have been approved by all accrediting bodies.

How to Build a Treatment Plan

The treatment plan is built around the problems that the patient brings into treatment. The problem list details each problem. It must take into account all of the physical, emotional, and behavioral problems relevant to the patient's care. It must take into account the patient's strengths and weaknesses. It must address each of the six dimensions that you are following.

The treatment plan details the therapeutic interventions, what is going to be done, when it is going to be done, and by whom. It must consider each of the patient's needs and come up with clear ways of dealing with each problem. The treatment plan flows into discharge planning, which begins from the initial assessments.

The Diagnostic Summary

After the interdisciplinary team members assess the patient, they meet and develop a summary of their findings. This is the diagnostic summary. This is where members of the clinical team—the physicians, nurses, counselors, psychologists, psychiatrists, recreational therapists, occupational therapists, physical therapists, dietitians, family therapists, teachers, pastors, pharmacists, and anyone else who is going to be actively involved with the patient's care—meet and develop a summary of the patient's current state and needs. The team members discuss each of the patient's problems and how to best treat it. From this meeting, the diagnostic summary is developed. This details what the problems are, where they came from, and what is going to be done about them. It is much better to do this as a team. As you see your team function, you will see how valuable it is to have many disciplines involved.

The Problem List

The treatment team will continue to develop the problem list as the patient moves through treatment. New problems will come up and be added. Nothing will stay the same. A problem list and treatment plan must be fluid. It must be modified as conditions change.

How to Develop a Problem List

A treatment plan must be measurable. It must have a set of problems and solutions that the staff can measure. The problems cannot be vague. They must be specific. A problem is a brief clinical statement of a condition of the patient that needs treatment. The problem statement should be no longer than one sentence and should describe only one problem.

All problem statements are abstract concepts. You cannot actually see, hear, touch, taste, or smell the problem. For example, low self-esteem is a clinical statement that describes a variety of behaviors exhibited by the patient. You can see the behaviors and conclude from them that the patient has low self-esteem, but you cannot actually see low self-esteem.

Problems are evidenced by signs (what you see) and symptoms (what the patient reports). A problem on the treatment plan should be followed by specific physical, emotional, or behavioral evidence that the problem actually exists. List the problem, add "as evidenced by" or "as indicated by," and then describe the concrete evidence you see that tells you that the problem exists.

Examples of a Problem List

Problem 1: Inability to maintain sobriety outside of a structured facility

As evidenced by: Blood alcohol level of .23
As evidenced by: The patient's family report of daily drinking
As evidenced by: Alcohol withdrawal symptoms
As evidenced by: Third DWI
As evidenced by: History of third treatment for chemical dependency

Problem 2: Depression

As evidenced by: Beck Depression Inventory score of 29
As evidenced by: Psychological evaluation
As evidenced by: Patient's two suicide attempts in the past 3 months
As evidenced by: Depressed affect

Problem 3: Acute alcohol withdrawal

As evidenced by: Coarse hand tremors
As evidenced by: Blood pressure 160/100, pulse 104
As evidenced by: Restless pacing; self-report of strong craving
As evidenced by: Profuse sweating; mild visual disturbances

Goals and Objectives

Once you have a problem list, you need to ask yourself what the patient needs to do to restore himself or herself to normal functioning. A person who has a drinking problem needs to stop drinking and must learn the skills necessary to maintain a sober lifestyle. A person who is depressed needs to reestablish normal mood. A person who is dishonest needs to get honest with himself or herself and others. Writing goals, objectives, and interventions in a treatment plan is made much easier for counselors by using *The Addiction Treatment Planner* or *The Addiction Treatment Planner With Disk* (Perkinson & Jongsma, 2001) plus the *TheraScribe 3.0* computer program. These plans conform to the highest standards set by accrediting bodies such as the Joint Commission on Accreditation of Healthcare Organizations (JCAHO, 1988).

How to Develop Goals

A goal is a brief clinical statement of the condition you expect to change in the patient or in the patient's family. You state what you intend to accomplish in general terms. Specify the condition of the patient that will result from treatment. All goals label a set of behaviors that you want to create.

Goals should be more than the elimination of pathology. They should be directed toward the patient learning new and more functional methods of coping. Focus on more than just stopping the old dysfunctional behavior. Concentrate on replacing it with something more effective.

Examples of Developing Goals

Instead of: The patient will stop drinking.
Use: The patient will develop a program of recovery congruent with a sober lifestyle. (The patient is learning something different.)
Use: The patient will learn to cope with stress in an adaptive manner.
Instead of: The patient will stop negative self-talk. (The patient does not learn or use something differently; the patient just avoids something that he or she already knows.)
Use: The patient will develop and use positive self-talk. (Now the patient learns something different that is incompatible with the old behavior.)
Use: The patient will develop a positive self-image. (The patient learns something new and more adaptive.)

The patient or the patient's family must be the subject of each goal. No staff member or staff intervention should be mentioned. Identify one goal and condition at a time. Make each goal one sentence.

Examples of Goals

1. The patient will learn the skills necessary to maintain a sober lifestyle.
2. The patient will learn to express negative feelings to his or her spouse.
3. The patient will develop a positive commitment to sobriety.
4. The patient will develop a healthy diet and begin to gain weight.
5. The patient will learn how to tolerate uncomfortable feelings without using chemicals.
6. The patient will learn to share positive feelings with others.
7. The patient will develop the ability to ask for what he or she wants.
8. The patient will develop the ability to use anger appropriately.
9. The patient will sleep comfortably on a regular basis.
10. The patient will learn healthy communication skills.

How to Develop Objectives

An objective is a specific skill that the patient must acquire to achieve a goal. The objective is what you really set out to accomplish in treatment. An objective is a concrete behavior that you can see, hear, smell, taste, or feel. An objective must be stated so clearly that almost anyone would know when he or she saw it. Goals usually are abstract statements that you cannot actually see happen. You cannot see someone learn or see his or her self-esteem. You can see an individual express 10 positive things about himself or herself. One way of seeing whether you have a goal or an objective is to use the "see Johnny" test developed by Arnold Goldman: "If you can see Johnny do it, then it's an objective; if you can't, then it's a goal." (Goldman [1989] gives lessons on treatment planning in *Accreditation and Certification: For Providers of Psychiatric, Alcoholism, and Drug Abuse Services* [P.O. Box 742, Bala Cynwyd, PA 19004]. Richard Weedman also has done a lot of work in this area. He wrote *Patient Records in Addiction Treatment: Documenting the Quality of Care* [JCAHO, 1992]. A copy can be obtained from the Joint Commission on Accreditation of Healthcare Organizations, One Renaissance Boulevard, Oakbrook Terrace, IL 60181. These materials should be read if you have problems with treatment planning.)

Remember, if you can see it, then it usually is an objective. If you cannot see it, then it usually is a goal.

Can you see the patient read about Step One in the "Big Book" (Alcoholics Anonymous, 1976)? Yes. (objective)

Can you see the patient understand the illness of chemical dependency? No. (goal)

Can you see the patient gain insight? No. (goal)

Can you see the patient improve his or her self-esteem? No. (goal)

Can you see the patient complete the Step One exercise? Yes. (objective)

Can you see the patient keep a daily record of his or her dysfunctional thinking? Yes. (objective)

Can you see the patient share his or her feelings in group? Yes. (objective)

All goals and objectives are aimed at change. Individuals must change how they feel, what they think, and/or what they do. Each goal should have one or more objectives. The best way of developing goals is to ask yourself these questions. How can you know for sure that the patient has achieved the goal? What must the patient say or do to convince you that the treatment goal has been completed?

State the goal aloud, add on the words "as evidenced by" or "as indicated by," and then complete the sentence describing the specific objectives that will tell you that the goal has been reached. Each goal will need at least one objective. Each goal and objective will need a number or a letter that identifies it. Each objective will need a completion date. This is the date by which you expect the objective will be completed. If the patient passes this date without completing the objective, then the treatment plan might have to be modified.

Examples

Goal A: The patient will develop a program of recovery congruent with a sober lifestyle, as evidenced by:

1. The patient will share in contracts group three times when he or she tried to stop drinking but was unable to stay sober.
2. The patient will make a list of the essential skills necessary for recovery.

Goal B: The patient will learn to use assertiveness skills, as indicated by:
1. The patient will discuss the assertive formula and will role-play three situations where he or she acts assertively.
2. The patient will keep an assertiveness log and will share the log with the counselor daily.
3. The patient will practice assertiveness skills in interpersonal group.

Objectives must be measurable. You must be able to count them. Thoughts, feelings, and actions all can be counted by you or the patient. The patient can count his or her thoughts by keeping a daily record of his or her thinking. The patient can count feelings by keeping a feelings log. You can keep a record of every time a patient acts angry around the unit.

To achieve the goal of maintaining a sober lifestyle, an alcoholic might need to develop one or more of the following skills:

1. Verbalize that he or she has a problem, or verbalize an understanding of the problem.
2. Develop and practice new behaviors that are incompatible with the problem. Read the Big Book.
3. Practice the Twelve Steps of AA.
4. Go to meetings.
5. Learn how to cope with uncomfortable feelings.
6. Develop a relapse prevention plan.

Patients who are depressed may need to develop one or more of the following skills:

1. Learn how to say positive things to themselves.
2. Develop recreational programs to add fun to their lives.
3. Grieve and learn how to accept the deaths of loved ones.
4. Get accurate in their thinking.
5. Improve the dysfunctional interpersonal relationships with their spouses.
6. Take antidepressant medication.

How to Develop Interventions

Interventions are what you do to help the patient complete the objective. Interventions also are measurable and objective. There should be at least one intervention for every objective. If the patient does not complete the objective, then new interventions should be added to the plan.

Interventions should be selected by looking at what the patient needs. They may include every treatment available from any member of the multidisciplinary team. They may include any therapy from any staff member such as group therapy, individual therapy, behavior therapy, cognitive therapy, occupational therapy, recreation therapy, or family therapy. The person responsible for the intervention needs to be listed below the intervention so that the staff knows who is responsible.

Examples

Intervention: Assign the patient to write a list of five negative consequences of his or her drug use.

*Responsible professional _____

Intervention: In a conjoint session, have the patient share the connection between drinking and marijuana use.

*Responsible professional _____

Intervention: In group, encourage the patient to share his or her anxious feelings.

Intervention: Have the patient develop a personal recovery plan that includes all of the activities that he or she plans to attend.

*Responsible professional _____

How to Evaluate the Effectiveness of Treatment

In treatment, it is vital to keep score of how you are doing. It is the only way in which you will know whether treatment is working. Feelings, thoughts, and behaviors need to be counted. The staff can count them, or the patient can count them. Thoughts and feelings, being internal states, must be recorded by the patient. Behaviors can be recorded by the patient or by the staff. Patients and the staff will record feelings, thoughts, and behaviors and keep a log of these data. The log of the staff is called the patient record or the chart.

How to Select Goals, Objectives, and Interventions

Goals, objectives, and interventions are infinite. It takes clinical skill to decide exactly what the patient needs to do to establish a stable recovery. Every treatment plan is individualized. Everyone is different, and every treatment plan is different. For the same goal, you may have widely different objectives. You need to ask yourself three questions:

1. What is this patient doing that is maladaptive?
2. What does the patient need to do differently?
3. How can I help the patient behave in a new way?

These questions, if asked carefully, will uncover your goals. Once you have your goals, ask yourself this question: What does the patient need to do to achieve these goals? These are your objectives. Then ask yourself what you can do to help the patient. Each patient will need to do the following three things:

1. Identify that he or she has a problem.
2. Understand exactly what that problem is and how it affects the patient.
3. Apply healthy skills that will reduce or eliminate the problem.

Examples of Goals, Objectives, and Interventions

Problem 1: Pathological relationship with alcohol, as indicated by a blood alcohol level on admission of .32, three DWIs, and family report of daily drinking

Goal A: Develop a program of recovery congruent with a sober lifestyle, as evidenced by:

Objective 1: Norman will identify with his counselor 10 times when alcohol use negatively affected his life by 6-1-00.

Intervention: Assign the patient the homework of making a list of 10 times when alcohol use negatively affected his life.

*Responsible professional _____

Objective 2: Norman will complete his chemical use history and share in group his understanding of his alcohol problem by 6-1-00.

Intervention: Assign the patient to complete a chemical use history exercise and then have him share his answers in group.

*Responsible professional _____

Objective 3: Norman will share his powerlessness and unmanageability with his group by 6-10-00.

Intervention: In a one-to-one counseling session, teach the patient about powerlessness and unmanageability and then have him share what he learned in group.

*Responsible professional _____

Objective 4: Norman will share in group his understanding of how he can use his Higher Power in sobriety by 6-15-00.

Intervention: Clergy will meet with the patient and explain how he can use a Higher Power in recovery.

*Responsible professional _____

Objective 5: Norman will take all medications as prescribed and report side effects to the medical staff.

Intervention: Physician will examine the patient and order medications as indicated while the medical staff monitors for side effects.

*Responsible professional _____

Objective 6: Norman will develop a written relapse prevention plan by 6-25-00.

Intervention: In a counseling session, teach the patient about relapse prevention and help him to develop a written relapse prevention program.

*Responsible professional _____

Objective 7: Norman will discuss his codependency with his wife by 6-30-00.

Intervention: In a conjoint session, help the patient to discuss his codependency with his wife and how this problem relates to substance abuse.

*Responsible professional _____

In developing goals and objectives, the patient must move through the following events:

1. Identify that he or she has a problem.
2. Understand how the problem negatively affects the patient.
3. Learn what he or she is going to change.
4. Practice the change.

Let's take another problem.

Problem 2: Poor impulse control, as indicated by numerous fights, abusiveness to spouse, and self-report that he loses control when angry

Goal A: Learn to use angry feelings appropriately, as evidenced by:

Objective 1: Thomas will discuss with his counselor five times when he used anger inappropriately by 7-2-00.

Intervention: Assign the patient the homework task of listing five times when he used anger inappropriately.

*Responsible professional _____

Objective 2: Thomas will share in group his understanding of what he needs to do differently to cope with his anger by 7-10-00.

Intervention: Have the patient share in group five tools he can use to cope with anger effectively.

*Responsible professional _____

Objective 3: Thomas will visit the staff psychologist to learn and practice stress management techniques by 7-2-00.

Intervention: Staff psychologist will teach the patient stress management techniques such as progressive relaxation, biofeedback, and systematic desensitization.

*Responsible professional _____

Objective 4: Thomas will keep a daily log of his angry feelings and discuss the log with his counselor once a week.

Intervention: Assign the patient to keep a daily log of angry feelings and to use subjective units of distress to rate each situation on a scale from 1 to 100.

*Responsible professional _____

Objective 5: Thomas will share his hurt and his angry feelings in group by 7-21-00.

Intervention: Encourage the patient to share his feelings log in group.

*Responsible professional _____

Objective 6: Thomas will practice sharing his hurt and his anger with his spouse in a conjoint session by 7-30-00.

Intervention: In a conjoint session, have the patient share his hurt and angry feelings with his wife, and make a written contract to separate and contact the sponsor or counselor when angry.

*Responsible professional _____

Objective 7: Thomas will attend a violence group once a week.

Intervention: Refer the patient to an anger management group and make the first appointment with the patient present.

*Responsible professional _____

Samples of a complete biopsychosocial, diagnostic summary, and treatment plan are given in Appendix 7.

Treatment Plan Review

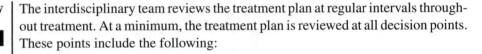

The interdisciplinary team reviews the treatment plan at regular intervals throughout treatment. At a minimum, the treatment plan is reviewed at all decision points. These points include the following:

1. Admission
2. Transfer
3. Discharge
4. Major change in the patient's condition
5. The point of estimated length of treatment

Most facilities have a daily staffing where the patient's progress is briefly discussed and a weekly review where the treatment plan is discussed. It is at these meetings that the treatment plan will be modified. Problems, goals, and objectives will change as the patient's condition changes. Treatment team review is where the staff finds out how the patient is doing in treatment and what changes need to be made.

Documentation

The staff keeps a journal of the patient's progress through treatment. This document is called the patient record, commonly called the chart. The staff keeps progress notes that document what happens to the patient during treatment.

Each progress note needs to be identified with one or more treatment objectives. For example, a progress note on Goal A, Objective 7, would begin with the notation *A(7)*. This helps the staff to keep track of how the patient is doing with each objective.

Progress notes include the following data:

1. The treatment plan
2. All treatment
3. The patient's clinical course
4. Each change in the patient's condition
5. Descriptions of the patient's response to treatment
6. The outcome of all treatment
7. The response of significant others to important events during treatment

How to Write
Progress Notes

Keep your progress notes short. They must include just enough detail to accurately describe what is going on with the patient. For the most part, describe things in behavioral terms. Any entry that includes your opinion or interpretation of events must be supplemented by a description of the actual behavior observed. What did you see, hear, smell, taste, or touch that led you to that conclusion? Describe exactly what the patient did or said. Direct quotations from the patient make an excellent progress note.

The patient's progress in meeting the goals and objectives must be recorded on a regular basis. The efforts of the staff in helping the patient to meet treatment goals and objectives are recorded. The progress notes will be used by the staff to see how the patient is doing. A person who has never met the patient should be able to know the patient's story by reading the patient record. Before you chart, ask yourself this question: If you were a counselor just coming in to take over this case, what would you need to know? It is a good idea to write a short progress note on each patient each day. This is not absolutely essential, but it will keep you thinking about the treatment plan and the patient's progress through the treatment plan on a daily basis.

Examples of Progress Notes

6-12-00 (10:30 a.m.)

B(3): Patty discussed her denial exercise in group. She verbalized an understanding of how denial had adversely affected her, stating, "I can't believe how dishonest I was to myself. I really didn't think I had a problem even after all that trouble. I lied to Andy too, about everything." The patient was able to see how denial was a lie to herself and to others. After the session, the patient was able to verbalize her need to get honest with herself and others. "I've been lying about everything. It's about time I got honest with myself."

6-14-00 (3:15 p.m.)

A(1): Patty was tearful in an individual session. She mourned the loss of her love relationship with her past partner. The group helped her to see how destructive the relationship had been for her. The treatment peers reinforced that Patty was worth being treated better than her partner was treating her. Patty expressed that she is extremely angry at her mother. "I hate her. She never spent any time with me. She only wanted me as a slave. She wanted a housekeeper, not me." It seemed to give Patty some relief to hear other patients express that they had similar feelings about their mothers. "I thought I was the only one who felt like that," Patty stated.

6-15-00 (11:00 a.m.)

C(2): Patty's facial expression is sad. She has been isolating herself. She didn't eat breakfast. She was seen crying alone in her room. I went in, and she was able to express her feelings. "I'm so ashamed of myself. I'll never be able to live this down." Patty expressed that she was feeling guilty about sharing with group her anger at her mother. I reassured Patty and told her to bring up her feelings in group this afternoon.

Formal Treatment Plan Review

Once a week, the staff will do a formal treatment team review. This requires a more detailed look at how the patient is doing in each problem area. The staff members present must be identified along with their credentials.

6-16-00 (11:45 a.m.)

Treatment plan review: Present, Dr. Roberts, M.D.; M. Smith, CCDC Level II; T. Anderson, R.N.; F. Mark, CCDC Level I; Dr. Thomas; M. Tobas, Ph.D.; E. Talbot, R.N.; A. Stein, L.P.N. The staff feels that Patty is adjusting well to treatment. She is more talkative and seems to feel more comfortable. She has made some friends with several treatment peers including her roommate. Her mother came to see her on Sunday, and Patty reported that this visit went well.

Problem 1: Patty continues on her Valium come-down schedule. She has reported only mild withdrawal symptoms. She is sleeping well. She continues to be mildly restless. She was encouraged to increase her level of exercise to 20 minutes daily.

Problem 2: Patty has completed her chemical use history and Step One exercise. She shared in interpersonal group her powerlessness and unmanageability. She was open in group, and she verbalized that she has accepted her disease of chemical dependency. She was somewhat more reluctant to accept her problem with Valium, but the group did a good job of explaining cross-tolerance. The patient should complete the cross-tolerance exercise and report her findings to the group.

Problem 3: The patient continues to take her iron supplement. Her hemoglobin is within normal limits.

Problem 4: The patient is over her cold. Problem 4 is completed.

Problem 5: The patient has written a letter to her mother and father describing how she felt about her childhood. The patient shared her letter in group, and she was surprised to find out that many of the other patients had similar experiences. The patient stated that she is feeling more comfortable sharing in group, and she appears to be gaining confidence in herself. Patty met with her counselor, and the counselor encouraged Patty to accept her new AA/NA group as the healthy family that she never had. Patty expressed hope in becoming involved with this healthy family.

Problem 6: Patty is working on the relationship skills exercise. She has been practicing asking for what she wants. It is still very difficult for her to share some of her feelings, particularly her anger, in group. When she shares her anger, she tends to feel guilty.

Problem 7: Patty completed the honesty exercise and the chemical use history that opened her eyes to how dishonest she has been. Patty made a contract with her group to be honest and asked the patients to confront her if they felt that she was being dishonest. Patty is keeping a daily log of her lies and when she is tempted to lie. She has been able to identify many lies she was telling in her life and is able to verbalize her understanding of how her lies keep her isolated from others.

Problem 8: Patty is working on the assertiveness skills exercise. She is practicing the assertive formula. She tends to feel guilty when she says no, but she is getting better at it. She will say no to someone five times a day for 3 days and keep a log of how she feels about each situation.

CHAPTER FOUR | Individual Treatment

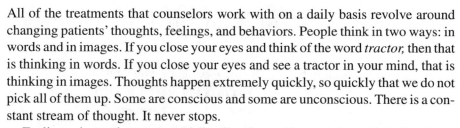

All of the treatments that counselors work with on a daily basis revolve around changing patients' thoughts, feelings, and behaviors. People think in two ways: in words and in images. If you close your eyes and think of the word *tractor,* then that is thinking in words. If you close your eyes and see a tractor in your mind, that is thinking in images. Thoughts happen extremely quickly, so quickly that we do not pick all of them up. Some are conscious and some are unconscious. There is a constant stream of thought. It never stops.

Feelings give us the energy and direction for problem solving. All feelings have a specific movement attached to them. The feeling of fear gives us the energy and direction to run away from an offending stimulus. The feeling of sadness gives us the energy and direction to recover a lost object. Good problem solving necessitates using feelings appropriately.

Behavior is movement. Anytime a person moves, he or she is exhibiting behavior. Speech is movement. Drinking is movement. Going to AA meetings is movement. These all are behaviors. Behaviors are the easiest things to see, count, and record. Whenever possible, conduct your treatment using the patient's behavior as your guide. Behavior will tell you whether your treatment is working.

The Therapeutic Alliance

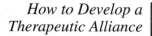

All individual treatment will revolve around the relationship that you have with your patients. This is called the therapeutic alliance. If the patients like and trust you, then they will listen to you and will want to change to please you.

How to Develop a Therapeutic Alliance

The therapeutic alliance should be growing and improving from the first moment you meet your patients. You need to be constantly encouraging and supportive. You should give the patients the feeling that you are going to walk with them through treatment. This relationship must be based on love and trust. The patients are afraid to tell anyone the truth. The patients probably never have told anyone the whole truth. You are going to be different. You are going to be confidential and consistently act in the patients' interest. You are going to show the patients unconditional positive regard. No matter what the patients do, you are going to be there for them when they need you. You are not always going to tell the patients what they want to hear; that would not be loving. You are going to tell the patients the truth, and you are going to encourage the patients to see the truth in themselves. You are going to expect the patients to improve, and you are going to act like it. You are going to encourage the patients to see the fact that they can recover if they work at a program of recovery. You believe that the patients have the resources necessary, or else you would not have accepted them as your patients. You believe that the patients can do it.

Patients will have great doubts about themselves. They have tried to lick their addictions many times before and always have failed. The patients hope that they can recover but do not have much self-confidence. Self-efficacy is where patients learn that they can do it. This confidence is carefully built over the weeks of treatment by constantly reinforcing the patients when they complete some small part of the program. This may be as little as coming to breakfast on time or as big as confronting their parents with their real feelings.

The solid basis of a good therapeutic alliance is to constantly be reinforcing. As the counselor, you look for good behavior from the patients. When you see the patients doing something right, you point it out and praise the patients for it.

How to Be Reinforcing

"Good job. I knew you could do it."

"You're doing great. I'm proud of you."

"That took great courage."

"This is going to pay off for you."

"Keep coming. You can do it."

These statements reinforce patients. You are going to support the patients warmly as often as you can. Touch the patients if you believe that this is a reinforcer, but do not force yourself on anyone. Be sensitive to the patients' needs. Constantly ask yourself this question: If you were in this patient's situation, how would you want to be treated? Then treat the patient that way.

Make good eye contact when you give praise or make a point. Patients have learned that they cannot trust anyone. The patients do not even trust themselves. You are going to prove to the patients, with your actions, that they can trust you.

Be gentle. Do not hammer your points home aggressively. That wounds the therapeutic alliance. Let the power of the truth work for you. A whisper of truth is much more powerful than an angry confrontation. Your patients are injured. They do not need to be attacked. They need to heal in an atmosphere of love and trust.

Aid patients in moving toward greater self-understanding. Help the patients to identify exactly how they have kept themselves isolated, and teach them new ways of reaching out to others. The patients have been hiding from themselves for a long time. They have been feeling lost and alone. They need to come out from the darkness created by the disease and into the light of the truth.

How to Use Empathy Empathy is understanding how someone feels from his or her frame of reference. Whenever you put yourself in someone else's position, you are practicing empathy. It often is helpful to recognize the feelings or thoughts of the patients that stimulate something from your own experience. You do not have to experience the same intensity of feelings that grips the patients, but you need to relate to the feelings and understand them. Feel yourself walking in the patients' shoes. What if this was happening to you? How would you feel? What would you be thinking? What would you need? What would you want? Your empathic responses will not always be correct—you can misperceive the patients—but they will improve over time. A good test of empathy is that your comments should deepen the patients' narrative flow (Havens, 1978). Empathic accuracy can be further determined by reflecting the patients' feelings. Repeat to the patients your understanding of what they have just said. The patients usually will clarify any misunderstanding. Their words and behavior should continually deepen your understanding of the patients (Bettet & Maloney, 1991).

Be sensitive to your own feelings. How are the patients affecting you? Are some of your own issues being triggered? How can this give you insight into yourself and the patients?

Transference and Countertransference

■

Transference is when patients respond to you with the same feelings, thoughts, and behaviors that they developed for other people in their lives. Countertransference is when you respond to patients in the same way that you responded to other people. We all have internal maps about how the world and people function. We trust these maps to help us navigate. We learned these maps from our primary caregivers and from significant others in our lives. If you had a father who was demanding, then you learned that people, particularly men, are demanding. If you had a mother who you could not trust, then you learned that people, particularly women, are not trustworthy. These maps profoundly affect therapy. Sometimes they are accurate, and sometimes they are inaccurate. You have to constantly check your maps, as well as the patients' maps, for accuracy.

There are counselors who are insensitive to themselves and others. These counselors can do great damage to their patients. They are impatient and demand immediate self-disclosure before their patients are ready. They are not sensitive enough to know that the patients are not ready to share. Patients should only be given the opportunity to share. They should never be forced or manipulated. The best intervention for someone who is keeping a secret is to tell that person that he or she can keep the secret; that is a person's right. An individual does not have to share everything with everyone, but there is a consequence for keeping secrets. If you cut someone off from the truth, then you cut yourself off from feeling close to that person. The formula is this: The more you can share, the closer you can get, and the closer you can get, the more you can share. Intimacy can occur only in an atmosphere of truth. It is impossible to love without truth.

Some of the keys to developing a positive therapeutic alliance are a forward-leaning posture, good eye contact, a reinforcing facial expression, good listening skills, unconditional positive regard, and the skill of engaging the patients on a feeling level. It helps if you can engage the patients using your own feelings. This increases the feeling of intimacy.

Examples of
Empathic Statements

"Bob, you scare me. I have to wonder how your wife and kids must feel when you raise your voice like that."
"I feel very close to you right now."
"I'm confused. What do you want from me right now?"
"That makes me feel really sad. I'm sorry that happened to you."
"I can feel that you're angry. What happened?"
"Ralph, I'm scared for you."

How to Be Confrontive

A good confrontation is where one individual states how another person is making him or her feel. The formula is as follows:

1. I think _____. (Describe the patient's behavior.) "That's the third time that you have said that nothing is wrong."
2. I feel _____. (Tell the patient how the behavior makes you feel.) "I feel a bit frustrated."
3. I want _____. (Describe exactly what you want the patient to do.) "I want you to describe how you are feeling."

These actions must be described in behavioral terms. Exactly what did the person do to make you have a certain feeling?

"I hear you deny you've been drinking. I feel frustrated. I want you to look at what's really been happening in your life. Didn't you just get your third DWI?"
"I feel scared when I hear you say that you want to hurt yourself. What are your alternatives?"
"When I see you sit there with that blank look on your face, I feel sad. You seem to want to cry. Can you tell me what you are thinking?"

A positive therapeutic alliance fosters mutual independence. It is an intense investment in energy. There is a lack of defensiveness and a sense of mutual positive regard. You develop similar modes of communication. You are on the same wavelength. You constantly affirm the patient's worth as an individual.

Behavior Therapy

In treatment, counselors concentrate on change. Patients have maladaptive feelings, thoughts, and behaviors that keep them from functioning normally. The patients are unable to reach their full potential in life because of something they are doing wrong. When there is something wrong with their actions, behavior therapy is used. All behavior is movement. Changing how patients move will help them to function better. Patients who always lash out in physical violence when they are mad are in for a world of hurt. They must understand how to do something different when they are mad. They must practice this new behavior until it becomes automatic.

How Patients Learn

To understand all types of therapy, you need to know how the brain works. The brain is like a jungle. Imagine, for a moment, that you have crash-landed an airplane in the jungle. There are thick branches and vines everywhere. All you see is thick vegetation. As you recover from the crash, you get thirsty. You hear a creek running to the right of the nose of the plane. You look for the easiest way of getting to the creek, but you only see jungle. The jungle is the same thickness in all directions. Finally, your thirst overcomes your fear, and you strike out for the creek. When you do, you make a pathway. It is not much, and it will not last long, but it is there. By passing through the jungle once, you have made a pathway of least resistance. Naturally, on the way back, you take that pathway again. It is the easiest way. As you go through again and again, you make more of a pathway until in time you have a nice smooth trail. Every time you go to the creek, you take the easiest way. That is exactly how the brain works, and that is how learning takes place.

Habits Humans are creatures of habit. Habits are learned behaviors. They are easy pathways in the brain. Habits must be practiced to remain an active part of the person's behavior. Suppose that someone has a drinking problem. This is a habit. The person has this wide pathway in the brain. We could call this the drinking pathway. When this person feels uncomfortable, he or she takes a drink. The person has been doing this for years. We need to teach this person another way of relaxing. The first time the person takes the new way in the brain, it is going to be difficult. Just like the jungle, there are thick vines and branches in the way, it hurts, and all the time the person has this other way tempting him or her back to drinking. The old pathway is better established. As the counselor, you encourage the patient to try something new. You support the patient, you reward the patient, and finally he or she tries the new way. It is not easy, but the patient does it. Now you encourage the patient to try it again and again. The patient begins to build a new pathway in the brain, and as he or she does, the old pathway gradually begins to grow over. It never will grow over completely. The patient may think about drinking. This will be tempting sometimes, but the more the patient takes the new pathway, the more it becomes the pathway of least resistance. Soon it will be the easiest way, and the patient will take the new way automatically.

You can see from this analogy that every time you go one way in the brain, it is important. Each time you go through the brain the same way, you are making a better and more long-lasting pathway.

Changing a Habit People drink for a reason. Let's say that they drink when they feel tense. Every time people feel tense, they reach for a drink. Once people come into treatment, they decide that they cannot drink anymore, but they still have times when they feel tense. They need to learn a new way of dealing with that tension. They need to learn a new skill. They may learn that every time they feel tense, they talk about it, they exercise, or they go to an AA meeting. The more patients practice the new behavior, the more comfortable and habitual it becomes. Soon the new behavior will become second nature. Every time the patients feel tense, they use the new skill.

What Is a Reinforcement? New behavior is learned by encouraging patients to try something new and then reinforcing them for the new behavior. Reinforcement increases the frequency of a behavior. It increases the chances that the new behavior will happen again. A reinforcer does one of two things for the patients:

1. It gives the patients something positive.
2. It allows the patients to escape from something negative.

Behavior does not exist, nor does it continue to exist, without reinforcement. If you take the reward away, then the behavior will vanish. It will extinguish.

What Is a Punishment? Punishment decreases the frequency of a behavior. It works in two ways:

1. It introduces something negative.
2. It removes something positive.

The best punishment for someone is to allow that person to suffer the natural consequence of his or her behavior. For example, someone who does a poor job of completing a step exercise has to do it over again. This usually is punishment enough. There are some bad things about punishment, so you need to use it sparingly. Punishment cannot teach someone a new behavior. It can only teach them to avoid an old behavior. Punishment takes the patient's mind off of what he or she did and puts it on to what you are doing. The patient can miss the point. Treatment centers need to be set up with a clear consequence for maladaptive behavior. The rules have to be carefully spelled out, and the consequence for breaking the rules must be specified.

The Behavior Chain

■

To understand people and behavior therapy, you need to understand the behavior chain. At every point along the chain, patients can change or can do something differently. Treatment is learning what to do and when to do it. These are the tools of recovery.

The first event in the chain is the *trigger*. This is the stimulus or event that triggers a patient's response. After the trigger comes *thinking*. Here the person evaluates what the stimulus means. Much of this thinking is so fast that it is not consciously experienced. The thoughts generate *feelings*. The feelings give energy and direction for action or *behavior*. All behavior has a positive or negative *consequence*. The behavior chain looks like this:

Trigger → Thinking → Feeling → Behavior → Consequence.

Let's take an example. Larry is addicted to cocaine. He is riding down the street and hears a particular song on the radio (trigger). He begins thinking about the "good old days" when he enjoyed using cocaine (thinking). This thinking leads him to crave cocaine (feeling). He decides to ride over to a drug dealer's house just to see how his "old friend" is doing (behavior). Larry uses cocaine (consequence).

Now let's plug in some tools of recovery. Larry is riding down the street and hears a particular song on the radio. He recognizes this song as one of his triggers. He tells himself that he no longer has the option of using cocaine (new thinking). He thinks about the misery that cocaine caused him (new thinking). He experiences some craving, so he decides to give his sponsor a call (new behavior). He goes to a meeting with his sponsor (new behavior). He does not use cocaine (new consequence).

The Importance of Reinforcement Every time you encourage people or pay attention to them, you reinforce them. You must try to reward patients only when they act in the way that you want them to act. If possible, you must ignore, or give a negative consequence for, all maladaptive behavior. Behavior therapy is going on constantly in treatment. You need to look for positive things to reinforce. Reward your patients as often as you can. See yourself as someone who is constantly looking for behavior to reinforce.

Examples of
Reinforcing Statements

"I liked what you did in group today."
"Thank you for joining in this afternoon."
"You look better after you exercise."
"You told the truth. That's great!"
"I saw you working on your assignments this afternoon. Good going."

How to Use Punishment | When maladaptive behavior is displayed, the first thing you need to do is share your feelings. Remember the formula. I feel _____ when you _____. I would prefer it if _____. This tells the patient how you are feeling, what the patient is doing that is causing you to have that feeling, and what you want the patient to do differently.

"Tom, I feel frightened when you raise your voice. I would prefer it if you speak more quietly."

If the maladaptive behavior continues, then warn the patient of an impending consequence.

"Tom, if you don't lower your voice, I'm going to leave the room."

If the behavior continues, then administer the consequence: Leave the room. Let's go through another example. Tim, an adolescent patient, begins to throw food.

"Tim, it makes me angry when you throw food. I would prefer it if you would eat normally."

Tim keeps throwing the food. He laughs with the other adolescents.

"Tim, if you don't stop throwing food, you will be restricted to your room for 1 hour."

Tim defiantly throws food again.

"Go to your room. You are restricted to your room for 1 hour."

When a Patient Breaks a Rule | If a rule is broken, then a consequence must be given. To let the behavior slide tells the patient that rules do not count. It is a common early mistake for counselors to want to avoid giving consequences. They do not want to hurt patients' feelings, and they want to be seen as the patients' friends. If you will examine this desire carefully, you will see how wrong it is. A good counselor does not want to teach people to do bad things. You do not want to let patients continue their maladaptive behavior. That would be helping them to stay sick.

Let's go through a few behavioral objectives. Remember that in behavior therapy you want to teach the patient to do something differently.

Objective 1: The patient will go to five treatment peers and share the feelings exercise with them. (This exercise comes with a built-in reward because sharing feelings brings people closer together. As the patient shares his or her feelings, the patient draws closer to others. This is a powerful reinforcement.)

Objective 2: The patient will list 10 times when he lost his temper with his children. He will discuss each situation with his counselor. He will verbalize other means of dealing with his anger (by 9-20-91). (In this objective, the patient also feels closer as he or she shares the truth. You also would want to reinforce the patient for being honest and ask the patient how he or she feels after the disclosure.)

Objective 3: The patient will keep a feelings log for the next 5 days (completed by 9-15-91). (In a feelings log, the patient charts his or her feelings. This allows the patient to keep up on his or her improvement. This is a powerful reinforcement.)

Objective 4: The patient will give a 20-minute speech to the group on his or her powerlessness and unmanageability (by 9-25-91). (Giving the group a talk is a good way of having the patient learn new material. If the patient is going to teach something to others, then the patient must first learn it himself or herself.)

Objective 5: The patient will meet with his or her counselor and spouse in five conjoint sessions before the end of treatment. (During each session, you would want to reinforce each person for building better communication skills. When someone compromises, reinforce him or her.)

Objective 6: The patient will ask two treatment peers a day for help with his or her program. The patient will record each situation and share weekly with his or her counselor. (A patient who is reluctant to ask for help needs practice in doing so. The illness tells the patient that he or she is not worth helping and that other people do not want to help the patient. Nothing works better to dispel these inaccurate beliefs than to actually have people help the patient.)

Objective 7: The patient will give three treatment peers a compliment each day. The patient will keep a log of each situation and discuss with his or her counselor (by 9-25-91). (By having a patient say reinforcing things to others, you set up a natural reinforcing situation. You need to talk with the patient about how the other people responded.)

Objective 8: The patient will keep an anger log and share weekly with his or her counselor (by 9-30-91). (Keeping an anger log will make the patient more aware of his or her anger. If the patient is more aware, then he or she can catch the anger earlier and use a specific skill to deal with the feeling. For example, every time the patient gets angry, he or she could back away from the situation until the patient can get accurate in his or her thinking. Then the patient can do something different such as talking about his or her anger.)

Why We Concentrate on Behavior Therapy

The reason why behavior therapy is so good is that you can see it happen. The new behavior either occurs or does not occur. The more you reinforce a new behavior, the quicker it develops into a habit. It is important to reinforce the behavior as quickly as you can after it occurs. Practice is important. The more a patient practices a behavior, the more of a habit it will become. You can role-play certain situations to solidify and practice the new skills. We ask for progress, not perfection. Most old behaviors fall away slowly. It will be months before the triggers stop creating old responses.

Do not drink or use drugs, read the "Big Book" (Alcoholic Anonymous, 1976), go to meetings, seek a Higher Power, call your sponsor, share how you feel, ask for what you want, be loving, tell the truth—all of these are essential parts of the program. They all can be placed in behavioral terms. They can be monitored. They can be changed and counted as they change. If you monitor behavior, then you will know exactly how your patients are doing in treatment.

Cognitive Therapy

Another essential element in chemical dependency treatment is how people think. Thoughts precede feelings, and feelings initiate action. Patients have to think about drinking before they drink. People think in words or in images. If I were to ask you to close your eyes and think about the word *wagon,* you could do that. If I were to ask you to close your eyes and see a wagon, you could close your eyes and see some sort of an image of a wagon. That is thinking in imagery.

How Chemically Dependent People Think

Patients who are chemically dependent do not think accurately. They have separated themselves from reality. They are distorting the truth to protect themselves. Most patients come into treatment in some form of denial.

"I don't think I have a drinking problem."
"I never had any problems with marijuana."
"Everybody I know drinks as much as I do."
"My husband is overly sensitive. His dad was a heavy drinker."
"Anybody can get a DWI."
"I may have an alcohol problem, but I'm not an alcoholic."

The patient who said these things had a severe drug problem. All of these thoughts were inaccurate. She was addicted to alcohol and cannabis. She was drinking and using cannabis all day every day.

The psychology of chemical dependency demands repressing the truth from consciousness. Repression is a mental process where we keep the facts hidden from ourselves. This information is kept secret to protect us from the painful reality of our situation. If drug addicts will see the whole truth, then they will see their addictions. The addicts will see that they are dying from chemical dependency. This truth creates tremendous fear. The addicted individuals protect themselves from experiencing this fear by not seeing reality. An addict might have gotten an eighth DWI but still does not think that he or she has a problem. The addict might see only half-truths. The addict might see that the police are out to get him or her or that the addict's spouse is overreacting. The addict does not see the whole truth or the seriousness of the addiction.

Defense Mechanisms   The illness of chemical dependency cannot operate without lies. Addicts must lie to themselves until they believe the lies or else the illness cannot continue. All of the lies are inaccurate ways of thinking. Cognitive therapy corrects the thoughts and gets the patients accurate. Cognitive therapy is a fearless search for truth.

Minimization distorts reality and makes it smaller than it actually is. Minimizing says, "It's not so bad." When an alcoholic pours whiskey, he or she does not use a shot glass; the alcoholic pours. If we take that poured drink and measure how many shots are in it, we might find four or five shots in the glass. To the alcoholic, this is *one* drink. But it is not one drink; it is five drinks. "I'm only having three," the alcoholic says innocently to himself or herself. "What's the problem?"

Rationalization is a good excuse for drinking or using drugs. Probably the most common excuse is that "I had a hard day." Therefore, for the addict, "Anyone who has had a hard day needs to relax." Therefore, "I need a few."

Patients can rationalize almost anything. Rationalization also can be called blaming.

"The police were out to get me."
"My wife doesn't understand me. That's why I drink."
"I've been having financial problems."
"I can't sleep if I don't drink."
"My boss really gets on my nerves. I need a drink."

The essential element here is that these patients are fooling themselves. They really believe that their behavior is not their fault. Something else is to blame. In treatment, these patients need to accept the responsibility for their own behavior. Being an adult means making all of your own decisions and living with the consequences.

Denial is the most common defense in chemical dependency. It is primitive and distorts reality more than does any other defense mechanism. In denial, patients refuse to experience the full impact of reality. Suppose that you are walking downtown on a hot summer day. Along the sidewalk, people are standing holding buckets of ice water. As you walk past, they throw the ice water in your face. You see the water and you see the people, but you do not experience the full shock of the water. Denial is a dissociated unreal world. A drug addict might be losing his or her spouse, children, job, friends, money, and freedom, but the addict does not experience the full impact of this reality. The addict does not see what everyone is worried about.

All patients who come into treatment are in some form of denial. They are not seeing what is right in front of their faces. It is incredible how strong denial can be. Patients can be at death's door and still believe that they are fine.

Applying Cognitive Therapy   Cognitive therapy is correcting the lies that patients have been telling themselves. It is the process of getting the thinking accurate. As the counselor, you help the patients to see the truth. First the patients need to see the lies in operation. Have a patient do the following exercise in your office or in group.

Place a chair in the center of the room and explain to the patient that he or she has an internal dialogue going on all of the time. The dialogue is between the illness and the healthy side of the patient. The illness wants to use alcohol or drugs. The healthy side wants to be healthy and happy. Have the patient sit in one chair and just be the illness. Have the illness side talk the healthy side into drinking or using drugs. It will be helpful if you model the exercise first. The dialogue will go something like this:

> "John, you've had a pretty hard day. Nobody is going to know if you have just a couple of beers. Your wife is not going to find out. Why don't you stop by the bar for just a couple? It would taste pretty good. You can handle a couple of beers. You can stop whenever you want to. Remember all the good times we had drinking. Remember the women. You can talk to them better if you've had a couple of beers. You don't have to call your wife. She won't know. You can hide it. It won't matter."

As the patient talks, you can see all of the lies he is telling himself:

1. "I've had a hard day."
2. "Nobody is going to know."
3. "Just a couple."
4. "You can handle it."
5. "You can stop."
6. "Remember all the good times."
7. "Remember the women. They liked you better when you were drunk."
8. "You can talk to women better when you've had a couple of beers."
9. "You don't have to call your wife."
10. "She won't know."
11. "You can hide it."
12. "It won't matter."

Now you challenge each of the patient's inaccurate statements.

"Do you think that having a hard day is worth risking your life for?"
"When is the last time you went in a bar and just had a couple of beers?"
"Haven't you proven to yourself that you can't stop? If you could stop, what are you doing in here?"
"How are you going to feel if you start hiding from your wife again?"

Again and again, patients' inaccurate thoughts have to be challenged. In treatment and in recovery, the patients must be committed to reality. They have to live in reality and solve problems using the whole truth.

Patients are inaccurate not only about their drugs but also about their self-images. They might call themselves stupid, inadequate, or ugly. They might have an exaggerated sense of their own importance. The best way of correcting these inaccurate thoughts is in group, but individual therapy also is valuable. Someone who thinks that he or she is worthless, helpless, or hopeless needs to see what is real. Many patients will argue with you about these things. The inaccurate thoughts seem to have a life of their own.

Patient: I can't live without Bob. I can't.

Counselor: You can't? What would happen to you if you were shipwrecked on an island in the South Pacific? There was no one on this island but you. You have plenty of food and water, but you're all alone.

Patient: Oh, I'd be okay.

Counselor: But Bob wouldn't be there. Wouldn't you die?

Patient: That's different. That's a different situation.

Counselor: No, it's not. You just said you *can't* live without Bob. Now you tell me you could live without anyone.

Patient: Well, I don't *want* to live without him.

Counselor: That's better, but that's not quite accurate either. Would you kill yourself if you didn't have Bob in your life? Is it really impossible to live without Bob?

Patient: No, it's possible to live without Bob, but I love Bob. I want Bob in my life.

Counselor: Good, that's accurate. You want Bob in your life. You don't need him in your life for survival. Seeing the relationship more accurately will give you more accurate feelings. If you need Bob for your survival and Bob leaves you, then you will die. That's pretty scary. It's too scary, and it's not accurate.

Automatic Thoughts

Thinking occurs extremely quickly. There is a never-ending stream of conscious and unconscious thought flowing though a person's mind. Most of this thought is not registered on the screen of consciousness. The more a behavior or thought process is practiced, the more unconscious and automatic it becomes. You do not have to think consciously of each of the hundreds of little decisions you make while driving a car. You make most of these decisions unconsciously out of habit—how to turn the wheel, when to put on the brake, when to speed up a little bit. These decisions all are made without conscious thought.

Beck, Rush, Shaw, and Emery (1979) found out that many people who were depressed were having certain thoughts that were leading them to feel depressed. It was the private way in which these individuals were interpreting events that were critical to their uncomfortable feelings. They were thinking inaccurate things that were involuntary, persistent, and plausible and that often contained a theme of loss. It was this thinking that was keeping them down. Most of these thoughts occurred automatically, totally out of the patients' awareness. The important thing to note here is that these thoughts profoundly affect feelings and behavior.

Beck (1967, 1972, 1976) reported that three elements were essential to the psychopathology of depression: the cognitive triad, silent assumptions, and logical errors.

The *cognitive triad* consists of the negative views of patients about themselves, their world, and their future. In general, depressives view themselves, their world, and their future as lacking something that is a prerequisite for happiness. For example, they may view themselves as inadequate, incompetent, and unworthy. They may view their environment as demanding and unsupportive. They may view the future as hopeless, frightening, and full of inevitable pain.

Silent assumptions are unarticulated rules that influence depressives' feelings, thinking, and behavior. For example, a patient may believe one or more of the following:

"I will only be happy if I'm good looking, intelligent, or wealthy."
"When I make a mistake, people think less of me."
"It is weak to ask for help."
"I have to please everyone all of the time."

These stable beliefs develop from early experience and influence the individual's responses to events. They give rise to automatic thoughts.

Logical errors are the inaccurate conclusions that patients draw from negative thinking. They can overgeneralize, drawing conclusions about their ability, performance, and worth from one incident.

"He doesn't love me, so I am unlovable."

Logical errors can magnify or minimize by exaggerating or diminishing the importance of an event.

"The class laughed. Everyone thinks I'm a fool."
"I got all A's this quarter, but 2 years ago I got a C."
"I can't do college work like other people."

How to Correct Inaccurate Thoughts	Let's go through an example of how to correct automatic thoughts. The first time that patients hear about interpersonal group, they usually feel frightened. The patients might not stop and think, "Why are we afraid?" They just feel scared. Feeling like this, the patients might try to do something to prevent themselves from going to group. They might fake that they are sick or tired.
Uncover the Thoughts and Feelings	Using cognitive therapy, you first would ask patients how they were feeling. Write each feeling down. Then ask, "What were you thinking between the time that you heard about interpersonal group and the feeling you felt? What thoughts came to mind?" The patients might be able to respond here, or you might have to suggest some thoughts. In cognitive therapy, you will have to constantly suggest to the patients thoughts that they could have been having. Do not stop until you have brought out a short list of thoughts such as the following:

"The people in group won't understand me."
"I'll make a fool of myself."
"This is going to be humiliating."
"They are going to put me on the hot seat."
"They are going to make me talk."

Pull on patients' automatic thoughts. Ask and then make suggestions. Remember, these are thoughts that the patients do not try to have. They are unconscious and happen automatically. Once you see the powerful negative message that these thoughts give the patients, you will understand why they feel afraid.

Score the
Inaccurate Feelings
It will help to have patients score each feeling on a scale of 1 (*as little as possible*) to 100 (*as much as possible*). Let's say that a patient felt fear at 90. Ask whether the patient was feeling any other feelings as well, and ask the patient to score each of these. Our patient also was feeling angry at a score of 50. The patient was angry because the group was going to try to "make me talk." The patient also was feeling sad at a score of 70 because "this is going to be humiliating. I'm going to make a fool out of myself. These people won't understand me." If we add up all of the negative feelings, the patient was feeling 210 units of distress.

Getting the
Thoughts Accurate
Now we help the patient to challenge his or her automatic thinking. We know that many of these thoughts are inaccurate.

> *Counselor:* Your thought was, These people won't understand me. What do you think is accurate?
>
> *Patient:* Well, they have the same problem as I do. They should be able to understand me. At least they'll try to.
>
> *Counselor:* How about, I'm going to make a fool out of myself.
>
> *Patient:* I don't really think I'm going to make a fool out of myself. It could be a little embarrassing.
>
> *Counselor:* Yeah, you could do something a little embarrassing. What do you think would happen if you did?
>
> *Patient:* I don't know.
>
> *Counselor:* Do you think the other patients might understand and be sympathetic?
>
> *Patient:* I think they would try to understand.
>
> *Counselor:* So, even if you did do something a little embarrassing, it wouldn't be the end of the world.
>
> *Patient:* No.
>
> *Counselor:* Now what about, "This is going to be humiliating." Do you think the group is going to humiliate you?
>
> *Patient:* No, I don't. I've met a few of the patients already, and they seem very nice. I do feel humiliated, though, just being here . . . you know, in treatment.
>
> *Counselor:* Do you think the other group members could relate to that?
>
> *Patient:* Sure.
>
> *Counselor:* How about, "They're going to put me on the hot seat."
>
> *Patient:* Well, they might. I've heard about these groups where they hound you, and attack you, until you spill your guts.
>
> *Counselor:* Let me assure you that the staff here doesn't work like that. We don't have a hot seat. We give people the opportunity to talk. If they don't want to talk, that's fine. What if it was one of those heavy confrontational groups. Could they make you talk if you didn't want to?
>
> *Patient:* Probably not.
>
> *Counselor:* So what's accurate here?
>
> *Patient:* I can talk if I want to. I really want to talk. I want to get better.

Counselor: Good. Let's go back and score your feelings again using accurate thoughts. You hear that there is an interpersonal group at 10 o'clock. You think, "These people are nice. They have the same illness as I do. They should be able to understand me. I want to talk and get better."

Scoring the Accurate Feelings

Counselor: Now, thinking accurately, how much fear do you feel?
Patient: About 35, I guess.
Counselor: How much anger?
Patient: None.
Counselor: How much sadness?
Patient: 40.

Compare Inaccurate and Accurate Thoughts and Feelings

Counselor: When you were thinking automatically, you were feeling 210 units of distress, but when you get accurate, your pain dropped to 75. That's a drop of 135 points.
Patient: Amazing.
Counselor: Yes, and these thoughts go on all the time. You automatically think the worst, so you feel bad. There is some real reason to feel uncomfortable—bad things could really happen—but if you get accurate, you can live in reality. You can feel the real world. You have been living and feeling in a world created by your distorted thoughts.

Uncovering the Themes

As patients keep track of their negative thoughts, you will see that their thinking ends up with certain themes. These are stable attitudes or beliefs that develop over time. They usually can be traced to early childhood experiences. These beliefs are very tenacious. A patient who believes that "I don't get along with people" might base that belief on something that happened to him or her as a small child. The inaccurate thinking keeps the person from seeing reality. Themes are based on evidence that patients have collected over a number of years. The patients act on these beliefs as if they were absolute facts. The patients no longer challenge them. The automatic thoughts are used as evidence from which these inaccurate conclusions are drawn. You must help the patients to uncover these distorted attitudes and beliefs. They are not accurate, and they need to be corrected.

Patients might believe that they are unlovable. The patients are convinced inside of their own thinking that this is a fact—"I am unlovable." These patients will begin to build evidence from their experience that will support this belief. The patients will begin to tell themselves things such as they are unlovable for various reasons—"I'm ugly," "I'm stupid," or "I'm bad." None of these things is true, but the patients believe that all are true. Naturally, this leads to uncomfortable feelings. Patients who think that they are unlovable feel depressed and lonely.

In cognitive therapy, your job is to get patients thinking accurate. Most of the patients' thinking is automatic, and you will have to train the patients to keep track of their thoughts. David Burns's book, *Feeling Good: The New Mood Therapy,* is an excellent overview of the various forms of cognitive therapy (Burns, 1980). Reading this is a good way of beginning to think in cognitive terms. In time, you will pick up patients' inaccurate thinking quickly. You rarely will want inaccurate thinking to pass by unnoticed. Stop patients at every opportunity and correct them.

Patient: I've messed my whole life.

Counselor: Your whole life?

Patient: Yeah.

Counselor: Is any part of your life still intact?

Patient: No. I've screwed up everything.

Counselor: You still have your job.

Patient: Well, yeah.

Counselor: You still have your wife and kids.

Patient: Yeah, they're still with me.

Counselor: And your boss is supporting your treatment.

Patient: Yeah.

Counselor: So, let's get accurate. You haven't messed up everything. You just feel like you have.

Patient: [Laughs.] Now that I think about it, I have a few things left. I still have my job, my wife, my kids, and my house.

Counselor: You have a lot of things. You haven't messed everything up. Why don't we make a list of the things you still have? Carry this list around with you and when you think you messed everything up, take out the list and read it to yourself.

This is cognitive therapy at its best. The patient corrects inaccurate thinking, develops accurate thoughts, and then practices accurate thinking.

Solidifying Accurate Thinking

It is helpful to have patients carry around note cards with accurate thoughts written on them. When they feel bad, they take out the cards and read them to themselves. Sometimes they need to look at themselves in the mirror and read the cards to themselves. Patients will not catch the inaccurate thinking at the thinking stage. Thinking happens too quickly. They will have to catch the inaccurate thoughts at the uncomfortable feeling stage and then backtrack to find out what the thoughts were. Have patients keep a feelings log in which they jot down every time they have a significant feeling and the situation that caused the feeling. Then have them score each feeling on the scale of 1 to 100. Once they have a few days of a log, call them in and begin to filter out what thoughts were occurring during the situation.

John came in with his feelings log. On Thursday at lunch, he felt hurt and angry when a treatment peer made the following comment about his sweater: "Where did you steal that?" John felt angry at 70 and hurt at 80. He felt 150 units of emotional distress.

Example of a Cognitive Therapy Session

Counselor: What were you thinking when he said that?

Patient: He doesn't like me.

Counselor: What else?

Patient: That's about it.

Counselor: Were you thinking that people don't like you very much?

Patient: Yeah, I was.

Counselor: Were you thinking that nobody likes you?

Patient: Exactly.

Counselor: Nobody has ever liked you?

Patient: [Nods his head.]

Counselor: How about, nobody will ever like you?

Patient: Well, I know that.

Counselor: Bob says to you, "Where did you steal that sweater?" and you think that he doesn't like you, nobody likes you, and nobody will ever like you.

Patient: Yes.

Counselor: Now, what's accurate? Bob says, "Where did you steal that sweater?" What do you think is an accurate way of thinking about that situation?

Patient: Bob was making a joke.

Counselor: So, to get you to like him, Bob tells a joke.

Patient: I think so.

Counselor: Why does Bob tell you a joke?

Patient: Because he wants me to like him.

Counselor: Right, Bob likes you and wants you to like him, so he tells you a joke. He ribs you about your sweater. Your automatic thinking takes over and says that he hates you, everyone hates you, and everyone will always hate you. Thinking these thoughts, you feel hurt and angry. Now thinking accurately, how do you feel?

Patient: I feel pretty good. Bob likes me.

Counselor: Right.

Interpersonal Therapy

■

Chemical dependency wounds relationships. Interpersonal therapy heals relationships and restores an atmosphere of love and trust. In recovery, patients are encouraged to love God, to love others, and to love themselves. If one of these relationships is not healed, then the patients will continue to feel uncomfortable and will be vulnerable to relapse.

How to Develop Healthy Relationships

In the AA/NA program, when we are talking about relationships, we are talking about spirituality. Spirituality is defined as the innermost relationship we have with ourselves and all else. The first thing that patients must do in developing a healthy relationship is to surrender. Step One demands an admission of powerlessness and unmanageability. Without surrender, the patients will continue to try to control themselves and other people. This leads to disaster as the "self will run riot" (Alcoholics Anonymous, 1976, p. 62).

The next step is to believe that a power greater than ourselves can restore us to sanity. This relationship with a Higher Power is an essential part of the AA/NA program. Patients must seek the God of their own understanding and establish a relationship with that Higher Power.

Relationships with a Higher Power, self, and others are based on love, trust, and commitment. Love is not a feeling. It is an action. Trust necessitates truth, and commitment takes consistency of action. Action without truth is not enough. Truth without action is not enough.

Building a Relationship With a Higher Power

In building a relationship with a Higher Power, patients must be willing to accept that some sort of a Higher Power is possible. The best way of showing this is to ask the patients a question. "Do you think that there is a power greater than yourself?" For most patients, this is enough. But for some, you have to demonstrate. "If you wanted to leave this room and the group was determined to keep you in, could you leave?" The answer here is obvious to even the most stubborn. The group has greater power.

Now, can patients *begin* to turn their wills and lives over to this new power? This will start with the group. Can the group be trusted? Does the group make good decisions? If the patients can begin to deal with doubt and faith in a group, then they have come a long way toward developing trust in a Higher Power. The patients must see the group members love each other. The patients must see the group be committed to the truth even when it hurts.

Much later in the program, patients are encouraged to begin thinking about a Higher Power. Willingness again is the key. If the patients will seek a Higher Power through prayer and meditation, then they will begin to make progress in this area. Some patients will want to do some reading about spirituality, and all of them need to talk with a clergy person who is familiar with the Twelve Steps.

Developing a Relationship With Self

The relationship with self begins to heal when patients begin to treat themselves well. They stop hurting themselves with drugs and alcohol. They stop saying bad things to themselves. They begin eating three meals a day. They sleep properly. They begin to get regular exercise. All of these simple skills have a profound effect on the patients' feeling of self-worth. People of great worth are worth treating well.

Building Relationships With Others

Interpersonal relationships heal when a patient uses good interpersonal relationship skills.

1. The patient must share how he or she feels.
2. The patient must ask for what he or she wants.
3. The patient must be honest.
4. The patient must be actively involved in the other person's individual growth.

If one of these skills is missing, then the relationship will be unstable. It will feel unstable, and the individuals involved will feel frightened. Each of these skills needs to be developed and practiced.

Patients must practice identifying and sharing their feelings. This takes education, individual therapy, and group work. There are only a few primary emotions. Plutchik (1980) theorized that there are eight:

1. Joy
2. Acceptance
3. Anticipation
4. Anger
5. Fear
6. Surprise
7. Disgust
8. Sadness

Other emotions are various combinations of the basic eight. For example, jealousy is feeling sad, angry, and fearful all at the same time. All feelings give energy and direction for movement. Feelings motivate behavior that is directly related to survival. For example, fear activates escape behavior. Escape protects the organism from a dangerous situation. Surprise activates orienting behavior. Sadness gives the organism the energy and direction to recover the lost object.

In therapy, you must educate patients about their feelings. For example, in many homes, anger is an unacceptable emotion. A child learns that anger is dangerous, so the child learns to repress anger. The child does not feel it. The child may feel fear every time that he or she feels angry. A patient needs to use all of his or her feelings to function normally. A person who cannot feel anger cannot express anger. A person who cannot express anger is handicapped. This person cannot adequately protect himself or herself. Anger is necessary to establish and maintain boundaries around ourselves. If a person cannot do this, then people will violate the person's boundaries and he or she will be victimized.

Have your patients list situations in which they felt each feeling and then discuss how the patients could have responded properly. You will find that cultural differences abound. For example, in the United States, women are not supposed to act angry, so when they feel angry, they cry. Men are not supposed to cry, so when they feel sad, they act angry.

As a counselor, you are teaching patients to use feelings in problem solving. When a patient has a feeling, he or she should listen to this feeling. What is the feeling telling the person to do? The patient should then consider options of action.

Patient: I got so mad.

Counselor: What did you do?

Patient: I just stood there. I didn't know what to do.

Counselor: What were your options?

Patient: I could have hit him.

Counselor: What else could you have done?

Patient: I could have walked away.

Counselor: What else?

Patient: I was so mad, I didn't know what to do.

Counselor: Could you have told him you were mad?

Patient: Oh, yeah, but he wouldn't have cared.

Counselor: You could have told him you were mad and what he did that made you mad.

Patient: What good would that have done?

Counselor: We have to hold people accountable for what they do. That's what anger is for. Anger gives us the energy and direction to fight for our rights. One of the best ways to use your anger is to tell people you're angry. That holds them accountable.

How Patients Use Feelings Inappropriately | Many patients use their feelings inappropriately. They make the wrong movements when they have feelings. People who are fearful can constantly be withdrawing. They shy away from everything. People who are angry can constantly be fighting. They fight everybody about everything. These patients need to learn how to use their feelings appropriately. Their feelings can get to be the problem. Some of these patients need behavior therapy. They need to learn how to act appropriately when they feel certain feelings. A patient who was abused and terrified by his father might respond to all people with fear. This patient needs to identify and understand how the relationship with his father influenced how he responds to everyone. He needs to understand that most people are going to treat him well.

How Patients Learn Relationship Skills
People learn what to expect from the world by the experiences they have had. It is from these experiences that we draw maps about what the world is like. We learn what to do in certain situations. Childhood experiences are very powerful. They condition us and give us attitudes about what the world is like. The most important relationship for us was with our primary caregiver. This person usually was the mother, but it could have been someone else. If this person was healthy and loved us, then we felt safe and important. We grew up feeling that the world was a safe and loving place. If our primary caregiver was not healthy, then we learned other things. We might have learned that the world was an abusive place or a sad place. The first relationship was very important. As the counselor, you must help patients to develop accurate maps of the world.

How to Change Relationships
In therapy, you will see patients' relationship maps in how they relate to you. The patients will react to you like they reacted to significant others in the past. This is called transference. When you react to the patients using your old maps, that is countertransference. As the patients respond to you, watch for the inaccurate ways in which they interpret what you do. If the patients act frightened of you when there is nothing to be frightened about, then you can be pretty sure that you are dealing with a transference issue. As you treat the patients with encouragement and love, they will have the opportunity to redraw their maps. Maybe the world is a safe place after all. In the relationship with you, the patients will see how healthy persons relate to each other. They will observe and be able to model after you. You will teach the patients how to communicate and how to relate to other people with love and trust.

Patients may have a relationship problem that they will need to address with some other person. In the family program, you will have the opportunity to work with the family. Here you can teach all of the family members healthy communication skills. You can teach them how to listen to each other and how to develop empathy for each other. Have them repeat each other's thoughts and feelings. This makes sure that each person understands what the others are saying. Teach them how to use "I feel" statements. Teach them how to reinforce each other. Teach them how to inquire for more information until they understand. Burns's (1990) *Feeling Good Handbook* has some communication exercises that can be helpful if you are interested in pursuing this therapy further.

How to Handle Grief
Grief issues can need attention in interpersonal therapy. When patients have lost significant others, they will have to work through the grief. The patients will have to experience pain and say good-bye to the lost loved ones. Having the patients talk about the good and bad times that they had with the lost loved ones is important. Have the patients write good-bye letters to the loved ones. Have them read the letters to you or to their interpersonal group. The patients need to gain the support of other people. The Higher Power concept can be greatly beneficial here. God

knows everything, and everything fits into God's plan. "Nothing, absolutely nothing happens in God's world by mistake" (Alcoholics Anonymous, 1976, p. 449). The patients can be encouraged to trust in a Higher Power's judgment. Step Three work and grief work go together. We turn our will and our lives over to the care of God as we understand God. Grief work is a good time to build a closer relationship with the Higher Power.

How to Choose the Therapeutic Modality

Individual therapy helps to prepare patients for group work. The patients will transfer what they learn from you in individual therapy to the group as a whole. From the group, the patients will transfer what they have learned to people in society. Individual therapy gives you an opportunity to discuss some things with your patients that are not appropriate for the group. There is no need for a patient to share every intimate detail in group. Some things are best left for individual therapy. Sexual abuse and other sensitive issues can generate a great deal of shame, and the group might not understand. If a patient decides to share something with you but does not want to share this issue with the group, then the patient should be given this opportunity, but remember that everything of importance must be discussed with the clinical staff. The patient does not have to talk to the staff, but you do. You need the help of your colleagues, particularly in sensitive situations.

Individual therapy gives patients the opportunity to have a healthy interpersonal relationship with another person. This is very healing. The patients finally will tell someone the whole truth and see that person's reaction. As you continue to care for the patients, even when they tell you the worst, it teaches the patients something that they never have known: They are persons who are worthy of love. Nothing battles the disease better than this fact.

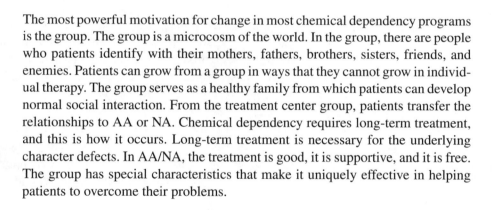

CHAPTER FIVE | Group Therapy

The most powerful motivation for change in most chemical dependency programs is the group. The group is a microcosm of the world. In the group, there are people who patients identify with their mothers, fathers, brothers, sisters, friends, and enemies. Patients can grow from a group in ways that they cannot grow in individual therapy. The group serves as a healthy family from which patients can develop normal social interaction. From the treatment center group, patients transfer the relationships to AA or NA. Chemical dependency requires long-term treatment, and this is how it occurs. Long-term treatment is necessary for the underlying character defects. In AA/NA, the treatment is good, it is supportive, and it is free. The group has special characteristics that make it uniquely effective in helping patients to overcome their problems.

Benefits of the Group Process

1. *Healthier members instill hope.* There are patients in the group who are further along in treatment. These patients look better and act better. They use effective communication skills. They do not deny their disease. They confront other patients gently and with the truth. They encourage each other. They are not afraid to share. This has great impact on patients coming into treatment. They see that people get better as they stay in treatment longer.

2. *Patients can model healthy communication skills.* They see members sharing their feelings and asking for what they want. Group members are not shamed for having feelings or thoughts. The world does not end if someone gets angry or cries. Patients watch as problems and feelings are worked through until they are resolved.

3. *Patients become aware that they are not alone in their pain.* They hear the stories of the other patients, and the stories are very similar. The group members

can laugh together about the mutual pain. No one else but fellow alcoholics would understand riding around the block waiting for the liquor store to open or hiding the bottle so well that even the alcoholic could not find it. It is a great relief for patients to hear someone else discuss a shameful situation that they have experienced themselves.

4. *Information is exchanged.* Patients share their experiences, strengths, and hopes. In these stories are examples of how to handle difficult situations. Group members learn from each other's experiences. If members never have relapsed, then it is informative to hear about someone who has had that experience.

5. *A feeling of family develops.* The group members feel close. They accept each other and try to love each other. Interpersonal trust and intimacy develops. Patients carefully keep each other's confidentiality and learn how to watch out for each other.

6. *Patients learn that they can be accepted for who and what they are.* Even when patients are at their worst, the other group members still accept them. They are supportive and loving. This comes into direct conflict with what patients always have believed—that if they told the truth, they would be rejected.

7. *Patients learn the power of the truth.* Using real feelings, in real situations, and with real people, patients learn to solve real problems. People do not go away from the group sulking or worse off than when they came in. They go away feeling loved and supported. As the counselor, it is your responsibility to make sure that every group ends in a positive light.

8. *Patients can express their feelings freely.* They can express their pain in a loving atmosphere. They can ventilate feelings and still feel accepted. They can practice sharing feelings to see whether they are appropriate to the situation. People who never have acted angry can act angry and see the positive effect of their anger.

9. *By listening to each other and sharing together, patients feel a new sense of self-worth.* They begin to feel worthy of the group's time and energy. The group members show each other that they all are worthwhile individuals.

10. *Patients learn what works, and what does not work, in interpersonal relationships.* They see what brings people together. They come to understand that the more they share, the closer they can get, and that the closer they can get, the more they can share.

Preparation for the Group

Before each group, you have someone read a statement about the group process. This sets the stage for group and prepares the members for the work ahead. It sets a few simple rules about how the group will operate.

The Preparation Statement

"Interpersonal group is an experience designed to help us learn more about how we feel, think, and act. Chemical dependency blinds us to the truth about ourselves. It keeps us from experiencing reality. We develop defenses that keep us from seeing ourselves as we really are. We present to the world a false front that we ourselves believe to be true. If we are ever going to accept ourselves and begin the process of recovery, then we must know who we are. We can do this only by learning how other people see us. The group members will act as mirrors, showing to us those parts of ourselves that we do not see. They will reflect our feelings, thoughts, and behaviors.

"The spirit of this group is love. We share, care, and help each other to grow as individuals. With all of our heart, we encourage you to share your experience, strength, and hope. Be open to listen and talk. Our experience has shown that only those who participate fully recover.

"A main focus of the group is feelings. Many of us never have dealt honestly with our feelings before. We know that doing this is frightening and painful, but it is necessary. You must be willing to be yourself. It is a tremendously rewarding experience to be accepted for who you really are.

"The group has only two rules. First, there will be no physical violence. We need to feel free to express ourselves without the fear of physical harm. The second rule is confidentiality. What you see here, what you hear here—let it stay here. We will now begin the session by introducing ourselves and stating why we are in treatment."

The reader of the preparation statement gives his or her first name and the reason why he or she is in treatment. For example, "I'm Shirley, and I'm an alcoholic." If someone in the group does not want to call themselves an alcoholic or chemically dependent, that is fine, but that person does have to give a reason why he or she is in treatment. For example, "I'm Frank, and I got a DWI."

The Agenda

As the counselor, you then have each group member choose an agenda and someone in the group to share it with. The agenda is a current matter of concern for the patient. It has to be a real problem that generates real emotion. Some patients will try to choose something easy, but do not let them. If they will not, or cannot, choose something important, then choose something for them. You write down all of the agenda items on the blackboard or a large pad for everyone to see.

Patient	Agenda	Share With
1. Bob	Feeling confused	Frank
2. Frank	Scared about family program	Shirley
3. Shirley	Mad at treatment peers	Tom
4. Tom	Disgusted with self	Jose
5. Jose	Fear about going to jail	Nancy
6. Nancy	Sad about loss of marriage	Francis
7. Francis	Angry at staff	Mory

How to Choose the Order of the Agenda Once the agendas are up on the board, you choose an agenda that seems to be the most therapeutic. Choose something that will generate emotion and will teach the patients about chemical dependency. The best agendas usually are those that deal with problems the group members are having with each other. It always is best to deal with the here and now rather than with the there and then.

The group members will start with the agenda item that you choose and will move as far through the list as they can. As the counselor, you choose the next agenda each time. You will have a pretty good idea which agendas need to be dealt with during a particular day. A patient starts off by telling her problem to the person with whom he or she has chosen to share the problem. For example, Shirley talks to Tom about being mad at her treatment peers. Tom answers first, and then anyone in the group can add what he or she feels is important. You watch for and reinforce appropriate feedback.

How to Give Good Feedback A person giving good feedback will do the following:

1. Talk about the specific behavior.
2. Give feedback in a caring manner.
3. Give the other person a chance to explain.
4. Avoid being judgmental.
5. Use "I feel" statements.
6. Share the positive as well.
7. Avoid giving advice.

How to Receive Feedback To receive feedback appropriately, a patient must do the following:

1. Ask for it.
2. Receive it openly.
3. Acknowledge its value.
4. Be willing to discuss it.
5. Make no excuses.
6. Indicate what he or she intends to do with it.
7. Listen to everyone.

How to Run the Group As the counselor, you should not talk much in group. You should intervene only when necessary to keep the group moving along therapeutically. So long as the truth is coming out and people are being loved for it, the group is doing well. It is a common early mistake for counselors to talk too much. This discourages the other members from sharing. Let the silent periods raise the group's anxiety. Someone will talk if you wait. If you always talk, then no one else will.

For the most part, the patients who are doing the most sharing are getting the most out of group. You must encourage quieter members to share. A simple question such as "Tom, how do you feel about that?" often is enough to get them started.

If someone is becoming a problem in the group, then let the group handle it. Do not try to handle everything yourself. That is what the group is for. Asking a question such as "How do the rest of you feel about Bob right now?" is enough to let the group work for you.

You need to make sure that no one gets harmed in the group process. If things are getting too hot and angry, then focus on the patient's pain. Hurt comes before anger, and it defuses anger to talk about the pain. If someone is getting hurt, then you must step in and give the group direction. Statements such as "How would you want to be treated right now?" go a long way toward giving the group solid direction.

How to Know Which Therapy to Use

Behavior, cognitive, and interpersonal therapy all can be used in a group setting. As the counselor, your skill is to know exactly which therapy is necessary and then to be able to plug the treatment into place. If a patient is moving in a way that is maladaptive, then behavior therapy comes into play. If the patient is thinking inaccurately, then cognitive therapy is necessary. If the problem is in a relationship, then interpersonal therapy is most appropriate.

The Honesty Group

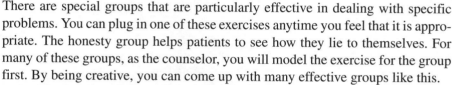

There are special groups that are particularly effective in dealing with specific problems. You can plug in one of these exercises anytime you feel that it is appropriate. The honesty group helps patients to see how they lie to themselves. For many of these groups, as the counselor, you will model the exercise for the group first. By being creative, you can come up with many effective groups like this.

In the honesty group, you might say, "Today we're going to see how the illness operates inside of your thinking. We all have a constant dialogue going on inside of our heads. This conversation is between the illness, who just wants to drink or use drugs, and the healthy side, who wants to get clean and sober." Place an empty chair in the center of the group. "We are going to put a chair in the center of the group. In this chair, we are going to put our illness. This is the side of us that wants to get high. In the chair that we are currently sitting in, we are going to put the healthy side of us, the side that wants to stay clean and sober. Now each of us is going to spend some time in each chair. We are going to start in the illness chair and try to convince the healthy side of us to drink or use drugs. I'm going to go first."

Example of the Honesty Group

The counselor, Judy, sits in the center chair and leans toward the empty chair in which she was just sitting. From the illness side of herself, she tries to talk herself into drinking or getting high. She might say something like this:

"Judy, you're doing great. I'm real proud of you. You've been sober for a long time. You've been going to meetings. That's great. You've got your life back together.

"You know, when you feel like it, I'd like to do something. I want to go for a ride in the car, maybe on a nice spring day. I'm not in any hurry. I can wait. I want to for a ride, relax, and drink three beers. No one is going to know. Nothing bad is going to happen. You need to relax, Judy. You've been working too hard. You deserve a break. Come on, it's just three beers. Remember all the good times we had drinking. Remember how good it felt."

Judy looks at the group. "That's how my illness still tries to get me drunk. Now, I'm going to trade chairs and answer the illness from the healthy side of me." She moves to her original chair and leans back. "Well, illness, you seem to forget a few things. You always forget. You remember selectively. See, I remember the misery. I remember trying to drink three beers and throw up three beers at the same time. I remember losing my husband and my kids. I remember the shame of losing my job." She sits forward in her chair. "I also remember that we have tried this before, about a hundred times. We have tried drinking only three beers, or two, or one, and it goes okay for a while, but sooner or later I get drunk and bad things happen. Illness, I know how good I feel in recovery. I have regained my self-respect. I have my children back. I have a good job that I'm proud of. I have found God for the first time in my life. And you want me to give all of this up for three beers. You keep your three beers. I don't want to have anything to do with you."

Now the patients should have the idea. The counselor picks someone who he or she thinks can do a good job, and the exercise is repeated. Most of the patients will not have as long a dialogue as the counselor, but it is important to see each person's illness at work. This exercise is excellent at uncovering who has a good recovery program and who is still struggling.

Patients usually will feel more comfortable in playing the illness role. This may show how little it is going to take the patient to go back to using. The counselor will see all manner of seductions perpetrated by the illness. It's good for the patients to see how they have been deceiving themselves.

Uncovering the Lies

About halfway through the group, hand each of the patients a blank piece of paper. Then tell them this. "It is important that you see how the illness works. The illness must lie to operate. It cannot exist in the truth. You must lie to yourself, and believe the lie, before you can ever go back to drinking or drugging. What we are going to do now is uncover the lies. Every time you hear the illness lie, I want you to wave your paper. This is your white flag of surrender. Wave it loud so it rattles." The counselor asks the next patient to start with his dialogue.

Bob smiles at the group and sits in the illness chair. "Well," says Bob, "you've had a hard day." (The group members rattle their papers.) "Why don't you stop by the bar and have a couple of beers? That's not going to hurt you." (The group members rattle their papers again.) "Your wife won't know." (The group members rattle their papers and laugh. Bob laughs with them.) "You can drink just a few." (Rattle.) "Just a couple." (Rattle.) "Remember all the good times we had." (Rattle.) "You need to relax and enjoy yourself." (Rattle.)

This is educational and fun. The patients never will forget those white flags going up after they speak to themselves. When the patients speak from their healthy side, the flags stay quiet. It is a sobering event to experience the lies try to work in front of treatment peers.

Have the group members discuss the exercise. In which role did they feel the most comfortable? Why? What are they going to do to keep from lying to themselves? How can they begin to keep the illness in check? How do they feel about the illness part of themselves and the healthy part of themselves? What is the goal of the illness? What is the goal of the healthy side? What is it like to have what seems to be two people in the same body?

How to End Each Group

End each group with a chance for the members to share the positive things that they learned about themselves. Keep this sharing time positive. At Keystone Carroll Treatment Center, we begin each group with the serenity prayer and end with the Lord's prayer. The group members put their arms around each other or hold hands as they pray.

The Euphoric Recall Group

This group examines euphoric recall and how it differs from reality. As the counselor, you stand at the blackboard and ask each patient to give an example of what drinking or using drugs did for him or her when that person first started using. You pull out all the positive things that the patients were getting from early use.

How to Uncover Euphoric Recall

"Tony, what did drinking do good for you? What was it giving you that was good?" the counselor asks.

"It made me relax," Tony responds.

"Good." The counselor writes "It made me relax" on the blackboard. Then the counselor moves to the next person in the group. "How about you, Sally? What did drugs do good for you?"

"It was easier for me to talk to people," Sally says.

"Okay, good." The counselor writes "It was easier to talk to people" on the blackboard.

As the counselor, you go around the group at least twice. You need a long list of the positive things that chemicals did for the group members. Do not put down the same thing twice. You should come up with a list that looks something like this:

1. It made me relax.
2. It was easier to talk to people.
3. I felt more intelligent.
4. I felt stronger.
5. It made me brave.
6. It made me feel wanted.
7. I felt more attractive.
8. I could sleep.
9. I felt happy.
10. I could be creative.
11. My problems did not bother me anymore.
12. I could get along.
13. I was funny.
14. I felt comfortable.
15. People liked me.
16. I could talk to women.

You make as long a list as the blackboard will allow and then state, "Now, here's some of the good things that drinking and drugs did for you. I assure you that we could make a longer list of the good things that chemicals gave us early in use. This is why we were drinking and using drugs."

How to Help the Patients See the Truth

You then draw a line down the middle of the blackboard. "Now let's see what happened to each of these things when chemical dependency set in. Tony, after you became an alcoholic, did alcohol still make you relax?"

"I was more tense. I couldn't relax," Tony says.

"How about it, Sally? After drug addiction took over, was it still easier for you to talk to people or did you feel more isolated?"

"Lonely. I felt lonely."

You write down what each person says. Be sure to read off what the patient got good out of early use before asking him or her what happened when drug addiction took over. What the group members are going to find out is that once chemical dependency set in, they ended up with the opposite of what they were using for. People who were drinking to sleep cannot sleep. People who were using to be social ended up alone. Your second list will look something like this:

1. I was more tense.
2. I couldn't talk to anyone. I was lonely.
3. I felt stupid.
4. I felt weak.
5. I felt inadequate.
6. I felt like no one wanted me.
7. I felt ugly.
8. I couldn't sleep.
9. I was very sad.
10. I couldn't think.
11. I had more problems.
12. I couldn't get along with anybody.
13. I wasn't funny anymore. I was sad.
14. I couldn't get comfortable.
15. I felt like no one liked me.
16. I couldn't talk to anybody.

The group members need to take a long look at both sides of the blackboard. You emphasize that the illness side of themselves will use euphoric recall to seduce them into using drugs and alcohol again. The patients have to get in the habit of seeing through the first use. They need to remember the painful consequences that come with continued use. The group members discuss what they learned for a brief period, and then you need to speak again.

"You see how the illness uses the good stuff to get you to use again. Now, what are you going to do when the illness side of you begins to gain strength? What are the tools of recovery that will put hurdles in the way of the first drink?"

"Call your sponsor," says Tony.

"Go to a meeting," says Bob.

"Turn it over," says Sally.

The counselor writes each of the new coping skills on the blackboard.

1. Call your sponsor.
2. Go to a meeting.
3. Turn it over to your Higher Power.
4. Get some exercise.
5. Talk to someone.
6. Read some AA/NA material.
7. Remember the bad stuff.
8. Remember how good you have felt when clean and sober.
9. Ask for God's help.
10. Do something else that you enjoy.

Help the patients to make a long list and then discuss it with the group.

The Reading Group

■

In reading group, patients read a portion of the "Big Book" (Alcoholics Anonymous, 1976) or the "Twelve and Twelve" (Alcoholics Anonymous, 1981) and discuss it with each other. It is necessary to have a counselor present to facilitate this discussion. Gently encourage all members of the group to share. People do not have to share, but if they do, they get more out of treatment. The first 164 pages of the Big Book, and all of the steps in the Twelve and Twelve, should be read during treatment. There will be patients who do not feel comfortable reading for one reason or another. Encourage all of them who can comfortably read to do so. If a patient feels too uncomfortable reading, then he or she can pass. This material can be taken chapter by chapter, paragraph by paragraph, or line by line. The patients discuss the subject matter to help them understand and internalize the material.

The Relapse Prevention Group

■

A relapse prevention group should be run once a week. This group concentrates on high-risk situations and develops coping skills for dealing with each situation. The first group introduces relapse and concentrates on the triggers that might trigger using. These are the environmental situations that make patients vulnerable to using drugs and alcohol. Patients are told that there is such a thing as lapse (the use of a mood-altering chemical) as well as relapse (continuing to use the chemical until the full-blown illness becomes evident again). For most patients, the time period between lapse and relapse is less than 30 days. If a lapse occurs, then immediate action must be taken to prevent relapse. All patients must develop coping skills for dealing with a lapse.

Hunt, Barnett, and Branch (1971) studied relapse rates following a variety of addiction programs. They found that 33% of patients lapsed within 2 weeks following treatment. Fully 60% lapsed within 3 months, and 67% lapsed within 12 months. This study should be reported to the patients, and the percentile figures should be placed on the blackboard. The patients typically are not happy when they see these figures. They may tend to think, "What's the use?" You must point out that most patients lapse early, within the first 3 months after treatment. This does not *have* to happen, but it *can* happen. If the patients use their new skills, then it will not happen. The patients cannot use their new skills and their drugs of choice at the same time. These behaviors are incompatible.

The Trigger Group

The five situations that trigger relapse are placed on the blackboard. These are the high-risk situations developed by Marlatt and Gordon (1985). To the side of each of these situations, you write the percentage of time that this event tends to trigger relapse.

1. Negative emotions—35%
2. Social pressure—20%
3. Interpersonal conflict—16%
4. Positive emotions—12%
5. Test personal control—5%

How to Uncover the Triggers

Each of these triggers needs to be carefully discussed with the group. The patients are asked to list the feelings that make them vulnerable to using. In what situations do they continue to use? How do they feel before they use? Are they more vulnerable when they are angry, frustrated, bored, lonely, anxious, happy, or joyful?

Social pressure can occur in one of two ways: direct social pressure or indirect social pressure. Direct social pressure is when someone directly encourages the patient to drink or use drugs. Indirect pressure is when the patient is in a social situation where people are drinking or using drugs.

The Drug Refusal Exercises

After discussing the triggers, the group goes through drug refusal exercises. One member of the group is encouraged to use by the other members while he or she tries to say no. The first time that a patient goes through this, anxiety and craving usually are generated. The first attempt at refusal tends to be rather pathetic, but with practice the patient gets better. Each patient needs to practice until he or she can say no and feel reasonably comfortable.

The group has a lot of fun with these exercises, but this role-playing delivers a powerful message: It is hard to say no and feel good about yourself. It is a new skill, and it has to be practiced until it feels reasonably comfortable. The exercise provides excellent protection against relapse if the patient can continue the exercises until he or she feels comfortable saying no. For each patient, try to reenact the exact situation that makes him or her the most vulnerable to relapse. For example, if the patient is vulnerable to a sexual situation, then set up this situation as exactly as you can. A situation in which a significant other encourages the patient to use is not difficult to set up. What is the patient going to say? What is the patient going to do? What if the other person gets mad? Have the patient go through each situation until the group members believe that he or she has developed the skills necessary to say no, and then have the group make a long list of the hurdles that the patient can put in the way of the first drink or use. What can the patient do that will prevent use even when in a high-risk situation?

The Inaccurate Thinking Group

The second group focuses on thinking. What thinking occurs between the trigger and the feeling of craving? This is where the patient's inaccurate thinking takes over.

"It won't hurt to have a couple of beers."
"No one will know."
"I can handle it."
"I never had any problem with pot."
"I can use a little pot."
"I never really had a problem anyway."
"I deserve a drink."
"I had a hard day."
"I'll show them."

All of these, and more, can be given as examples of inaccurate thinking at work.

Have group members discuss what they think about before they use chemicals. How is the sick part of themselves trying to trick them into thinking that they can still drink or use drugs normally? Use the chair technique again. Have the patients talk to the empty chair and talk the healthy side of themselves into using drugs or alcohol. Each of these thoughts must be placed on the board and exposed for the lie that it is. Discuss the inaccurate thoughts carefully until the patients understand that they all are lies. Then replace the inaccurate thoughts with accurate thoughts and have the patients practice the accurate thinking. Go over exactly what new thoughts the patients are going to use. They all are taught a sentence to plug into their thinking whenever they feel the desire to use alcohol or drugs:

"Drinking (or using drugs) is no longer an option for me."

Have patients practice thinking this sentence to themselves several times. Have them write it down and carry it with them. Every time they feel craving in treatment, they are to first think this new thought and log the situation that triggered the craving. These triggers can be discussed in further groups. Every time patients are in a high-risk situation, they will think the new thoughts and then consider the other options for dealing with the situation. Drinking and using drugs no longer are an option, so what are they going to do? If they are in a high-risk situation, then they need to use their new coping skills. Have the group put on the blackboard a variety of options available other than drinking or using. It will end up looking something like this:

1. Call someone.
2. Turn it over to your Higher Power.
3. Think "That is no longer an option for me."
4. Call your sponsor.
5. Go to a meeting.
6. Think through the first use.
7. Think about how good you feel in recovery.
8. Remember how miserable you were before treatment.
9. Exercise.
10. Call the treatment center.

The Feelings and Action Group

The third group focuses on feelings and behaviors. The group members need to know that most chemically dependent persons are particularly vulnerable to anger and frustration. How are they going to handle these feelings in sobriety?

Feelings are used to give the patients energy and direction for problem solving. Have the group members discuss the feelings that make them vulnerable to relapse, and come up with coping skills to deal with each feeling. Any number of positive or negative feeling states can lead to relapse. The patients need to learn how to cope with good and bad feelings without chemicals.

When patients are having intense feelings, they need to share these feelings with others. This allows the patients to feel accepted and supported. They need to develop better problem-solving skills and to practice problem solving in treatment. The following steps need to be followed when solving a problem:

1. Stop and think. Exactly what is the problem?
2. Consider the options. What is the best thing you can do for yourself and/or the other person right now?
3. Develop an action plan.
4. Carry out the plan.
5. Evaluate the effect of your action.

The Lapses Group

The fourth group is a lapses group. What are patients going to do to prevent a lapse, and what are they going to do if they have a lapse? How are they going to feel?

What are they going to do specifically? What hurdles are they going to put in the way after the first use to prevent continued use? Remember that for most patients, the elapsed time between lapse and relapse is less than 30 days.

Group members put on the blackboard the actions they are going to take to prevent a lapse. Make a long list and have all patients copy the list to take home with them.

1. Work a daily program of recovery.
2. Attend regular meetings.
3. Read AA/NA material.
4. Do daily meditation.
5. Have daily contact with sponsor or other AA/NA member.
6. Get daily exercise.
7. Develop enjoyable hobbies.
8. Attend church or work on spiritual program.
9. Say daily prayer.
10. When wrong, promptly admit it.
11. Be honest. Do not lie.
12. Eat right.
13. Get enough sleep.
14. Take a daily personal inventory.

Have each patient make an emergency card of phone numbers to call if he or she is feeling vulnerable. Have the patient carry this card in a wallet or purse at all times. The phone numbers should include those of the following: sponsor, several AA/NA group members, the treatment center, the local AA/NA hotline, a religious contact, and any other person who may be able to respond to the person positively.

In group, patients should role-play calling these numbers and practice asking for help. This is a very difficult skill for some people, and they need to be desensitized to the situation. Have someone else in the group play the other party. A patient needs to get in the habit of calling someone when he or she feels uncomfortable. Just out of treatment, the patient should call someone every day until he or she feels comfortable. The patient should make every attempt to go to an AA/NA meeting every day for 90 days. The first 3 months out of treatment are when the patient is the most vulnerable to relapse. Every effort should be made to stay sober during these first 90 days. After the 3 months, the patient can discuss with his or her sponsor and aftercare group how and when to cut back on meetings.

Signs and symptoms of impending relapse developed by Gorski (Gorski, 1989; Gorski & Miller, 1986) should be given to a patient and his or her significant others. Each symptom should be discussed so that the patient understands and can identify the symptom. These warning signs include the following:

1. Apprehension about well-being
2. Denial
3. Adamant commitment to sobriety
4. Compulsive attempts to impose sobriety on others
5. Defensiveness
6. Compulsive behavior
7. Impulsive behavior

8. Tendencies toward loneliness
9. Tunnel vision
10. Minor depression
11. Loss of constructive planning
12. Plans beginning to fail
13. Idle daydreaming and wishful thinking
14. Feeling that nothing can be solved
15. Immature wish to be happy
16. Periods of confusion
17. Irritation with friends
18. Easily angered
19. Irregular eating habits
20. Listlessness
21. Irregular sleeping habits
22. Progressive loss of daily structure
23. Periods of deep depression
24. Irregular attendance at meetings
25. Development of an "I don't care" attitude
26. Open rejection of help
27. Dissatisfaction with life
28. Feelings of powerlessness and helplessness
29. Self-pity
30. Thoughts of social use
31. Conscious lying
32. Complete loss of self-confidence
33. Unresolved resentments
34. Discontinuing all treatment
35. Overwhelming loneliness, frustration, anger, and tension
36. Start of controlled using
37. Loss of control

Patients and their significant others should be given a copy of the warning signs. It is possible to prevent relapse. In taking a daily inventory, the patients should list any relapse symptoms that they saw in themselves and come up with a plan for dealing with the symptoms as soon as possible. Any symptoms resistive to change should be discussed with a patient's sponsor or AA/NA group.

Patients might not recognize the early warning signs, so someone else needs to check them. That is why a sponsor, the aftercare group, and regular attendance at meetings are so essential. The patients need to listen to everyone. A closed mind is a sure way of ending up in trouble.

Patients must understand that relapse is a process. It does not begin with using alcohol or drugs. Some of the symptoms will occur long before actual drug use begins. The one symptom that everyone should pick up on is a decrease in attendance at meetings. Any decrease in attendance at meetings should be carefully discussed with a patient's family, sponsor, and group.

The Spirituality Group
■

Spirituality group should be conducted every week. This group should be run by a clergy person trained in the group process or by a member of the counseling staff who has a solid spiritual program. At the beginning of each group, the group leader (or someone the leader has chosen) reads the following to prepare the group for the spiritual process.

Group Preparation

"Spirituality is the innermost relationship we have with ourselves and all else. Religion and spirituality are different. Religion is an organized system of faith and worship. Spirituality deals with three intimate relationships. We will explore how to improve our relationship with ourselves, with others, and with a Higher Power. We are going to call this Higher Power 'God.' You may call your Higher Power something else if you like. We only ask that you be willing to consider the possibility that there is a power greater than yourself. We will begin the group by giving our names and the reason why we are here."

How to Develop a Healthy Relationship

The first group discusses the concept of a healthy relationship. What are the essential components of a good relationship? What are the patients' past experiences with relationships with self, others, a Higher Power, and religion? What hurdles seem to stand in the way of these relationships? What makes them worse? What makes them better? Many patients see a Higher Power as punitive. They see a Higher Power as they saw their fathers or mothers. These transferences, attitudes, and beliefs need to be discussed with the group. The pastor or counselor should be free to discuss his or her own relationships with self, others, and the Higher Power of his or her own understanding.

As the counselor, you must be willing to accept how other people experience a Higher Power. You will see a wide variety of individual beliefs. This is good. Each person has his or her own understanding of what the Higher Power is like and what the Higher Power can do. In the atmosphere of unconditional acceptance, the group members can freely explore their own concepts of a Higher Power. They must see that a Higher Power and religion are not going to be shoved down their throats in this program.

It is a mistake to allow formal religious doctrine to enter into this group. Do not allow one group member to try to convince others about some religious principle or belief. Neither AA nor NA has any religious affiliation. People can talk about their religious preferences, but for the most part, they should discuss spirituality rather than religion. They need to talk about their own spiritual journeys.

How to Develop a Healthy Relationship With a Higher Power

The second group specifically delves into the relationship with a Higher Power. The group members write letters to a Higher Power in which they ask for what they want and share how they feel. They may come up with questions that they would ask a Higher Power if the power was sitting next to them. The group members share this material with each other. The group is encouraged to view the relationship with the Higher Power as essential to the program. Patients are encouraged to share their knowledge of a Higher Power with each other. What do they want a Higher Power to be like? What does a Higher Power want from them? How can people have a relationship with a Higher Power?

The group needs to process through how God communicates with them. The relationship with God needs to be presented as a simple dialogue between two people. Patients can be taught to contact God in a variety of ways. Nature, scripture, prayer, meditation, church, and other people all are ways in which God can speak to them. Each of these ways needs to be discussed, and patients in the group should give examples of when they felt close to or far away from a Higher Power.

The Eleventh Step Group

The third group seeks ways of improving conscious contact with God. Prayer and meditation are defined and discussed. Prayer is described as talking to God, whereas meditation is described as listening for knowledge of God's will. Patients are encouraged to begin to talk to God. They need to discuss various methods of prayer and meditation. They are encouraged to look for God in themselves and in each other. What do they see in themselves that is loving and good? Patients explore the moral law. We all know what is right and wrong. Why do we all have the same laws? Is it possible that some life force gives us these laws? If that is possible, then who might that force be? Patients are asked to explore several philosophical questions. If there is a God, then why didn't God make Himself more knowable? If there is a God, and if God is all good, then how come bad things happen?

The Meditation Group

The fourth group does an exercise in an attempt to contact God directly. The patients are told that God may communicate with them in many different ways, thoughts, feelings, images, other people, scripture, music, nature, and so on. God often communicates with them inside of their own minds. God may contact them in words or in images inside of their own thinking. The patients are told that the group members will try to establish a conscious contact with God, as they understand God, and that they will try to receive a direct communication from God. It is explained that God may communicate with them in one of three ways:

1. In words inside of their thinking
2. In images inside of their thinking
3. In no words or images, but the communication will be known

Give the group members a piece of paper and tell them to write down any communications they receive. Then play some soft music and take the group members through an imagery exercise. You can take them through the exercise yourself, or you can order a book, *God Talks to You* (Perkinson, 2000), and a meditation tape, *A Communication From God,* on the Web (www.godtalkstoyou.com). If you want to do it yourself, then speak these words slowly and rhythmically:

"Close your eyes and concentrate on your breathing. Just feel the cool air coming in and the warm air going out. As you concentrate on your breathing, you will begin to relax. Your arms and legs will begin to feel heavy and warm. See, as completely as you can in your own way, an image of ocean waves. Don't worry about how you are seeing these waves. Just try and see them as completely as you can. See the waves build, as you inhale, and wash upon a shore as you exhale. There is no right way or wrong way to do this exercise. There is just your way. God knows exactly what you need to experience. Feel yourself relax more as you see the waves build and wash upon the shore. You begin to feel more at peace.

"Picture an island, inside of your mind, with palm trees and lush green vegetation. See yourself standing on a white sandy beach watching the ocean, watching the waves. There is a trail on this island, and you see yourself turn and take this trail. You walk under the palm trees. You are not in a hurry. You have plenty of time. You walk to a hill that is covered with wildflowers. You climb the hill, and as you do, you become more tired. Your arms and legs feel heavy.

"At the top of the hill is a huge field of flowers. You can see all the way down to the sea. You sit in the center of the field and feel yourself relax in the sun. You call out for the Higher Power of your choice three times. You may call out for God, or Jesus, a Higher Power, you choose, but call out three times.

"A person dressed in white walks out of the trees and begins to walk to you. The person is looking right into your eyes. You know who this person is. This is your Higher Power. The person comes to you, and you stand up and embrace God. You have waited for God all your life. God sits across from you, takes your hands, and looks you right in the eyes. God has a communication for you. Open yourself up in every way you know how and receive the communication from God. I will give you 5 minutes to receive the communication. I will count off the minutes for you."

You then are silent and speak only to count off the minutes. At 2 minutes, you state, "If you are receiving only silence, then stretch yourself into the silence and seek your communication." At 4 minutes, you state, "You may have questions for God. Ask them and God may answer them for you."

At the end of the 5 minutes, you state, "Now stand up in the field and place God into your heart, where your Higher Power will stay. Walk down the hill and back to the beach. Watch the ocean waves. Feel yourself in your chair. Wiggle your toes and your fingers. Feel your eyelids flutter, and when you feel comfortable, go ahead and open your eyes and write down the communication you received."

After the patients have written down their communications, go around the group and have each of them share what he or she received. If a patient received no communication, then have that person discuss what happened when things were silent. How did the patient feel? What did the patient think? What did the patient see in his or her mind?

When everyone has shared his or her communication, have the group members decide whether or not they believe that this communication came from God. Have them describe the characteristics of the person who delivered the message. What was that person like? Do they believe that this is a person who can be trusted?

All of the spirituality groups should begin with the serenity prayer and end with the Lord's prayer. Those patients who do not feel comfortable praying can remain silent. At all points in spirituality group, you need to concentrate on spirituality and not on religion. You must be willing for each patient to find his or her own unique relationship with God. Each patient is seeking the God of his or her own understanding.

If this is done properly, then it will be the most important turning point for most of your patients in treatment. Alcoholics Anonymous (1976) says that (a) we were alcoholics and could not manage our own lives, (b) probably no human power could have relieved our alcoholism, and (c) God could and would if God was sought. Following God's plan for us is the only way of getting and keeping the peace that AA calls serenity. Addicts need personal experiences with a Higher Power. They need to walk into the presence of a Higher Power and feel the incredible joy of a Higher Power's love that is so much better than any drug. For more information about this procedure, I highly recommend you get my book *God Talks to You* (Perkinson, 2000). The text will tell you how to help patients make conscious contact with God and then to help patients make progress along the spiritual journey.

The Childhood Group

In the childhood group, patients come to understand how they developed the tendency to lie about themselves. They come to understand the great lie. The great lie is that if you tell people the whole truth about yourself, then they will not like you. The truth is the opposite of this: If you do not tell people the truth about yourself, then they cannot like you. Most of the patients have been living their lives as though the great lie were the truth. They need to hear that they were created in perfection in the image of God. There is no reason for them to lie. The group members need to see that they could not be themselves and that they pretended to be someone else. They wore a variety of social masks and played a variety of roles. They thought that it was the only way in which they could ever be loved.

How to Explore Early Parental Relationships

The group explores early parental relationships. The patients had to pretend to be someone else to their parents. They knew that their parents would not love them for who they were. This belief system resulted in the patients feeling empty and unloved. They did not get what they wanted from their homes of origin. Chemical dependency is an attempt to avoid this empty feeling. Most chemically dependent persons come out of their childhoods feeling inadequate and unloved by parents and others.

Have the group members write a letter to their parents. This work is based on some of the work of Bradshaw (1990). As the counselor, you introduce the exercise like this. "Write a letter to your parents using your nondominant hand. This makes the letter look like a small child wrote it. Write them about how you felt as a child growing up. Tell them how you were feeling and what you wanted that you didn't get."

After the group members write their letters, have each patient read his or her letter to the group. Then have the other members of the group respond, each in turn, as if they were the *healthy* parent hearing the letter. If the patient feels comfortable, then have the group members reach out and touch the patient as they respond. The group should sound something like this.

John reads his letter. "Dear Mom and Dad. Mom, I wanted you and Dad to stop fighting. I wanted you to pay more attention to me. Dad, I wanted you to take me fishing and tell me you loved me. I wanted you to stop drinking. I wanted you to tell me everything was going to be all right. I was afraid."

Joyce, a group member, reaches out and touches John's arm. She speaks as if she is John's healthy mother. "John, I'm sorry your dad and I were fighting. We were having problems. It wasn't your fault. I love you."

Meg, another group member, leans over to John. She too plays the role of a healthy mother. "I'm sorry your dad and I were fighting. We didn't mean to frighten you. We both love you very much."

Frank speaks as the healthy father. "John, I'm sorry I was drinking. I'm sick. I'm going to try and get some help. I'd love to go fishing with you."

How to Begin to Heal Early Childhood Pain

After all of the group members have read their letters, you take the group through this imagery exercise. This exercise must be positive. It must emphasize that the patients are now going to be their own champions in recovery. They are going to take over the parental role. They are going to try to forgive their parents and reach for their Higher Power. You should speak very slowly, pausing briefly after each sentence.

"Close your eyes and relax. Feel yourself becoming more comfortable. See yourself drifting back through time. See your high school. What was that building like—was it brick or wood? See yourself walking the halls of that school. How did you feel at that time in your life? Did you feel happy? Did you feel frightened? Feel the feelings that you were feeling then. See your grade school. See the playground. See a special friend. What is your friend wearing? See yourself playing a favorite game with your friend. How did you feel in that school? Reexperience the feelings that you were having at that time.

"See yourself walk up the street where you lived as a small child. See your house up ahead. You walk up the front walkway and peek in your window. Which room was yours? Go inside your house and see yourself as a small child. How did you feel in that house? Did you feel safe? Did you feel loved? Feel the feelings you were feeling then. See your mother. How did you feel when she was there? See your father. How did you feel about him?

"Walk over to yourself as a child and smile. Imagine that the child looks up at you. Tell the child, 'I am from your future. I am going to be your champion from now on. You can trust me. I am going to keep you safe. I am going to see to it that good things happen to you. You are important. You matter to me. I want to listen to how you feel. I care for what you want.' Tell the child that it is time for you to leave. You are growing up. You are not going to blame your parents anymore. That would not do any good. They were trying as hard as they could to love you. You pick the child up, and the child wraps his or her arms around you. You carry the child out of the house. Your parents come out on the porch and wave good-bye. Your Higher Power appears beside you. Your new AA/NA group members are ahead. 'Come on,' they say. 'You can do it. We'll help you.' You walk up the street feeling confident, trusting yourself, trusting your Higher Power, trusting your new support group. You feel happy and at peace. Everyone is smiling. You and the child are laughing together. You take the child and place him or her into your heart, where the child will stay. You feel yourself coming back to this time, back to the treatment center, back to your chair. Take a deep breath. Feel your toes wiggle and your eyelids flicker. When you feel comfortable, open your eyes."

The group then discusses the exercise. It is important that the group not delve deeply into old childhood pain. If you keep pulling on these memories, they can overwhelm patients. Most of these wounds need to be left to the second year in recovery. Patients in early recovery need to concentrate on working a self-directed program of recovery. Once their program is stable, usually in the second year, they can begin to work through some of the origin issues. In early recovery, you want to connect the patients to their feelings and not work through every issue. You want them to feel supported by their new group and their Higher Power. This will give them new hope that even the old pain can be resolved.

The Men's Group/ Women's Group

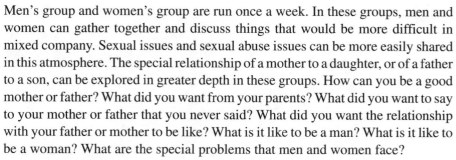

Men's group and women's group are run once a week. In these groups, men and women can gather together and discuss things that would be more difficult in mixed company. Sexual issues and sexual abuse issues can be more easily shared in this atmosphere. The special relationship of a mother to a daughter, or of a father to a son, can be explored in greater depth in these groups. How can you be a good mother or father? What did you want from your parents? What did you want to say to your mother or father that you never said? What did you want the relationship with your father or mother to be like? What is it like to be a man? What is it like to be a woman? What are the special problems that men and women face?

The group needs to discuss how to have healthy relationships with the opposite sex. They need to consider addictive, dependent, and normal relationships as well as how they differ. Women can discuss the premenstrual syndrome that may make some of them more vulnerable to relapse. Men need to discuss anger and how to use it appropriately. Men and women can role-play various situations. Both groups need to discuss boundaries and how to establish and maintain appropriate boundaries around themselves.

The Community Group

Community group is where the patient population meets to discuss problems that they are having with each other or the staff. This group usually is run first thing in the morning and lasts for only a few minutes. Some programs run this group daily and some weekly. A daily group is best if the patients feel supported.

A daily meditation should be read during this group. Any rules of the treatment center that have been broken need to be outlined and discussed. Have the group members join hands or put their arms around each other and commit themselves to helping each other through treatment.

The Personal Inventory Group

At the end of every treatment day, the patients have personal inventory group. In this group, they evaluate their day. They need to consider how they grew in the program and how they slipped backward. At a minimum, they need to consider each of the following points:

1. What did I do to love myself today?
2. What did I do to love others today?
3. What did I do to love my Higher Power today?
4. Was I honest?
5. What uncomfortable feelings did I have?
6. What did I do with my feelings?
7. What character defects caused me problems?
8. How have I been doing in my program?
9. What am I grateful for?
10. What do I need to do differently tomorrow?

Once patients have considered their personal inventories, they need to share positive experiences from the day. Then they need to go through a relaxation exercise to wind down. This exercise can be taped or given by the counselor. Have the patients sit in a comfortable place and pay attention to their breathing. Then have them imagine a relaxing scene. They can imagine that they are at the beach, in the mountains, down by a river, or in the desert. Take them through the scene for about 20 minutes and call it a night.

The Contracts

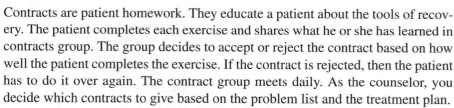

Contracts are patient homework. They educate a patient about the tools of recovery. The patient completes each exercise and shares what he or she has learned in contracts group. The group decides to accept or reject the contract based on how well the patient completes the exercise. If the contract is rejected, then the patient has to do it over again. The contract group meets daily. As the counselor, you decide which contracts to give based on the problem list and the treatment plan.

Contracts can be listed as specific objectives. They help a patient to identify a problem, understand the problem, and learn new skills to overcome the problem. These are tools of recovery that are individualized for each patient. The types of contracts are infinite. You will want to develop some of them on your own. There are a few contracts that you will use more often. There are some, such as the Chemical Use History, that you will use on every patient. This chapter discusses the contracts that you will use most often. You can order a wide variety of other contracts from treatment facilities (e.g., Hazelden, Educational Materials, P.O. Box 176, Center City, MN 55012).

**The Chemical
Use History**

The Chemical Use History (Appendix 8) is designed to give patients and their counselors a detailed account of the patients' use of drugs and alcohol. This is an excellent way of breaking through the patients' denial. It is very beneficial for the patients to see the whole thing written down at one time. There is nothing like writing down the history of the patients' chemical abuse and presenting it in front of their treatment peers for breaking through the denial system.

Patients need to address each drug that they took and process through any problems that the drug caused them in their lives. They need to identify specifically when they started using and detail their patterns of use. Where do they use and with whom? What happens when they use? What are the consequences? Each problem caused or exacerbated by use needs to be identified and discussed with the group.

Most patients will hedge, at least to some degree, in presenting their Chemical Use History. Remember that these patients come into treatment in denial. They do not know what the truth is. You and the group need to be ready to press a patient when group members feel that the patient is not being completely honest. The group members can give examples of how they answered certain questions when they came into treatment. This solidifies that the patient is not trying to lie. The patient is just fooled by the denial process.

As you work through the Chemical Use History, you will be able to firm up patients' diagnoses. Periods of intense intoxication; blackouts; withdrawal symptoms; using to avoid symptoms of withdrawal; and all consequences in the home, work, and school are covered. The feeling of shame and humiliation needs to be identified, and the group needs to support the patients when they have these feelings. The patients need to feel like they are not alone. Now the patients are with their brothers and sisters in this program.

Honesty

The Honesty exercise (Appendix 9) helps patients to see how they have been distorting reality. All patients use denial, in its many forms, to keep themselves from experiencing the pain that the truth would bring. If they were to see the whole picture about themselves, then they would realize that they were deathly ill and needed treatment. This fact would create tremendous fear in the patients, and they would have to do something about their problems.

Patients keep from feeling this fear by minimizing, rationalizing, denying, blaming, distorting, projecting, intellectualizing, diverting, and countless other ways of not seeing the truth. The other patients in contracts group will need help with this exercise. Patients cannot uncover unconscious denial without help from the group. The Honesty exercise just gets them started in this process. Treatment should be an endless search for the truth.

It is an eye-opening experience for patients to realize just how much they have been lying to themselves and to others. Patients usually feel guilty about lying to others, but they do not realize that the persons to whom they have lied the most were themselves.

Patients need to process how they feel about themselves when they lie and learn the consequences of dishonesty. If patients lie, then they will be lonely and will not be able to solve problems in the real world. They need to understand why dishonesty leads to empty relationships. If you tell people lies about yourself, then people cannot know the real you and you will feel unloved, empty, and alone. If patients lie to themselves about the real world, then they cannot use the facts to solve problems. If problems are not solved, then they escalate until the patients go crazy, get sick, and/or use drugs.

Love, Trust, and Commitment

The Love, Trust, and Commitment exercise (Appendix 10) builds self-esteem. Patients come into treatment not understanding what love is. They might have love confused with sex. Patients need to develop a new positive relationship with themselves. They have been saying bad things to themselves for a long time. "I'm no good. I'm bad. I'm stupid. I'm ugly. I'm unlovable." These thoughts dominate the patients' thinking and keep them feeling discouraged, depressed, and anxious.

Using the Love, Trust, and Commitment exercise, patients build a positive relationship with themselves and others. For this, they will need to understand the essential ingredients in a healthy relationship. They need to understand where their original feelings of inadequacy and rejection come from. They need to explore their first relationships with their parents or primary caregivers and how these relate to their current relationships with themselves and others.

Patients need to learn what it means to trust themselves and to commit themselves to their own individual growth. What do they need to see from themselves that will show them that they are trustworthy? What do they need to see from themselves that will show them that they are committed to their own recovery?

Patients need to learn how to be loving to themselves and to others. They need to say positive loving things to themselves. They need to give themselves a lot of praise whenever they try to do something well. These skills will need to be practiced on a daily basis.

Many patients will have considerable difficulty in working through this exercise. Some might even fight and say that there is nothing positive to say about themselves. They have a hard time thinking up anything good to say about themselves. These patients need the help of the group. Each group member might have to come up with something positive to say about such a patient. It might be a long time before the patient believes these things, but if he or she keeps trying, then the new ideas will begin to take hold.

Patients need to develop a personal plan that will help them to treat themselves well. They need to act as if they are persons worthy of good things. They need to learn how to praise themselves and others, and they need to practice this skill. A compliments group often is helpful to get this process started. In this group, each member comes up with positive things to say about each other member.

Feelings

The Feelings exercise (Appendix 11) is designed to help patients identify their feelings and use them appropriately to solve problems. The patients are told that all feelings are motivators. Feelings give energy and direction for movement. Each feeling is connected to a specific motor activity. Fear gives the energy and direction to run away from danger. If patients cannot use their fear, then they cannot run and they are handicapped. Similarly, if they cannot act appropriately on their anger, then they are more vulnerable to the world. If patients cannot feel, then they cannot adapt to their environment.

Chemically dependent people treat their feelings with drugs or alcohol. They do not use their feelings to solve problems. The Feelings exercise takes the patients through each feeling, connects them with the physical cues that accompany each feeling, and teaches them how to problem solve.

The main point that patients need to get is this: Each feeling needs to be carefully processed. Patients need to stop, think, and plan before they act. Each feeling is directing the patients to take some sort of action. The patients must have the skill of identifying each feeling and understand what each feeling is directing them to do. Then the patients need to process through their options of action, decide which is the best, and act.

Patients in treatment need a lot of practice in properly identifying their feelings. They have old skills that will constantly get in the way. For example, when men feel hurt or frightened, they often act angry. That is confusing. Once the patients are able to identify the real feeling—the pain—they can address the problems more accurately.

Women often cry when they are angry. This is confusing to them and to others, and it muddies the waters of problem solving. Their husbands might react to the tears when in fact the real problem is that the women are angry. You and the group help the patients to get at the core feeling and then process through the feeling to resolve the problem.

Bob might come to group acting angry and sullen. When it comes time for him to talk, he might not talk about the anger at all. He might talk about his fear. Bob might not even be aware that he is angry. Perhaps in his home of origin, he could not get angry or else he would incur the wrath of his father. As a child, it was dangerous for Bob to feel angry, so he did not feel it. He repressed it and felt scared instead. The group might need to teach Bob how he is really feeling by processing the situation with him. What happened to Bob that caused the feeling? How would the rest of the group have felt in a similar situation? Bob's anger is reflected to him by one group member: "Bob, you say you feel scared, but you look angry."

Patients who have felt feelings for the first time in their lives can express their feelings in group in a nonthreatening environment. They are not rejected for their feelings. They are accepted and loved no matter how they feel.

Patients need to know that all of their feelings are friendly and are great and wise counselors that need to be listened to and acted on. Acting too quickly on feelings is a mistake. This causes impulse control problems, which make the patients vulnerable to relapse. Feelings need to be processed carefully and acted on rationally. That takes a lot of practice.

Relationship Skills

■

Patients who are chemically dependent have poor interpersonal relationship skills. They manipulate, distort, accuse, blame, shame, project, sulk, rage, and harbor deep-seated resentments. They are trying to control the world and everyone in it, and they are furious when everything is not going their way. The Relationship Skills exercise (Appendix 12) has been designed to teach and practice healthy interpersonal relationship skills.

Patients learn that love is not a feeling. It is an action in truth. You cannot love and lie. Love is the interest in and active involvement in people's individual growth. Self-love is the interest in and active involvement in your own individual growth. To love, you have to be there for yourself or for the other people when they need you. Chemically dependent people cannot do this. Sometimes they are too intoxicated or hung over. No drug addict is completely trustworthy.

Patients are taught that commitment means stability over time. Commitment is developed by working a daily program of recovery. Patients must take the time necessary to nourish themselves and others.

Patients need to be encouraging and reinforcing to themselves and others. They practice the skill of giving praise. Some patients will need specific social skills training. They need to learn how to do simple things such as making good eye contact and standing at an acceptable interpersonal distance. As the patients practice good interpersonal skills, it is important that they recognize how they feel when they are using healthy skills compared to the old skills they have been using.

It is inevitable that patients will use their old methods of coping with conflict while in treatment. When this happens, you and the group can help these patients to stop and use their new skills. Nothing solidifies learning better than watching the consequence of the old behavior compared to the new behavior. The patients will see that the new skills work better and result in better problem solving. The old skills tend to make the problem worse.

Patients will need a lot of practice in sharing how they feel and in asking for what they want. Most of them are trying to tell people what they want to hear rather than the truth. This results in the patients feeling unknown. They need to share their feelings and watch the other members of the group respond appropriately.

Many patients are reluctant to share their feelings. They never have asked for what they wanted. They have been taught that this is selfish or that other people simply do not care. It is a new experience for these patients to see the power of the truth.

Compromise is necessary for healthy relationships. Patients have to practice working through issues until every party is satisfied with the result. This is called the "win-win scenario." Each party in a conflict shares how he or she feels, and what he or she wants, until the problem is resolved. New options have to be constantly thrown out by the group for consideration. The primary principle is this: Treat other people the same way in which you want to be treated.

Patients are taught that all people need to be respected equally regardless of race, color, creed, education, or belief system. Healthy relationships demand caring for how other people feel and caring for what they want.

Addictive Relationships
■

Many patients coming through treatment for chemical addiction are just as addicted to some other person as they are to their drugs of choice. Addictive relationships can be as destructive as alcohol or drugs. They leave the patients feeling empty, abandoned, and unlovable. People can be so hooked on other people that they cannot see the truth.

The Addictive Relationships exercise (Appendix 13) is designed to teach patients the difference between healthy and addictive relationships. It teaches them what they need to do if they are in relationships that are addictive. These unhealthy relationships are fueled by powerful sexual feelings that the patients mistake for love. The patients become caught up in the excitement of emotionally chaotic relationships.

Addictive relationships are characterized by the same loss of reality as is involved in chemical dependency. The patients are unaware that these relationships are bad for them and are convinced that they are the best things that have ever happened in their lives. Lies permeate these relationships, which are filled with feelings of intense fear, anger, and pain.

An addictive relationship must use lies to keep going. The partners must feel that they have to stay in the relationship to feel normal. They fear that without the relationship, they will be lonely forever. "I will never have anything as good as this. I can't live without her."

Addictive relationships are filled with verbal and physical abuse. They are demoralizing and end in feelings of anger and abandonment. Patients who have addictive relationships typically will have a pattern of these relationships rather than just one.

Patients use these relationships in a similar way as they use drugs. The relationships distract them from their real pain and fill their lives with something to obsess about. The patients will need to make the decision either to get out of these addictive relationships or to take the relationships into long-term treatment.

Communication Skills

■

The Communication Skills exercise (Appendix 14) teaches healthy communication skills. It is essential that these skills be practiced in group as well as in individual sessions. The patients need to be constantly reminded to use these skills.

Basically, good communication necessitates being able to listen well and speak clearly. Active listening pulls out more of a person's communication until all of the message is perceived.

Words are symbols for thoughts and feelings. They are accompanied by nonverbal cues that often are more accurate than the words themselves. Patients who tell you that they are doing well with flat unemotional voices and downcast eyes are telling you with their words that they are fine, but with their actions they are telling you another thing entirely.

To develop good listening skills, patients need to practice repeating what the other person said. People often have different communication patterns, or family rules, that other people do not understand. In certain cultures, for example, friends argue vehemently about things. That is just how they communicate. In other cultures, this behavior might be considered insulting. Patients who are used to using an angry tone of voice to get their point across need to hear how it adversely affects other people. They might not know how scary it is.

Many patients need to develop empathy skills. They have to practice understanding and personally relating to how other people are feeling. This will take a lot of trial-and-error practice. Patients must try to relate personally to what other people are saying by directly relating it to their own personal experience.

As patients watch you validate the other members of the group, they will begin to be more reinforcing to each other. Patients need to be encouraged to use "I feel" statements when they speak. Many chemically dependent persons constantly blame others for their problems. "You" is perceived as the problem rather than "I." Statements that begin with "You" usually are headed for trouble. In the great scheme of things, we know much more about "I" than we do about "you."

Patients need to be reminded to be positive in their interactions with each other. A positive attitude needs to be soundly reinforced by all staff members. Patients who are not positive need to see how their attitude clouds their whole day. They need to practice saying positive things to themselves and others, even if they do not feel positive.

Patients with poor communication skills need to go through the Communication Skills exercise with at least five of their treatment peers. These skills have to be practiced over and over again until they are used automatically. The more the patients practice, the better communicators they will become.

Self-Discipline

■

The Self-Discipline exercise (Appendix 15) is for those individuals who have a difficult time in delaying gratification and accepting responsibility for their own actions. They constantly blame other people for their problems. They think that they would be fine if other people would leave them alone. Patients with these problems often have antisocial traits. They have had no experience with success. They never have worked at a goal long enough to reach the goal.

These individuals need to see themselves achieve objectives in gradually escalating steps. They can accomplish things if they settle down and try. Most of these individuals have a low frustration tolerance, and they have serious problems with impulse control. They act out too quickly on their feelings, particularly anger and frustration.

Begin with a simple task, such as one of the contracts, and walk the patients through it. Do not get frustrated with them when they procrastinate. That is all they know how to do. Have them sit down for a few minutes at a time and work through a page of the exercise. When they have accomplished something, reinforce them. Tell them that they can do it if they try and that you have confidence in them. These patients need to see themselves be successful. They need to feel like they can do things that are difficult. Self-discipline is not an easy skill, and many times it will be frustrating. But remember that if the patients get reinforced for doing something, then the behavior will increase.

Patients need to see how poor self-discipline leads to failure. To accomplish this objective, the patients need to process through several of their problems with you. Take a problem that caused them quite a bit of pain, such as getting arrested or failing at something they really wanted, and walk them through the problem. Where did they go wrong? What else could they have done? Who was responsible?

Let's take someone who got arrested for drunk driving. This person might be blaming the police. "They have always been out to get me." But who was drunk? Did the police make this person drive drunk? In what way is the patient responsible?

Patients must understand that if other people are responsible for everything bad that happens to them, then other people are in control of their lives. They need to re-achieve control by taking back the responsibility for their own behavior.

Patients with poor self-discipline do not understand the rules. They break the rules of society to get their own way. They do not understand that the rules are there to keep them safe. The spiritual part of the program can be a benefit here. The patients need to understand that God did not make the rules to keep us from having a good time. God made the rules so that we could be safe and happy. The same thing goes for the laws of the state. The legislature makes the rules to protect its citizens.

These patients usually will break some rules in treatment and will blame others for their rule breaking. You must walk them through these violations and help them to see that it was their choice to break the rules. Breaking the rules resulted in their getting caught and experiencing pain. If they could learn how to obey the rules, then they would feel better all of the time.

Patients with self-discipline problems have poor problem-solving skills. They go for the pleasure first, being unable to delay gratification long enough to achieve long-term goals. They need to process several problems with you while in treatment. If they want job training, how are they going to get that? What are they going to have to do specifically? If they want to stay sober, how are they going to get that? They must learn and practice working on a problem on a daily basis until the problem is solved. These individuals usually have such low frustration tolerance that they are unable to feel much pain without acting impulsively. People who can tolerate little pain cannot work at anything for very long. They must see themselves take off a small piece of a problem and work on it until the whole problem is resolved.

Impulse Control

■

Patients who have impulse control problems act too quickly on their feelings. They need only a little of a feeling to move into action. If they feel angry, then they act angry immediately. This leaves them vulnerable to relapse. Craving is a feeling. If they move too quickly when they crave, then they will relapse into using substances. The Impulse Control exercise (Appendix 16) helps the patients to develop control over their feelings.

These patients need to stop, think, and plan before they act. This takes a great deal of practice, particularly when the patients are feeling strong emotions.

Patients must be able to identify each feeling, understand why they are having the feeling, consider the options of action, plan their response, and then act. When they are having strong feelings, the patients need to stop and analyze their feelings carefully. They cannot continue to act too quickly on their feelings. That leads to disaster.

Patients need to understand the behavior chain and practice analyzing their behavior carefully. They need to understand how their poor impulse control led to excessive drinking or drug use. They have developed a habit of moving immediately from craving to drug use. They will need to develop another plan and practice that plan many times in treatment.

These individuals are particularly vulnerable when they are feeling angry and frustrated. They have a low frustration tolerance, and they desire immediate gratification. They need to understand how this has led them into trouble. Most of them will have to work through the Self-Discipline exercise.

These individuals will need to learn assertiveness skills and will need to role-play interpersonal conflict. When they act impulsively in treatment, they need to process through the situation until they understand how they could have handled it better.

As patients become more skilled at identifying their feelings, they can begin to address the real feelings. What underlies most anger is pain. As the patients begin to solve real problems in real time and with real people, they feel less frustrated and more in control.

When angry, these patients must take a "time out" and walk away from such situations. They cannot stay in situations where they have lost control before. Teach them and their significant others to use the "time out" sign of a referee when they are feeling too angry. They also can say "time out" as they make the sign. Their partners then agree to say nothing except "okay, time out." The patients then leave these situations to get their thinking accurate. They might have to call other people to process the problem with a third party before they come back into the original situations. The patients must promise to come back within a previously specified length of time to continue to work on the problems. Both members of a couple need to write this plan down and follow it every time they have a significant conflict. Everyone who gets angry knows when he or she is beginning to "lose it." At the earliest possible opportunity, someone needs to make the "time out" sign and then follow the prearranged contract.

All anger, fueled by pain, is there to make the pain stop. To be angry, patients must establish other people to blame. They must think that the other people purposely did things wrong that hurt them. This rarely is accurate. Other people are just trying to meet their needs. They rarely are trying to hurt others.

Patients with impulse control problems will need to come up with a written plan that they carry with them at all times. When they are feeling strong emotions, they need to carry out the plan. They can call their sponsors, go to meetings, read some AA/NA material, turn the situations over, talk with friends, and so on.

Relapse Prevention

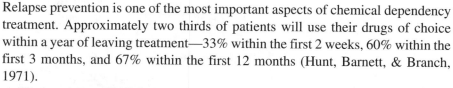

Relapse prevention is one of the most important aspects of chemical dependency treatment. Approximately two thirds of patients will use their drugs of choice within a year of leaving treatment—33% within the first 2 weeks, 60% within the first 3 months, and 67% within the first 12 months (Hunt, Barnett, & Branch, 1971).

Most patients (60%) lapse within 3 months of leaving treatment. This is the period of highest risk, and it needs the greatest attention. The patients must be willing to do almost anything to prevent relapse during this period of time. They need to see themselves as clinging to an ice-covered cliff with their recovery group holding the only rope. The most important thing that they can do is go to meetings. Patients who are working a daily program of recovery will not relapse. They cannot work the program and use at the same time. The two are incompatible.

Relapse is a process that begins before the first use. A patient begins to feel under stress. The patient's new tools of recovery are not used, so the problems continue to escalate. The patient reaches a point where he or she thinks that the only option is to drink or use drugs.

The Relapse Prevention exercise (Appendix 17) uses the works of Gorski and Miller (1986) and Marlatt and Gordon (1985) to develop a relapse prevention plan. Relapse prevention takes working a daily program of recovery. The patient must take his or her personal inventory at the end of every day. If any of the relapse symptoms become evident, then immediate action must be taken.

Gorski and Miller (1982) developed a list of 37 relapse warning signs. The patient checks this every day for symptoms that he or she is having problems. The patient must have a written plan detailing the exact thing that he or she is going to do if the patient gets into trouble. The patient carries an emergency card full of telephone numbers of people he or she can call if problems arise.

Other people need to be encouraged to check the patient daily for relapse warning signs. This is a good reason to go to daily meetings and to hang around other recovering persons. Other people often can see what the patient is unable to see for himself or herself.

Patients need to identify high-risk situations that may trigger relapse and develop coping skills to deal with each situation. The more patients can practice these skills, the better off they will be. In groups, patients need to role-play high-risk situations and help each other make relapse prevention plans.

Each patient will be different, but Marlatt and Gordon (1985) found that most relapse occurs when patients are experiencing the following high-risk situations:

1. Negative emotions
   a. Particularly anger and frustration but also negative emotions such as boredom, jealousy, depression, and anxiety
2. Social pressure
   a. Being in a social situation where people are using or being directly encouraged to use by someone
3. Interpersonal conflict
   a. Can be conflict with a parent, spouse, child, boss, friend, and so on

4. Positive emotions
   a. The patient wanting to celebrate after something positive happening such as a promotion, wedding, birth of a child, or graduation
5. To test personal control
   a. Using to find out whether the patient can control the alcohol or drug again

Using the relapse exercise, patients develop the skills necessary to deal with each of the high-risk situations and practice the skills until they become skilled at them. All patients must role-play drug refusal situations until they can say no and feel relatively comfortable. They must examine and experience all of their triggers, see through the first use, and learn about euphoric recall.

All patients must develop a plan for a lapse. What are they going to do if they use again? Who are they going to contact? What are they going to say? This must be role-played in group so that the patients can see that the people on the other end of the phone are not going to be angry at them.

Patients must understand the behavior chain and develop skills for changing their thoughts, feelings, and actions when they have craving. Using imagery and drug paraphernalia, the patients need to experience craving and learn experientially that craving will pass if they move away from their drugs of choice.

When you are discussing relapse with patients, you need to discuss the benefits of medications that cut relapse rates. Naltrexone and Acamprosate both reduce the craving for alcohol and decrease some of the reinforcing properties of drinking. These medications consistently cut the relapse rates in half. Naltrexone is an opioid antagonist that is helpful in many patients, particularly those with chronic histories of relapse. Naltrexone blocks some of the reinforcing properties of alcohol by blocking the action of endorphins (opium-like chemicals that exist naturally in the brain to kill pain). Endorphins give addicts the euphoric effects that trigger craving. Several studies have shown that alcoholics who take Naltrexone daily can decrease relapse rates by 50%. The alcoholic still may drink, but the intense craving is not triggered, so he or she can bring the drinking under control more quickly (O'Malley et al., 1992; Volpicelli, Alterman, Hayashida, & O'Brian, 1992).

Acamprosate soon will be Food and Drug Administration approved and now is approved for use in many European countries. This medication works by affecting gamma-aminobutyric acid (GABA) and excitatory amino acid (glutamate) neurotransmission rather than affecting the endogenous opioid system. It has been studied extensively and consistently cuts the craving for alcohol and reduces relapse rates (Littleton, 1995, 1996). One of these two medications should be encouraged to be used in everyone who can afford it. These drugs must be used in addition to working a program.

Stress Management
■

The Stress Management exercise (Appendix 30) helps patients to cope with stress. The inability to deal with stress effectively fuels chemical dependency. The patients have been using chemicals to deal with the uncomfortable feelings caused by stress.

Stress is the physiological response of the organism to a stressor. A stressor is any demand made on the body. This can include psychological or physiological loss, absence of stimulation, excessive stimulation, frustration of an anticipated reward, conflict, or the presence or anticipation of painful events (Zegans, 1982).

Selye (1956) found that if rats were presented with a problem to which there was no solution, they got sick. There was a generalized stress response that affected most organ systems. Initially, the body's response to stress is adaptive, but chronic stress is damaging. Severe stress has been linked with many diseases including kidney impairment, malignant high blood pressure, atherosclerosis, ulcers, anxiety, depression, increased infections, and cancer (Selye, 1956; Zegans, 1982).

To learn how to deal with stress more effectively, chemically dependent patients need to do three things: relax twice a day, maintain regular exercise, and learn coping skills for dealing with stressors (Benson, 1975).

Many patients resist developing these programs, and some will be unable to do so, but as many as possible need to be encouraged to practice these techniques. The patients who have the most trouble will have problems with self-discipline. They have not learned how to work toward a long-term goal. They will moan and complain whenever you mention the exercise or relaxation program. What they are really complaining about is they do not want to be told what to do. What is behind that is the inability to stick to things that they want to do. They have just failed too much and are unwilling to go to any length to stay clean and sober. Many of these patients will have antisocial traits. You have to show them, over and over again, why it is important to develop these programs.

If people relax twice a day for 10 to 20 minutes, they reap many benefits. They learn how to control their feelings, decrease tension, and decrease psychosomatic problems. In general, these people are happier and healthier. They learn that there is something that they can do to make themselves feel normal (Benson, 1975).

Patients can go through one of the formal relaxation techniques listed in the Stress Management exercise, or they can pray and meditate quietly twice a day. The important thing is that they practice relaxing. The more they do this, the better they will feel.

Once patients know what it feels like to relax, they can develop techniques to stay more relaxed during the day. If something stresses them, then they can use one of the techniques to recapture their serenity. The Higher Power can be used as an adjunct to this process. The patients can turn things over and relax.

It is very difficult to get some chemically dependent individuals to maintain an exercise program. This is like pulling teeth for some people, but you should encourage them. Research has shown that exercise is important, not only for cardiovascular fitness but also for a sense of psychosocial well-being (Folkins & Sime, 1981; Greist et al., 1979; Ledwidge, 1980; Stern & Cleary, 1981).

It has been demonstrated that hospitalized alcoholics can increase fitness levels in as little as 20 days. This increase enhances not only their physical fitness but also their self-concepts (Gary & Guthrie, 1972). A strong exercise program is important for developing a new sense of self-efficacy. Many chemically dependent people come into treatment thinking that they cannot do anything. When they see their strengths develop, they feel a new sense of power and control. They feel like they can do it. This is a key, particularly to adolescent patients who are concerned about their body images.

Rigorous exercise produces natural opioids in the body that will give patients a natural high (Appenzeller, Standefer, Appenzeller, & Atkinson, 1980). They feel better all day after working out. The patients must be encouraged to develop a stretching, strength, and cardiovascular fitness program. The exercise or recreational therapist will help them to individualize the program.

In learning new coping skills, patients need to learn assertiveness skills, social skills, and how to increase their involvement in pleasurable activities. The patients need to be shown what they are doing that makes their lives difficult. If they are frowning at everybody all of the time, they are not getting positive responses from the world. They need to learn how to be pleasant and how to ask for what they want. They need to practice sharing how they feel.

The Stress Management exercise helps patients to develop more pleasurable activities in their lives. They need to learn how to have fun clean and sober. They must be encouraged to reach out and try different things. If they sit at home and wait for the wonders of sobriety to overtake them, then they are going to be disappointed. They must reach out to others and become actively involved in their AA/NA groups and communities.

Many of these patients do not know how to have fun without chemicals. Chemicals have been their whole lives, and they are all that they know. The patients need to be shown that sobriety can be fun. This will be very difficult for many patients when they are grieving the loss of their drugs of choice. The pleasure of the drugs must be replaced by pleasure from the environment. This requires doing something new.

The best way of getting patients motivated is to show them that drugs and alcohol are no fun for them anymore. Once chemical dependency clicks in, the drugs lose their ability to make the patients feel better. The patients feel miserable when intoxicated and when clean. A new lifestyle must be developed to help the patients to enjoy their sobriety. New hobbies and interests have to be tried until the patients develop a leisure program that fits.

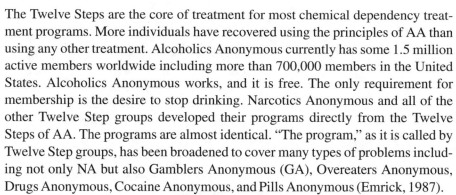

CHAPTER SEVEN | The Steps

The Twelve Steps are the core of treatment for most chemical dependency treatment programs. More individuals have recovered using the principles of AA than using any other treatment. Alcoholics Anonymous currently has some 1.5 million active members worldwide including more than 700,000 members in the United States. Alcoholics Anonymous works, and it is free. The only requirement for membership is the desire to stop drinking. Narcotics Anonymous and all of the other Twelve Step groups developed their programs directly from the Twelve Steps of AA. The programs are almost identical. "The program," as it is called by Twelve Step groups, has been broadened to cover many types of problems including not only NA but also Gamblers Anonymous (GA), Overeaters Anonymous, Drugs Anonymous, Cocaine Anonymous, and Pills Anonymous (Emrick, 1987).

Treatment programs differ as to which steps they address in treatment. Some programs address only Step One, some address Steps One to Three, and others address Steps One to Five. This must be individualized. Some patients will be able to embrace only the First Step, and that is fine if they do a good Step One. For most patients, it is beneficial to complete at least Steps One to Three while in treatment. The more steps the patients can complete, the better off they are in recovery and the further along they are in the program. Working through the Fifth Step takes a great burden off of patients. If they complete the Fifth Step, then they will not have to carry the burden of guilt into early sobriety.

If your center works only on the First Step, then that will give you more time to work on powerlessness and unmanageability. This chapter teaches you how to take the patient through Steps One to Five, assuming that some inpatient programs will go this far. Rare is the program that goes further than Step Five.

As you take patients through the steps, you must make sure that they are internalizing the material. The patients must be able to identify each problem, understand the problem, and learn coping skills for dealing with the problem. They must be able to verbalize to you a solid understanding of each step and how they are going to apply the step in their lives.

You will be able to tell when patients are complying and when they are understanding and internalizing the material. The level of commitment to sobriety will be evident in their behavior, in what they do, and in what they say. If you watch how they act with you and with their treatment peers, then you will have a good idea as to whether they are internalizing the information or not. If you are hearing one thing in individual sessions and a patient's peers are hearing another thing, then one of you is not getting the truth. The patient has to be confronted in group with the inconsistency of his or her behavior.

The Committee

■

Patients are constantly torn between the side of themselves that wants to use alcohol and drugs and the side that wants to get clean and sober. There often is a constant, and often turbulent, internal war going on inside of a patient's head. Each side tries to take control over the patient's behavior. Each side has its good and bad arguments. Sometimes it is hard for the patient to know who he or she is or what he or she wants. It feels as though there is more than one person talking to the patient inside of his or her head.

It is useful to label the three voices. Freud called them the id, the ego, and the superego. In treatment, we call these voices the disease, God, and me. One train of thinking is the disease process. This side only wants patients to use drugs or alcohol, and it does not care how it gets the patients to do it. If the patients feel miserable, this is all the better. Another voice is the voice of God. God only wants the patients to love themselves and others and to reach for their full potential in life. This voice is incredibly supportive and loving. The third voice is the patients' own thinking. Here the patients are trying to figure out things for themselves.

As you move patients through the steps, you must be careful not to continue to the next step until they have a solid foundation in the steps below. If the patients have not embraced a good Step One, then there is no use in moving on to Step Two. If you have to work on Step One the whole time the patients are in treatment, that is fine, but do not try to move up in the steps until the patients have a firm foundation of the steps below. The steps must be built one on top of the other. The first building block is Step One.

Step One

■

"We admitted we were powerless over alcohol—that our lives had become unmanageable" (Alcoholics Anonymous, 1976, p. 59). Read the Step One exercise (Appendix 18) before continuing on with this chapter.

It is vital that all patients complete a solid Step One in treatment. Step One is the most important step. Without it, recovery is impossible. Step One necessitates a total surrender. Patients must accept as true that they are chemically dependent and that their lives are unmanageable so long as they use mood-altering chemicals. Until this conscious and unconscious surrender occurs, the patients cannot grow. So long as they believe that they can somehow bring their lives under control and learn to use alcohol or drugs normally, they have not accepted their disease, they are stuck in the illness, and they cannot break free.

Step work is mainly group work. Patients complete the Step One exercise and present the exercise in group. The group members help the patients with the step, ask questions, and help you decide whether or not the step is completed successfully. You usually should not make this decision without the support of the group. Particularly in an inpatient setting, things go on in treatment that you, as the counselor, are not aware of. The patients may be complying with treatment and may be pretending that they are working when, in face, they really are not internalizing anything. The treatment peers are more likely to see these lies. They see the patients in casual interaction and pick up on the inconsistencies.

In Step One, patients must learn to accept as fact that they are chemically dependent, that they are powerless, and that their lives are unmanageable. They must understand that they cannot live normally so long as they use mood-altering substances.

The best way of convincing patients to surrender is to show them over and over again that they get into trouble when they drink or use drugs. They do not get into trouble every time, just sometimes, but they never can predict when the trouble is going to occur. They might drink a couple of beers and go home, or they might drink more and get arrested for drunk driving. The patients must process through many of their problems in detail until they realize that they never have been able to predict when they were going to have drug or alcohol problems. This is one of the primary reasons for processing through Step One.

How do patients feel about having blackouts? It is very scary for patients to know that they were awake doing things and that they cannot remember what they did. Did the patients do embarrassing things while intoxicated? What were they, and how do the patients feel about what they did? How do they feel about not doing things with their families, at school, or at work because they were too intoxicated or hung over? You must get at the real stories—exactly what happened—and examine how the patients feel. Talk about the shame, humiliation, depression, and anxiety caused by the drinking or drug use. How depressing is it to know that the patients' families are falling apart? How did it feel to be unable to keep promises?

Sometimes patients used chemicals more, or for a longer period of time, than they originally had intended. Once they began using, the addiction took control. Even when they promised themselves that they were going to stop or cut down, they kept on using. The patients must understand that once they start using, they never know what they are going to do.

Most chemically dependent patients want to hold onto the delusion that they still are in control. Patients do not want to admit that they are powerless and that their lives are unmanageable. They were having problems sometimes, they think, but only occasionally. The fact is that when the patients had problems, the problems almost always were directly related to chemical use. The patients got into trouble obtaining the substances, using the substances, or recovering from the substance use. Chemically dependent persons do things when they are intoxicated that they never would do when sober. They need to take a look at each of these things and see the painful consequences of their addictions. They need to take a careful look at their chemical use histories—at the lies, the crimes, the inconsistencies, and the people they have hurt. They need to understand that so long as they use drugs or alcohol, they will hurt.

Step Two

■

"[We] came to believe that a power greater than ourselves could restore us to sanity" (Alcoholics Anonymous, 1976, p. 59). Read the Step Two exercise (Appendix 19) before continuing on with this chapter.

The beginning of patients' spiritual program is Step One. This is the surrender step, and it is essential to accept powerlessness and unmanageability before the patients reach toward a Higher Power. The essential ingredient of Step Two is willingness. Without willingness to seek a power greater than themselves, the patients will fail. "There is one thing more than anything else that will defeat us in our recovery; this is an attitude of indifference or intolerance toward spiritual principles" (NA, 1988, p. 18). The patients have admitted that they are powerless and that their lives are unmanageable. They must now see the insanity of their disease and search for an answer to their problem.

The word *sanity* in AA means soundness of mind. To have a sound mind, a person must be able to see and adapt to reality. The person must be able to see what is real. No person who is chemically dependent sees reality accurately. The person is living in a deluded world of his or her own creation. The mind of a chemically dependent person is irrational. The person cannot see what is real, so he or she cannot adapt to reality.

In Step Two, patients take a look at their insane behavior. They see how crazy they were acting and reach for an answer. They must conclude that they cannot hold onto their old ways of thinking. If they do, then they will relapse into old behavior.

How to Help Patients Accept a Higher Power

Many patients rebel at the very idea of a Higher Power. They must be gently encouraged to open the door just a little and to seek. They must be encouraged to be honest, open-minded, and willing. They need power. They are powerless. They need someone else to manage. Their lives are unmanageable.

At first, you encourage patients to see that some sort of a Higher Power can exist. The patients must look at their interpersonal group and see that the group has more power than they do. You can say something like this to a patient: "If you wanted to leave this room, and the group wanted to keep you in, do you think you could leave?" The matter becomes obvious. The group could force the patient to stay inside of the room. It might take some wrestling, but the group has more physical power than the patient does. The patient could then be asked if he or she is willing to place his or her trust in the Higher Power of the group.

Trust is a difficult issue for most chemically dependent persons, and they will need to process their lack of trust with the group. This is a good issue for group work. If patients cannot trust the group as a whole, can they trust anyone in the group? If they cannot trust anyone, can they trust themselves? Are they willing to try to trust—to be open to the possibility? If they are unable to trust themselves and are unable to trust anyone else, then they are lost. They will have to start somewhere. This reality will have to be driven home. The patients cannot really trust themselves. That should be obvious. There were times when they were out of control, they were powerless, and their lives were unmanageable.

The best way of having patients learn to trust the group is to develop a loving group. This is a group in which the members are actively interested and involved in each other's growth. They gently help each other to search for the truth. The group members are kind, encouraging, and supportive. The group members never are hostile and aggressive. They do not put each other down. That is counterproductive. If you have an aggressive and highly confrontive group, then you will destroy trust. People must learn to confront each other in an atmosphere of love and unconditional positive regard. It is your job to teach the group this process.

Once patients trust the group, they can begin to transfer this trust to the AA/NA group. The patients should attend as many meetings as possible while in treatment. Gradually, the patients will feel safe and will begin to share. This builds trust. As the group members are interested in a patient, and as they show love to the patient, the patient's confidence in the group grows. This probably is the first time in the patient's life when he or she has told someone the absolute truth. When the group does not abandon the patient, it is a tremendous relief. This will show on the patient's face and will be etched into his or her heart.

Patients see people further along in the program doing better. These people look better and sound better. The patients cannot miss the power of the group process. It changes people right in front of their eyes. They will see new members come in frightened or hostile, and they will watch them turn around. They will watch the power of group support. Soon they will be offering new patients encouragement. They will learn how helpful it is to share their experiences, strengths, and hope.

Once patients see how insane they were acting and accept that the group has the power to restore them to sanity, they have come a long way toward embracing Step Two. By trusting the group, the patients open the door to a Higher Power. This basic building block of trust is vital to good treatment. Patients can miss seeing a Higher Power in others. These patients, on discharge, might feel that a Higher Power is the only answer they need. They might think that they do not have to go to meetings so long as they have a good spiritual program. These patients will not work a program of recovery, and they ultimately will relapse. All patients must be encouraged to trust the group process. They need other people to flag for them what they do not see in themselves.

Step Three

■

"[We] made a decision to turn our will and our lives over to the care of God *as we understood Him*" (Alcoholics Anonymous, 1976, p. 59). Read the Step Three exercise (Appendix 20) before continuing on with this chapter.

Most patients will have some difficulty with Step Three. They need to be reminded to turn problems over to their Higher Power. Chemically dependent people are self-centered, and they need to learn how to be God-centered. Patients can be so self-centered that they constantly set themselves up for unnecessary pain. They think that the whole world, and everyone in it, should revolve around them. When people do not cooperate with their self-aggrandizing plans, they are furious. They think that their spouses, children, and friends always should obey their every whim. Previous relationships in which their partners have been involved are seen as humiliating and self-degrading. They believe that everything should go exactly the way in which they want it to go. They believe that they are deserving of special honor and privileges. They care very deeply about what they want and how they feel, but their ability to empathize with others is seriously impaired (B. Carr, personal communication, 1992).

A patient might get furious when someone does something simple such as turn up the heat or fail to fix the car. When the world does not cooperate by doing exactly what the patient wants, he or she goes into a rage. A more serious form of this character defect is called narcissistic personality disorder.

Patients correct this defect by learning empathy for others and turning their will and their lives over to the care of a Higher Power. Our program is a set of spiritual principles through which we are recovering from a seemingly hopeless state of mind and body (NA, 1988, p. xvi).

The worst thing that you can do is push patients faster than they are ready to go. The decision to turn things over is the patients' decision. All you can do is encourage them.

You have one big thing going for you in Step Three. When the patients finally do turn things over, they feel immediate relief. They feel this relief emotionally, and this is the most powerful way of learning. They will feel that the stress of trying to figure out the problem is reduced. The pressure will be off, and they will feel better. Nothing works better than to show the patients how this tool of recovery works. If you give a chemically dependent person a good feeling, then he or she will want to re-create the feeling. That is what the person was doing with chemicals—seeking immediate relief from pain. The Third Step is the new answer that patients have been waiting for. They must experience it to believe it.

Many patients will stubbornly resist Step Three. Even people who have been in the program for years have difficulty with Step Three. Meetings are full of people talking about turning over the controls and then taking them back. Step Three is a decision that must be made every day.

There is a great hope here for patients in Step Three, and they will feel it. If there is a God, and if God loves them and will help them, that is great.

This newfound hope must not be shattered by religion. Religion can make people feel excluded. Religious doctrine must be kept out of the program as much as possible. If patients want to use a religious structure, that is encouraged so long as it sets the patients free and does not immerse them in guilt and remorse. The Higher Power is presented to the patients in an atmosphere of forgiveness.

How to Help Patients Embrace Step Three

The key to Step Three is willingness. Once patients are willing to seek a Higher Power of their understanding, they have come a long way toward completing Step Three. The patients will find relief in talking about a God that loves them and forgives them.

When you hear patients say that they are willing to turn it over, you can tell them that they are well on their way to recovery. The problems might not be solved immediately, but the patients are moving in the right direction.

Patients need to trust and turn things over to the group. The group has more collective wisdom than the patient, and the group members can be helpful in solving problems. As the patients use the power and support of their group, they are learning about how to turn things over to their Higher Power.

Some patients have serious problems with the word *God,* and that is fine. They do not have to use the word if they do not want to. Many patients have had the word *God* crammed down their throats for so long—since they were children—that they are sick of it. If you try to do the same thing, then they will revolt. Remember that even God gives total freedom of thought and action.

Step Four

"[We] made a searching and fearless moral inventory of ourselves" (Alcoholics Anonymous, 1976, p. 59). Read the Step Four exercise (Appendix 21) before continuing on with this chapter. Much of this exercise was developed by Lynn Carroll during his years at Hazelden and at Keystone Treatment Center.

Step Four is where patients make a thorough housecleaning. They rid themselves of the guilt of the past and look forward to a new future. Detail is important here. You must encourage the patients to be specific. They must put down exactly what they did. The patients will share their Step Four with someone of their choice in Step Five. They will go over the assets part of the Fourth Step in group. The assets part of the Fourth Step allows the patients to share the good things about themselves with their treatment peers. This keeps them from decompensating into a negative attitude. Step Four can be very painful for many patients, and they must be encouraged to look at the good parts of themselves.

Step Four was developed directly from spiritual principles. To get rid of guilt, if someone admits his or her wrongs and asks God for forgiveness, then God wipes the slate clean. You should discuss the grace of the Higher Power with your patients. They need to know that there is no way of earning God's forgiveness. God offers it for free. God wants to set us free and give us an opportunity to start over again.

To do this, patients must be honest. They must share their wrongs with God, with themselves, and with one other person. The other person is necessary because patients need to see a non-shaming face respond to their wrongs. Remember that the illness has been telling them that if they tell anyone the whole truth about themselves, then they will be rejected. The only way of proving this to be wrong is to do it. The patients no longer will be excessively burdened with guilt if they do their Steps Four and Five properly. They might have a difficult time forgiving themselves, but God will forgive them. Faith can do for them what they cannot do for themselves.

There will be a tendency for patients to leave things they consider bad out of the Fifth Step. The "Big Book" (Alcoholics Anonymous, 1976) says that this is not a good idea. "Time after time, newcomers have tried to keep to themselves certain facts about their lives. Trying to avoid the humbling experience, they have turned to easier methods. Almost invariably, they got drunk" (pp. 72-73).

Patients are encouraged to share everything that they think is important no matter how trivial it might seem to be. If it causes them any degree of guilt or shame, then it needs to be examined. The patients need to come face-to-face with themselves. All of the garbage of the past must be cleaned out. Nothing can be left to fester and rot. The patients who leave things out will feel unforgiven.

The Fourth Step is where patients identify their character defects. Once identified, the patients can work toward resolution. Patients often will come upon material suppressed for years. As memory tracks are stimulated, deeper unconscious material will surface.

Patients need to concentrate on the exact nature of their wrongs rather than accuse or blame other people. This is a time to take full responsibility. They do not make excuses. They ask for forgiveness. Yes, there likely were mitigating circumstances, but this is not a time to find out who was right and who was wrong. It is the time to dump the guilt and the shame.

The illness of chemical dependency projects on the screen of a patient's consciousness his or her wrongs. This makes the patient feel bad. By drowning in his or her guilt and shame, the patient cannot pull free. The patient wallows in self-pity.

Patients who get too depressed doing their Fourth Step need to stop and concentrate on their good qualities. It is not all bad. They need to be shown that they are valuable persons who deserve to be accepted and loved. Some patients might have to wait quite a while before doing their Fifth Step. Absolute honesty is a requirement of their readiness.

Some patients are so used to being negative about themselves that they cannot come up with their assets. These patients need to have the group help them to see the positive things about themselves.

Step Four must be detailed and specific. The patients must cover the exact nature of their behavior. This is the only way for them to see the full impact of their disease. They should not color their stories to make themselves seem less guilty or responsible.

Most of all, Step Four, like all of the steps, is a time of great joy. The patients finally face the whole truth about themselves. The truth is that they are wonderful creations of God. As they rid themselves of the pain of the past, they are ready to move forward to new lives filled with hope and recovery.

Step Five

"We admitted to God, to ourselves, and to another human being the exact nature of our wrongs" (Alcoholic Anonymous, 1976, p. 57). Read the Step Five exercise (Appendix 22) before continuing on with this chapter.

As the counselor, your job in Step Five is to help a patient match up with the right person with whom to share the Step Four inventory. Who this person is, and what he or she is like, is vitally important. This person stands as a symbol of God and all of the people on earth. This step directly attacks the core of the disease of chemical dependency. If it is done properly, then the patient will be free of the past. The person chosen should be in the clergy, if at all possible, because a minister better symbolizes a Higher Power. Someone else in the program will do if he or she is chosen carefully and has a good spiritual program. The person chosen needs some experience in hearing Fifth Steps, and this person must have an attitude of acceptance and unconditional positive regard. The person must be nonjudgmental and strictly confidential. It is helpful if this person is working a Twelve Step program. The person should not look uncomfortable when the patient is sharing sensitive material. If this person looks uncomfortable, then the patient may take this negatively. The patient needs to see a non-shaming face.

The purpose of the Fifth Step is to make things right with the self, with others, and with God. Patients should see themselves accurately—all of their positive and negative points—all at the same time. At the core of the illness of chemical dependency is this firmly held belief: "If I tell anyone the truth about me, they won't like me." This is not accurate, but the patients have been living as if it were true. They have not been honest with themselves and others for a long time, perhaps since childhood. They have pretended to be someone else to get the good stuff in life. The only way of proving to people that this held belief is wrong is to show them. This is the purpose of having another person hear the Fifth Step. If this person does not reject the patient, then the belief is proved wrong. A new accurate thought replaces the old one: "I have told someone the truth, and that person still likes me." This is a tremendous relief to the patient, who has been living his or her life convinced that he or she was totally unacceptable to others. This is a deeply held conviction, and it causes great pain. The patient must come to realize that unless he or she tells the truth, the patient never will feel loved.

In the Fifth Step, patients must come to realize that they are good people. They have made mistakes and have done bad things. But they are not bad; they are good. God will forgive them, and they can forgive themselves. They can start over, clean and new. Patients have varying degrees of spirituality and religious beliefs. You and the clergy must help the patients see that forgiveness has taken place. All religious systems provide for the forgiveness of sin.

Many patients will be tempted to hold something back in their Fifth Step. They do not want to share some part of their past. They do not think anyone can understand. The patients must be warned against this tendency. If they hold anything back, then the illness is still winning. All the illness needs to stay in operation is something important kept secret. All major wrongs must be disclosed. The whole truth must come out. The patients must stop living double lives.

After the Fifth Step, most patients experience a feeling of relief. The truth sets them free. In time, the patients will need to process the feelings with you. Some patients feel no immediate relief, but if they are honest, then they feel the relief later. Sometimes this takes a little while to sink in. The Fourth and Fifth Steps are a profoundly humbling experience, but once they are over, there is a profound feeling of relief. The person giving the Fifth Step should be encouraged to end the step with a prayer asking for forgiveness. The person listening to the step also should end the session in prayer. The person who has heard the step should tell the patient that he or she understands what the patient has said, that God forgives the patient, and that he or she believes in the patient's basic goodness.

CHAPTER EIGHT | The Lectures

Once or twice a day, patients go to lecture. The lectures last 30 minutes to an hour. All professional staff members will take their turn in educating the patients about the program. The physician will lecture on medical aspects, the psychologist on psychological aspects, the dietitian on diet aspects, and so on. As the counselor, you will be responsible for lecture topics relevant to chemical dependency. You can use any of the exercises in this book to come up with your speech. If the patients hear the material more than once, that is all the better. Each of the Twelve Steps should be presented in lecture. Other topics might include the disease concept, spirituality, relapse, feelings, relationship skills, communication skills, and defense mechanisms, to name a few.

Many of these topics have been discussed already, and it would be redundant to present them again. You can use any of this information in developing your lecture program.

The lecture schedule should be flexible enough to allow for something that the current patient population needs. You should read the "Big Book" and the *Twelve Steps and Twelve Traditions* (Alcoholics Anonymous, 1976, 1981) to round out your lectures. It is not difficult to talk to the patient population, and you soon will learn to breeze through the lectures. Those of you who are frightened of public speaking will need to make an outline of each talk and follow it carefully. The structure will give you the confidence you need.

Examples of several lectures are presented in what follows, but it is important to develop your own personal style. You must use your creativity. Only the important points of each lecture are given. Your job is to fill in the lecture with examples and stories of your own. It is best to speak from personal experience. You can use your own stories or stories that you have learned from patients. The patients do not need to hear a lot of confusing research in these lectures. They will be less confused if you put forth the facts in a simple and straightforward manner. Begin each lecture with the Serenity Prayer and end the lecture with the Lord's Prayer, just like at a meeting.

The Disease

This morning we are going to talk about the disease concept of chemical dependency. It is important for you to know that you have an illness. This illness has a certain set of signs and symptoms. No one of you asked to be chemically dependent. It's not your fault. You should not feel guilty. That would be unduly hard on yourself. You would not blame someone for having cancer or heart disease, even though some of their behaviors may have contributed to their disease. If you eat a certain way or smoke cigarettes, then you increase your chances of coronary artery disease. If you drink or use drugs, then you increase your chances of becoming chemically dependent.

Chemical Dependency Is Not a Moral Problem

Dorland's Illustrated Medical Dictionary (1965, p. 428) defines disease as "a definite morbid process having a characteristic train of symptoms; it may affect the whole body or any of its parts, and its etiology, pathology, and prognosis may be known or unknown." During the late 1940s, E. M. Jellinek began to study alcoholism in more than 2,000 members of AA. He found that alcoholism had a characteristic set of signs and symptoms and that it had a definite progressive course. In 1956, the American Medical Association formally recognized alcoholism as a disease. Up until that time, medical science, and society in general, thought that someone who was chemically dependent was a person with a moral problem or someone with a weak will.

Chemical Dependency Is Not Due to a Weak Will

Please do not think that a weak will had anything to do with your chemical dependency. We find that alcoholics and drug addicts are strong and resourceful people. More than 90% of chemically dependent persons are able to keep functioning even when they are deathly ill. You know how it goes. You come to work and you've got this incredible hangover, your head is throbbing, and you feel like you are going to throw up. Your co-worker comes in and asks how you are doing. "Fine," you say cheerfully. You are there, you feel terrible, but you made it to work. That takes a person with a strong will.

Chemical Dependency Has Genetic Links

There is no major psychiatric disease that does not have genetic links. We all are genetically predisposed to certain physical and mental illnesses. We are more likely to acquire the same diseases that the members of our families have had. Cancer and coronary artery disease run in families, depression and anxiety run in families, and chemical dependency runs in families. For example, cells are programmed at birth to do certain things when alcohol is in the body. Many sons of alcoholics need to drink more before they feel intoxicated. They have a programmed need to drink more before they get the same effect. You may have noticed in your drinking or drug use that you could use more than other people could. This is because some people who are predisposed to chemical dependency metabolize drugs differently. It seems that many people who are chemically dependent were predisposed to the illness before they were born (Anthenelli & Schuckit, 1994; Woodward, 1994).

Chemical Dependency Is a Social Problem

To be chemically dependent, you need to use chemicals. This is a psychosocial issue. In some societies, drinking and drug use are not tolerated. For example, Muslims and Mormons have a strong religious belief against the use of drugs. They consider use to be a sin. There is less chemical dependency in these groups.

In France, drinking is a regular part of life. It is not uncommon for a French person to have wine with breakfast, lunch, and dinner. Understandably, France has a higher incidence of alcoholism.

Chemical Dependency Is a Psychological Problem

Certain psychological factors also have to come into play. There is no specific alcoholic personality, but people do have to drink to become alcoholic. Alcohol is reinforcing to some people, and to other people it is not. You have to like drinking to drink. Drinking behavior naturally increases if it is reinforced.

Chemical dependency is a biopsychosocial disease. It has biological components, psychological components, and social components. Two or more of these elements appear to be necessary for chemical dependency to exist.

Someone has a drug problem if he or she continues to use a drug despite persistent physical, psychological, or social problems associated with that drug. Anyone who continues to use despite persistent problems is an abuser. Obviously, if you get into trouble when you use chemicals, then you shouldn't use chemicals.

Chemical Dependency Is a Physiological Problem

Chemical dependency is characterized by tolerance and withdrawal symptoms. As you use cocaine, the cocaine tells your brain to wake up. The cells of your body gradually catch onto this abnormal wake-up signal, and they produce chemicals that tell the brain to go to sleep. The cells counteract the drug. Ultimately, it will take more of the drug to produce the same effect. As you take in more of the drug, the cells counteract even further. This is a vicious cycle called tolerance. You will find that you are using more of the drug now than when you started.

People who are having a chemical problem know it—at least on some level—and they try to cut down. They might change from beer to wine or from hard liquor to beer. They might decide to use only after 5 o'clock or only on weekends. They might even move or change jobs.

The Obsession

People who are having problems with chemicals will find that more and more of their time is taken up using the substance. People on cocaine first use only recreationally. They occasionally use at parties. As their illness progresses, however, they find themselves using more often, during the week, even when they are alone. More and more of their time is spent in getting cocaine, using cocaine, and withdrawing from cocaine. The more they use, the more they need. The more they need, the more they use.

People who are chemically dependent find themselves intoxicated or hung over when they need to do something else. The homemaker might be high when she is supposed to be taking care of the children. She might be drunk at work. She might have to call in sick because she is too hung over to work. More and more, the disease takes over, usually over a long period of time. The drug becomes the center of the universe. Dinner time revolves around those first drinks. There begins a morning hung-over ritual and an evening get-high ritual. Eventually, the person gives up normal activities. The person doesn't go fishing or camping. The person quits school or gets fired. Sexual activity decreases. Recreational activity decreases. Time with the children decreases. Any activity can go, but the drug stays and grows more and more important.

The Problems

Sooner or later, problems begin to develop. There are social consequences caused by the drug use, problems with the spouse, problems with the law, problems at school, problems with friends, and problems with parents. The problems begin to mount, but the chemically dependent person keeps dealing with the problems in the same way. The person gets relief the only way he or she knows how, with the drug of choice. The drug becomes the person's best friend. It's the only thing the person can count on. It always helps to ease the pain. It works, and it works every time.

By this time, people around the chemically dependent person are complaining. They are warning that something is wrong. Someone might even have the unmitigated gall to talk to the person about the problem. When someone does this, the chemically dependent person hammers that person to the floor. "It's not my problem," the addict shouts. "It's your problem." The lies escalate, and the addict begins to get caught in the lies. People challenge the addict with the truth. All of this leads to more drug use, and the cycle goes on.

Finally, some crisis breaks through the lies the addict has been telling himself or herself. Some glimmer of the truth seeps in, and the person comes into treatment. The person is still in denial. This person is still lying to himself or herself. The person still can't see the full impact of the disease. But here this person is in treatment.

Chemical dependency is the third leading cause of death in this country. Most people who are chemically dependent die because of it. Very few make it into treatment. Of those who do make it into their first treatment, most will achieve a stable program of recovery. Either you will abstain from drugs and alcohol, or you will die.

You will find this treatment center dedicated to the truth. We must tell the truth to get clean and sober. We must give up all that control we have been working on and turn our will and our lives over to the care of others. If you work this program, then you will find relief. If you hang onto your old ways, then you will be miserable. The choice is yours.

Defense Mechanisms
■

Today we are going to talk about where all the lies come from. How did we end up being such liars? In chemical dependency, we tell incredible lies. We lie when we think we have to, and we lie when we don't have to. We lie to get out of trouble, and our lies get us into more trouble. We lie to increase our pleasure, and we lie to wallow in our self-pity.

This illness must lie, and it must continue to lie, or it cannot exist. The illness cannot live in the light of the truth. You can't tell the truth to yourself and continue to be chemically dependent. With the truth, you would realize your problem and get some help for it.

All of the lies exist to protect us from a painful truth. The truth is that we are out of control, and if we keep up the addictive behavior, then we are doomed. The truth causes us great anxiety, so we defend ourselves from the truth. We distort the truth just enough to feel like nothing is wrong.

Minimization

The first lie we tell ourselves is called minimization. This is where we take reality and make it smaller. We think the problem is not that bad. If an alcoholic takes an 8-ounce glass, fills it up with ice, takes a shot glass full of whiskey and pours it over the ice, and holds the glass up to the light, the alcoholic will be disappointed. A shot glass full to the brim with whiskey makes a disgustingly small splash in an eight ounce glass.

If you are an alcoholic, you are not going to use a shot glass. If you have a shot glass at home, it is gathering dust. You are going to pour your whiskey until you see some color in that glass. Now, if we were to take this drink and measure how many shots are in it, we are going to find four, maybe five, shots in the glass. Here's how we minimize. We think, and believe, that this is a drink—one drink. But it's not one drink; it's four drinks.

We can do the same thing with beer cans. If you are a beer drinker, you probably have a considerable collection of empty beer cans at the end of the week. When you take out the garbage, you have got maybe two big plastic trash bags full of cans. As you are taking out the garbage, you may think, "Boy, I hope the garbage person doesn't think I'm drinking all this beer." At that time, you may put one of the bags on your garbage pile, and the other one on your neighbor's pile.

Those of you who are into cocaine, remember when you have just picked up your stash. You have this nice big pile of cocaine on your kitchen table. You feel self-satisfied. You have more than enough. Your treasure chest is full. You are content. You feel a great peace. This is going to last a long time. But the next morning, you are wondering who got into your stash. Where did it all go? You used it all; that's where it went.

We can minimize about our mounting problems. Everyone gets a couple of DWIs, right? Almost everybody gets a divorce. It's not so bad to spend a couple of nights in jail. We're good persons. We're not bad. We were just unlucky; the cops were after us. We take what is real and make it look smaller. We lie to ourselves, and we believe the lie.

Rationalization

The next lie we tell is called rationalization. This is where we have a good excuse. Probably the most commonly used excuse for drinking is "I had a hard day." It follows, then, that if I had such a hard day, I deserve to get blasted. Anyone who had the hard day that I had would need to relax. Let's have a few beers or a couple of joints. In rationalizing, we might blame our problems on someone else. "If you would just lighten up," we might say, "I could straighten things out." We might think remorsefully of all that we could have been if we had been born wealthy or been given the right breaks. We look at all of those successful people, and we hate them. We never had such a chance, we tell ourselves. There's no God. If there was a God, then where was God when we needed Him?

Denial

The last type of lie that we tell ourselves—and this one is the most characteristic of chemical dependency—is denial. Denial is a stubborn and angry refusal to see the truth. Here we refuse to see what is right before our eyes. We block out what is real until we really don't see it at all. The best way of showing you how this works is to give you an example. You are walking down the street on a very hot day. It's 95 degrees in the shade. Sweat is pouring down your face. As you walk up the road, watching the heat waves rise up off of the asphalt, people are standing along the side of the road with pails full of ice water. As you pass each of them, they throw their buckets full of reality in your face. "Your wife's divorcing you! That's your third DWI! The boss won't put up with you anymore! You're in trouble with your parents again!" You see the pails of water, you see the people throw them in your face, and you hear the words that are shouted at you, but you don't experience the full reality of what's happening. You don't get the full emotional impact of the problems. With your whole life falling apart, you are walking up the street as if nothing was happening at all. The people around you are amazed. Why don't you see? Why don't you understand? Why can't you see what's happening to you?

How to Begin to Live in the Truth

You can't see what's happening to you because you are lying to yourself. You can't see the truth because you are believing the lies. You are completely fooled. In treatment, the full reality of what has been happening to you will be before you. It will be painful, but the truth will set you free. Treatment is an endless search for the truth, and you must be willing to listen to what others say. You must try to be open to what people tell you about yourself. We will reflect to each other what we see. We will try to find the truth together. What we cannot do alone, we can do together.

The Great Lie

It is important for you to know how the psychology of chemical dependency gets going. During childhood, we come to believe in the great lie. This lie is at the core of chemical dependency. We do not hear this lie from our parents or from our friends. We don't hear it from our teachers or from television. It is more powerful than that. We hear this lie inside of our own thinking, inside of that most personal part of ourselves. The lie is this: If we tell people the whole truth about ourselves, then they won't like us.

Once we hear this lie and believe this lie, we know that we never will be loved for who we are. Therefore, to get any of the good stuff out of life at all, we have to pretend to be someone that we are not. We try to be someone else. We watch those people who are popular, and we copy them. We are very careful about what kind of clothes we wear. We copy people's mannerisms and their fine little gestures. We find ourselves cocking our heads in a certain way when we laugh or smile. We are hoping to fool the people. We hope that they cannot see our real selves. We want them to see our pretend selves.

How the Great Lie Works

As this coping behavior occurs, it works. Some people do like us for the new selves we are trying to be. We become pleased to know that we are not going to be alone. The people we are fooling will love us. We begin to wear specific costumes and to play certain roles. We might wear the nice girl costume or the cowhand costume. We might wear the hippie costume or the yuppie costume. We know that it is a costume—we know it's not us—but the people are fooled and the lie goes on.

We Never Feel Accepted

You must look carefully at what is happening. We have fooled people into liking us, but they don't really like us. They don't know us. We are keeping who we are secret. As we keep doing this—making this effort to be loved—our emptiness grows and our pain increases. We try hard. We copy everyone who looks cool. We put on the best false front that we can, but in time we realize that it isn't going to work. We feel more and more lonely and isolated. We have known all along that we weren't going to be loved, not for the real us. No one was going to love us.

The Promise of the Disease

When we are lonely enough in this process, when we are isolated enough, and when we are hurting enough, the illness comes along and offers us a smorgasbord of answers to our pain. Sex, money, power, influence, drugs, gambling, and alcohol all are there, and more, and we begin to feed from this cafeteria of behavior. For a while, things get better. All of these things relieve the pain for a little while. We find ourselves irresistibly drawn to this table of wrongs. We spend more time doing it. We eat, drink, stuff, cram, push, and shove. We find that more and more of our lives center around the use of these things. We get up on the table and stuff ourselves. We begin to lose our morals and values. We eat, consume, vomit, and stuff ourselves even more. In time, there never is enough. There is not enough sex. There is not enough money. There is not enough power. There is not enough booze. Alcoholics Anonymous says that one drink is too much and that a thousand never is enough.

Truth

Finally, you begin to get sick from this cafeteria of wrongs. You realize an awful fact: The answer is not in these things. It is a terrible point of grief when you finally realize that the answer is not in your drug of choice. This is not a happy time, but by now you are addicted. You can't stop. You might be addicted to sex, and you want to stop what you are doing, but you can't stop. You might be addicted to money, and you want to stop chasing money, but you can't stop. You want to stop drinking. You promise yourself that you'll stop, but you can't stop. You're addicted.

Somehow, by the grace of God, you finally come to treatment. Maybe you are ready to surrender. I hope so, because if you aren't, then you are in for a lot more misery. If you are ready to surrender, and if you are ready to try something new, then this program is for you.

A Program of Rigorous Honesty

One of the things that you must be willing to do is tell the truth all of the time. Nothing else will stop the great lie. The truth will set you free. You are enslaved to your addiction, but the truth will set you free of your chains.

In treatment, probably for the first time in your life, you will have the opportunity to get honest. If you do not, and if you hold anything back, then you will return to chemicals. You don't have to tell everyone the truth, but there is a psychological law at work. The law is this: The more you can share, the closer you can get; the closer you can get, the more you can share. As intimacy grows, you tell more of the truth. In your Fifth Step, you will tell someone the whole truth at one time. You will tell that person exactly what happened. Time after time, we have had new comers decide to hold something back in their Fifth Step. They didn't want to tell that one thing. Invariably, these people get drunk because they don't prove to themselves that people will like them if they tell the whole truth. They keep the emptiness, loneliness, and isolation. The pain grows, and sooner or later they relapse.

It is vitally important that you find out the truth about yourself. God created you in perfection. You are God's masterpiece. You were created in the image of God. God loves you and wants you to be happy. For some of you, this will be difficult to hear and difficult to believe. How could God love you? Where was God when you needed God? If there is a God, then where is God? These are the questions that you will seek the answers to in this program.

Normal Development

Today we are going to talk about normal development and how things go wrong for people who are chemically dependent. As infants, we can't see very well. Our eyes are developing, and everything looks hazy. An infant knows only when it feels comfortable and uncomfortable. When it feels uncomfortable enough, it cries. It cries out in the only way it knows how. This cry is at such a pitch and timbre that parents cannot ignore it. Those of you who have heard the cry of an infant know what I'm talking about. The infant cries out into the haze, "Help me! Help me!" It's the only thing the infant can do. Without someone coming to help, the infant will die.

The Primary Caregiver

But out of the haze, someone comes, and that someone meets our needs, and we feel comfortable again. In healthy homes, this someone always comes, at all hours of the day and night, and as we grow older, this someone has a particular sight, sound, taste, and smell. Later still, it has a name—mother.

A great trust develops between mother and child. We learn that whenever we cry out, mother will come. It happens time and time again. It happens every time, and we learn to trust in mother. She is always there.

The Struggle for Independence

As we grow older, we begin to struggle for independence. We begin to do things for ourselves. We reach out and grasp things. We learn language, and we ask for things. During the second year, we learn the power of the word *no*. Mother can be all ready to go home, she can have her hands full of packages, she can be walking out the door, and we can say no. Oh, the power of that word. The whole world seems to stop and revolve around us. "No!" People get very upset with that word. It is very powerful.

The Fear of Abandonment

Somewhere between 3 and 5 years of age—and this depends on the maturity of the child—we learn a terrifying fact: Other people can say no too. This fact strikes terror in a child's heart. We know that we need other people for survival. What will happen if we cry out in the night and someone doesn't come? We develop a new fear—the fear of abandonment. We never get over this fear. We carry it with us for the rest of our lives. It is the fear of life and death itself. When something goes wrong in our lives, this fear can come back very intensely. Lovers and spouses panic when one partner attempts to leave the other. They fear that if that person leaves, then they will die. You hear them say things such as "I can't live without her" and "I can't live without him."

Learning the Rules

As a frightened child, we go to our parents and search out an answer. "Mom, Dad, how can I be sure that when I cry out, you will always come?"

"These are the rules," the parents say. "These are the rules about how to be a good boy and a good girl. If you obey the rules and you cry out, we will come. But if you are a bad boy or girl, and if you break the rules, we might not come." As a child, we nod our head reverently. We want to live!

The Development of Insecurity

Now the parents hit us with a crippling blow, and from this blow we will get another new feeling—insecurity. They don't tell us all the rules. The rules are too complicated, and the rules keep changing. Sometimes things are against the rules, and sometimes they are not. Sometimes we get punished for things, and sometimes we do not get punished for the same things. We spend the rest of our lives trying to learn the rules. In every situation, the rules are a little different. It is very complicated, and it causes a great deal of anxiety.

The Peer Group | As we move out of the home and into the peer group, things are very different. The peer group does not love us just because we are a part of the family. The peer group loves us because we have a function. We are a good leader or a good follower, we are funny, we laugh, we are strong, or we are loyal. If we do not have a function in the group, then we are rejected.

Little boys and little girls are very different by this age. Boys struggle for power, and girls struggle for connection. Boys work to control, and girls work to cooperate. Boys work at being the ones who can solve the problem, and girls work toward who is the closest to whom. It's not that either of these personality styles is better or worse. They are just different. Both are necessary for healthy family roles.

If we have been told how wonderful we are every day of our lives, then we might be ready for school by 6 years of age. In the best of circumstances, school is a struggle. It's a totally new situation with a new set of rules. We are not rewarded for our individuality or our creativity. We are rewarded for our ability to cooperate. We are supposed to be quiet and stay still. It goes against everything that a child is, but we try to cooperate, we try to be quiet, we try to stay still. We remember that we don't want to be abandoned.

Adolescence | Adolescence is a time of great change. There is a huge hormone dam. It leaks, cracks, and finally breaks, releasing a flood of chemicals into our bodies. These hormones say one thing—mate. They say this loud and clear. We begin to mate in our dreams, in class, and in every waking moment. The opposite sex becomes exciting, irresistible, and new. We try even harder than ever to fit in because with all these changes going on, it is even more critical to be accepted. We struggle to fit in much more than we struggle for our individuality.

Society tells us to prepare to leave our parents, who have been at the very core of our survival. We begin to question the morals and values of our parents. We begin to make decisions on our own. We prepare ourselves for the commitment of adulthood. We must know who and what we are. We try out many different things in an attempt to find ourselves.

For most chemically dependent persons, it is here, during early adolescence, that chemical use gets going. Here we first try chemicals, and they make us feel good. Soon we begin to use chemicals to deal with our problems. Here is where our emotional development stops. If we treat our feelings with chemicals, then we don't learn to use our feelings to solve problems. If we continue to use mind-altering chemicals, then we do not have our real feelings anymore. Most chemically dependent persons are emotionally stuck in adolescence. They still do not know how to use their feelings appropriately to solve problems.

Adulthood | The dividing line between adulthood and adolescence is the ability to make long-term commitments. Adults are emotionally stable and mature. They can commit to career, family, and home. They can build a nest and rear healthy young. Adulthood should really be a long smooth ride. It is a gradual building of knowledge and skill. Financial problems fall to the wayside as we reach our full economic potential.

Somewhere during our 60s, the decision comes: Should we retire? If we like our work, and if it gives us joy, then of course we should keep working. If we don't like our work, then we should retire and do something that we do enjoy. We deserve it.

During later life, there inevitably will come a time of terminal illness. We will acquire a disease from which we will not recover. This usually is coronary artery disease or cancer, but it can be many others. If we are close to God, then this is not such a scary time. We will have the hope of eternal life. If we do not know God, then this time may be more difficult. But in normal life, everyone dies.

We have discussed the normal life cycle, and we have seen where it usually goes wrong in chemical dependency. The illness can occur at any stage in life, but it usually gets started in adolescence. The moment we begin to use chemicals to excess, we cannot live a normal life. It is impossible. We cannot use our feelings in real time, and with real people, to solve life's real problems. In treatment, you will learn the skills necessary for living a normal life. These are the tools of recovery. If you learn these skills, then your life will stabilize and you ultimately will live a normal life again.

Physical Addiction and Recovery

This morning we are going to talk about the physical changes that occur in chemical dependency. The cell is the basic building block of the body. It has a cell wall that protects the cell from harm, a nucleus that is the brain of the cell, and a variety of other specialized parts with specialized functions called organelles. The nucleus is made up of deoxyribonucleic acid, or DNA, and it decides how the cell is made and how the cell works. It is the manager of the cell in the same way as the brain manages your body. The cell wall is an actively selective membrane that chooses what comes into and out of the cell.

How Drugs Affect the Cell

Drugs pass through the cell wall in a variety of ways and influence how the cell operates. This is a very involved process, and we do not know exactly what each drug does. What we know, however, is important, and you must understand some of this in your recovery program. Alcohol is a drug. One of its effects is that it dehydrates protoplasm. It sucks water out of the cell. This prevents the cell wall from operating properly. This happens in every cell in the body, but it has its most noticeable effect on the central nervous system. It suppresses higher cortical centers in the brain. This reduces people's normal ability to perceive the environment. It tells the brain to go to sleep. This inability to perceive accurately makes us feel less inhibited. We lose the normal constraints that the world puts on us. We miss the subtle cues. It makes us feel free.

The brain of the cell picks this up as a problem and changes things in the cell to correct the problem. Alcohol tells the brain to go to sleep. The cell tells the brain to wake up. At first, these changes are transient chemical changes or subtle changes in metabolism that will quickly return to normal after alcohol leaves the body. But if the alcohol keeps coming, then the cell produces permanent changes in the cell wall. One way in which it does this is by making tunnels, or chloride channels, through the cell wall. This provides for easier transport of atoms across the cell wall. The more that alcohol stays around, the more of these chloride tunnels are needed.

How Drugs Affect Behavior

Now let's see what is happening to you behaviorally. You start drinking, and one beer gets you that feeling you are after. One beer is all that you need, but sooner or later, the cell produces those changes and you need two beers to get that same feeling. In a few weeks, or months, or years, you are going to need three beers, and then four, and five, and six, and so on. The more beer you drink, the more the cell corrects with those chloride channels. This is called tolerance. You need more and more of the drug to get the same effect. All chemically addicting drugs create this physiological pattern.

Tolerance

It is important for you to know that these changes in the cell may take years to develop, but once tolerance is there, it is there permanently. The cell never changes back completely the way it was before. It never forgets. That is why you never can use drugs normally again. You have developed permanent changes in the cells in your body. If you were drinking a fifth a day, stay sober for 20 years, and then start drinking again, you will be drinking a fifth a day within 30 days. It took you years to develop tolerance, but this time it is there already. This never will change. You can recover completely from some of the psychological and social effects of this disease, but you never can recover from the physical changes that have taken place in your cells. Your cells never forget.

Cross-Tolerance

This is why cross-tolerance is such a problem. Alcohol, pot, sedatives, and sleeping pills all tell the brain to go to sleep, and the cells counteract that drug in some of the same ways. If you develop tolerance for one of these drugs, then you will develop tolerance for all of them. You can't leave treatment and say to yourself, "Well, I'm sure glad I got that alcohol problem licked, but I never had any problem with pot. I can have a little pot now and then." This would spell disaster for you. Taking a little pot is like taking a little alcohol because of the cross-tolerance.

What we find in chemical dependency treatment is that once you are addicted to one mood-altering chemical, you are addicted to all of them. You have learned things physically, psychologically, and socially that will cross over to any other mood-altering chemical. If your drug of choice is whiskey, and if you go out of here and smoke a little dope, then you will be back to the whiskey very soon.

Withdrawal

The cells produce all of these short- and long-term changes to counteract what the drug is doing, so you can guess what happens when the drug is removed. All of these cellular changes are still there and the drug is gone. The cells are producing wake-up signals to the brain to counteract the go-to-sleep signals that the alcohol is producing, and all of a sudden there is no alcohol. What happens is called acute alcohol withdrawal. The cells are screaming for you to wake up, and no alcohol is telling you to go to sleep. Acute withdrawal has been driving alcoholics to the liquor store every day. They go to sleep under the effects of alcohol and in a few hours they wake up feeling nervous and restless. They can't sleep. Their stomachs feel upset. They have headaches. Their hands shake. All of these are withdrawal symptoms.

Some of you learned that what you needed was a drink or a Valium to get you back to sleep, but if you have that drink or that pill, then the cycle starts all over again. Acute withdrawal is not fun. It produces the opposite effect of the drug that you are using. If you were using a sedative drug, then withdrawal will tell you to wake up. If you were using a stimulant drug, then the withdrawal symptoms will tell you to go to sleep.

The length of acute withdrawal differs depending on the drug you were taking. With alcohol, withdrawal usually is over within a few days. With cannabis or certain of the benzodiazepines, it can be weeks or even months. Once acute withdrawal is over, protracted withdrawal extends the problems for about 2 years. Protracted withdrawal is characterized by random mood swings, sleep problems, and generalized feelings of stress. These symptoms will wax and wane over the next few months. Don't think that you are crazy or think that anything is wrong. Just recognize the symptoms for what they are (Geller, 1994).

The first 3 months out of treatment will be the hardest for you because of the extended withdrawal syndrome. This is where people tend to relapse, so do everything in your power to work a daily program of recovery in early sobriety. The daily program will put hurdles in the way of the first use.

How We Learn

Drug use is a habit. We get into the habit of drinking or using in certain situations or when having certain feelings. A habit is some movement or thought that is so practiced that it has developed a nice smooth pathway in the brain. Whenever we even randomly approach that area in the brain, we are very likely to take that pathway because it is so well traveled and easy to follow.

You have developed certain habits in your drinking or drug use. You might use when you celebrate, or when you feel angry, or when you are frightened or sad. You might always drink after work or always drink a certain kind of beer. These pathways in your brain are well developed. What treatment is all about is teaching you to get what you want by doing something else other than using your old behavior. It is a process of learning new behaviors. For example, if you want to feel less angry, then you will need to talk to someone about how you feel and try to work through the problem. The second you realize that you are on one of your old pathways, you need to stop and change direction. Drinking or drug use no longer is an option for you. You need to find other methods for dealing with your problems.

Alcoholics Anonymous

■

The idea behind Alcoholics Anonymous got started in 1935. Bill Wilson, one of its founders, had gotten drunk again. He was at the end of his rope. He was afraid to go home. He was afraid he was going to kill himself. He hated himself. His spouse was still sticking by him, but he couldn't trust himself anymore. He had tried to quit drinking countless times, in countless ways, and he had always ended up drunk. Here he was in the hospital again. He didn't know whether he wanted to live or die, but he knew that he didn't want to live this way anymore. Medical science had given up on him as hopeless. He had nowhere to go. He was trapped.

A Spiritual Awakening

In his room alone, feeling totally powerless, Bill looked up toward Heaven, and he cried out, "If there is a God, show me. Give me some sign." At that moment, Bill's room filled with a great white light. He felt incredibly filled with new hope and joy. "It was like standing on a mountaintop with a strong clear wind blowing through me. But it was not a wind of the air. It was a wind of the spirit." Bill felt like he had stepped into another world full of goodness and grace. There was a wonderful feeling of presence that he had been seeking all of his life. He never felt so complete, so satisfied, and so loved. Bill had finally surrendered, and when he surrendered, God came into his life. Notice that God came into his life with such power and force that Bill never denied God again.

Bill never took another drink, but his spiritual awakening didn't fully resolve his problem. He still had a craving for alcohol. One day, he passed a bar and felt himself being pulled into it. He thought that if he could just talk to another drunk, he might be able to pull himself back together. He got on the phone and, after making a few calls, finally found one, Dr. Bob Smith. Dr. Bob was a hopeless alcoholic. He had destroyed his medical practice, and he was waiting to die. He reluctantly agreed to see Bill, but he had no hope that Bill could help him. Dr. Bob would have no nonsense. He had talked about his alcohol problem with the best, and now here was some other guy—a drunk—who was coming over to try to help him. He was in no mood for help.

Two Alcoholics Talking to Each Other

When Bill got there, Dr. Bob was surprised to learn that Bill wasn't there to keep him sober. "No," Bill said, "I'm not here to keep *you* sober. I'm here to keep *me* sober." Well, this was the new concept—one alcoholic talking to another to keep himself (or herself) sober. Dr. Bob was going to give Bill only a few minutes, but they talked easily, and Bill stayed for hours. Dr. Bob began to open up and speak as frankly as Bill was doing. Having common experiences, they could speak to each other without shame. They talked about the helplessness and hopelessness that they had been feeling—the feeling of total powerlessness. They talked about all of the problems that alcohol had caused them. Bill told Dr. Bob about the spiritual experience that he felt had saved him.

These two persons became great friends, and AA was born. They began to meet with other alcoholics. They began to carry the program to others. Dr. Bob got drunk one more time—when he was away at a convention—but when he returned he was more determined than ever to stay sober.

A bunch of alcoholics began getting together to help each other stay sober. To everyone's amazement, it worked. Hopeless cases began to recover. Of course, the group members had their setbacks, but the way to recovery had been found. The group wouldn't have the name Alcoholics Anonymous for 4 more years.

The Big Book

Bill dictated most of the first chapters to his secretary. He had considerable resistance when he came up with the Twelve Steps. Some of the group members were adamantly opposed to including so much God talk in the program. They didn't want to scare drunks away with all of the spiritual talk. Bill listened quietly, but he knew that he was right. The only concession he made was to add the phrase "God *as we understood Him.*" That made some members of the group feel more comfortable.

As the program developed and people began to stay sober, Bill was offered a job as the first alcohol counselor. A hospital wanted to incorporate the program and use it to help alcoholics. The group was opposed. Group members were afraid that it would make the program commercial and that this would destroy an essential element of the group. This time Bill agreed, and AA remained a free self-supporting program.

Another problem was money. The group needed money to pay for expenses and to reach out to alcoholics who were still suffering. They went to John D. Rockefeller, and he gave the group $5,000. They had asked for $50,000, but Rockefeller felt that financial backing would weaken the program.

With the individual stories written by the new groups, Bill completed the Big Book in 1939. The groups ordered 5,000 copies to be printed. They didn't sell many until an article written by Jack Anderson appeared in the *Saturday Evening Post* (Anderson, 1941). This gave AA national exposure, and the mail began to pour in. Alcoholics Anonymous now has more than 1 million members and has meetings all over the world.

The Twelve Steps

The program is made up of Twelve Steps. You will hear these steps read at every meeting:

1. We admitted we were powerless over alcohol—that our lives had become unmanageable.
2. [We] came to believe that a power greater than ourselves could restore us to sanity.
3. [We] made a decision to turn our will and our lives over to the care of God *as we understood Him.*
4. [We] made a searching and fearless moral inventory of ourselves.
5. [We] admitted to God, to ourselves, and [to] another human being the exact nature of our wrongs.
6. [We] were entirely ready to have God remove all these defects of character.
7. [We] humbly asked Him [God] to remove our shortcomings.
8. [We] made a list of all persons we had harmed and became willing to make amends to them all.
9. [We] made direct amends to such people whenever possible except when to do so would injure them or others.
10. [We] continued to take personal inventory, and when we were wrong promptly, [we] admitted it.
11. [We] sought through prayer and meditation to improve our conscious contact with God *as we understood Him,* praying only for His will for us and the power to carry that out.
12. Having had a spiritual awakening as a result of these steps, we tried to carry this message to alcoholics and to practice these principles in all our affairs. (Alcoholics Anonymous, 1976, pp. 59-60)

There are many slogans in AA that will help you to reorganize your life and your thinking—slogans such as "one day at a time," "easy does it," "keep it simple," "live and let live," and "let go and let God." These slogans have great meaning, and they will help to keep your program on track.

Meetings

It is hoped that, after treatment, you will attend a lot of AA or NA meetings. The more meetings you attend, the greater your chances of achieving a stable recovery. You need to ask someone further along in the program to be your sponsor. That person will guide you though the steps and will be there for you in times of need.

You will find this program to be a healthy family. The regular meeting that you attend will be called your home group. There is a stable set of rules. People will care about you. They will respond to how you feel. They will care for what you want. They will be there for you when you need them.

The choice is yours. We strongly recommend that you throw yourself into this program with all the enthusiasm and courage you can muster. Tell your group the truth. Don't hold back. Alcoholics Anonymous says, "Rarely have we seen a person fail who has thoroughly followed our path."

Feelings

Most chemically dependent people have difficulty with their feelings. They do not know how to identify their feelings and don't know to use their feelings effectively. All feelings give us motivation. They give us specific energy and direction for movement. If you cannot use your feelings effectively, then you cannot adapt to the changes in your environment.

The reason why we, as chemically dependent persons, don't use feelings appropriately is we learned not to trust our feelings. We learned that there was something wrong with our feelings. We learned this from watching people respond to us when we were having feelings. When we were children and we were feeling afraid, we heard, "There's nothing to be afraid of." When we were angry, we learned that we were bad. "There's nothing to be angry about," our parents said.

Look at what this does to us as children. We begin to think, "I am having feelings that I shouldn't be having. I am afraid when there is nothing to be afraid of. I am angry when there is nothing to be angry about." We believe our parents. We can reach only one conclusion: Something is wrong with us. We are not feeling right, or we are having the wrong feelings at the wrong time.

We might be further confused when we get to school and are teased when we have feelings. The other kids tease us when we cry. They don't take us seriously when we are in love. We all know that feelings are one of the most basic things about us. It is one of the things that make us who we are. If there is something wrong with our feelings, then there is something wrong with us. "Something is wrong with me," we think. "I can't trust myself."

Once we can't trust who we are, we have to become someone else. We begin to search for that person who we want to be. We copy other people who we respect. We imitate various roles to see whether the roles fit us. Whatever we do, we don't share our feelings. We have been taught not to do that. We keep our feelings more and more to ourselves until sometimes we don't know how we feel anymore. Boys aren't supposed to cry, so they get angry instead. Girls aren't supposed to get angry, so they cry when they are angry. More and more, we separate from ourselves. We become more isolated.

Feelings Are Adaptive

Each feeling has a specific action attached to it. Fear gives us the energy to run away. Anger gives us the energy to fight. Acceptance gives us the energy to move closer. You may have more than one feeling at the same time, and this can be confusing. But if you break the feelings down into their basic units, then you always can figure out what the feelings are telling you.

There are eight primary feelings: anger, acceptance, anticipation, joy, disgust, sadness, surprise, and fear. There are more complicated emotions, but they are only combinations of the basic eight feelings. For example, jealousy is when you feel sad, angry, and fearful all at the same time. When you feel jealous, you have to break the feelings down into their smaller units. Each feeling has to be identified and dealt with. What exactly are you frightened of, and what can you do to relieve your fear? What exactly are you angry at, and what can you do with your anger to make the situation more tolerable? What makes you so sad, and what action can you take to help you feel more comfortable? As each of the feelings is addressed, you will have a more complete picture of the problem.

Remember that all feelings have movement attached. Fear moves you away from an offending stimulus. So does disgust. Sadness gives you the direction to recover the lost object. Anger gives you the direction to fight. Anticipation and surprise are orienting responses that prepare your body for action. Joy and acceptance give you the direction to move closer and stay with the object that gives you those feelings.

You must learn how to identify your feelings and use them to help you take action. It is a mistake to keep your feelings quiet. Sharing your feelings is an essential skill in interpersonal relationships. You cannot be close to someone if you don't know how that person feels and vice versa. You don't have to act on all of your feelings—that wouldn't be wise—but you do have to process or deal with each feeling that is important to you.

How to Be Assertive

In treatment, we are going to learn the assertive formula. This is an excellent way of dealing with your feelings appropriately. This is what we are going to say when we have an uncomfortable feeling:

I feel _____

when you _____.

I would prefer it if _____.

Start by describing your feelings. That will be one or more of the eight feelings that we discussed. Then describe the behavior of the other person that triggered that feeling. Exactly what did they do or say that made you feel uncomfortable? Then tell that person what you would prefer him or her to do.

Let's say that your husband is an alcoholic and that he is 2 hours late from work. You are scared and angry. He could be drunk again. He could have been involved in an accident. He could be having an affair. Just as your worry reaches its peak and you begin to call the police, he comes home. Using the assertive formula, you would say, "I feel scared and angry when you come home late. I would prefer it if you would call me and let me know where you are." Now this statement gives him knowledge about how you are feeling, what he did to give you that feeling, and what he can do to improve things. This is good communication.

What if you feel as though someone in your group is in denial and lying to himself or herself? You might say something like this: "I feel sad when I hear you say you don't have a drinking problem. I would prefer it if you would try to see the truth about what you are doing to yourself."

In group, you will have people reflect your feelings to you. They aren't trying to hurt you. They are trying to get you to see the truth. They might tell you that they experience you as mad or sad when you don't really know how you feel. It is important to listen to your group members and to try to see what they see. Maybe they can see a side of you that you can't see.

It is vitally important for you not to feel ashamed of your feelings. You can have your feelings whether or not you have a good reason for having them. They don't have to be logical and make sense to be important. You will learn how to trust your feelings in treatment. You will learn that all of your feelings are great and wise counselors.

CHAPTER NINE | Special Problems

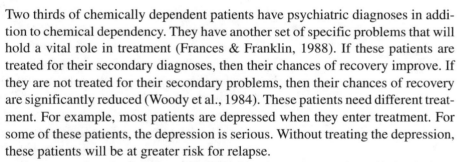

Two thirds of chemically dependent patients have psychiatric diagnoses in addition to chemical dependency. They have another set of specific problems that will hold a vital role in treatment (Frances & Franklin, 1988). If these patients are treated for their secondary diagnoses, then their chances of recovery improve. If they are not treated for their secondary problems, then their chances of recovery are significantly reduced (Woody et al., 1984). These patients need different treatment. For example, most patients are depressed when they enter treatment. For some of these patients, the depression is serious. Without treating the depression, these patients will be at greater risk for relapse.

One way of evaluating these clinical phenomena is to make a distinction between the primary and secondary diagnoses. The disorder that occurred first is called primary, and the problem that appeared second is called secondary. When the disorder appearing first is abuse of substances, it is highly likely (but not always true) that the secondary problems will improve rapidly (within days or weeks) once abstinence is achieved (Schuckit, 1994).

The Psychiatric/ Psychological Assessment

All patients need to be carefully screened for psychiatric/psychological problems during the initial assessment process. This screening must be done by a psychiatrist or a psychologist with the special skills necessary for this examination. The assessment must include the following:

1. A systematic mental status examination with special emphasis on immediate recall and recent and remote memory
2. A determination of current and past psychiatric/psychological abnormality
3. A determination of the dangerousness to self or others
4. A neurological assessment (if indicated by the psychiatric/psychological assessment)

5. An evaluation of cognitive functioning including any learning impairment that might influence treatment

This assessment will signal to the staff problems that need further treatment. The psychologist/psychiatrist will flag for you serious psychopathology, but you still need to keep him or her informed if you believe that something else is going on other than chemical dependency. You see the patient on a daily basis, and you are the most likely to know when things are not going well. Sometimes more of the patient's abnormal behavior will become evident as he or she moves through the treatment program.

How to Develop the Treatment Plan

■

Once the patient is diagnosed with a secondary problem, the treatment team will develop a treatment plan. Sometimes you will not be formally involved in the treatment (the psychiatrist or psychologist may do it), but you will deal with the problem on some level, so you need special skills. If you ever feel that you are in over your head with a patient, then you must inform the staff. You might need to refer the patient for further consultation. Do not strike out on your own with these patients. Use the treatment team to guide you.

It would be beyond the scope of this book to cover all of the psychopathology that you will experience as a counselor, but we discuss what you will see most often. You should familiarize yourself with the latest edition of the *Diagnostic and Statistical Manual of Mental Disorders (DSM,* American Psychiatric Association, 1994). Keep this manual close to you for reference. It is not your job to diagnose these patients, but you should be alert for the major problems you will see and become familiar with methodologies to treat the problems.

All of the major psychiatric diseases, like chemical dependency, have a biological component, a psychological component, and a social component. You must consider all three parts of the problem in developing a treatment plan.

Some psychiatric diseases require psychotropic medication. There is an old idea in AA/NA that all medications are bad. This no longer is appropriate. Many patients need their medication to survive. For example, a certain type of depression is treated very well with antidepressant medication. If you deprive these patients of the treatment they need, then some of them will die. Fully 15% of people who have serious depression eventually kill themselves (Hirschfeld & Goodwin, 1988). The schizophrenic patient and the patient with bipolar affective disorder are other examples of persons who need their medication for normal functioning. Let the physician make this decision. Once the decision is made to treat the patient with medication, it is vital that you support this decision.

The Depressed Patient

■

By far the most common secondary diagnosis related to chemical dependency is depression. Depression is a whole body illness that involves a patient's body, mood, and thinking. It affects the ways in which patients eat and sleep, feel about themselves, and think about things. There is a consistently high rate of depression in substance abusers (Dorus, Kennedy, Gibbons, & Raci, 1987; Hesselbrock, Meyer, & Kenner, 1985). Most chemically dependent individuals will come into treatment with some degree of measurable depression.

Excessive use of alcohol and other chemicals results in depressed mood. This depression can be organic, psychological, or interpersonal. You will first pick up depression in the mental status examination or in the psychological testing. Patient depressed mood can range from mild to severe. The best way of measuring the severity is to use a psychological instrument such as the Beck Depression Inventory (Appendix 31). A score lower than 10 indicates mild depression, a score of 10 to 20 indicates moderate depression, and a score higher than 20 indicates severe depression. Any depressive score higher than 10 should be followed. The average Beck score of patients coming into inpatient treatment is 16.

The primary symptom of depression is the inability to experience pleasure. This is called anhedonia. Depression clouds the patients' whole lives. The anhedonia is persistent and pervasive. The patients feel as though life is dead. The joy is gone. They feel sad or down most of the day almost every day. They sleep poorly; they either undersleep or oversleep. Their appetites are off. They have a diminished ability to concentrate. They might feel helpless, hopeless, worthless, or excessively guilty. When people feel this bad, they might think that they would be better off dead. They may be suicidal.

How to Assess Depression

To assess depression, you will have the Beck score, the mental status examination, the history of the present problem, and the past history. The patient is asked, "Have you ever felt sad or down most of the day, almost every day, for more than 2 weeks?" If the answer to this question is yes, then the patient needs to see someone on the staff experienced in depression. As the counselor, do not try to evaluate the extent of the depression yourself. It gets complicated and takes quite a bit of diagnostic skill. You should be familiar with the types of depression listed in the *DSM*. Some depressions are chronic and mild, and some can be acute and life threatening.

How to Treat Depression

Depression can be treated by you if you work with the clinical team. Depression is treated in three ways: with antidepressant medication, with psychotherapy (e.g., behavior therapy, cognitive therapy), and with interpersonal therapy. If the patients are placed on medication, then you need to be supportive of these decisions and encourage the patients to comply. In behavior therapy, you will encourage the patients to change their actions. For example, you will help the patients to develop leisure time activities that will increase their opportunity to experience joy. What the patients do will change how they feel. In cognitive therapy, you will help the patients to correct their inaccurate thinking. In interpersonal therapy, you will help the patients to resolve interpersonal conflicts.

Chemotherapy

The biology of depression is centered around a chemical problem in the brain. Certain neurotransmitter systems (e.g., norepinephrine, dopamine, serotonin) become deregulated or out of balance. This chemical problem can be corrected chemically with medication. There are four groups of antidepressant medications commonly used in treating depression: selective serotonin reuptake inhibitors (SSRIs), tricyclics, monoamine oxidase inhibitors (MAOIs), and lithium. Lithium, carbamazepine, and valproic acid are the current treatments for bipolar affective disorder. The doctor might have to try a variety of antidepressant medications or a combination of medications before finding the right one. Depression has strong genetic links, and certain genes predispose some people to manic or depressive episodes. Affective disorders can be caused by physical, psychological, or interpersonal problems, or they can occur without environmental precipitant.

There is not always a psychological or social cause of the disease, but it always has psychological and social effects that need treatment.

If the physician decides to put the patient on antidepressant medication, there usually will be a 3- to 6-week delay before the patient begins to feel better. You must encourage the patient during this period. Keep telling the patient that the depression is going to get better. This encouragement will instill hope in the treatment and will increase patient compliance. There are side effects of antidepressants that the patient needs to discuss with the physician. Mostly, this will be mild sedation and an overall drying effect experienced as dry mouth, urinary retention, and constipation. Some of the newer antidepressants can cause an increase in anxiety and loss of appetite. Be sure to chart any symptoms that the patient reports and to discuss them with the clinical team.

Because it takes these drugs 3 to 6 weeks to work, you might not see the antidepressants take effect in every patient. The patient might respond only after he or she has left treatment. Once you see this change take place, however, you will be totally convinced. The dramatic effect that these drugs produce will win you over. They contribute in a major way to the treatment of depression.

Medication never should be the only treatment for depression. Studies have consistently shown that patients that undergo medication plus psychotherapy have a better prognosis (Beitman, Carlin, & Chiles, 1984; Conte, Plutchik, Wild, & Karasu, 1986).

The two major psychological treatments for depression are behavior therapy and cognitive therapy. In the biopsychosocial, you will try to uncover any psychosocial stressors that may have precipitated the depression. Certain depressions are caused by specific environmental events such as a death in the family or a divorce. If you can determine what caused or exacerbated the depression, then you will have come a long way toward knowing where to concentrate treatment.

Behavior Therapy   Behavior therapy of depression centers around teaching the patient new skills and increasing positive reinforcers in the patient's environment. This increase in pleasure-oriented activity elevates mood. Studies have shown that depressed people do not do fun things. They tend to sit and feel helpless, hopeless, and depressed. Your behavioral intervention will increase the patients' activities. You will have them begin an exercise program; increase social interaction with treatment peers; and become more involved in games, sports, and hobbies. You must be specific in what you are recommending, and you must make sure that the patients are following through with your recommendations.

Monitor depression with a weekly Beck Depression Inventory. You can give this test daily if it is necessary. As the patient gets better, the Beck score will drop. You want that score to drop to 10 or lower before the patient leaves the treatment center. If the patient levels off for a few weeks at a score higher than 10, then you will have to adjust the treatment plan.

A word about psychological testing is appropriate here. Testing will give you a general indication of what is going on. A test is not able to be absolutely certain about anything. The scores need to be considered in light of the total clinical picture. You need to trust your clinical judgment more than you trust a psychological test. If the tests show that the patient is not depressed and you believe that he or she is depressed, you could be right. This is an issue that needs to be discussed with the clinical team. You will make more accurate judgments together.

An increase in goal-oriented behavior is essential to behavioral treatment of depression. Depressed persons have a difficult time in doing anything, and they will need encouragement to set goals. If they need to increase their level of social interaction, then you can get them to go through a communication exercise with one or two peers each day. You can get them to play pool or cards with someone once a day. The contracts are very helpful here, and most of these patients will need to work through the contracts with you or with a treatment peer. Relaxation skills and stress reduction skills will be important to some of these patients. Depressed patients might need to learn assertiveness skills. *Control Your Depression* (Lewinsohn, Munoz, Youngren, & Zeiss, 1978) is an excellent, highly structured, skill training program for depression. You can work through this text with your patients and come up with specific behaviors for the patients to learn.

In groups, depressed patients will need to be encouraged to talk in both individual and group sessions. They need to talk about how they feel, and they need to detail what they are going to do to feel better. You cannot let these patients ruminate about how bad they feel. They need to be encouraged to do something different. Have them go for a bike ride, take a walk, play basketball, play pool, swim, talk to someone, call a friend, become involved in a hobby, listen to music, read pleasant material, breathe the clean air, pray, meditate, eat something good, listen to the sounds of nature, give a gift, help someone in the program, do a job until it is well done, take a hot bath, or kick the leaves. You can have fun coming up with new ideas for them to try.

As the patients try these new fun behaviors, they will naturally begin to feel better. When they do, you need to reinforce them and show them that it is what they are doing that is influencing how they feel. You must chart the new behaviors and the responses of the patients. Place some quotations in their charts regarding what the patients say about their new behaviors.

Cognitive Therapy Cognitive therapy concentrates on how a patient thinks. This therapy was developed by Albert Ellis during the early 1960s (Ellis, 1962). It was further refined for depressed patients by Aaron Beck and colleagues (Beck, Rush, Shaw, & Emery, 1979). These researchers found that many depressed feelings come from negative self-talk. This tends to be inaccurate thinking, and it needs to be corrected. All patients who are depressed should read *Coping With Depression* (Beck & Greenberg, 1974). This monograph will explain cognitive therapy and will get the patients started.

Using the technique developed by Beck et al. (1979), the patients keep a daily record of their dysfunctional thinking. This is accomplished by having the patients write down each situation that makes them feel uncomfortable during the day. The patients need to be specific about this situation, stating exactly what happened that triggered the uncomfortable feelings. Then the patients make a list of each uncomfortable feeling that they had following the situation. Did the patients feel fear, sadness, disgust, or anger? Then the patients rate the intensity of each feeling on a scale from 1 (*as little of that feeling as possible*) to 100 (*as much of that feeling as possible*). These numbers are called subjective units of distress. Only the negative feelings are of interest to you. The patients add up the scores—the total of the subjective units of distress that they felt during the situation.

Now you help the patients to determine what they were thinking between the situation and the negative feelings. Ask the patients what they were thinking and then be willing to make suggestions. The patients will not be able to come up with all of these thoughts by themselves because the thinking is out of their awareness. The thoughts that you are after are negative, and they lead directly to uncomfortable feelings. Pull for as many of these negative thoughts as you can, and write all of them down. This is uncovering the automatic thinking that occurred between the situation and the uncomfortable feelings. It must be emphasized that the patients do not try to think these thoughts. They are automatic and come without conscious effort.

Once you have a list of the negative thoughts and feelings, have the patients go back and develop accurate thoughts. Go over what happened again and help the patients to decide what they should have been thinking. What would have been an accurate judgment of that situation? Once you have a list of the accurate thoughts, re-rate each of the feelings based on an accurate evaluation of the situation. You will come up with new subjective units of distress based on accurate thoughts rather than inaccurate thoughts.

The patients will be amazed at how their inaccurate thinking directly causes their uncomfortable feelings. The patients need to keep actively involved in cognitive therapy the whole time that they are in treatment. Each time the patients go though an uncomfortable situation, they need to keep a record of the thinking. In time, the patients will be able to catch themselves in inaccurate thinking, stop this thinking, and get their thinking accurate. Once the patients are accurate, they will feel much better.

An Example of Cognitive Therapy   Let's go though an actual cognitive therapy session. In this session, the counselor uses the first time that the patient hears about interpersonal group as the situation that caused uncomfortable feelings. The first time that any patient hears about this group creates quite a bit of anxiety. The patient is Kim, a 17-year-old female who is rather shy and avoidant. Her Beck depression score is 24, which puts her in the severely depressed range.

The counselor introduces the cognitive therapy session.

Counselor: Kim, I want you to begin to get accurate in your thinking. When you do this, you will feel more comfortable. What we are going to do now is go through an actual situation and see if we can uncover some of your inaccurate thoughts. The first time you heard about interpersonal group, how did you feel?

Kim: Scared.

Counselor: How scared did you feel on a scale of 1 (*as little scared as possible*) to 100 (*as scared as possible*)?

Kim: I don't know.

Counselor: We're just going to guess. How scared do you think you were feeling on a scale of 1 to 100?

Kim: [Pauses.] About 85, I guess.

Counselor: Great, 85. How else were you feeling?

Kim: Oh, I don't know.

Counselor: Were you feeling angry?

Kim: No, I wasn't feeling angry.

Counselor: Were you feeling sad?

Kim: Yeah, I guess I was.

Counselor: How sad were you feeling on a scale of 1 (*as little sad as possible*) to 100 (*as sad as possible*)?

Kim: About 60.

Counselor: Good. How else were you feeling?

Kim: [No response.]

Counselor: Were you feeling surprised?

Kim: No.

Counselor: Were you feeling any anticipation?

Kim: No. . . . I was feeling discouraged.

Counselor: How discouraged?

Kim: About 75.

Counselor: Good. Now if we add up all those negative feelings, we get 230 subjective units of distress. When you hear about interpersonal group, you feel 230 units of uncomfortable feelings. Now, what were you thinking between hearing about interpersonal group and the feelings you felt? What thoughts ran through your mind?

Kim: I won't fit in.

Counselor: Great. What else were you thinking?

Kim: I'll be treated like an outcast.

Counselor: What else?

Kim: They will think I'm a psycho.

Counselor: Okay, what else?

Kim: They will get the idea that I'm not serious about treatment.

Counselor: What else were you thinking?

Kim: That's about it.

Counselor: Were you thinking, "They're not going to like me"?

Kim: Yeah, I was.

Counselor: Okay, let's put that down. Were you thinking, "I'll have to talk"?

Kim: Yes.

Counselor: Were you thinking, "They'll make me talk about things I don't want to talk about"?

Kim: Definitely.

Counselor: Any other thoughts?

Kim: They won't understand me.

Counselor: Good. Now I have written down all of your automatic thoughts. It is important to recognize that these thoughts came to you automatically. You didn't try to think these thoughts. They came on their own. You will find that before you have negative feelings, you will always have rapid thoughts before the feelings. This is where you make assumptions or judgments about the situation. It's where you internally evaluate the situation and how it directly applies to you. Do you understand?

Kim: Yeah.

Counselor: Good. Now we need to get accurate. Go back to the situation and think about it. You hear about interpersonal group. What is accurate thinking about that situation?

Kim: They might be able to help me in group.

Counselor: That's right. That's what they are there for. What else is accurate?

Kim: I won't have to talk if I don't want to.

Counselor: Good. What else is accurate?

Kim: I'll try to fit in. We all have problems in common.

Counselor: That's right. What else?

Kim: They'll try to make me feel like a part of the group.

Counselor: Yes. What else?

Kim: They have some of the same problems as I do.

Counselor: That's very true. What else?

Kim: That's all I can think of.

Counselor: How about, "They'll try to be supportive of me"?

Kim: Yeah, that's true.

Counselor: How about, "If I want to get help, I should try and share as much as I can"?

Kim: That's right.

Counselor: Okay, now let's go back and rate each of the negative feelings we rated before. You hear about interpersonal group, but this time you think accurately. You think, "They will try to make me feel like a part of the group. They might be able to help me. They will try to support me. They will try and understand me. I won't have to talk, but if I want help here, I should try and share as much of myself as I feel comfortable sharing." How much fear do you feel when you are thinking accurately?

Kim: About 20.

Counselor: How sad do you feel?

Kim: I don't feel any sadness.

Counselor: How discouraged?

Kim: About 5.

Counselor: Great. Now let's see. When you are thinking automatically and inaccurately, you score 230 units of distress. But when you stop and get accurate, you feel only 25 units of uncomfortable feelings. How do you feel about that?

Kim: That's amazing.

Counselor: Yes, it is. Many of these inaccurate thoughts come out of childhood. We judge situations automatically as if our inaccurate thoughts are accurate. No wonder you were feeling bad about interpersonal group. You were thinking, "I won't fit in. I'll be treated like an outcast. They will think I'm a psycho." What we are going to do over the next few weeks, Kim, is to keep account of each situation that makes you feel uncomfortable. Then we are going to uncover the inaccurate thinking that leads to your uncomfortable feelings. Then we are going to challenge these thoughts and get accurate. You need to live in the real world. You can no longer live in the painful world of your inaccurate thinking. You need to commit yourself to reality.

In cognitive therapy, you can decrease your patients' negative feelings substantially if you get the patients accurate. You must make this therapy formal. The patients will be unable to do this therapy on their own. They will not be able to uncover their inaccurate thoughts or to get accurate without your help. You will need to make suggestions. As the patients understand that they have been getting their depressed feelings from inaccurate thoughts, they will feel better and their depression will begin to lift.

As the patients bring in their dysfunctional thoughts, you will begin to see patterns in their thinking. Some of the same thoughts will come up over and over again. These thoughts give the patients false information from which they make false assumptions. They collect the inaccurate thoughts and reach conclusions based on false information. These conclusions must be challenged with accurate information. It is not uncommon for patients to reach conclusions such as "I'm stupid," "I'm ugly," "I'm unworthy," "No one will ever love me," "I'm inadequate," and "Everyone is better than I am." They live their lives as if these false conclusions were true.

You will have some interesting therapy sessions with these patients. Many of their false assumptions are held onto quite rigidly. You might have to get the support of the group to help convince the patients that they are wrong. It is not uncommon for a strikingly beautiful person to think that he or she is ugly. Many patients will fight to hold onto their inaccurate opinions of themselves.

Trust in you and in the group is important here. The patients will need to trust others to make accurate judgments. This is difficult. The old ideas die hard; they seem to have lives of their own. With work, the patients will get more accurate. You should see the patients in cognitive therapy at least once a week. The more the patients keep up on their thinking, the more rapidly they will improve.

Interpersonal Therapy

Interpersonal therapy of depression has been outlined by Klerman, Weissman, Rounsaville, and Chevron (1984). This therapy seeks to heal interpersonal problems that leave the patients feeling depressed. For example, many patients will come into treatment with abnormal grief reactions. They have had a loss of a love object or self-esteem that they have not dealt with. Some patients are involved in interpersonal disputes. These unresolved conflicts leave the patients feeling lost and depressed. Some patients are in a role transition that they cannot deal with. Some patients are impoverished. They have no socially reinforcing situation from which they can gain pleasure.

Grief

Patients in an abnormal grief reaction need to work through the grief process. Normal grief is much like depression, but it lifts without treatment within 2 to 4 months. The persons gradually deal with the loss and move on with their lives. Sometimes the persons suffering a loss do not grieve until much later. This is a delayed grief reaction. They postpone the grief because they cannot deal with it at the time of its occurrence. Persons with a delayed grief reaction will feel numb at the actual loss. It is only later that they begin to experience the pain.

Some patients will drink or use drugs that prevent them from feeling the pain. Grief can be unresolved for years. When patients come into treatment with a significant loss of a close family member or friend, you must consider how they handled the grief process. Did they work the death through, or do they still have grief work to do? Is the issue resolved, or are the patients still stuck in the grief process? Many persons who have had abortions have unresolved grief to work through.

Normal grief runs through a range of highly charged feeling states. The loss of a loved one leads to at least 1 year of disturbance, and 3 years of disturbance is not uncommon. Normal bereavement reactions include states of shame, guilt, personal fear of dying, and sadness. In normal grief, anger at the person who died, at the self, and at persons who are exempted from the tragedy are common. In pathological grief, the patient becomes frozen in one or more of these stages for weeks, months, or years (Karasu, 1989).

People in the unresolved grief process need to talk about their grief. To accept the reality of their loss, they need to experience their pain. They need to talk about it in individual sessions and in group. They need to share the good and bad memories. They need to discuss the events prior to, during, and after the loss. They need to gradually adjust to a new environment. This may include coming to terms with living alone, managing finances, learning to do the chores, facing an empty house, and changing social relationships. They need to begin to withdraw emotionally from the lost person, reinvest in new relationships, and acquire new interests to substitute for the loss. They need to be reassured that they have a program full of people, which makes it impossible that they ever will be lonely again. They need to see what they lost accurately, with all of the good and bad qualities. People who see only the good things will not work through the grief.

These patients need to develop new relationships in the program. They need to be encouraged to increase their social interaction with treatment peers. Do not let them huddle up in your office bemoaning their fate. Get people further along in the program to stick with them and keep them out with the patient population.

Interpersonal Disputes Patients in interpersonal disputes will have to work toward resolving the interpersonal problems. In chemical dependency treatment, you often will see spouses who are being rejected by their significant others. The drinking and drugging have taken their toll, and the spouses have emotionally or physically left their relationships. The patients may come into treatment in a frantic attempt to save their relationships. These patients may feel hopeless and solely responsible for the problems.

Treatment begins with helping the patients to identify the problems. The patients need to plan what they are going to do. What are all of the possible actions that the patients can take regarding the problems? The patients will need to improve communication skills. They should work through the Relationship Skills exercise (Appendix 12) and the Communication Skills exercise (Appendix 14). They will need to practice these skills with their peers before they bring these skills into play in their current conflicts. If possible, you need to meet with the patients and the significant others to work toward resolution.

At times, the patient will need only to renegotiate a dispute with a significant other. This is the easiest type of conflict to resolve. First, you need a commitment from each party to work on the problem. At times, there is an impasse, where one member of the couple is not willing to cooperate. You cannot do much here except to encourage the patient to hope that in recovery this other person will change. Often a spouse needs to see recovery to know that it is real. Many marriages reconnect after a few months or years of sobriety. The patient must understand that the other person has been devastated by the disease. It is the disease that is the problem. The best thing that the patient can do now is to get into a stable program of recovery and turn the situation over to the Higher Power. "God grant me the serenity to accept the things I cannot change, the courage to change the things I can, and the wisdom to know the difference."

Suicide | Most patients who are depressed consider suicide to relieve their pain. There is a 15% mean suicide rate in alcoholics (Talbott, Hales, & Yudofsky, 1988). Suicidal ideation begins with patients thinking that everyone would be better off if they were dead. Remember that the primary symptom of depression is the absence of pleasure. When all of life's pain remains, and all of the pleasure leaves, it is logical for the patients to consider death. The incidence of suicide is about 20 times higher in drug abusers (Blumenthal, 1990). Patients who are a suicide threat will move through three phases of increasing lethality.

1. They will have increasing suicidal thoughts.
2. They will plan their suicide.
3. They will carry out their plan.

As the counselor, your job is to recognize the process and reestablish hope. No patients commit suicide if they can see that they can live lives that have meaning and worth. All patients who are depressed need to hear that depression is an illness from which people recover. Depression is treatable and curable. The depression is not their fault. It is a sickness that happened to them. It is not a punishment.

On the Beck Depression Inventory, Question 2 assesses hopelessness and Question 8 assesses suicidal ideation. Both of these questions, when answered positively, should be taken seriously. The higher the score, the greater the risk.

In the mental status examination, all patients are formally assessed for suicidal risk, but you also can ask the suicidal questions anytime during treatment when you believe that they may be important. The questions are as follows:

1. Have you ever wanted to go to sleep and not wake up? (If the answer is yes, then ask the patient about that. What was going on?)
2. Have you ever thought about hurting yourself? (If the answer is yes, then ask the patient what was happening.)
3. If you were to hurt yourself, how would you do it? (If the patient has a suicidal plan, then write it down.)
4. If the above answer is yes, have you carried any of that plan out? (Carefully assess any actions the patient has taken to arrange for or to commit suicide.)

These four questions accurately assess suicidal risk in escalating order of severity. Patients who have suicidal ideation, have an active plan, and have carried out any part of the plan should be transported to a psychiatric unit. These patients are in danger of hurting themselves and need more structure. A psychiatric facility has rooms and wards that are specifically designed to reduce the possibility of suicide.

Patients who are suicidal usually are afraid of themselves or are resigned to their death. Each of these signs is an ominous indicator of serious intent.

Most patients who come in for chemical dependency treatment have thought about suicide but do not have an active plan. If they do have a plan, then it is one that they worked out outside of the treatment center. Patients who have been actively considering suicide, and who have been considering a plan in treatment, need to be transported. Do not leave these patients alone, not even for a second. Wait until you turn them over to the care of professionals.

Do not make decisions about suicidal patients by yourself. This is outside of your level of expertise. All of these patients need to be examined as soon as possible by appropriate mental health professionals. This covers you and your staff, and it will give you confidence in the decisions reached.

Patients who are experiencing suicidal ideation with no plan can stay in treatment. They will need extra support, and they will need to be watched more carefully than will other patients. You do not want these patients isolating themselves. You want them to be with people who are supporting and encouraging them. These patients need to feel that they are in a safe environment, and they need to be certain that the staff is going to respond to their needs. Once these patients begin to feel hope, their suicidal ideation will subside.

The Angry Patient ■

Anger and resentments are poison for chemically dependent persons. "Resentments is the 'number one' offender. It destroys more alcoholics than anything else" (Alcoholics Anonymous, 1976, p. 64). It is not very far from that burning angry feeling to the chemicals. Anger has a lot of energy behind it. This angry energy is going to have to go somewhere, and it is important that it is directed positively into the recovery program. Anger at the illness can be constructive.

Anger necessitates blame. Patients must believe that someone purposely did something wrong that ended up hurting them or else the anger cannot continue. Each of these beliefs must be checked out for accuracy. The patients must stop and think before they act.

How to Handle a Violent Patient

Patients who are actively violent do not belong in the normal chemical dependency treatment center. Like the actively suicidal patient, these patients belong in a more secure psychiatric facility. Psychiatric hospitals have the equipment and the staff to deal with violent patients. Most chemical dependency centers do not have this expertise. If your patient makes overt attempts, acts, or threats of substantial bodily harm to himself or herself or other persons, then the patient should be transferred. Keep as many staff members with this patient as necessary to transport him or her safely. Do not hesitate to call the police. Apprise the officers carefully of your situation, and tell them to bring enough backup to manage the situation. Get an immediate consultation from your psychiatrist or psychologist, and follow his or her orders carefully. The doctor can order chemical or mechanical restraints if this becomes necessary.

How to Handle an Angry Patient

Patients who are feeling angry, or are verbally acting angry, usually can be managed in your facility. It is rare for a patient to go through treatment without expressing anger. Most of your patients have unresolved anger issues. Chemically dependent persons tend to harbor deep anger and resentments. They boil and fume for years over some real or imagined slights. This all comes from the desire to be in control. "Each person is like an actor who wants to run the whole show; [the actor] is forever trying to arrange the lights, the ballet, the scenery, and the rest of the players in his [or her] own way" (Alcoholics Anonymous, 1976, pp. 60-61). When people do not do what chemically dependent people want them to do, the latter become furious.

The treatment for angry patients revolves around having them complete the Anger Management exercise (Appendix 33), where the patients learn about their anger problem and learn specific skills to deal with angry feelings. Most people feel sad and fearful along with the anger. All of the feelings need to be expressed. The patients need to verbalize how they see the whole situation while you support them. Do not argue with angry patients. Stay out of their reach and use a calm voice. Do not stand in the way of an exit. Let them rant and rave if they want to do so. The patients need to feel that they are important. If you listen to them, even when they are angry, it validates them as people.

Angry patients are feeling afraid and will need a lot of reassurance. The patients often feel that their anger is so repulsive that they will be rejected for expressing it. You need to show them that their anger is friendly so long as it is used appropriately. Anger exists to help us establish and maintain boundaries around ourselves. It keeps us from being violated. Anger is adaptive. People who cannot get angry will have their boundaries violated.

Help your patients to see that all anger comes from hurt. Anger is there to make the pain stop. First something violates the patients physically or emotionally, and then they get angry. If the patients learn to hold people accountable by expressing all of their feelings, then they might not even get angry.

Assertiveness Skills

Patients do not have to act aggressively to show that they are angry. They need to be taught assertiveness skills. They need to see that assertiveness skills work and bring people closer together. Aggressive skills, on the other hand, are controlling and drive people away. The book, *Your Perfect Right* (Alberti & Emmons, 1995), is an excellent resource for you and your patients. If your patients need assertiveness training, then they can read assigned parts of this book as homework. Assertiveness skills need to be practiced over and over again in individual sessions, in role-playing, and in group.

The Importance of Forgiveness

Patients with an anger problem must learn how to forgive. They can use the Higher Power for this if they cannot forgive themselves. They want to be forgiven, and God will forgive them as they learn to forgive others.

Forgiveness is difficult. Patients never will forget what happened, but they can understand the persons who hurt them by understanding their own disease. "We realized that the people who wronged us were perhaps spiritually sick. Though we did not like their symptoms and the way they disturbed us, they, like ourselves, were sick too. We asked God to help us show them the same tolerance, pity, and patience that we would cheerfully grant a sick friend" (Alcoholics Anonymous, 1976, p. 67).

All patients who are angry and resentful need to read the following passage from the "Big Book":

And acceptance is the answer to *all* my problems today. When I am disturbed, it is because I find some person, place, thing, or situation—some fact of my life—unacceptable to me, and I can find no serenity until I accept that person, place, thing, or situation as being exactly the way it is supposed to be at this moment. Nothing, absolutely nothing happens in God's world by mistake. Until I could accept my alcoholism, I could not stay sober; unless I accept life completely on life's terms, I cannot be happy. I need to concentrate not so much on what needs to be changed in the world as on what needs to be changed in me and in my attitudes. (Alcoholics Anonymous, 1976, p. 449)

Have patients who are angry keep an anger diary. Take them through some cognitive therapy. Every time they feel angry, they should write down the situation and uncover their automatic thoughts. As these inaccurate thoughts are uncovered, the patients will see why they have been so angry. They take the slightest look or word as an attack. They need to work through the impulse control exercise and begin to practice the assertive formula over and over again.

I feel _____

when you _____.

I would prefer it if _____.

| *How to Teach the Patient to Recognize Anger* | These patients need to learn the specific changes in their bodies when they are getting angry. They need to learn how this feels. Do they feel a tightness in their chests? Do their faces feel flushed? As early in the anger process as possible, the patients need to back out of the situation and use their new assertiveness skills. The initial response needs to be delayed until they can stop, think, and plan. This requires a lot of practice. Have the patients write down every time they use assertiveness skills and every time they lapse back into aggressive behavior. You will be able to show them the damage that they are doing to relationships with their old behavior. You also will show them how assertiveness skills bring people closer together. |

| *Disengagement* | It often will help angry patients to disengage from the current situation and detach as if the situation is happening to someone else. It is here that the patients can step back from themselves and see themselves as if they were their own counselors. |

"I'm feeling some anger."
"This is interesting."
"I need to check this out."
"What's going on with me right now?"

By stepping out of themselves and checking out the anger, patients will be more likely to get accurate and make better judgments. They can even laugh at themselves. They can recognize their anger, smile at themselves, and realize that getting angry is a silly thing to do to themselves. The patients can then take two deep breaths, breathing in slowly through the nose and out slowly through the mouth. As they exhale, they feel a warm wave of relaxation move down their bodies. The patients should practice this technique in your individual and group therapy sessions.

Time Out   Patients who have a tendency to become verbally or physically violent must move away from an escalating situation as soon as possible. They must move away from the situation as far as necessary to recover their normal feelings. One useful technique to use if the anger happens in a family is to develop a "time out" contract. This is a written contract between two or more people in which they agree that either party can say "time out" at any time. Once one person has said "time out," the other party can only say "okay, time out." At this point, the couple separates and agrees to return in an hour to further process through the problem. When they are separated, it is important that they do not rehash the argument over again in their minds. Otherwise, they might come back even more furious than when they left. When separated, it is important that they both tell themselves certain things to get their thinking more accurate (McKay, Rogers, & McKay, 1989).

1. No one is completely right or wrong.
2. It is okay to disagree.
3. The other person is not trying to hurt me. The other person is trying to meet his or her needs.
4. Do I need to call someone and talk about this? If I do, then I need to do that right now.
5. I will turn this situation over to my Higher Power.

The patients need to keep with them a list of these statements along with several numbers of people to call at all times.

How to Keep Your Cool as a Counselor   It is not easy dealing with people who are angry. They may verbally abuse you, and you need to keep calm. The worst thing that you can do is to lose your temper. Anger from the counselor can do a lot of damage. Concentrate on feeling yourself relax. Feel your arms and legs become heavy. Focus on your breathing and breathe slowly. If you are getting angry, then excuse yourself and take a few minutes outside of the room. Let someone else take over for a while. The best thing that you can do for angry patients is to remain calm and take good care of yourself.

The Homicidal Patient   Patients who are experiencing homicidal ideation need to ventilate their feelings and then process through their options. They are not thinking clearly. They need help in processing through their problem to a logical conclusion. It is not unusual for patients to feel like killing someone, even someone they love. You will find homicidal thoughts to be a common element in dealing with angry patients. Most patients are just blowing off steam, thinking about homicide, wanting the ultimate revenge.

The Duty to Warn   If staff members determine that a patient presents a serious danger of violence to another person, then they have the obligation to protect the intended victim (*Tarasoff v. Regents of the University of California,* 1976). This is an unusual event, but it does happen, and it should be carefully discussed with the clinical staff. There is a delicate balance between duty to warn and confidentiality.

Whenever you have a patient seriously threatening another person, it is necessary to staff the problem and document the staff decision in the patient record. This patient might have to be transferred to a more secure facility, or the threatened person might have to be warned.

Persons who have homicidal ideation usually can be reasoned with if they can be guided to see the truth. What is going to really happen if they kill someone? They need to process through the whole idea from beginning to end. Is killing someone taking good care of themselves? What good is going to come of homicide? Is murder going to do the world any good? Is it going to do the patients any good? What does God want from them? These persons will need to be encouraged to turn the situation over to the perfect judge—God.

Homicidal intent is assessed in escalating order of severity:

1. Have you ever thought about hurting anyone or anything like that? (If yes, ask the patient who. Ask what happened.)
2. If you were to hurt that person, how would you do it? (If the patient has a plan, then write it down.)
3. Have you carried out any of that plan? (Get the details of the patient's behavior.)

Patients with homicidal ideation who have a plan and have carried out any part of that plan must be considered seriously homicidal. They must be watched. They must not be discharged or allowed to leave without being processed by the clinical staff. If the patients are imminently harmful to others by overt attempts, acts, or threats within the past few hours, then they might have to be detained against their will and transported to another facility. A psychiatrist, psychologist, physician, and/or police officer are necessary for these decisions. Your job is to keep the appropriate personnel informed of the patients' conditions. Let them take over the responsibility for these patients when they can.

Personality

■

Personality is composed of two basic parts: temperament and character. Temperament is the general level of physiological responsivity to the environment. Some people are more sensitive to incoming stimulation. Some people seem dull and unresponsive. Character is what we learn about what to do and how to behave. It is shaped by the family and the social environment. Temperament and character are the primary elements in all personality disorders (Millon, 1981).

What Is Personality?

Personality is the enduring way in which a person thinks, feels, and acts. Personality is stable, well learned, and resistive to change. Personality makes up the total person. It is the pattern of behavior that a person evolves as the style of his or her life or how the person adapts to the environment.

A state is a person's current condition. This is transient, flexible, and easily manipulated by environmental stimulation. A person may feel sad, or even depressed, by the loss of his or her car keys. Once the keys are found, the person immediately returns to his or her normal state of thinking, feeling, and acting.

A trait is a long-standing tendency to react in a particular way to a set of circumstances. A trait is fixed and resistant to change. This is how a person has acted for years. A person might feel frightened of social interaction. This person fears doing something to embarrass or humiliate himself or herself in a group. This tendency may be persistent.

Personality disorders are patterns of inflexible and maladaptive traits that cause significant impairment. These patterns are not time limited. They are chronic. Personality disorders become evident by late adolescence and often last lifelong. The symptoms of personality disorder can be relieved. The patient can learn how to function better and more comfortably.

The Antisocial Personality

■

The Impulsive Temperament

You will see many antisocial personality disorders in your career. There is a higher incidence of this disorder in substance abusers (Khantzian & Treece, 1985; Weiss, Mirin, Griffin, & Michaels, 1988). This personality disorder has at its biological base the tendency to act impulsively. These patients have a diminished capacity to delay or inhibit action, particularly aggressive action (Siever & Davis, 1991; Siever, Llar, & Coccaro, 1985). These patients act too quickly on their feelings. They have a tendency to act before they think. They do not feel the same arousal levels that normal people feel, so they can push the limits further (Eysenck & Eysenck, 1976). These biological tendencies leave these individuals vulnerable to a variety of problems. When most people break the rules, they are afraid of getting caught. Antisocial persons do not feel this fear as much. They have difficulty in anticipating the effects of their behavior and learning from the consequences of their past.

A Disorder of Empathy

Antisocial patients do not feel normal empathy. They can break the rules of society to get their own way. They can openly defy authority and break the law without suffering much guilt or remorse. They do not feel at fault, and they have a tendency to blame others for their faults. They lack insight and fail to learn from past experience. This is easy to understand. If they do not feel responsible for their actions, why should they change?

Antisocial patients begin to get into trouble with society by their early teens. They are in trouble at home, at school, and often with the police. As they grow older, they are unable to sustain work, and they fail to conform to the social norms with respect to lawful behavior. This is one of the most difficult disorders to treat. These patients can spend more time trying to outwit the staff than trying to work the program.

How to Treat the Antisocial Personality

Treatment for these patients revolves around teaching them the consequences of their behavior and learning how to think in a new way. They need to stop blaming others and accept responsibility for their own actions. They must see how their choices lead directly to painful consequences. At every opportunity, you need to show them how their decisions and actions got them into trouble. (An excellent resource for corrective thinking is the Truthought Corrective Thinking Process listed in Appendix 55. An excellent manual can be obtained from Truthought, P.O. Box 222, Roscoe, IL 61073 (815) 389-0127.) They will love to argue the point so that they can place the blame on someone else, but you are not going to allow them to do this. You are going to constantly direct them to see the truth.

You may hear these kinds of statements from a patient with an antisocial personality:

"I didn't know that was a rule."
"She didn't explain it properly to me."
"He did it. I didn't do it."
"I was just standing there. What are you looking at me for?"

These patients are used to lying their way out of everything. They need to keep a daily log of their honesty and work hard at learning from their behavior. Each time they do something wrong, take them aside and take them through the behavior chain. Cover the trigger, thoughts, feelings, actions, and consequences carefully. They need to see their patterns over and over again.

Working with the antisocial personality can be a frustrating experience, but these patients can do well in recovery. They will need a lot of structure in early sobriety. A halfway house or some other facility can be helpful during those first few months out of treatment.

These patients have little self-discipline and have poor impulse control (Appendix 15 and 16). They will need to work through each of these problems in treatment. They need to stop, think, and plan before they act. This will be learned only with practice. The patients need to learn to stick to a task until it is completed. The contracts in treatment give them an opportunity to learn this new skill. They are notorious for procrastinating at their work or for doing barely enough to get by. The group will have to reject these poorly done contracts, and put up with these patients' anger, to show the patients what is required. Sobriety necessitates a long-standing commitment.

How to Deal With a Rule Violation

You need to be familiar with the rules of your facility. These patients will push the limits and will argue that they are right. If they can find a way around a rule, then they will break the rule. Rather than being totally negative, this provides the staff with an opportunity to intervene and teach these patients. The patients need to see what is causing their pain. The rules do not exist to keep them from having a good time. The rules exist to keep them safe. They need to practice turning things over rather than trying to manipulate everything.

If an antisocial patient is caught breaking a rule, have him or her write a report on the incident and present it to the group. This is not intended to shame the patient. It is intended to help the patient see the consequences of this behavior. The group encourages the patient and supports him or her in trying to bring the antisocial behavior under control. The group and the counselor should constantly reinforce prosocial behavior.

Learning empathy and appropriate guilt is a difficult skill. An antisocial patient will do most of this work in group. When someone in the group is having a strong feeling, the antisocial patient can be asked to relate to the feeling. Have the patients ever felt in a similar way? The patient tries to match his or her experience with the feeling of the other person. If the feelings can be matched, then empathy will begin to develop.

When an antisocial patient takes advantage of someone in treatment (this is inevitable), he or she needs to see the other person's pain. Take the patient through the behavior chain that revolved around the incident.

Moral Development

Moral development occurs in stages.

1. It is right so long as I can get away with it. (no rules)
2. It is right if it is within the law. (rules outside of self)
3. It is right because I believe it is right. (rules internalized)

Antisocial patients are stuck in the first stage of moral development. A spiritual program can do wonders for these patients. If they can see that a Higher Power is there and watching, then they can begin to develop some external control.

Cognitive therapy is helpful with these patients, but they must learn to be honest. Sometimes they will deny or hide what they are thinking to prevent reprisals. It is very important for these patients to know that you understand them and do not blame them for their antisocial thinking. The patients need to feel like they can share their antisocial thoughts and acts with you. Patients must never be shamed for their thinking. They are held accountable only for their actions.

It is very easy to get into a "bad guy" role with antisocial patients. They might feel like you are pushing them around or being unnecessarily controlling. They want you to be the problem. That is why the rules, and the consequences of breaking the rules, need to be very clear from the outset. Then when the patient breaks a rule, all you have to say is, "It's not me doing this to you. It's you doing this to yourself. You knew the rule and you broke it. There is a consequence for that. I hope that next time you will think before you act."

How to Deal With the Family of an Antisocial Patient

The family of an antisocial patient usually is in chronic distress. The family members need to be educated in how the patient manipulates them. Communication patterns need to be improved. The family must hold the patient accountable for his or her actions. This means allowing the patient to suffer the consequences. This means no more enabling.

Antisocial patients are not used to being loved, and they often are suspicious of anyone who tries to get close to them. They wonder what you really are after. They look for the hidden motive. Once they see you consistently act on their behalf—even when they are being difficult—they will begin to come around. The worst thing that you can do with these patients is to constantly get angry with them. This is playing their game, and they know it better than you do. They are used to dealing with people's anger. The know just how to manipulate this situation. They will just blame you.

If you establish a good therapeutic alliance, there will come a time when antisocial patients will want to please you. This gives you great power as a reinforcer. By carefully selecting when to give positive reinforcement, you can effectively shape the patients' behavior. A day without a violation of the rules should be soundly reinforced, perhaps by congratulating the patients in front of the staff or the patient population. A day without a lie is cause for celebration. The more positive attention you can give these patients for prosocial behavior, the further along they will be in their treatment program.

The Borderline Patient

The biological component of borderline personality disorder is a tendency to act impulsively plus emotional instability. The affective instability is characterized by rapidly changing moods that are overly reactive to environmental emotional stimulation (Siever & Davis, 1991; Siever et al., 1985). These patients overreact when they encounter emotional events such as relationship problems, separation, criticism, and frustration. They have much of the feelings and carry the feelings too long. When having extreme feelings, it is very difficult to think normally. The emotional shift can be quick and extreme, rarely lasting more than a few hours. It is common for borderline patients to attempt to control these affective shifts with self-damaging behavior such as suicide attempts, sexual acting out, and overusing mood-altering chemicals (Widiger & Frances, 1989). These patients grow up immature and unstable. They experience their feelings as being outside of their own control, controlled by environmental events. The environment becomes a major regulator of self-esteem and well-being. The boundaries between the patients and their environment become blurred (Siever et al., 1985). These patients do not feel safe and do not trust others because whenever they have trusted in the past, bad things inevitably occurred. Many of these patients have a history of childhood physical or sexual abuse.

Interpersonal Relationships

When borderline patients sense supportive relationships with other persons, counselors, staff members, or loved ones, they feel uncomfortable. At first they adopt an engaging, clinging, overly dependent style of relating. You are the greatest counselor in the world here, and you can do no wrong. You are the only person who can help them. When the relationship is threatened through normal treatment, whether real or imagined, the patients shift to angry manipulation. Then you become the worst person in the world, and you cannot help anyone. The patients may become self-destructive to regain control. The clinging dependency is rapidly replaced by devaluation of the goodness and worth of the other person (Gunderson & Zanarine, 1987).

Borderline patients tend to throw temper tantrums and will attempt to pit one staff member against another. They seem to flourish in an atmosphere of conflict, splitting people into having all good or all bad characteristics. This split often occurs with the same person hour by hour. At times the other person is the best, and at times the other person is the worst. This can be very difficult for you to deal with, but remember that these patients need to feel safe. Staff members need to work together to prevent the patients from manipulating. Constantly ask the patients, "What do you need to feel safe right now?" Then try to support the patients. After they calm down, try to help them to see the emotionally charged situation more accurately.

Affective Dysregulation

Borderline patients have extreme feeling shifts and act impulsively on their feelings. They repeatedly become involved in self-destructive behavior. They have chronic abandonment fears. They have a difficult time distinguishing who they are at any point in time. They often have attempted to hurt themselves, and they tend to become involved in dangerous activities such as shoplifting, sex, substance abuse, and reckless driving. They lack a life plan. They chronically feel empty and bored.

How to Treat the
Borderline Patient

Borderline patients bring all of this psychopathology into the treatment program. They can act out of control, and they can be very disruptive. You must provide a stable framework from which they can grow. They are emotionally immature and unstable. They will try your patience and push the limits of their relationship with you.

You must remain alert and active in their treatment. They need a lot of direction and input. They need to be confronted on their maladaptive behavior. Use the group if the patients are not under control. Meet with the patients and the whole staff if necessary. The patients need to identify the feelings and motivations behind their acting out. Often this comes as a shock to them. Self-destructive behavior will become unwanted if you draw the patients' attention to the consequences. They need to get real about what they are doing and what happens when they do it. They seem to always be in a mess, and they rarely believe that the problem is their fault. They need to see how their behavior affects what happens.

Setting Limits

Treatment centers around setting limits, learning impulse control, and developing skills for dealing with feelings. The staff will have to keep up on these patients to make sure that they do not pit one staff member against another. Often a borderline patient will believe that one staff member is the enemy and someone else is a trusted friend. Without staffing this patient, two staff members might end up in confrontation with each other. In such a situation, the staff needs to bring the patient in during staffing. Here everyone can get the same story at the same time.

Dealing With Transference

Transference and countertransference can be a real problem with these patients. They seem to have a way of creating strong feelings and relationships among staff members. You might end up feeling angry, guilty, or frustrated. You might feel helpless. At first the patients might see you as their savior, and then they might see you as their persecutor. It feels like an emotional roller-coaster ride. It is common for some to see these patients as "poor little things" who just need nurturing and for other staff members to see these patients as angry manipulators who need limits. Consultation with other staff members is essential. This will keep you in balance. This is the patients' problem, not yours. Borderline patients can form overly intense relationships with their counselors. You need to carefully maintain your boundaries. Do not become overly involved. Do not do anything for borderline patients that you would not normally do for someone else.

Coping With
the Intense Feelings

When borderline patients are feeling uncomfortable, they need to do something. They need a specific plan of action when they have strong feelings. They can exercise, talk to someone, turn it over to a Higher Power, become involved in something else, go to a meeting, read recovery material, and so on. They should not always talk to you when they are upset; this fosters dependency. It is notorious for borderline patients to say that they have to talk to you right now. You need to teach them that they cannot always come to you. You cannot always be there for them. They need to develop other coping skills.

Cognitive therapy is important. Patients need to be able to see a person's good and bad qualities at the same time. When the patients are extremely angry at someone, help them to see the person's positive characteristics. Borderline patients would rather be joined in attacking someone, but you should encourage them to look for the good. The patients need to see themselves and others more realistically. Cognitive therapy will help them to uncover their unconscious thoughts and motivations. They need to see why they feel and act the way they do. What are they after? How can they get what they want more appropriately?

Dealing With the Family

Two family issues may be important with the borderline patient. The family may be overinvolved and need to let go, or the family may have a history of abuse or neglect. Both of these issues need further counseling than you can provide in an inpatient program. They will need long-term psychotherapy. You can just help the family to get started. The family members must be referred to make sure that they address the problems in continuing care. The borderline patient often has clinging dependency needs or extreme anger at his or her family members.

Everyone in a borderline patient's family needs to be educated about the patient's diagnosis and become actively involved in treatment. They will be relieved to know that there is an illness called borderline personality disorder, and they need to understand the signs and symptoms. Most family members will be amazed that other people have this disease.

Behaviorally, patients need to work through the Impulse Control exercise (Appendix 16), the Relationship Skills exercise (Appendix 12), and the Communication Skills exercise (Appendix 14). They need to practice these skills with their treatment peers. They need to rehearse and role-play problem situations in interpersonal group.

Borderline patients are a challenge for you and the staff. They take a lot of energy. It is important to remember that these patients have an illness. They did not ask for their disease, nor did they create it themselves. They are frantic for love and affection with no idea about how to get it. They should work through the Love, Trust, and Commitment exercise (Appendix 10) to help them understand exactly what love is. They need to practice establishing relationships without unrealistic expectations.

These patients will need to be referred to outpatient psychotherapy in continuing care. They might need the structure of a halfway house or some other long-term facility. Long-term involvement with AA/NA is very beneficial to these patients. They can learn to function reasonably well over the years.

The Narcissistic Patient

Narcissistic patients can be difficult to deal with emotionally. They have a grandiose sense of their own self-importance. They feel as if they are the ruler of the earth and that everyone should treat them as if they were special. They think that they have special talents, beauty, power, or abilities. If you do not treat them in a special way, they get mad and reject you, destroying the therapeutic alliance. It is very difficult for them to hear the truth about themselves because they cannot tolerate criticism. They are excessively sensitive to having any flaws. When they are confronted with a problem that they have, they tend to dissolve into shame and worthlessness. When they become extremely angry and resentful, it is called narcissistic rage. Narcissistic patients do not think they need to learn anything from you. They know everything already. They tell everyone else what to do.

These patients spend a lot of time with big plans and schemes for unlimited success or power. They want to rule over others rather than be one of the common people. They believe that they deserve to be treated special due to their outstanding achievements, brilliance, beauty, or ability. They believe that only the special people of the world, those of a similar high caliber, can understand them. They think that they should interact only with the beautiful people.

It is very easy to countertransfer with these patients and get angry, but if you do, then you will destroy your therapeutic alliance and they will think of you as inadequate. The best way of treating these patients is as if they really were the ruler. If you treat them as if they are the ruler and you are the servant, then you will go a long way toward getting them to listen. They often need to see that you are special too, with special powers and abilities. After all, only the greatest professional could help them. Once they see that you are wonderful, you can then show them that you have faults and that you have made some mistakes. If you and these patients can agree that both of you are wonderful but that both of you have made some mistakes, the patients are beginning to get accurate in their thinking.

Give these patients the Narcissism exercise (Appendix 34), which allows them to learn about their narcissistic traits. The most important thing for narcissistic patients to do is get honest with themselves and others. After they do that, they need to turn their wills and their lives over to the Higher Power. This is very difficult for them to do because they have been playing God for a long time.

Narcissistic patients grew up as the kings or queens of their households. They were in control. Their every whim was met. One of their primary caregivers was a servant doting on their every word, loving them, and telling them that they were wonderful. The adults in their homes used these children to build their own inadequate self-esteem. If their children were wonderful, then they were wonderful.

Narcissistic patients are interpersonally exploitative because they are only interested in their own needs. They are not capable of understanding how other people feel. Their relationships start off in a blaze of glory but end in despair. A high relapse trigger for them is sex, and they often fall in love in treatment. They can become convinced that any new relationship, no matter how bad it might seem to others, is going to be ideal and wonderful. It is as if they are blind to the truth, making the same mistakes over and over again. They need love and attention so much that when they get it, they tend to idealize the other persons, and this sets these relationships up to fail.

Narcissistic patients need to spend time developing empathy for others. In group, when someone is having a feeling, have the narcissistic patient try to connect with the other patient's feeling.

Most of the time, you inevitably will end up disappointing narcissistic patients. You will not be empathic in the right way, in the right amount, or at the right time, and they ultimately will decide that you are not enough for them. Every relationship ends up this way. That is why the Higher Power concept is the only one that works. God is the one that can be enough. God always is available. God has all the power. God is smart enough. When you feel these patients' disappointment, carefully explain the ABCs of AA: (a) that we were alcoholic and could not manage our own lives, (b) that probably no human power could have relieved our alcoholism, and (c) that God could and would if God were sought. When narcissistic patients see that no one can meet their needs except God, things can change. It is to be hoped that the patients will begin a genuine search for their Higher Power.

The Anxious Patient ■

Anxiety is a vague generalized fear. Some children are born with a nervous system that is more sensitive than others (Kagan, 1989; Kagan, Reznick, & Gibbons, 1989; Kagan, Reznick, & Snidman, 1987). This increased physiological responsivity can heighten the sensation of unpleasant experience. These children have a low threshold for subjective fear and a high arousal in anticipation of adverse consequences (Siever & Davis, 1991). Children with such a heightened response to the environment can become shy and inhibited. It takes less of an adverse experience to upset them (Rosenbaum, Biederman, Hirshfeld, Bolduc, & Chaloff, 1991).

Anxious patients are afraid, but they are not sure why. These individuals are hypervigilant and tense. They look for the impending disaster. They believe that the ax is falling. They feel a sense of dread and impending doom. Most of these patients are avoidant. They avoid social situations. They feel uncomfortable in groups and fear doing something that will humiliate them.

There is a high percentage of anxiety disorders in patients who end up abusing central nervous system depressants (Dorus et al., 1987; Hesselbrock et al., 1985). Patients attempt to reduce their anxious feelings with drugs that suppress central activity.

How to Measure Anxiety

Anxiety can be tested with a variety of psychological tests or rating scales similar to the Beck Depression Inventory (Beck, 1978). The test scores will help you to determine the effectiveness of your treatment. The Self-Rating Anxiety Scale (Zung, 1971), the Hamilton Anxiety Rating Scale (Hamilton, 1959), and the State-Trait Anxiety Inventory (Spelberger, 1983) can be used to measure anxiety. The tests are simple and can be given as often as necessary.

Multiple somatic complaints accompany anxiety. Patients may feel sweaty palms, a pounding heart, trembling, light-headed, dizzy, or numb. They may feel as though their lives are threatened. They may think that they are having a heart attack. The anxiety may go on for a few minutes, or it may last most of the day.

There are nonaddictive medications that can suppress or block certain forms of anxiety. Panic disorder is virtually eliminated with certain antidepressant medication. Feel relieved when doctors order medication for your patients. Physicians can be trusted to treat these patients with medication appropriately.

Outside of the chemical dependency field, anxiety often is treated with benzodiazepines. These central nervous system depressants are contraindicated in chemically dependent persons because they can be highly addictive. Patients who come into chemical dependency treatment taking these drugs will have to be withdrawn.

The Psychological Component of Anxiety

The psychological part of anxiety disorders centers around an inaccurate perception of threat. This threat can be real or imagined, but it is exaggerated to the point where it interferes with normal functioning. To these patients, all of the fears are real. The intensity of the fear is preparing them to escape a dangerous situation. Patients can be immobilized by fear. They can freeze and be unable to move. This is no joke, and you will get nowhere pretending that these patients have nothing to worry about. You must try to relate to, and understand, the intense fear that these patients are feeling. Patients can be intensely afraid of spiders even if there are no spiders. They can be terrified of a group even if there is no logical reason to be afraid. These patients need gentle support and encouragement. They need to feel as though someone understands them.

There are many forms of anxiety disorders, and the feared objects are incredibly variable, but you can approach all anxiety in the same general way. You need to know the following things about an anxious patient:

1. What is the patient afraid of?
2. Where did the fear seem to come from?
3. Is the fear accurate or inaccurate?
4. What can the patient do to reduce the fear?

Anxiety disorders are not character disorders. In character disorders, the patients blame everyone else for everything. In anxiety disorders, the patients blame themselves for everything.

How to Use Relaxation Techniques

Anxious patients need to learn how to relax. They cannot be anxious and relaxed at the same time. The two physiological states are incompatible. The patients will have to be taught how to relax using relaxation techniques. There are many relaxation tapes on the market. You can use relaxing music, sounds of nature, or imagery. Get a few and have the patients listen to a relaxation exercise twice a day. You can take patients through a relaxation exercise yourself by doing the following exercise.

Make sure that you will not be interrupted. Have the patients sit or lie down in a quiet comfortable place. Read these words in a quiet slow voice:

"Close your eyes and pay attention to your breathing. Feel the cool air coming in and the warm air going out. As you focus your attention on your breathing, feel yourself beginning to relax. There is no right way or wrong way to do this exercise. There is just your way. Feel yourself becoming calm. Your arms and legs are feeling more heavy. Inside of your mind, as completely as you can, in your own way, see ocean waves. Don't worry about how you are seeing these waves. Just see them as completely as you can. Match the waves with your breathing. As the wave builds, you inhale, and as the wave washes on a shore, you exhale. See yourself standing on an island, on a white sandy beach, looking at the waves. You are feeling at peace. With each breath and each wave, you feel more relaxed. It is warm, and you can feel the sunshine on your cheeks and on your arms. You are on an island. This is your island inside of your own mind. You are safe here. There is no one else on the island except you. There are palm trees and lush green vegetation on the island. There is a trail on the island, and you turn and see yourself take that trail. You are not in a hurry. You have plenty of time. You are walking slowly. There are flowers along the trail of every imaginable color and hue. You begin to walk up a hill, and as you walk up the hill, you become tired. Your arms and legs feel heavy. You come to a ridge that overlooks a lush green valley filled with waterfalls. You wander for as long as you like in this valley feeling at peace."

You can add any other relaxing scene to modify this exercise. When the patients have been relaxing for 10 to 20 minutes, you need to bring them out of the state of relaxation. Say something like this:

"You walk out of the valley and down the trail. You walk back on the beach and watch the waves. They build and wash on the shore. You feel yourself becoming more awake and aware of yourself. You wiggle your toes and fingers. You feel yourself in this room and in your chair. Your eyelids begin to flicker. When you feel comfortable, open your eyes and become fully awake."

While the patients are relaxed, you can give them some positive affirmations. The patients are good persons. They have talents. They have a Higher Power. They have people who support them. How the patients feel is important. They are going to take care of themselves. The patients are going to commit themselves to being honest. They should help you to develop these positive self-statements. Use this exercise to build a more positive self-image.

The Daily Log | These patients will need to score the level of relaxation after each exercise from 1 (*as little as possible*) to 100 (*as much as possible*). They also need to keep a log of their daily anxiety using the same scale. The patients score their general anxiety level at the end of each day. The patients should log any situation that caused or exacerbated their anxiety. This, plus the psychological testing, will give you a good idea of where the patients are in working their program.

Cognitive Therapy | Anxious patients need to see you in individual sessions at least twice a week. You will take the anxious situations and go through the same cognitive therapy suggested for depression. The patients can read *Coping With Anxiety and Panic* (Beck & Emery, 1979) or *Panic Attacks* (Greenberg & Beck, 1987) to introduce them to the cognitive techniques. (These pamphlets can be ordered from the Foundation for Cognitive Therapy, 133 South 36th Street, Room 602, Philadelphia, PA 19104.)

Anxious patients often exaggerate the level of threat by inaccurately perceiving and judging the situation. There are a lot of ways in which they can do this. They may make any of the following cognitive distortions:

1. Catastrophizing
   "I'm going to pass out."
   "I'm going crazy."
   "I'm losing control."
2. Exaggerating
   "This is the worst thing that could happen."
   "I fail at everything."
   "I'll make a fool of myself."
3. Ignoring the positive
   "They hate me."
   "Nobody likes me."

Each of these patients' inaccurate thoughts needs to be challenged for accuracy. The patients will need to keep track of their automatic thinking while in treatment. You cannot just do this for a few days. Cognitive therapy takes weeks of concentrated effort.

If it is medically possible, these patients need to exercise for 20 minutes a day at a training heart rate (220 minus age times 0.75). The patients might have to build up to this level of fitness. The exercise will burn off excess stress hormones that the patients are producing. They will be more relaxed for 24 hours following the exercise.

Anxious patients need to understand what triggers their anxiety and prepare for anxious moments with accurate thinking and relaxation techniques. These patients must learn that they can cope with anxiety using the tools of recovery. They are not going to die or go crazy from anxiety. They need to slow the anxiety cycle by stopping and thinking when they feel anxious. What are they thinking? Is it accurate? Then they replace negative thinking with positive thinking. At any time, they can use a relaxation technique to block the anxious symptoms.

Panic Attacks

If these patients come to you when they are having a panic attack, you need to be calm and reassuring. Have them look at you and slow their breathing—slow deep breaths. Then begin one of your relaxation techniques to distract the patients from their feelings. Tell them the anxiety will pass. You might want to take them on a walk and have them look at the scenery—at the blue sky and the clouds. You might have them contact their Higher Power and have the Higher Power begin to fill them with peace. Have the patients float in their anxiety and go with it. Reassure them that nothing bad is going to happen and that you are going to stay with them until they feel comfortable.

These patients will need to practice distracting themselves when feeling anxious. They can notice some fine details in the room or in the environment. They can look for styles of clothing or shoes. They can read something or estimate the cost of things. They need to develop a simple coping imagery, such as a trip to the beach, to replace the fearful thoughts. The coping fantasy can be any relaxing situation in which the patients feel comfortable and in control.

Anxious patients usually are easy to work with. They are frightened, but they are responsible individuals. They are willing to do almost anything to get better. These patients need a lot of love. It will be hard for them to accept your rewards. They often do not feel worth it, but you should give reinforcers lavishly. When they feel praised by their treatment peers for their work in group, it is a triumph.

The Psychotic Patient

Psychotic patients persistently mistakenly evaluate reality. They have disturbances in cognitive/perceptual organization. They are unable to perceive important incoming stimuli, process this information in relation to past experience, and select appropriate responses (Siever & Davis, 1991). This mistaken evaluation of experience results in tenacious false beliefs (Klein, Gittelman, Quitkin, & Rifkin, 1980). If you walked into a restaurant and a person turned around and looked at you, you would not think much about it. But a psychotic patient might mistakenly evaluate this situation and think, "That person is after me." This mistaken evaluation has the force of reality, and it results in distorted conclusions. "The mob sent that person to kill me."

Hallucinations and Delusions

Psychosis is characterized by hallucinations and delusions. Hallucinations are false perceptions. They can seem to come from any sense organ. Patients may hear voices, see visions, have a strange taste or smell, or feel something unusual on or under their skin. To psychotic patients, these false perceptions are as real as reality itself.

Delusions are false beliefs that are intractable to logic. The patients may believe that they are being watched by someone, that they have strange or unusual powers, or that one of their body organs is not operating properly. No rational argument will deter them from this irrational belief. Some patients have social or cultural beliefs that might seem odd, but if they occur in a normal social context, they are not considered psychotic. For example, someone could believe that he or she has the power to read minds, but that person has been trained culturally in this belief. Psychosis is a persistent mistaken perception of reality that is not accounted for by social indoctrination or normal life experiences.

All psychotic states are due to an abnormal condition of the brain. Chronic disorders, such as schizophrenia and schizoid personality disorder, seem to result from a core vulnerability expressed in a relative detachment from the environment, often with defects in reality testing. This seems to be due to inherited neurointegrative dysfunction. These individuals do not develop normal interpersonal relationships. They lack empathy and a sense of connectedness. Their relationships are shallow and not satisfying (Siever et al., 1985).

Acute organic brain syndromes, including intoxication and withdrawal, can produce psychotic symptoms. Many other psychiatric conditions, such as schizophrenia and major depression, can create psychosis. Acute organic brain syndrome must be ruled out first because it can be life threatening. Psychosis can be transient, as in some forms of acute alcohol withdrawal, or it can be chronic in some forms of schizophrenia.

How to Treat the Psychotic Patient

In psychotic patients, there is a mix of psychotic and real perception being evaluated. Your job is to respond to, and reinforce, the healthy side of these patients. Rarely will you respond to a psychotic statement other than to reassure the patients and point out reality to them. Even in the most florid psychotic states, patients have some hold on reality and do remember what happened. The environment of a patient having active hallucinations needs to be reduced to its lowest level of stimulation. A quiet room, without a radio or television, is best. Keep calm yourself. There is no reason for you to be afraid. A conversation with a psychotic patient might go something like this:

The patient, Mary, is lying in her bed, covers drawn up to her chest. She is looking at the walls with a frightened look on her face. The counselor walks over and sits in a chair beside the bed.

Counselor:　How are you doing, Mary?

Mary:　Okay, I guess. . . . I keep seeing colors. The walls seem to be moving, like they're breathing.

Counselor:　That's withdrawal, Mary. We're treating you for that. It will pass. Just hang in there.

Mary:　And I see spiders on the wall.

Counselor:　I know that seems real to you, but the bugs are not real. They are coming from the withdrawal. There are no spiders on the wall.

Mary:　But I see them.

Counselor: It seems real, doesn't it? Shows you how tricky the mind can be. You're going to be feeling a lot better soon. I'm proud of you coming into treatment. That took a lot of courage.

Mary: Thanks.

Counselor: Can you tell me a little bit about your drinking?

The counselor did not try to prove to the patient that there were no spiders. The counselor just told the patient the truth and reassured her. Then the counselor began to get some history of the patient's problems.

There may be patients who will have psychotic symptoms throughout treatment. These patients might need to be treated with antipsychotic medications that are the mainstay of the treatment for psychosis. The psychotic symptoms probably will gradually decrease in intensity over time. The hallucinations will go first, with the delusions gradually decreasing over the next several months. Some of the delusional material may be persistent, lasting for years or even the patient's entire life. Once these beliefs are set, they are very tenacious to change.

Do not allow psychotic symptoms to trouble the other patients. Psychotic patients rarely are dangerous. For the most part, you can ignore the symptoms in group. If they do come up, a frank explanation might be necessary. The other patients will understand so long as they know there is nothing to be frightened of. The group can be helpful in assisting the patient to test reality and to gain social skills.

Diseases such as schizophrenia and mania can be difficult to manage. Patients who are not in good control will need to be transferred to a more structured psychiatric facility. The psychotic patients that you work with will, for the most part, be having mild perceptual and thought disturbances. It is useless to argue with patients about their delusional material. These beliefs are well defended and intractable. For the most part, you will reassure, support, and try to take them through your program.

Many psychotic patients will have an unusual affect. The range of feelings may be flat, or the patients may have a strange feel to them. Their behavior might not fit the circumstances. They may have little or no motivation. With the flat affect, you can help the patients to identify and use their feelings. Motivation can be improved by having the patients do many small tasks that can be separately reinforced. Do not set the patients up to fail by asking them to do things that are too difficult for them.

These patients usually need social skills training. They might have to be taught how to sit, walk, talk, smile, and use eye contact. They might have to learn what is appropriate conversation and what is not. They might need to practice communication skills and interpersonal relationship skills.

Patients who are chronically mentally ill will need help in becoming acquainted with community resources. They need to be referred to the appropriate agencies for follow-up. Social, vocational, and housing needs all will have to be appropriately addressed.

Insight-oriented therapy, or therapy that is highly confrontive, is contraindicated with these patients. If painful material is uncovered, then the psychotic symptoms may worsen. With these patients, it is best to stay with the here and now.

The patients will need to learn problem-solving skills in treatment and will need to practice these skills. They need to identify the problem, consider the options, plan their actions, and carry out the plan. The patients should check the problem later to see whether their plan has been successful.

The Family of the Psychotic Patient

The patient's family will have to meet with the staff to be educated about the disease. The psychologist or psychiatrist should do this because he or she knows more about the psychopathology. If you do not have anyone on staff who has this expertise, then you might need to refer the patient to an outside agency. The family is important in preventing a relapse with the patient. A family that is emotionally unstable will increase the patient's chance of relapse (Brown, Monck, Carstairs, & Wing, 1962). A family needs to be educated to keep criticism and overinvolvement to a minimum.

The great healer in any good treatment program is love. You can actively care for and respond to these patients even though they make you feel a little uncomfortable. They are just people who have a difficult disorder. They need all of the love and encouragement that you can give them. It is incredibly rewarding to see these people improve.

Acquired Immune Deficiency Syndrome

Some patients in need of treatment for chemical dependency will have acquired immune deficiency syndrome (AIDS), will have AIDS-related complex (ARC), or will test positive for HTLV-III antibodies. Needle sharing among intravenous drug users places them at high risk for contracting this disease. AIDS can affect the central nervous system, and it can affect thinking, feeling, and behavior, even in the absence of other symptoms (Gabel, Barnard, Norko, & O'Connell, 1986; Perry & Jacobsen, 1986). Patients with AIDS can develop a psychosis characterized by delusions, hallucinations, bizarre behavior, affective disturbances, and mild memory or cognitive impairment. The cause of this psychosis is yet to be established (Harris, Jeste, Gleghorn, & Sewell, 1991).

Approximately 30% of all AIDS cases are intravenous drug users. They are the second leading risk group for infection for transmission of the disease to the adult heterosexual population (Centers for Disease Control, 1990).

More than one third of AIDS patients develop symptoms of AIDS dementia complex. This organic brain disease may complicate the diagnosis and treatment of chemically dependent individuals because of the complicated cognitive, emotional, and behavioral changes that can occur. The course of AIDS-related dementia is variable. Early signs and symptoms may be subtle. AIDS dementia complex generally progresses to severe global impairment within months. Depression and psychosis are frequent complications (Perry & Jacobsen, 1986).

The High-Risk Patient

All high-risk patients, homosexuals, intravenous drug users, and sexual partners of high-risk individuals should be routinely screened for HIV infection, particularly if they present with signs of organic or psychotic impairment, fever, or weight loss. Informed consent should be obtained before testing. Patients who are seropositive without active symptoms of AIDS can be safely taken through the program.

AIDS patients will have special issues revolving around their disease. Uncertainty of diagnosis, guilt about the previous lifestyle, fear of death, exposure of lifestyle, changes in self-esteem, and alienation from family and friends all can be important elements in treatment. The catastrophic nature of this illness will have to be dealt with on an individual basis. If possible, the patients need to be referred to a facility that specifically deals with AIDS for continuing care.

The AIDS and Chemical Dependency Committee (1988) of the American Medical Society on Alcoholism and Other Drug Dependencies recommends that treatment be provided for these patients. The patients need to be assessed on a case-by-case basis and referred for follow-up by a physician familiar with AIDS. All staff members should be educated with the latest AIDS-related data. Patients with AIDS do *not* require isolation techniques any different from patients with active hepatitis B. Hepatitis B precautions should be followed carefully. Caps, gloves, masks, and other kinds of protective wear are *not* necessary in routine contact (e.g., blood pressure checks, group therapy). The principle of confidentiality is particularly important in protecting these patients (AIDS and Chemical Dependency Committee, 1988).

The Patient With Low Intellectual Functioning ■

Patients with low intellectual functioning have defects in learning and in adaptive skills. Most of these patients will have low average to borderline intelligence. You occasionally will see someone in the mildly mentally retarded range. Intelligence below this is not amenable to the normal treatment program.

How to Treat the Patient With Low Intelligence

Some of these patients will need a specialized treatment plan. These patients have difficulty with abstract reasoning. Their program will have to be tangible and concrete. Many of them will have deficiencies in social skills that will need remediation.

Abstract thought is complicated. To have normal abstract thought, patients must easily shift from one aspect of a situation to another, keeping in mind simultaneous aspects of the situation. They must be able to grasp how the parts fit into a whole. They must be able to separate the parts and put them back together again mentally. Patients with good abstract thought can plan ahead and think in complex symbols.

Concrete thought is immediate and tangible. It is set in the current situation without the ability to generalize to other situations. Use of complex symbols or the ability to see all of the parts is not present. The ability to effectively plan and understand complicated issues is impaired if the patient can think only concretely.

The Patient Who Cannot Read

Some of these patients cannot read or do the written exercises. Most of the reading material in the AA/NA program is written at a sixth-grade level. Patients with reading levels two or more grades below this are going to have difficulty. The psychologist can help you to determine the extent of these problems and can give you advice on how to present the program. If the patients can read a little, then they should be encouraged to do so. The encouragement and praise that they receive will more than offset minor problems.

If the patients cannot read, then the program will have to be presented to them in oral form. They can watch videos and hear AA/NA material on tape. Every treatment center has audiovisual material around for just such a purpose. The patients will need more individual attention and additional support in group. Some of the group sessions will be over their heads, and that is okay so long as they are getting the basic program. The program can be made simple enough for most anyone to follow.

You will have to do a lot of repeating with these patients, and you need to keep asking them to repeat what you said. This is the only way of being sure that they understand. Many of these patients learn to be great head-nodders when they do not understand. If they can repeat the program to you, then they are learning it. Give them a few key phrases to learn by heart. Check on them from time to time to see whether they are learning the phrases and understanding what they mean. "Don't drink. Go to meetings. Turn it over to your Higher Power."

These patients may need occupational rehabilitation in continuing care. They may qualify for locally supported programs. They may need a halfway house or other structured facility in continuing care. The Division of Vocational Rehabilitation is an excellent program for many of these patients.

The Family of the Patient With Low Intelligence	The family of a person with low intelligence might not know of their loved one's disability. The family will need to be informed about the patient's liabilities. These patients can be some of the best AA/NA members. They can be fiercely loyal and consistent. They often are willing to do jobs that other members find distasteful. It is very reinforcing to watch them bond with the group and find a place for themselves.

The Elderly Patient

Most counselors do not realize how prevalent addiction is among the elderly. A recent study revealed that substance abuse was the third-ranked mental disorder in a large geriatric mental health population (Reifler, Raskind, & Kethley, 1982). The elderly are vulnerable to becoming addicted to a variety of over-the-counter or prescription medications, and they tend to take a variety of medications without proper medical supervision. Any medication or illicit drug tends to have more effect on the elderly than on younger persons. Drugs usually have one third more power in older individuals for a variety of physiological factors. There appears to be no age-related change in liver detoxification, but there is a decline in brain cells that results in higher concentration of alcohol and other substances. With normal aging, there is a decline in extracellular and intracellular fluid and an increase in body fat that result in a greater effect of many drugs on the central nervous system (Gambert, 1992).

Elderly patients often have outlived their psychosocial support system. Their spouses may have died or been incapacitated, and their children may be unable to care for them. Loss of family and friends, coupled with retirement and loss of job and self-esteem, may lead elderly patients into a depressive state where substances are used to ease the pain. A study at the Mayo Clinic's inpatient alcohol unit found that 44% of elderly patients were compromised organically from chronic alcohol or drug use but that they went through treatment with no appreciable difference in treatment outcome (Morse, 1994). Only 10% of elderly patients have a dementia that is serious enough to hamper them in retaining a recovery program. Many patients suffer from mild cognitive defects including impairment of orientation, concentration, short-term memory recall, and abstract thinking.

Atkinson and Kofed (1984) found a number of risk factors that contributed to the vulnerability of the elderly to substance abuse. Biological sensitivity to chemicals, loneliness, pain, insomnia, depression, and grief all were predisposing factors.

Symptoms of substance abuse often are overlooked in the elderly in medical settings because they suffer from multiple pathological conditions. Changes in cognition or behavior may be blamed on an illness or old age rather than on substance abuse.

For a variety of reasons, the elderly may start drinking heavily after they retire. They have more time on their hands, and drinking or drug use can easily become a habit using relatively small amounts of substances. It is most common for these patients to drink or use alone. Like any addict, there is a strong desire for the patients to hide their use. This may be easy to do when they live alone and have no one to check on them periodically.

The good thing about recovery is that it gives patients a new family. They do not have to live alone anymore. The patients can use their support group to reestablish social connections and develop new leisure activities. They develop a sense of belonging by helping other addicts, and this improves their self-worth. This gives elderly patients, who often are ready to die, a reason to live. The patients have to know that their recovery group needs them. God trained them in addiction, they have grown wise over the years, and now they need to heal. They can do this by going to meetings and sharing their experience, strength, and hope. It might take a while before elderly persons realize this truth. The best way of having them learn it is to have them help someone in treatment. They can help someone go through detox or can help someone earlier in recovery. Once they see that their lives have meaning and worth for others, they are on the road to recovery.

The Patient With Early Childhood Trauma

■

Many chemically dependent patients were raised in severely dysfunctional families, and some of them were abused as children. For the most part, you need to leave severe early childhood trauma for treatment later in the recovery. The patients will need to maintain a stable recovery before they tackle the intense pain of these issues. To immerse themselves too deeply in the old trauma now is not appropriate.

If patients disclose abuse in individual sessions or in group, they need to be supported. They need to hear that it was not their fault. Little children are not responsible for what adults do. If a patient who discloses abuse is an adolescent, then the situation will have to be reported to the proper authorities. This is to protect the child from further harm. Do not do this without consulting with the clinical staff and carefully documenting it in the patient record.

How to Deal With Sexual Abuse

If a patient is stuck in treatment because of this pain, then it will have to be addressed to relieve the pressure. This is a clinical decision. If the patient is too vulnerable for this issue, then he or she will feel anxious and you will feel uneasy yourself. If you can, transfer this issue to the psychiatrist or psychologist. You might have to refer the patient to an outside mental health professional. Patients with posttraumatic stress disorder from childhood trauma will need to reexperience the trauma in a safe environment. They will need to tell their stories many times. Details are important. The stories need to include the events before, during, and after the trauma. Therapy begins with a safe relationship with the therapist.

Patients may decompensate when this material comes out. If staff members are loving and supportive, this should not last long. The patients may experience feelings of derealization or depersonalization. This can be frightening to an unskilled counselor. If at any time you feel that you are in over your head, stop and get the help of someone more experienced.

Sexual abuse is not a topic for most groups. The material is too disturbing and explosive. These matters need to be addressed in individual sessions. Events such as rape and insults to self-esteem and security are particularly likely to cause long-term problems. The more extreme and long-lasting the trauma, the more likely the events are to cause psychological damage.

These patients ultimately need to see the past events in a new context and attempt to forgive themselves and the offenders. The patients no longer are children, and these things are unlikely to happen again. The patients now have power and control that they did not have before. They will need to see themselves as competent and capable of handling stressful situations now. You can role-play situations for them and help them to develop skills for getting themselves out of trouble. "If that happened to you now, at your present age, what would you do?" The patients can learn that they can take care of themselves.

People who were involved in traumatic events often become anxious when they have to deal with similar situations in their current life situations. A spouse who was sexually abused as a child may feel frightened or numb when called on to perform sexually in his or her marriage. This patient may need some of the techniques you used with the anxious patient.

Cognitive Therapy

Cognitive techniques are necessary to correct the negative self-talk of these patients. They often call themselves bad or evil in their own thinking. They think that no one will like them because they have been bad. This negative self-talk will have to be exchanged for positive affirmation.

These patients will need to develop trust. The Love, Trust, and Commitment exercise (Appendix 10) is a good one for them to start with. First, they need to reestablish a trusting relationship with themselves and then hopefully with you. This trust ultimately can be transferred to the group. The patients need to be encouraged to see their new support group as the healthy home that they never had. The home group will be there for them when they need it. The group has a stable set of rules that do not change.

These patients need to learn interpersonal relationship skills and to practice these skills with their treatment peers. They need to work on honesty. The cocoon of individual therapy is important here, and the patients must know that they can trust you. You need to be consistent and nonjudgmental. You need to be honest about how you feel about the abusive issues.

How to Learn Forgiveness

As these patients develop a good spiritual program, they need to try to forgive the perpetrators. By seeing the abusers as spiritually sick, the patients are relieved of some of the anger and the feeling of responsibility. When the patients are ready, they can be encouraged to pray for the perpetrators. They can turn the judgment over to the perfect judge. God will judge all humankind. The judgment will be perfect because God sees into everyone's heart.

Small steps in trust will be beneficial with these patients. You may find the patients sharing their abuse with other patients who have had similar experiences. The Fifth Step is tremendously beneficial for these patients. If the step is done properly, they will feel relieved of the guilt and rage.

Love in the Treatment Center

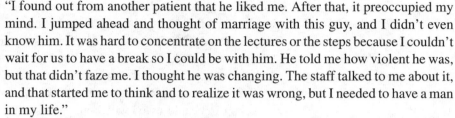

"I found out from another patient that he liked me. After that, it preoccupied my mind. I jumped ahead and thought of marriage with this guy, and I didn't even know him. It was hard to concentrate on the lectures or the steps because I couldn't wait for us to have a break so I could be with him. He told me how violent he was, but that didn't faze me. I thought he was changing. The staff talked to me about it, and that started me to think and to realize it was wrong, but I needed to have a man in my life."

These thoughts and feelings are all too familiar. Two patients, during those fragile first few weeks of sobriety, have become romantically involved. These patients can lose the focus of treatment. They do not respond well to the interventions of the staff who are trying to get them to see the mistake they are making. They are in love, and to them it is real. It is difficult for these patients to realize that what they are feeling is not love at all and that the intense feelings they are experiencing are sexual. In their passion for each other, they are confused. It feels like love, it feels like the real thing, it is heaven, and it is the answer to what they have been looking for. They came into treatment feeling totally worthless and unimportant, and this other person has restored their sense of value. They have been made whole again. These patients do not realize that they are particularly vulnerable to such feelings in early sobriety. Feelings, which were deadened by chemicals before treatment, are just beginning to blossom new and untested. Their whole treatment program is at stake.

One patient described the consequences of love in the treatment center like this: "After treatment, we had sex right away, and it all went downhill from there fast. He got too jealous. I was totally bending over backward for him, buying him cigarettes and pop. Even when I told him I only wanted to be friends, he wanted me back. He got drunk and threatened to kill me, so I went back with him for a while. I finally got the courage to tell him the truth. When he finally left, I felt so guilty."

The Importance of the Unit Rules

It is prudent for treatment programs to develop a set of unit rules that discourage these relationships from developing. The rule that only three or more patients may pair off together at any one time is a valuable one. Then if staff members see two patients pairing off, they can intervene.

How to Deal With Patients in Love

The first intervention attempted should be individual counseling with each patient. These sessions should focus on educating the patients about what love is and what it is not. The patients can explore the addictive relationships exercises (Appendix 13) with you and use this opportunity to learn and grow in treatment. They must be helped to see the reality of the situation. With assistance, they can begin to see the situation accurately. Is this really the best time for romance? Is this the partner who they want to spend the rest of their life with? What is their history? The patients and counselor must carefully collect all the evidence possible. They must get accurate and explore all of the options available. What is going on? Why? What do the patients hope to gain? What does it mean to the patients? Can they get their needs met in another way? Do they see the danger? What is love? What are romance and sexual attraction? How do they differ? How are they alike? The complexities of the feelings and motivations must be thoroughly explored. The dangers of this relationship at this time must be emphasized and addressed.

Disciplinary action might become necessary to prevent further problems. Considerable clinical skill is necessary here. Transference and countertransference issues may arise. The patients may resist your attempt to end the relationship that they see as beneficial. The staff must be sensitive to how in love these patients feel. Disapproving looks and derogatory comments will tend to intensify the feelings and draw the patients closer together.

The next intervention that you might need is conjoint counseling. Here the relationship can be addressed with both parties at the same time. If the patients have separate counselors, then both counselors should be involved in this session. The patients should be warned that they are placing each other's treatment at risk. It is not loving to risk someone else's sobriety. If the problem persists, then it becomes an issue for the group. Now everyone's treatment is threatened, and the patient population needs to respond. If the group cannot stop it, then the transfer of one patient to another facility, or dismissal from treatment, becomes a viable option.

Love in the treatment center is a crisis from which all patients can grow. They can learn more about themselves. They can learn more about how to develop healthy relationships and the challenges that will confront them in sobriety. They must be encouraged to focus on their own recovery. The patients need to concentrate on loving themselves.

The Pathological Gambler

"Gamblers Anonymous (GA) has been, and is, the single most effective treatment modality for the pathological gambler" (Custer, 1984a). This point continues to be true today. The American Psychiatric Association's *Treatments of Psychiatric Disorders* states, "In general, an approach which utilizes several treatment modalities, including participation in Gamblers Anonymous, appears warranted at this time" (Karasu, 1989, p. 2466).

Gamblers Anonymous is a Twelve Step program modeled after the Twelve Steps of AA. The program provides hope to recovering individuals. Many patients recover by going to GA alone, but some patients, particularly those with concomitant psychiatric disorders, need the structure of inpatient or outpatient treatment (Custer, 1984b; Karasu, 1989).

All patients with gambling issues need to be thoroughly assessed for their gambling problem and take the South Oaks Gambling Screen (Appendix 54). Gamblers tend to leave things out of their gambling history, so you must be careful to collect all of the problems caused by gambling. It helps to use the financial forms (Appendix 52) to assess the amount of debt.

Patients who have entered gambling treatment need to do a minimum of three things to begin recovery: (a) get honest with themselves, (b) embrace the first few steps of GA, and (c) develop a good relapse prevention program. These steps provide the foundation for recovery. The contracts presented in this book are patient homework. They educate about the disease of pathological gambling, teach the tools of recovery, and have patients apply the tools in their daily lives. Each patient completes each exercise and shares his or her answers with the contracts group. The group decides by majority vote to accept or reject the contract based on how well the patient completes the exercise. If the contract is rejected, then the patient has to do it over again.

Contracts help a patient to identify the problem, understand the problem, and learn coping skills for dealing with the problem. The types of contracts are infinite. You will want to develop some on your own, but there are a few exercises that you will use with nearly every patient. The following contracts are the ones that you will use most often. If there is no pressure relief group in your local GA chapter, then you will have to help the patient make a payback plan using the pressure relief group and financial forms in Appendix 52.

Honesty

The Honesty for Gamblers exercise (Appendix 35) helps patients to see how they have been distorting reality. All patients use denial, in its many forms, to keep from experiencing the pain of the truth. But if they see the whole picture about themselves, they hurt. They realize that they are sick and need help. This creates tremendous fear. Patients keep from feeling this fear by minimizing, rationalizing, denying, blaming, distorting, projecting, intellectualizing, diverting, and dozens of other ways of not experiencing the truth.

Patients cannot uncover unconscious denial without getting help from others. The Honesty for Gamblers exercise gets them started in this search for the truth. It is the job of the counselor and treatment center to set up an atmosphere of love and trust and then to give patients the opportunity to search for, and share, the truth with each other. It is the truth that sets people free. Treatment is an endless search for truth.

Working through the Honesty for Gamblers exercise is an eye-opening experience for patients. They come to realize how much they have been lying to themselves and to others. They feel guilty about lying to others. But patients usually do not realize that they have lied to themselves more than to anyone else. This comes as a startling revelation.

Patients need to process how they feel about themselves when they lie, and they need to learn the negative consequences of dishonesty. First, if they lie, then they will hurt. If they do not tell people the truth, then they will not be known or feel loved. Second, without truth, patients cannot solve problems accurately. To solve problems, you need the facts.

The Twelve Steps should be the core of treatment for pathological gambling. More individuals have recovered using the principles of GA than using any other treatment. Gamblers Anonymous works, and it is free. The only requirement for GA membership is the desire to stop gambling.

Treatment programs differ in terms of the steps that they address. Some programs address Step One, some address Steps One to Three, and others address Steps One to Five. This must be individualized. Some patients will be able to work only through Step One, and that is fine if they do a good Step One. For most patients, it is a benefit to complete at least Steps One to Three while in treatment. The more patients can do, the better off they will be in recovery. Working through the Fifth Step takes a great burden off of the patients. If they complete the Fifth Step, then they will not have to carry as much guilt and shame into abstinence from gambling.

If your program works only on the First Step, that will give you more time to work on powerlessness and unmanageability.

As you take patients through the step exercises, make sure that they are internalizing the material. They must be able to identify the problem, understand the problem, and learn coping skills for dealing with the problem. They must be able to verbalize a solid understanding of each step and how they are going to apply each step in their lives.

You will be able to tell when patients are just complying and when they are actually understanding and internalizing the material by their level of commitment to remain free of gambling. This will be evident in their behavior. If you watch how patients act with you and with their treatment peers, you will have a good idea of whether they are internalizing the information or not. If you are hearing one thing in individual sessions and a patient's peers are hearing another thing around the treatment center, then someone is not getting the truth. This patient needs to be confronted with the inconsistency of his or her behavior.

Patients often feel torn between various parts of themselves. There seems to be a side that wants to gamble and a side that wants to stop. There seems to be a side that wants to love and a side that wants to hate. There is a constant, and often turbulent, internal war going on inside the patients' thinking. Each side tries to take control of the patients' behavior. Sometimes it is hard for a patient to know who he or she really is. It feels as though there is more than one person talking inside the patient's own head.

Freud (2000) called these internal voices the id, ego, and superego. Berne (1964) called them the child, adult, and parent. In recovery, we call the voices the illness, self, and Higher Power. One train of thinking is the thought process of the disease. This side only wants the patients to gamble, and it does not care how it gets them to do it. If the patients feel miserable, that is all the better. Another voice is that of the Higher Power. The Higher Power wants the patients to love themselves, others, and the Higher Power. This voice is supportive and loving. The third voice is the patients' own thinking.

As you move these patients through the steps, do not move a patient to the next step until he or she has a solid foundation of successfully completing the step below. If the patient has not embraced a good Step One, then there is no use in moving to Step Two. If you have to work on Step One the whole time that the patient is in treatment, that is fine. Some patients do that. But do not try to move up in the steps too quickly. The steps must build on top of each other. The first building block is Step One.

Step One | "We admitted we were powerless over gambling—that our lives had become unmanageable" (Gamblers Anonymous, 1989b, p. 38).

It is vital that all patients complete a solid Step One for Gamblers (Appendix 36) in treatment. Step One is the most important step because without it, recovery is impossible. Step One necessitates a total surrender. The patients must accept as true that they are pathological gamblers and that their lives are unmanageable. Until this conscious and unconscious surrender occurs, these patients cannot grow. So long as patients think that they can bring the gambling under control, they will not accept their disease. "The idea that somehow, some day, we will control our gambling is the great obsession of every compulsive gambler. The persistence of this illusion is astonishing. Many pursue it into the gates of prison, insanity, or death" (Gamblers Anonymous, 1989a, p. 2).

Step work is mainly group work. The patients complete the step exercise and present the exercise in group. The group helps the patients with the step by asking questions, giving constructive comments, and deciding whether or not the step is successfully completed. As the counselor, you usually should not make the decision to clear the step without the support of the group. Particularly in an inpatient setting, things go on in treatment that you are not aware of. The patients may be only complying with treatment, pretending that they are working, when in reality they are not internalizing the information. The treatment peers sometimes are more likely to see this manipulation. The peers see the patients in casual interaction, and they may pick up on the inconsistencies.

In Step One, the patients must learn to accept that they are pathological gamblers and that they are powerless over gambling. Their lives are unmanageable. They also must understand that they cannot live normally so long as they gamble.

The best way of convincing patients to surrender is to show them that they get into trouble when they gamble. They do not get into trouble *every* time, but they cannot predict when the trouble is going to occur. They may place a few bets and go home, or they may gamble away the farm. The key point is inconsistency once they place the first bet.

Patients need to process through many of their problems until they realize that they cannot predict their behavior. Have patients share exactly what happened when their gambling got out of control. Talk about the fear, shame, humiliation, and depression caused by gambling. How depressing was it to know that their families were falling apart? How did it feel to be unable to keep promises?

Sometimes the patients gambled more, or for a longer period of time, than they originally had intended. Once they began gambling, the addiction took control. Even when they promised themselves that they were going to stop or cut down, they kept on gambling. Patients must understand that once they place the first bet, they do not know what they are going to do.

Most gamblers want to hold onto the delusion that they are still in control. They do not want to admit that they are powerless and that their lives are unmanageable. Sure, they were having problems sometimes, but they think that they were having problems only occasionally. The fact is that when patients had serious problems, they almost always were related to gambling. Gamblers do things when they are gambling that they never would do otherwise. They need to take a look at each of these behaviors and see the painful consequences of their addiction. They need to take a careful look at their gambling histories—at the lies, the crimes, the inconsistencies, and the people they have hurt. They need to understand that so long as they gamble, they will be in pain.

Step Two | "[We] came to believe that a power greater than ourselves could restore us to a normal way of thinking and living" (Gamblers Anonymous, 1989b, p. 39).

The beginning of the patients' spiritual program is Step One or the surrender step. It is essential to accept powerlessness and unmanageability before the patients reach toward a Higher Power. The essential ingredient of Step Two for

Gamblers (Appendix 37) is willingness. Without being willing to seek a power greater than themselves, the patients will fail. They have admitted that they are powerless over gambling and that their lives are unmanageable. Now the patients need to see the insanity of their disease and search for an answer.

In Step Two, the patients look at their insane behavior. They see how crazy they were acting and reach for an answer. They must conclude that they cannot hold onto their old ways of thinking and behaving. If they do, then they will relapse.

Many patients rebel at the very idea of a Higher Power. They are encouraged to open the door, just a little, and seek a Higher Power of their own understanding. They are encouraged to be honest, open-minded, and willing. They need power; they are powerless. They need someone else to manage; their lives are unmanageable.

At first, you encourage the patients to see that a Higher Power can exist. The patients are encouraged to look at their interpersonal group and see that the group has more power than they do. You can say something like this to a patient: "If you wanted to leave this room but the group wanted to keep you in, do you think you could leave?" It soon becomes obvious to this patient that the group members could force the patient to stay inside the room if they so desired. The patient is then asked to try to place his or her trust in the Higher Power of the group.

Trust is a difficult issue for most gamblers, and they need to process their lack of trust with the group. This is good group work. If patients cannot trust the group as a whole, can they trust anyone in the group? If they cannot trust anyone, can they trust themselves? Are they willing to try? If they are unable to trust others, then they are lost. Patients who obviously cannot trust themselves are out of control.

The best way of helping patients learn to trust the group is to create a loving group. This is a group in which the members are actively interested in each other. They are involved in each other's recovery. They gently help each other to search for the truth. The group members are kind, encouraging, and supportive. They are confidential. The group members never are hostile or aggressive. They do not put each other down. This is counterproductive. If you have an aggressive, highly confrontational group, you will destroy trust. People must learn to confront each other in an atmosphere of unconditional positive regard. It is the counselor's job to teach the group this process.

Once the patients trust the group, they can be encouraged to transfer this trust to the GA group. The patients in treatment should attend as many regular meetings as possible. Gradually, they will feel safe enough to share. This builds trust.

As the group becomes involved in the patients' growth, confidence in the group process grows. This probably is the first time in these patients' lives when they have told someone the whole truth. When the group does not reject these patients, the patients feel a tremendous relief. This will show on their faces and be etched in their hearts.

The patients also see people further along in the program doing better. These people look better and sound better. The patients cannot miss the power of the group process. It changes people. Patients see new members come in frightened or hostile and watch them turn around. Patients watch the power of group support. Soon the group will be offering the new patients encouragement. Patients learn how helpful it is to share their experiences, strengths, and hopes. Once these patients see how insane they are acting and accept that the group has the power to restore them to a healthy way of thinking and living, they have embraced Step Two. By trusting the group, the patients open the door to a Higher Power. This basic building block of trust is vital to good treatment. Patients who move too quickly to the concept of God miss out on the power of the group. They miss seeing the Higher Power in others. These patients sometimes believe that God is the only answer they need. They might think that they do not have to go to meetings so long as they have a good spiritual program. These patients might not work a program of recovery, and they probably will relapse. All patients are encouraged to trust the group process.

Step Three | "[We] made a decision to turn our will and our lives over to the care of this power of our own understanding" (Gamblers Anonymous, 1989b, p. 40).

Most patients have difficulty with Step Three for Gamblers (Appendix 38). They need to be reminded to turn problems over to their Higher Power. Patients can be so self-centered that they set themselves up for pain. They think that the whole world should revolve around them. When people do not cooperate with their plans, they are furious. They think that their spouses, children, and friends should obey them. They believe that everything should go exactly the way in which they want events to go. They believe that they are deserving of special honor and privileges. They care very deeply about what they want and how they feel, but their ability to empathize with others is seriously impaired. Patients correct this defect in treatment by learning empathy for others and turning their will and their lives over to the care of a power greater than themselves.

The worst thing that a counselor can do in the Third Step is to push patients faster than they are ready to go. The decision to turn things over is the patients' decision. As the counselor, all you can do is encourage, educate, and support. However, you have one big thing going for you in Step Three. When patients turn something over, they feel immediate relief. They feel this relief emotionally, and this is a powerful way of learning. Nothing works better than showing patients how this tool of recovery works. If you give gamblers a good feeling, they will want to re-create that feeling. That is why they were gambling. The Third Step is the answer that these patients have been waiting for. They must experience it to believe it.

Many patients resist Step Three. Even people who have been in GA for years have difficulty with it. Meetings are full of people talking about turning things over and then taking them back. Step Three is a decision that is made every day.

There is great hope for patients in Step Three, and they usually feel it. This new-found hope must not be confused with religion. Religion is an organized system of faith and worship. Spirituality is the innermost relationship that you have with yourself and all else. If the patients want to use a religious structure, that is encouraged so long as it sets the patients free and does not immerse them in guilt or remorse.

The key to Step Three is willingness. Once patients are willing to seek a Higher Power of their own understanding, they have come a long way toward completing Step Three. As soon as you hear patients say that they are willing to turn it over, they are well on their way to recovery. Patients need to trust and turn things over to the group. The group has more collective wisdom than does the individual patient, and the group can be helpful in solving problems. As patients use the power and support of their group, they learn how to turn things over.

Some patients have serious problems with the word *God*. They feel better if they use the words *good orderly direction* (for each letter in *God*). Patients do not have to use the word *God* if they do not want to. Many patients have had God and religion crammed down their throats for so long, they are sick of it.

Step Four | "[We] made a searching and fearless moral and financial inventory of ourselves" (Gamblers Anonymous, 1989b, p. 42). Much of this exercise was developed by Lynn Carroll during his years at Hazelden and at Keystone Treatment Center. The material has been expanded and adapted for use with gamblers.

Step Four for Gamblers (Appendix 39) is where patients make a thorough housecleaning. They rid themselves of the guilt of the past and look forward to a new future. Detail is important here. You must encourage patients to be specific. They must put down exactly what they did. The patients will share their Fourth Step inventory with someone in the Fifth Step. Another part of Fourth Step group work involves each patient's assets. This work allows patients to share good things about themselves with their peers.

To do a good Step Four, patients must be honest. They will relieve themselves of the guilt if they do their Steps Four and Five properly. They might have a difficult time in forgiving themselves, but they can feel that their Higher Power has forgiven them. Faith can do for them what they cannot do for themselves.

There is a tendency for some patients to leave something bad out of the Fifth Step. This is not a good idea. Patients are encouraged to share everything that they think is important, no matter how bad it might seem. If it causes them guilt or shame, then it needs to be shared. Patients need to come face-to-face with themselves. All the garbage of the past must be cleaned out. Nothing can be left to fester and rot.

The Fourth Step is where patients identify their character defects. Once these defects are identified, the patients can work toward resolution. Often patients will come upon material suppressed for years. As memory tracks are stimulated, deeper unconscious material may surface.

Patients need to concentrate on the exact nature of their wrongs. Do not let them accuse or blame someone else. This is a time to take responsibility. They should not make excuses. They should just ask for forgiveness. Yes, there were mitigating circumstances. But this is not a time to find out who was right and who was wrong. It is time to dump the shame.

Patients who get depressed doing their Fourth Step need to concentrate on their good qualities. These patients are not all bad. They need to be shown that they are valuable persons who deserve to be loved. Some patients might have to wait quite a while before doing their Fourth Step. Absolute honesty is a requirement.

Some patients are so used to being negative about themselves that they cannot come up with their assets. These patients need to have the group help them to see the positive things about themselves.

Step Four must be detailed and specific. Patients must cover the exact nature of their behavior. This is the only way for them to see the full impact of their disease. They should not color their stories to make themselves seem less guilty or responsible.

Most of all, Step Four (like all of the steps) is a time of great joy. Patients finally face the whole truth about themselves. The truth is that they are wonderful. As they rid themselves of the pain of the past, they are ready to move forward to new lives filled with hope and recovery.

Step Five | "[We] admitted to ourselves and to another human being the exact nature of our wrongs" (Gamblers Anonymous, 1989b, p. 44).

As the counselor, your job in Step Five for Gamblers (Appendix 40) is to help the patient to match up with the right person to share with. Who this person is, and what each is like, is vitally important. This person stands as a symbol of the Higher Power and all people on earth. This step directly attacks the core of the disease. If it is done properly, the patient will be free from the past. The person chosen should be someone who understands the program and who has experience in hearing Fifth Steps. This person needs an attitude of acceptance and unconditional positive regard. The individual must be nonjudgmental and strictly confidential. It is helpful if this person is working a Twelve Step program himself or herself. The person should not look uncomfortable when a patient is sharing sensitive material. The patient needs to see a non-shaming face.

The purpose of the Fifth Step is to make things right with self, others, and the Higher Power. The patients should see themselves accurately—the positive *and* negative points, all at the same time. At the core of the illness is this firmly held belief that if the patients tell anyone the truth about themselves, then that person will not like them. This is not accurate, but the patients have been living as if this were the truth. The patients have not been honest with themselves and others for a long time, perhaps since childhood. The patients have pretended to be somebody else to get the good stuff in life. The only way of proving to these patients that their held belief is wrong is to show them. This is the purpose of having another human being hear the Fifth Step. If this person does not reject the patients, then the inaccurate thinking is proved wrong. A new accurate thought replaces the old one: The patients can tell the truth, and people will still like them. This is a tremendous relief to patients. They have been living their lives convinced that they were unacceptable to others. This is a deeply held conviction, and it causes great pain. Patients must come to realize that unless they tell the truth, they never will feel loved.

In the Fifth Step, patients need to come to realize that they are good persons. They have made mistakes. They have done bad things. But they are not bad; they are good. They need to forgive themselves and start over, clean and new. Patients have varying degrees of spirituality and religious beliefs. You must help each patient see that forgiveness has taken place.

Many patients will be tempted to hold something back in the Fifth Step. They do not want to share some part of their past. They do not think that anyone can understand. Patients must be warned against this tendency. If they hold anything back, then the illness will win. All major wrongs must be disclosed.

After the Fifth Step, most patients experience a feeling of relief. The truth sets them free. In time, patients will need to process these feelings with you. Some patients feel no immediate relief. But if they were honest in the step, they will feel the relief later. Sometimes it takes a while to sink in. Steps Four and Five are profoundly humbling experiences. But once they are over, there is a profound feeling of relief.

Relapse Prevention

Relapse prevention is one of the most important aspects of treatment. In a study of many different addictions, approximately two thirds of patients relapsed within the first year of leaving treatment. Fully 33% relapsed within the first 2 weeks, 60% relapsed within the first 3 months, and 67% relapsed within 12 months (Hunt, Barnett, & Branch, 1971).

Most patients relapse within 3 months of leaving treatment. This is the period of highest risk. Patients must be willing to do almost anything to prevent relapse. They need to see themselves as clinging to an ice-covered cliff with their recovery support group holding the only rope. The most important thing that they can do is go to meetings. Patients who are working a daily program of recovery will not relapse. You cannot work the program and gamble at the same time. These behaviors are incompatible.

Relapse is a process that begins long before making the first bet. If the new tools of recovery are not used and problems begin to escalate, then patients reach a point where they think that their only option is to gamble.

The Relapse Prevention for Gamblers exercise (Appendix 41) uses the works of Gorski and Miller (1986) and Marlatt and Gordon (1985) to develop a relapse prevention plan. Some of this work was done with alcohol or other addictions, but it is applicable for any compulsive behavior.

Relapse prevention requires that patients work a daily program of recovery. The patients must take their personal inventory at the end of every day. If any of the relapse symptoms become evident, then immediate action must be taken.

Gorski and Miller (1982), working with alcoholics, developed a list of 37 relapse warning signs. Patients check these every day for symptoms that they are having problems. Patients must develop written plans detailing the exact things that they are going to do if they get into trouble.

Other people need to check patients daily for relapse warning signs. This can be done by family members, sponsors, or co-workers. This is a good reason for patients to go to daily meetings and hang around other recovering persons. Often other people can see what patients are unable to see for themselves.

The patients need to identify high-risk situations that might trigger relapse and to develop coping skills to deal with each situation. The more patients can practice these skills, the better off they will be in recovery. In group, patients need to role-play high-risk situations and help each other to develop relapse prevention plans.

Each patient will be different. But Marlatt and Gordon (1985) found that most relapses occur when patients are experiencing the following high-risk situations:

1. *Negative emotions:* These include particularly anger and frustration. They also can be negative emotions such as boredom, jealousy, depression, and anxiety.
2. *Social pressure:* This is being in a social situation where people are gambling or being directly encouraged to gamble by someone.
3. *Interpersonal conflict:* This can be a conflict with a parent, spouse, child, boss, friend, and so on.
4. *Positive emotions:* Something positive happens and the patient wants to celebrate. This can be a promotion, wedding, birth of a child, graduation, and so on.
5. *Testing personal control:* The patient gambles to find out whether he or she can control the gambling.

Using the Relapse Prevention for Gamblers exercise, patients develop the skills necessary to deal with each of the high-risk situations and then practice the new skills until they become good at them. All patients must role-play gambling refusal situations until they can say no and feel relatively comfortable. They must examine and experience all of their triggers, see through the first use, and learn how to deal with euphoric recall.

Patients must develop a plan for a lapse. What are they going to do if they gamble again? Who are they going to contact? What are they going to say? This must be role-played in group to give the patients practice.

The patients must understand the behavior chain. They also must develop skills for changing their thoughts, feelings, and actions when they have problems. Using imagery, the patients need to experience craving and learn experientially that craving will pass if they move away from the situation and use their new tools of recovery. No gambler should carry money in early recovery. It is a relapse trigger. Someone else, such as a spouse, has to manage the patient's money and give him or her only enough to buy the essentials, such as lunch, that they need each day. This is a humbling experience for most gamblers but is necessary to prevent relapse.

| # Adolescent Treatment

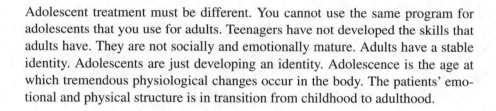

Adolescent treatment must be different. You cannot use the same program for adolescents that you use for adults. Teenagers have not developed the skills that adults have. They are not socially and emotionally mature. Adults have a stable identity. Adolescents are just developing an identity. Adolescence is the age at which tremendous physiological changes occur in the body. The patients' emotional and physical structure is in transition from childhood to adulthood.

The Normal Adolescent

Studies have shown that most adolescents are well adjusted. They get along well with their peers, teachers, and families (Block, 1971; Csikszentmihalyi & Larson, 1984; Douvan & Adelson, 1966; Offer & Offer, 1975; Offer, Ostrov, & Howard, 1981; Vaillant, 1977; Westley & Epstein, 1969). Adolescence should be understood as a transitional stage that allows individuals to gradually adjust to growth, development, and change. Each cycle of life brings new challenges and opportunities, but all of the changes will be incorporated into the basic personality structure. At the end of high school, the majority of American adolescents enter a new phase of life called young adulthood (Offer, 1986).

Normal adolescents do not feel inferior to others. They do not believe that other people treat them badly. They feel relaxed. They believe that they can control themselves, and they have confidence that they can handle novel situations. They feel proud of their body image and physical development. They feel strong and healthy. They have embraced the work ethic. They feel good when they do a good job. They are not afraid of their sexuality, and they like the recent changes in their bodies. They do not perceive any major problems between themselves and their parents. They are hopeful about the future, and they believe that they will be successful. They do not believe that they have major problems (Offer, 1986).

There are three alternative routes through normal adolescence. About 23% of adolescents develop continuously through adolescence, 35% show developmental spurts alternating between periods of some conflict and turmoil, and 21% experience more severe turmoil (Offer & Offer, 1975).

These three groups have been labeled the continuous growth group, the surgent growth group, and the tumultuous growth group. Those in the continuous group are characterized by excellent genetic and environmental backgrounds. They have strong egos and are able to cope well with internal and external stimuli. They have mastered previous developmental stages without serious problems. They accept social norms and feel comfortable in society at large. The adolescents in the surgent growth group are different in that their genetic and environmental backgrounds are not as free of problems and traumas. Both of these groups are free of adolescent turmoil, and they comprise 80% of the adolescent population (Offer, 1986).

Ages 13 to 16 Years	The period of ages 13 to 16 years brings an enormous change in physical and psychological development. Throughout adolescence, girls remain about 2 years ahead of boys in their level of maturity. Some adolescents bloom early, and some bloom late, each having a different psychological challenge. Early bloomers may be expected to perform with individuals of their size, whereas late bloomers suffer from the problems of self-esteem that result from looking more immature than their peers.

Adolescents of this age group experience a great deal of ambivalence and conflict, and they often blame the outside world for their discomfort. As they struggle to develop their own identity, dependence on parents gives way to a new dependence on peers. These adolescents struggle to avoid dependence and may disparage parents, devaluing past attachments. These early teens often find a new ego ideal that leads to idealization of sports figures or entertainers. Adolescents at this stage are particularly vulnerable to people who they would love to emulate.

The development of a self-concept is crucial at this stage. These adolescents must explore their own morals and values, questioning the accepted way of society and family to gain a sense of self. They make up their own minds who they are and what they believe in. They must reassess the facts that were accepted during childhood and must accept, reject, or modify these societal norms as their own. The here-and-now thinking of earlier childhood gives way to a new capacity for abstract thought. These adolescents may spend long periods abstractly contemplating the "meaning of life" and who they are.

Ages 16 to 19 Years	In our culture, we expect a gradual development of independence and self-identity by 19 years of age. The physical manifestations of approaching adulthood require numerous psychological adjustments, in particular the development of how one views the self in relation to others. The vast majority of adolescents attain their adult size and physical characteristics by 18 years of age, and the earlier differences between early and late bloomers no longer are evident. The process of abstract thinking changes along with physical development, becoming more complex and refined. Late adolescents are less bound by concrete thinking. A sense of time emerges where these individuals can recognize the differences among past, present, and future. They can adopt a future orientation that leads to the capacity to delay gratification. These individuals develop a sense of equality with adults.

Self-certainty and an internal structure develop while teens experiment with different roles. By 19 years of age, most adolescents are considering occupational choices and have begun to develop intimate relationships (Weedman, 1992).

The Chemically Dependent Adolescent

The tumultuous group of adolescents comprises 20% of the adolescent population. These adolescents come from family backgrounds that are not stable. There often are histories of mental illness in these families, the parents often have marital conflicts, and the families often have economic difficulties. The moods of these adolescents are not stable, and these individuals are more prone to depression. They have significantly more psychiatric disturbances, and they do well only with the aid of intense psychotherapy. They do not grow out of it (Masterson & Costello, 1980; Offer, 1986). It is in the tumultuous growth group that chemical dependency often develops.

In this country, the average first use of mood-altering chemicals for boys is 11.9 years and for girls is 12.7 years (U.S. Department of Justice, 1983). Adolescents almost always use alcohol or drugs for the first time under peer pressure. They want to be accepted and to be a part of the group. Children are likely to model after the chemical use of their parents. Children with alcoholic parents are at greater risk for becoming chemically dependent (Spalt, 1979).

Adolescents who continue to use will increase drinking to a regular pattern (usually weekends). They may experiment with other drugs. They begin to use drugs to communicate, to relate, and to belong. With regular drinking, tolerance develops. The adolescents need more of the drug to get intoxicated. Emotional changes may first be noticed here by their families. The adolescents may become irritable and more noncommunicative. They may begin to spend more time alone in their rooms. They may begin not caring for themselves or for others. Polarization of parents and children begins to occur (Morrison & Smith, 1990).

As chemical dependency further develops, adolescents no longer can trust themselves when using chemicals. The choice to use these drugs no longer is available to them; they have to use to feel normal. The continued use of chemicals eliminates the ability to think logically and rationally. Rationalization, minimization, and denial cut the adolescents off from reality (Soujanen, 1983).

Chemically dependent adolescents gradually change their peer group to include drinking and drug-using friends. They begin to use chemicals to block out the pain. They no longer use for the euphoric effect. They drink to escape pain. Blackouts and drinking alone are strong indicators of chemical dependency in the adolescent population. With the progression of the disease, family conflicts increase. The adolescents may run away, withdraw, or act out at home and at school. They withdraw from family and community activities. Problems with the police and school officials increase and become serious. The adolescents may become verbally abusive to parents and more rebellious to authority figures. Life begins to center around alcohol or drugs. Daily use begins, and these individuals begin to use to maintain rather than to escape. The adolescents make attempts to cut back or quit, but they are unable to stay clean and sober. Physical deterioration begins. Hiding and lying about drugs becomes more common. The adolescents feel more intensely isolated and alone. Concern is now openly expressed by parents, teachers, and even peers. Gradually, the adolescents lose all self-esteem and depression begins. Persistent chemical use leads to incarceration, institutionalization, or death (Chatlos & Jaffe, 1994; Morrison & Smith, 1990).

Chemical dependency halts emotional development. To develop normally, people must learn to use their feelings to give them energy and direction for problem solving. When feelings are consistently altered by alcohol or drugs, this no longer is possible. The major coping skill of chemically dependent persons is chemical use.

Adolescent chemical dependency can occur extremely quickly—within weeks—because these individuals' emotional development is immature. Adolescents do not have the internal structure to bring themselves and their lives under control. They cannot delay the onset of chemical dependency for years as can adults.

The Adolescent Chemical Dependency Counselor

■

Working with adolescents can be among the most rewarding work in the field. By making an early intervention in these persons' lives, you can save them years of misery. Adolescents can be frustrating, but to see them blossom from hurting children into people who can laugh is a wonderful thing to watch. Just being a part of their recovery will make you feel good about yourself.

Becoming an adolescent counselor is not for everybody. These patients have a lot of energy, and the counselor has to tolerate a certain amount of disorder without feeling uncomfortable. As the counselor, you must be able to withstand people challenging you face-to-face and toe-to-toe. You must have good impulse control. If you have a weak spot, these patients will find out what it is and use it against you. They are expert manipulators. It is normal for them to want to manipulate you and the system.

Adolescents almost never decide to come into treatment on their own. They most often are forced into treatment by other people, their parents, or the courts. Most of their homes are extremely dysfunctional, and many have chemically dependent parents. These patients come into treatment angry and resistive. Where most adults are ready to surrender, most adolescents are ready to fight. The staff must be willing to endure this initial resistance. These patients gradually will change their attitudes about chemicals as they process more of the facts.

Unlike adults, adolescents are not frightened by the physical consequences of chemical dependency. It does little good to threaten them with talk about chemical dependency being a deadly disease. The adolescents need more time before they will pay attention to this information. They tend to think that they are invincible when it comes to physical problems.

Adolescents are resistive to the initial part of the program, and they need more structure in treatment. This allows them to learn self-discipline and social responsibility. A good way of adding structure is to develop a level system (Appendix 23) in which the patients move up in rank as they progress through the program. At each level change, the patients earn increased freedom and responsibility. A point system can be used in conjunction with the level system to increase the structure. In the point system, the patients earn points for working the program and lose points for resisting. Points can be given for a clean room, a neat appearance, level of commitment, participation in group, completion of exercises, positive interaction with treatment peers, and so on. Whether you have a level system or a point system depends on your patient population. More resistive adolescents will need more structure (Davidson & Seidman, 1974; Phillips, 1968).

The Point System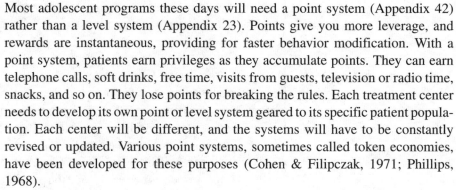

Most adolescent programs these days will need a point system (Appendix 42) rather than a level system (Appendix 23). Points give you more leverage, and rewards are instantaneous, providing for faster behavior modification. With a point system, patients earn privileges as they accumulate points. They can earn telephone calls, soft drinks, free time, visits from guests, television or radio time, snacks, and so on. They lose points for breaking the rules. Each treatment center needs to develop its own point or level system geared to its specific patient population. Each center will be different, and the systems will have to be constantly revised or updated. Various point systems, sometimes called token economies, have been developed for these purposes (Cohen & Filipczak, 1971; Phillips, 1968).

A level system is sufficient for most adolescent programs, but if you need more structure, then a point system can be added (Herbert, 1982; Lynch & Ollendick, 1977; Wolf, Philips, & Fixsen, 1975). In the point system, the patients earn points for each goal that they complete during the day. Points can be given or taken away as the staff desires. For example, patients will be required to keep their rooms clean. They will be given points for completing this goal or will lose points for failing to complete the goal. They can earn or lose 10 points per day for keeping their rooms clean. They can be scored on participation in group or on commitment to treatment. If 10 behaviors are scored, then patients can earn up to 100 points per day.

The staff must make sure that most reinforcers are positive. The patients turn in points for positive reinforcers, candy, television time, or trips to the recreation room. The patients can earn greater privileges by saving points. For example, a "fun" video might cost 75 points. A telephone call to a friend might cost 200 points. This teaches the patients self-discipline and how to delay gratification. Patients with serious conduct disorders need this kind of structure (Graziano & Mooney, 1984; Herbert, 1982; Ollendick & Cerny, 1981).

A point system adds structure because it gives the staff more control over reinforcers. This tends to shape behavior more quickly. Token reinforcement programs for adolescent patients have existed for a long time and have a proven track record. For further information about such a point system, see Cohen, Filipczak, and Bis (1965); Davidson and Seidman (1974); and Phillips (1968).

The Primary Elements in Adolescent Treatment

The most important thing that occurs in adolescent treatment is the change in perceptions, attitudes, and behaviors that revolve around addictive chemicals. The patients must come to realize that they have a problem, come to understand the problem, and develop tools of recovery. Adolescents must be habilitated rather than rehabilitated. They have never developed the skills necessary to lead a normal sober lifestyle. They need to learn these skills for the first time. They must stop using chemicals so that they can grow and mature normally. Healthy role models are essential to this process. The staff on any adolescent unit must show the patients how to deal with problems. Patients further along in the program also will model coping skills. Patients must be shown how to treat each other with respect at all times.

The Rules | Adolescents will constantly test the rules and each staff member. The staff must rigidly adhere to the rules of the treatment center. It is a manipulation for an adolescent to try to get special privileges from you. If they can get you to bend a rule even a little, then they have got you right where they want you. Your rules do not mean anything if they can be manipulated.

Communication Skills | Adolescents need to focus on developing communication skills. They need to practice identifying their feelings and sharing their feelings with their treatment peers. They must practice telling each other the truth. As the patients develop new skills, they can transfer this behavior to their families.

As open communication begins, the patients build trust. They usually transfer trust from the treatment peers, to you (the counselor), and to the parents, in that order. Mutual respect is necessary, and the patients must hear you be positive about treatment. A positive attitude will take you a long way with these patients.

It is important for you to know that adolescents are not acting out to personally hurt you. They are not mad at you. They are just mad at their lives. Most of their anger is transferred from the family and environment from which they came. If they act out, then you must provide the structure of consequences. Do not hesitate to give these consequences. They are learning tools. Explain to the adolescents that it is not you who is doing this to them. It is the adolescents who are doing this to themselves. They knew the rules, and they broke them.

It is normal for adolescents to push the limits and break the rules. They will try to manipulate their environment just like they did at home and at school. This is all that they know how to do. You cannot blame them for using the old skills that have worked for them. Treatment will teach them what is wrong with the old skills, and it will teach them new skills to get what they want more appropriately.

Honesty | Lying is a good example of an old behavior. Adolescents have learned how to lie to get their way. They lie to get out of trouble. They lie to get what they want. This works for them, at least to some degree, and the lying increases. As the lying grows, they feel more lonely and isolated. What they do not understand, and what they need to learn, is that the lying and loneliness are directly connected; one causes the other. If they lie, then they will be lonely. Most adolescents do not understand this, but they will learn it with education. Once they learn why they are telling the truth, they will be motivated to be honest.

Adolescents need to practice honesty. Just because they understand the principle does not mean that the behavior changes. They must practice it over and over again. They need to experience the natural rewards that come when they use a new skill. As the patients set up natural reinforcers, the behavior ultimately will become automatic.

Exercise | Adolescents need a challenging exercise program. They need to exercise at a training heart rate at least once a day. They need to be actively involved in sports and other athletic events. Weight training and jogging are excellent accompaniments to any program. These are exercises where the adolescents can see their gains and feel good about them.

Fun in Sobriety	Adolescents need to learn how to have fun in sobriety. One of the things that they are worried about is that they will not be fun if they stop using drugs and alcohol. They do not want to be boring to their friends. They need to see that they can feel good without chemicals. The only way of doing this is to take the patients out on recreational activities and have them experience firsthand that they can still enjoy themselves. Trips to the zoo, an amusement park, a dance hall, a movie, a pizza parlor, an ice cream parlor, or a video arcade all can be used to show the adolescents that they can still have fun in sobriety.
The Reinforcers	Adolescents are very concerned about how they look and how they get along with others socially. If you are searching for a reinforcer, you always can hook into one of these. Adolescents desperately want to be loved, no matter what they might say. These children are starving for genuine love, compassion, help, attention, encouragement, and praise. They need people to listen to them, and they need a chance to prove what they can do. Most of these patients feel like failures in the real world, and they are mad about it. They are mad at themselves, and they are mad at everyone else. They have felt overwhelmed by their dysfunctional home situations. Many of these children come from homes of severe abuse and neglect. They have been beaten down by society, and many of them have given up. You will see these patients flourish in an environment of love. You will see the real children blossom. It is a beautiful thing to watch.
Spirituality	Adolescents have more difficulty with spirituality than do adults. Most adolescents still have their health, and they are not as ready to surrender. They need to be shown a Higher Power is there for them. This takes a spiritual program of action rather than of words. You need to seek a clergy person with particular skills in working with adolescents. The patients should trust this person and not feel intimidated by him or her. The patients need to actively explore spirituality in spirituality group. The best way of hooking adolescents into a Higher Power is to have them directly experience a Higher Power's presence. This is done using the meditation exercise discussed in Chapter 5. Some of the adolescents will resist a Higher Power, but they cannot deny their own experiences. Some of these patients have been involved in Satanism, and it takes a great deal of skill to get them to a place where they can be open to a Higher Power. The best therapist here often is another peer. Peers have a way of trusting each other about this sensitive issue. Adolescents will explore spirituality if they do not feel as though they will be shamed by their peers. A peer further along in the program is an excellent model.
Group Therapy	Group therapy with adolescents is different. The level of sharing at first is more shallow. Adolescents are inexperienced with their deeper feelings. They do not have the skills necessary to share openly. They feel just as deeply as adults, but most of them never have practiced communicating their feelings. Early attempts to share feel clumsy and awkward, and the adolescents fear being humiliated in group. Once older members of the group begin sharing, the way is paved for new members. Role-playing works well for adolescents. They do not feel as vulnerable when playing a role. They can role-play drug refusal situations or parent-child conflicts.

Adolescents need to be active in group. If they are not talking, then they need to be doing something else that is constructive to treatment. For example, you can hold denial court for those patients who remain in denial. This is an active group. The adolescents enjoy and benefit from the experience. In denial court, the patients divide up and play the roles of defense attorney, prosecuting attorney, judge, and jury. The patient who is in denial is called to the stand and is examined and cross-examined by the attorneys. The patient tries to prove to the court that he or she is not chemically dependent. The group holds the trial and reaches a verdict.

The patients can act out the thoughts that exist inside of someone's head at certain decision points. One patient can pretend to be the illness while another pretends to be the healthy side. The two sides try to get the adolescent in question to behave in certain ways. These three—the illness, the healthy side, and the person—can be placed in a variety of situations to see how all sides respond. Use your creativity and come up with group exercises. What you are after is active participation by all of the group members. Once the group members start talking, let them go, with only occasional guidance from time to time. The best treatment will be between the patients further along in the program and those just coming into the program. Once they get the hang of it, the adolescents will enjoy group. It draws them closer together. They feel supported, listened to, and understood. They lose that sense of separateness that has haunted them all of their lives.

Peer Pressure

Peer pressure is vitally important to adolescents, and they can easily be swayed to use drugs by their peer group. Peer pressure comes in two forms: being in a social situation where chemicals are available and being actively encouraged to use chemicals by friends. The adolescents need to spend a lot of time role-playing drug refusal exercises. They need to practice exactly how they are going to say no. Most of the adolescents will need to work through the Peer Pressure exercise (Appendix 24). Sometimes the adolescents will attempt to gang up on the staff because of something that happens between a staff member and a patient. In one way, this is a good sign because the group members begin to function together. This process should be encouraged, and the staff should carefully listen to the complaint. Try to compromise and reach a decision that is agreed on by all. The center rules must not be broken or manipulated in the process, but the situation can be explored to determine exactly what happened and who is responsible. This can be a difficult process, but once the whole truth comes out, it will be clear where the patient or staff member went wrong. Everyone makes mistakes, and Step Ten says, "When we were wrong, we promptly admitted it" (Alcoholics Anonymous, 1976, p. 59). This goes for the staff as well as for the patients. It is a great learning experience for the patients to see the staff struggle to be fair and impartial. It is not easy.

Continuing Education

Continuing education is necessary for adolescents, even those who have dropped out of school. They should have a thorough educational assessment, including an examination of school records, and psychological testing. From these data, schoolteachers develop individual plans for educating the patients. Some patients will need intensive remedial work, and some can continue regular assigned schoolwork. School is an excellent opportunity to develop self-discipline. The patients need to determine what they want from further education, and they need to help develop a plan for reaching their goals. Do not allow patients to slough off school because they are dropouts. Quitting is old behavior. All adolescents need continuing education.

| *Continuing Care* | Continuing care is essential for adolescent patients. They do not have the internal structure necessary to stick to a recovery program on their own. Just going to meetings is not enough. Adolescents need to move from an inpatient program into an extensive aftercare program. This will necessitate the patients coming in for aftercare as much as is needed to keep them in stable recovery. The content of the aftercare program must be individualized. Some patients will need a daily aftercare program. Most will need at least three aftercare sessions per week. The aftercare program should continue to teach the tools of recovery and also show the patients that they can have fun in sobriety. The group members need to go on outings and do fun things together. They can attend concerts or go to the zoo, parks, games, dances, and so on. This establishes a new peer group and solidifies recovery. |

The Parents Support Group

As the adolescents are going through treatment, the parents attend at least two groups per week. Again this is individualized and based on the needs of their families. All parents attend a parents support group and a weekly conjoint session with the patients. The parents support group encourages the parents, supports them emotionally, and teaches them the tools of recovery. This is a Twelve Step group. The patients' families concentrate on working the steps, developing healthy communication skills, and learning a behavior program to follow in aftercare.

The Behavioral Contract

The behavioral contract (Appendix 25) is the primary method by which patients and their families hold each other accountable for their actions. The contract is necessary to show the patients and families that they can function together in an atmosphere of mutual support. A point system will be necessary for more seriously disturbed adolescents. All parents need to be taught behavioral contracting and the point system.

Using the approach of Alexander and Parsons (1973), the parents negotiate a behavior contract with the adolescent. The contract is jointly developed by the patient, the family, and you (the counselor). The family is taught how to negotiate future contracts on its own. The benefit of behavioral contracting has been widely confirmed by a variety of studies (Alexander, 1974; Sanders & Glynn, 1981; Wells & Forehand, 1981, 1984).

If the adolescent is a more serious behavior problem, then the parents will need to develop a point system. The parents will need intensive training and practice in this procedure before the child comes home. The training is divided into three phases. In the first phase, the parents are taught basic social learning concepts (Patterson, 1977; Patterson & Gullion, 1976). In the second phase, they are taught how to define, track, and record deviant and prosocial behaviors. In the third phase, the parents learn how to develop a point system where the adolescent earns or loses points contingent on positive and negative behaviors. Points are exchanged *daily* for rewards previously selected by the child. The parents are taught to use positive social reinforcers (e.g., smiles, pats on the back) for appropriate behaviors and "time out" procedures for inappropriate behaviors. As the counselor, you must work closely with the parents, particularly shortly after discharge. Daily phone calls might be necessary to make sure that the parents are following the program. The parents and the patient need to attend aftercare for at least 6 months following treatment. Some will attend for years depending on their specific needs.

Phases of Adolescent Treatment

Adolescent treatment seems to go in phases. When the adolescents come into treatment, most of them are angry. This may be expressed overtly or covertly. They may be overly aggressive toward the staff, or they may be quiet and sulk. This defiant period is a good indication that the patients have been out of control. They are attempting to use old skills to bring order to a new situation.

In 1 or 2 weeks, the adolescents will begin to comply with the staff, but they still have not begun to internalize the program. They have learned how to get along in treatment, but they do not think that they have a problem, and they are planning to go back to their old behavior when they leave treatment.

As the adolescents begin to feel the genuine love of the staff and the group, they begin to take a real look at themselves. They see the negative consequences of their chemical use. They realize that they do not want to go on living like that. This is positive movement, and it depends primarily on trusting other people. Many of these patients never have trusted anyone, but as they open up to the group and continue to be accepted, they soften. When they behave at their worst and the staff still sticks with them, a light comes on in their heads. The adolescents, who came into treatment defiant and trusting no one, begin to reach out to others. They feel loved and understood for the first time in their lives.

As trust develops, denial becomes more evident. The patients begin to see the truth. The patients are encouraged to transfer this trust of the group to trust of their new AA/NA group. Many adolescent patients hate group when they come into treatment, but in time they learn to like it. It is the only time in their lives when people have dealt with real feelings. The patients are encouraged to see their new AA/NA group as a healthy family. In this family, the patients can grow and develop normally. The goal is to stay involved with AA or NA for life.

CHAPTER
ELEVEN

The Family Program

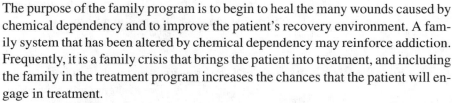

The purpose of the family program is to begin to heal the many wounds caused by chemical dependency and to improve the patient's recovery environment. A family system that has been altered by chemical dependency may reinforce addiction. Frequently, it is a family crisis that brings the patient into treatment, and including the family in the treatment program increases the chances that the patient will engage in treatment.

You should carefully evaluate the patient's social system and move it toward being supportive of recovery. If anyone in the family needs long-term intervention, it is your job to refer that person to the appropriate professionals.

If the family is not supportive, then you should intervene with education and counseling to change the attitudes and behaviors that will make the patient's recovery possible. It should be obvious that the patient will do better in recovery when supported by his or her family.

Each primary relationship needs to be examined carefully. You should send each significant person the Family Questionnaire (Appendix 26). This will give you a good idea of how the family members are functioning and explore what they think about the patient and his or her chemical dependency.

By the end of the family program, you should know how each person is functioning and how the family is functioning as a unit. You need to gather enough data to show you how the family members are coping with their environment. Many families will need financial aid or therapy of some sort in continuing care.

The First Contact

The patient's family should be contacted within the first few hours of the patient's admission. Once you have met the patient, you need to meet the family members, either in person or over the phone. You need to speak to them and light a spark of hope about recovery. The family members will be relieved to have the patient in treatment, but they will feel frightened that treatment might not work. Do not give them unrealistic expectations, but reassure them that the patient is safe and has a

187

new opportunity to recover. The family members should be immediately encouraged to begin attending Al-Anon meetings. Give them a list of meetings in their area and stress that they need some support right now. The best place to feel understood is with people who are in recovery.

How to Handle the Early AMA Risk

The family must be warned that the patient may attempt to leave treatment early against medical advice. It is not uncommon for patients to want to go home after the first few hours in treatment.

You want to reduce the possibility that the patient will call the family and have someone come and pick the patient up. You need to make it clear that this is very common and is to be expected in early recovery. It is not a matter of concern so long as it is handled properly. Tell the family to say a firm no along with some gentle encouragement. That usually is enough to keep the patient in treatment. If the patient is a serious AMA risk, you might have to plan an in-house intervention with the family. Some patients come into treatment not yet ready to surrender to the disease.

The family members may have a lot to tell you over the phone, but you want them to save this information for the forms that you will be sending them. The first contact with them is to reduce fear and to support their decision for treatment. The forms take a history of the problem and give the family members an opportunity to provide input into the treatment process.

The Family Problems

No one can grow up in an alcoholic family, or live in one, without it changing him or her. Patients who live in chemically dependent homes live in a whirlwind. These patients grasp at anything that will help them to regain control. Their environment has been totally out of control for a long time. They do not know what is going to happen next. They cannot predict or trust anyone. They desire, more than anything else, to achieve stability in their families.

Codependency

A codependent person is obsessed with controlling the person who is out of control (Beattie, 1987; Weinhold & Weinhold, 1989). Chemical dependency adversely affects everyone in the home. Codependents, adult children of alcoholics, and children of alcoholics are some of the names given to these suffering persons.

These people have been seriously damaged by chemical dependency. They have learned to live in a chemically dependent world, and this takes certain maladaptive skills. They learn to stuff their feelings, to never ask for what they want, and to keep secrets. They focus their lives totally on the chemically dependent persons. They do not have time for themselves and their own needs.

Codependents are as blinded and reality distorted as are chemically dependent persons. They do not think about their own problems because their own problems are too painful. They would rather think about other people. Their whole lives revolve around the sick persons. Codependents become so obsessed with helping and controlling the other persons that they lose the ability to think. They cannot see reality. Over the years, in an unbearable situation for most, they have developed an incredible tolerance for neglect and abuse. They keep thinking that if they just do enough—if they figure it out—then everything will work out.

Guilt | Family members often feel incredible guilt. They think that they are at fault. The chemically dependent person keeps denying responsibility, and someone must be held accountable, so the family members often take the blame. The spouse might feel that everything would be okay if he or she could just be the right kind of husband or wife or could just do the right thing.

These people attempt to control their out-of-control environment in any way they can. They whine, wheedle, threaten, cry, bemoan, seek counseling (for themselves), manipulate, and lie. Each attempt at control works to some degree, and it is kept tucked away in their behavioral repertoire to be used later.

The wife might start calling her husband to make sure that he got to work. She feels responsible for her husband getting to work on time, and her anxiety builds as the time approaches for him to be there. The little boy of the family might try to do especially well in school in hopes that the drinking or drug use will stop. The child is anxious because he feels a direct relationship between his grades and the family problems. Family members will go to incredible lengths to control the chemical dependency. They pour out bottles. They threaten using friends. They scold, argue, cry, get depressed, get anxious, go to church, talk to the boss, and make excuses. They chase drinking or using friends away from the house. They talk to the family physician or their clergy person in trying to get support.

Loss of Control | As more and more energy is expended in trying to control someone else, the family members lose contact with themselves. They become so involved in the addicted person that they lose who they are. They do not know what they want. They do not know how they feel. They cannot ask for what they want. They cannot share how they feel. This leaves their interpersonal relationships unstable and unfulfilled. They cannot use their real feelings to solve problems. Therefore, their problems escalate out of control. They are on a treadmill, frantically trying to keep the family together.

Shame | Codependency is deeply rooted in the feeling of shame. The family members feel as though something is wrong with them. They believe that the reason why the family is in such a mess is that they are not doing enough. They are not working hard enough or long enough. If they could just figure this whole thing out, then things would be better. They are battered and beaten. They keep trying, but they keep failing. They never can keep up with the increasing nightmare.

Caretaking | Family members of an addicted person learn to be caretakers. They are obsessed with taking care of the chemically dependent person. In their frantic attempt to take care of someone else, they lose contact with their own needs. In group, they will be able to tell you how the chemically dependent person is feeling, but they will be unable to tell you how they themselves are feeling. Their whole lives are caught up in taking care of the other person. This happens to divert the family members from feeling the pain in their lives. In group, you must redirect the family members to stop concentrating on the other person and to explore their own pain.

Enabling | The family members will have a long history of making excuses for the chemically dependent person. They have been protecting the addicted individual from facing the severity of the problem. They help the addicted individual get out of trouble. They will lie because they are ashamed of the reality of their family life. Children will lie to friends, the spouse will call the boss, the father or mother will make excuses, and the siblings will pretend that nothing is wrong. Enabling is the major way in which the family members protect themselves from the reality of the situation. They fear that if they do not enable, then their world will collapse. The truth is that they are living with an addictive individual and their lives are out of control, but they keep the family from falling into disaster by shoring up the situation.

The family members must realize that they have kept the illness alive by protecting the chemically dependent individual from the reality of his or her behavior. By their constantly getting the addicted individual out of trouble, the addicted individual could not learn the truth. To protect themselves, the family members allowed the illness to go unchecked. They fed into the denial of the disease.

Inability to Know Feelings

People in chemically dependent homes are so separated from reality that they do not know how they feel. Their feelings have been suppressed for so long that all they feel is numb. They have let go of the pain and live in lives full of false beliefs. They have learned to keep their feelings hidden because they fear that if they expressed themselves, the drug addict will punish them. It is not unusual to find family members who have been subjected to incredible abuse who think that they feel relatively fine.

Inability to Know Wants

The family members do not know what they want. Their lives are centered around the chemically dependent individual. They only know what the addict wants. That is the focus of attention. Most family members are trying to hold onto their sanity and to keep themselves, and the family, from going under. They have no time for the superficial wishes and wants of normal people. They only have vague hopes that everything can be better. They are so used to the broken promises that they do not listen anymore.

Lack of Trust

The family members have learned to trust no one. The people who they trusted ultimately abandoned them. Therefore, they lie to everyone—parents, friends, brothers, sisters, neighbors, and fellow employees. They tell no one the secret. They never trust that they will be safe and comfortable again. They have had their dreams shattered so often that they are afraid to dream anymore.

People Pleasing

The family members of the chemically dependent person learn to be people pleasers. They will do anything to prevent someone from feeling bad. This comes from the attempt to be responsible for other people's pain. If someone is hurting, then they feel anxious. The pain is their fault, and they have to do something about it. They feel that their wants and wishes always are secondary to the needs of someone else. They get to the point where they feel guilty when they get anything; someone else might be deprived.

Feelings of Worthlessness

The family members feel worthless. They feel as though no one cares for how they feel or for what they want. They feel profoundly inadequate and unlovable. They feel rejected by others. They do not feel as though they have a fair chance in life, and somehow they feel as though this is fair—that it is all their fault anyway. This would not be happening to them if they were better persons. This is all they deserve. This is the best they can get.

Dependency | Codependent persons do not trust their own decisions. They feel incapable of dealing with life. Something always goes wrong with their plans. The very thought of leaving the addicted individual terrifies them. They cling to that person. The more they try to control things, the more things lapse out of control. They develop a profound sense of inadequacy and indecisiveness that keeps them locked in to an intolerable situation.

Poor Communication Skills | The family members have poor communication skills. They learned a long time ago the credo of the chemically dependent family: "Don't talk, don't trust, and don't feel." These individuals do not talk to their friends or other family members. They are cut off from everyone. They feel afraid of open communication. If they talked openly, then the truth might come out and the family would be destroyed. They constantly tell other people what they think these people want to hear rather than how or what they really think or feel.

How to Treat Family Members

Before reading this section, read the Codependency exercise (Appendix 27). The exercise will show you basically what the family members need to work on in treatment. It must be emphasized that each family, and each family member, must be treated individually. No one intervention works for everyone. All families will need individually developed treatment plans. No two families are the same.

The first thing that the family members need is support. They need to feel listened to, known, and understood. They need to be encouraged to share the reality of their lives. They need to feel as though they are in a safe, loving place where others care for how they feel and will respond to what they want. These people are not used to being cared for; they are used to caring for someone else. Some of them will resist any attempt by you to help them. They will tell you that they are fine. They want you to help their loved one, not them. They have identified that person as the "sick" one.

In treatment, the family members will need to realize that they have a problem. Each member of the family will work through the Codependency exercise (Appendix 27). This should open their eyes to what they have been doing, which is maladaptive. This exercise gives basic information about codependency and helps each family member to identify the problems that he or she is having.

These individuals have been living in an addicted world, and they are suffering whether they realize it or not. They have learned survival skills that are inappropriate for normal living. They will need to examine exactly what they are doing wrong and learn how to do it in another way. They need to practice the tools of recovery in the family groups and with the patient.

Many families, or family members, will have to be referred to outside agencies for continuing therapy. They have severe marital and family problems that need further treatment. It is your job to refer them to appropriate therapists.

The family members need to understand that they are powerless over the disease and that their lives have been unmanageable. If they think that they can still control things, then they might try to work the patient's program for him or her, and that is a setup for relapse. The family members need to admit to the patient that they have problems too. The family members need to identify exactly what the problems are, understand the problems, and learn what they are going to do differently in recovery.

Some family members come into the program ready to unload and blame the patient for everything. This is not going to do anybody any good. Chemical dependency is a family disease. Everyone is affected, and everyone needs to bear some responsibility. Everyone needs to keep the focus on what he or she can do to make things better. All of the eight core feelings need to be explored. Do not let the family get by with sharing only the feelings with which they feel comfortable.

Do not think that you can handle all of the family problems in treatment. All that you can do is start the family members off in the right direction and give them some practice in the tools of recovery. You will see the family members in conjoint sessions. In these sessions, try to get the family members to share the whole truth with each other. If a family member withholds the truth or lies, then the illness will have a foothold and, just like a cancer, will grow until it ends in relapse.

Each family member needs to write a letter to the patient stating exactly how the person feels and what he or she wants. The patient does the same thing for each family member. The family will read each other these letters in the conjoint sessions. It is from these letters, and from the questionnaires, that you will get a good idea of what needs to be worked on in the conjoint sessions. Only with the whole truth can you help the family to move closer to a healthy lifestyle.

The only truth that can be withheld is something that will injure someone. Use your best judgment here. Alcoholics Anonymous (1976) says, "[We] made direct amends to such people wherever possible, except when to do so would injure them or others" (p. 59). Sometimes a truth is too painful or harmful to the patient or to others to disclose.

After the family members have been involved in the family program long enough to break through initial resistance, they should be given the Codependency exercise to complete at home. Each family member will then read his or her answers to the group. As the family members do this, they will begin to bond together and understand how chemical dependency has affected them.

The Family Program Schedule ■

The family program in most facilities lasts for 1 week. This gives the family members enough time to get started in their own recovery. The family group meets separately from the patients for the first few sessions. The family members are oriented to the program and hear several lectures. They learn about the disease concept of chemical dependency and how it affects families and codependency. The family members need to see people talk about their problems rather than keep them secret.

The family program members need to share their experiences, strengths, and hopes with each other. A family group, without the patients, should meet at least once a day. Here each family member needs to tell his or her story in brief autobiographical form. This helps to remove the intense shame and guilt that the family members have been feeling. The counselor should continue to educate them about chemical dependency and codependency in the groups. The family members need to see how the tools of recovery offer better solutions to their problems.

Many times, family members are so beaten up by the disease that it is difficult for them to share. If you wait and extend the silence, then they will begin talking. They really want to talk. They have been closed up for a long time, and they long for closeness. These people are people pleasers, and they will want to please you.

They feel uncomfortable and anxious in extended silence. If you ask a question and remain quiet, then someone will get the idea and start sharing. Once the ice is broken, it will become easier for others.

The group needs to be introduced to the Al-Anon program and should attend an Al-Anon group once a day throughout the family week. It is essential that the family members bond with their new Al-Anon group as quickly as possible. This will happen only with regular attendance at meetings. Each family member should receive a copy of *Alateen: A Day at a Time* or *One Day at a Time in Al-Anon* (Al-Anon Family Group Headquarters, 1973, 1995). They should be encouraged to begin daily meditation. (These books and other literature can be ordered from Al-Anon Family Group Headquarters, P.O. Box 862, Midtown Station, New York, NY 10018-0862.) Samples of literature should be on display in the family program meeting area.

As the family group members share, they will feel understood and supported by the group. Most groups begin to bond after 1 or 2 days. Many tears will be shed as they hear each other's stories. Once the group of family members has bonded, the patients can be brought into the group. This must not be done until the family members are supporting each other. The patients have bonded in treatment, and they are supporting each other. The family members need a similar support system. The groups with the family members and chemically dependent patients in them will be able to address the problems more fully.

How to Work With the Family in Group

■

You cannot solve each family problem in these groups. You need to concentrate on the process. Help the family members to gain support from each other and eliminate dysfunctional communication skills. You should have each person share and work toward group acceptance. This is the first time in years that these people have had anyone listen to them.

You should not let one family member interrupt, manipulate, or speak for another. You must explain how these techniques are used for control. With group support and encouragement, the patients and their family members will have the opportunity to express themselves fully. Quiet family members, who have been intimidated at home, will find new strength from the group. This group work prepares the family members for flowing smoothly into continuing care.

Family members are encouraged to keep a daily journal during the family program. At the end of the day, they write down the important things that they learned. They write down how they did that day, and they make plans for what changes they need to make the next day. This is their daily inventory. What do they need to do next? How can they be more actively involved in uncovering the truth? This log can be shared periodically in group.

The family members will need to learn and practice healthy communication skills and healthy interpersonal relationship skills. They can work through each of the exercises, just like the patients did. You will develop a mini-treatment plan for each family. What does this family need specifically? The family members need to identify that they have a problem, understand the problem, and learn skills to deal with the problem. They must see that they have a problem or else they will not continue to go to aftercare and support groups.

The Conjoint Session

Once the family has practiced the tools of recovery for a few days, you will begin to see the family in conjoint sessions. This is where you meet with the family members and work out a specific recovery plan. You may want to meet with the spouse more regularly, but you need at least one session with the whole family. All family members need to hear the plan of recovery and understand their responsibility. They need to know exactly what they are expected to do. This is a family disease, and everyone will have to do things differently.

In the conjoint sessions, the family members will read the letters that they have written to the patient. Each family member will share how that person feels and will ask for what he or she wants from other family members. All of them need to understand that they are developing a program of recovery. Every family member is responsible to act in a manner that is conducive to recovery. Not all of the problems are going to be solved now. First, the family members must enter into a personal recovery program. They need to take one day at a time. They are not going to address all of the problems now.

You occasionally will get resistance from the family. Some family members are not willing to cooperate. Some are chemically dependent or are not interested in recovery. Some individuals have an investment in keeping the patient sick. They might fear that if the sick person gets well, their role in the family will be threatened. These people only want to show the family that they are in recovery; they really want things to stay the same. The family needs to see the truth about this dynamic, and the problem needs to be worked through. The family members who want the patient to remain sick cannot see that everyone will be better off in recovery. They are trying to meet their own needs inappropriately. Once they see the truth, you will see these family members turn around. If they continue to deny that a problem even exists, then they will continue to be a detriment to recovery.

At the end of the family program, there will be a short grieving process whereby the family members say good-bye to each other. For the first time in their lives, they have felt unconditionally loved. They do not want to leave this warm supportive atmosphere. If you have encouraged them to seek this support in their outside Al-Anon meetings, this will not be overly difficult, but some pain will be involved. They need to transfer this good feeling to their new support group. All of the family members will need continuing care, and some will need further counseling or treatment. This must be arranged before the family goes home.

To see the family members come into the family program frightened and sad, and then to see them go out with new hope, is a very rewarding experience. The family members never will forget the major role that you played in their lives.

CHAPTER
TWELVE | # The Clinical Staff

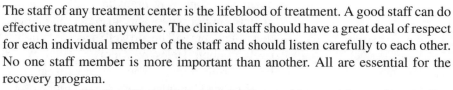

The staff of any treatment center is the lifeblood of treatment. A good staff can do effective treatment anywhere. The clinical staff should have a great deal of respect for each individual member of the staff and should listen carefully to each other. No one staff member is more important than another. All are essential for the recovery program.

A good staff is fun. The staff members enjoy working together and supporting each other in the war against chemical dependency. A good staff laughs a lot. Sometimes you have to laugh to keep the full impact of the disease from getting you down.

Everyone has input into the patients' treatment plans, but everyone has his or her own area of specialization. Professional boundaries are important and should be respected and guarded. To question another person's skills or decisions when you do not know what these skills are is silly. If you stay within your own boundaries—the boundaries of the chemical dependency counselor—then you will be a lot better off, you will feel better, and you will give better quality treatment. All staff members are experts in their chosen fields. They are licensed by their respective boards, and you have to assume that they know what they are doing.

The Physician

The medical doctor is in charge of all treatment. This physician has the most training in the total disease process. A physician completes a bachelor's degree in pre-medicine, 3 or 4 years of advanced medical training, and at least 1 year of internship. Many physicians go on to specialize in one or more areas of medicine. Physicians can have a specialty in addiction called addictionology.

All patients must have a complete history and physical examination given by the physician. If you have any questions about any type of physical disease or medical treatment, then the physician is the person to rely on. It is important to establish a professional working relationship with the physician. He or she is a wealth of information. Do not be intimidated by professionals with advanced degrees. They are just people like you—fallible and human.

The physician will be in close contact with you, particularly if your patient has a medical condition that requires treatment. Close consultation with the physician will prevent you from assuming that behavior caused by an organic disease is a psychological problem.

The physician is in charge of any medication order. If you believe that your patient needs pharmacological treatment, then you need to tell the physician or nurse. Once you have discussed this issue carefully with the medical staff, your job is over. The physician will examine the patient and make the determination based on his or her own clinical judgment. Do not argue with the physician or the nurse about what they are doing. They know more about it than you do. Trust them to do their job.

The Psychologist/ Psychiatrist

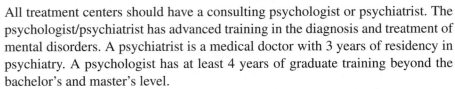

All treatment centers should have a consulting psychologist or psychiatrist. The psychologist/psychiatrist has advanced training in the diagnosis and treatment of mental disorders. A psychiatrist is a medical doctor with 3 years of residency in psychiatry. A psychologist has at least 4 years of graduate training beyond the bachelor's and master's level.

Two thirds of chemically dependent patients have a concomitant psychiatric diagnosis (Frances & Franklin, 1988). They have problems such as depression, anxiety, and/or personality disorders in conjunction with their chemical dependency. Patients will not do well in recovery unless these disorders are treated effectively (Talbott, Hales, & Yudofsky, 1988; Woody et al., 1984). It is important to have a professional in your center who can deal with these coexisting problems.

The Joint Commission on Accreditation of American Hospitals requires that all patients in inpatient treatment receive a psychiatric/psychological evaluation. This examination includes a mental status examination, a determination of current and past psychiatric/psychological abnormality, a determination of the degree of danger to self or others, and a brief neuropsychological assessment. It is from this examination that you will learn about any secondary diagnosis and will develop a treatment plan. The psychiatrist or psychologist will tell you what to do. Follow his or her directions as precisely as you can. Use this professional as a valuable information source. This professional understands the development of personality and the forces that motivate behavior. If you are confused by a patient, talk the situation over carefully with the psychiatrist or psychologist.

The Nurse

There are two types of nurses: registered nurses and licensed practical nurses. Registered nurses complete a registered nurse's degree from an accredited institution. Most go on for a bachelor's degree. Licensed practical nurses complete a 1-year vocational-technical program in nursing.

Nurses are frontline medical personnel. They take responsibility for the patient in the absence of the physician. In an inpatient setting, they usually are available 24 hours a day. There is a tendency in some centers for there to be some conflict between the nursing staff and the counseling staff. This is a boundary issue, and it is a big mistake for all concerned. A good clinical staff has little of these turf battles. Each staff member should know and feel comfortable with his or her unique function in the treatment setting.

Nurses are second-in-command in medical treatment. Only the doctor has more authority. The physician writes the orders, and the nurses carry them out. In many facilities, there are standing orders that allow nurses to make medical decisions. This is necessary to reduce response time and to prevent the physician from being called every time a decision is made. If a nurse tells you to do something, then you should carry out this order as if it came from the physician.

Nurses will listen to you and help you. You will find them to be very supportive. They tend to be caring people who are willing to go the extra mile to provide good quality care. They are used to charting and usually are wonderfully self-disciplined.

The Clinical Director ■

The clinical director has the primary responsibility for making sure that the clinical team provides good treatment. This individual hires the professional staff and develops and implements the treatment program. He or she has advanced training and experience in treating chemical dependency. The clinical director makes sure that the team is working well together and is accomplishing its goals. The director decides who does what, when, how, and with whom. This person directs the treatment program. The clinical director has administrative experience. This individual usually does not see many patients himself or herself and usually works with the staff. All program and policy changes go through the clinical director.

The Clinical Supervisor ■

The clinical supervisor is a chemical dependency counselor with several years of experience in counseling and supervision. This individual's primary responsibility is to supervise the counseling staff. The clinical supervisor will be doing some hands-on work with the patients and will be sitting in on some of your groups. He or she makes up the work schedule and will see you for supervision. This is a person who you should use often. The clinical supervisor is meant to be your mentor. This person will set a good example for how to take a patient through treatment effectively. If you have any questions about treatment planning, charting, or therapy, then this is the first person to ask. You should receive continuing education from the supervisory personnel. If you feel as though you have any weak points in your training, then ask them for in-service training sessions to build your expertise.

The clinical supervisor will be going over your charts to be sure that you are treating the patients according to Joint Commission on Accreditation of Healthcare Organizations (JCAHO) standards. JCAHO requires specific standards of care to be met before it will allow a facility to receive accreditation. (You can order a copy of the standards by contacting the Joint Commission on Accreditation of Healthcare Organizations, 875 North Michigan Avenue, Chicago, IL 60611.)

The Chemical Dependency Counselor ■

Chemical dependency counselors must meet state standards set by a certification board. They take specialized college courses and work for at least 1 year in a treatment setting under a qualified supervisor. In most states, they have to pass a national examination and are state certified. Counselors must show competency in 12 core function areas: screening, intake, orientation, assessment, treatment planning, counseling, case management, crisis intervention, client education, referral, reports and record keeping, and consultation. Many counselors are involved in their own recovery programs, but many are not. It does not seem to matter. It is the on-the-job training in addictions and personal experience that gives addictions counselors their unique professional character. They are excellent health care professionals.

The Rehabilitation Technician or Aide

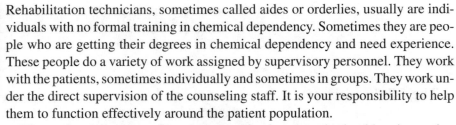

Rehabilitation technicians, sometimes called aides or orderlies, usually are individuals with no formal training in chemical dependency. Sometimes they are people who are getting their degrees in chemical dependency and need experience. These people do a variety of work assigned by supervisory personnel. They work with the patients, sometimes individually and sometimes in groups. They work under the direct supervision of the counseling staff. It is your responsibility to help them to function effectively around the patient population.

There often is some conflict about how far these people should go in treating patients. For the most part, the care they offer should be highly structured and supervised by someone on the clinical staff. You will find that much of the real work in treatment is offered by these individuals. You must see to it that they offer quality care. The only way of doing this is to listen to them, talk to them, and educate them. They might be in recovery and know the AA/NA program well, but you can still improve their skills by extending yourself.

The Activities Coordinator

The activities coordinator is in charge of getting the patients involved in constructive leisure time activities. This individual will be doing an activities assessment to see what the patients are doing for entertainment, play, or fun. The activities coordinator will develop an exercise program for each patient. Most chemical dependency patients have lost the capacity to have fun in sobriety. They need to be encouraged to develop healthy recreational activities and hobbies. They need to learn how to have fun clean and sober. It is important that you encourage your patients to become active in pleasure-oriented activities in recovery. The patients who enjoy sobriety will be more likely to stay sober. One of the most important things that patients can do in their recovery program is to establish regular exercise habits. All patients should be encouraged to exercise on a daily basis.

Clinical Staffing

The clinical staff makes up the treatment team. The staff usually meets once a day to discuss the patients' current status. Once a week, the staff meets for a more formal clinical staffing. Here the patients will be discussed in more detail, and each problem on the problem list will be evaluated.

The staff must be constantly kept informed about how the patients are doing in treatment. In these meetings, treatment plans will be updated. A multidisciplinary staff can take patients through treatment much more effectively. More expertise comes into play, and several heads are better than one.

Clinical staffing is your opportunity to discuss a patient with the whole team. You can get advice and help from everyone at the same time. The patient is reassessed throughout treatment to determine current clinical problems, needs, and responses to treatment. The assessment includes major changes in the patient, family, or life events that could complicate or alter treatment. A patient could have just learned that his wife is divorcing him or that he is being prosecuted for a crime.

Someone in the patient's immediate family could die or become ill. All changes in treatment need to be documented in the patient record.

The atmosphere of clinical staffing is a professional one. The principal matter of concern is the patients. You must assume that all members of the professional staff are willing and able to help. The staff members should be very supportive of each other. Treating chemical dependency is emotionally draining, and everyone occasionally will make mistakes. The atmosphere in clinical staffing should be one of mutual respect. You should enjoy clinical staff meetings. They should be educational, and they should help you to develop your professional skills.

How to Present a Patient

You will present each of your patients to the clinical staff and will discuss how treatment generally is going. If you have any questions, now is the time to ask them. The first time that you present a patient, you need to be thorough. As the patient remains in treatment, you need to cover just the pertinent issues. An outline for case presentation is handy to use your first few times. The outline might look something like this:

1. Identifying data
2. Present illness
3. Past history
4. Family history
5. Social history
6. Medical history
7. Mental status examination
8. Most likely diagnosis
9. Formulation
    a. Predisposing factors
    b. Psychosocial stressors
    c. Stress that precipitated treatment
10. Further assessment you propose
11. Treatment plan
12. Prognosis

Your presentation should sound something like this:

"Mr. Roberts is a 43-year-old Black male who just got his third DWI. He has been drinking heavily for the past 20 years. He is divorced with two children. He lives alone. He came to treatment after spending the night in jail. He is working on his chemical use history and problem assessment form. He is doing well around the unit so far. He is in good physical health except for some mild withdrawal. He seems to be getting along well with his treatment peers. In group, he did admit to a drinking problem. I think he is committed to treatment. He says he doesn't want to go on living this way anymore. I talked to his oldest son this morning, and the family is supportive of treatment. He is in some withdrawal, but he seems to be handling that okay. He needs to take the Minnesota Multiphasic Personality Inventory and visit with the psychologist to rule out other psychiatric disorders. He is somewhat depressed. His diagnosis is alcohol dependence, severe. He will be working through the steps, and we will probably address his depression depending on the psychologist's report."

The case presentation globally advises the treatment team of the patient's condition and describes how the patient is doing in treatment. After you present the patient, each member of the treatment team can comment. The physician or the nursing staff may have something to share about withdrawal or the medical condition for which the patient is being treated. The dietitian may make a report on the patient's diet. The recreational therapist may have a comment on how the patient has been using his or her leisure time. The other counselors may have something to say about what they see. As the primary counselor, you collate this material and enter the staff's input into the patient record. These progress notes do not have to be very long, but they do have to show that the treatment team is reassessing the patient and changing the treatment plan where necessary.

Team Building

A good staff is constantly building the team. These staff members are actively encouraging each other and reinforcing each other's work. When you see someone do a good job, you say so. "You did a good job with Mark this morning. I was impressed with how you handled yourself." These comments are very reinforcing to fellow staff members. The staff members often put so much energy into the patients that they forget that they have needs too. This is emotionally difficult work, and everyone needs support. A good team knows this. Each member goes out of his or her way to treat each other well.

New team members are welcomed and are assisted in adjusting to the flow of treatment. Every treatment center is different, and new staff members need orientation on both an intellectual and an emotional level. A good team's members constantly talk each other up to insiders as well as outsiders. They never talk someone on the staff down. You can share the truth about someone without damaging his or her reputation. The members of a good staff communicate well together. They share openly how they feel and what they think. They work together as a group. If a personal problem develops between staff members, then the problem is handled by a supervisor.

A good staff's members never gossip about each other. Gossip is one of the most harmful things that can occur in any staff organization. Gossip will cause a team to fail. Everyone's life outside of the center should be private. Unless someone decides to confide in you, keep out of the issue. Do not spread damaging rumors about anyone. A good way of checking yourself is to refuse to repeat anything unless you have okayed it with the person you are talking about.

Good staff members get support, not treatment, from their fellow staff members. It is a mistake for someone in recovery to think that they no longer need their AA/NA meetings because they have the support of the clinical team. The clinical staff does not exist to treat you; it exists to treat the patients. If you want to see someone on the staff for a brief consultation about a problem, that is fine, but keep it short. Do not be afraid to seek outside help for your problems. Your mental and physical health directly affect your job performance. If your problems are bogging you down, then you cannot be effective. Becoming involved in a good program of recovery will make you a better counselor and a better person. One of the best ways of learning about good therapy is to go to a good therapist. Make sure that this therapist is highly qualified in his or her field.

A good clinical staff does not "subgroup" against each other. This is where a smaller group of staff members gets together and talks about the other members.

This is very common, and it is a disaster for the clinical team. If you are having problems with a staff member, then go to that staff member first and try to work the issue through. If you are unable to resolve the problem, then go to your supervisor and get him or her to help you. If you and the supervisor cannot handle the problem, then it needs to be addressed before the clinical staff as a whole. Do not let problems fester. The only way of resolving problems is to get everyone together and have each person share how he or she feels. Any problem can be solved in an atmosphere of love and truth. The staff needs to practice what it preaches to the patients.

The following guidelines are excellent for maintaining productive staff interaction.

Commitment to Co-workers | As your co-worker with a shared goal of providing excellent care to our patients, I commit myself to the following:

1. I will accept responsibility for establishing and maintaining healthy interpersonal relationships with you and every member of this staff. I will talk to you promptly if I am having a problem with you. The only time I will discuss it with another person is when I need advice or help in deciding how to communicate to you appropriately.
2. I will establish and maintain a relationship of functional trust with you and every member of this staff. My relationships with each of you will be equally respectful, regardless of job titles or levels of educational preparation.
3. I will not engage in the "3 B's" (bickering, back-stabbing, and bitching) and will ask you not to do as well.
4. I will not complain about another team member and ask you not to do as well. If I hear you doing so, I will ask you to talk to that person.
5. I will accept you as you are today, forgiving past problems, and ask you to do the same with me.
6. I will be committed to finding solutions to problems, rather than complaining about them, and ask you to do the same.
7. I will affirm your contribution to quality patient care.
8. I will remember that neither of us is perfect and that human errors are opportunities, not for shame or guilt but rather for forgiveness and growth. (Manthey, 1991)

Boundaries | Everyone on the clinical team needs to know and respect each other's professional boundaries. You need to know what each person's function is in treatment. Once you know that a part of treatment is not in your area of expertise, stay out of that area. Everyone on the staff wants to hear what you think—that is helpful—but do not concern yourself with patient care outside of your area of specialization. You are a chemical dependency counselor, not a physician or a nurse. You should not concern yourself with who gets aspirin. Many counselors spend long hours worrying about whether or not their patients are being properly treated by the medical staff. If you worry that your medical staff is inadequate, then work somewhere else. Never accept a job in an institution that gives substandard care. Once you decide to accept a position, act as if your staff is the greatest. Be grateful for all of the good work the staff is doing.

Most staff problems are attitude problems, and attitudes can change. You need to keep a positive attitude about you and your co-workers. This will go a long way toward making your day more pleasant and enjoyable. If you see your attitude slipping, then talk about this with your supervisor. Check your own life. How are you doing? Many times, a negative attitude flags personal problems that need to be addressed outside of the treatment center.

Staff-Patient Problems

■

The staff and the patients will constantly have problems with each other. It is the nature of transference and countertransference that there will be conflict. As the patients' maladaptive attitudes and behaviors come into play, the staff can teach new methods of dealing with problems.

Never agree that a patient has been treated unfairly by a staff member until you first talk with the staff member. Patients will attempt to use you in a manipulative way against someone else. You must not subgroup with patients against staff members. This decreases the effectiveness of the entire staff. You must prevent patients from using their old manipulative skills. If a patient is having a problem with a staff member, then arrange for the staff member and the patient to meet to see whether they can resolve the issue together. You are teaching the patient how to resolve interpersonal problems. If the patient has a problem with someone, then he or she has to go to that person to resolve the issue.

Certain patients will try to pit the staff members against each other. This is common for borderline and antisocial patients. This must be resolved by the staff as a whole. A patient usually attempts this by telling different staff members different things. The only way of making this manipulation stop is to call everyone together at the same time. This way, the patient cannot continue to manipulate. Any other means of trying to solve this problem will not work because the lies will continue to operate. Once everyone gets together, you will have a more accurate picture of what the problem is and how to resolve it.

What to Do When a Patient Does Not Like a Counselor

Sometimes a patient will want to change counselors. This patient needs to share how he or she feels with the current counselor. Something might be going wrong with the therapeutic alliance. This matter needs to be discussed with the counselor and the patient who are having the problem. It should be rare for a patient to change primary counselors while in treatment. Most of these problems revolve around lack of trust, and this is a common problem for chemically dependent persons.

Many staff-patient problems result from miscommunication. It is common for two people to misinterpret each other's behavior. Only by bringing the parties together and having them check out their interpretations will the problems be resolved. Each person needs to ask for, and listen to, the other person's thoughts and feelings.

Sometimes patients will want the counselor to do too much. It is as though the patients want the counselor to do all of the work for them. When the counselor balks at this, the patients feel resentful. These patients need to accept the responsibility for their own behavior. They cannot count on someone else to work the program for them. They must work it for themselves.

A patient who is having a problem with a staff member might need more time in individual sessions. The patient needs to get his or her thinking accurate. Trust issues are of paramount importance in recovery. Trust is essential for the development of a good therapeutic alliance. If a patient is having trust problems with the staff, you can bet that the patient has this same problem outside of the treatment setting. The patient might need to track his or her lack of trust to earlier situations, perhaps during childhood. Things that happened early can convince a patient to trust no one. Keep asking the patient if he or she ever felt these feelings at an earlier time. These situations will have to be explored in depth and worked through. The patient needs to see that the situation has changed. The patient is not in the original situation anymore. He or she is in a new situation that demands a new level of trust. What about the new situation leads the patient to feel that he or she cannot trust? What is the most rational decision for the patient to make? Trust issues must be resolved for the patient to move forward in treatment. The patient will remain stuck until he or she can trust someone. Once the patient trusts one person, the patient can transfer the trust to someone else, the group, and then the Higher Power.

What to Do When a Patient Complains About a Rule

Many staff-patient problems revolve around rule violations. Patients will say that they did not break the rule, and they may have a very good story to tell about the situation. You must support other staff members in the consequences they give out. If you do not, then those staff members will be unable to discipline the patients. If the patients learn that the rules can be manipulated, then all of the rules become meaningless. Bring all members involved in the situation together and talk the issue through. In very rare instances, the person who leveled the consequence may remove the consequence or change it to something more appropriate. This should be done only by the person who leveled the consequence.

No chemically dependent persons want to obey the rules, but the rules exist to protect them from harm. Once they understand that the rules are for them rather than against them, they will be more likely to obey the rules. Patients who are breaking the rules need to see how this tendency feeds into their chemical dependency. If they learn how to follow the rules, particularly the rules of AA/NA, then this is recovery.

The Work Environment

A treatment center should be a fun place to work. People who come into recovery at their worst are at their best in a few short weeks. This is an extremely rewarding environment. It is a place full of great joy. Real love abounds in a good treatment center. Patients and staff alike enjoy their days. If you do not genuinely enjoy your work, then you are at the wrong treatment center or you are in the wrong business. Chemically dependent persons are a lot of fun to work with. They laugh and have a good time. They have been the life of the party. The staff can learn how to have fun at work. If the staff members work together and love each other, then they can grow from each work day.

Good treatment must be done in an atmosphere of love and trust. Staff members must support each other through the good times as well as the bad times. The old saying applies: When the going gets tough, the tough get going. Even during periods of stress, the well-functioning staff pulls together and works things out. Humor often saves the day, and a genuine caring for each other smoothes the rough spots for staff members. Remember that you are in this field not only for your patients but also for yourself. You are actively involved in your own individual growth.

CHAPTER THIRTEEN

Discharge Summary and Aftercare

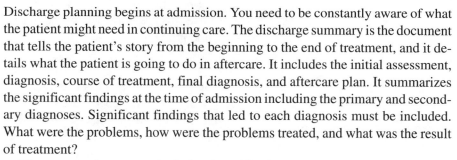

Discharge planning begins at admission. You need to be constantly aware of what the patient might need in continuing care. The discharge summary is the document that tells the patient's story from the beginning to the end of treatment, and it details what the patient is going to do in aftercare. It includes the initial assessment, diagnosis, course of treatment, final diagnosis, and aftercare plan. It summarizes the significant findings at the time of admission including the primary and secondary diagnoses. Significant findings that led to each diagnosis must be included. What were the problems, how were the problems treated, and what was the result of treatment?

The course of treatment includes detoxification and withdrawal, any medical treatment, and all treatment provided by the clinical team. You will follow each problem on the problem list, detailing what the problem is and how the problem was treated. You will discuss how the treatment affected the problem. Make sure that you concentrate on behaviors. Include any changes in the treatment plan and the reasons for those changes as well as the family's response to treatment.

The final assessment of the patient's current condition must include how the patient is functioning at discharge compared to how he or she was functioning before treatment and during treatment. The changes in feelings, thoughts, and behaviors should be detailed. The aftercare plan should be laid out, and the patient must agree to follow the aftercare plan. If the patient needs to see someone for further treatment in continuing care, then this person must be named in the discharge summary. If the patient is on any medication at discharge, then this medication should be listed along with a follow-up plan for continuing or discontinuing this medication.

All patients must meet the discharge criteria developed by the American Society of Addiction Medicine (Mee-Lee, Gartner, Miller, Shulman, & Wilford, 1998).

Outpatient Discharge Criteria

For adult and adolescent outpatient discharge, the patient must meet one of the following conditions:

I. The patient is assessed, postadmission, as not having met the *Diagnostic and Statistical Manual of Mental Disorders (DSM)* criteria for a substance use disorder (American Psychiatric Association, 1994); or

II. The patient must meet at least one of the following criteria:

1. All of the following:
   a. The patient is not intoxicated or in withdrawal.
   b. The patient does not manifest symptoms of protracted withdrawal syndrome.
   c. The patient does not meet any of the Level I continued stay criteria.

2. One of the following:
   a. The patient's medical problems, if any, have diminished or stabilized to the point where they can be managed through outpatient appointments.
   b. There is a biomedical condition that is interfering with treatment and requires treatment at another setting.

3. One of the following:
   a. The patient's emotional behavioral problems have diminished or stabilized to the point where they can be managed through outpatient appointments.

4. One of the following:
   a. The patient's awareness and acceptance of an addiction problem and commitment to recovery are sufficient to expect maintenance of a self-directed recovery plan as evidenced by the following:
      (1) The patient is able to recognize the severity of his or her relationship with alcohol or drugs.
      (2) The patient has an understanding of his or her self-defeating relationship with alcohol or drugs.
      (3) The patient is applying the essential skills necessary to maintain sobriety in a self-help fellowship and/or with further posttreatment care.
   b. The patient has consistently failed to achieve treatment goals, and no further progress is likely to be made.

5. One of the following:
   a. The patient's therapeutic gains that address cravings and relapse issues have been learned and internalized.
   b. The patient is experiencing an exacerbation in drug-seeking behavior or craving that necessitates treatment in a more intense treatment setting.

6. One of the following:
   a. The patient's social system and significant others are supportive of recovery to the point where the patient can be expected to adhere to a self-directed treatment plan.

    b. The patient is functioning adequately in assessed deficiencies in life areas of work, social functioning, or primary relationships.

    c. The patient's social system remains nonsupportive or has deteriorated, and the patient is at risk for relapse. The patient needs placement in a higher level of care to prevent relapse.

Inpatient Discharge Criteria

■

Adults and adolescents in inpatient treatment are ready for discharge if they do not meet the *DSM* criteria for substance use disorder or when they meet the specifications in one of the following six dimensions:

1. One of the following:
   a. The patient is not intoxicated or in withdrawal or the symptoms have diminished to the point where the patient can be managed in a less intense level of care.
   b. The patient has protracted withdrawal symptoms that no longer require 24-hour monitoring.
   c. The patient meets criteria for a more intensive level of treatment.

2. One of the following:
   a. The patient's biomedical problems, if any, have diminished or stabilized to the extent where daily availability of a 24-hour medical staff no longer is necessary.
   b. There is a biomedical condition that needs treatment in another setting.

3. One of the following:
   a. The patient's emotional/behavioral problems have diminished or stabilized to the point where a 24-hour staff no longer is necessary.
   b. An emotional/behavioral problem exists that needs treatment in another setting.

4. One of the following:
   a. The patient's awareness and acceptance of an addiction problem and commitment to treatment are sufficient to expect compliance in a less intensive setting as evidenced by the following:
      (1) The patient is able to recognize the severity of his or her addictive problem.
      (2) The patient understands his or her self-defeating relationship with alcohol and other drugs and also understands their triggers that lead to use.
      (3) The patient accepts continued care and has participated in the development of an aftercare plan.
      (4) The patient does not meet any of the Level III continuing care dimensions.
   b. The patient has consistently failed to meet treatment goals even with changes in the treatment plan, and no further progress is expected.

5. One of the following:
   a. The patient is capable of following and completing a continuing care plan, and the patient is not at substantial risk for relapse.

b. The patient is not committed to continuing care and has achieved the maximum benefit from all attempts to have the patient see that he or she needs an aftercare plan.

6. One of the following:
   a. Problem aspects of the patient's social and interpersonal environment are responding to treatment, and the environment is now supportive enough to transfer the patient to a less intense level of care.
   b. The social and interpersonal environment has not changed or has deteriorated, but the patient has learned skills necessary to cope with the situation or has secured an alternative environment.
   c. The social environment has deteriorated, and the patient has not learned the skills necessary to cope. An extended care environment has been secured, but the patient is unwilling to be transferred.

How to Develop a Discharge Summary

The discharge summary must be entered into the patient record within 15 days following discharge. It must summarize the following things about the patient's treatment:

1. The significant findings of the clinical staff including the problem list and the initial primary and secondary diagnoses
2. The course of treatment through each identified problem
3. The final assessment of the patient's current condition
4. The recommendations and arrangements for further treatment and aftercare
5. The final primary and secondary diagnoses

The aftercare plan details how the patient is going to continue treatment after he or she leaves the treatment center. Each patient will have an aftercare plan that will list the specific arrangements for continuing care.

Each patient will need an AA/NA contact person. It is this person's job to see to it that the patient gets to the new AA/NA group and is introduced around. The contact person stays close to the patient until the patient chooses a sponsor. You will want to carefully build up your AA contact list over the years and get the other counselors to help you. Try to match the patient and the contact person carefully. Some patients will need contact persons who are hard and pushy, and some will need just the opposite. The AA/NA contact is an important link from you to the new group. This contact will keep you informed if anything goes wrong.

The aftercare plan is developed in accordance with the patient's identified needs at the time of discharge. The plan is developed with the full participation of the patient. The patient must agree to abide by the aftercare plan. There is no use in developing a great aftercare plan if the patient has no intention of following it.

Patients will need a variety of care following treatment, and you need to find the least restrictive environment for the patients. Each of the following methods of continuing treatment needs to be considered in developing an aftercare plan:

1. *Inpatient treatment.* If patients' recovery is still shaky and they have serious medical or psychological problems, then the patients might need further inpatient care.

2. *Halfway house.* Some patients will need the structure of a halfway house to help them stay clean and sober. These patients will not function well on their own. They might have poor social skills, or they might need someone else to be in control of their environment. A good halfway house will structure the patients' days and usually will have AA/NA meetings held at the house. Everyone eats together and shares the responsibilities of cooking and cleaning. This is a good alternative for many patients who are shaky in early recovery. If you feel uncomfortable about a patient's ability to maintain a recovery program, then this is something you should encourage.

3. *Outpatient treatment.* Some patients need further treatment, but they can handle treatment in an outpatient setting. Outpatient programs usually offer 1 to 3 days of structured treatment per week. The patients come in and move through an individualized outpatient program. This is much like inpatient treatment, but it is not nearly as intensive or as structured. These patients must be able to stay abstinent between appointments.

4. *Aftercare.* All patients who come through treatment will need an extended care program to make sure that they are following through with their recovery plan. This program will need to be at least once a week for a year. Ideally, a program should offer aftercare so long as it is necessary. It is not unusual for patients to stay in aftercare for over a year.

The Personal Recovery Plan (Appendix 28) describes the patient's goals in recovery. It is another treatment plan developed with the patient's input. If the patient still has problems that need to be addressed in continuing care, then each of these problems will need a treatment plan. You cannot send a patient out of treatment with an unstable psychiatric or family problem without making arrangements for the patient to receive treatment for this problem.

The Discharge Summary

You have collected the data necessary, and you are ready to do your discharge summary. You have the patient's record before you. Remember that this is a summary. You do not have to put in everything, just the significant findings and the course of treatment. You will keep the personal recovery plan in the chart and give a copy to the patient to take home. A sample discharge summary is given in Appendix 29.

After you have completed the discharge summary, write a letter to each of the people to whom you are referring the patient. These letters are important to maintain good communication between your facility and the other professionals in the community. You will need to telephone all of these professionals and tell them about the patient. You might want to send each of them a copy of the discharge summary.

The patient's employer may request an exit interview. You should call the employer and let him or her know that the patient is getting out of treatment and tell the employer how the patient is doing. Employers are an important referral source for your facility, and they have an interest in the patient's recovery.

Saying Good-Bye

When your patients walk down that hallway for the last time, they are going to have mixed feelings. Probably for the first time in their lives, the patients have had a group of people consistently act on their behalf. The patients will not want to leave a good program. They will be feeling some fear of what is going to happen on the outside. For the first time in weeks, they are going to be on their own. It will be easy to get back to the old self-destructive behaviors, and the patients should know this. Alcohol and drugs will be easily accessible. The patients do not know whether they are going to make it. It is a long walk out that front door.

You need to be smiling and offering your patients encouragement all the way. Tell them that you are available if they have difficulty. Explain that you want to see them at the alumni functions that your center will be sponsoring. Tell the patients that they can make it and that you have faith in them. Tell them that no matter what happens out there, you care for them. You will be there for them if they need you. If they have trouble, they can call you or come back to the treatment center. Most of all, you need to give these patients a hug. You have walked with them through one of the most difficult and rewarding periods of their lives.

CHAPTER
FOURTEEN | The Drugs

All psychoactive drugs of abuse alter feelings, thoughts, and behavior. They directly affect the brain or the central nervous system (CNS). The specific actions of these drugs are highly complex. Feelings are altered when the drugs affect neurotransmitters and intercellular communications that seek a balance between excitatory and inhibitory functions. Every organism is driven toward establishing a balance between these two systems that is called homeostasis.

It is widely believed by many experts in the field that the level of drug use in the United States is the highest in the industrialized world. An estimated 14.8 million Americans used a drug illegally during the month prior to being surveyed in the 1999 National Household Survey on Drug Abuse (Appendix 43). Among youths ages 12 to 17 years, 10.9% had used an illicit drug during the past 30 days. Nearly half of Americans age 12 years or over had used alcohol, 20.2% were binge drinkers, and 30.2% smoked cigarettes. The number of people admitted to emergency rooms following cocaine use increased four times over the 5-year period between 1985 and 1989 (Adams, Blanken, Ferguson, & Kopstein, 1990).

Specific drug action depends on the route of administration, the dose, the presence or absence of other drugs, and the clinical state of the individual. In general, psychoactive drugs can be classified by their primary action on the CNS (Hardman, Limbird, Molinoff, Ruddon, & Gilman, 1996).

CNS Depressants

The CNS depressants depress excitable nervous tissue at all levels of the brain and nervous system. The CNS depressants include all sleeping medications, anti-anxiety drugs (also called minor tranquilizers), opium derivatives, cannabis, and inhalants (Hardman et al., 1996; Schuckit, 1984).

CNS Stimulants

The CNS stimulants achieve their effect either by the stimulation of nervous tissue through blocking the actions of inhibitory cells or releasing transmitter substances from the cells or by the direct action of the drugs themselves. These drugs include all of the amphetamines and cocaine. Nicotine and caffeine also stimulate nervous tissue, but to a much lesser degree (Hardman et al., 1996; Schuckit, 1984).

The Hallucinogens

The effect of these drugs is the production of an altered perception, thought, or feeling that cannot be experienced otherwise except in dreams. The hallucinations usually are of a visual nature. These drugs have no known medical usefulness. The most common hallucinogen currently found on the street is LSD (Carroll & Comer, 1998; Jaffe, 1980).

The Reinforcing Properties of Drugs

Drugs of abuse are powerful reinforcers. Animals quickly learn to self-administer most of these drugs for their rewarding properties. Animals will press a lever more than 4,000 times to get a single injection of cocaine. They will continue to self-administer for weeks, alternating between self-imposed abstinence and drug administration. These animals generally die of drug toxicity and lack of food. They would rather use drugs than eat (Wise & Kelsey, 1998).

When given continuous access to drugs of abuse, animals show patterns of self-administration strikingly similar to those of human users of the same drug. These drugs are strongly reinforcing even in the absence of physical dependence (Thompson & Pickens, 1970; Woods & Carney, 1977).

Tolerance and Dependence

Tolerance and physical dependence develop after chronic administration of any one of a wide variety of mood-altering substances. With increasing tolerance, the individual needs more of the drug to get the same effect. Tolerance and dependency develop as the nerve cells chemically and structurally counteract the drug's psychoactive effects. Tolerance is a complex generalized phenomenon that involves many independent physiological and behavioral mechanisms. It leaves the chemically dependent individual physiologically and psychologically craving the drug. The individual becomes obsessed with obtaining the drug for a sense of well-being. The chemically dependent person becomes inflexible in his or her behavior toward the drug despite adverse consequences. The intensity of this felt "need" or dependence may vary from a mild craving to an intense overwhelming obsession. At severe levels, the individual becomes totally preoccupied with the drug (Kalant et al., 1978; Nestler, 1998; Wilcox, Gonzales, & Erickson, 1994).

Physical dependence is characterized by withdrawal symptoms. Withdrawal develops in an addicted individual when the drug is discontinued too quickly. Physical dependence occurs throughout the entire nervous system (Smith, 1977). The withdrawal symptoms are a rebound effect in the physiological systems modified by the drug. For example, alcohol depresses the CNS, whereas withdrawal stimulates the CNS. In studying the effects of withdrawal, look for the opposite effect that the drug was used for initially. Amphetamines are used to stimulate or to give energy, so amphetamine withdrawal causes depression and a lack of energy. The time required to produce physical dependence can vary. Withdrawal symptoms can develop in a day with large quantities of CNS depressants (Alexander, 1951). For most drug users, development of physical dependence is gradual, occurring over weeks, months, or years of chronic administration.

Cross-Tolerance The ability of one drug to suppress withdrawal symptoms created by another drug is referred to as cross-dependence or cross-tolerance. Cross-tolerance may partially or completely remove symptoms of withdrawal. All drugs of abuse cause intoxication and induce a psychological dependency. The individual is self-administering the drug to change his or her level of consciousness or to increase psychological comfort (Schuckit, 1984).

Alcohol

No one knows when alcohol was first produced. If any watery mixture of vegetable sugars or starches is allowed to stand long enough in a warm temperature, alcohol will make itself. Nature alone cannot produce anything stronger than 14% alcohol, but by distillation, the percentage can be increased to 93% (Kinney & Leaton, 1987).

Alcohol is the most used and abused psychoactive chemical in the United States. Approximately half of Americans have had a drink during the past 30 days, and 20% had five or more drinks on one occasion during the past 30 days. About 90% of children use before they leave high school, and 20% have consumed more than five drinks on one occasion during the past 30 days (U.S. Department of Health and Human Services, 1999). It is estimated that alcoholism costs Americans nearly $100 billion and results in 100,000 deaths per year (National Institute on Alcohol Abuse and Alcoholism, 1993, 1997).

The early detection of alcohol abuse and dependency is complicated by denial that is found in the individual, in the family, and in society. Long-term alcohol dependence has profound effects on personality, mood, cognitive functioning, and a variety of physiological problems involving virtually all organ systems. The interaction of alcohol and other drugs may lead to fatal overdoses (Frances & Franklin, 1988).

Alcoholism is the result of a complex interaction of biological vulnerability and environmental factors. Environmental factors such as childhood experience, parental attitudes, social policies, and culture strongly affect the vulnerability to alcoholism. Genetic variables significantly influence the disease. There probably is no personality style that is predictive of alcoholism (Goodwin, 1985; Vaillant, 1984).

Alcohol-Induced Organic Mental Disorders

Alcohol Intoxication

Alcohol intoxication is the most frequent organic-induced mental disorder. It is time limited, and it may occur with varying amounts of ingested alcohol. The intoxicated individual exhibits maladaptive behavioral changes due to recent ingestion. These changes may include aggressiveness, impaired judgment, impaired attention, irritability, euphoria, depression, emotional liability, and other manifestations of impaired social functioning. Although alcohol is basically a CNS depressant, its initial effects disinhibit the individual. Early in intoxication, the person may feel stimulated with an exaggerated sense of well-being. With further use, the person may slow down and become depressed, withdrawn, and dull. The person may even lose consciousness (Spitzer, 1987; Woodward, 1994).

Alcohol Amnestic Disorder (blackout)

Alcohol amnestic disorder, or a blackout, is a period of amnesia during periods of intoxication. The person may seem fully conscious and normal when observed by others, but the person is unable to remember what happened or what he or she did while intoxicated. The disorder may last for a few seconds or for days. The severity and duration of alcoholism correlate with the frequency of occurrence of these blackouts (Goodwin, 1971; Goodwin, Crane, & Guze, 1969).

Wernicke-Korsakoff Syndrome

Wernicke-Korsakoff syndrome is a neurological emergency that should be treated by the immediate parenteral administration of thiamine. The symptoms begin with a sudden change in organic functioning. The patient becomes ataxic with a wide-based unsteady gait. The person may be unable to walk without support. The patient is mentally confused and unable to transfer memory from short- to long-term memory. The patient may be disoriented, listless, inattentive, and indifferent to the environment. Questions directed at the patient may go unanswered, or he or she may fall asleep while being examined. The etiology of this syndrome involves a thiamine deficiency due to dietary, genetic, or medical factors. All patients with compromised mental functioning or a deficit in memory need to be examined by the medical staff as soon as possible to prevent further brain damage (Braunwald et al., 1987).

Alcoholic Idiosyncratic Intoxication

Alcoholic idiosyncratic intoxication is a marked behavior change, usually to aggressiveness, due to recent ingestion of small amounts of alcohol. There usually is amnesia for the period of intoxication. The behavior is unusual for the person when he or she is not drinking. With one drink, the person may become belligerent or assaultive or may manifest other unusual behavior (Spitzer, 1987).

Alcohol Withdrawal

Alcohol withdrawal symptoms relate to a relative drop in alcohol blood levels. Withdrawal can occur when the individual is still drinking. The classic withdrawal symptom is a coarse fast frequency tremor observed when the patient's hand or tongue is extended. The tremor is made worse by motor activity or stress. The patient may experience nausea and vomiting, malaise, weakness, elevated pulse and blood pressure, anxiety, craving, depressed mood, irritability, transient hallucinations, headache, and insomnia. These symptoms follow several hours after cessation or reduction in alcohol intake and peak within 72 hours. They almost always disappear within 5 to 7 days of abstinence. The patient in alcohol withdrawal is treated with a cross-tolerant drug similar in pharmacological effects to alcohol, usually one of the benzodiazepines. This stabilizes the patient in a mild withdrawal syndrome (Mayo-Smith, 1998; Schuckit, 1984).

Alcohol Withdrawal Seizures   Withdrawal seizures may occur 7 to 38 hours after the last alcohol use in chronic drinkers. The tendency to seizure peaks within 24 hours (Adams & Victor, 1981; Mayo-Smith, 1998).

Alcohol Withdrawal Delirium   One third of patients with seizures go on to develop alcohol withdrawal delirium
(delirium tremens)   or delerium tremens. This is characterized by confusion, disorientation, fluctuating or clouded sensorium, and perceptual disturbances (Adams & Victor, 1981; Mayo-Smith, 1998). Typical symptoms include delusions, vivid hallucinations, agitation, insomnia, mild fever, and marked autonomic arousal. The patient frequently reports visual hallucinations of insects, small animals, and other perceptual disturbances. The patient may be terrified. The delirium typically subsides after a few days, but it can continue for weeks (Gessner, 1979).

Sedatives, Hypnotics, and Anxiolytics
■

Benzodiazepines and barbiturates are useful medications with a potential for abuse and dependence. They are medically useful for a variety of symptoms such as insomnia and anxiety. Approximately 15% of the population uses a benzodiazepine each year (Gottchalk, McGuire, Haser, et al., 1979). About 16% of patients abuse the sedatives that are prescribed by their physicians (Richels, Case, Downing, & Winokur, 1983). In 1977, 18% of young adults reported nonmedical use of sedatives (Abelson, Fishburne, & Cisin, 1977). There are no sharp lines that can be drawn among appropriate use, abuse, habituation, and addiction. Both the patient and the physician might not recognize symptoms of dependence. Both might assume that the anxiety, tremulousness, and insomnia that develop when the drug is discontinued is a return of the original anxiety (Jaffe, 1980). Low-dose benzodiazepine dependence is very common today. Some of these patients have been on a succession of various benzodiazepines for years. When the medication is withdrawn, anxiety symptoms may increase for months. These patients must be followed by someone experienced in treating anxiety disorders. The therapist can work to reduce the anxiety symptoms while the patient is experiencing withdrawal (Burant, 1990; Geller, 1994; Juergens, 1994).

Diagnosis of sedative abuse may prove to be difficult. The abuse can start in the context of medical treatment for anxiety, medical disorders, or insomnia. Physical dependence can develop to low doses over several years or to high doses over a few weeks (Dietch, 1983). Intoxication, withdrawal, withdrawal delirium, and amnestic disorder are similar to those found with alcohol. Benzodiazepines have a much longer half-life, so withdrawal might not be evident until 7 to 10 days after cessation of use. The patient may have a protracted withdrawal that can last for months (Geller, 1994). Alcohol and opioid CNS depression may interact with sedative hypnotics and potentiate the depression. Adding small amounts of alcohol or opioids to the sedatives can quickly lead to overdose (Frances & Franklin, 1988). Treatment for sedative, hypnotic, or anxiolytic withdrawal is similar to that for alcohol withdrawal. A cross-tolerant sedative is administered to prevent severe withdrawal symptoms. This medication is gradually decreased until the patient is clear of the drug.

Opioids

During the late 1960s, the use of heroin increased in the United States. Once centered in large urban areas, the use of heroin infiltrated smaller communities. Members of lower socioeconomic groups continue to be overrepresented in this patient population, but the use of heroin is now observed with greater frequency among affluent members of society. A survey in 1977 indicated that 2% to 3% of young adults had tried heroin at some time in their lives. A large proportion of the individuals recently beginning heroin use are young. It is estimated that 125,000 children had their first heroin use between 1996 and 1998. The existence of opioid addiction among physicians, nurses, and health care professionals is many times higher than that of any group with a comparable educational background (Gilman, Goodman, & Gilman, 1980; U.S. Department of Health and Human Services, 1999).

Rapid intravenous injection of an opioid produces a warm flushing of the skin and sensations in the lower abdomen described by addicts as similar to orgasm. This lasts for about 45 seconds and is known as the "kick" or "rush" (Jaffe, 1980). Tolerance to this high develops with repeated use. Physical signs of intoxication include constricted pupils, marked sedation, slurred speech, and impairment in attention and memory. Daily use over days or weeks will produce opioid withdrawal symptoms on cessation of use. The withdrawal symptoms are intense but generally not life threatening. Withdrawal starts approximately 10 hours after the last dose (Frances & Franklin, 1988). Mild opioid withdrawal presents as a flu-like syndrome with symptoms of anxiety, yawning, dysphoria, sweating, runny nose, tearing, pupillary dilation, goosebumps, and autonomic nervous system arousal. Severe symptoms include hot and cold flashes, deep muscle and joint pain, nausea, vomiting, diarrhea, abdominal pain, and fever. Protracted withdrawal may extend for months (Gold, 1994b; Kosten, Rounsaville, & Kleber, 1985).

The treatment of opioid addiction can be grouped into opioid maintenance with methadone versus abstinence approaches. Choice of the proper treatment depends on the patient's characteristics. The course of heroin addiction typically involves a 2- to 6-year interval between the start of regular heroin use and the seeking of treatment. The need to participate in criminal activity to procure the drug predisposes the addict to further social problems. Treatment takes total psychosocial rehabilitation.

Many heroin addicts cannot or will not give up using opioids. Methadone maintenance programs can return them to a productive lifestyle. Methadone substitutes long-acting methadone for short-acting heroin. Methadone has a half-life of 24 hours and can be taken once a day, whereas heroin has a half-life of 4 to 6 hours and must be taken several times a day. Longer acting synthetic opioids are available (e.g., LAAM [levo-alpha-acetylmethadol]) that have a half-life of 72 hours. These medications can be taken several times a week.

Worldwide, methadone maintenance remains the major modality for the treatment of opioid dependency. The research supporting methadone's benefits to the heroin user are well documented (Institute of Medicine, 1995; Lowinson, Marion, Herman, & Dole, 1992). Methadone has been found to be medically safe even when used continuously for 10 years or more (Leshner, 1998). Methadone is administered to the patient orally at established methadone clinics. Although a mainstay of treatment, these programs reach only 20% to 25% of addicts, with program retention rates from 59% to 85% (Stimmel, Goldberg, Rotkopf, et al., 1977). Opioid detoxification should be slow to avoid relapse. The drug should be removed by as little as 10% per week. Total abstinence might be the only alternative for many patients.

A new medication that has not yet been approved by the Food and Drug Administration is buprenorphine. In a large clinical trial, buprenorphine tablets (either buprenorphine alone or the combination with naloxone) were shown to be superior to placebo treatment in reducing opiate use (Fudala, Yu, Macfadden, Boardman, & Chiang, 1998). Additional clinical studies have shown that the addition of naloxone to the buprenorphine tablets decreases the response to buprenorphine when the combination is injected under controlled conditions. This means that when persons attempt to dissolve the tablets and inject them, they will experience either withdrawal or a diminished buprenorphine effect. These properties will make buprenorphine combined with naloxone undesirable for diversion to illicit use, especially when compared to other existing illegal and legal opiate products.

Pharmacologically, buprenorphine is related to morphine but is a partial agonist that possesses both agonist and antagonist properties. Partial agonists exhibit ceiling effects; increasing the dose has effects only to a certain level. Therefore, partial agonists usually have greater safety profiles than do full agonists such as heroin, morphine, and certain analgesic products chemically related to morphine. This means that buprenorphine is less likely to cause respiratory depression, the major toxic effect of opiate drugs, in comparison to full agonists such as morphine and heroin. This should translate into a greatly reduced chance of accidental or intentional overdose and death. Another benefit of buprenorphine is that the withdrawal syndrome seen on discontinuation with buprenorphine is mild to moderate and often can be managed without administration of narcotics.

Cocaine and Amphetamines

Moderate doses of the psychoactive stimulants produce an elevation in mood, a sense of increased energy and alertness, and decreased appetite. Task performance that has been impaired by boredom or fatigue improves. Some individuals may become anxious or irritable. Cocaine addicts describe the euphoric effects of cocaine in a way that is indistinguishable from that of amphetamine addicts. In the laboratory, research participants familiar with cocaine cannot distinguish between the two drugs when both are given intravenously (Fischman et al., 1976). Animals use the drugs in a similar fashion, and the toxic and withdrawal syndromes of the drugs are indistinguishable. There is a difference in the half-lives of the drugs' effects. Cocaine's effects tend to be brief, lasting a matter of minutes, whereas amphetamine effects last for hours (Griffith, Cavanaugh, Held, & Oates, 1972; Wesson & Smith, 1977).

The user of a psychoactive stimulant at first feels increased physical strength, mental capacity, and euphoria. The person feels a decreased need for sleep or food. A sensation of "flash" or "rush" immediately follows intravenous administration. It is described as an intensely pleasurable experience similar to an orgasm. With time, tolerance develops and more of the drug is necessary to produce the same effects. With continued use, toxic symptoms appear. These include gritting the teeth, undue suspiciousness, and a feeling of being watched. The user becomes fascinated with his or her thinking and the deeper meaning of things. Stereotypical repetitive behavior is common. The individual may become preoccupied with taking things apart and then putting them back together. The mixture of another CNS depressant drug, such as an opioid (speed-ball) or alcohol, can be used to decrease irritable side effects. The patient often becomes addicted to both drugs (Wesson & Smith, 1977).

Pattern of Use

Stimulants may be injected or taken intranasally every few minutes to every few hours around the clock for several days. Such a "speed run" usually lasts until the individual has exhausted the drug supply or is too paranoid or disorganized to continue. Stopping administration is followed within a few hours by deep sleep. On arising, the individual feels hungry and lethargic. Sometimes the individual is depressed. Cocaine is inhaled, smoked, or injected intravenously. Cocaine users who try to maintain the euphoric state will ingest the drug every 30 to 40 minutes (Wesson & Smith, 1977). Animals given free access to stimulants develop weight loss, self-mutilation, and death within 2 weeks (Jaffe, 1980). Given a choice between food and cocaine, monkeys consistently choose cocaine (Aigner & Balster, 1978).

A toxic psychosis may develop after weeks or months of continued stimulant use. A fully developed toxic syndrome is characterized by vivid visual, auditory, and tactile hallucinations. There are paranoid delusions with a clear sensorium (Griffith et al., 1972). Unless the individual continues to use the drug, these psychotic symptoms usually clear within a week. The hallucinations are the first symptom to disappear (Jaffe, 1980). Craving for the drug, prolonged sleep, general fatigue, lassitude, and depression commonly follow abrupt cessation of chronic use (Post, Kotin, & Goodwin, 1974).

The National Institute on Drug Abuse (1986) estimated that between 25 million and 40 million Americans had tried cocaine by 1986. Adolescent cocaine abuse leads to more rapid and severe consequences than does adult cocaine abuse. The time from first use to addiction is reduced from 4 years in adults to 1.5 years in adolescents (Washton, Gold, & Pottash, 1984). Cocaine's price has decreased to the point where it costs as little as $5 to get high. During the mid-1980s, the distribution of the ready-to-smoke free-base cocaine known as "crack" spread nationwide (Featherly & Hill, 1989). With the potent free-base form, there is an almost instantaneous euphoric high that is extremely desirable (Frances & Franklin, 1988). Cocaine's half-life is less than 90 minutes, but the euphoric effect lasts for only 15 to 30 minutes (Jaffe, 1980).

The Cocaine Abstinent Syndrome

The cocaine abstinent syndrome has three phases. The first phase is the crash, where the individual reports depression, anhedonia, insomnia, anxiety, irritability, and intense cocaine craving. These symptoms can last up to 3 days. In the second phase, low-level cocaine craving continues along with irritability, anxiety, and decreased capacity to experience pleasure. Over several days, the negative consequences of cocaine use fade, the person feels more normal, and the craving for cocaine increases, especially in the context of environmental cues. The third phase consists of several weeks of milder episodic craving triggered by environmental stimuli. Many patients will appear to have a major depression shortly after cessation of cocaine or amphetamine use. These patients may become suicidal. Most of these symptoms will clear, but some symptoms, such as sadness and lethargy, can last for months (Gawin & Kleber, 1986a; Schuckit, 1984).

The treatments for stimulant rehabilitation are similar to the treatment for alcoholism. The euphoria that stimulants offer needs to be replaced by more adaptive achievements. Stimulant intoxication can be managed with the benzodiazepines or propranolol. Amphetamine or cocaine psychosis might have to be treated with antipsychotic medication. Patients in psychosis need to be kept in a quiet place, supported, and reassured. Antidepressants such as desipramine may ease the withdrawal syndrome (Gawin & Kleber, 1986b).

Phencyclidine (PCP)

■

Phencyclidine (PCP) is an anesthetic initially manufactured for animal surgery. For a short time, it was used as a general anesthetic for humans. Street use of PCP became widespread during the 1970s, when it was introduced as a drug to be smoked or snorted (Jaffe, 1980). It is still epidemic in certain eastern American cities (Caracci, Megone, & Dornbush, 1983).

In humans, small doses of PCP produce a subjective sense of intoxication with staggering gait, slurred speech, and numbness of the extremities. The user may experience changes in body image and disorganized thought, drowsiness, and apathy. There may be hostile or bizarre behavior. Amnesia for the episode may occur. With increasing doses, stupor or coma may occur, although the eyes may remain open (Domino, 1978). Animals will self-administer PCP for its reinforcing properties (Balster & Chait, 1978). Psychoactive effects of PCP generally begin within 5 minutes and plateau in 30 minutes. In contrast to the use of hallucinogens, the use of PCP may lead to long-term neurological damage (Davis, 1982).

Few drugs are able to produce more wide a range of subjective effects than can PCP. Among the effects that users like are increased sensitivity to external stimuli, stimulation, mood elevation, and a sense of intoxication (Carroll & Comer, 1994). Other effects, seen as unwanted, are perceptual disturbances, restlessness, disorientation, and anxiety. Smoking marijuana cigarettes laced with PCP is the most common form of administration (Frances & Franklin, 1988). PCP produces several organic mental disorders including intoxication, delirium, delusional mood, and flashback disorders (Spitzer, 1987). Acute adverse reactions to this drug generally require medication to control symptoms. Benzodiazepines usually are the drug of choice, but antipsychotics might become necessary.

Hallucinogens

■

There is no sharp line that divides the psychedelics from other psychoactive drugs that cause hallucinations. Anticholinergics, bromides, antimalarials, opioid antagonists, cocaine, amphetamines, and corticosteroids can produce illusions and hallucinations, delusions, paranoid ideation, and other alterations in mood and thought similar to psychosis. What seems to distinguish the psychedelic drugs from the others is the unique characteristic to produce states of altered perception that cannot be experienced except in dreams (Carroll & Comer, 1994; Jaffe, 1980).

The psychedelic most available in the United States is lysergic acid diethylamide (LSD). The psychedelic psilocybin has long been used in religious ceremonies by Southwest American Indians. In 1982, 21% of 18- to 25-year-olds had tried a psychedelic at least once (Miller, 1983). Fortunately, the use of this drug is on the decline.

Hallucinogens are not reinforcing to animals, and in humans use is infrequent. Using more than 20 times is considered chronic abuse. Hallucinogens produce a variety of organic brain syndromes including hallucinogen hallucinosis, delusional disorder, mood disorder, and flashback disorder (Spitzer, 1987). Flashbacks may occur in as many as 25% of users (Naditch & Fenwick, 1977). Chronic delusional and psychotic reactions, and rarely schizophrenoform states, have been reported in some psychedelic users (Vardy & Kay, 1983).

The Psychedelic State

During the psychedelic state, there is an increased awareness of sensory input often accompanied by a sense of clarity. There is a diminished ability to control what is experienced. The user experiences unusual and vivid sensory sensations. Hallucinations are primarily visual. Colors may be heard, or sounds may be seen. Frank auditory hallucinations are rare. Time seems to be altered. The user frequently feels like a casual observer of the self. The environment may be experienced as novel, often beautiful, and harmonious. The attention of the user is turned inward. The slightest sensation may take on profound meaning. There commonly is a diminished ability to differentiate the boundaries of objects and the self. There may be a sense of union with the universe. The state begins to clear after about 12 hours (Freedman, 1968). The intoxicated patient generally can be talked down without sedation. This patient needs to be placed in a quiet environment free of excess stimulation. A sedative occasionally may be necessary to calm the patient (Frances & Franklin, 1988).

Cannabis

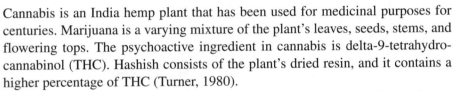

Cannabis is an India hemp plant that has been used for medicinal purposes for centuries. Marijuana is a varying mixture of the plant's leaves, seeds, stems, and flowering tops. The psychoactive ingredient in cannabis is delta-9-tetrahydro-cannabinol (THC). Hashish consists of the plant's dried resin, and it contains a higher percentage of THC (Turner, 1980).

Marijuana remains the most commonly used illegal drug in the United States, used by 75% of illicit drug users (U.S. Department of Health and Human Services, 1999). Surveys reveal that 31% of teenagers, 40% of young adults, and 10% of older adults have tried marijuana. It is generally acknowledged that marijuana use among adolescents peaked during the 1970s. Daily users of marijuana dropped from 10.2% in 1978 to 5.0% in 1984 (Frances & Franklin, 1988).

Cannabis produces effects on mood, memory, motor coordination, cognitive ability, sensorium, time sense, and self-perception. Peak intoxication with smoking generally occurs within 10 to 30 minutes. Most commonly, there is an increased sense of well-being or euphoria, accompanied by feelings of relaxation and sleepiness. Where individuals can interact, there is less sleepiness and there often is spontaneous laughter (Hollister, 1974; Jones, 1971). Physical signs of use include red eyes, strong odor, dilated pupils, and increased pulse rate. With higher doses, short-term memory is impaired, and there develops a difficulty in carrying out actions that require multiple mental tasks. This leads to a tendency to confuse past, present, and future. Depersonalization develops with a strange sense of unreality about the self (Melges, Tinklenberg, Hollister, & Gillespie, 1970). Balance and stability of stance are affected even at low doses (Evans et al., 1973). Performance of simple motor skills and reaction times are relatively unimpaired until high doses are reached (Hollister, 1974; Jones, 1971).

Marijuana smokers frequently report an increase in hunger, dry mouth and throat, an increase in vivid visual imagery, and a keener sense of hearing. Subtle visual and auditory stimuli may take on new meanings (Cloptin, Janowsky, Cloptin, Judd, & Huey, 1979). Higher doses can produce frank hallucinations, delusions, and paranoid feelings. Thinking becomes confused and disorganized, and depersonalization and altered time sense increase. Anxiety to the point of panic may replace euphoria. With high enough doses, the patient presents with a toxic psychosis with hallucinations, depersonalization, and loss of insight. This syndrome can occur acutely or after months of use (Chopra & Smith, 1974; Nahas, 1973; Thacore & Shukla, 1976).

Chronic smoking of marijuana and hashish has long been associated with bronchitis and asthma. Smoking affects pulmonary functioning even in young people. The tar produced by marijuana is more carcinogenic than that produced by tobacco (Secretary of Health, Education, and Welfare, 1977). Individuals using marijuana chronically exhibit apathy; dullness; and impairment of judgment, concentration, and memory. They lose interest in personal appearance, hygiene, and diet. These effects have been observed in young users who regularly smoke a few marijuana cigarettes a day. These chronic effects take months to clear after cessation of use (Jaffe, 1980; Tennant & Grossbeck, 1972).

The pharmacological effects of marijuana begin within minutes after smoking. Effects may persist for 3 to 5 hours. THC and its metabolites can be found in the urine for several days or weeks after a single administration. THC is highly lipid soluble, and its metabolites tend to accumulate in the fat cells. They have a half-life of approximately 50 hours (Hollister, 1974; Secretary of Health, Education, and Welfare, 1977). Tolerance to and dependence on marijuana develop, and abrupt cessation after chronic use is followed by headache, mild irritability, restlessness, nervousness, decreased appetite, weight loss, and insomnia. Tremor and increased body temperature may occur (Gold, 1994a; Jones, Bennowitz, & Bachman, 1976; Wikler, 1976). Because the withdrawal symptoms tend to be mild, detoxification usually is not necessary (Frances & Franklin, 1988).

Inhalants

Inhalants include substances with diverse chemical structures used to produce a state of intoxication—gasoline, airplane glue, aerosol (spray paints), lighter fluid, fingernail polish, typewriter correction fluid, a variety of cleaning solvents, amyl and butyl nitrate, and nitrous oxide. Hydrocarbons are the most active ingredients in these substances. In 1980, 10% of 12- to 17-year-olds reported using inhalants at least once (Frances & Franklin, 1988).

Several methods are used to inhale the intoxicating vapors. Most commonly, a rag soaked with the substance is applied to the mouth and nose, and the vapors are breathed. The individual may place the substance in a paper or plastic bag and inhale the gases. The substance also may be inhaled directly from containers or sprayed into the mouth or nose (Spitzer, 1987).

Dependent individuals may use inhalants several times per week, often on weekends and after school. Inhalants sometimes are used by children as young as 9 to 13 years of age. These children usually use with a group of friends who are likely to use alcohol and marijuana as well as the inhalant. Older adolescents and young adults who have inhalant dependence are likely to have used a wide variety of substances (Spitzer, 1987).

Whereas high doses of these agents produce CNS depression, low doses produce an increase in CNS activity and a brief period of intoxication. Intoxication can last from a few minutes to 2 hours. Impaired judgment, poor insight, violence, and psychosis may occur during the intoxicated period. Inhalants are easily and cheaply acquired, and they can be attractive to children who cannot drink legally.

Animals will self-administer inhalants for a reinforcement. There is a strong cross-tolerance with inhalants and the CNS depressants. Studies of inhalers have found indications of long-lasting brain damage (Cohen, 1979; Sharp & Brehm, 1977; Sharp & Carroll, 1978). Long-term damage to the bone marrow, kidneys, liver, and brain also has been reported (Frances & Franklin, 1988). There have been a number of deaths among inhalant abusers attributable to respiratory depression or cardiac arrhythmia. These deaths often appear to be accidental (King, Smialick, & Troutman, 1985).

Nicotine

Crew members who accompanied Columbus to the New World were the first Europeans to observe the smoking of tobacco. They brought the leaves and the practice of smoking back to Europe. Tobacco addiction is the number one preventable health problem in the United States. Approximately 66.8 million Americans currently use tobacco products (U.S. Department of Health and Human Services, 1999). Cigarettes are responsible for more than 434,000 deaths each year in the United States (Centers for Disease Control, 2000). About 4,000 different compounds are generated by the burning of tobacco, but tobacco's main psychoactive ingredient is nicotine. Nicotine produces a euphoric effect and has reinforcing properties similar to cocaine and the opioids (Henningfield, 1984). Tolerance to some of the effects of nicotine quickly develops, but even the chronic smoker continues to exhibit an increase in pulse and blood pressure after smoking as little as two cigarettes. Nicotine has a distinct withdrawal syndrome characterized by craving for tobacco, irritability, anxiety, difficulty in concentrating, restlessness, increased appetite, and increased sleep disturbance (Hughes & Hatsukami, 1986; U.S. Surgeon General, 1979).

Tobacco addiction has many properties similar to opioid addiction. The use of tobacco usually is an addictive form of behavior (Frances & Franklin, 1988). Tobacco produces a calming euphoric effect, particularly on chronic users. Nicotine in cigarette smoke is suspended on minute particles of tar, and it is quickly absorbed from the lungs with the efficiency of intravenous administration. The compound reaches the brain within 8 seconds after inhalation. The half-life for elimination of nicotine is 30 to 60 minutes (U.S. Surgeon General, 1979).

Chronic use of tobacco is causally linked to a variety of serious diseases ranging from coronary artery disease to lung cancer. The likelihood of developing one of these diseases increases with the degree of exposure that is measured by the number of cigarettes per day. Cigarette-smoking men have a 70% higher death rate than do nonsmoking men. Smoking in women is increasing along with smoking-related diseases (Braunwald et al., 1987).

It is estimated that 42 million Americans have stopped smoking. Approximately 30% of smokers make an attempt to quit smoking each year, and 8% of these attempts succeed. More than 90% of successful quitters do so on their own without participating in an organized cessation program. Smokers who quit "cold turkey" are more likely to remain abstinent than are those who decrease their daily consumption of cigarettes gradually, switch to cigarettes with lower tar or nicotine, or use special filters or holders. Quit attempts are nearly twice as likely to occur among smokers who receive nonsmoking advice from a physician. Heavily addicted smokers, or those who smoke more than 25 cigarettes per day, are more likely to participate in an organized cessation program (Pierce, Fiore, Novotny, Hatziandreu, & Davis, 1989).

As addiction specialists, all counselors need to advise their patients against smoking and help them to quit. Smokers can and do quit. All smokers should consult with the staff physician for advice on not smoking. Self-help material can be presented to the patients who request more information. A pharmacological alternative, such as gum containing nicotine or a nicotine patch, can be substituted to ease withdrawal. Formal smoking cessation programs, such as the American Lung Association's "Freedom From Smoking" clinic, may be beneficial for heavier smokers (Glynn, 1990). The Twelve Steps can be useful in giving smokers support in their attempts to quit. Some patients will want to quit smoking while in treatment. This should be highly encouraged and supported.

Polysubstances ■

Few drug abusers abuse only one drug. There is a strong correlation between misuse of heroin and alcohol problems, abusers of stimulants frequently use depressants to cut irritable side effects, and alcoholics are at a higher risk for abusing other depressants and stimulants (Schuckit, 1984).

In Western society, youths begin drug use with caffeine, nicotine, and alcohol. If they go on to use other drugs, then the next drug of choice most likely will be marijuana, followed by one of the hallucinogens, depressants, or stimulants. These drugs first are taken on an experimental basis. They are reinforcing and lead to few serious consequences. Marijuana is seen as a step on the road to the use of other substances. Once the illegal barrier is crossed, it becomes easier to take a second and a third drug (Gould & Keeber, 1974; Kandel, 1978).

The effects of a drug may be either increased or decreased by adding an additional drug. Depressants taken together may potentiate the effect of either drug taken alone. Depressants and stimulants taken together may decrease the level of side effects encountered when one of the drugs is used alone. Marijuana has been shown to potentiate the effects of alcohol; it may increase the likelihood of a flashback from hallucinogen use (Schuckit, 1984). More than half of the patients presenting to a polydrug clinic report the use of three or more substances (Cook, Hostetter, & Ramsay, 1975).

The most common multiple drug withdrawal syndromes are those seen following concomitant use of multiple depressants or depressants and stimulants. Depressants produce the most severe and life-threatening withdrawal symptoms. When depressants and stimulants are used together, the withdrawal syndrome more closely follows the clinical picture of depressant withdrawal, but it probably includes greater levels of sadness, paranoia, and lethargy (Shuckit, 1984).

Treatment Outcome ■

The Treatment Outcome Prospective Study (TOPS) is the largest and most comprehensive study of drug abuse treatment ever completed. It collected data on more than 10,000 patients admitted for chemical dependency treatment nationwide. The patients were in 37 different programs that varied from methadone maintenance, to residential, to outpatient treatment. The major finding was that treatment works. Drug abuse is significantly reduced after treatment, and the amount of decrease is greater in patients who remain in treatment longer. Patients needed to remain in treatment at least 6 months before a significant impact on drug abuse was achieved. Associated problem behaviors decreased (e.g., criminal behavior, family problems, suicidal thoughts). This study found that drug addiction is a chronically relapsing condition usually requiring prolonged or repeated treatment (Hubbard et al., 1989).

The overwhelming weight of evidence from a large number of outcome studies and epidemiological studies indicates that treatment contributes significantly to positive behavior change in chemically dependent patients (Anglin & Hser, 1990; Gerstein & Harwood, 1990; Hoffmann, 1994; Hubbard, 1992).

The Institute of Medicine's Committee for the Study and Treatment and Rehabilitation Services for Alcoholism and Alcohol Abuse (1990) and many individual reviewers (e.g., Anglin & Hser, 1990; Hubbard & DesJarlais, 1991; Sisk et al., 1990) have concluded that chemical dependency treatment changes patients for the better. Other studies confirm that the benefits of these changes considerably outweigh the costs of treatment (e.g., Hubbard, 1992).

Follow-up studies of proprietary programs reviewed by the Institute of Medicine (1989) found abstinence rates between 40% and 60% during the first year after treatment. Similar results were found in studies of state and private programs (Hoffman & Harrison, 1987; Hubbard & Anderson, 1988; Institute of Medicine, 1989).

Comprehensive Assessment and Treatment Outcome Research (CATOR) is the largest independent evaluation service for the chemically dependent field in the United States. Since 1980, CATOR has collected data on more than 50,000 adults and 10,000 adolescents who have entered treatment programs. CATOR finds that there are large differences in the clinical characteristics of patients admitted to inpatient programs versus outpatient programs. Cocaine dependence is much higher in the inpatient group; marijuana and stimulant dependence also is higher. Half of the inpatients are dependent on illicit drugs, whereas only one third of the outpatients are so addicted. Nearly 20% of inpatients admit to using at least two drugs other than alcohol on a weekly basis, whereas only 8% of outpatients admit to such heavy use. Recent ingestion is more common in the inpatient population, with 44% using alcohol or drugs within the past 24 hours of admission, compared to 23% of outpatients.

Detailed analysis of the CATOR research has encouraging words for chemical dependency counselors. A patient who completes treatment—either outpatient or inpatient—has a 50% chance of staying clean and sober for the year following treatment. If the patient completes treatment and attends AA/NA once a week for the next year, then he or she has a 70% chance of staying sober. If the patient completes treatment and attends one AA/NA meeting and one aftercare session per week, then he or she has a 90% chance of remaining sober for the next year. These are fantastic results: Fully 90% of patients can stay sober if they complete treatment and attend AA/NA and aftercare on a regular basis (Hoffmann, 1991, 1994).

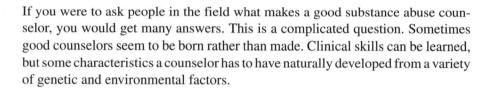

CHAPTER
FIFTEEN | # The Good Counselor

If you were to ask people in the field what makes a good substance abuse counselor, you would get many answers. This is a complicated question. Sometimes good counselors seem to be born rather than made. Clinical skills can be learned, but some characteristics a counselor has to have naturally developed from a variety of genetic and environmental factors.

Being Loving

Good counselors are, first of all, loving. They are interested and actively involved in other people's interpersonal growth. They care for how people feel, and they care for what people want. They feel this not only at work but in their social lives as well. They instinctively believe that their patients have great worth. They help their patients to grow by gently guiding them. They do not hammer their patients; hurting their patients would deeply hurt them. They do not constantly confront patients with their faults; rather, they praise patients for their strengths. They build on patients' strengths rather than concentrating on patients' weaknesses. They focus their attention on helping their patients grow in the way that they want to grow. They never push their own values and moral beliefs on their patients. They constantly encourage their patients to see the truth about themselves and others. They want their patients to be fully themselves and to reach for their full potential.

Loving Counselors Enjoy Their Work

Loving counselors do not feel burdened by their work. They feel that their work is a great privilege. It is an honor to have people share the intimate details of their lives with them. By loving others in this program, the counselors will have love turned back on them. They will feel loved and important. Thomas Merton said that "happiness is unselfishly giving to others." Loving counselors give freely of themselves and expect nothing in return.

Loving Counselors
Do Not Become
Overly Involved

Loving counselors do not become overly involved with their patients because to do so would not be loving; it would be self-serving. To be loving, you have to be healthy in your life. You have to be reasonably comfortable with who you are, where you are, what you do, and who you are with. If you have unmet needs, these will be a roadblock to you in becoming a good counselor. It is not that you have to be completely problem free—no one ever is—but you have to have a strong support system within yourself and outside of the treatment center. You have to be able to meet your own needs. If you ever think that patients can meet your needs, then you are in for trouble. Counselors who are in the field to heal their own problems will feel angry and frustrated. Patients are too sick to help you. They need to concentrate on their own recovery.

Loving Counselors
Do Not Lie

Loving counselors never lie. Love necessitates action in truth. Without truth, love cannot occur. It never is loving to lie. You can tell a patient that you do not want to talk about an issue, but you never should make up a story, even if you think it is for the patient's own good. It never is in the patient's good to lie. Lies cut the patient off from reality.

Loving Counselors
Are Gentle

Loving counselors are gentle and kind. They are sensitive to their patients' pain. To cause unnecessary pain is inexcusable. The truth also may cause patients some pain, but without the truth, the patients never will recover. Good counselors can give consequences because they know that it is for the patients' own good.

Gentle means that you encourage the patient to see the truth. Never yell or call the patient names. You may get angry—that is normal—but try to use your anger appropriately. The patient might have a very difficult time in dealing with your anger. It can permanently damage the therapeutic relationship. When you are angry, it is useful to be angry at the illness rather than at the patient. If the patient understands this, then he or she can join you in feeling angry at the disease. It might hurt the patient some to give him or her a consequence, but it will feel good in the long run. You are doing the right thing by helping the patient to learn from his or her maladaptive behavior.

Good Counselors
Love Themselves

Good counselors love themselves. They nourish themselves. They cultivate stable loving relationships with family and friends. They spend quality time alone. If they are in recovery, then they work a daily program of recovery. Good counselors do not overwork, and they do not become overly involved. When they leave work, they do not bring the problems home.

Sensitivity

Good counselors must be sensitive to other people's feelings. This seems to be an inborn trait. Some people have this sensitivity naturally, and other people do not. Some sensitivity can be learned, but the sensitivity that counselors need cannot. You need a hypersensitive autonomic nervous system for this. To be sensitive, you need to feel other people's pain almost as if it is your pain. When they hurt, you hurt. When they feel joy, you feel joy. This is called empathy. With empathy, you perceive, feel, and understand other people's experiences.

The Sixth Sense

The more sensitive you are, the better counselor you are going to be. The sensitivity will enable you to know where a patient is emotionally. This gives you accurate information about your patients' motivation. The patients might not know how they feel. They may be cut off from their feelings. In a sense, you need to be ahead of the patients. You will feel the feelings as they are feeling them, but you will feel the feelings before they have processed them. There will be those few seconds when you know where they are going. You know because that sixth sense of yours has picked it up. Remember, feelings give us energy and direction for movement. If you know how other people feel, then you can predict what they are going to do.

You can learn sensitivity to some degree by trial and error. Constantly ask patients how they are feeling to check yourself. Most patients will correct you if you are wrong. As you reflect their feelings and they correct you, you will develop more sensitivity. This skill will develop and become more accurate over the years of your career. As you learn what people want and how they feel, you will be able to help them to move forward more quickly. You will make mistakes, but you will learn many things about people. You will learn that no one really wants to do a bad thing. People do bad things because they see the good in them. If you understand this, then you will be able to understand your patients. Child abuse can occur simply because the parent wanted the child to be quiet. The parent did not want to hurt the child for the joy of seeing someone in pain.

Your supersensitivity will help you to know what motivates patients. Borderline or schizophrenic patients are very difficult to understand unless you understand how they are feeling and what they are thinking. These are patients whom you have to explore until you understand how they perceive the world.

Good Counselors Do Not Become Overly Emotional

Some counselors seem to be overly sensitive. They become overly emotional. This is countertransference. These are the counselors who weep openly with most clients and at family sessions. They encourage their patients to call them at home, anytime. They call patients after they leave treatment just to see how they are doing. They encourage patients to drop by their homes. These counselors have a need to be liked, and they are transferring their need to their patients. Some of these counselors have unresolved psychological problems that are driving them. Their desire to help, please, and take care of others is out of control. These counselors get hurt, frustrated, and angry because they learn that the patients do not want a friend; they want a counselor. Many of these counselors burn out and eventually leave the profession. They never seek the professional help that they need to get their work in perspective.

You cannot be too sensitive if you use your sensitivity correctly. This supersensitivity will give you accurate direction. You will be able to say the right thing at the right time. You will just know what to say. You will know what you would want to hear. Best of all, this supersensitivity will give you great timing. You will be able to say the right thing at the right time. This is almost a magical experience. It will happen to you more and more as you grow in your counseling career.

Active Listening

■

Good counselors listen. They know when to be quiet and focus on what their patients are saying. They are interested in how the patients perceive things. They want to know what the patients are thinking and how they are feeling. They desire to become a part of the patients' world. Counselors who are good listeners will have patients tell them that they are good. The patients feel understood.

Good Counselors Do Not Talk Too Much

A common mistake of new counselors is to talk too much. If they recorded themselves in group or in individual sessions, then they would see that they do most of the talking. They think that they have a lot to say, and the patients have a lot to learn, so why not just teach them? Counseling with these individuals is more like going to a lecture. Good counselors ask a lot of questions, and they listen carefully for the answers. They are attentive to the patients' verbal and nonverbal behavior. If they see the patients saying one thing with their words and another thing with their behavior, they believe the behavior.

Active listeners will reflect how the patients are feeling and wait for feedback. Even with supersensitivity, you never know exactly what other people are experiencing. You have to ask and listen. Nothing helps patients feel more understood than to be listened to attentively. As you focus your attention on the patients, they feel important. They feel as though someone cares for them and knows them. Active listening takes a lot of energy. It is not easy. You have to listen with every fiber of your being. If you do not listen, then your patients never will feel loved. Counselors with poor listening skills hear their patients say, "You don't understand me." Good counselors rarely hear these words. If patients do not feel understood, then they will be frustrated, their treatment will suffer, the therapeutic alliance will be shaky, and the patients will not trust. To trust you, the patients must feel known.

Boundaries

Good counselors know their boundaries. They know who they are as people, and they will not allow other people to violate them. You will have patients in treatment who will try to threaten you or throw their weight around. You will use the group with these patients to give you the support you need. Angry patients are using the only skill that they know how to use. It is your job to teach them how to get what they want in some other way.

You must know your professional boundaries and not cross them. You must use only techniques that you have learned through professional training and experience. You never should use a technique if you have only heard about it. Watch a skilled person use the technique a few times, and then have that person watch you. Use only the skills that you have been trained to use. You must be able to demonstrate, through professional education and experience, that you know what you are doing.

If you feel comfortable with yourself and your training, it is a relief to let the rest of the staff members do their own thing. You do not have to question their skills. The professional staff organization will accept that responsibility. You can relax and enjoy your role as the counselor. That is plenty of work. You do not have to do everyone's job, just your own.

Boundaries include keeping your relationships with your clients professional. Good counselors never take advantage of their relationships with patients. They never act on romantic feelings or become involved in business dealings with their clients. If you do these things, it will be confusing to you and your patients. The patients are in a vulnerable situation, and you are their confidant—their hero. If you use these relationships for your own gain, then you are going to hurt your patients. The relationships with your patients are special. Do not take advantage of them.

Patience

Good counselors are patient. They treat chemically dependent people at those individuals' own pace. They know that different patients come into treatment with different levels of readiness for treatment. Some patients are ready to disclose the truth very fast—the first day—and some patients will be reluctant to share the truth. It never helps to threaten or push patients to disclose information. All you can do is to give the patients the opportunity to share in a loving environment. You teach the patients the consequences of not sharing. If the patients understand and see unconditional positive regard, then they will share. If they cannot share with you, then they can share in their Fifth Step. If they cannot share the truth there, then encourage them to share at a later date. You cannot make people talk. If you try, you will be in trouble. People will view you as abusive and harmful. Your job is to provide a loving atmosphere in which people want to talk.

You need to give the patients the chance to grow at their own pace. You must take them through treatment at a pace that they can follow and understand. The patients must recognize the severity of their illness, understand their self-defeating relationship with substances, and apply the tools of recovery. They must see their new behaviors work.

Some patients will not do written work well, or they will not get things if they read them. Learning disabilities can handicap some patients. These patients have to be treated differently. If you try to push them to do something that they cannot do, then you will fail. Many people have physical, emotional, or social roadblocks to learning. You must recognize when patients are struggling and intervene as soon as possible. You must do something differently to make the program more understandable.

Interpersonal Relationship Skills

Good counselors have good interpersonal relationship skills. They are good communicators. They tell people how they feel and what they think. They do not keep their feelings to themselves. They use their feelings appropriately to help them solve problems. They are trustworthy and reliable. If they tell the patients that they are going to do something, then they do it. They are there for the patients when they are needed. If a patient asks for help, then good counselors stop what they are doing and focus on the patient. This might take only a few minutes. If the discussion is going to take longer, then they can make an appointment to see the patient later.

Good counselors never manipulate to get their way. They never say one thing and mean another. They never plot or plan against a patient or against a member of the professional staff. Manipulation necessitates lies, and this is a program of rigorous honesty. Good counselors will not become involved in dishonest communication.

Good counselors are assertive, not aggressive. They do not use the power of their positions or their personalities to make the patients do things. They share with the patients how they feel and ask for what they want. If the patients have broken the rules and consequences are required, then the consequences are leveled without excessive guilt or remorse. Good counselors never attack, assault, abuse, yell, scream, chastise, torment, scold, assail, batter, shame, berate, condemn, lay into, insult, tongue-lash, intimidate, threaten, terrorize, force, violate, oppress, sneak, defame, or belittle. They treat the patients the same way in which they would want to be treated.

Good counselors suspect when patients are transferring energy from a previous relationship to the therapeutic relationship. They help the patients to understand and work through the transference. Good counselors always keep patients informed about what they are thinking and how they are feeling. The patients never feel left in the dark.

Good counselors treat patients with honor and respect. They believe that it is a privilege to work with all patients no matter who they are. If they have a patient who they cannot work with, then they refer the patient to someone else. They care for how patients feel and for what patients want. They want to help patients to feel comfortable.

Good counselors are constantly reinforcing. They are fun to be around. They enjoy life. They like giving people praise. They look for things to reinforce. These counselors try to see the good in everything. They always are reaching for the positive. They praise people for the little things. They notice when someone does something right, and they point it out. Good counselors rarely are punitive; they do not like to punish. When they are giving good things to others, they feel the best about themselves.

Sound Code of Ethics

■

Good counselors have a good code of ethics. This is what you need to do to maintain the highest in ethical principles:

1. You respect the dignity and worth of each patient and strive to protect individual human rights.
2. You are committed to patients understanding themselves and reaching their full potential.
3. You protect the welfare of those who seek your services as a professional.
4. You do not permit patients' skills to be misused.
5. You accept the responsibility for the consequences of your actions. When you are wrong, you promptly admit it.
6. You make sure that your services are used appropriately.
7. You avoid relationships that may create a conflict of interest.
8. You try to prevent distortion or misuse of your findings.
9. You present material objectively, fully, and accurately.
10. You know that your work bears a heavy responsibility because your recommendations and actions may alter the lives of others.
11. You accurately represent your competence, education, training, and experience.
12. You recognize the need for continuing education and are open to new procedures and changes.
13. You recognize the differences among people of different races, sexes, cultures, creeds, ethnic backgrounds, and socioeconomic statuses. When necessary, you are willing to obtain special training in how to deal effectively with such persons.
14. If you use assessment tools, then you are responsible for knowing the reliability and validity of such instruments.

15. You recognize that personal problems may interfere with your professional effectiveness. You refrain from becoming engaged in an activity where your personal problems may have an influence. If you have serious problems, then you have a responsibility to seek appropriate professional assistance.

16. You obey the law.

17. You do not condone practices that you perceive as being inhumane or unjust.

18. When announcing professional services, you do not make claims that cannot be demonstrated by sound research.

19. You present yourself accurately, avoiding misrepresentation of you or your findings.

20. You respect the confidentiality of all information obtained within the context of your work.

21. You reveal such information only with the written permission of the patient or the patient's legal representative, except when the patient is a clear danger to self or others.

22. When appropriate, you inform the patient of the legal limits of confidentiality.

23. You discuss information obtained in professional relationships only for professional purposes and only with persons clearly concerned with the case.

24. You ensure that appropriate provisions are made for maintaining confidentiality in the storage and disposal of the patient record.

25. You recognize your own needs and are cognizant of your potential to influence clients and subordinates.

26. You make every effort to avoid relationships that could impair your professional judgment or increase the risk of exploitation. This includes, but is not limited to, treatment of employees, close friends, or relatives.

27. You understand that sexual intimacies with patients are unethical.

28. You make arrangements for payment of services that safeguard the best interest of the client.

29. You terminate your services when it is reasonably clear that the patient is not benefiting.

30. You understand the areas of your competence and make full use of other professionals who will serve the best interests of your patient.

31. You cooperate fully with other professionals.

32. If a person is receiving a similar service from another professional, then you carefully consider that relationship and proceed cautiously, protecting the other professional and the patient.

33. If you employ or supervise other professionals or professionals in training, then you accept the obligation to facilitate the professional development of these individuals. You provide appropriate working conditions, timely evaluations, constructive consultation, and continuing education.

34. You do not exploit your professional relationships with patients, supervisees, students, or employees sexually or otherwise. You do not condone or participate in any form of sexual harassment.

35. When you know of an ethical violation by another counselor, if it seems appropriate, you bring this violation to the attention of the counselor. If

this behavior is not corrected, then you bring the information to the appropriate local, state, or national board.

Are you a good counselor? I hope so. If you are, you have chosen a field that will give you indescribable joy. You will see people at their worst and at their best. You will see them crying, and you will see them laughing. You will help people to change for the better. You will be there to help put broken families back together again. You will see, in the eyes of your patients, the love and appreciation that they will feel for you. You will experience a deep love for others. You will learn to appreciate people for their uniqueness. You will savor the fact that no two people are the same. You will travel with men and women who are addicted as they struggle toward new hope and new lives. Their hope is in you because you are the chemical dependency counselor.

List of Appendixes

1. Cognitive Capacity Screening Examination
2. Short Michigan Alcoholism Screening Test (SMAST)
3. CAGE Questionnaire
4. *DSM-IV* Psychoactive Substance Use Disorder
5. Clinical Institute Withdrawal Assessment of Alcohol Scale
6. Narcotic Withdrawal Scale
7. Sample Biopsychosocial Interview
8. Chemical Use History
9. Honesty
10. Love, Trust, and Commitment
11. Feelings
12. Relationship Skills
13. Addictive Relationships
14. Communication Skills
15. Self-Discipline
16. Impulse Control
17. Relapse Prevention
18. Step One
19. Step Two
20. Step Three
21. Step Four
22. Step Five
23. Adolescent Unit Level System
24. Peer Pressure
25. The Behavioral Contract
26. Family Questionnaire

27. Codependency
28. Personal Recovery Plan
29. Sample Discharge Summary
30. Stress Management
31. The Beck Depression Inventory
32. Biopsychosocial Assessment
33. Anger Management
34. Narcissism
35. Honesty for Gamblers
36. Step One for Gamblers
37. Step Two for Gamblers
38. Step Three for Gamblers
39. Step Four for Gamblers
40. Step Five for Gamblers
41. Relapse Prevention for Gamblers
42. Adolescent Unit Point System
43. National Household Survey on Drug Abuse, 1999
44. Drug Categories for Substances of Abuse
45. Adult Inpatient Program Schedule
46. Adolescent Inpatient Program Schedule
47. Adult Outpatient Program Schedule
48. Adolescent Outpatient Program Schedule
49. Gambling Inpatient Program Schedule
50. Gambling Outpatient Program Schedule
51. Intensive Outpatients/Partial Care/Day Treatment Program Schedule
52. Pressure Relief Group Meeting and Budget Forms
53. Heroin: Abuse and Addiction
54. South Oaks Gambling Screen
55. Barriers in Thinking

Appendix 1

Cognitive Capacity Screening Examination

Examiner _____ Date _____

Instructions: Check items answered correctly. Write incorrect or unusual answers in the space provided. If necessary, urge the patient once to complete task.

Introduction to patient: "I would like to ask you a few questions. Some you will find very easy, and others may be very hard. Just do your best."

1. What day of the week is this? _____
2. What month? _____
3. What day of the month? _____
4. What year? _____
5. What place is this? _____
6. Repeat the numbers 8 7 2. _____
7. Say them backward. _____
8. Repeat the numbers 6 3 7 1. _____
9. Listen to the numbers 6 9 4. Count 1 through 10 out loud, then repeat 6 9 4.
       (Help if needed. Then use numbers 5 7 3.) _____
10. Listen to the numbers 8 1 4 3. Count 1 through 10 out loud, then repeat 8 1 4 3. _____
11. Beginning with Sunday, say the days of the week backward. _____
12. 9 plus 3 is _____
13. Add 6 (to the previous answer or to 12). _____
14. Take away 5 (from 18). _____

    Repeat these words after me and remember them. I will ask for them later: *hat, car, tree, twenty-six.*

15. The opposite of fast is slow. The opposite of up is _____
16. The opposite of large is _____
17. The opposite of hard is _____
18. An orange and a banana are both fruits. Red and blue are both _____
19. A penny and a dime are both _____
20. What are those words I asked you to remember? (*hat*) _____
21. (*car*) _____
22. (*tree*) _____
23. (*twenty-six*) _____
24. Take away 7 from 100, then take away 7 from what is left and keep going: 100 minus 7 is _____
25. Minus 7 _____
26. Minus 7 (Write down the answer. Check correct subtraction of 7.) _____
27. Minus 7 _____
28. Minus 7 _____
29. Minus 7 _____
30. Minus 7 _____
        Total Correct _____
Patient was:
    Cooperative _____

Uncooperative _____
Depressed _____
Lethargic _____
Other _____

If the patient's score is less than 20, then some diminished cognitive capacity is present. Therefore, an organic mental syndrome should be suspected, and the medical staff should be notified.

_____

Reproduced, with permission, from Jacobs, J. W., Bernhard, M. R., Delgado, A., & Strain, J. J. (1977). Screening for organic mental syndromes in the medically ill. *Annals of Internal Medicine, 86,* 40-46.

Appendix 2

Short Michigan Alcoholism Screening Test (SMAST)

1. Do you feel that you are a normal drinker? (By *normal,* we mean that you drink less than or as much as most other people.) (no)
2. Does your wife, husband, parent, or other near relative ever worry or complain about your drinking? (yes)
3. Do you ever feel guilty about your drinking? (yes)
4. Do friends or relatives think that you are a normal drinker? (no)
5. Are you able to stop drinking when you want to? (no)
6. Have you ever attended a meeting of Alcoholics Anonymous? (yes)
7. Has drinking ever created problems between you and your wife, husband, parent, or other near relative? (yes)
8. Have you ever gotten into trouble at work because of your drinking? (yes)
9. Have you ever neglected your obligations, your family, or your work for 2 or more days in a row because you were drinking? (yes)
10. Have you ever gone to anyone for help about your drinking? (yes)
11. Have you ever been in a hospital because of drinking? (yes)
12. Have you ever been arrested for drunken driving, driving while intoxicated, or driving under the influence of alcoholic beverages? (yes)
13. Have you ever been arrested, even for a few hours, because of other drunken behavior? (yes)

Answers related to alcoholism are given in parentheses after each question. Three or more of these answers indicate probable alcoholism, two answers indicate the possibility of alcoholism, and fewer than two answers indicate that alcoholism is not likely.

Reprinted with permission. Selzer, M., Winokur, A., & van Rooijen, C. (1975). A self-administered Short Michigan Alcoholism Screening Test. *Journal of Studies on Alcohol, 36,* 117-126. Copyright © by Journal of Studies on Alcohol Inc., Rutgers Center of Alcohol Studies, New Brunswick, NJ 08903.

Appendix 3

CAGE Questionnaire

1. Have you ever felt that you ought to **C**ut down on your drinking?
2. Have people **A**nnoyed you by criticizing your drinking?
3. Have you ever felt bad or **G**uilty about your drinking?
4. Have you ever had a drink first thing in the morning (**E**ye-opener) to steady your nerves or to get rid of a hangover?

Two or more affirmative answers indicate probable alcoholism. Any single affirmative answer flags further evaluation.

Reprinted with permission from the *Journal of the American Medical Association, 252,* 1905-1907 (1984). Copyright © 1984, American Medical Association, 515 North State Street, Chicago, IL 60610.

Appendix 4

DSM-IV Psychoactive Substance Use Disorder

I. Diagnostic Criteria for Psychoactive Substance Abuse

    A. A maladaptive pattern of substance use leading to clinically significant impairment or distress, as manifested by one (or more) of the following occurring within a 12-month period:

        1. Recurrent substance use resulting in a failure to fulfill major role obligations at work, school, or home (e.g., repeated absences or poor work performance related to substance use; substance-related absences, suspensions, or expulsions from school; neglect of children or household)

        2. Recurrent use in situations in which it is physically hazardous (e.g., driving while intoxicated or operating a machine when impaired by substance use)

        3. Recurrent substance-related legal problems (e.g., arrests for substance-related disorderly conduct)

        4. Continued use despite knowledge of having persistent or recurrent social or interpersonal problems caused or exacerbated by the effects of the substance (e.g., arguments with spouse about consequences of intoxication, physical fights)

    B. Never met the criteria for psychoactive substance dependence for this substance

II. Diagnostic Criteria for Psychoactive Substance Dependence

    A. A maladaptive pattern of substance use leading to clinically significant impairment or distress, as manifested by three (or more) of the following occurring at any time in the same 12-month period:

        1. Tolerance, as defined by either of the following:

            a. A need for markedly increased amounts of the substance to achieve intoxication or desired effect

            b. Markedly diminished effect with continued use of the same amount of the substance

        2. Withdrawal, as manifested by either of the following:

            a. Characteristic withdrawal syndrome of the substance

            b. The same (or a closely related) substance taken to relieve or avoid withdrawal symptoms

        3. Substance often taken in larger amounts or over a longer period of time than was intended

        4. A persistent desire or unsuccessful efforts to cut down on or control substance use

        5. A great deal of time spent in activities necessary to get the substance (e.g., visiting multiple doctors, driving long distances), use the substance (e.g., chain smoking), or recover from its effects

        6. Important social, occupational, or recreational activities given up or reduced because of substance use

        7. Substance use continued despite knowledge of having a persistent or recurrent social, psychological, or physical problem that is likely to have been caused or exacerbated by the use of the substance (e.g., keeps using heroin despite family arguments about it, cocaine-induced depression, having an ulcer made worse by drinking)

Specify if:

With physiological dependence: Evidence of tolerance or withdrawal

Without physiological dependence: No evidence of tolerance or withdrawal

---

Used with permission. *Diagnostic and Statistical Manual of Mental Disorders* (4th ed., 1994). Washington, DC: American Psychiatric Association.

Appendix 5

Clinical Institute Withdrawal Assessment of Alcohol Scale

Patient _____ Date _____ Time _____

Pulse or heart rate taken for 1 minute _____

Blood pressure _____ / _____

Nausea and Vomiting

Ask "Do you feel sick to your stomach? Have you vomited?"

Observation:

0 No nausea and no vomiting

1 Mild nausea with no vomiting

2

3

4 Intermittent nausea with dry heaves

5

6

7 Constant nausea, frequent dry heaves, and vomiting

Tremor

Arms extended and fingers spread apart

Observation:

0 No tremor

1 Not visible but can be felt fingertip to fingertip

2

3

4 Moderate, with arms extended

5

6

7 Severe, even with arms not extended

Proximal Sweats

Observation:

0 No sweat visible

1 Barely perceptible sweating, palms moist

2

3

4 Beads of sweat obvious on forehead

5

6

7 Drenching sweats

Anxiety

Ask "Do you feel nervous?"

Observation:

0 No anxiety, at ease

1 Mildly anxious

2

3

4 Moderately anxious or guarded, so anxiety is inferred

5

6

7 Equivalent to acute panic states, as seen in severe delirium or acute schizophrenic reactions

---

Agitation

Observation:

0 Normal activity

1 Somewhat more than normal activity

2

3

4 Moderately fidgety and restless

5

6

7 Paces back and forth during most of the interview or constantly thrashes about

---

Tactile Disturbances

Ask "Have you had any itching, pins-and-needles sensations, burning, or numbness? Do you feel bugs crawling on or under your skin?"

Observation:

0 None

1 Very mild itching, pins and needles, burning, or numbness

2 Mild itching, pins and needles, burning, or numbness

3 Moderate itching, pins and needles, burning, or numbness

4 Moderately severe hallucinations

5 Severe hallucinations

6 Extremely severe hallucinations

7 Continuous hallucinations

Auditory Disturbances

Ask "Are you more aware of sounds around you? Are they harsh? Do they frighten you? Are you hearing anything that is disturbing to you? Are you hearing things that you know are not there?"

Observation:

0 Not present

1 Very mild harshness or ability to frighten

2 Mild harshness or ability to frighten

3 Moderate harshness or ability to frighten

4 Moderately severe hallucinations

5 Severe hallucinations

6 Extremely severe hallucinations

7 Continuous hallucinations

Visual Disturbances

Ask "Does the light appear to be too bright? Is the color different? Does it hurt your eyes? Are you seeing anything that is disturbing to you? Are you seeing things that you know are not there?"

Observation:

0 Not present

1 Very mild sensitivity

2 Mild sensitivity

3 Moderate sensitivity

4 Moderately severe hallucinations

5 Severe hallucinations

6 Extremely severe hallucinations

7 Continuous hallucinations

Headache, Fullness in Head

Ask "Does your head feel different? Does it feel like there is a band around your head?" Do not rate dizziness or lightheadedness. Otherwise, rate severity.

Observation:

0 Not present

1 Very mild

2 Mild

3 Moderate

4 Moderately severe

5 Severe

6 Very severe

7 Extremely severe

Orientation and Clouding of Sensorium

Ask "What day is this? Where are you? Who am I?"

Observation:

0 Oriented and can do serial additions

1 Cannot do serial additions or is uncertain about date

2 Disoriented about date by no more than 2 calendar days

3 Disoriented about date by more than 2 calendar days

4 Disoriented about place and/or person

Total Score _____

Rater's Initials _____

Maximum Possible Score = 67

A score higher than 25 indicates severe withdrawal (impending delirium tremens). If score is lower than 10 after two 8-hour reviews, then monitoring can stop. If score is higher than 20, then the patient should be assessed hourly until the symptoms are under control.

Appendix 6

Narcotic Withdrawal Scale

There are four major stages in narcotics withdrawal:

Grade I: Lacrimation (teary eyes)
   Rhinorrhea (runny nose)
   Diaphoresis (sweating)
   Yawning
   Restlessness
   Insomnia (difficulty sleeping)

Grade II: Dilated Pupils
   Piloerection (goosebumps on skin)
   Muscle twitching
   Myalgia (muscle pain)
   Arthralgia (joint pain)
   Abdominal pain

Grade III: Tachycardia (pulse or heart rate higher than 100)
   Hypertension (high blood pressure)
   Tachypnea (rapid breathing)
   Fever
   Anorexia (loss of appetite)
   Nausea
   Extreme restlessness

Grade IV: Diarrhea
   Vomiting
   Dehydration
   Hyperglycemia (high blood sugar)
   Hypotension (low blood pressure)
   Curled-up position

Used with permission. Fultz, J. M., & Senay, E. C. (1975). Guidelines for the management of hospitalized narcotics addicts. *Annals of Internal Medicine, 82,* 815-818.

Appendix 7

Sample Biopsychosocial Interview

DATE: 6-2-01

PATIENT NAME: Patty Jean Robbins

DEMOGRAPHIC DATA: This is a 28-year-old single White female. She is childless. She lives in Watertown, South Dakota, by herself. She has lived in Watertown for the past 5 years. She has a high school education. She is employed as a beautician at The Cut Above.

CHIEF COMPLAINT: "I couldn't go on drinking the way I was."

HISTORY OF THE PRESENT ILLNESS: This patient's father died when she was an infant. She was raised by an overly demanding alcoholic mother. Her mother had strict rules and made the patient work hard to keep the house clean. The patient never made an emotional connection with her mother. "I grew up feeling left out, abandoned, lost, and alone. I think I was loved, but I wasn't shown it." In school, she continued to feel isolated from her peers. She began drinking during her early teens. In high school, the patient did not date a lot, but when she did, she fell immediately in love. She began a series of addictive relationships with men. In these relationships, she was able to experience the affection she had always longed for. The patient was "devastated" when her boyfriends would go out with someone else. She would frantically "keep grasping" to hold onto these relationships. After high school, the patient had an affair with a married man. This man was demonstrative in his affection, and this fooled the patient into thinking that he "really loved me." The patient was unable to disengage from this relationship, even though the man was married and emotionally and physically abusive. The patient's drinking began to increase. Her tolerance to alcohol increased. She had blackouts. The patient began to use Valium for sleep. Her dose of Valium has more than doubled. She currently is drinking at least a six-pack of beer and taking 30 milligrams of Valium every night. The patient currently is suffering from acute alcohol and anxiolytic withdrawal. Her withdrawal will probably be protracted because she has been on Valium for 5 years. In withdrawal, she reports that she feels restless and is sleeping poorly. The patient has few assertive skills and can be excessively dependent. She enjoys men who are powerful and controlling. The patient has few healthy relationship skills, and she is dishonest. The patient is accepting of treatment and has a strong desire to get help for her chemical dependency.

PAST HISTORY: This patient was born in Livingston, South Dakota, on June 28, 1963. She reports a normal birth and normal developmental milestones. She was raised with her mother and two younger sisters. Her father died when she was too young to know him. Her ethnic heritage is Irish. She describes her home of origin as "I didn't like it. I felt alone." In grade school, "I was timid, not very outgoing." In high school, "I was scared to relate." The patient denies ever serving in the military. Her occupational history includes a 5-year stint as a secretary. She has held her current job as a beautician for 10 years. She is happily employed. Sexually, the patient is heterosexual. She has a complex history of addictive relationships with men who have been abusive both verbally and physically. The patient currently is involved with a new boyfriend. She has been seeing him for the past few months. She reports that this relationship is going well. Her friends and family support her coming into treatment. Spiritually, the patient believes in God. She was raised in the Lutheran Church. She attends church regularly. She denies any legal difficulties. For strengths, the patient identifies that "I'm caring. I get along with people real well. I think that I'm intelligent." For weakness, the patient states that "I have a drinking problem." For leisure activities, the patient enjoys biking and jogging. Her leisure activities have been only mildly affected by her chemical use.

MEDICAL HISTORY:

- Illnesses: Measles, mumps, chicken pox
- Hospitalizations: None
- Allergies: None
- Medications at present: 5 milligrams of Valium three times a day for withdrawal

FAMILY HISTORY:

- Father: Age of death, "in his 20s"; cause of death, unknown; patient does not remember her father
- Mother: Age, 53, in good health; history of alcoholism; described as "quiet, demanding"
- Other relatives with significant psychopathology: None

MENTAL STATUS: This is a tall, thin, 28-year-old White female. She has short, curly, light brown hair and blue eyes. She has a broad smile and a freckled face. She was dressed in white jeans and a white sweatshirt. Her sensorium was clear. She was oriented to person, place, and time. Her attitude toward the examiner was cooperative, friendly, and pleasant. Her motor behavior was mildly restless. The patient fidgeted in her chair. She made good eye contact. Her speech was spontaneous and without errors. Her affect was mildly anxious. Her range of affect was within normal limits. Her mood was mildly anxious. Her thought processes were productive and goal directed. Suicidal ideation was denied. Homicidal ideation was denied. Disorders of perception were denied. Delusions were denied. Obsessions and compulsions were denied. The patient exhibited an above average level of intellectual functioning. She could concentrate well. Her immediate, recent, and remote memories were intact. She exhibited fair impulse control. Her judgment was fair. She is insightful about her alcohol problem and is in minimal denial about her drinking. She is in more denial about her problem with Valium.

DIAGNOSTIC SUMMARY

DATE: 6-10-01

PATIENT NAME: Patty Jean Robbins

This is a 28-year-old single White female. She is childless. She lives in Watertown, South Dakota, by herself. She has lived in Watertown for the past 5 years. She has a high school education. She currently is employed as a beautician at The Cut Above. She comes to treatment with a chief complaint of a drinking problem. The patient's father died when she was an infant. She was raised by an emotionally distant alcoholic mother. Patty grew up feeling a profound sense of abandonment. All her life, she has felt empty and lost. She could gain her mother's approval only by being a hard worker. In grade school, the patient was timid and shy. In high school, she began a series of addictive relationships with men. Patty gets love and sex mixed up. She is starved for attention and affection. She is vulnerable to manipulation. She had an affair with a married man. Her relationships with men have been dysfunctional and abusive. The patient has few assertive skills. She cannot ask people for what she wants or share how she feels. She is dishonest. She lies to get what she wants. Patty began drinking during her early teens. After high school, her drinking began to increase. Her tolerance to alcohol increased. She has had multiple blackouts and has suffered withdrawal symptoms. She is drinking at least a six-pack of beer per day. Patty has been taking Valium for sleep for the past 5 years. She has increased her tolerance to Valium, and she has more than doubled her bedtime dose. The patient currently is experiencing symptoms of alcohol and Valium withdrawal. She has been anemic for the past several years. She is being treated with vitamins. She has cold symptoms and is taking aspirin and an antihistamine. She has a history of arthritis, but she exhibits no current symptoms. She has a history of a heart murmur. The patient is highly motivated for treatment, and her relapse potential is low. She is psychologically minded and is opening up well in group. She shows minimal resistance to treatment. Her current recovery environment is poor. She has no social support system except for her boyfriend of the past 2 months. The psychological testing shows that Patty is emotionally unstable and manipulative. She will break the rules of society to get her own way. She will openly defy authority. She is suffering from mild depressive symptoms, and she is experiencing significant daily anxiety. These symptoms seem to directly relate to the patient's chemical dependency.

DIAGNOSIS:

Axis I: 303.90 Alcohol dependence

304.10 Anxiolytic dependence

291.80 Alcohol withdrawal

292.00 Anxiolytic withdrawal

Axis II: V 71.09 No diagnosis Axis II

Axis III: Anemia, mild cold symptoms

Axis IV: Severity of psychosocial stressors, personal illness, Severity 3 (moderate)

Axis V: Current global assessment of functioning: 50

Highest global assessment of functioning past year: 70

PROBLEM LIST AND RECOMMENDATIONS:

Problem 1: Extended withdrawal from alcohol and Valium, as evidenced by autonomic arousal and elevated vital signs

Problem 2: Inability to maintain sobriety outside a structured program of recovery, as evidenced by patient having tried to quit using chemicals many times unsuccessfully

Problem 3: Anemia, as evidenced by a chronic history of low red cell counts

Problem 4: Upper respiratory infection, as evidenced by sore throat and rhinitis

Problem 5: Fear of rejection and abandonment, as evidenced by patient feeling abandoned by both her mother and her father and now clinging to relationships even when abusive

Problem 6: Poor relationship skills, as evidenced by patient not sharing the truth about how she feels or asking for what she wants, leaving her unable to establish and maintain intimate relationships

Problem 7: Dishonesty, as evidenced by patient chronically lying about her chemical use history

Problem 8: Poor assertiveness skills, as evidenced by patient allowing other people to make important decisions for her, inhibiting her from developing a self-directed program of recovery

TREATMENT PLAN

Problem 1: Inability to maintain sobriety outside a structured program of recovery, as evidenced by repeated unsuccessful attempts to remain abstinent as well as increased tolerance and withdrawal symptoms

Goal A: Acquire the skills necessary to achieve and maintain a sober lifestyle.

Objective 1: Patty will discuss three times when she unsuccessfully attempted to stop drug and alcohol use with her counselor by 6-15-00.

Intervention: Assign the patient to list three times when she unsuccessfully attempted to stop or cut down on her drug and alcohol use, and have her discuss this in a one-to-one session.

*Responsible professional: Carla Smith, C.C.D.C., Level II

Objective 2: Patty will verbalize her powerlessness and unmanageability in group by 6-15-00.

Intervention: Encourage the patient to share her powerlessness and unmanageability in group.

*Responsible professional: Carla Smith, C.C.D.C., Level II

Objective 3: Patty will verbalize her understanding of her chemical dependency with her group by 6-15-00.

Intervention: Assign the patient to complete her chemical use history, and encourage her to share her story in group.

*Responsible professional: Robert Johnson, C.C.D.C., Level III

Objective 4: Patty will share her understanding of how to use Step Two in recovery with her counselor by 6-20-00.

Intervention: Assign the patient to meet with her clergy person to discuss how to use a Higher Power in recovery.

*Responsible professional: Father Larry Jackson

Objective 5: Patty will log her meditation daily and will discuss how she plans to use the Third Step in sobriety with her clergy person by 6-25-00.

Intervention: The staff will administer medications as ordered and monitor for side effects.

*Responsible professional: Margaret Roth, R.N.

Objective 6: Patty will develop a written relapse prevention plan by 6-30-00.

Intervention: Help the patient to develop a written relapse prevention plan.

*Responsible professional: Carla Smith, C.C.D.C., Level II

Objective 7: Patty will develop an aftercare plan with her counselor by 7-5-00.

Intervention: Have the aftercare coordinator help the patient to develop an aftercare program.

*Responsible professional: Martha Riggs, C.C.D.C., Level I

Problem 5: Chronic fear of abandonment, as evidenced by fear of losing all interpersonal relationships

Goal B: To alleviate the fear of abandonment by connecting the patient to her Higher Power and her AA/NA support group

Objective 1: In one-to-one counseling, Patty will share her feelings of abandonment by her parents and how this relates to her chemical dependency by 6-15-00.

Intervention: In a one-to-one session, encourage the patient to share her feelings of abandonment by her parents, and help her to connect this to her chemical dependency.

*Responsible professional: Carla Smith, C.C.D.C., Level II

Objective 2: Patty will share her feelings of fear, loneliness, and isolation with her group by 6-20-00.

Intervention: Assign the patient to share her feelings of fear, loneliness, and isolation in group.

*Responsible professional: Carla Smith, C.C.D.C., Level II

Objective 3: Patty will discuss her fear that the group will abandon her and receive feedback from the group by 6-25-00.

Intervention: In group, encourage the patient to share her fears that the members of the group will abandon her.

*Responsible professional: Carla Smith, C.C.D.C., Level II

Objective 4: In one-to-one counseling, the patient will discuss accepting her AA/NA group as her new support system by 6-28-00.

Intervention: Teach the patient about how her recovery group can be her new support system.

*Responsible professional: Carla Smith, C.C.D.C., Level II

Objective 5: Patty will write a letter to her father and mother telling them how she felt as a child, and she will share this letter with her counselor and in group by 6-20-00.

Intervention: Assign the patient to write a letter to her father and mother telling them about the abandonment she felt as a child, and have her read this letter to her primary counselor and the group.

*Responsible professional: Carla Smith, C.C.D.C., Level II

Problem 6: Poor interpersonal relationship skills, as evidenced by inability to share emotions, wishes, and wants with others

Goal C: To develop healthy interpersonal relationship skills

Objective 1: Patty will verbalize an identification of her problem with relationships with her counselor by 6-15-00.

Intervention: Teach the patient about interpersonal relationship skills and how her addiction affected her ability to have healthy relationships.

*Responsible professional: Carla Smith, C.C.D.C., Level II

Objective 2: Patty will ask five treatment peers for something she wants and share with them how she feels, keeping a log of each conversation and sharing this with her counselor by 6-15-00.

Intervention: Assign the patient to ask five treatment peers for something she wants and share how she feels, and have her log each event and share in a one-to-one session.

*Responsible professional: Carla Smith, C.C.D.C., Level II

Objective 3: Patty will complete the Addictive Relationships exercise (Appendix 13) and share her understanding of the differences in addictive and healthy relationships with her counselor by 6-20-00.

Intervention: Assign the patient to complete the Addictive Relationships exercise, and teach her the difference between addictive and healthy relationships.

*Responsible professional: Carla Smith, C.C.D.C., Level II

Objective 4: Patty will use and log 10 "I feel" statements a day until the end of treatment, and she will share her daily feeling log with her counselor weekly by 6-25-00.

Intervention: Assign the patient to log 10 feeling statements a day and to share in one-to-one sessions.

*Responsible professional: Carla Smith, C.C.D.C., Level II

Objective 5: Patty will discuss her normal and addictive relationships with her group by 6-30-00.

Intervention: In group, encourage the patient to share her understanding of addictive relationships and the tools she can use to develop and maintain healthy relationships in recovery.

*Responsible professional: Carla Smith, C.C.D.C., Level II

Problem 7: Dishonesty, as evidenced by chronic lying about chemical use

Goal D: To develop a program of recovery based on rigorous honesty

Objective 1: Patty will complete the Honesty exercise (Appendix 9) and verbalize in group 10 times when she was dishonest about her chemical use by 6-15-00.

Intervention: Assign the patient to complete the Honesty exercise, and in group have her verbalize 10 times when she was dishonest about her addiction.

*Responsible professional: Bill Thompson, M.S.W.

Objective 2: Patty will discuss in group how her alcohol use contributed to her dishonesty by 6-20-00.

Intervention: In group, have the patient discuss the connection between addiction and dishonesty.

*Responsible professional: Bill Thompson, M.S.W.

Objective 3: Patty will keep a daily log of the times when she lies in treatment and will share this log with her counselor weekly by 6-25-00.

Intervention: Help the patient to keep a daily log of the lies she tells in treatment, and discuss with her how it feels to lie and how it feels to tell the truth.

*Responsible professional: Carla Smith, C.C.D.C., Level II

Objective 4: Patty will give a 20-minute speech to her group about why it is important to be honest in recovery by 6-25-00.

Intervention: Assign the patient to write a 20-minute speech about why it is important for her to get honest, and then encourage her to read her paper in group.

*Responsible professional: Carla Smith, C.C.D.C., Level II

Objective 5: In a conjoint session with her mother, Patty will share her chemical use history by 6-30-00.

Intervention: In a family session, have the patient share her chemical use history with her mother.

*Responsible professional: Ronda Vocal, L.M.F.T.

Objective 6: Patty will discuss how dishonesty separated her from her Higher Power with the clergy by 6-20-00.

Intervention: Have clergy meet with the patient and discuss how her lies kept her away from her Higher Power.

*Responsible professional: Pastor Steve Schultz

Problem 8: Poor assertiveness skills, as evidenced by being too passive and allowing other people to make important decisions

Goal E: To develop assertiveness skills

Objective 1: In group, Patty will verbalize an identification of her problem of being passive and will directly relate her passivity to her chemical use by 6-20-00.

Intervention: The psychologist will help the patient to understand passive traits and how this relates to addiction.

*Responsible professional: Frank Rockman, Ph.D.

Objective 2: Patty will verbalize an understanding of how her passive behaviors lead directly to increased chemical use with her group by 6-15-00.

Intervention: Assign the patient to discuss in group how her passive traits lead to chemical use.

*Responsible professional: Carla Smith, C.C.D.C., Level II

Objective 3: Patty will practice the assertiveness formula with two treatment peers per day, keeping a daily log of each interaction by 6-20-00.

Intervention: The psychologist will teach the patient the assertiveness formula and, using behavior rehearsal, will role-play several assertiveness situations.

*Responsible professional: Frank Rockman, Ph.D.

Objective 4: Patty will have weekly individual sessions with the psychologist in which she will role-play assertiveness situations by 6-30-00.

Intervention: The psychologist will meet with the patient weekly to role-play assertiveness situations.

*Responsible professional: Frank Rockman, Ph.D.

Appendix 8

Chemical Use History
Robert R. Perkinson, Ph.D.

This exercise will help you to become more aware of how chemicals have affected your life and the lives of those around you. Using alcohol, or any other mood-altering substance, is considered to be chemical use. Answer the questions as completely as you can. It is time to get completely honest with yourself. Write down exactly what happened.

1. How old were you when you had your first drink? Describe what happened and how you felt.

2. List all of the drugs you have ever used and the age at which you first used each drug.

3. What are your drug-using habits? Where do you use? With whom? Under what circumstances?

4. Was there ever a period in your life when you used too much or too often? Explain.

5. Has using chemicals ever caused a problem for you? Describe the problem or problems.

6. When you were using, did you find that you used more, or for a longer period of time, than you had originally intended? Give some examples.

7. Do you have to use more of the chemical now to get the same effect? How much more than when you first started?

8. Did you ever try to cut down on your use? Why did you try to cut down, and what happened to your attempt?

9. What did you do to cut down? Did you change your beverage? Limit the amount ("I'll only have three tonight")? Restrict your use to a certain time of day ("I'll only drink after five o'clock")?

10. Did you ever stop using completely? What happened? Why did you start again?

11. Did you spend a lot of time intoxicated or hung over?

12. Did you ever use while doing something dangerous such as driving a car? Give some examples.

13. Were you ever so high or hung over that you missed work or school? Give some examples.

14. Did you ever miss family events or recreation because you were high or hung over? Give a few examples.

15. Did your use ever cause family problems? Give some examples.

16. Did you ever feel annoyed when someone talked to you about your drinking or use of drugs? Who was this person, and what did they say? Give some examples.

17. Did you ever feel bad or guilty about your use? Give some examples.

18. Did using ever cause you any psychological problems such as being depressed? Explain the problem or problems.

19. Did using ever cause you any physical problems or make a physical problem worse? Give a few examples.

20. Did you ever have a blackout? How old were you when you had your first blackout? Give some examples of blackouts.

21. Did you ever get sick because you got too intoxicated? Give some examples.

22. Did you ever have a real bad hangover? Give some examples about how you felt.

23. Did you ever get the shakes or suffer withdrawal symptoms when you quit using? Describe what happened to you when you stopped using.

24. Did you ever use chemicals to avoid symptoms of withdrawal? Give some examples of when you used a substance to control withdrawal symptoms.

25. Have you ever sought help for your drug problem? When? Who did you see? Did the treatment help you? How?

26. Why do you want to continue to use? Give five reasons.

27. Why do you want to stop using? Give 10 reasons.

28. Has alcohol or drug use ever affected your reputation? Describe what happened and how you felt.

29. Describe the feelings of guilt you have about your use. How do you feel about yourself?

30. How has using affected you financially? Give a few examples of how you wasted money in your addiction.

31. Has your ambition decreased due to your use? Give an example.

32. Has your addiction changed how you feel about yourself? Give some examples.

33. Are you as self-confident as you were before?

34. Describe the reasons why you want treatment now.

35. List all of the chemicals you have used in the past 6 months.

36. List how often, and in what amounts, you have used each chemical in the past 6 months.

37. List the life events that have been affected by your chemical use (e.g., school, marriage, job, children).

38. Have you ever had legal problems because of your use? List each problem.

39. Have you ever lost a job because of your use? Describe what happened.

40. Do you want treatment for your chemical problem? List a few reasons why.

Appendix 9

Honesty
Robert R. Perkinson, Ph.D.

This is an exercise to help you get honest with yourself. In recovery, it is essential to tell the truth. As you will hear at every AA meeting, this is a program of rigorous honesty. "Those who do not recover are people who cannot or will not completely give themselves to this simple program, usually men and women who are constitutionally incapable of being honest with themselves" (Alcoholics Anonymous, 1976, p. 58).

Why is it so important to be honest? Because dishonesty to self and others leads to the fear and the fear leads to drug and alcohol use. "Rigorous honesty is the most important tool in learning to live for today" (Narcotics Anonymous, 1988, p. 92). You never will solve problems if you lie. You need to live in the facts. In sobriety, you must commit yourself to reality. This means accepting everything that is real.

People who are chemically dependent think that they cannot tell the truth. They believe that if they do, they will be rejected. The facts are exactly the opposite; unless you tell the truth, no one can accept you. People have to know you to accept you. If you keep secrets, then you never will feel known or loved. An old AA saying states, "We are only as sick as our secrets." If you keep secrets from people, then you never will be close to them.

You cannot be a practicing alcoholic or drug addict without lying to yourself. You must lie, and believe the lies, or else the illness cannot operate. All the lies are attempts to protect you from the truth. If you had known the truth, then you would have known that you were sick and needed treatment. This would have been frightening, so you kept the truth from yourself and from others. "Let's face it; when we were using, we were not honest with ourselves" (Narcotics Anonymous, 1988, p. 27).

There are many ways you lied to yourself. This exercise will teach you exactly how you distorted reality, and it will start you toward a program of honesty. Answer each of the following questions as completely as you can.

1. *Denial:* Telling yourself or others, "I don't have a problem." Write down a few examples of when you used this technique to avoid dealing with the truth.

2. *Minimizing:* Making the problem smaller than it really was. You might have told yourself, or someone else, that your problem was not that bad. You might have told someone that you had a couple of beers when you really had six. Write down a few examples of when you distorted reality by making it seem smaller than it actually was.

3. *Hostility:* Becoming angry or making threats when someone confronted you about your chemical use. Give a few examples.

4. *Rationalization:* Making an excuse. "I had a hard day. Things are bad. My relationship is bad. My financial situation is bad." Give a few examples of when you thought that you had a good reason to use chemicals.

5. *Blaming:* Shifting the responsibility to someone else. "The police were out to get me. My wife is overreacting." Give an example of when you blamed someone else for a problem you caused.

6. *Intellectualizing:* Overanalyzing and overthinking about a problem. This avoids doing something about it. "Sure I drink some, but everyone I know drinks. I read this article, and it said that this is a drinking culture." Give an example of how you use intellectual data and statistics to justify your use.

7. *Diversion:* Bringing up another topic of conversation to avoid the issue. Give an example.

8. Make a list of five lies that you told to someone close to you about your drinking or drug use.

    1. _____
    2. _____
    3. _____
    4. _____
    5. _____

9. Make a list of five lies that you told yourself about your drug problem.

    1. _____
    2. _____
    3. _____
    4. _____
    5. _____

10. Make a list of 10 people you have lied to.

    1. _____
    2. _____
    3. _____
    4. _____
    5. _____
    6. _____
    7. _____
    8. _____
    9. _____
    10. _____

11. How do you feel about your lying? Describe how you feel about yourself when you lie.

12. What do you think will change in your life if you begin to tell the truth?

13. How do you use lies in other areas of your life?

14. When are you the most likely to lie? Is it when you have been drinking or using chemicals?

15. Why do you lie? What does it get you? Give five reasons.

    1. _____

    2. _____

    3. _____

    4. _____

    5. _____

16. Common lies of chemical dependency are listed below. Give a personal example of each. Be honest with yourself.

    A. Breaking promises:

    B. Pretending to be sober when you are intoxicated:

    C. Blackouts; pretending you remember when you do not:

    D. Minimizing use: Telling someone you drink no more than others:

    E. Telling yourself that you were in control when you were not:

    F. Telling someone that you rarely get high:

    G. Hiding morning drinking:

    H. Hiding your supply:

    I. Substituting alcohol for food and telling someone that you were not hungry:

    J. Saying that you had the flu when you were really hung over or sick from using:

    K. Having someone else call in to work to say that you are too sick to come to work:

    L. Pretending not to care about your drug problem:

People who are chemically dependent lie to avoid facing the truth. Lying makes them feel more comfortable, but in the long run they end up feeling isolated and alone. Recovery demands living in the truth. "I am an alcoholic. My life is unmanageable. I am powerless over alcohol. I need help. I can't do this alone." All of these are honest statements from someone who is living in reality.

Either you will get real and live in the real world, or you will die in a fantasy world of your own creation. If you get honest, then you will begin to solve real problems. You will be accepted for who you are.

Wake up tomorrow morning and promise yourself that you are going to be honest all day. Write down in a diary when you are tempted to lie. Watch your feelings when you lie. How does it feel? How do you feel about yourself? Write it all down. Keep a diary for 5 days and share it with your group. Tell the group how it feels to be honest.

Take a piece of paper and write the word *truth* on your bathroom mirror. Commit yourself to rigorous honesty. You deserve to live a life filled with love and truth. You never need to lie again.

Appendix 10

Love, Trust, and Commitment
Robert R. Perkinson, Ph.D.

It seems that going through life, we should be taught a few simple things about relationships. After all, we have a relationship first with ourselves and then, if we so choose, with others. How can we trust ourselves? How can we trust others? When are we committed? When do we love? This exercise will start you thinking about these essential parts of a relationship. Use this exercise to ask yourself some important questions.

THE FIRST RELATIONSHIP

An infant learns about love, trust, and commitment from its primary caregiver. This usually is the mother. When the infant cries out, someone comes and addresses its needs. The baby cannot see very well, so this someone comes out of a haze, seemingly out of nowhere. Whenever the baby cries, this someone comes. This someone comes every time, and a great trust develops between the infant and its mother. As the infant grows older, it becomes aware that this someone has a particular sight, smell, sound, taste, and feel. Soon this someone has a name—mother.

Sometime during childhood, the child learns that the mother does not have to come; she chooses to come. Why does she come? Why, at all hours of the day or night, does she choose to come? She comes because she is bonded with her child. Her child's pain is her pain, and her child's joy is her joy. She cannot ignore her child's pain because when her child hurts, she hurts. In this bonding or joining of mother and child, there is love, trust, and commitment. "Mother will always be there for me." The child knows this. The child's very life depends on it.

It is from this first relationship that we learn what to expect from all of our other relationships. We expect relationships to have certain core characteristics. If the relationships are healthy, they will have love, trust, and commitment as essential building blocks.

TRUST

How do you know that you can trust yourself? What are you going to do to prove to yourself that you are trustworthy? First, you will need to develop consistency of action in your own behalf. If you act consistently in a manner that is in your best interest, then you have gone a long way toward learning how to trust yourself. You must be consistent even when times get rough. You need to learn that no matter what, you are going to do things that are good for yourself. You are trustworthy to someone else when you consistently act in that other person's interest.

COMMITMENT

Commitment means that you are faithful and loyal for an extended period of time. It means that on a daily basis, you can count on yourself to follow through. You have plans to be good to yourself, and you are going to stick with these plans. You are going to hammer away at the things you want day by day. You are not going to give up. These same elements apply when you commit yourself to someone else.

LOVE

A good definition for love is that love is the interest in, and the active involvement in, a person's individual growth. Love for someone else needs trust and commitment, but it needs something more. It needs empathy. You must feel the other person's feelings as if they were your own. Empathy is the feeling that you share with another person. It is being on the same wavelength. "I feel your feelings. When you feel sad, I feel sad. When you feel joy, I feel joy. To help you is to help myself. To love you is to love myself."

Perhaps somewhere along the way, you have lost the ability to experience normal relationships. Maybe you never developed a trustworthy, committed, loving relationship with your primary caregiver. It could be that you never really felt accepted the way in which you needed to be. Children need a lot of encouragement when they try things, and they need a lot of praise. This makes them feel accepted, cherished, and loved. If you take children and sit on their beds every day of their lives and tell them how wonderful they are, then maybe by the time they are 6 years old they will be ready for school. Children need a lot of encouragement to develop a sense of self-worth.

HOW TO BE LOVING TO YOURSELF

To be loving to yourself, you must give yourself a lot of encouragement and a lot of praise. If you missed this as a child, then your challenge is to reinforce yourself. Treat yourself the way in which you wanted to be treated. Be your own mother and your own father. Give yourself all of the love you wanted.

Imagine for a moment that you are a very young child with a fragile and impressionable mind. Write down 10 things that you would need to see from your parents.

1. _____
2. _____
3. _____
4. _____
5. _____
6. _____
7. _____
8. _____
9. _____
10. _____

Only you know what you need. It is up to you to give to yourself everything you wanted. Give to yourself all of the love you need.

RELATIONSHIP WITH SELF

List the things that you need to see from yourself that will prove you can be trusted to act in your own best interests.

1. _____
2. _____
3. _____
4. _____
5. _____
6. _____
7. _____
8. _____
9. _____
10. _____

List the things that you need to see from yourself that will show that you are committed to your own growth. This is a day-by-day commitment.

1. _____
2. _____
3. _____
4. _____
5. _____
6. _____
7. _____
8. _____
9. _____
10. _____

List the things that you will need to see from yourself that will show that you love yourself.

1. _____
2. _____
3. _____
4. _____
5. _____
6. _____
7. _____
8. _____
9. _____
10. _____

HOW TO FIND OUT THE GOOD THINGS ABOUT YOURSELF

List the things about yourself that you feel good about or are proud of. Start with physical appearance. What are some of your good physical qualities? List as many as you can think of. Start with your hair and move downward to the tips of your toes. Admire the color, size, shape, feel, smell, sound, or whatever you can think of. Do not let the old stinking thinking keep you feeling bad about yourself. Get accurate.

Physical appearance: What do you like about how you look?

1. _____
2. _____
3. _____
4. _____
5. _____
6. _____
7. _____
8. _____
9. _____
10. _____

Personality: List all of the personality characteristics that you like and admire about yourself. What do people seem to like about you? What do you like about yourself?

1. _____
2. _____
3. _____
4. _____
5. _____
6. _____
7. _____
8. _____
9. _____
10. _____

You need a lot of encouragement and praise. Now you have a lot of accurate things to say to yourself that make you feel good about yourself.

Things you enjoy: List the things you enjoy doing. How do you play? What do you do for fun or entertainment? What would you like to start doing?

1. _____
2. _____
3. _____
4. _____
5. _____
6. _____
7. _____
8. _____
9. _____
10. _____

People you enjoy: List some of the people you enjoy being around. Write down what makes them feel special to you.

1. _____
2. _____
3. _____
4. _____
5. _____
6. _____
7. _____
8. _____
9. _____
10. _____

Take a long look at what you have written. See how wonderful you really are.

SAY GOOD THINGS TO YOURSELF

Now you have all of these good things to say to yourself. Start with 10 things and write them down on note cards. Carry these cards with you and read them to yourself periodically throughout the day. Look at yourself in the mirror and say these things to yourself. Practice until you have these 10 memorized then take 10 more. Constantly bombard yourself with positive self-talk. When you find yourself speaking harshly to yourself, stop and self-correct. Get out the note cards if you have to, but do not continue to treat yourself poorly.

DO GOOD THINGS FOR YOURSELF

You are saying good things to yourself. That is healing and treating yourself well. Now what can you do for yourself today that is really special? Maybe take a long hot bath or go for a relaxing walk? Could you spend some time with a friend who you enjoy? How about getting some ice cream or just reading and taking a nap? Come up with a few special things to do for yourself today. Write all of these things down and do them. When you are doing these things, think of why you are doing them: because you are a person of great worth. Do this every day. Before you get up in the morning, commit yourself to treating yourself well and then get up and get busy, enjoy life, and feel the pleasure of being alive. You deserve it.

RELATIONSHIP WITH OTHERS

You have some things that you want from a partner, a friend, or a lover. It is your responsibility to ask for what you want. Be specific and give that person a lot of encouragement when he or she tries to give these things to you. You know the secret. Be reinforcing, give encouragement, and shower the person with praise—it is contagious. If you give more often, then you will get more often. Happiness is created when we unselfishly give to others.

HOW TO FIND OUT IF A RELATIONSHIP IS GOOD FOR YOU

What are the things you need to see from someone that will show you that he or she is trustworthy, committed, and loving to you?

1. _____
2. _____
3. _____
4. _____
5. _____
6. _____
7. _____
8. _____
9. _____
10. _____

HOW TO GET WHAT YOU WANT IN A RELATIONSHIP

If you have a friend or partner, then you must ask that person for what you want. The person cannot guess what you want or need; you must tell him or her. Remember to give the person a lot back when he or she gives you something. Ask the person for what he or she wants, and do your best to give it to this person. As you give to this other person, you will feel good about yourself and you will get more of your needs met in return. The more you give, the more you will get.

After completing this exercise, you should be treating yourself well. You should know what you need to see from yourself, and from others, to make you feel good. You have learned that you directly influence how you feel. You are not helpless to others or to your environment. You can love yourself. You are special. You are worth it. Others can love you. You can love others. You can feel whole, healthy, and complete. You have all of the skills that you need.

Appendix 11

Feelings
Robert R. Perkinson, Ph.D.

Chemically dependent persons have a difficult time with their feelings. They never have learned how to use their feelings appropriately. They have been chemically altering their feelings for years. They do not know how they feel, and they do not know what to do, when they do feel. Many chemically dependent people were shamed for having normal feelings when they were children. When they were afraid, they were told that there was nothing to be afraid of. When they were angry, they were told that there was nothing to be angry about. Children who are taught these things learn that their feelings cannot be trusted. They learn that there is something wrong with their feelings. This exercise will help you to identify your feelings and use your feelings appropriately.

THE PURPOSE OF FEELINGS

Feelings or emotions are physiological states that motivate action. Each feeling gives you specific energy and direction for movement. This is how problems are solved. First, there is a situation that triggers thought. The thoughts create feelings, which motivate action. This is how all problems are solved. A person becomes involved in a problem, thinks about the problem, has feelings generated by the thoughts, acts on the feelings, and hopefully resolves the issue.

THE CORE FEELINGS

There are only a few core feelings. More complicated feelings are various combinations of the primary ones. Plutchik (1980) studied feelings and found that there were eight primary emotions:

1. Joy	5. Fear
2. Acceptance	6. Anger
3. Anticipation	7. Disgust
4. Surprise	8. Sadness

Each of these feelings gives us specific energy and direction for movement. We need to discuss each feeling carefully and have you learn specifically what each feeling is like. Then you can recognize when the feeling occurs, and you will know what the feeling is telling you to do. You need practice in experiencing the subtle physiological changes that differentiate each feeling from the others.

Joy

Joy is that feeling we experience when we reach a goal that we have been striving for. The harder we have been working for the goal, and the more important the goal is to us, the more joy we feel. List five times when you felt joy in your life. As you write down each situation, take a moment to reexperience the feeling you had at that moment in your life. Feel the situation as if you were actually there.

1. _____
2. _____
3. _____
4. _____
5. _____

Joy gives us the energy and direction to celebrate and enjoy. It directs us to seek more of whatever is giving us this pleasure.

Acceptance

Acceptance is the feeling we get when someone likes us or approves of us. List five times in your life when you felt accepted. Allow yourself to feel the feeling as you remember each situation.

1. _____
2. _____
3. _____
4. _____
5. _____

The feeling of acceptance gives us the energy and direction to stay involved with the person or group that is accepting. It is a feeling that bonds people together.

Anticipation

Anticipation is the feeling we get when we prepare ourselves for change. It mobilizes us for something new. We can anticipate something good or bad. List five times when you felt an intense sense of anticipation. Reexperience the feeling of each situation.

1. _____
2. _____
3. _____
4. _____
5. _____

Anticipation gives us the energy and direction to mobilize ourselves for change. We prepare ourselves for something exciting.

Surprise

Surprise is the feeling we get when something unexpected happens. Surprise give us the energy to orient ourselves to a new situation. List five times when you felt surprised. Feel the feeling that you felt each time.

1. _____
2. _____
3. _____
4. _____
5. _____

Surprise mobilizes our bodies to take in the new situation as quickly as possible. The brain is very quickly deciding how to respond.

Fear

Fear is the feeling we have when something is perceived as dangerous. List five times when you felt fear. Allow yourself to feel the feeling generated by each situation.

1. _____
2. _____
3. _____
4. _____
5. _____

Fear gives us the energy and direction to withdraw or escape from a dangerous situation. It mobilizes us to get away from the offending stimuli.

Anger

Anger is the feeling we feel when we are violated. This violation may be real or imagined. List five times when you were angry. Feel the anger you felt in each situation. Concentrate on the physical changes that occur when you get angry.

1. _____

2. _____

3. _____

4. _____

5. _____

Anger gives us the energy and direction to fight. It helps us to reestablish the boundaries around ourselves. Anger is necessary to prevent people from violating us.

Disgust

Disgust is the emotion we feel when something repels us. We loathe it; it is repugnant. List five times when something disgusted you. Allow yourself to reexperience the feeling of each situation.

1. _____

2. _____

3. _____

4. _____

5. _____

Disgust gives us the energy and direction to withdraw from the offending stimulation. We need to move away from the object that repels us.

Sadness

Sadness is the feeling we get when we have lost something. We can lose a love object or self-esteem. List five times when you felt sad. Feel the sad feeling. Sense the subtle physiological changes that occur when you feel sad.

1. _____

2. _____

3. _____

4. _____

5. _____

Sadness gives us the energy and direction to recover the lost object. If we are unable to recover the object, then the sadness can deepen. Sadness can immobilize an organism so that healing can begin to take place. The organism does not move or do new things. It stays still and recovers from the loss.

HOW TO USE FEELINGS APPROPRIATELY

Feelings can be used appropriately or inappropriately. They can be based on accurate or inaccurate information. They can lead to adaptive behavior or maladaptive behavior. It is important to know how you feel and what to do when you have a feeling. Feelings will help you to solve problems. Without using your feelings appropriately, you never will be able to solve problems well.

When you feel, you will be experiencing one or more of the eight primary feelings. Jealousy is feeling fearful, angry, and sad all at the same time. Each feeling needs to be addressed for full resolution of the problem.

If you feel confused, then you are feeling many feelings at the same time. Some of these feelings may be in conflict with each other, and you may be torn about what to do. When confused, you must separate each feeling and examine it carefully. What is each feeling telling you to do? What is the most rational thing to do?

When you have a feeling, you must decide how to act. The feeling is motivating you to take action. Feelings need to flow naturally and spontaneously into adaptive action. The actions must be appropriate to the situation. To always fight when you are angry is not appropriate. Most of the time, it is necessary to stop and think before you act. You want to use your feelings. When you are having an intense feeling, always ask yourself two questions:

1. What is the best thing I can do for myself?
2. What is the best thing I can do for the others?

For the most part, you must practice thinking and planning before you act. Plan carefully how you are going to act when you have each feeling, and practice this action until it flows naturally.

Your feelings are important. They are great and wise counselors that need to be listened to. You do not need to hide from your feelings. You need to listen and learn.

Appendix 12

Relationship Skills
Robert R. Perkinson, Ph.D.

There are certain skills that are necessary to establish and maintain close interpersonal relationships. The skills seem simple, but some of them can take great courage. Love is not a feeling; it is an action. We must love in action and in truth. To love someone, you must be actively involved in that other person's individual growth. Love is not self-oriented; it is other-oriented. There also is the love that you show yourself. This is when you are involved in your own growth.

HOW TO LOVE

The first skill is love. Love is an action. You are interested in and actively involved in the other person's individual growth. You are there for that other person when he or she needs your help. You respond to how the person feels and what he or she wants. You tell the truth all of the time. You are willing to spend your time and energy being involved in the other person's well-being.

List five times when you were not there for someone when he or she needed you. Then list what you could have done, or should have done, to help that other person at that moment.

1. _____
   _____
2. _____
   _____
3. _____
   _____
4. _____
   _____
5. _____
   _____

List five times when you lied to someone you loved. Love cannot exist where there are lies.

1. _____
2. _____
3. _____
4. _____
5. _____

HOW TO COMMIT

The second skill is commitment. You must commit yourself, on a daily basis, to work on building the relationship. This means that you work to provide a safe atmosphere in which the relationship can grow. This is an atmosphere full of love and trust. You dedicate yourself to the relationship. You must take the time necessary to nourish yourself, the other person, and the relationship. You consistently ask yourself what you can do for the other person, and then you do it. Now make a plan. What are you going to do to make your relationship grow?

1. _____
2. _____
3. _____
4. _____
5. _____

HOW TO BE ENCOURAGING

The third skill is being encouraging. You must encourage the other person to reach his or her full potential in life. This takes a lot of reinforcement and praise. No one needs to be punished and criticized. This dampens the spirit and weakens interpersonal bonds. People need soothing and encouraging words. They need to know that you have faith in them, that you trust them, and that you will help them to grow. People need their good points praised. They need to hear what they are doing right. Encourage five people today. Write down each of their names and the situation below. Watch their reactions and make note of how you feel.

1. _____
   _____
2. _____
   _____
3. _____
   _____
4. _____
   _____
5. _____
   _____

HOW TO SHARE

The fourth skill is sharing. You must practice sharing how you feel and what you think. You must ask for what you want. You cannot keep these things to yourself. The relationship will falter if you withhold the truth. As children, we are taught that asking for what we want is selfish. But it is not selfish in a loving relationship; it is necessary. Happiness is unselfishly giving to others. How can your partner give to you if you do not tell him or her what you want? How can the other person be encouraged to grow and change unless you hold the person accountable for his or her actions? If you keep your feelings and wants to yourself, then your relationship will not work. Your partner cannot guess what you want. The other person is not capable of that. List 10 important things you want from your relationship, and decide how you are going to ask for these things.

1. _____
2. _____
3. _____
4. _____
5. _____
6. _____
7. _____
8. _____
9. _____
10. _____

Now list the feelings that you have difficulty sharing with your partner. What feelings do you tend to keep inside?

1. _____
2. _____
3. _____
4. _____
5. _____

Make yourself a promise: The next time you have a sharing time with someone, you are going to share how you feel and think. You are going to ask for what you want.

HOW TO COMPROMISE

The fifth skill is Compromise. No one is going to get exactly what he or she wants in a relationship. You have to create an atmosphere of give and take. You must be willing to respond to how the other person feels and what he or she wants. Always ask yourself what you would want if you were in the other person's position. Compromise creates an atmosphere of fairness and equality. List five areas in your life where you have stubbornly wanted to have things your own way. What are you going to do to be more flexible in those situations?

1. _____
2. _____
3. _____
4. _____
5. _____

HOW TO SHOW RESPECT

The sixth skill is establishing a relationship filled with respect. This means that you show the other person that he or she is important to you. You do things that make the person feel special. You care for how the person feels and for what he or she wants. This person matters to you. This person counts. You do not treat this person poorly; you love him or her too much for that. You want this person to be happy. When this person feels happy, you feel happy. List five ways in which you can show someone that he or she is special and important to you.

1. _____
2. _____
3. _____
4. _____
5. _____

These relationship skills need practice. They will not come easily. You need to work at telling the truth all of the time. You need to practice being encouraging. You need to practice sharing how you feel and asking for what you want. You need to develop the skill of commitment. You will struggle when you compromise. You need to work at showing someone that he or she is important.

Keep a log every day for the next week. Detail how you did on each skill and watch for the other person's reaction. Look carefully at how the other person's response changes how you feel about yourself.

THE DAILY PLAN

1. Encourage someone today.
   a. Write down the situation. Exactly what happened?
   b. How did the person feel when you encouraged him or her?
   c. How did you feel?

2. Ask for something you want.
   a. How did it work?
   b. Did you get what you wanted?
   c. How did you feel about asking?
   d. How did the other person respond?
3. Share your feelings.
   a. What was the situation?
   b. How did you feel about yourself?
   c. What response did you get?
4. Tell someone that he or she is important to you.
   a. How did you feel about doing this?
   b. How did the other person feel?
5. Evaluate yourself on honesty.
   a. Did you lie or withhold truth today?
   b. How do you feel about what you did?
6. Help someone and watch his or her reaction.
   a. How did the person respond?
   b. How did you feel?
7. Give something to someone without expecting anything in return.
   a. How did you feel about yourself?
   b. How was your gift accepted?
8. Compromise with someone.
   a. How did you feel?
   b. How did the other person feel?
   c. What was the result of your compromise?

The more you practice these skills, the more proficient you will become. If you hit all of the skills accurately, then your relationships will be stable. If you leave one skill out, then your relationships will be shaky and you will feel frightened. These skills are just like riding a bicycle. The first few times you try to use some of them, they feel awkward and clumsy and you may be worried about getting hurt. But with practice, they will get easy and you will be able to relax and enjoy yourself.

Appendix 13

Addictive Relationships
Robert R. Perkinson, Ph.D.

Relationships are our greatest challenge. Even the best relationships have periods of intense strain. It takes hard work to consistently get along. You have to be willing to give and to think of the other person's needs first. This is not easy. Chemically dependent persons often are just as addicted to their partners as they are to their drugs of choice. Sometimes that "love" feeling is the drug. This should not surprise you. Sexual feelings are created by powerful chemicals in the body called hormones. These chemicals can be just as addictive as any drug, and they can be just as destructive.

Addictive relationships are very different from normal ones. You need to be able to tell which is which. For stability and happiness, you want to get in and stay in a healthy relationship. You want to get out of or treat an addictive one.

THE CYCLE OF ADDICTIVE RELATIONSHIPS

The addictive relationship begins with strong feelings. These feelings may fool you because most of us are taught that these feelings are love. They are not love; they are sexual feelings. These first feelings are extremely powerful, and they draw you, seemingly irresistibly, toward that other person. These are the "love at first sight" feelings. But do not be fooled; it is not love. We can feel these feelings with a movie star or even with someone's picture. In an addictive relationship, you see someone across a crowded room. Your eyes are drawn to that person. Sexual acting out can occur quickly because these feelings are so powerful.

The feelings are so good that you will do anything to keep them. Here is where addictive relationships begin to get sick. You are so thrilled and enchanted with your new "love" that you begin to lie to keep the relationship going. You say things that you do not mean, and you do things that you do not want to do. You just want to keep the feelings flowing. This can be subtle, but it is the clearest difference between addictive and normal relationships. In addictive relationships, you lie. In normal relationships, you tell the truth.

People have an instinctive way of knowing when someone is being dishonest with them. It might take them a while to catch on, but lies begin to tell. Fear begins to build. This feels uncomfortable, and the partners begin to test each other to check for the truth. Jealousy begins to rear its head, and the partners begin to accuse each other of being dishonest and unfaithful. They may begin to suspiciously keep track of each other. "Where were you? Who were you with? What did you do?" Over and over again, the accusations fly back and forth. All of this craziness gets its fuel from the lies. That is the problem. There are lies to uncover, and both people feel it.

Sooner or later, there is an explosion. The fear, jealousy, and accusations reach a fever pitch, and the relationship shatters. There is a violent argument. This usually is verbally abusive and possibly physically abusive. The feelings are so intense—both the pleasure and the pain—that things explode. There usually is screaming and name calling. Demands are made as these two individuals try to reestablish their individual boundaries and resolve the aching fear.

After the explosion, there is a short cooling-off period, and then the two are back to the good feelings again. It is make-up time. The sex is just as good as it was before, maybe even better. "How could we have fought? We love each other so much. What could we have been thinking about?" This is the real thing. It feels so good.

This vicious cycle repeats itself over and over again. There is incredible pain in addictive relationships. You constantly feel desperately in love, scared, and angry. It feels like a roller-coaster out of control. The intensity of the feelings and the lies are the primary factors that keep this sick relationship going—round and round in the agony and the ecstasy.

NORMAL RELATIONSHIPS

A normal relationship begins when you meet someone who interests you as a friend. There is no intense sexual desire at first. You just want to spend time together because you enjoy each other's company. There is no reason to lie, so you tell each other the truth.

Sharing the truth, you gradually draw closer together. The intimacy begins to grow. The more you share, the closer you get. The closer you get, the more you share.

There is a genuine concern for each other. This relationship is based on trust and friendship. There is no reason to be afraid. In this safe atmosphere, surrounded by real love, the sexual feelings come and romance begins.

LOVE

Love is an action. It is not a feeling. We must love in action and in truth. Love is the active involvement in someone's individual growth. If you love yourself, then you will actively participate in your own growth. Similarly, if you love someone else, then you will be actively involved in that person's growth. It is time to find out where you are in your relationship. Is this relationship addictive or normal? Take out a piece of paper and at the top of it write "LIES." Now list all of the lies you can think of that exist in the relationship. Start with the big lies, such as infidelity, and work down from there. You will immediately get the idea if there are major lies in your relationship. A normal relationship cannot exist on a foundation of lies. Such a relationship will falter, crumble, and fail.

Get another piece of paper and label it "FEAR." Write down some things you are afraid of in your relationship. Are you afraid of infidelity? Why? Do you have any information that your partner has been unfaithful? If you do, what is it? Strong fears of infidelity are one of the core components in addictive relationships. These fears can be based on good evidence or can be completely groundless. It does not matter what causes the fear; it is the fear itself that is the damaging factor. Are you verbally or physically afraid of your partner? Abusive relationships are extremely damaging. Abusive relationships need treatment. Verbal and physical abuse are very common in addictive relationships.

Label another piece of paper "FIGHTS." Here describe three major fights you have had with your partner. Pick the worst ones that you can remember. What were the fights about? How did they progress? Were the problems resolved, or did you tend to fight about the same things over and over again? How do you fight? What words are said? How do each of you act when you are very angry?

The next page will deal with "LOVE." Does your partner consistently care about how you feel? Does your partner change what he or she does because of how you feel? Is your partner interested and involved in what you want? Is your partner committed to your individual growth? Some individuals are so caught up in their own needs that they will not become involved in their partners' needs. These people may be incapable of love.

Now go over this information with your counselor or group. Do you believe that you are involved in an addictive relationship? If you are, then you must do one of two things: You must get out of the relationship entirely or get treatment. Both people must go to treatment. If you continue on the way you are going, then you are in for more misery. You now know what love is and what a normal relationship is like. You deserve a relationship filled with love. Do not settle for less.

Appendix 14

Communication Skills
Robert R. Perkinson, Ph.D.

In developing good communication skills, you need to learn how to listen and how to share. You need to understand where the other person is coming from, and you need the ability to express yourself clearly. People communicate with words and actions. Tears or an angry voice can say a lot. You need to be sensitive to both verbal and nonverbal behavior.

EMPATHY

Empathy is the ability to put yourself in another person's shoes. You understand how the person feels. You are on the same wavelength. To develop empathy, you practice paraphrasing what the other person has said until you get the communication correct. The other person needs to be encouraged to correct your mistakes until you have the message correct.

Repeat what the other person said as exactly as you can—both the verbal and the nonverbal message. Continue to repeat the message until the person agrees that you have it right. This might take a few tries, but you will get better as you practice. Include the verbal and nonverbal parts of the message. You might have to ask questions as you go along. Try to be genuine, not sarcastic or punitive. Act as a mirror, reflecting exactly what the other person is saying and how he or she is feeling. Practice getting the total communication correct. As time goes on, you will need to ask for clarification less often—only when you are unsure of certain parts of the communication.

VALIDATION

The other person has a right to his or her opinion, and that opinion always should be important to you. This is an essential element in healthy communication. The other person needs to know that you value and will try to understand him or her. People need to be validated often, particularly when they disagree with you. Not everything that a person says is wrong. Find the areas that you agree on and emphasize those areas. Always pick out the things you have in common and bring out those points for discussion.

HOW TO USE "I FEEL" STATEMENTS

Practice beginning many of your communications with "I feel." You might not know what is right or wrong in a given situation, but you always know how you feel. Start with your feelings and then fill in what you think is creating those feelings. If you are feeling confused, then you are having many feelings at the same time. Try to break down the feelings and address each one separately. The "I feel" statements prevent you from concentrating on the other person. Communications that begin with "You" can be accusatory and punitive. Instead of pointing out what the other person is doing, concentrate on how you feel and what you think.

BE POSITIVE

Always try to find something positive to say to the other person. Even when you are disagreeing, you need to show the other person that you are going to be reinforcing. This shows the other person that you respect and care about him or her. Be genuine in your compliment; do not say something that is not true. Continue to be positive throughout your communications with others. Being positive is contagious; the more you look at the bright side of things, the better things actually become. A positive attitude can go a long way toward improving communication skills. People like being around someone who is positive. It gives them a lift, and they will want to be around you again.

HOW TO USE PHYSICAL PROXIMITY

One of the most important elements in whether a person will like you or not is physical proximity. People who you are around more often are more likely to be attracted to you. When you are talking with someone, stand or sit at a comfortable distance from that person. In the United States, this is a little more than an arm's length apart. In other countries, this distance can be different, so you must be up on the social norms. Do not have a piece of furniture or something else between you and the other person as you communicate; this increases interpersonal distance. Be conscious of how the other person is feeling. If the person seems uncomfortable, then back up a little.

HOW TO USE TOUCH

Touch is a very powerful communication tool. It is hard to act angry at someone you are touching. Touch increases intimacy and decreases fear. It shows the other person that you value him or her and the relationship. You often can touch someone during a conversation. Try to find that opportunity and take it. Even a simple touch on the arm is a powerful message that says "I care."

HOW TO USE EYE CONTACT

Good communication necessitates good eye contact. If you do not look at the other person, then you will miss a good deal of what the person is saying. Eye contact is a lot like touch; it shows the person that you are interested. It also shows the person that he or she is important enough to warrant your full attention.

BE REINFORCING

Compliment the other person. Say something nice. Tell the person how much you appreciate him or her. Try to be patient and kind. Give the person your full attention. Try to understand the person's point of view. Dress appropriately, and take good care of your appearance and personal hygiene. All of these make you a reinforcing person.

HOW TO PRACTICE COMMUNICATION SKILLS

Find two people and ask them to do the following exercise with you. Watch each of the communication skills in action as you go through the exercise. All of the information disclosed during your conversation should be kept confidential. Each person should have the opportunity to respond to each statement before continuing on to the next item.
Sit close to each other and make eye contact before you speak. Read the first part of the sentence and fill in the rest with your own words.

1. My name is . . .
2. My current hometown is . . .
3. My marital status is . . .
4. My occupation is . . .
5. The reason I am here is . . .
6. Right now, I am feeling . . .

Developing Empathy

1. When I think about the future, I see myself . . .
2. The second person repeats what the first person said until the first person agrees that he or she has been heard correctly.
3. When I am in a new group . . .
4. The second person repeats what the first person said until the first person agrees that he or she has been heard correctly.
5. When I enter a room full of people, I usually feel . . .
6. The second person repeats.
7. When I am feeling anxious in a new situation, I usually . . .

8. For the rest of the exercise, the second person will repeat or question only if he or she does not understand the communication.
9. In groups, I feel the most comfortable when . . .
10. When I am confused, I . . .
11. I am happiest when . . .
12. The thing that turns me on the most is . . .
13. Right now, I am feeling . . .
14. The thing that concerns me the most is . . .
15. When I am rejected, I usually . . .
16. I feel loved when . . .
17. A forceful person makes me feel . . .
18. When I break the rules . . .
19. The thing that turns me off the most is . . .
20. Toward you right now, I feel . . .
21. When I feel lonely, I usually . . .
22. Make a listening check. Have the second person repeat the last communication. "What I hear you saying is . . ."
23. I am rebellious when . . .
24. Take a few minutes to discuss the exercise so far. How do you feel you are doing? Is the level of sharing deep enough? How can you improve the level of sharing? Are you getting to know each other?
25. The emotion I find the most difficult to control is . . .
26. My most frequent daydreams are about . . .
27. My weakest point is . . .
28. I love . . .
29. When I feel jealous, I . . .
30. I am afraid of . . .
31. I believe in . . .
32. I am the most ashamed of . . .
33. Right now, I am the most afraid to discuss . . .
34. Reach out and touch the person on the arm.
35. When I touched you, I felt . . .

Take some time to evaluate each other's communication skills. Talk about what you did well and what you need to work on. Ask for help in developing your skills. Discuss one or two other issues together (e.g., politics, religion, sports, work, family).

Appendix 15

Self-Discipline
Robert R. Perkinson, Ph.D.

Life is full of problems that need to be solved. We can reach our full potential in life only when we meet our problems head-on, accept the responsibility for them, and work toward resolution. Problems cause us to feel pain. This pain is not bad; it is good. It is a motivation for change. It gives us energy and direction for action. We can solve problems only if we learn how to endure this pain. If we always seek immediate pain relief, then we never will stretch ourselves and grow. If we can learn how to delay the instant pleasure, then we can get higher quality and more enduring pleasure later. To get an *A* on an English test next week, we have to study this week. Studying hurts. We must learn how to endure the pain of work to get what we want later. This is the pathway to excellence.

DELAYED GRATIFICATION

Self-discipline requires training and practice. Work does not feel good. If it did, then it would be called play. Work is the expenditure of energy. When we expend energy, things change.

We all want to be champions, but to be champions, we have to work. Professional athletes train every day. It is the only way of excelling. They cannot win a race every day, but they can train for a race every day. They must constantly keep in excellent physical and mental condition. They must be so practiced in their sport that they do things automatically. So it is with us. To do something well, we must practice and learn how to set long-term goals.

Take a piece of paper and write down some things you wanted in your life that you did not get because you did not work hard enough. Perhaps you wanted to go to college or to get a certain job. Did you want a particular car or a certain house? Did you want to go out with someone special? Did you want to play a musical instrument? Find five things you wanted that you did not get. Write those down and take a long look at each of them.

1. _____
2. _____
3. _____
4. _____
5. _____

What would it have taken for you to achieve each of these goals? What work needed to be done that you did not do? Nothing reasonable is out of your grasp if you work hard enough. Write down the steps you needed to take to achieve that goal. Spend time thinking about exactly what needed to be done and think about why you did not do it.

Suppose that you wanted to be a mechanic. The first thing that you would need is training. You need the skills of a mechanic. Where would you get those? You could start with the yellow pages, or you could call an employment service and ask. Now this is work, and nobody likes it. You are having to move and expend energy. It is not fun. It hurts. But you want the job as a mechanic, and you will have to work to get it. It will happen one step at a time, not all at once. You cannot just wish it to be true. You need to be patient. You need to go through the pain first.

Okay, suppose that you look in the yellow pages and find a mechanics school. Now you have to get an application, fill it out, and mail it in. This is getting to be hard work. It is not fun, but it will pay off. You will not get what you want if you do not work for it. If you quit, then you will get nothing, so do not quit. Keep trying. Stay committed for what you want. You deserve the best. Do not settle for less.

THE IMPULSIVE TEMPERAMENT

Some people have a harder time with discipline because they have an impulsive temperament. They are born needing only a little of a feeling to initiate action. For example, they do not need to feel much anger before they act angry. Are you that kind of a person? Do you feel anger easily and act angry quickly? Do you do things impulsively that you feel sorry for later? Impulsive people respond too quickly to their feelings. This can be a problem because they do not naturally stop and think problems through. These individuals do not solve problems well, and they tend to have poor self-discipline.

What would you do if you came home and saw the person you love making love with someone else? "I'd kill them," you might say. This is a typical impulsive response. It went immediately from feeling to action. Now stop and think about it. What good is it going to do you to kill two people? Is this going to really help you? Are you going to feel better? Is your problem solved? You may get transient relief, but what is the long-term consequence? The result of a double homicide will be years of imprisonment. You will experience pain for a long time. If you are a person with an impulsive temperament, then you need to learn how to endure feelings before you act. You need to stop, think, and plan before you act. Until you do this, you will be helpless to circumstances.

These new skills do not come easily. They take practice. When you feel a feeling, particularly an intense one, stop and think the problems through, consider your options, plan your response, and then act. For the next week, keep a log of five situations that give you strong feelings. Write down the situation and the thoughts and feelings you had during the situation. Did you respond appropriately, or did you act impulsively? Learn from your mistakes. Practice.

RULES

Rules do not exist to deny you pleasure. They exist to protect you from pain. If you break the rules, then you will hurt. It is as simple as that. Consistently obeying the rules takes self-discipline. You must decide that the rules are for your own good. The legislature did not make the speed laws to deny you the pleasure of driving fast. They made the rules to keep you safe.

Many of us who have a difficult time with self-discipline were raised in homes where the rules were inconsistent. This is confusing to children. Sometimes our parents would enforce the rules, and sometimes they would not. Sometimes we would get punished (even abusively punished), and sometimes we would get no punishment at all. Sometimes our parents would do the same things they told us not to do. For example, they would tell us not to hit others, and then they would hit us. This teaches children that rules are not important.

A person without rules is a person with no self-respect. It is only when we respect ourselves that we set limits on what we will and will not do. Children know that people who love them set limits for them. There is no one more unhappy than a child with no rules. This child is allowed to be the ruler of the home. This monarch of the house will demand more and more until the child makes himself or herself miserable. Are you important enough to keep safe? If you are, then you need rules.

Get a piece of paper and write down some rules that you have broken. For example, write down three times when you lied or three times when you stole. Write down each situation as completely as you can. You had some good reasons for doing that thing, didn't you? Why did you do it? What good came out of it?

1. _____
2. _____
3. _____

Now write down the consequence of breaking each of those rules. How did you feel about yourself? How did you feel about the other people? What happened?

1. _____
2. _____
3. _____

Now look at each situation and ask yourself this question: Did breaking this rule help me to grow and reach my full potential as a person. Did I honor myself, others, and my Higher Power? You will find that breaking rules results in pain—your pain. Take lying as an example. We lie to avoid getting into trouble. Now, in the short run this works, but in the long run it is interpersonal disaster. We want people to love us. If we lie, then people do not know us, so they cannot love us. In the long run, if you lie, then you will be lonely and you will hurt.

To love, you must be self-disciplined. Love is an action, not a feeling. Love is work. Love takes time, energy, and commitment. To do unto others as you would have them do unto you is not always easy, but you will not experience joy unless you love like this. To love, you must be consistent. If you are selfish, and if you always come first, then you will hurt and you will be deprived of the joy of giving unselfishly to others.

Many parents love without discipline. They do not take time with their children, and they do not solve problems with their children. It is important for children to see their parents hurt with them when the children have a problem. The family members feel the pain together, and they buckle down to solve the problem together. In healthy homes, the family members have confidence that if they work together, they can solve the problem.

HOW TO SOLVE PROBLEMS

Life is an endless puzzle of problems that need to be solved. Problem solving is challenging, necessary, and fun. It needs to be practiced enough times that it gets to be automatic. Get a piece of paper and write down a problem of yours, and we will go through the problem-solving steps together.

1. Write down the problem. What is the problem exactly? How do you feel about it? What do you want to see happen?

2. Make a list of options. What are all of the possible ways in which you can deal with this problem? Get input from others you trust. Ask other people to give you alternatives of action. You will be surprised. Other people will come up with good ideas that you did not have.

3. Consider each option carefully and decide which choice will help you to grow into the person you want to be. If another person is involved, remember to treat that person the same way in which you would want to be treated.

4. Put the option you have chosen into action.

5. Evaluate the effect of your action on the original problem. This gives you information about how to solve future problems.

Problem → Options → Decision → Action → Evaluation

Work through several problems with your counselor or group. Get in the habit of writing down the problem and getting advice on options.

RESPONSIBILITY

To solve a problem effectively, you must accept that problem as *your* problem. If you blame the problem on something else, then you are helpless. It is easy to feel this way, but it is self-defeating. "I would be okay if they would just leave me alone" is a common cry in treatment. This is the cry of someone who is defeated by life. Blaming other people for your problems never is effective. There always is something you can do to make things better. You have great power and influence over your own life. If you sit and do nothing, then nothing will change.

Take a piece of paper and write down five times when you got into trouble. Maybe you were arrested or got into trouble at home or at school.

1. _____

2. _____

3. _____

4. _____

5. _____

Think about your choices that led to this problem. What did you do that ended up getting you in trouble? Think about all of the choices you made along the way that led to the problem. Do not blame anyone else. Just look at your own behavior. Use your counselor and group to help you. If you look closely, you will see that a series of choices—*your* choices—led to these events. Accidents do happen, but most of what happens to you is a result of your choices. Think of how scary the world would be if some other person had the power to make you happy or unhappy. No one has that power but you.

Think of yourself as a gift to the world. There never has been anyone like you. There never will be anyone like you again. You owe the world only one thing—to be different. Only you can do this. Only you can be responsible for what you do. You will change the course of history because you were here. Maybe you will change things for the good, maybe for the bad. Maybe you will change things a little, maybe a lot, but you definitely will change things. Things will be different because you were here. You have a great responsibility to be yourself.

Appendix 16

Impulse Control
Robert R. Perkinson, Ph.D.

You have problems controlling your impulses if you act too quickly on your feelings. You constantly suffer negative consequences because you act without careful thought. If you had stopped to think, you would not have gotten into all that trouble. Maybe you ended up in jail, struck someone you cared for, or just got drunk. This set of exercises is for those people who lose control over their behavior. It outlines the skills necessary to overcome problems with impulse control.

The first thing you have to understand is that you are held accountable in our society only for what you do. You are not held accountable for what you think or for how you feel. Your movements are what count. That is what people see. That is how people judge you. You can think about robbing a bank all day long, and you will not get arrested. But if you rob a bank, then you have committed a crime and might be in big trouble. To control your impulses, you must learn to control your movements.

HOW TO UNDERSTAND YOUR FEELINGS

To control your impulses, you need to understand your feelings. Feelings are impulses, and feelings motivate action. They are a powerful force. They direct behavior. Each feeling is connected to a specific activity. Let's examine several feelings and the actions they stimulate. There are only a few basic feelings. Fear, anger, and sadness are a few of them. Fear motivates you to run, anger motivates you to fight, and sadness motivates you to recover a lost object. Examine each feeling and the movement to which it is attached. Learn that each feeling motivates a specific action, and learn what each feeling is and the action it initiates.

HOW TO DEVELOP GOALS

Now it is time to take a close look at exactly what you want to change. Remembering that behavior is movement, take a piece of paper and detail exactly what you want to do differently. For example, someone who physically abuses his or her spouse or kids would want to write down something like this: "I want to stop hitting my spouse and children."

Study each of your goals. Is it reasonable that you can attain this goal? Make sure that the goal is written in behavioral terms. It needs to be a movement you can see, hear, or feel.

Now that you have the specific behavior you want to change, we can look at exactly how you are going to change.

THE BEHAVIOR CHAIN

Behavior can be analyzed by studying the behavior chain. This chain starts with a stimulus or trigger that initiates a thought, the thought initiates a feeling, and the feeling motivates action. All behavior results in a consequence. This consequence may be positive or negative. The behavior chain looks like this:

Trigger → Thought → Feeling → Behavior → Consequence

There are many points along a behavior chain where you can do things differently. Look at it like this: If you are on a train that is going to Kansas and stay on that train, then you are going to end up in Kansas. Likewise, if you initiate an old behavior chain and continue on that chain, then you are going to end up with the same consequence. Now maybe that behavior got you into a lot of trouble, and maybe you do not want to repeat the behavior. Next time, you want to do something different. The key word here is *doing*. You have to do something different if things are going to change.

Trigger

Let's take a close look at the behavior chain and see where you can change. Behavior will surface under certain situations or triggers. Marlatt and Gordon (1985) grouped relapse triggers into several categories. The first trigger is negative emotions. Old behavior often returns when you are experiencing negative feelings, particularly anger and frustration. You may return to the old behavior under social pressure or when you are in an interpersonal conflict. You may go back to that old behavior when feeling good. Let's list the high-risk situations and spend some time on each one.

1. Negative feelings
2. Social pressure
3. Interpersonal conflict
4. Positive feelings

Negative Feelings

Start by getting out a clean piece of paper and writing the heading "NEGATIVE FEELINGS" at the top of the page. Under this heading, write all of the negative feelings you can think of that lead to the behavior you want to change. Maybe you lapse into the old behavior when you are angry, bored, lonely, happy, embarrassed, frustrated, irritable, or excited. Write down the feelings that seem to precede the action you want to change.

Social Pressure

Make another heading, "SOCIAL PRESSURE," and list all of the social situations in which you are likely to lapse into the old behavior. Remember that social pressure can be direct (e.g., someone actively encouraging you to act in the old way) or indirect (e.g., a social situation in which the behavior might normally occur). Maybe you will be more likely to get back to the old behavior when you are with certain friends or at certain places or events. Write down every social situation in which you feel you will be vulnerable.

Interpersonal Conflict

The "INTERPERSONAL CONFLICT" heading comes next. Make that heading, and under it write every situation you can think of where a conflict with someone else leads to the behavior you want to change. Try to include the total situation. Who said what and how? What happened? When did you lose control? What preceded your behavior?

Positive Feelings

Now write "POSITIVE FEELINGS" as a heading, and list the times when you acted in that old way when feeling good, to celebrate, or to increase the good feeling. Detail each situation and carefully study what you were after and what feelings you wanted to enhance.

Thought

We will analyze thoughts next. These get a little tricky, so pay careful attention to them. Beck, Rush, Shaw, and Emery (1979) developed cognitive therapy for depression. Burns (1980) further developed this technique. Many thoughts are very quick—so quick that they occur out of your awareness. These thoughts are called automatic thoughts because they do not come from anything you try to think. You think them automatically.

Take another piece of paper and near the top write down a situation where you lost control. Write the specific situation in as much detail as you can. Now explore how you were feeling in that situation. Remember that the eight primary feelings are anger, acceptance, joy, sadness, anticipation, fear, surprise, and disgust. Write down each feeling, and score the intensity of the feeling on a scale of 1 to 100 (1 = *as little of the feeling as possible,* 100 = *as much of the feeling as possible*).

Let's take an example. Frank came home, and his spouse angrily asked him where he had been. He was late coming home from work. Frank felt hurt at an intensity of 45, angry at 90, and frightened at 75.

Now it is your turn. You have the situation and all of the feelings you had during that situation. You have scored how intense you were feeling each feeling. Now carefully process with your counselor what you were thinking between the situation and the feelings. This will take some time, so take it slow. Try to think of all the thoughts that came to mind between the event and the feelings. Let's see how Frank did. "My wife asked me where I had been. I thought the following: 'Here we go again. She's mad. She thinks I've been drinking again. She's always mad at me. She never trusts me. She doesn't love me. She has never loved me.'"

Make as long a list of these thoughts as you can. You will be surprised at how many thoughts you can have in a short period of time. Next, look at the thoughts and check them out for accuracy. Which thoughts are accurate and which thoughts are inaccurate? Frank decided that his spouse was mad and that she was worried that he had been drinking again. Those thoughts were accurate, but she was not always mad at him and she trusted him plenty of times. She does love him, and she has loved him for a long time. These thoughts were inaccurate.

With your counselor or with your group, discover which thoughts are accurate and which thoughts are inaccurate. On another sheet, write down the situation again. Write only the accurate thoughts you were having and then score all of the feelings you had listed on the previous page.

Frank did it like this. "My wife asked me where I had been. She was frightened that I had been drinking again and a little angry just at the thought of it. She is very concerned for me. She loves me very much, and she is afraid for my health. That doesn't hurt me at all, so I'd put the hurt at 0. It still makes me a little mad, but much less, so I would put that at 20. That doesn't scare me at all, so I would rate the fear at 0."

Now add up your scores on each sheet, coming up with a total score of all the feelings when you were thinking inaccurately and when you were thinking accurately. This is Frank's sheet:

	Inaccurate Thinking	Accurate Thinking
Hurt	45	0
Angry	90	20
Fear	75	0
Total	210	20

You can now see what we are after. Many of your thoughts are automatic, are inaccurate, and lead to uncomfortable feelings. Some of these feelings are unnecessary because they are inaccurate assessments of reality. Obviously, if you see a situation inaccurately, then you will react inaccurately. If you develop the skill of stopping and assessing the situation accurately, then you will feel more comfortable and be able to deal with the situation with more precision and skill.

For the next few days, keep a running account of any situation that makes you feel uncomfortable and do this exercise again. After a few days, you will notice patterns in your thinking. You will see that you think the same inaccurate thoughts in many different situations. These are thoughts that need to be challenged in treatment. Address them carefully with your group and your counselor, and begin to watch out for them. When they resurface, stop and correct yourself. Try to keep your thinking accurate.

Feelings

All feelings are friendly, even the painful ones. They help us adapt to our environment and give us energy and direction for action. The skill necessary for dealing with feelings appropriately is to learn exactly what coping skills to use when having a particular feeling. Feelings should not be ignored; they should be acted on. Which action to take is the skill you want to learn. You need to spend some time with a few feelings and learn coping skills for dealing with these feelings. Then you must practice the new skills until they become automatic. You cannot just learn what to do. You must practice the actual behavior until it becomes second nature. This will take a lot of time and practice. Do not try to do this perfectly; just make progress.

Anger

Anger gives chemically dependent persons more problems than does any other feeling. You can relapse into old behavior when you feel angry and frustrated. Anger gives you the energy and direction to fight. Anger is good, and fighting is good, so long as the actions are appropriate. The problems arise when we fight all the time or at inappropriate times.

Anger is friendly. It needs to be listened to and expressed. You need to learn how to use your anger assertively rather than aggressively. Much of this work is taken from *Your Perfect Right,* an assertive guide by Alberti and Emmons (1986). They found that verbal and physical aggression rarely is necessary and can even be harmful. Acting on your anger assertively is a much more effective means of getting what you want. Here is an assertive formula that you should memorize and practice until it becomes automatic.

I feel _____

when you _____.

I would prefer it if _____.

When you feel angry with someone, you start by describing how you feel. Then, in behavioral terms, describe what the person did that led to your feelings. Then, again in behavioral terms, tell the person what you want him or her to do. Let's try it in a situation to show how the assertive formula works.

The Aggressive Response

Bob comes home from work 1 hour late. Barbara, his spouse, is hurt and angry.

Barbara: Where have you been? You're such an incredible jerk!

How is Bob going to be feeling—attacked, hurt, angry, defensive? He might retaliate and say something like this:

Bob: What a nag! You're always mad at me!

The Assertive Response

Barbara: I feel hurt and angry when you're late. I would prefer it if you would call me and tell me when you're not going to be on time.

The assertive formula gives the other person accurate information that he or she can use to remedy the situation. The person knows what he or she did and knows what to do differently.

Try the assertive formula at least two times today. After each use, write down the situation and how it turned out. Notice the feelings that you have. If you are like most people, you will feel much more in control of your feelings. You also will get more of what you want. This will lead to less anger.

Fear

Fear is another difficult feeling for people. Fear motivates you to run or withdraw from a dangerous situation. Fear is friendly. Withdrawal is friendly, and it can be adaptive, but it also can be inappropriate. It is important to think accurately and consider the consequences before you withdraw. What are the pros and cons of withdrawing from the situation? It is not appropriate to run from all of your problems even if they are scary. If you did, then you would not solve many of them. You must learn to stand your ground even in a painful situation. That way, you can work a problem through to resolution. If you find that you always are running away, then you must find other coping skills to use when you feel frightened. The same assertive formula works here. "I feel _____ when you _____, I would prefer it if _____" works as well with fear as it does with anger. If people know you are frightened, they often will respond positively to your fear. It even helps to share your fear with someone who is not involved with the immediate situation. Remember to share your feelings. This is a major coping skill. It can be used with all feelings.

Behavior

By now you know that using the right behavior at the right time is the real secret to success when dealing with impulse control problems. It is the movements—the behavior—that people are responsible for, so you must practice not moving quickly. You have to delay action until you have time to think and plan. Some people have to back away from the situation entirely to give themselves the time to think. They might have to go for a walk, a run, or a drive. They might have to leave the house, or the places of conflict, and give themselves some space.

You know yourself the best, and you know beforehand when you are getting ready to lose control. You must practice catching this increase in your feelings before you lose control. At this point, you must move away from the situation. You cannot stay there and hope to achieve control. That is too dangerous. Do not worry. You are going to come back to the problem and the situation is going to be addressed, but you need some time away from the problem. If you stay in a situation where you have lost control, then you are playing with fire. Do not do that to yourself.

Exactly what coping skills to use in a particular situation will take some planning. This planning must take place before the situation, and it must be practiced until it becomes automatic.

Get out another piece of paper and write down the situation you are having difficulty with. Now brainstorm with your counselor and your group. What else could you do in that situation? For example, Barbara is trying to control her tendency to hit her children. She made this plan when she feels angry with them again:

When I'm getting angry, I'm going to do the following:

1. Recognize my anger.
2. Step back from the situation as far as necessary to feel the anger go down and then:
   a. Go into another room.
   b. Go for a walk.
   c. Go for a drive.
   d. Go to my mother's house.
   e. Go talk to a friend next door.
   f. Call my sponsor.
3. When I'm thinking clearly, I will plan my response. I might have to do this with someone I trust.
4. Come back to my children and try my plan.
5. If I get too angry again, I will go back and repeat the whole procedure.

Consequence

It is important to take a careful look at the consequence of your behavior. You will not learn from your actions unless you see clearly what happens when you act in a certain manner. On another piece of paper, write briefly what happened each time you lost control of your actions. Under each situation, write down the negative consequence that resulted from that loss of control. This must be done in great detail. Take a lot of time and think. Do not blame anyone else for what happened. Concentrate on your own actions. Use every situation you can think of. The more clearly you can see the negative consequence of your behavior, the more you will tell yourself never to act that way again. You can learn from your behavior if you stop, think, and plan before you act.

We have looked carefully at the behavior you want to change. We have studied the trigger, thought, feeling, behavior, and consequence. Now let's go over what you are going to do when you are in a high-risk situation. What is your plan when you feel impulsive? First, think of the word *STOP.*

S = *stop:* Stop and commit yourself to a rational response.

T = *think:*
1. What is the situation?
2. What is at stake?
3. Get your thinking accurate.

O = *options:*
1. What are the options?
2. What are the pros and cons of each option?
3. Choose the best option.

P = *plan:* Carry out the plan.

With your counselor and group, work through the situations and feelings that you are having the most difficulty with. If you are having a difficult time with anger, then discuss your anger carefully in individual sessions and in group. Come up with specific coping skills to deal with each feeling. Exactly what are you going to do? List options available to you, and carry them in your pocket or purse. Now practice, practice, practice. When you lapse into the old behavior, do not give up. Use the lapse as an education. What happened? What coping skill could you have used? How can you do things differently next time? You can do this. You no longer have to be a slave to your impulses. You can change your behavior. You have all of the necessary skills.

Appendix 17

Relapse Prevention
Robert R. Perkinson, Ph.D.

There is some bad news and some good news about relapse. The bad news is that many patients have problems with relapse in early sobriety. About two thirds of patients coming out of addiction programs relapse within 3 months of leaving treatment (Hunt, Barnett, & Branch, 1971). The good news is that most people who go through treatment ultimately achieve a stable recovery (Frances, Bucky, & Alexopolos, 1984). Relapse does not have to happen to you, and even if it does, you can do something about it. Relapse prevention is a daily program that can prevent relapse. It also can stop a lapse from becoming a disaster. This exercise has been developed using a combination of the models of Gorski and Miller (1986) and Marlatt and Gordon (1985). This uses the disease concept model in combination with a behavioral approach.

RELAPSE IS A PROCESS

Relapse is a process that begins long before you use drugs or alcohol. There are symptoms that precede the first use of chemicals. This exercise teaches you how to identify and control these symptoms before they lead to actual drug or alcohol use. If you allow these symptoms to go on without acting on them, then serious problems will result.

THE RELAPSE WARNING SIGNS

All relapse begins with warning signs that will signal for you that you are in trouble. If you do not recognize these signs, you will decompensate and finally use chemicals. All of the signs are a reaction to stress, and they are a reemergence of the disease. They are a means by which your body and mind are telling you that you are in trouble. Gorski and Miller (1982) recognized 37 warning signs in patients who had relapsed. You might not have all of these symptoms, but you will have some of them long before you actually use chemicals. You must determine which symptoms are the most characteristic of you, and you must come up with coping skills for dealing with each symptom.

Listed below are the 37 warning symptoms. Circle the ones that you have experienced before you used drugs or alcohol.

1. Apprehension about well-being
2. Denial
3. Adamant commitment to sobriety
4. Compulsive attempts to impose sobriety on others
5. Defensiveness
6. Compulsive behavior
7. Impulsive behavior
8. Loneliness
9. Tunnel vision
10. Minor depression
11. Loss of constructive planning
12. Plans beginning to fail
13. Idle daydreaming and wishful thinking
14. Feeling nothing can be solved
15. Immature wish to be happy
16. Periods of confusion
17. Irritation with friends
18. Easily angered

19. Irregular eating habits
20. Listlessness
21. Irregular sleeping habits
22. Progressive loss of daily structure
23. Periods of deep depression
24. Irregular attendance at meetings
25. Development of an "I don't care" attitude
26. Open rejection of help
27. Dissatisfaction with life
28. Feelings of powerlessness and helplessness
29. Self-pity
30. Thoughts of social use
31. Conscious lying
32. Complete loss of self-confidence
33. Unreasonable resentments
34. Discontinuing all treatment
35. Overwhelming loneliness, frustration, anger, and tension
36. Start of controlled using
37. Loss of control

WHAT TO DO WHEN YOU EXPERIENCE A WARNING SIGN

When you recognize any of these symptoms, you need to take action. Make a list of the coping skills you can use when you experience a symptom that is common for you. This will happen. You will have problems in recovery. Your task is to take affirmative action. Remember, a symptom is a danger signal. You are in trouble. Make a list of what you are going to do. Are you going to call your sponsor, go to a meeting, call your counselor, call someone in AA/NA, tell someone, exercise, read the "Big Book" (Alcoholics Anonymous, 1976), pray, become involved in an activity you enjoy, turn it over, or go into treatment? Detail several plans of action.

Plan 1. _____
Plan 2. _____
Plan 3. _____
Plan 4. _____
Plan 5. _____
Plan 6. _____
Plan 7. _____
Plan 8. _____
Plan 9. _____
Plan 10. _____

You need to check each warning symptom daily in your personal inventory. You also need to have other people check you daily. You will not always pick up the symptoms in yourself. You might be denying the problem again. Your spouse, your sponsor, and/or a fellow AA/NA member can warn you when they believe that you might be in trouble. Listen to these people. If they tell you that they sense a problem, then take action. You might need professional help in working the problem through. Do not hesitate to call and ask for help. Anything is better than relapsing. If you overreact to a warning sign, you are not going to be in trouble. But if you underreact, you might be headed for real problems. Chemical dependency is a deadly disease. Your life is at stake.

THE HIGH-RISK SITUATIONS

Marlatt and Gordon (1985) found that relapse is more likely to occur in certain situations. These situations can trigger relapse. They found that people relapsed when faced with life situations that they could not cope with except by using chemicals. Your job in treatment is to develop coping skills for dealing with each high-risk situation.

Negative Emotions

About 35% of people who relapse do so when feeling a negative feeling that they cannot cope with. Most feel angry or frustrated, but some feel anxious, bored, lonely, or depressed. Almost any negative feeling can lead to relapse if you do not learn how to cope with the feeling. Feelings motivate you to take action. You must act to solve any problem.
Circle any of the following feelings that seem to lead you to use chemicals.

Loneliness	Envious	Selfish	Scared	Irritated
Anger	Exhausted	Restless	Spiteful	Overwhelmed
Rejection	Bored	Weak	Sorrowful	Panicked
Emptiness	Anxious	Sorrowful	Helpless	Trapped
Annoyed	Ashamed	Greedy	Neglected	Unsure
Sad	Bitter	Aggravated	Grief	Intimidated
Exasperated	Burdened	Exasperated	Confused	Distraught
Betrayed	Foolish	Miserable	Crushed	Uneasy
Cheated	Jealous	Unloved	Discontented	Guilty
Frustrated	Left out	Worried	Restless	Threatened

A Plan to Deal With Negative Emotions

These are just a few of the feeling words. Add more if you need to do so. Develop coping skills for dealing with each feeling that makes you vulnerable to relapse. Exactly what are you going to do when you have this feeling? Detail your specific plan of action. Some options are talking to your sponsor, calling a friend in the program, going to a meeting, calling your counselor, reading some recovery material, turning it over to your Higher Power, and getting some exercise. For each feeling, develop a specific plan of action.

Feeling _____

    Plan 1. _____

    Plan 2. _____

    Plan 3. _____

Feeling _____

    Plan 1. _____

    Plan 2. _____

    Plan 3. _____

Feeling _____

    Plan 1. _____

    Plan 2. _____

    Plan 3. _____

Continue to fill out these feeling forms until you have all of the feelings that give you trouble and you have coping skills for dealing with each feeling.

Social Pressure

About 20% of people relapse in a social situation. Social pressure can be direct (where someone directly encourages you to use chemicals) or indirect (a social situation where people are using). Both of these situations can trigger intense craving, and this can lead to relapse. More than 60% of alcoholics relapse in bars.

Certain friends are more likely to encourage you to use chemicals. These people do not want to hurt you. They want you to relax and have a good time. They want their old friend back. They do not understand the nature of your disease. Perhaps they are chemically dependent themselves and are in denial.

High-Risk Friends

Make a list of the friends who might encourage you to use drugs or alcohol.

1. _____
2. _____
3. _____
4. _____
5. _____

What are you going to do when they offer you drugs? What are you going to say? In group, set up a situation where the whole group encourages you to use chemicals. Look carefully at how you feel when the group members are encouraging you. Look at what you say. Have them help you to develop appropriate ways of saying no.

High-Risk Social Situations

Certain social situations will trigger craving. These are the situations where you have used chemicals in the past. Certain bars or restaurants, a particular part of town, certain music, athletic events, parties, weddings, family events—all of these situations can trigger intense cravings. Make a list of five social situations where you will be vulnerable to relapse.

1. _____
2. _____
3. _____
4. _____
5. _____

In early sobriety, you will need to avoid these situations and friends. To put yourself in a high-risk situation is asking for trouble. If you have to attend a function where there will be people using chemicals, then take someone with you who is in the program. Take someone with you who will support you in your sobriety. Make sure that you have a way to get home. You do not have to stay and torture yourself. You can leave if you feel uncomfortable. Avoid all situations where your sobriety feels shaky.

Interpersonal Conflict

About 16% of people relapse when in a conflict with some other person. They have a problem with someone and have no idea of how to cope with the problem. The stress of the problem builds and leads to drinking or using drugs. This conflict usually happens with someone who they are closely involved with—wife, husband, child, parent, sibling, friend, boss, and so on.

You can have a serious problem with anyone—even a stranger—so you must have a plan for dealing with interpersonal conflict. You will develop specific skills in treatment that will help you to communicate even when you are under stress.

You need to learn and practice the following interpersonal skills repeatedly.

1. Tell the truth all of the time.
2. Share how you feel.

3. Ask for what you want.
4. Find some truth in what the other person is saying.
5. Be willing to compromise.

If you can stay in the conflict and work it out, that is great. But if you cannot, then you have to leave the situation and get help. You might have to go for a walk, a run, or a drive. You might need to cool down. You must stop the conflict. You cannot continue to try to deal with a situation that you believe is too much for you. Do not feel bad about this. Interpersonal relationships are the hardest challenge we face. Carry a card with you that lists the people who you can contact. You might want to call your sponsor, minister, or counselor or a fellow AA/NA member, friend, family member, doctor, or anyone else who may support you.

In an interpersonal conflict, you will fear abandonment. You need to get accurate and reassure yourself that you have many people who still care about you. Remember that your Higher Power cares about you. A Higher Power created you and loves you perfectly. Remember the other people in your life who love you. This is one of the main reasons for talking with someone else. When the other person listens to you, that person gives you the feeling that you are loved.

If you still feel afraid or angry, then get with someone you trust and stay with that person until you feel safe. Do not struggle out there all by yourself. Any member of AA or NA will understand how you are feeling. We all have had these problems. We all have felt lost, helpless, hopeless, and angry.

Make an emergency card that lists all of the people who you can call if you are having difficulty. Write down their phone numbers and carry this card with you at all times. Show this card to your counselor. Practice asking someone for help in treatment once each day. Write down the situation and show it to your counselor. Get into the habit of asking for help. When you get out of treatment, call someone every day just to stay in touch and keep the lines of communication open. Get used to it. Do not wait to ask for help at the last minute. This makes asking more difficult.

Positive Feelings

About 12% of people relapse when they are feeling positive emotions. Think of all the times you used drugs and alcohol to celebrate. That has gotten to be such a habit that when something good happens, you will immediately think about using. You need to be ready when you feel like a winner. This may be at a wedding, birth, promotion, or any event where you feel good. How are you going to celebrate without drugs and alcohol? Make a celebration plan. You might have to take someone with you to a celebration, particularly in early recovery.

Positive feelings also can work when you are by yourself. A beautiful spring day can be enough to get you thinking about drinking or using. You need an action plan for when these thoughts pass through your mind. You must immediately get accurate and get real. In recovery, we are committed to reality. Do not sit there and recall how wonderful you will feel if you get high. Tell yourself the truth. Think about all of the pain that chemical dependency has caused you. If you toy with positive feelings, then you ultimately will use chemicals.

Circle the positive feelings that may make you vulnerable to relapse.

Affection	Joy	Lazy	Silly	Ecstatic
Bold	Free	Loving	Vivacious	Upbeat
Brave	Glad	Peaceful	Adequate	Splendid
Calm	Glee	Pleasant	Efficient	Yearning
Capable	Happy	Pleased	Successful	Bliss
Cheerful	Honored	Sexy	Accomplished	Excited
Confident	Horny	Wonderful	Hopeful	Exhilarated
Delightful	Infatuated	Cool	Cheery	Proud
Desire	Inspired	Relaxed	Elated	Aroused
Enchanted	Kinky	Reverent	Merry	Festive

A Plan to Cope With Positive Feelings

These are the feelings that may make you vulnerable to relapse. You must be careful when you are feeling good. Make an action plan for dealing with each positive emotion that makes you vulnerable to using chemicals.

Feeling _____
    Plan 1. _____
    Plan 2. _____
    Plan 3. _____
Feeling _____
    Plan 1. _____
    Plan 2. _____
    Plan 3. _____

Feeling _____
    Plan 1. _____
    Plan 2. _____
    Plan 3. _____

Continue this planning until you develop a plan for each of the positive feelings that make you vulnerable.

TEST PERSONAL CONTROL

About 5% of people relapse to test whether they can use chemicals again. They fool themselves into thinking that they might be able to use normally. This time they will use only a little. This time they will be able to control themselves. People who fool themselves this way are in for big trouble. From the first use, most people are in full-blown relapse within 30 days.

Testing personal control begins with inaccurate thinking. It takes you back to Step One. You need to think accurately. You are powerless over mood-altering chemicals. If you use, then you will lose. It is as simple as that. You are physiologically, psychologically, and socially addicted to mood-altering chemicals. The cells in your body will not suddenly change no matter how long you are clean and sober. You are chemically dependent in your cells. This never will change.

HOW TO SEE THROUGH THE FIRST USE

You need to look at how the illness part of yourself will try to convince you that you are not chemically dependent. The illness will flash on the screen of your consciousness all the good things that drugs and alcohol did for you. Make a list of these things. In the first column, marked "Early Use," write down some of the good things that you were getting out of using chemicals. Why were you using? What good came out of it? Did it make you feel social, smart, pretty, intelligent, brave, popular, desirable, relaxed, or sexy? Did it help you to sleep? Did it make you feel confident? Did it help you to forget your problems? Make a long list. These are the good things that you were getting when you first started using. This is why you were using.

Early Use	*Late Use*
1. _____	1. _____
2. _____	2. _____
3. _____	3. _____
4. _____	4. _____
5. _____	5. _____
6. _____	6. _____
7. _____	7. _____
8. _____	8. _____
9. _____	9. _____
10. _____	10. _____

Now go back and place in the second column, marked "Late Use," how you were doing in that area once you became chemically dependent. How were you doing in that same area right before you came into treatment? Did you still feel social, or did you feel alone? Did you still feel intelligent, or did you feel stupid? You will find that a great change has taken place. The very things that you were using for in early use, you get the opposite of in late use. If you were drinking for sleep, then you could not sleep. If you were using to be more popular, then you felt more isolated and alone. If you were using to feel brave, then you were feeling more afraid. This is a major characteristic of chemical dependency.

Take a long look at both of these lists and think about how the illness is going to try to work inside of your thinking. The addicted part of yourself will present to you all of the good things you got in early use. This is how the disease will encourage you to use. But you must see through the first use to the consequences that are dead ahead.

Look at that second list. You must see the misery that is coming if you use chemicals. For most people who relapse, there are only a few days of controlled use before loss of control sets in. There usually are only a few hours or days before all of the bad stuff begins to click back into place. Relapse is terrible. It is the most intense misery that you can imagine.

LAPSE AND RELAPSE

A lapse is the use of any mood-altering chemical. A relapse is continuing to use the chemical until the full biological, psychological, and social disease is present. All of the complex biological, psychological, and social components of the disease become evident very quickly.

THE LAPSE PLAN

You must have a plan in case you lapse. It is foolish to think that you never will have a problem again. You must plan what you are going to do if you have a problem. Hunt et al. (1971), in a study of recovering addicts, found that 33% of patients lapsed within 2 weeks of leaving treatment, and 60% lapsed within 3 months. At the end of 8 months, 63% had used. At the end of 12 months, 67% had used.

The worst thing you can do when you have a lapse is to think that you have completely failed in recovery. This is inaccurate thinking. You are not a total failure. You have not lost everything. You have made a mistake, and you need to learn from it. You let some part of your program go, and you are paying for it. You need to examine exactly what happened and get back into recovery.

A lapse is an emergency. It is a matter of life or death. You must take immediate action to prevent the lapse from becoming a full relapse. You must call someone in the program, preferably your sponsor, and tell that person what happened. You need to carefully examine why you had a problem. You cannot use drugs and alcohol and the tools of recovery at the same time. Something went wrong. You did not use your new skills. You must make a plan of action to recover from your lapse. You cannot do this by yourself. You are in denial. You do not know the whole truth. If you did, you would not have relapsed.

Call your sponsor or a professional counselor and have that person develop a new treatment plan for you. You may need to attend more meetings. You may need to see a counselor. You may need outpatient treatment. You may need inpatient treatment. You have to get honest with yourself. You need to develop a plan and follow it. You need someone else to agree to keep an eye on you for a while. Do not try to do this alone. What we cannot do alone, we can do together.

THE BEHAVIOR CHAIN

All behavior occurs in a certain sequence. First there is the *trigger*. This is the external event that starts the behavioral sequence. After the trigger, there comes *thinking*. Much of this thinking is very fast, and you will not consciously pick it up unless you stop and think about it. The thoughts trigger *feeling,* which gives you energy and direction for action. Next comes the *behavior* or the action initiated by the trigger. Last, there always is a *consequence* for any action. Diagrammed, the behavior chain looks like this:

Trigger → Thinking → Feeling → Behavior → Consequence

Let's go through a behavioral sequence and see how it works. On the way home from work, Bob, a recovering alcoholic, passes the local bar. (This is the trigger.) He thinks, "I've had a hard day. I need a couple of beers to unwind." (The trigger initiates thinking.) Bob craves a beer. (The thinking initiates feeling.) Bob turns into the bar and begins drinking. (The feeling initiates behavior.) Bob relapses. (The behavior has a consequence.)

Let's work through another example. It is 11 p.m. and Bob is not asleep (trigger). He thinks, "I'll never get to sleep tonight unless I have a few drinks" (thinking). He feels an increase in his anxiety about not sleeping (feeling). He gets up and consumes a few drinks (behavior). He gets drunk and wakes up hung over and unable to work the next morning (consequence).

How to Cope With Triggers

At every point along the behavior chain, you can work on preventing relapse. First you need to carefully examine your triggers. What environmental events lead you to using chemicals? We went over some of these when we examined high-risk situations. Determine what people, places, or things make you vulnerable to relapse. Stay away from these triggers as much as possible. If a trigger occurs, then use your new coping skills.

Do not let the trigger initiate old behavior. Stop and think. Do not let your thinking get out of control. Challenge your thinking and get accurate about what is real. Let's look at some common inaccurate thoughts.

1. It is not going to hurt.
2. No one is going to know.
3. I need to relax.
4. I am just going to have a couple.
5. I have had a hard day.
6. My friends want me to drink.
7. I never had a problem with pot.
8. It is the only way I can sleep.
9. I can do anything I want to.
10. I am lonely.

All of these inaccurate thoughts can be used to fuel the craving that leads to relapse. You must stop and challenge your thinking until you are thinking accurately. You must replace inaccurate thoughts with accurate ones. You are chemically dependent. If you drink or use drugs, then you will die. That is the truth. Think through the first drink. Get honest with yourself.

How to Cope With Craving

If you think inaccurately, then you will begin craving. This is the powerful feeling that drives compulsive drug use. Craving is like an ocean wave; it will build and then wash over you. Craving does not last long if you move away from your drug of choice. If you move closer to the drug, then the craving will increase until you are compelled to use. Immediately on feeling a desire to use, think this thought:

"Drinking (or drug use) no longer is an option for me."

Now drinking and using drugs no longer is an option. What are your options? You are in trouble. You are craving. What are you going to do to prevent relapse? You must move away from your drug of choice. Perhaps you need to call your sponsor, go to a meeting, turn it over, call the AA/NA hotline, call the treatment center, call your counselor, go for a walk, run, or visit someone. You must do something else other than thinking about chemicals. Do not sit there and ponder using. You will lose that debate. This illness is called the great debater. If you leave it unchecked, it will seduce you into using chemicals.

Remember that the illness must lie to work. You must uncover the lie as quickly as possible and get back to the truth. You must take the appropriate action necessary to maintain your sobriety.

DEVELOP A DAILY RELAPSE PREVENTION PROGRAM

If you work a daily program of recovery, then your chances of success increase greatly. You need to evaluate your recovery daily and keep a log. This is your daily inventory.

1. Assess all relapse warning signs.
   a. What symptoms did I see in myself today?
   b. What am I going to do about them?
2. Assess love of self.
   a. What did I do to love myself today?
   b. What am I going to do tomorrow?
3. Assess love of others.
   a. What did I do to love others today?
   b. What am I going to do tomorrow?
4. Assess love of God.
   a. What did I do to love God today?
   b. What am I going to do tomorrow?
5. Assess sleep pattern.
   a. How am I sleeping?
6. Assess exercise.
   a. Am I getting enough exercise?
7. Assess nutrition.
   a. Am I eating right?
8. Review total recovery program.
   a. How am I doing in recovery?
   b. What is the next step in my recovery program?
9. Read the *24 Hours a Day* book (Walker, 1992).
10. Make conscious contact with God.
    a. Pray and meditate for a few minutes.
    b. Relax completely.

Fill out this inventory every day following treatment, and keep a journal about how you are doing. You will be amazed as you read back over your journal from time to time. You will be surprised at how much you have grown.
Make a list of 10 reasons why you want to stay clean and sober.

1. _____
2. _____
3. _____
4. _____
5. _____
6. _____
7. _____
8. _____
9. _____
10. _____

Never forget these reasons. Read this list often, and carry a copy with you. If you are struggling in sobriety, then take it out and read it to yourself. You are important. No one has to live a life of misery. You can recover and live a clean and sober life.

Appendix 18

Step One

We admitted that we were powerless over alcohol—that our lives had become unmanageable.

—Alcoholics Anonymous (1976, p. 59)

Before beginning this exercise, read Step One in *Twelve Steps and Twelve Traditions* (Alcoholics Anonymous, 1981).

No one likes to admit defeat. Our minds rebel at the very thought that we have lost control. We are big, strong, intelligent, and capable. How can it be that we are powerless? How can it be that our lives are unmanageable? This exercise will help you to sort through your life and make some important decisions. Answer each question that applies to you as completely as you can. This is an opportunity for you to get accurate. You need to see the truth about yourself.

Let's pretend for a moment that you are the commander in a nuclear missile silo. You are in charge of a 10-megaton bomb. If you think about it, this is exactly the kind of control you want over your life. You want to be in control of your thinking, feeling, and behavior. You want to be in control all of the time, not just some of the time. If you do something by accident or do something foolishly, you might kill a lot of people. You never want to be out of control of your behavior, not even for a second.

People who are powerless over alcohol or drugs occasionally will be under the influence of the chemical when they are doing something physically hazardous. They may be intoxicated or hung over when they are at work, using dangerous equipment, or driving. About 25,000 Americans are killed each year driving while intoxicated. If you have ever done anything like this, then you have been out of control. You have risked your own life and the lives of others. Surely you cannot drive better when you are intoxicated than when you are sober. Now it is time to get honest with yourself.

POWERLESSNESS

1. Have you ever been intoxicated when you were doing something dangerous? For example, have you ever driven a car when you were using? Give some examples.

_____

_____

_____

2. Did you think that you were placing your life and the lives of others in jeopardy? What were you thinking?

_____

_____

_____

3. Whose lives did you risk? Make a list of those people you endangered.

_____

_____

_____

4. How do you feel about what you did?

_____

_____

_____

People who are powerless occasionally will do things while intoxicated or hung over that they feel bad or guilty about later. They might act foolishly at a party, act out sexually, get angry, or say things they do not mean. Have you ever done anything while intoxicated that you felt guilty or bad about later? Make a list of the things that made you feel the most uncomfortable.

1. _____
2. _____
3. _____
4. _____
5. _____

People who are powerless gradually will lose respect for themselves. They will have difficulty in trusting themselves. In what ways have you lost respect for yourself due to drug or alcohol use?

1. _____
2. _____
3. _____

People who are powerless will do things that they do not remember doing. If you drink enough or use enough drugs, you cannot remember things properly. You might have people come up to you after a party and tell you something you did that you do not remember doing. You might wake up and not know where you are. You might not remember how you got home. This is a blackout, and it is very scary. You could have done anything. Most blackouts last a few minutes, but some can go on for hours or days.

1. Describe any blackouts you have had.

_____

_____

_____

2. How does it feel to know that you did something that you do not remember?

_____

_____

_____

3. Think for a minute of what you could have done. You could have done anything, and you would not have known it.

People who are powerless cannot keep promises that they make to themselves or others. They promise that they will cut down on their drinking, and they do not. They promise that they will not use, and they do. They promise to be home, to work, to be at the Cub Scout meeting, or to go to school, but they do not make it. They cannot always do what they want to do because sometimes they are too intoxicated or hung over. They disappoint themselves, and they lose trust in themselves. Other people lose trust in them. They can count on themselves some of the time, but they cannot count on themselves all of the time.

1. Did you ever promise yourself that you would cut down on your drug or alcohol use?

    Yes _____ No _____

2. What happened to these promises?

    _____

    _____

    _____

3. Did you ever promise yourself that you would quit entirely?

    Yes _____ No _____

4. What happened to your promise?

    _____

    _____

    _____

5. Did you ever make a promise to someone that you did not keep because you were intoxicated or hung over? Give a few examples.

    _____

    _____

    _____

6. Are you reliable when you are intoxicated?

    Yes _____ No _____

People who are powerless have accidents. They fall down, or have accidents with their cars, when they are intoxicated. Evidence proves that drugs profoundly affect thinking, coordination, and reaction time.

Have you ever had an accident while intoxicated? Describe each accident.

_____

_____

_____

People who are powerless lose control of their behavior. They do things that they would not normally do when they are clean and sober. They might get into fights. They might hit or yell at people they love—a spouse, child, parent, or friend. They might say things that they do not mean.

Have you ever gotten into a fight when you were intoxicated? Describe each instance.

_____

_____

_____

People who are powerless say things that they do not mean. They might say sexual or angry things that they feel bad about later. They might not remember everything they said, but the other people do remember.

Have you ever said something you did not mean while intoxicated? What did you say? What did you do?

_____

_____

_____

People are powerless when they have feelings that they cannot deal with. They might drink or use drugs because they feel frightened, angry, or sad. They medicate their feelings.

Have you ever used drugs to cover up your feelings? Give a few examples.

_____

_____

_____

What feelings do you have difficulty dealing with?

_____

_____

_____

People are powerless when they are not safe. What convinces you that you no longer can use drugs or alcohol safely?

_____

_____

_____

People are powerless when they know that they should do something but they cannot do it. They may make a great effort, but they just cannot seem to finish what they started out to do.

1. Could you cut down on your drug or alcohol use every time you wanted and for as long as you wanted?
   Yes _____ No _____

2. Did being intoxicated or hung over ever keep you from doing something at home that you thought you should do? Give some examples.

_____

_____

_____

3. Did being intoxicated or hung over ever keep you from going to work? Give some examples.

_____

_____

_____

4. Did you ever lose a job because of your drinking or drug use? Write down what happened.

_____

_____

_____

People are powerless when other people have to warn them that they are in trouble. You may have felt like you were fine, but people close to you noticed that something was wrong. It probably was difficult for them to put their finger on just what was wrong, but they were worried about you. It is difficult to confront someone when the person is wrong, so people avoid doing so until they cannot stand the behavior anymore. When addicts are confronted with their behavior, they feel annoyed and irritated. They want to be left alone with the lies that they are telling themselves.

Has anyone ever talked to you about your drinking or drug use? Who? How did you feel?

_____

_____

_____

People are powerless when they do not know the truth about themselves. Addicts lie to themselves about how much they are drinking or using. They lie to themselves about how often they use. They lie to themselves about their problems, even when the problems are obvious. They blame others for their problems. Here are some common lies they tell themselves:

"I can quit anytime I want to."
"I only had a couple."
"The police were out to get me."
"I only use when I need it."
"Everybody does it."
"I was drinking but I wasn't drunk."
"Anybody can get arrested for drunk driving."
"My friends won't like me if I don't use."
"I never have problems when I drink beer."
"I won't drink until after 5 o'clock."
"From now on, I'll only smoke pot."
"I'm going to cut down to five pills a day."

Addicts continue to lie to themselves to the very end. They hold onto their delusional thinking, and they believe that their lies are the truth. They deliberately lie to those close to them. They hide their use. They make their problems seem smaller than they actually are. They make excuses for why they are using. They refuse to see the truth.

1. Have you ever lied to yourself about your chemical use? List some of the lies you told yourself.

_____
_____
_____

2. List the ways in which you tried to convince yourself that you did not have a problem.

_____
_____
_____

3. List some of the ways in which you tried to convince others that you did not have a problem.

_____
_____
_____

UNMANAGEABILITY

Imagine that you are the manager of a large corporation. You are responsible for how everything runs. If you are not a good manager, then your business will fail. You must carefully plan everything and carry out those plans well. You must be alert. You must know exactly where you are and where you are going. These are the skills you need to manage your life effectively.

Chemically dependent persons are not good managers. They keep losing control. Their plans fall through. They cannot devise and stick to things long enough to see a solution. They are lying to themselves, so they do not know where they are and they are too confused to decide where they want to go next. Their feelings are being medicated, so they cannot use their feelings to give them energy and direction for problem solving. Problems do not get solved; they escalate.

You do not have to be a bad manager all of the time to be a bad manager. It is worse to be a bad manager some of the time. It is totally confusing. Most chemically dependent persons have flurries of productive activity when they work too much. They work themselves to the bone, and then they let things slide. It is like being on a roller-coaster. Sometimes things are in control; sometimes things are out of control. Things are up and down, and they never can predict which way things are going to be tomorrow.

People's lives are unmanageable when they have plans fall apart because they were too intoxicated or hung over to complete them. Make a list of the plans you failed to complete because of your chemical use.

_____

_____

_____

People's lives are unmanageable when they cannot manage their finances consistently.

    1. List any money problems you are having.

_____

_____

_____

    2. Are any of these problems the result of your chemical dependency? Explain how chemicals have contributed to the problems.

_____

_____

_____

People's lives are unmanageable when they cannot trust their own judgment.

    Have you ever been so intoxicated that you did not know what was happening? Explain.

_____

_____

_____

    Did you ever lie to yourself about your chemical use? Explain how your lies contributed to your being unable to manage your life.

_____

_____

_____

    Have you ever made a decision while intoxicated that you were sorry about later? Explain.

_____

_____

_____

People's lives are unmanageable if people cannot work or play normally. Addicts miss work and recreational activities because of their drug use. They make excuses, but the real reason that they missed these events was that they were too intoxicated or hung over.

    Have you ever missed work because you were too intoxicated or hung over? List the times.

_____

_____

_____

Have you ever missed recreational or family activities because you were too drunk or hung over? List the times.

_____

_____

_____

People's lives are unmanageable if they are in trouble with other people or society. Chemically dependent persons will break the rules to get their own way. They have problems with authority.

Have you ever been in legal trouble when you were drinking or using drugs? Describe the legal problems that you have had.

_____

_____

_____

Have you ever had problems with your parents because of your drinking or using drugs? Explain.

_____

_____

_____

Have you ever had problems in school because of your chemical use? Explain.

_____

_____

_____

People's lives are unmanageable if people cannot consistently achieve their goals. Chemically dependent people reach out for what they want, but something keeps getting in the way. It does not seem fair. They keep falling short of their goals. Finally, they give up completely. They may have had the goal of going to school, getting a better job, improving their family problems, getting in good physical condition, or going on a diet. No matter what the goals are, something keeps going wrong. Chemically dependent people always will try to blame other people, but they cannot work hard enough or long enough to reach their goals. Alcoholics and drug addicts are good starters, but they are poor finishers.

List the goals that you had for yourself that you did not achieve.

_____

_____

_____

People's lives are unmanageable if people cannot use their feelings appropriately. Feelings give us energy and direction for problem solving. Chemically dependent people medicate their feelings with drugs or alcohol. The substance gives them a different feeling—a chemically induced feeling. Chemically dependent people become very confused about how they feel.

What feelings have you tried to alter with the use of chemicals?

_____

_____

_____

What feelings are created by your drug of choice? How do you feel when you are intoxicated or hung over?

_____

_____

_____

People's lives are unmanageable if they violate their own rules or when they violate their own morals and values. Chemically dependent persons compromise their values to continue using chemicals. They have the value not to lie, but they lie anyway. They have the value not to steal, but they steal anyway. They have the value to be loyal to their spouses or friends, but when they are intoxicated or hung over, they do not remain loyal. Their values and morals fall away, one by one. They end up doing things that they do not believe in. They know that they are doing the wrong thing, but they do it anyway.

Did you ever lie to cover up your chemical use? How did you feel about yourself?

_____

_____

_____

Were you ever disloyal when using chemicals? Explain.

_____

_____

_____

Did you ever steal to get your drugs? Explain what you did and how you felt about yourself later.

_____

_____

_____

Did you ever break the law when intoxicated? What did you do?

_____

_____

_____

Did you ever hit someone you loved while intoxicated or hung over. Explain.

_____

_____

_____

Did you treat yourself poorly by refusing to stop drinking or using drugs? Explain how you were feeling about yourself.

_____

_____

_____

Did you stop going to church? How did this make you feel about yourself?

_____

_____

_____

People's lives are unmanageable when they continue to do things that give them problems. Chemicals create physical problems: headaches, ulcers, nausea, vomiting, cirrhosis, and many other physical problems. Even if chemically dependent persons are aware of physical problems caused by chemicals, they keep on using anyway.

Chemicals cause psychological problems. They can make people feel depressed, fearful, anxious, or overly angry. Even if alcoholics or drug addicts are aware of these symptoms, they will continue to use.

Chemicals create relationship problems. They cause family problems such as family fights and verbal and physical abuse. They cause interpersonal conflicts at work, with family, and with friends. Chemically dependent persons withdraw and become more isolated and alone. Even if they believe that the problems are caused by the alcohol or drugs, they continue to use.

Did you have any persistent physical problems that were caused by your chemical use? Describe the problems.

_____
_____
_____

Did you have any persistent psychological problems, such as depression, that were caused by your chemical use? Describe the problems.

_____
_____
_____

Did you have a persistent interpersonal conflict that was exacerbated by your chemical use? Describe this problem.

_____
_____
_____

You must have good reasons to work toward a clean and sober lifestyle. Look over this exercise and list 10 reasons why you want to continue to remain clean and sober.

1. _____
2. _____
3. _____
4. _____
5. _____
6. _____
7. _____
8. _____
9. _____
10. _____

After completing this exercise, take a long look at yourself.

1. Have there been times when you were powerless over drugs or alcohol?

   Yes _____   No _____

2. Have there been times when your life was unmanageable?

   Yes _____   No _____

Appendix 19

Step Two

[We] came to believe that a power greater than ourselves could restore us to sanity.
—Alcoholics Anonymous (1976, p. 59)

Before beginning this exercise, read Step Two in *Twelve Steps and Twelve Traditions* (Alcoholics Anonymous, 1981).

In Step One, you admitted that you were powerless over drugs or alcohol and that your life was unmanageable. In Step Two, you need to see the insanity of your disease and seek a power greater than yourself. If you are powerless, then you need power. If your life is unmanageable, then you need a manager. Step Two will help you to decide who that manager can be.

Most alcoholics and drug addicts who see the phrase *restore to sanity* revolt. They think that they may have a drinking or drug problem, but they do not feel as though they have a mental illness. They do not think that they have been insane.

In AA and NA, the word *sanity* means being of sound mind. Someone with a sound mind knows what is real and knows how to adapt to reality. A sound mind feels stable, safe, and secure. Someone who is insane cannot see reality and is unable to adapt. A person does not have to have all of reality distorted to be in trouble. If you miss some reality, then you ultimately will get lost. It only takes one wrong turn to end up in the ditch.

Going through life is like going on a long journey. You have a map given to you by your parents. The map shows the way in which to be happy. If you make some wrong turns along the way, then you will end up unhappy. This is what happens in chemical dependency. Searching for happiness, you make wrong turns. You find out that your map is defective. Even if you followed your map to perfection, you still would be lost. What you need is a new map.

Both AA and NA give you this new map. It puts up 12 signposts to show the way. If you follow this map as millions of people have done, then you will find the joy and happiness that you have been seeking. You have reached and passed the first signpost, Step One. You have decided that your life is powerless and unmanageable. Now you need a new power source. You need to find someone else who can manage your life.

This is a spiritual program, and it directs you toward a spiritual answer to your problems. It is not a religious program. Spirituality is the intimate relationship you have with yourself and how you relate to everything else. Religion is an organized system of faith and worship. Everyone has spirituality, but not everyone has religion.

You need to explore three relationships very carefully in Step Two: the relationships with yourself, with others, and with a Higher Power. This Higher Power can be any Higher Power of your choice. If you do not have a Higher Power, do not worry. Most of us started that way. Just be willing to consider that there is a power greater than you in the universe.

To explore these relationships, you need to see the truth about yourself. If you see the truth, then you can find the way. First you must decide whether you were insane. Did you have a sound mind or not? Let's look at this issue carefully.

People are insane when they cannot remember what they did. They have memory problems. They do not have to have memory problems all of the time, just some of the time. People who abuse chemicals might not remember what happened to them when they were intoxicated.

List any blackouts or memory problems you have had while drinking or using drugs.

_____

_____

_____

People who are insane lose control over their behavior. They do things when they are intoxicated that they never would do when they are sober.

List three times when you lost control over your behavior when intoxicated.

1. _____
2. _____
3. _____

List three times when you could not control your drinking or drug use.

1. _____
2. _____
3. _____

People who are insane consider self-destruction.

Did you ever consider hurting yourself when you were intoxicated or hung over?

Yes _____   No _____

Describe what happened.

_____
_____
_____

People who are insane feel emotionally unstable.

Have you ever thought that you were going crazy?

Yes _____   No _____

Describe this time.

_____
_____
_____

Have you felt emotionally unstable recently?

Yes _____   No _____

Describe how you have been feeling.

_____
_____
_____

People who are insane are so confused that they cannot get their lives in order. They may frantically try to fix things, but problems stay out of control.

List some personal, family, work, or school problems that you have not been able to control.

_____

_____

_____

People who are insane cannot see the truth about what is happening to them. People who are chemically dependent hide their drinking and drug use from themselves and from others. They minimize, rationalize, and deny that there are problems.

Do you believe that you have been completely honest with yourself?

Yes _____   No _____

List some of the lies that you have told yourself.

_____

_____

_____

People who are insane cut themselves off from healthy relationships. They might find that they do not communicate with their spouses as well. They might not see their friends as often. More and more of their lives center around alcohol or drugs.

List three people you have cut yourself off from.

1. _____

2. _____

3. _____

As your drinking and drug use increased, did you go to church less often?

Yes _____   No _____

List any relationships you have damaged in your drinking and drug use.

_____

_____

_____

People who are insane cannot deal with their feelings. Alcoholics and drug addicts cannot deal with their feelings. They do not like how they feel, so they medicate their feelings. They may drink or use drugs to feel less afraid or sad. They may drink to feel more powerful or more friendly.

List the feelings that you tried to change by drinking or using drugs.

_____

_____

_____

Now look back over your responses. Get out your Step One exercise and read through it. Look at the truth about yourself. Look carefully at how you were thinking, feeling, and behaving when you were drinking or using drugs. Make a decision. Do you think that you had a sound mind? If you were unsound at least some of the time, then you were insane. If you believe this to be true, then say this to yourself: "I am powerless. My life is unmanageable. My mind is unsound. I have been insane."

A POWER GREATER THAN YOURSELF

Consider a power greater than yourself. What exists in the world that has greater power than you do—a river, the wind, the universe, the sun?

List five things that have greater power than you do.

1. _____

2. _____

3. _____

4. _____

5. _____

The first Higher Power that you need to consider is the power of the group. The group is more powerful than you are. Ten hands are more powerful than two. Two heads are better than one. Both AA and NA operate in groups. The group works like a family. The group process is founded in love and trust. All members share their experiences, strengths, and hopes in an attempt to help themselves and others. There is an atmosphere of anonymity. What you hear in group is confidential.

The group acts as a mirror reflecting you to yourself. The group members will help you to discover the truth about who and what you are. You have been deceiving yourself for a long time. The group will help you to uncover the lies. You will come to understand the old AA saying, "What we cannot do alone, we can do together." In group, you will have greater power over the disease because the group will see the whole truth better than you can.

You were not lying to hurt yourself. You were lying to protect yourself. In the process of building your lies, you cut yourself off from reality. This is how chemical dependency works. You cannot recover from addiction by yourself. You need power coming from somewhere else. Begin by trusting your group. Keep an open mind.

You need to share in your group. The more you share, the closer you will get and the more trust you will develop. If you take risks, then you will reap the rewards. You do not have to tell the group everything, but you need to share as much as you can. The group can help you to straighten out your thinking and can help restore you to sanity.

Many chemically dependent persons are afraid of a Higher Power. They believe that a Higher Power will punish them or treat them in the same way as their parents did. They might fear losing control. List some of the fears that you have about a Higher Power.

_____

_____

_____

_____

_____

Some chemically dependent persons have difficulty in trusting anyone. They have been so hurt by others that they do not want to take the chance of being hurt again. What has happened in your life that makes it difficult for you to trust?

_____

_____

_____

_____

_____

What are some of the things that you will need to see from a Higher Power that will show you that the Higher Power can be trusted?

_____

_____

_____

_____

_____

Who was the most trustworthy person you ever knew?

Name _____

How did this person treat you?

_____

_____

_____

_____

What do you hope to gain by accepting a Higher Power?

_____

_____

_____

Alcoholics Anonymous wants you to come to believe in a power greater than yourself. You can accept any Higher Power that you feel can restore you to sanity. Your group, your counselor, your sponsor, and nature all can be used to give you this restoration. You must pick this Higher Power carefully. It is suggested that you use AA or NA as your Higher Power for now. Here is a group of millions of people who are recovering.

Millions of chemically dependent persons have recovered because they were willing to reach out for a Higher Power. Alcoholics Anonymous makes it clear that nothing else will remove the obsession to use chemicals. Some of us have so glorified our own lives that we have shut a Higher Power out. Now is your opportunity. You are at a major turning point. You can begin to open your heart and let a Higher Power in, or you can keep it out.

Remember that this is the beginning of a new life. To be new, you have to do things differently. All that the program is asking you to do is to be open to the possibility that there is a power greater than yourself. Alcoholics Anonymous does not demand that you believe in anything. The Twelve Steps are but suggestions. You do not have to swallow all of this now, but you need to be open. Most recovering persons take Step Two a piece at a time.

First you need to learn how to trust yourself. You must learn how to consistently treat yourself well. What do you need to see from yourself that will show you that you are trustworthy?

_____

_____

_____

_____

Then you need to begin to trust your group. See whether the group members act consistently in your interest. They will not always tell you what you want to hear. No real friends would do that. They will give you the opportunity and encouragement to grow. What will you need to see from the group members that will show you that they are trustworthy?

_____

_____

_____

_____

Every person has a unique spiritual journey. No one can start this journey with a closed mind. What is it going to take from a Higher Power to show you that a Higher Power exists?

_____

_____

_____

_____

Step Two does not mean that we believe in God as God is presented in any religion. Remember that religion is an organized system of worship that is made by humans. Worship is just a means of assigning worth to something. Many people have been so turned off by religion that the idea of God is unacceptable. Describe the religious environment of your childhood. What was it like? What did you learn about God?

_____

_____

_____

_____

How did these early experiences influence the beliefs you have today?

_____

_____

_____

_____

What experiences have caused you to doubt a Higher Power?

_____

_____

_____

_____

Your willingness is essential to your recovery. Give some examples of your willingness to trust in a Higher Power of your choice. What are you willing to do?

_____

_____

_____

_____

Describe your current religious beliefs.

_____

_____

_____

_____

Explain the God of your understanding.

_____

_____

_____

_____

List five reasons why a Higher Power will be good for you.

1. _____
2. _____
3. _____
4. _____
5. _____

If you asked the people in your AA/NA group to describe a Higher Power, you would get a variety of answers. Each person has his or her own understanding of a Higher Power. It is this unique understanding that allows a Higher Power to work individually for each of us. A Higher Power comes to each of us differently.

Appendix 20

Step Three

[We] made a decision to turn our will and our lives over to the care of God as we understood Him.

—Alcoholics Anonymous (1976, p. 59)

Before beginning this exercise, read Step Three in *Twelve Steps and Twelve Traditions* (Alcoholics Anonymous, 1981).

You have come a long way in the program, and you can feel proud of yourself. You have decided that you are powerless over mood-altering chemicals and that your life is unmanageable. You have decided that a Higher Power of some sort can restore you to sanity. In Step Three, you will reach toward God—the God of your own understanding. You will consider using God as your Higher Power. This is the miracle that you have been searching for. It is the major focus of the AA/NA program. This is a spiritual program that directs you toward the ultimate truth. It is important that you be open to the possibility that there is a God. It is vital that you give this concept room to blossom and grow. The "Big Book" says, "That probably no human power could have relieved our alcoholism. That God could and would if He were sought" (Alcoholics Anonymous, 1976, p. 60).

Step Three should not confuse you. It calls for a decision to correct your character defects under spiritual supervision. You must make an honest effort to change your life.

The AA program is a spiritual program. About the Big Book, it states, "Its main object is to enable you to find a power greater than yourself that will solve your problem" (Alcoholics Anonymous, 1976, p. 45). Both AA and NA clearly state that the God of your understanding is the answer. If you are willing to seek God, then you will find God. That is God's promise.

UNDERSTANDING THE MORAL LAW

All spirituality has, at its core, what is already inside of you. You do not have to look very far for God. Your Higher Power lives inside of you. Inside of all of us there is inherent goodness. In all cultures, and in all lands, this goodness is expressed in what we call the moral law. The law demands love in action and in truth. It is simply stated as follows: Love God all you can, love others all you can, and love yourself all you can. This law is very powerful. If some stranger were drowning in a pool next to you, then this internal law would motivate you to help. Instinctively, you would feel driven to help, even if it put your own life at risk. The moral law is so important that it transcends our instinct for survival. You would try to save that drowning person. This moral law is exactly the same everywhere and in every culture. It exists inside of everyone. It is written on your heart. Even among thieves, honesty is valued.

When we survey religious thought, we come up with many different ideas about God and how to worship God, but if we look at the saints of the various religions, they are living practically indistinguishable lives. They all are doing the same things with their lives. They do not lie, cheat, or steal; they believe in giving to others before giving to themselves; and they try not to be envious of others. To believe in your Higher Power, you must believe that this good exists inside of you. You also must believe that there is more of this goodness at work outside of you. If you do not believe in a living and breathing God at this point, do not worry. Every one of us has started where you are.

All people have a basic problem: We break the moral law, even if we believe in it. This fact means that there is something wrong with us. We are incapable of following the moral law as we want to. Even though we would consider it unfair for someone to lie to us, occasionally we lie to someone else. If we see someone dressed in clothes that make the person look terrible, we might tell that person that he or she looks good. This is a lie, and we would not want other people lying to us like that. In this and other situations, we do not obey the very moral law that we know is good. We might even stand there and watch that person drown.

You must ask yourself several questions. Where did we get this moral law? How did these laws of behavior get started? Did they just evolve? The program of AA/NA believes that these good laws come from something good and that there is more of this good at work in the universe. People in the program believe that people can communicate with this good, and they call this good *God.*

We do not know everything about the Higher Power. Much of God remains a mystery. If we look at science, we find the same thing: Most of science is a mystery. We know very little about the primary elements of science such as gravity, but we can make judgments about these elements using our experience. No one has ever seen an electron, but we are sure that it exists because we have some experience of it. It is the same thing with the Higher Power. We can know that there is a power greater than ourselves if we have some experience of this power. Both science and spirituality necessitate a faith based on experience.

There emerges in people, as naturally as the ability to love or hate, the ability to experience God. The experience cannot be taught. It is already there, and it must be awakened. It is primal, already planted, and awaiting growth. God is experienced as a force that is alive. This force is above and more capable than humans. God is so good, pure, and perfect that God obeys the moral law all of the time. The experience of the Higher Power brings with it a feeling of great power and energy. This can be both attractive and frightening, but mainly you will find that God is loving. God has contacted humans through the ages and has said, "I am. I exist."

Instinctively, people know that if they can get more of this goodness, then they will have better lives. Spirituality must be practical. It must make your life better or else you will discard it. If you open yourself up to the spiritual part of the program, then you will feel better immediately.

God knows that if you follow the law of love, then you will be happy. God makes love known to all people. It is born in everyone. The consequence for breaking the law is separation from God. This separation is experienced as deep emotional pain. We feel isolated, empty, frightened, and lonely.

God tells us that He is hungry for your love. God desires a deep personal relationship with you. All people have a similar instinctive hunger for God. By reading this exercise, you can begin to develop your relationship with God. You will find true joy here if you try. Without some sort of a Higher Power, your recovery will be more difficult. A Higher Power can relieve your chemical dependency problem like nothing else can. Many people achieve stable recovery without calling their Higher Power *God.* That certainly is possible. There are many wonderful atheists and agnostics in our program, but the AA/NA way is to reach for some sort of a God of your own understanding.

You can change things in your life. You really can. You do not have to drown in despair any longer. No matter who you are, God loves you. God is willing to help you. Perhaps God has been waiting for you for a long time. Think of how wonderful it is. There is a God. God created you. God loves you. God wants you to be happy. Open yourself up to this experience.

THE KEY TO STEP THREE

The key to working Step Three is willingness—the willingness to turn your life over to the care of God as you understand God. This is difficult for many of us because we think that we are in control. We are completely fooled by this delusion. We believe that we know the right thing to do. We believe that everything would be fine if others would just do things our way. This leads us to deep feelings of resentment and self-pity. People would not cooperate with our plans. No matter how hard we tried to control everything, things kept getting out of control. Sometimes the harder we worked, the worse things got.

You are not in control, and you never have been in control. Your Higher Power is in control. God is the only one that knows about everything. God created you and the universe. Chemically dependent persons, in many ways, are trying to be God. They want the universe to revolve around them. "Above everything, we alcoholics must be rid of this selfishness" (Alcoholics Anonymous, 1976, p. 62).

HOW TO TURN IT OVER

To arrest chemical dependency, you have to stop playing God and let your Higher Power take control. If you sincerely want this and you try, it is easy to do so. Go to a quiet place and talk to your Higher Power about your chemical dependency. Say something like this: "God, I am lost. I can't do this anymore. I turn this situation over to you." Watch how you feel when you say this prayer. The next time you have a problem, stop and turn the problem over to your Higher Power. Say something like this: "God, I can't deal with this problem. You deal with it." See what happens.

As you ask for God's will to be done, you will find the right direction. God knows the way for you. If you follow your Higher Power, then you never will be lost again. God will encourage you to see the truth, and then God will leave the choices up to you. You always can decide. God wants you to be free. God wants you to make all of your own decisions, but God wants to have input into your decisions. Your Higher Power wants to show you the way. If you try to find the way by yourself, then you will constantly be lost. God promises that if you will follow God's plan, then God will see to it that you receive all of the desires of your heart. God knows exactly what you need.

Step Three offers no compromise. It calls for a decision. Exactly how you surrender, and turn things over, is not the point. The important thing is that you are willing to try. Can you see that it is necessary to give up your self-centeredness? Do you see that it is time to turn things over to a power greater than yourself?

List the things that you have to gain by turning your will and your life over to a Higher Power.

1. _____
2. _____
3. _____
4. _____
5. _____

Why do you need to turn things over?

1. _____
2. _____
3. _____
4. _____
5. _____

We should not confuse organized religion with spirituality. In Step Two, you learned that spirituality deals with your relationship with yourself, others, and God. Religion is an organized system of faith and worship. It is person-made, not God-made. It is humans' way of interpreting God's plan. Religion can be very confusing, and it can even drive people away from God. Are old religious ideas keeping you from God? If so, then how?

_____

_____

_____

A great barrier to your finding God may be impatience. You may want to find God right now. You must understand that your spiritual growth is set by God and not by you. You will grow spiritually when God thinks that you are ready. Remember that we are turning this whole thing over. Each person has his or her own unique spiritual journey. Each person must have his or her own individual walk. Spiritual growth, not perfection, is your goal. All you can do is seek the God of your understanding. When God knows that you are ready, God will find you. Total surrender is necessary. If you are holding back, then you need to let go absolutely. Faith, willingness, and prayer will overcome all of the obstacles. Do not worry about your doubt. Just keep seeking in every way you know how.

List 10 ways in which you can seek God. Ask your friends or counselor to help you.

1. _____
2. _____
3. _____
4. _____
5. _____
6. _____
7. _____
8. _____
9. _____
10. _____

What does the saying "Let go and let God" mean to you?

_____
_____
_____
_____

What are some ways in which you can put Step Three to work in your life?

_____
_____
_____
_____

What things in your life do you still want to control?

_____
_____
_____
_____

How can these things be handled better by turning them over to your Higher Power?

_____
_____
_____
_____

List five ways in which you allowed chemicals to be the God in your life.

1. _____
2. _____
3. _____
4. _____
5. _____

How did your chemical use separate you from God?

_____
_____
_____
_____

What changes have you noticed in yourself since you entered the program?

_____
_____
_____
_____
_____

Of these changes, which of them occurred because you listened to someone else other than yourself?

_____
_____
_____
_____
_____

Make a list of the things that are holding you back from turning things over.

1. _____
2. _____
3. _____
4. _____
5. _____

How do you see God caring for you?

_____
_____
_____
_____
_____

How do you understand God now?

_____
_____
_____
_____
_____

HOW TO PRAY

Pray by reading the Step Three prayer once each day for a week. Say the words carefully out loud, and listen to yourself as you speak. Feel God's presence with you, and when you are ready, begin to talk to God. Make prayer a dialogue, not a monologue. Talk to God and then listen for God's answer to come to you inside of your thinking.

"God I offer myself to Thee—to build with me and to do with me as Thou wilt. Relieve me of the bondage of self, that I may better do Thy will. Take away my difficulties, that victory over them may bear witness to those I would help of Thy Power, Thy Love, and Thy Way of Life. May I do Thy will always!" (Alcoholics Anonymous, 1976, p. 63).

Listen for God in others. God may speak to you through them. Look for God's actions in the group, in the weather, and in nature. Read scripture and seek God through your reading. Ask your counselor or your clergy person for some suggestions.

HOW TO MEDITATE

Take time to meditate each day. Sit in a quiet place for about 10 to 20 minutes and pay attention to your breathing. Ask God to come into your thinking and then empty your mind. Ask God this question: "God, what is the next step in my relationship with you?" Do not be nervous if there is only silence for a while. Listen for God's message for you. Write down any words or images that come into your mind. Keep a log of each meditation for a week.

Day 1. _____

_____

_____

Day 2. _____

_____

_____

Day 3. _____

_____

_____

Day 4. _____

_____

_____

Day 5. _____

_____

_____

Day 6. _____

_____

_____

Day 7. _____

_____

_____

Write down your spiritual plan. What are you going to do on a daily basis to help your spiritual program grow?

_____

_____

_____

Trust that if you are seeking God, then God will find you—no matter who you are, no matter where you are. God loves you more than you can imagine. You are God's perfect child, created in God's image. God has great plans for you.

Appendix 21

Step Four

[We] made a searching and fearless moral inventory of ourselves.
—Alcoholics Anonymous (1976, p. 59)

Before beginning this exercise, read Step Four in *Twelve Steps and Twelve Traditions* (Alcoholics Anonymous, 1981).

You are doing well in the program. You have admitted your powerlessness over chemicals, and you have found a Higher Power that can restore you to sanity. Now you must take an inventory of yourself. You must know exactly what resources you have available, and you must examine the exact nature of your wrongs. You need to be detailed about the good things about you and the bad things you have done. Only by taking this inventory will you know exactly where you are. Then you can decide where you are going.

In taking this inventory, you must be detailed and specific. It is the only way of seeing the complete impact of your disease. A part of the truth might be, "I told lies to my children." The complete truth might be, "I told my children that I had cancer. They were terrified and cried for a long time." These two statements would be very different. Only the second statement tells the exact nature of the wrong, and the patient felt the full impact of the disclosure. You can see how important it is to put the whole truth before you at one time—the truth that will set you free.

The Fourth Step is a long autobiography of your life. Read this exercise before you start and underline things that pertain to you. You will want to come back and cover each of these issues in detail as you write it down. If the problem does not relate to you, then leave it blank. Examine exactly what you did wrong. Look for your mistakes even though the situation was not totally your fault. Try to disregard what the other person did and to concentrate on what you did. In time, you will realize that the person who hurt you was as spiritually sick as you were. You need to ask your Higher Power to help you forgive that person or to show that person the same forgiveness that you would want for yourself. You can honestly pray that the other person finds out the truth about what he or she did to you.

Review your natural desires carefully and think about how you acted on them. You will see that some of them became the Higher Powers of your life. Sex, food, money, relationships, power, influence, education, and many others can become the major focus of your life. The pursuit of these desires can take total control and can become the center of our existence. That is when we insult God. We say that these objects can make us happy and save us.

In working through the inventory, you will experience pain. You will feel angry, sad, fearful, ashamed, embarrassed, guilty, and lonely. The Fourth Step is a grieving process. As you see clearly your wrongs, you may feel that no one will ever love you again, but remember that God created you in perfection. You are God's perfect child, God's masterpiece, and God's work of art. There is nothing wrong with you. You have everything that you need to be happy, joyous, and free. Sure, you made some mistakes. That is an essential part of life. You learn from your mistakes. Once you clean house, you can begin to purify yourself by shedding your defects. They will not go away easily, and you might feel the old behaviors fight for life. You have grown comfortable in the lies, and now you are walking into the truth. You are walking out of the darkness and into the light—out of the fear and into the peace that AA calls serenity.

Now let's take a basic look at right and wrong. We cover the following areas.

1. Did God come first in your life? Did you seek and follow God's will at all times?

   a. What were your idols—money, fame, position, alcohol, drugs, sex, power, relationships?
   b. Have you honored God with your language?
   c. Have you always set aside a day to improve your relationship with God?
   d. Have you loved, honored, and respected your parents?
   e. Do you have unresolved hate, anger, and resentments?
   f. Were you ever guilty of adulterous acts or thoughts?

g. Have you ever cheated, misrepresented, made pressure deals, or had bad debts?

h. Have you ever been guilty of slander or spreading gossip?

i. Have you ever wanted something that belongs to someone else or felt envious or overly competitive?

2. Take a close look at any false pride.

a. Egotistical vanity is too great an admiration of yourself. Pride makes you your own law, moral judge, and Higher Power. It produces the following:

   (1) Boasting or self-glorification
   (2) Love of publicity
   (3) Hypocrisy or pretending to be better than others
   (4) Hardheadedness or refusal to give up your will
   (5) Discord or resenting anyone who crosses you
   (6) Quarrelsomeness or quarreling whenever another person challenges your wishes
   (7) Disobedience or refusal to submit your will to the will of superiors or to God

3. Take a close look at any greed.

a. Do you desire wealth, such as money or other things, as an end in itself rather than as a means to an end? In acquiring wealth in any form, do you disregard the rights of others? Do you give an honest day's work for an honest day's pay? How do you use what you have? Are you stingy with your friends and family? Do you love money and possessions for these things in themselves? How excessive is your love of luxury? Do you stoop to devices such as fraud, perjury, dishonesty, and sharp practices in dealing with others? Do you try to fool yourself in these regards? Do you call questionable business "Big Business"? Do you call unreasonable hoarding "security"? Will you do almost anything to attain these things and kid yourself by giving your methods innocent names?

4. Take a close look at any lust.

a. Lust is inordinate love and desire of the pleasures of the flesh. Are you guilty of lust in any of its forms? Do you tell yourself that improper or undue indulgence in sexual activities is okay? Do you treat people as objects of your desire other than as God's perfect creations? Do you use pornography or think unhealthy sexual thoughts? Do you treat other people sexually the same way in which you would want to be treated? Do you love others the same way in which you want them to love you?

5. Take a close look at any envy.

a. Do you dislike seeing others happy or successful, as though they had stolen something from you? Do you resent those who are smarter than you are? Do you criticize the good done by others because you secretly wish that you had done it yourself? Are you ever envious enough to try to lower another person's reputation by starting or engaging in gossip about that person? Do you call religious people "hypocrites" because they go to church and try to be religiously good even though they are subject to human failings? Do you ever accuse the educated, wise, or learned of being highbrow because you envy their advantages? Do you genuinely love other people, or do you find them distasteful because you envy them?

6. Take a close look at any anger.

a. Do you ever fly into a rage of temper, become revengeful, or entertain urges to "get even" or an "I'll not let him get away with it" attitude? Do you ever resort to violence, clench your fists, or stomp about in a temper flare-up? Are you touchy, unduly sensitive, or impatient at the smallest slight? Do you ever murmur or grumble even in small matters? Do you ignore the fact that anger prevents development of personality and halts spiritual progress? Do you realize that anger often ruins good judgment? Do you permit anger to rule you when you know that it blinds you to the rights of others? Do you permit yourself to become angry when others are weak and become angry with you? Do you find yourself in a rage when someone criticizes you even for small things?

7. Take a close look at any overindulgences.

   a. Do you weaken your moral and intellectual life by excessive use of food and drink? Do you generally eat to excess and, thus, enslave your soul and character to the pleasures of the body beyond the reasonable needs of the body? Did you ever, when drinking or using drugs, become nauseated and vomit, only to immediately return and drink or use some more? Did you use so much that your intellect and personality deteriorated? So much that memory, judgment, and concentration were affected? So much that personal pride and social judgment vanished? So much that you developed a spirit of despair?

8. Take a look at any laziness.

   a. Are you finding yourself being lazy or given to idleness, procrastination, nonchalance, and indifference in material things? Are you lukewarm in prayer? Do you hold the self-discipline of others in contempt? Are you fainthearted in performance of those things that are morally or spiritually difficult? Are you ever listless with aversion to effort in any form? Are you easily distracted from things spiritual, quickly turning to things temporal?

PERSONALITY DEFECTS

1. Selfishness

   a. This is taking care of one's own needs without regard for others.

      (1) Example: The family would like an outing. Dad would like drinking, golf, or fishing, or he has a hangover. Who wins?

      (2) Example: Your child needs a new pair of shoes. You put it off until payday but get a fifth that same night.

      (3) You are afraid to dance because you might appear awkward.

2. Alibis

   a. This is the highly developed art of justifying our chemical use and behavior through excuses such as the following:

      (1) "A few will straighten me out."

      (2) "Starting tomorrow, I'm going to change."

      (3) "If I didn't have a wife and family . . ."

      (4) "If I could start all over again . . ."

      (5) "A drink will help me think."

      (6) "Nobody cares anyway."

      (7) "I had a hard day."

3. Dishonest thinking

   a. We take truths or facts and twist them to come up with the conclusions we need, such as in the following examples:

      (1) My secret love is going to raise the roof if I drop her. It is not fair to burden my wife with that sort of knowledge. Therefore, I will hang on to my girlfriend. This mess isn't her fault.

      (2) If I tell my family about the $500 bonus, it will all go for bills. I've got to have some drinking money. Why start a family argument? I'll leave well enough alone.

      (3) My spouse dresses well and eats well, and the kids are getting a good education. What more do they want from me?

4. Shame

   a. This is the feeling that something irreparable is wrong with us.

      (1) No matter how many people tell you that it is okay, you continue to berate yourself.

      (2) You keep going over and over your mistakes, wallowing in what a terrible person you are.

5. Resentment

    a. This is displeasure aroused by a real or imagined wrong or injury accompanied by irritation.

        (1) You are fired from work. You hate the boss.

        (2) Your sister warns you about excessive drinking. You get fighting mad at her.

        (3) A co-worker is doing a good job and gets accolades. You have a drug record and fear that this co-worker might have been promoted over you. You hate his guts.

        (4) You may have a resentment toward a person or a group of people, or you may resent an institution, a religion, and so on.

    b. Anger and resentment lead to bickering, friction, hatred, and unjust revenge. It brings out the worst in our immaturity and produces misery for ourselves and all concerned.

6. Intolerance

    a. This is the refusal to put up with beliefs, practices, customs, or habits that differ from our own.

        (1) Do you hate other people because they are of another race, come from a different country, or have a different religion?

        (2) Did you have any choice in being born a particular color or nationality?

        (3) Isn't our religion usually "inherited"?

7. Impatience

    a. This is an unwillingness to calmly bear delay, opposition, pain, or bother.

        (1) A chemically dependent person is someone who jumps on a horse and gallops off madly in all directions at the same time.

        (2) Do you blow your stack when someone keeps you waiting over the "allotted time" you gave that person?

        (3) Did anyone ever have to wait for you?

8. Phoniness

    a. This is a manifestation of our false pride or the old false front.

        (1) I present my love with a present as evidence of my love. Just by pure coincidence, it helps to smooth over my last binge.

        (2) I buy new clothes because my business position demands it. Meanwhile, the family also could use food and clothes.

9. Procrastination

    a. This is putting off or postponing things that need to be done—the familiar "I'll do it tomorrow."

        (1) Did little jobs that were put off become big and almost impossible later?

        (2) Do you pamper yourself by doing things "my way"?

        (3) Can you handle little jobs that you are asked to take care of, or do you feel picked on?

        (4) Little things, done for God, make them great. Are you doing the little things for God?

10. Self-pity

    a. These people at the party are having fun with their drinking. Why can't I be like that? This is the "woe is me" syndrome.

    b. If I had that guy's money, then I would not have any problems. This is a similar attitude.

11. Feelings too easily hurt

    a. I walk down the street and say hello to someone. The person does not answer. I am hurt and mad.

    b. I am expecting my turn at the AA meeting, but the time runs out. I feel rejected.

12. Fear

    a. This is an inner foreboding, whether real or imagined, of doom ahead. We suspect that our use of chemicals, behavior, negligence, and so on are catching up with us. We fear the worst.

        (1) When we learn to accept our powerlessness, ask our Higher Power for help, and face ourselves with honesty, the nightmare will be gone.

13. Depression

    a. This is feeling sad or down most of the day.

        (1) You keep going over all of the things that are going wrong.

        (2) You tend to think the worst.

14. Feelings of inadequacy

    a. This is feeling as though you cannot do it.

        (1) You hold on to a negative self-image even when you succeed.

15. Perfectionism

    a. You have to do everything perfect all of the time.

        (1) Even when you have done a good job, you find something wrong with it.

        (2) Someone compliments you on something. You feel terrible because it could have been better.

PHYSICAL LIABILITIES

1. Diseases, disabilities, and other physical limitations about how you look or how your body functions
2. Sexual problems or hang-ups
3. Negative feelings about your appearance
4. Negative feelings about your age
5. Negative feelings about your sex.

TIME OUT

If you have gone through the exercise to this point without coming up for air—it figures. We did our drinking and drugging the same way. Whoa! Easy does it! Take this in reasonable stages. Assimilate each portion of the exercise thoughtfully. The reading of this is important, but the application of it is even more important. Take some time to think and rest, and let all of this settle in. Develop some sort of a workable daily plan. Include plenty of rest.

When chemically dependent people stop using, part of their lives is taken away from them. This is a terrible loss to sustain unless it is replaced by something else. We cannot just boot the chemicals out the window. They meant too much to us. They were how we faced life, the key to escape, and the tool for solving life's problems. In approaching a new way of life, a new set of tools is substituted. These are the Twelve Steps and the AA/NA way of life.

The same principle applies when we eliminate our character defects. We replace them by substituting assets that are better adapted to a healthy lifestyle. As with substance use, you do not fight a defect. You replace it with something that works better. Use what follows for further character analysis and as a guide for character building. These are the new tools. The objective is not perfection but rather progress. You will be happy with the type of living that produces self-respect, respect and love for others, and security from the nightmare of chemical dependency.

THE WAY TO RECOVERY

1. Faith

    a. This is the act of leaving that part of our lives to the care of a power greater than ourselves with assurance that it will work out. This will be shaky at first, but with it comes a deep spiritual connection.

(1) Faith is acquired through application—acceptance, daily prayer, and meditation.

(2) We depend on faith. We have faith that the lights will come on, that the car will start, and that our co-workers will handle their end of things.

(3) Spiritual faith is the acceptance of our gifts, limitations, problems, and trials with equal gratitude, knowing that God has a plan for us. With "Thy will be done" as our daily guide, we will lose our fear and find ourselves.

2. Hope

a. Faith suggests reliance. We came to believe that a power greater than ourselves would restore us to sanity. We hope to stay clean and sober, regain our self-respect, and love our families. Hope resolves itself into a driving force. It gives purpose to our daily living.

(1) Faith gives us direction, and hope gives us the steam to take action.

(2) Hope reflects a positive attitude. Things are going to work out for us if we work the program.

3. Love

a. This is the active involvement in someone's individual growth.

(1) Love must occur in action and in truth.

(2) In its deeper sense, love is the art of living realistically and fully, guided by spiritual awareness of our responsibilities and our debt of gratitude to God and to others.

Analysis. Have you used the qualities of faith, hope, and love in your past? How will they apply to your new way of life?

WE STAY ON TRACK THROUGH ACTION

1. *Courtesy:* Some of us are actually afraid to be gentle persons.

2. *Cheerfulness:* Circumstances do not determine our frame of mind. We do. "Today I will be cheerful. I will look for the beauty in life."

3. *Order:* Live today only. Organize one day at a time.

4. *Loyalty:* Be faithful to whom you believe in.

5. *Use of time:* Use your time wisely.

6. *Punctuality:* This includes self-discipline, order, and consideration for others.

7. *Sincerity:* This is the mark of self-respect and genuineness. Sincerity carries conviction and generates enthusiasm. It is contagious.

8. *Caution in speech:* Watch your tongue. We can be vicious and thoughtless. Too often, the damage is irreparable.

9. *Kindness:* This is one of life's great satisfactions. We do not have real happiness until we have given of ourselves. Practice this daily.

10. *Patience:* This is the antidote to resentments, self-pity, and impulsiveness.

11. *Tolerance:* This requires common courtesy, courage, and a "live and let live" attitude.

12. *Integrity:* This includes the ultimate qualifications of a person—honesty, loyalty, and sincerity.

13. *Balance:* Do not take yourself too seriously. We get a better perspective when we can laugh at ourselves.

14. *Gratitude:* The person without gratitude is filled with false pride. Gratitude is the honest recognition of help received. Use it often.

Analysis. In considering the little virtues, where did I fail and how did that contribute to my accumulated problem? What virtues should I pay attention to in this rebuilding program?

PHYSICAL ASSETS

1. *Physical health:* How healthy am I despite any ailments?
2. *Talents:* What am I good at?
3. *Age:* At my age, what can I offer to others?
4. *Sexuality:* How can I use my sexuality to express my love?
5. *Knowledge:* How can I use my knowledge and experience to help myself and others?

MENTAL ASSETS

1. Despite your problems, how healthy are you emotionally?
2. Do you care for others?
3. Are you kind?
4. Can you be patient?
5. Are you basically a good person?
6. Do you want to help others?
7. Do you try to tell the truth?
8. Do you try to be forgiving?
9. Can you be enthusiastic?
10. Are you sensitive to the needs of others?
11. Can you be serene?
12. *Sincerity:* Are you going to try to be sincere?
13. *Self-discipline:* Are you going to try to bring order and self-control into your life?
14. Are you going to accept the responsibility for your own behavior and stop blaming others?
15. How are you going to use your intelligence?
16. Are you going to seek the will of a Higher Power?
17. *Education:* How might you improve your mind in furthering your education?
18. Are you going to be grateful for what you have?
19. *Integrity:* How can you improve your honesty and reliability?
20. *Joy:* In what areas of your life do you find happiness?
21. Are you humble and working on your false pride?
22. Are you seeking the Higher Power of your own understanding?
23. *Acceptance:* In what ways can you better accept your own limitations and the limitations of others?
24. *Courage:* Are you willing to trust and follow the Higher Power of your understanding?

THE AUTOBIOGRAPHY

Using this exercise, write your autobiography. Cover your life in 5-year intervals. Be brief, but try not to miss anything. Tell the whole truth. Write down exactly what you did. Consider all of the things that you marked during the exercise. Read the exercise again if you need to do so. Make an exhaustive and honest consideration of your past and present. Cover both assets and liabilities carefully. You will rebuild your life on the solid building blocks of your assets. These are the tools of recovery. Omit nothing because of shame, embarrassment, or fear. Determine the thoughts, feelings, and actions that plagued you. You want to meet these problems face-to-face and see them in writing. If you wish, you may destroy your inventory after completing the Fifth Step. Many patients hold a ceremony in which they burn the Fourth Step inventory. This symbolizes that they are leaving the old life behind. They are starting a new life free of the past.

Appendix 22

Step Five

[We] admitted to God, ourselves, and to another human being the exact nature of our wrongs.

—Alcoholics Anonymous (1976, p. 57)

Before beginning this exercise, read Step Five in *Twelve Steps and Twelve Traditions* (Alcoholics Anonymous, 1981).

With Steps One to Four behind you, it is now time to clean house and start over. You must free yourself of all the guilt and shame and go forward in faith. The Fifth Step is meant to right the wrongs with God. You will develop a new attitude and a new relationship with your Higher Power. You have admitted your powerlessness, and you have identified your liabilities and assets in the personal inventory. Now it is time to get right with God. You will do this by admitting to God, to yourself, and to another person the exact nature of your wrongs. You are going to cover all of your assets and liabilities in the Fifth Step. You are going to tell someone the whole truth at one time. This person is important because he or she is a symbol of God and all of humanity. You must watch this person's face. The illness has been telling you that if you tell anyone the whole truth about you, that person will not like you. That is a lie, and you are going to prove that it is a lie. The truth is this: Unless you tell people the truth, they cannot like you. You must see yourself tell someone the truth and watch that person's reaction.

It is very difficult to discuss your faults with someone. It is hard enough just thinking about them yourself, but this is a necessary step. It will help to free you from the disease. You must tell this person everything, the whole story, all of the things that you are afraid to share. If you withhold anything, then you will not get the relief you need to start over. You will be carrying around excess baggage. You do not need to do this to yourself. God loves you and wants you to be free of guilt, shame, and hurt. God wants you to be happy and to reach your full potential.

> Time after time, newcomers have tried to keep to themselves certain facts about their lives. Trying to avoid this humbling experience, they have turned to easier methods. Almost invariably, they got drunk. Having persevered with the rest of the program, they wondered why they fell. We think the reason is that they never completed their housecleaning. They took inventory all right but hung on to some of the worst items in stock. They only *thought* they had lost their egotism and fear; they only *thought* they had humbled themselves. But they had not learned enough of humility, fearlessness, and honesty, in the sense we find necessary, until they told someone else *all* their life story. (Alcoholics Anonymous, 1976, pp. 72-73)

By finally telling someone the whole truth, you will rid yourself of that terrible sense of isolation and loneliness. You will feel a new sense of belonging, acceptance, and freedom. If you do not immediately feel relief, do not worry. If you have been completely honest, then the relief will come. "The dammed-up emotions of years break out of their confinement and miraculously vanish when they are exposed" (Alcoholics Anonymous, 1981, p. 62). You can be forgiven, no matter what.

The Fifth Step will develop within you a new humbleness of character that is necessary for normal living. You will come to clearly recognize who and what you are. When you are honest with another person, it confirms that you have been honest with yourself and with God.

The person with whom you will share your Fifth Step has been chosen carefully for you. You will meet with this person several times before you do the step. You need to decide whether you can trust this person. Do you believe that this person is confidential? Do you feel comfortable with this person? Do you believe that this person will be understanding and loving?

Once you have chosen that person, put your false pride aside and go for it. Tell this person everything about yourself. Do not leave one dark corner unturned. Tell this person about all of the good things as well as all of the bad things you have done. Share the details, and do not leave anything out. If it troubles you even a little, then share it. Let it all hang out to be examined by God, by yourself, and by that other person. Every good and bad part needs to be revealed. When you are finished, say a prayer to your Higher Power. Tell God that you are sorry for what you have done wrong, and commit yourself to a new way of life following the God of your understanding. Many patients like to say the Seventh Step prayer.

My Creator, I am now willing that you should have all of me, good and bad. I pray that you now remove from me every single defect of character which stands in the way of my usefulness to you and my fellows. Grant me strength, as I go out from here, to do your bidding. (Alcoholics Anonymous, 1976, p. 76)

Appendix 23

Adolescent Unit Level System

Patients participating in the adolescent program will be involved in the Freedom Level System. This system is a simple three-level program designed to be a guide in the development of appropriate treatment attitudes and behaviors. This program is for your benefit, and it is the primary means by which you will move forward into a stable program of recovery. You will enjoy more freedom and responsibility as you move up in levels. All we ask is that you try to be honest, open-minded, and willing to participate in your treatment.

FREEDOM LEVEL 1

All adolescents entering treatment will begin on Freedom Level 1. To be eligible for advancement to Level 2, you must accomplish the following list of goals in a satisfactory manner and identify and implement positive behaviors and attitudes toward treatment.

Treatment Goals

1. Complete the process of orientation to the unit with the assistance of the staff and assigned treatment peer.
2. Participate and cooperate with staff in completing all aspects of the assessment phase of treatment including clinical and psychological assessments.
3. Review general unit rules with the staff or treatment peer and abide by these rules.
4. Cooperate with the staff schoolteacher in developing a workable school program. Review and follow all school rules, and willingly participate in your continuing education.
5. Become actively involved in all scheduled activities.
6. Complete all written assignments in a timely manner.
7. Verbally participate in groups and begin to take risks.
8. Exhibit a positive attitude both verbally and behaviorally toward the staff and treatment peers.
9. Satisfactorily complete all unit assignments and duties such as keeping your room, and the entire unit, clean and organized.

Level 1 Privileges

1. You are able to watch "fun" videos.
2. You may watch television during free time.
3. You may have recreation room privileges as scheduled.

FREEDOM LEVEL 2

Adolescents who have satisfactorily completed the goal requirements listed under Level 1 will be promoted to Level 2. Patients on this level may enjoy the Level 1 privileges in addition to the Level 2 privileges. To maintain Level 2 status, patients must continue to live up to the Level 1 goals. To advance to Level 2, patients must demonstrate the following.

Treatment Goals

1. Increase participation in all groups. Take significant risks by being open and honest and providing appropriate feedback.
2. Complete all school assignments and cooperate in all aspects of the school program.

3. Act as a positive role model to your treatment peers by refusing to participate in negative talk or behaviors. Confront your peers regarding their inappropriate behaviors.
4. Verbalize an understanding of chemical dependency and the components of a recovery program.

Level 2 Privileges

1. You may have radios, tape players, and tapes.
2. You are eligible to be a patient sponsor to a new patient.
3. You will be eligible to be the unit sheriff.
4. You may accompany staff members away from the facility to help pick out "fun" videos.
5. You have snack bar privileges.
6. You may leave the unit unescorted with staff approval, and you may escort a Level 1 peer to the nurses station or to other functions and appointments in the facility.

FREEDOM LEVEL 3

Adolescents who have satisfied all goal requirements listed under Levels 1 and 2 are eligible for Level 3. All Level 3 patients must complete the following goals.

Treatment Goals

1. Continue to demonstrate the desire to work a program of recovery.
2. Consistently show, by words and actions, that you are working on the Twelve Steps.
3. Be a good role model to other patients.

Level 3 Privileges

1. You may participate in scheduled weekend outings with the staff and other eligible treatment peers.
2. You are eligible to make one supervised telephone call to a friend each week. Phone calls will have a 10-minute maximum and must be made to an individual approved by your primary counselor.
3. You may leave the dining room and return to the unit unescorted.

PROBLEM BEHAVIORS AND CONSEQUENCES

1. Think Table
   a. The adolescent is restricted totally to the Think Table for a length of time determined by the staff. The patient does not attend any activities. No peer visitors are allowed.

2. Time out
   a. The adolescent is restricted to the "time out" room for at least 1 hour. Patient is not allowed peer visitors.
   b. The adolescent loses recreation period and all breaks.

3. Loss of free time—24 hours or longer, as determined by the staff
   a. The adolescent has to spend all recreational time at the Think Table.

4. The buddy system
   a. When a new patient comes into treatment and is on Freedom Level 1 or 2, a Level 3 patient may be assigned to orient the patient to the unit. This would involve introducing the new patient to the other patients and staff members and showing the patient around the center. The buddy should help the new patient to feel more comfortable on the unit.
5. Major consequence
   a. The adolescent who receives a major consequence will automatically be dropped a level.
   b. The adolescent will be assigned other consequences as determined by the staff.

6. Minor consequence
    a. The adolescent who receives three minor consequences will be dropped a level as well as receive consequences determined by the staff.

Adolescents are encouraged to work on respecting themselves, others, and property. They need to be working toward knowing and understanding themselves and toward developing appropriate and positive social relationships. They need to learn how to identify and deal with their feelings appropriately. All patients are encouraged to develop a sense of responsibility for their actions. The following problem behaviors and consequences deal with these principles.

MAJOR CONSEQUENCE

1. Adolescents will not use or have in their possession any mood-altering substances during treatment except those prescribed by the physician.
    a. *Consequence:* Use or possession of mood-altering substances is a serious violation and may result in extended treatment or discharge from the program. If adolescents are not discharged, then they will be placed at the Think Table for at least 1 hour, will be placed on a behavioral contract, and will be returned to Freedom Level 1.

2. Adolescents are not permitted to be verbally aggressive to the staff or peers. Each behavior will be assessed individually by the staff member involved to determine whether it is a major or minor consequence.
    a. Adolescents involved in a major consequence will drop a freedom level, face possible discharge, and sit at the Think Table for at least 1 hour.

3. Adolescents are not permitted to be destructive to or deface any treatment center property.
    a. *Consequence:* Adolescents involved in this behavior on a major scale (e.g., putting holes in walls, throwing and damaging items) will become involved in working off the damage by doing jobs around the center. They will be dropped one freedom level. The behavior also may result in the Think Table or time out. Patients will present a written report on the incident in contracts group and give a copy of the written report to their primary counselor.

4. Adolescents will not engage in any form of sexual activity while in treatment (e.g., kissing, necking, foreplay, intercourse). Forming romantic relationships in treatment is not permitted (e.g., holding hands, arms around each other, flirting, inappropriately hugging or touching each other).
    a. *Consequence:* Engaging in sexual contact is a serious violation of unit policy, and patients who engage in this activity may be discharged from the program. Adolescents not discharged will sit at the Think Table for at least 1 hour. They will complete a written assignment that they will share with their primary counselor. They may have their time in treatment extended. They will be placed on a behavioral contract. They will lose one freedom level.

5. Adolescents are not permitted to act in a physically aggressive manner toward the staff or treatment peers. Anger outbursts (e.g., slamming doors, yelling, angrily getting up and leaving a scheduled activity before it is completed) are prohibited. Physical or verbal aggression toward the staff or peers (e.g., fighting, throwing items, making verbal threats of harm) is not permitted.
    a. *Consequence:* Adolescents involved in physical or verbal aggression may be discharged from the program. Adolescents not discharged from the program will sit at the Think Table for at least 1 hour. They will make a verbal presentation in contracts group. A written copy of the presentation will be given to their primary counselor. The adolescents will lose at least one freedom level.

6. Adolescents are expected to cope with their problems in a more constructive way than running away from the treatment center.
    a. Adolescents who verbally threaten to run away, or who are believed to be at risk for running away, will be placed on AMA (against medical advice) precautions until decided otherwise by their primary counselor with input from the clinical team. Adolescents who leave the center AMA and are returned will sit at the Think Table for at least 1 hour or time out. They will be returned to Freedom Level 1. This may result in discharge from treatment or extension of treatment. A urine specimen will be obtained from all patients who inappropriately leave the treatment center.

7. Adolescents are expected to fulfill any consequences that they may obtain in a time frame organized by the staff.
   a. Adolescents who do not fulfill their consequences will receive loss of free time or sit at the Think Table until the consequences are fulfilled.

MINOR CONSEQUENCE

1. Adolescents are not allowed to use verbally abusive language to the staff or peers (e.g., profanity, hostile language).
   a. Adolescents involved in being verbally abusive will lose free time for up to 24 hours and make a verbal presentation in contracts group. A written copy of the presentation will be given to their primary counselor.

2. Adolescents are not to be involved in "horseplay" activities (e.g., wrestling, pushing, shadow boxing). Aggressive horseplay or practical jokes may be a major consequence. This will be determined by the staff member involved.
   a. Adolescents involved in horseplay activities will lose free time for up to 24 hours and make a verbal presentation to contracts group. A written copy will be given to their primary counselor.

3. Honesty is a vital part of adolescents' treatment and recovery. Being dishonest is not permitted.
   a. Involvement in dishonest behavior will result in loss of free time or 1 hour at the Think Table. A verbal presentation to contracts group will be required. A copy of this presentation will go to the primary counselor.

4. Adolescents who have possession of unauthorized articles will lose free time for up to 24 hours.

5. Radios and tape players must be kept to an acceptable volume. If they can be heard outside of the room, then they are too loud. Radios and tape players that are played too loud will be confiscated for 24 hours.

6. Adolescents who are late for a scheduled activity will be given a minor consequence. Three such consequences will result in the loss of free time for 24 hours. These patients will be dropped one freedom level.

7. Patients who do not participate in group will be given a minor consequence. They will present to the next group their reasons for not participating.

Appendix 24

Peer Pressure
Robert R. Perkinson, Ph.D.

You want your friends to accept you. Sure you do. That is normal. You want to be liked. You want to be loved and accepted by your peers. In treatment, it is important to learn about peer pressure, where it comes from, what is good about it, and what can be dangerous about it. There are things that you need to watch out for in recovery. If you are not careful, then the pressure of your peer group can get you back to drinking or using drugs. Your friends are not trying to hurt you. They just want their old friend back. These friends may have a chemical problem themselves. They may see your recovery as a threat to them.

HOW PEER PRESSURE EVOLVED

The roots of peer pressure evolved in the birds. Birds learned that they were safer if they gathered together in flocks. They could warn others of danger more easily if they stuck together. In a group, they were less likely to be singled out as prey. Birds learned how to stay together for safety. Because this worked so well, over thousands of years, birds developed a feeling of wanting to be together. They developed social skills used to keep them together. They began to make noises to keep together. Anyone who has heard a flock of geese fly overhead will testify to the active communication patterns of these birds. Communications became more complicated over the years. The birds developed a particular sound for relaxation and a particular sound for danger. They developed the feeling of wanting to be together in groups. It felt better to be together. These feelings are what we now call emotions.

Higher ordered social activity continued to evolve in mammals. Baboons, for example, have very complicated social rituals. These animals groom each other to keep the troop together. The grooming serves to rid them of irritating insects, and it helps them to feel closer together. It is like a back scratch; it says, "If you scratch my back, then I'll scratch yours." These social rituals hold a group of animals together. When you go to the zoo, you will see animals rubbing and stroking each other. You will see mothers holding and licking their babies. As such, the species becomes bonded together.

Acceptance is a very important feeling because animals depend on acceptance by the group for survival. If they are rejected by the herd, then they have a higher chance of being killed by predators. All animals are safer if they are in a group.

As we move up the evolutionary scale, we finally get to humans. Early people, as we know them, were social creatures. They gathered together in groups or tribes for safety. A tribe could function better with people together. Tribe members could specialize and reap the benefits of other people's expertise. It was easier to hunt, fish, and gather food if the tribe members worked together. Some would do the hunting, and some would make arrowheads. Each tribe member specialized in a particular function. It was very important for early people to be accepted by their tribes. If they were banished, then they would have to fend for themselves. Being alone in the world would put individuals at great risk. So, humans developed a desire, a wish, or a need to be liked and to be accepted. This was very important for survival.

THE IMPORTANCE OF PEER PRESSURE

You are beginning to see why peer pressure is so important. If you are rejected by the group, you fear death. Without the acceptance of the group, people feel more vulnerable to the world. Now you can see why we try so hard to get our friends to like us. We need our friends so that we can feel safe.

It is very clear that being liked and being accepted by the group is important and good. It is important for all of us to learn the skills necessary to establish and maintain close interpersonal relationships. These are the skills that keep the group together.

There often are symbols or gestures that identify groups. Groups may have flags or uniforms. Group members all may ride a certain kind of motorcycle or wear a particular hat. Every group has a particular language that is unique to that group. Medical doctors do not use the same words as do auto mechanics.

HOW PEER PRESSURE CAN RISK YOUR SOBRIETY

There are a few things about peer pressure that can get you into trouble. Groups can get you to do things that you would not normally do. They might talk you into doing something that you do not want to do—things such as stealing, drinking, and even playing a practical joke on someone. If we always follow the group, then we can be led into behavior that we know is wrong.

List five times when you were talked into doing something that you did not really want to do.

1. _____
2. _____
3. _____
4. _____
5. _____

HOW THE GROUP USES PEER PRESSURE

The group will have a means of pressuring you into cooperating. In formal society, there are laws that govern group behavior. In most groups, members are subject to ridicule or even group expulsion if they do not cooperate. "Don't be chicken! What are you scared of?" There are any number of ways of encouraging individuals to do what the group wants them to do.

List some of the ways in which your friends try to get you to cooperate with them.

1. _____
2. _____
3. _____
4. _____
5. _____

HOW TO COPE WITH PEER PRESSURE

It is important to stay in the group, but it also is important for you to make your own decisions. If you do not make all of your decisions, then you will be held accountable for the decisions of others.

Here is a new concept for you. The only thing that you owe anyone else is to be different. You must be different from anyone that ever was or anyone that ever will be. You were created for your individuality. The only way in which you can reach your full potential in life is to make all of your own decisions. If you always follow a group, then you cannot be yourself. It is important for you to have the skill to say no. You need to be able to go against the group sometimes. If you are going to be an adult, then you have to make all of your own decisions and live with the consequences. That is the only way in which you can take your own direction. You must think about every choice you make. You cannot let other people make your decisions for you.

When you decide to do something that is different from what the group wants, the group will apply peer pressure. The group will try to get you to conform. The group members may threaten you or make fun of you. They may get angry at you. But remember that it is your responsibility to yourself, and to everyone else, to sometimes be different. Once you make a decision and you believe in it, you must be able to stick to it. If you cannot do this, then the group always will manipulate your choices. You need to develop the skill of going your own way, even in the face of group opposition.

You do not have to have a good reason for not doing what the group wants. It can just be your choice. You do not have to explain yourself or your opinions to anybody. You do not need an excuse. You can simply say "because I want to." This is reason enough.

You must keep the group informed about how you are feeling if it tries to pressure you. This holds the group members accountable for their behavior. If the group members are causing you to feel uncomfortable, then you must express this feeling. This will keep their behavior in line. "It makes me feel uncomfortable when you ask me to drink when you know that I'm recovering." Honest statements such as this usually will bring people under control. You must constantly keep people informed about how you are feeling and what you want from them. "I don't want any pot. I would prefer it if you would stop asking me." A simple "no" or "no thank you" is enough in most circumstances. Say no and stand your ground. You do not have to explain yourself further. If the group continues to coerce you even after you have said no, then you might have to leave the situation. If the group members do not respect your wishes, you do not want to be with those people anyway. Just excuse yourself and go home. You have not lost anything. If the group does not care for how you feel, then it is not the group for you.

People always can get you to feel a certain way if they try. They can get you to feel angry or guilty if they work at it, but even if they have some control over your feelings, they cannot control your actions. That is up to you. If they can get control over your actions by controlling your feelings, then they have a slave in you. They can get you to do anything. Group members often will try to lay guilt on you if you do not cooperate with them, but they cannot make you do anything with this guilt. You are in control of your actions.

MAKE A PLAN TO SAY NO

List 10 ways in which you are going to say no to alcohol and drugs.

1. _____
2. _____
3. _____
4. _____
5. _____
6. _____
7. _____
8. _____
9. _____
10. _____

Here are some important points to remember. The desire to be accepted by the group is normal and very powerful. The feeling of wanting to be accepted exists deep inside all of us, and this feeling helps us to gather together in groups for everyone's mutual gain. Being a part of a group feels good, but our primary responsibility to ourselves and to everyone else is to be different—to be one of a kind. Therefore, it is crucially important that you take your own direction, make all of your own decisions, and be yourself.

Appendix 25

The Behavioral Contract
Robert R. Perkinson, Ph.D.

Behavioral contracting has been found to be a powerful means of directly influencing behavior (Stuart, 1971). Developing a behavioral contract and living within its limits will create a stable family situation for you and your child. Behavior is defined as any movement. When anyone acts or speaks, it is behavior. Counselors often are asked by frustrated parents, "Why doesn't my child cooperate?" The answer to this question is simple: No behavior exists, nor does it continue to exist, without reward. Children get good things for their behavior. They might get more freedom by arguing than they do by behaving in a more sociable manner. Many children have been reinforced for antisocial behavior. Parents do not mean to do this. It seems to happen on its own. But psychological laws are at play in all learning.

REWARD AND PUNISHMENT

A reward is anything that increases the frequency of a behavior. Behavior is reinforced when it gets children something they want or removes something they do not want. A reward might be money, praise, or free time. You cannot always tell what is reinforcing to children. You have to watch the behavior to determine this. If the behavior increases, then you can assume that what you have done is reinforcing. To most children, a hug is reinforcing. But to some children, it is not reinforcing and might even be punitive.

A punishment decreases the frequency of a behavior. You can punish children by giving them something they do not want or taking away something they do want. You can verbally reprimand them, send them to their room, or take away their use of the family car. Again, you have to watch the behavior to see what is a punishment. If the behavior decreases, then you can assume that you have punished it. The problem with punishment is that you cannot teach children anything new and that you get the children's minds off of what they did and onto what you are doing to them. If you want to change children, reinforcement is much more powerful.

HABITS

If children are reinforced for a behavior over a period of time, then the behavior will get to be a habit. It will develop a life of its own. This behavior will not go away easily. It will stick like glue. It will take time for new behavior to replace it. In behavioral contracting, you teach children new behavior by carefully scheduling when they get reinforced. You want to think before you act. Give the children good things when they are acting the way in which you want them to act. This means that your behavior must change as well as theirs.

The family is a powerful force in teaching children new behavior. All children want to be loved, and you can use this desire to develop the behavior you want. A behavioral contract is a means by which you control the exchange of positive reinforcement. The contract specifies who is going to do what, for whom, and under what circumstances. The contract makes explicit the expectations of each party. It gives the parent and the child the opportunity to get the things they want. It clarifies the benefits of cooperation by making each person's role in the family clear. The contract makes it more likely that each person will live up to his or her responsibilities. This leads to family harmony and stability.

LOVE

Love is the active involvement in someone's individual growth. To be loving, you must be actively involved in your children reaching their full potential. Rewards must be earned. They should not be given randomly. If you give your children good things just because they exist, then you give them no direction and you do not teach them what works in life. They will think that the world owes them things. This is not fair to the children, and it is not an accurate view of the world.

Each member in a family has rights and duties to each other, and rewards must be exchanged equally. Many times, parents feel that they are doing all of the giving and the children are doing all of the taking. This is a mistake. Happiness comes from giving to others. If parents do not teach their children to give, then the children will not be happy.

In a healthy family, if you give something, then you get something in return. The more you give, the more you get. Each member of a family should want to give all that he or she can. In the behavioral contract, if children act responsible, they earn specific rewards. Some examples of rewards include free time, time with friends, television time, spending money, and use of the family car. Each child will have a different set of rewards, and the child should actively ask for what he or she wants.

HOW TO DEVELOP A BEHAVIORAL CONTRACT

The behavioral contract details the behavior necessary for earning each reward. Let's say that you are having problems with your child coming home from school on time. For a variety of reasons, the child is late and you worry about him or her. You decide to put this behavior into the behavioral contract. If the child gets home from school every day on time, then he or she earns a certain amount of television time. If the child misses coming home, then he or she does not earn that privilege. Behaviors of interest might include minimum school attendance and performance, curfew hours, and completion of household chores. The responsibilities required must be monitored. You must be able to see whether the behavior is occurring. It would be useless for you to forbid your child from seeing a person at school because you could not monitor the behavior. If you want your child to be at school on time and to cooperate with school authorities, then you can have the teacher keep track for you. You could check with the teacher each week to be sure of compliance. You could send a school performance chart with your child to give to the teacher each day. It might look something like this.

The School Performance Chart

Name of Student _____ Date _____

To keep my parents informed about my school progress, I am asking all of my teachers to complete this form at the end of each class period. Thank you.

Subject _____

	Yes	No
1. Student was on time for class	_____	_____
2. Student completed homework assignment (Mark only if applicable)	_____	_____
3. Student obeyed class rules	_____	_____
4. Student was attentive to task	_____	_____
5. Student was cooperative with teacher	_____	_____

You must be sure that you are giving your child enough rewards to keep him or her cooperating with the contract. If the child believes that the contract is not good for him or her, then the child will resist the whole idea. All parties in the contract must have a full say about what they want, and everyone must be willing to compromise. All parties must agree to the contract and sign it. You must include the consequences that will occur if the child does not comply with the terms of the contract.

Make sure that you verbally reinforce your child as he or she complies. We are striving for progress, not perfection. Statements such as "Good job! You're doing great! I'm proud of you!" go a long way toward getting your child to cooperate cheerfully.

Detailing What Each Party Wants

The first thing you need to do is determine what all parties want from the family. The child might want to go out on weekend nights and stay out until 11 o'clock. The child might want to use the family car. The child might want to go out without explaining where he or she is going. The child might want a new bike. The child might want to choose his or her own clothes or hairstyle without your input. Brainstorm with your child about what he or she wants from you. Then decide what you want from your child. You might want the child to improve in school. You might want the child to come home on time. You might want the child to keep you informed about where he or she is. You might want the child to help out with the household chores.

Write down all of these things. With the counselor, work out what each person is willing to give to get what he or she wants from the others. It is important that each person gets the reasonable things that they want from the contract. All parties mutually exchange things that they want from each other. The contract might look something like this.

A Sample Contract

Privilege	Responsibility
In exchange for the privilege of going out one weekend night of the week at 7 p.m. and coming home by 11 p.m.	Robert agrees to maintain a weekly B average in school
In exchange for going out one weeknight at 7 p.m. and returning by 10 p.m.	Robert agrees to wash the family car once a week
In exchange for the privilege of using the family car once a week	Robert agrees to wash the dishes at dinner and take out the garbage
In exchange for the privilege of having Robert cut the grass	Mr. and Mrs. Jones agree to pay him $5 each week

Consequence	
If Robert is 1 to 10 minutes late coming home	Robert agrees to come home 30 minutes earlier the next time he goes out
If Robert is 10 to 30 minutes late coming home	Robert will lose the privilege of going out one weekend night

In this contract, the parents will need to keep a written record of when Robert comes home, and Robert will have to provide the parents with a school performance chart each day.

The contract can include anything you want so long as everyone agrees to it. Let the primary counselor help you. If you have any problems with the contract, then you can discuss the issues in the aftercare group.

Appendix 26

Family Questionnaire
Robert R. Perkinson, Ph.D.

Your name _____ Date _____

Patient name _____ Relationship _____

Address _____

Home phone _____

Work phone _____

Best time for you to be contacted by the family program counselor _____

Chemical dependency affects everyone it touches. Chemically dependent persons and everyone close to them are adversely affected. No one wants a loved one to be sick, so the family members pretend that the disease is not there. The average chemically dependent person has been ill for years before the family finally realizes that there is a problem. After the problem has been identified, there are even more years before the average chemically dependent person receives treatment.

The person you care for is in treatment. That is great! You can relax and know that this person is safe. This person stands at the turning point, and there is an excellent chance that he or she will achieve a stable sobriety. The person might have further problems, but this is a major step in the right direction. You have done the right thing, and you can feel good about it.

The patient might not feel good about coming to treatment right now. The patient might feel angry or rejected. The patient might still believe that he or she does not have a problem. This is denial. It is very common, and it is one of the best signs that the disease is present. Chemical dependency demands that these people lie to themselves. They are fooled into believing that they are okay even when their lives are falling apart.

It is important for you to understand that it is not only the chemically dependent person who is having problems. If you have lived close to a chemically dependent person, then you are having problems too. All of these problems have, at their source, subtle distortions of reality. Family members change reality into something that does not make them so nervous. Trying to keep the reality of chemical dependency hidden is like hiding an elephant in your living room. The problem is there, and it is big. It takes large distortions of reality to keep it hidden. The family tries to pretend that there is not a problem. As the problem gets bigger, it takes distortions of reality to keep it secret.

The distorting begins with minimizing. Family members pretend that the problem is not so bad. They believe that other people have more problems than they do. They think that the drinking is not that bad. It could be worse. They minimize to the point where they cannot see the real effect of the illness on themselves and on the other family members. But the problem is big. They focus on the chemically dependent person, and as they do, they become cut off from their own feelings. They have no time for themselves. This sinks the family deeper into an unreal world.

The next lie that families tell themselves is that there is a good excuse for the problem. This is called rationalization. It is not the drugs. It is the job, the boss, or maybe even me. The family members, even the children, may feel responsible for the chemically dependent person's drinking or drug use. They blame themselves, other people, institutions, money, whatever it takes to take their minds off of the real problem. The family actually believes that it is these other things that are the problem. It is not the chemicals.

The last distortion of reality is called denial. This is where the family members do not experience the full impact of their lives. They have developed such a tolerance for the craziness that they think it is normal. Their lives may be coming apart, but they still think that things are under control.

Now is the time for the patient to get honest with himself or herself. Do not make things seem smaller than they were. Do not make excuses. Write down exactly what happened.

Why did the patient decide to seek treatment at this time?

_____

_____

_____

What mood altering chemicals does the patient currently use? Mark all that apply.

Chemical	*Amount Used per Day*
_____ Alcohol	_____
_____ Tranquilizers	_____
_____ "Sleeping pills"	_____
_____ Marijuana (pot)	_____
_____ Cocaine	_____
_____ Amphetamines (speed)	_____
_____ Pain medications	_____
_____ Hallucinogens (LSD)	_____
_____ Inhalants (e.g., gas, paint, glue)	_____
_____ Over-the-counter medications	_____
_____ Narcotics	_____

What is the pattern of use?

_____ Continuous (daily)

_____ Periodic (fairly regular pattern)

_____ Sporadic (off and on with no pattern)

What is the problem as you see it?

_____ Alcohol

_____ Illegal/Street drugs

_____ Prescription drugs

_____ Combination of alcohol and drugs

_____ Emotional problems

_____ Family problems

What is the problem as the patient sees it?

_____ Alcohol

_____ Prescription drugs

_____ Illegal/Street drugs

_____ Combination of alcohol and drugs

_____ Emotional problems

_____ Family problems

What is the patient's awareness of the problem?

_____ No awareness: "I don't have a problem. It's no worse than anyone else."

_____ Minimal awareness: "Sure I've had a problem, but I can take it or leave it."

_____ Moderate awareness: "I have a problem, but I can handle it on my own."

_____ Admits to a problem and accepts the responsibility for change.

What is the duration of the problem?

_____ 0 to 6 months

_____ 6 months to 1 year

_____ 1 to 2 years

_____ 2 to 5 years

_____ More than 5 years (specify number of years: _____)

What is the longest period of abstinence?

_____ Days

_____ Weeks

_____ A month at a time

_____ 6 to 12 months at a time

When the patient was abstinent, what was the reason why he or she stopped using?

_____

_____

_____

Which of the following symptoms of dependency apply to the patient?

_____ Blackouts (cannot remember what he or she did while drinking)

_____ Hides or protects supply of drugs or alcohol

_____ Cannot stop once he or she starts

_____ Makes excuses for using alcohol or drugs

_____ Has a physical problem associated with use (e.g., tremors, nausea, headache)

_____ Personality changes while using

_____ Other (explain: _____)

Which of the following behaviors has the patient demonstrated?

_____ Violent, aggressive, or abusive behavior

_____ Unreasonable resentments (e.g., holds grudges)

_____ Changing type of friends (e.g., changing to friends who use)

_____ Poor school or work performance

_____ Unable to join in family activities

_____ Unable to do things that he or she should do (e.g., unable to keep appointments or to get things done at home or at work)

How does the patient obtain money to buy alcohol or other drugs?

_____

_____

_____

How much do you think the patient spends on alcohol or other drugs? Has this created a problem for you, your family, or the patient?

_____

_____

_____

How has the chemical use changed family activities?

_____
_____
_____
_____

What does the patient think about AA/NA?

_____ Critical of AA/NA members

_____ "Good program, but it's not for me"

_____ AA/NA is the answer to the problem

_____ Has no knowledge of AA/NA

Previous treatment: Has the patient participated in any of the following treatments for chemical dependency?

_____ Attended a few AA/NA meetings

_____ Participated regularly for a brief period

_____ General hospital

_____ Psychiatric treatment

_____ Outpatient treatment

_____ Inpatient treatment

Give a brief history of treatment dates.

_____
_____
_____
_____

Are there any other problems in connection with or related to the chemical problem?

_____ Not to my knowledge

_____ School problems

_____ Work problems

_____ Legal problems

_____ Financial problems

_____ Family problems

_____ Psychiatric problems

Explain:

_____
_____
_____
_____

Have you or other family members experienced any of the following?

_____ Health problems

_____ School/Work problems

_____ Legal problems

_____ Financial problems

_____ Difficulty in expressing feelings

Explain:

_____

_____

_____

_____

What treatment have you sought for yourself and your family?

_____ AA/NA

_____ Al-Anon/Alateen

_____ Counseling

_____ Psychiatric visits

Explain:

_____

_____

_____

_____

Have any of your children been referred to the following:

_____ Social services

_____ Juvenile detention center

_____ Court services

_____ Psychological services

_____ Chemical dependency treatment

Explain:

_____

_____

_____

_____

Can you see anything that might interfere with the evaluation or treatment of your family member(s)?

_____

_____

_____

_____

_____

What do you believe are the problem areas that need to be addressed while the patient is in treatment?

_____

_____

_____

_____

_____

In addition to the questions that have already been covered, is there any other information that we should know about the patient?

_____

_____

_____

_____

Which types of abuse have occurred in your current family?

_____ Emotional

_____ Verbal

_____ Physical

_____ Sexual

Explain:

_____

_____

_____

_____

Did any of the following types of abuse occur in your family when you were growing up?

_____ Emotional

_____ Verbal

_____ Physical

_____ Sexual

Explain:

_____

_____

_____

_____

Do you believe that chemical dependency is a disease?

Yes _____   No _____

Explain how the chemical problem has affected your relationship with the patient.

_____

_____

_____

_____

Write down the names of all members of your family and rate them on how they use mood-altering chemicals. No use = 0; infrequent use = 2; social use = 3; misuse/abuse = 4; dependency = 5.

Family Member	*Chemical Used*	*Rating*
Yourself _____		
Present spouse _____		
Former spouse _____		
Children _____		
_____		
_____		
_____		
Your father _____		
Your mother _____		
Your brothers and sisters _____		
_____		
_____		
_____		
Other family members _____		
_____		
_____		

Appendix 27

Codependency
Robert R. Perkinson, Ph.D.

Codependency is what happens to someone who is trying to control someone else. If your loved one is chemically dependent, then you probably have tried to help him or her. You have attempted to fix the problem. But you could not fix it any more than you could fix your loved one if he or she had cancer. Chemical dependency is a disease for which no one is to blame. The causes of chemical dependency are so varied and complex that no one has been able to figure it all out. It is too complicated.

In your love for the patient, you might have done some things that were not good for you. It is very common for codependent persons to take better care of the other persons than they do of themselves. You may have been so concentrated on the other person's problems that you had no time for your own. This is a mistake. This is your turn to stop and concentrate on yourself. What has happened to you in your struggle against this disease? Our experience shows us that the family member who looks at his or her own life will immeasurably help the patient to achieve a stable recovery. If only the patient is treated, then the chance of success is reduced.

There are a variety of codependent traits. These are maladaptive thoughts and behaviors that have been learned in response to the chemically dependent person. It is important that you take a look at each of these traits because they inhibit you from being able to live a normal life. You cannot solve problems accurately when these traits are at work. They distract you. They keep you from seeing the truth.

DEFENSE MECHANISMS

Defense mechanisms are mental states where we refuse to see reality. We cut ourselves off from reality because the real world is too painful for us. We need to live in a fantasy world of our own creation. The more we use defense mechanisms, the more cut off from reality we are. We feel lonely and helpless because no one can reach us in our self-deceived world.

Minimization

It begins with minimization. When we minimize, we take reality and make it smaller than it really is. We pretend that the problem is not bad when it is bad. We may have become so deluded that we think that drinking a six pack of beer every night is normal. Doesn't everyone drink like this? We may minimize about the financial problems. They do not seem so bad either. Doesn't everyone struggle like this? We minimize about verbal and physical abuse. This person was just mad, out of control, or drunk. That was not really him or her. This person is not really like that. We may minimize by telling ourselves that the addicted person just overdid it at the party. This individual is really a good person. He or she did not mean it. When we minimize, we tell ourselves that we have no reason to feel afraid. If the problem were bad, then we would have to be frightened and do something about it. But it is not so bad, so we can relax.

List five times when you told yourself that things were not bad when they really were.

1. _____
2. _____
3. _____
4. _____
5. _____

Rationalization

The next defense mechanism we use is rationalization. This is where we make an excuse for the patient. The patient is drinking or drugging because he or she has had a hard life, had a fight with his or her mother, had a bad childhood, got fired, has financial problems, has problems with a sibling, or just is not understood. Codependents can think of a million reasons why the person is using, but the real reason is that the person is chemically dependent. The person is sick and needs help. We do not want to see this truth because it is frightening. We do not want to believe that our loved one is ill. We want to believe that this person is just fine or is only having temporary difficulty.

A rationalization is a lie. It is an excuse for the real problem. Did you ever make an excuse for the chemically dependent person? Did you ever tell the boss that this person was sick or tell the children that the person was not feeling well when you knew that he or she was intoxicated or too hung over to function? If you did, you may have believed some of this yourself.

List five times when you made an excuse for the patient's behavior.

1. _____
2. _____
3. _____
4. _____
5. _____

You can see what is happening to the family. By minimizing and rationalizing, family members get more and more cut off from reality. They cannot accurately see what is going on anymore. They are using the defense mechanisms to cut themselves off from the painful truth.

Denial

The most characteristic form of defense used in chemical dependency is denial. This is where the mind refuses to experience the full emotional impact of what is happening. Your family is falling apart. Your relationship is shot. You cannot talk to your family anymore. You are in severe financial trouble, and you still think that you can fix these things. You still think that all of these problems are something else other than chemical dependency. You might even be so fooled that you think that the problems are your fault. If you were a better wife, husband, child, or parent, then the chemically dependent person would not be having problems.

List the worst things that have happened during the past few years while the chemically dependent person was using drugs or alcohol.

1. _____
2. _____
3. _____
4. _____
5. _____

In each of these situations, what were you telling yourself that convinced you that things were all right?

1. _____
2. _____
3. _____
4. _____
5. _____

CARETAKING

Codependent people focus on the other person. They are obsessed with taking care of the chemically dependent person to the point where they lose contact with reality. They actually think that everything will be all right if they do the right things. They plan everything for everyone. They scold and control. They read self-help books. They feel responsible for everyone's feelings. They go to extraordinary lengths to help. They feel totally drained, as if there is not enough time in the day. They threaten, cry, lie, scream, blame, and shame. They seek counseling, pray, and manipulate. All of these behaviors, and many more, are designed to bring control to an out-of-control situation. Codependent people think that they can fix things if they just work hard enough. The fact of the matter is that they cannot control someone else's behavior, no matter how much they try. The more they try, the more frustrating it becomes.

List five ways in which you tried to control the chemically dependent person.

1. _____
2. _____
3. _____
4. _____
5. _____

ENABLING

In treatment, you must understand that you cannot control anyone but yourself. You are responsible for only your own actions. If you keep the chemically dependent person out of trouble, then you keep that person from suffering the natural consequences of his or her behavior. If you call the boss and make excuses, then the patient does not learn from his or her mistakes. This is called enabling. By protecting the patient from the consequences of his or her addiction, you help the patient stay sick. You must stop protecting the patient from his or her maladaptive behavior. You must not pay the patient's bad checks or debts, make excuses, or smooth over ruffled feathers. You must let the patient be responsible.

By caretaking and enabling, codependent people constantly get the chemically dependent person out of trouble. They protect the patient from the consequences of his or her actions. They may call the boss and say that the patient is sick when, if fact, the patient is too intoxicated or hung over to come to work. They may tell the children that their dad or mom needs to rest when, in fact, the patient has passed out on the couch. They may pay the bail or the bad checks. They may call the creditors who are clamoring for payment. They may comfort abused family members and try to make everything better.

List five times when you got the chemically dependent person out of trouble.

1. _____
2. _____
3. _____
4. _____
5. _____

You were taking the responsibility for someone else's behavior. By protecting the patient from the logical consequences of his or her own actions, you helped the patient avoid the pain of the disease. This prevented the patient from learning that he or she was sick and needed help. You enabled the illness to stay hidden. You helped the patient to avoid reality. By protecting the patient from pain, you prevented him or her from seeing the severity of the problem. This has got to stop. Each person in a family has to accept the responsibility for his or her own behavior. Everyone must make his or her own decisions and live with the consequences.

INABILITY TO KNOW FEELINGS

People who are codependent do not know how they feel. They are so focused on the other person's feelings that they ignore their own. They know how the other person is doing, but they do not know much about themselves. For the most part, codependent people think that they are fine, but what they are really feeling is frustrated, frightened, and depressed. They are desperately trying to bring order to disorder and confusion.

People who live in a chemically dependent home do not trust how they feel. They feel as though something is wrong with them. They try to block out the reality of the nightmare that they are living. They might even make up what their family is like. Bradshaw (1988, 1990) described this as a fantasy bond. Children or family members create an idealized family in their minds. They might feel that their father is warm and loving when, in fact, he is actually abusive. They might feel their mother is a good mother when, in fact, she always is away drinking at the bar.

In chemically dependent homes, family members learn that feelings are dangerous. If they share how they feel, then bad things will happen. They keep their fear, sadness, anger, disgust, and hurt to themselves. They keep the secrets, sharing them with no one.

List some situations where you kept your real feelings to yourself. Who were you trying to protect by keeping these feelings secret?

1. _____
2. _____
3. _____
4. _____
5. _____

INABILITY TO KNOW WHAT YOU WANT

Codependent people are so obsessed with the wants and wishes of the chemically dependent person that they lose what they want for themselves. They become experts at manipulating the family to get the sick person what he or she wants, but they become less and less skilled at getting what they themselves want. They believe that they have no wants. They are trying so desperately to control the situation that they have no time for their own needs.

Stop and think for a minute. What do you want out of life? List five things that you want.

1. _____
2. _____
3. _____
4. _____
5. _____

Now write a letter to the chemically dependent person telling him or her how you feel. Ask this person for what you want. Be thorough. Do not leave out any of your feelings or wants. Be completely honest with yourself and the other person. When you have the letter written, put it aside. We will use it later.

LACK OF TRUST

Family members from a chemically dependent home have been living in a situation where they could not trust anything or anyone. They did not know what was going to happen. Family rules changed when the chemically dependent person was intoxicated or hung over. A father who was loving could turn into a monster. A mother who was quiet could turn loud, aggressive, and pushy. Someone who usually was happy could sob hopelessly. There was nothing that the family could trust. Alcohol or drugs could change any rule at any time. This is an atmosphere permeated by fear. The family members live in a constant state of tension. When they come home, they do not know what to expect. When the car drives up in the driveway, they do not know what is going to happen. Things can get out of control in a hurry, and the behaviors can be life threatening. The chemically dependent person and the people around that person constantly lie about what the addicted person is doing. They hide how much the addicted person is using. They lie about what the addicted person is doing. No one in the home can be trusted. No one knows the truth.

This lack of trust builds an atmosphere heavy with fear. The family members are constantly worried about what is going to happen next. What makes this even worse is that they try to hide the family secret from everyone. This increases their feelings of isolation and helplessness.

List five things that happened in your family that convinced you that you could not trust your family members.

1. _____
2. _____
3. _____
4. _____
5. _____

PEOPLE PLEASING

Codependent people are people pleasers. They will do virtually anything to keep someone else happy. They feel personally responsible for the other person's feelings. People pleasers never are interested in what they themselves want. They are interested in what the other person wants. They want to keep the other person happy. They do not care about how they themselves feel. People pleasers will go to incredible lengths to keep the other person feeling comfortable. They tell people that they are feeling fine when, in fact, they are coming apart at the seams. They have a smile for everybody. They are nice, nice, nice. They rarely, if ever, go against the flow of things. They are almost incapable of saying no. If they say no, then they feel guilty. They will allow people to violate their boundaries. They never rock the boat.

List five times when you did something you did not want to do just to please some other person.

1. _____
2. _____
3. _____
4. _____
5. _____

FEELINGS OF WORTHLESSNESS

Codependent persons feel worthless compared to other people. They do not feel as though they deserve the good stuff. They have been treated so badly, been taken advantage of so many times, and given of themselves without getting anything back so often that they have given up. They are tired. They feel burdened. It is like carrying the world around on their shoulders. Somewhere, deep down in a secret part of their minds, they fear that they deserve to be treated poorly. They feel like they are small persons of little worth. They feel like they do not matter. They are not important. These codependent people think that they are stupid, unattractive, inadequate, and incompetent. They do not feel capable of dealing with the world. They feel vulnerable, lost, and alone.

When you look at yourself in the mirror, what do you see? Circle all that apply.

1. I am stupid.
2. I am ugly.
3. I am old.
4. Other people are smarter than I am.
5. I never get the breaks.
6. I hate myself.
7. No one loves me.
8. No one knows me.
9. God made a mistake when God made me.
10. I am inadequate.

We could go on with the negative self-statements, but you get the idea. Codependent people constantly bombard themselves with negative self-talk. The talk is inaccurate and extremely self-damaging. If you use any of the preceding statements, you must feel terrible about yourself.

Treatment is a time to get accurate. You must learn to live in the real world and to see the positive as well as the negative. List 10 positive things about yourself. If you have difficulty, then ask someone who knows you to help you.

1. _____
2. _____
3. _____
4. _____
5. _____
6. _____
7. _____
8. _____
9. _____
10. _____

Write these down on a piece of paper and tape it to your mirror. Read them to yourself at least once a day.

DEPENDENT

Codependent persons are overly dependent. They feel incapable of making good decisions. They do not trust themselves. They get their self-worth from someone else. They may coerce and threaten to leave an addicted spouse, but the thought of leaving fills them with panic. They feel overly vulnerable to the world and everything in it. They do not feel as though they can do things on their own. Even if a spouse is incapacitated from the disease, a codependent person can still feel dependent on the spouse. "What would I do on my own? What would happen to the children? How would I support myself?" These all are serious questions, and it leaves codependent persons stuck in an intolerable situation. They cannot stay, and they cannot leave. Dependency is fueled by deep-seated feelings of inadequacy and shame. Codependent persons do not feel capable of doing anything other than holding on.

Do you feel competent to handle life on your own?

_____

_____

_____

POOR COMMUNICATION SKILLS

Codependent people have poor communication skills. They cannot ask for what they want or share how they feel. This leaves them incapable of communicating effectively. They are so concerned with how the other person feels, and with what the other person wants, that they do not even think about their own needs. Closeness in interpersonal relationships depends on the ability to share the whole truth with someone. You have to be able to tell that person how you feel and ask him or her for what you want. To be a good communicator, you have to be a good listener. You have to probe and question the other person to bring out the whole truth. Codependents do not want to know the truth. The truth is too painful. They are busy keeping the truth from themselves and from everyone else. If they knew the whole truth, then they would be terrified.

Codependents feel lonely because they feel as though no one knows them. They feel as though no one understands them. They try to communicate but feel as though the message never really gets across. They feel isolated and trapped.

When is the last time you felt really understood by anybody? Describe the time and person and what it meant to you.

_____

_____

_____

Do you believe that the patient understands you?

Yes _____   No _____

Explain

_____

_____

_____

What are the roadblocks in the way of your communicating openly with others?

_____

_____

_____

THE TOOLS OF RECOVERY

In treatment, you will learn the tools of recovery. The first of these tools is honesty. Without rigorous honesty, this program will not work for you. You must tell the truth all of the time. You will need to hold family members accountable by constantly sharing your feelings. This takes practice. In treatment, you must accept your powerlessness over the disease. If you still think that you can figure it out or work it out, then you are still acting codependent.

Alcoholics Anonymous says that probably no human power can remove this disease. The second tool of recovery is a Higher Power. You must turn the problem over to a power greater than yourself. If you continue to try to handle the problem by yourself, then you will fail. If you turn the problem over to God, then you will succeed. Practice whenever you are faced with a problem. Stop and seek God's will in that matter. Do not try to figure it out for yourself. Ask for God's guidance.

The third tool of recovery is going to meetings. You must attend regular Al-Anon meetings to continue your recovery. If you think that it is only the chemically dependent person who needs to attend meetings, then you are off track. You have problems too. You need treatment to get back on track. Al-Anon groups will give you the support, encouragement, and education that you need for continued recovery.

The fourth tool of recovery is using good interpersonal relationship skills. This means that you have to share how you feel and ask for what you want. You have to listen and take the time that is necessary to develop healthy communication skills. This will not come easily. You have many habits to overcome. You no longer can just do what the other person wants. You no longer can live to please the other person in your life. You must accept the responsibility for your own behavior and allow the other person to accept the responsibility for his or her own behavior. You must allow the person to suffer the consequences for his or her actions. You have to stop living for the other person and start living for yourself.

Many of you are thinking, "How selfish!" You were taught to always let the other person come first. You were taught that it is not right to ask for what you want. But you have to love yourself to be happy. If you leave yourself out, then you will suffer. God says to love God all you can, love yourself all you can, and love others all you can. That is all that we are asking you to do. Bring this exercise and the letter to your family member to the family program.

Appendix 28

Personal Recovery Plan

Name: _____   Home Phone: _____

Admission Date: _____   Work Phone: _____

Discharge Date: _____

Name of Concerned Other: _____   Phone: _____

It is important to your recovery to continue to work through your problems on discharge. Your recovery never can stand still. You must be constantly moving forward in your program. Working with your counselor, you must detail exactly what you need to do following inpatient treatment. Each psychological problem or family problem will need a specific plan of action. You must commit yourself to following this recovery plan to the letter. Do not think that just because you have completed treatment, your problems are over. Your recovery is just beginning, and you need to work diligently to stay clean and sober.

Make a list of the problems that you need to address in continuing care. Any emotional, family, legal, social, physical, leisure, work, spiritual, or school problem will have to have a plan. How are you going to address that problem in recovery? What is the goal? What do you want to achieve? Develop your personal recovery plan with your counselor's assistance.

A. Treatment plan for continued sobriety

    1. Problem 1: _____

         Goal: _____

         Plan: _____

         _____

         _____

         _____

    2. Problem 2: _____

         Goal: _____

         Plan: _____

         _____

         _____

         _____

    3. Problem 3: _____

         Goal: _____

         Plan: _____

         _____

         _____

         _____

4. Problem 4: _____

      Goal: _____

      Plan: _____

      _____

      _____

      _____

5. Problem 5: _____

      Goal: _____

      Plan: _____

      _____

      _____

      _____

B. Relapse

In the event of a relapse, list the specific steps that you will take to deal with the problem.

_____

_____

_____

_____

C. Support in recovery

Indicate the AA/NA meetings that you will attend each week after discharge. We recommend that you attend at least three meetings per week for the first few months following discharge.

Day	Time	Location
_____	_____	_____
_____	_____	_____
_____	_____	_____
_____	_____	_____
_____	_____	_____

D. Indicate when you will attend aftercare group.

Day	Time	Location
_____	_____	_____

E. Who is the AA/NA contact person or persons who can provide you with support in early recovery?

Name: _____ Phone: _____

Name: _____ Phone: _____

Name: _____ Phone: _____

F. If you have any problems or concerns in sobriety, you always can call the treatment center staff at the following number:

_____

G. If you and your counselor have arranged for further counseling or treatment following discharge, then complete the following:

Name of Agency: _____

Address: _____ Phone: _____

First Appointment: Day _____ Time _____

H. Make a list of the things that you are going to do daily to stay clean and sober.

1. _____
2. _____
3. _____
4. _____
5. _____
6. _____
7. _____
8. _____
9. _____
10. _____

I. You are changing your lifestyle. It will be important to avoid certain people and situations that will put you at high risk. List the people and places you need to avoid in early recovery.

1. _____
2. _____
3. _____
4. _____
5. _____

STATEMENT OF COMMITMENT

I understand that the success of my recovery depends on adherence to my recovery plan. The aftercare program has been explained to me, and I understand fully what I must do in recovery. I commit to myself that I will follow this plan.

Patient's Signature: _____

Staff Member's Signature: _____

Date: _____

Appendix 29

Sample Discharge Summary

IDENTIFYING INFORMATION: Mary Louise Roberts is a 45-year-old, married White female. She has two children. She lives in Thomas, Maryland, with her husband, Mark, and her two daughters. She has lived in Thomas for the past 5 years. She is currently employed as a secretary for Morton Electronics. She was admitted to Keystone Treatment Center on 9-9-01. She was referred by Marcie Frankle, a counselor at the Mandel Mental Health Clinic.

CHIEF COMPLAINT: "Drinking."

ASSESSMENT OF PROBLEM AREAS: The following problems were identified by the clinical staff as needing to be addressed in treatment.

Problem 1: Pathological relationship to alcohol

Problem 2: Depression

Problem 3: Poor interpersonal relationship skills

Problem 4: Unresolved grief

Problem 5: Borderline personality disorder

The following problems were identified and treated by the medical staff.

Problem 2: Depression

Problem 6: Fractured finger

MEDICAL REPORT (this report is completed by the medical staff): Mary's admission lab work and urinalysis were within normal limits. An admission physical was completed with no significant findings noted. While in treatment, Mary hit a door with her right hand. An X ray was taken on 9-15-01, and it found evidence of a transverse hairline fracture on the radial side of the distal neck of the right fifth metacarpal. No specific treatment was needed. At discharge, Mary voiced no physical complaints. Her hand was observed to be healing. In treatment, the patient received a daily multivitamin. We have recommended that the patient continue her multivitamin therapy for at least 6 months following discharge.

Problem 2: Depression

> *Progress notes:* For her major depression, Mary was started on Prozac (20 mg q.d.) on 9-22-01. No side effects were noted. The medication was reviewed with the patient prior to discharge, and a 1-week supply of Prozac was sent home with her. We have recommended that the patient continue to take the medication daily and to see Dr. Frank Smith of the Mandel Mental Health Clinic in Thomas, Maryland. She has an appointment on 10-5-01 at 3:45 p.m. for a follow-up visit.

TREATMENT PLAN AND PROGRESS NOTES:

Goal 1: Begin a program of recovery congruent with a sober lifestyle.

> *Progress notes:* When Mary first entered treatment, she minimized her drinking behavior and denied the need to be in treatment. She stated that she did not have a problem with alcohol that was severe enough to require treatment. She completed the Honesty exercise (Appendix 9), and she began to see how she was deceiving herself about the extent of her alcohol problem. She was able to trace the family problems that were a direct cause of her drinking behavior. The patient was able to see that the DWI (driving while intoxicated arrest) she received last year was directly related to her drinking. In her first step, Mary was able to share her powerlessness to quit drinking on her own and the unmanageability of her life. Mary began to accept her alcoholism during the second week of treatment. She rec-

369

ognized that she would have to change her attitudes and behaviors if she was going to be able to maintain a sober lifestyle. A major stumbling block to Mary's treatment was her lack of trust. It was difficult for her to trust her interpersonal group for the first few weeks of treatment. As Mary was able to share more in group, she was able to see that the group could be trusted. This was a great relief to the patient, and this was a significant move forward in her treatment program. Mary struggled with the same trust issue when she worked through her Second Step and Third Step. She began to practice prayer and meditation in treatment, and this convinced her that there was a Higher Power called God. She completed a Fifth Step with the staff clergy, and this significantly relieved her. She stated that this was the first time that she had ever told anyone the whole truth. Mary was able to carefully assess high-risk situations for relapse by working through the Relapse Prevention exercise (Appendix 17). Her situation of greatest risk appears to be her tendency to become depressed, and this leads her to further drinking. The patient has committed herself to call this treatment center, her sponsor, or her therapist if she begins to feel depressed in continuing care. Mary does state a sincere desire to maintain a sober lifestyle and to live a happy life without alcohol.

Goal 2: Alleviate symptoms of depression.

Progress notes: Mary stated on admission that she had been feeling severely depressed for the past 6 months. She had experienced suicidal ideation and had made two suicide attempts before coming into treatment. While in treatment, she visited with the staff psychologist and took the Beck Depression Inventory weekly. She read *Coping With Depression* (Beck & Greenberg, 1974) and logged her dysfunctional thoughts. The patient's negative thinking centered around thinking that she was ugly, stupid, and inadequate. Once these thoughts were challenged for accuracy, the patient could see that she was pretty; bright; and a capable wife, mother, and secretary. The patient was placed on medication for her depression. Mary is aware that she has to stay on this medication for at least 6 months. Two weeks after starting the medication and working on correcting her thinking, Mary's Beck depression scores began to improve. Her score dropped from severe depression to mild depression over her 4 weeks of treatment. Mary still shows some excessive sadness, and she continues to feel overly tired and fatigued. She is sleeping through the night.

Goal 3: Learn and practice healthy interpersonal relationship skills.

Progress notes: Mary has been unable to establish and maintain healthy interpersonal relationships. Her relationship with her husband has been dysfunctional for a number of years. Mary tends to become quickly attracted to men and to think that they are the answer to her problems. When she gets closer to them, she realizes that they have as many problems as she does. She has been involved in several extramarital affairs. In one-to-one counseling, Mary was able to see how alcohol played a significant role in her relationship problems. When she was drunk, she usually fought with her husband and became involved with other men at the bar. The patient was able to see how her parents taught her to keep her feelings to herself. She learned never to ask for anything. The patient completed the Relationship Skills exercise (Appendix 12) and began to use these skills with her treatment peers. Mary was able to share her feelings with her interpersonal group. Again the trust issue was a hurdle for her. Gradually, she was able to ask for what she wanted without feeling guilty. She found out that other people in the program were trustworthy and loyal to her; they could keep information in confidence. Mary was able to work though the Communication Skills exercise (Appendix 14) and was able to improve her active listening skills. She began to stop manipulating to get what she wanted and began to ask for what she wanted. She worked on developing assertiveness skills and was able to confront people in group about behavior that troubled her. Mary was able to establish many meaningful relationships while in treatment.

Goal 4: Identify her losses and share her feelings with others. Develop an understanding of the grief process, and learn healthy ways of coping with her grief.

Progress notes: Mary lost her mother to cancer 2 years ago and lost her brother to an automobile accident last March. It became clear to the clinical staff that Mary had not appropriately grieved through these losses in her life. The pain was still very evident in Mary's behavior whenever she would talk about her mother or brother. She would cry for long periods of time whenever these issues were discussed in group. Mary talked about her grief and began to share her feelings in one-to-one counseling and in interpersonal group. Several of her treatment peers had similar losses to report, and Mary began to take an active role in getting them to talk about their losses. As she was able to share her pain with the group, Mary's grief began to ease. She wrote letters of closure to her mother and brother and read these letters to several treatment peers. Mary spoke on several occasions with the staff clergy about the deaths, and she began to turn the situation over to the care of God. She began to believe that God was taking good care of her mother and brother and that she would see them again. Mary stated that she felt that her mother and brother would want her to continue with her life and to let go of the grief she was feeling. At the end of treatment, Mary was able to talk about the deaths in her family without crying and with new hope about her dependence on God.

Goal 5: Learn coping skills for dealing with symptoms of borderline personality disorder.

Progress notes: Mary has had a persistent affective problem all of her life. She experiences rapid extreme shifts in her feelings, from feeling relatively normal to feeling severely angry, depressed, or frightened. The patient had been drinking to relieve herself of these uncomfortable feelings. Her interpersonal relationships have been severely dysfunctional, and the patient has felt chronically empty and bored. Mary becomes suicidal and has cut her wrists and arms to relieve herself of her intense psychic pain. During treatment, Mary met regularly with the staff psychologist. She learned to identify her feelings and learned what action to take when she was feeling intense feelings. The patient practiced talking to a staff member or a treatment peer when she was angry or frightened. She learned to get some exercise when she was feeling intense feelings. The patient worked through the Relationship Skills exercise (Appendix 12) and the Communication Skills exercise (Appendix 14). She learned how to effectively communicate with others. The patient met with her husband once a week with her primary counselor to work on her marital problems. The patient was referred to Dr. Frank Smith, a psychiatrist who will follow the patient once a week in continuing care.

FAMILY PROGRAM: Mary's husband, Mark, and her two children, Kathy and Tina, attended the family program. Mary participated in all of the family sessions. Mark shared that he has been very frightened by Mary's drinking behavior. He tends to keep his feelings to himself and to not share what he wants from his wife. Mark expressed that he thought that Mary would come around if he could get her to address her alcohol problem. Mark was able to make significant progress in sharing his feelings in the family program. He was able to tell Mary of the hurt and fear that he had been feeling when she would go out and stay out all night. He expressed how angry he was at the extramarital affairs, one of which was with his best friend. Mark often openly wept as he shared his feelings. Kathy, the oldest child (age 10 years), was able to share how she had to take care of her younger sister when Mary was passed out on the couch. She explained how frightening it was to see her mother intoxicated and out of control. Kathy had witnessed one of her mother's suicide attempts and had to call the police to get Mary under control. This child had been more of a mother to Mary than Mary had been to her. It was obvious in the family sessions that this was a very responsible little girl. The youngest child, Tina (age 6 years), was very quiet during the sessions. She was able to express how frightened she was seeing her father and mother fight. She also had witnessed the suicide attempt. The family had problems severe enough that these family members were referred to the Mandel Mental Health Clinic for further family counseling. They have an appointment with Marcie Frankle, a marriage and family counselor, on 10-31-01 at 4 p.m.

SUMMARY: While in treatment, Mary completed the Steps One to Five of AA's Twelve Step program. She has been introduced to Steps Six to Twelve. She has worked a daily program of recovery while in treatment, and she understands what she needs to do to stay sober. Mary has developed a good understanding of her disease and has made significant changes in her attitudes and behaviors that can be used in a sober lifestyle. She is more honest with herself and with others, and she has learned good problem-solving skills. Mary can now use her feelings to help her solve problems. Mary has begun to resolve her depression and will continue to work on her psychological problems in continuing care. Her marriage is more stable, and she is going to continue marriage counseling. She knows how to cope with her feelings without drinking. She has worked though her grief issues and has established conscious contact with her Higher Power. Mary is willing to take the responsibility for her own life and behavior.

PROGNOSIS: The patient's prognosis is good. Mary has a positive attitude toward recovery. She made progress in treatment in many areas, and she worked hard. She has shown that she is willing to work to maintain her sobriety. She established many supportive relationships in treatment, and she plans to build on these friendships in recovery. She has plans to attend AA meetings with a good friend of hers who has 12 solid years of sobriety. Mary will need positive reinforcement in recovery, and she will have to address her depression until it clears. She will need to continue family counseling to stabilize her relationship with her husband and children. She is aware that she will need to stick close to AA to stay in recovery.

AFTERCARE:

1. Maintain complete abstinence from all mood-altering chemicals.
2. Attend AA meetings on a regular basis and get an AA sponsor who she can relate to. Mary does have an AA contact person, Cheryl M., 336-2281.
3. Attend aftercare group for a minimum of 6 months on Monday evenings at 7 p.m. at the Thompson Alcohol and Drug Center, 303 Fuller Lane, Thomas, Maryland. Her first appointment has been set with Charlene Schultz on 10-25-01 at 1 p.m.
4. Continue to work on a daily spiritual program that she began in treatment. Mary will attend church at the Good Faith Lutheran Church. Reverend Bob Luce is the pastor.
5. Continue to check the relapse symptoms daily and work a daily program of relapse prevention.
6. Develop honest and open relationships with others who can aid her in recovery.
7. Avoid people and places that could trigger relapse symptoms.
8. Continue Prozac therapy and continue to see Dr. Frank Smith for psychotherapy for her depression. Her first appointment is on 10-22-01 at 2:30 p.m. at the Mandel Mental Health Clinic, 12 Tigar Street, Thomas, Maryland.
9. Continue family counseling with Marcie Frankle of the Mandel Mental Health Clinic, 12 Tigar Street, Thomas, Maryland. The first appointment is on 10-22-01 at 1:30 p.m.
10. Continue to trust and praise herself in recovery. Practice self-affirmations daily.

DSM-IV-R DIAGNOSIS:

Axis I:	303.90 Alcohol dependence, severe
	296.25 Major depression, single episode in partial remission
Axis II:	301.83 Borderline personality disorder
Axis III:	Asthma
Axis IV:	Severity of psychosocial stressors: Personal illness, death in the family, Severity 4 (severe)
Axis V:	Current global assessment of functioning: 70

Appendix 30

Stress Management
Robert R. Perkinson, Ph.D.

Unresolved stress fuels chemical dependency. Addicted individuals deal with stress by using chemicals rather than using other more appropriate coping skills. Everyone has stress, and everyone needs to learn how to manage stress in daily life. Stress is the generalized physiological response to a stressor. A stressor is any demand made on the body.

A stressor can be anything that mobilizes the body for change. This can include psychological or physiological loss, absence of stimulation, excessive stimulation, frustration of an anticipated reward, conflict, and presentation or anticipation of painful events (Zegans, 1982).

The stress response is good and adaptive. It activates the body for problem solving. Stress is destructive only when it is chronic. The overly stressed body breaks down. Initially, the body produces certain chemicals to handle the stressful situation. Initially, these chemical changes are adaptive. But in the long run, they are destructive. Severe or chronic stress has been linked to irreversible disease including kidney impairment, high blood pressure, arteriosclerosis, ulcer, and a compromised immune system that can result in increased infections and cancer (Selye, 1956).

When animals encounter an unsolvable problem, they ultimately get sick. They fall victim to a wide variety of physical and mental disorders. Under chronic stress, these organisms ultimately die.

It seems that everyone has a genetic predisposition to break down in a certain organ system when under chronic stress. Some people get depressed, some get ulcers, and some become chemically dependent.

In treatment, you must learn how to deal with stress in ways other than by using chemicals. You must learn to use the stress signals that your body gives you to help you solve problems. If you cannot solve the problem yourself, then you need to get some help.

Most people who are chemically dependent are dealing with unresolved pain that they never have worked through. They begin drinking or using chemicals to ease the pain, and soon they become chemically dependent. Addiction is a primary disease. It takes over people's lives and makes everything worse.

Stress management techniques help addicted individuals to regain the control they have lost in their lives. By establishing and maintaining a daily program of recovery, they learn how to cope with stress. If you are dealing with stress better, then you are not as likely to relapse. There are three elements necessary to reduce your overall stress level: a regular exercise program, regular relaxation, and a change in lifestyle.

RELAXATION

For centuries, people have relaxed to quiet their minds and reach a state of peace. When animals have enough to eat and they are safe, they lie down. People do not do that because humans are the only animals that worry about the future. Humans fear that if they relax today, then they will be in trouble tomorrow.

Benson (1975) showed that when people relax twice a day for 10 to 20 minutes, it has a major impact on their overall stress levels. People who do this have fewer illnesses, feel better, and are healthier. Illness such as high blood pressure, ulcers, and headaches can go away completely with a regular relaxation program.

Benson maintained that the relaxation technique is simple.

1. Sit or lie down in a quiet place.

2. Pay attention to your breathing.

3. Every time you exhale, say the word *one* over quietly to yourself. It is normal for other ideas to come, but when they do, just return to the word *one.*

4. Do this for 10 to 20 minutes twice a day.

You do not have to use the word *one.* You can use any other word or phrase of your choice, but it has to be the same word or phrase repeated over and over again. You can get some relaxation tapes or music that you find relaxing. You can pray or meditate. The most important thing is to relax as completely as you can. If you do this, then your stress level will be lower and you will be better able to mobilize yourself to deal with stress when it occurs.

As you practice relaxation, you will learn how it feels to be relaxed. Try to keep this feeling all day long. When you feel stressed, stop and take two deep breaths. Breathe in through your nose and out through your mouth. As you exhale, feel a warm wave of relaxation flow down your body. Once you have regained your state of relaxation, return to your day and move a little slower this time. Remember, nothing is ever done too well or too slowly. You do not have to do things quickly to succeed.

When you come to something new that you think you need to do, ask yourself several important questions.

1. Do I have to do this?
2. Do I have to do it now?
3. Is this going to make a difference in my life?

If the new stressor is not that important, perhaps you should not do it at all. Do not decide to overly stress yourself. That does not make any sense. Know your limits. Achieve a state of relaxation in the morning, and listen to your body all day long. If anything threatens your serenity, turn it over and let God deal with it.

For the next week, set aside two times a day for relaxation. Go through the meditation exercise we discussed or some other relaxation exercise. Score the level of relaxation you achieved from 1 (*as little as possible*) to 100 (*as much as possible*). Then score your general stress level during the day in the same way. Write down any comments about your stress. List the situations when you felt the most tension.

DAY 1

Relaxation Score _____

Daily Stress Score _____

Comments _____

_____

_____

DAY 2

Relaxation Score _____

Daily Stress Score _____

Comments _____

_____

_____

DAY 3

Relaxation Score _____

Daily Stress Score _____

Comments _____

_____

_____

DAY 4

Relaxation Score _____

Daily Stress Score _____

Comments _____

_____

_____

DAY 5

    Relaxation Score _____

    Daily Stress Score _____

    Comments _____

    _____

    _____

DAY 6

    Relaxation Score _____

    Daily Stress Score _____

    Comments _____

    _____

    _____

DAY 7

    Relaxation Score _____

    Daily Stress Score _____

    Comments _____

    _____

    _____

EXERCISE

The role of exercise in the treatment of chemical dependency has been well established. Significant improvements in physical fitness can occur in as short a period as 20 days. People who maintain a regular exercise program feel less depressed and less anxious, improve their self-concepts, and enhance the quality of their lives (Folkins & Sime, 1981).

Most chemically dependent people come into treatment in poor physical and mental shape. They gave up on exercise a long time ago. Even if they were in good physical condition at one time in their lives, the chemicals have taken their toll. These people are unable to maintain a consistent level of physical fitness. The mind and body cannot maintain a regular exercise program when a person chronically abuses drugs or alcohol.

An exercise program, although difficult to develop, can be fun. You get a natural high from exercise that you do not get in any other way. It feels good, and it feels good all day.

A good exercise program includes three elements: stretching, strength, and cardiovascular fitness. The exercise therapist will assist you in developing an individualized program specific to you.

Stretching means that you increase a muscle's range of motion until you become supple and flexible. Never stretch your muscles to the point of pain. The body will warn you well before you go too far. Let the exercise therapist show you how to stretch each major muscle group. Get into a habit of stretching before all exercise.

In a strength program, you gradually lift more weight until you become stronger. Do not lift more often than every other day. The muscles need a full day of rest to repair themselves. Soon you can increase the load. Three sets of 10 repetitions each is a standard exercise for each muscle group. The exercise therapist will show you how to complete each exercise. Correct technique is very important.

Endurance training means that you exercise at a training heart rate for an extended period of time. This is where the cardiovascular system gets stronger. Your training heart rate is calculated by taking your age, minus the number 220, multiplied by .75.

Cardiovascular fitness is attained when you exercise at a training heart rate, for 20 minutes, three times a week. Have the exercise therapist help you to determine your training heart rate and develop a program in which you gradually increase your cardiovascular fitness. Usually, you will be increasing your exercise by 10% each week.

Many forms of exercise can be beneficial for cardiovascular training. The key point is this: It must be sustained exercise for at least 20 minutes. It cannot be a stop-start exercise such as tennis or golf. It must be something that you can sustain. These include exercises such as jogging, walking, swimming, and biking.

After you have worked out your exercise program, keep a daily log of your exercise. Reinforce yourself when you reach one of your goals. You might have a goal of running a mile by the end of the month. If you reach your goal, then buy yourself something you want or treat yourself to a movie to celebrate. Write down your exercise schedule for the next month.

EXERCISE PROGRAM

Date _____ Training Heart Rate _____

Strength

_____
_____
_____

Stretching

_____
_____
_____

Cardiovascular Fitness

_____
_____
_____

CHANGING YOUR LIFESTYLE

Along with maintaining a regular relaxation and exercise time, you must change other aspects of your life to improve your stress management skills.

Problem-Solving Skills

You need to be able to identify and respond to the problems in your life. Unsolved problems increase your stress level. Problems are a normal part of life, and you need specific skills to deal with them effectively. For each problem that you encounter, work through the following steps:

1. Identify the problem.
2. Clarify your goals. What do you want?
3. Consider every alternative of action.
4. Think through each alternative, eliminating one at a time, until you have the best alternative.
5. Act on the problem.
6. Evaluate the effect of your action.

Work through several problems with your counselor or group while in treatment. See how effective it is to seek the advice and counsel of others. You need to ask for help.

Developing Pleasurable Activities

One of the things that chemically dependent people fear the most is not being able to have fun when clean and sober. Chemicals have been involved in pleasurable activities for so long that they are directly equated with all pleasure. To look forward to a life without being able to have fun is intolerable.

You do not give up fun in sobriety. You change the way in which you have fun. You cannot use chemicals for pleasure anymore. This is not good for you. But you can enjoy many pleasant activities without drugs or alcohol. If you think about it, this is real fun anyway. The fun you are missing is based on a false chemically created feeling. Once you see how much fun you can have when clean and sober, you will be amazed.

Increasing pleasurable activities will elevate your mood and decrease your overall stress level. If you are not feeling well in recovery, it is likely that you are not involved in enough pleasurable activities. If you increase the level of pleasure, then you will feel better and be less vulnerable to relapse.

First, identify the things that you might enjoy doing, and then make a list of the things that you are going to do more often. Make a list of the activities that you plan to do for yourself each day. Write down your plan. The more pleasurable things you do, the better you will feel.

1. Being in the country
2. Wearing expensive clothes
3. Talking about sports
4. Meeting someone new
5. Going to a concert
6. Playing baseball or softball
7. Planning trips or vacations
8. Buying things for yourself
9. Going to the beach
10. Doing artwork
11. Rock climbing or mountaineering
12. Playing golf
13. Reading
14. Rearranging or redecorating your room or house
15. Playing basketball or volleyball
16. Going to a lecture.
17. Breathing the clean air
18. Writing a song
19. Boating
20. Pleasing your parents
21. Watching television
22. Thinking quietly
23. Camping
24. Working on machines (e.g., cars, bikes, motors)
25. Working in politics
26. Thinking about something good in the future
27. Playing cards
28. Laughing
29. Working puzzles or crosswords
30. Having lunch with a friend or an associate
31. Playing tennis
32. Taking a bath
33. Going for a drive
34. Woodworking
35. Writing a letter
36. Being with animals
37. Riding in an airplane
38. Walking in the woods
39. Having a conversation with someone
40. Working at your job
41. Going to a party
42. Going to church functions
43. Visiting relatives
44. Going to a meeting
45. Playing a musical instrument
46. Having a snack
47. Taking a nap
48. Singing
49. Acting
50. Working on crafts
51. Being with your children
52. Playing a game of chess or checkers
53. Putting on makeup or fixing your hair
54. Visiting people who are sick or shut in
55. Bowling
56. Talking with your sponsor
57. Gardening or doing lawn work
58. Dancing
59. Sitting in the sun
60. Sitting and thinking
61. Praying
62. Meditating
63. Listening to the sounds of nature
64. Going on a date
65. Listening to the radio
66. Giving a gift
67. Reaching out to someone who is suffering
68. Getting or giving a massage or back rub
69. Talking to your spouse
70. Talking to a friend
71. Watching the clouds
72. Lying in the grass
73. Helping someone
74. Hearing or telling jokes
75. Going to church
76. Eating a good meal
77. Hunting
78. Fishing
79. Looking at the scenery
80. Working on improving your health

81. Going downtown
82. Watching a sporting event
83. Going to a health club
84. Learning something new
85. Horseback riding
86. Going out to eat
87. Talking on the telephone
88. Daydreaming
89. Going to the movies
90. Being alone
91. Feeling the presence of God
92. Smelling a flower
93. Looking at a sunrise
94. Doing a favor for a friend
95. Meeting a stranger
96. Reading the newspaper
97. Swimming
98. Walking barefoot
99. Playing catch or with a Frisbee
100. Cleaning your house or room

101. Listening to music
102. Knitting or crocheting
103. Having house guests
104. Being with someone you love
105. Having sexual relations
106. Going to the library
107. Watching people
108. Repairing something
109. Bicycling
110. Smiling at people
111. Caring for houseplants
112. Collecting things
113. Sewing
114. Going to garage sales
115. Water skiing
116. Surfing
117. Traveling
118. Teaching someone
119. Washing your car
120. Eating ice cream

Social Skills

What you do socially can turn people off or turn them on. If you do any of the following, you might be turning people off.

1. Not smiling
2. Failing to make eye contact
3. Not talking
4. Complaining
5. Telling everyone your troubles
6. Not responding to people
7. Whining
8. Being critical
9. Poor grooming
10. Not showing interest in people
11. Ignoring people
12. Having an angry look
13. Using nervous gestures
14. Feeling sorry for yourself
15. Always talking about the negative

You are turning people on if you do the following.

1. Smiling
2. Looking people in the eyes
3. Expressing your concern
4. Talking about pleasant things
5. Being reinforcing
6. Telling people how nice they look
7. Being appreciative
8. Telling people that you care
9. Listening

10. Touching
11. Asking people to do something with you
12. Acting interested
13. Using people's names
14. Talking about the positive
15. Grooming yourself well

To have good social skills, you have to be assertive. You cannot be passive or aggressive. All this means is that you have to tell people how you feel and ask for what you want, even if it makes people feel uncomfortable. You must tell the truth at all times. If you withhold or distort information, then you never will be close to anyone.

Do not tell other people what to do; instead, ask. Do not let other people tell you what to do; instead, negotiate. Do not yell; instead, explain. Do not throw your weight around. When you are wrong, promptly admit it. Happiness is giving to others. The more you give, the more you get.

In the AA/NA program, you never have to be alone. Your Higher Power always is with you. Learn to enjoy the presence of God, and communicate with God as if God were standing right beside you. Call someone in the program every day. Go to a lot of meetings. Reach out to those who are still suffering. There are many people in jails or hospitals who need your help. Volunteer to work on the AA/NA hotline. Ask people out for coffee after meetings. Do not worry if you are doing all of the asking at first. The reason you are doing this is for you. Most people, particularly men, feel very uncomfortable asking others to go out with them. But do not let that stop you. If you do not ask, then you will not have the experience of someone saying yes.

Using the pleasant activities list, make a plan for how you are going to increase your social interaction this month. Write all of it down and reward yourself when you make progress. Here are a few hints to get you going.

1. Read the activities and entertainment section of your local newspaper. Mark down events that fit into your schedule and attend them.
2. Offer to become more involved in your AA/NA group.
3. Ask the local chamber of commerce for information about groups and activities in the area.
4. Spend your weekends exploring new parts of town.
5. Smile.
6. Join another self-help support group such as an Adult Children of Alcoholics group or a singles group.
7. Join a church and get involved. Tell the pastor that you want to do something to help.
8. Volunteer your services with a local charity or hospital. Help others and share your experiences, strengths, and hopes.
9. Join a group that does interesting things in the area—hiking, skydiving, hunting, bird watching, theater group, sports club, senior center, and so on. Check the local library for a list of such clubs and activities.
10. Ask someone in the program for interesting things to do in the area.
11. Go to an intergroup dance.
12. Go to an AA/NA conference.

The most important thing to remember is that you are in recovery. You are starting a new life. To do this, you must take risks. You must reach out like you have never done before.

Appendix 31

The Beck Depression Inventory

Instructions. On this questionnaire are groups of statements. Please read each group of statements carefully. Then pick out the one statement in each group that best describes the way you have been feeling the *past week including today.* Circle the number beside the statement you picked. If several statements in the group seem to apply equally well, then circle each one.

Be sure to read all of the statements in each group before making your choice.

1. 0   I do not feel sad.
   1   I feel sad.
   2   I am sad all of the time, and I can't snap out of it.
   3   I am so sad or unhappy that I can't stand it.

2. 0   I am not particularly discouraged about the future.
   1   I feel discouraged about the future.
   2   I feel that I have nothing to look forward to.
   3   I feel that the future is hopeless and that things cannot change.

3. 0   I do not feel like a failure.
   1   I feel that I have failed more than the average person.
   2   As I look back on my life, all I can see is a lot of failure.
   3   I feel that I am a complete failure as a person.

4. 0   I get as much satisfaction out of things as I used to.
   1   I don't enjoy things the way I used to.
   2   I don't get real satisfaction out of anything anymore.
   3   I am dissatisfied or bored with everything.

5. 0   I don't feel particularly guilty.
   1   I feel guilty a good part of the time.
   2   I feel quite guilty most of the time.
   3   I feel guilty all of the time.

6. 0   I don't feel that I am being punished.
   1   I feel that I may be punished.
   2   I expect to be punished.
   3   I feel that I am being punished.

Used with permission: A. T. Beck, C. H. Ward, M. Mandelson, et al. (1961), An inventory for measuring depression, *Archives of General Psychiatry, 4,* 561-571. Copyright © 1961, American Medical Association.

7. 0   I don't feel disappointed in myself.
    1   I am critical of myself for my weaknesses or mistakes.
    2   I blame myself all of the time for my faults.
    3   I blame myself for everything bad that happens.

8. 0   I don't have any thoughts of killing myself.
    1   I have thoughts of killing myself, but I would not carry them out.
    2   I would like to kill myself.
    3   I would kill myself if I had the chance.

9. 0   I don't cry any more than usual.
    1   I cry more now than I used to.
    2   I cry all of the time now.
    3   I used to be able to cry, but now I can't cry even though I want to.

10. 0   I am no more irritated now than I ever am.
    1   I get annoyed or irritated more easily than I used to.
    2   I feel irritated all of the time now.
    3   I don't get irritated at all by the things that used to irritate me.

11. 0   I have not lost interest in other people.
    1   I am less interested in other people than I used to be.
    2   I have lost most of my interest in other people.
    3   I have lost all interest in other people.

12. 0   I make decisions about as well as I used to.
    1   I put off making decisions more than I used to.
    2   I have greater difficulty in making decisions than before.
    3   I can't make decisions at all anymore.

13. 0   I don't feel that I look any worse than I used to.
    1   I am worried that I am looking old or unattractive.
    2   I feel that there are permanent changes in my appearance that make me look unattractive.
    3   I believe that I look ugly.

14. 0   I can work about as well as before.
    1   It takes an extra effort to get started at doing something.
    2   I have to push myself very hard to do anything.
    3   I can't do any work at all.

15. 0   I can sleep as well as before.
    1   I don't sleep as well as I used to.
    2   I wake up 1 or 2 hours earlier than usual and find it hard to get back to sleep.
    3   I wake up several hours earlier than I used to and cannot get back to sleep.

16. 0   I don't get more tired than usual.

     1   I get tired more easily than I used to.

     2   I get tired from doing almost anything.

     3   I am too tired to do anything.

17. 0   My appetite is no worse than usual.

     1   My appetite is not as good as it used to be.

     2   My appetite is much worse now.

     3   I have no appetite at all anymore.

18. 0   I haven't lost much weight, if any, lately. I have been trying to lose weight _____ Yes _____ No

     1   I have lost more than 5 pounds.

     2   I have lost more than 10 pounds.

     3   I have lost more than 15 pounds.

19. 0   I am no more worried about my health than usual.

     1   I am worried about physical problems such as aches and pains, upset stomach, and constipation.

     2   I am very worried about physical problems, and it's hard to think of much else.

     3   I am so worried about my physical problems that I cannot think about anything else.

20. 0   I have not noticed any recent change in my interest in sex.

     1   I am less interested in sex than I used to be.

     2   I am much less interested in sex now.

     3   I have lost interest in sex completely.

Score _____

Appendix 32

Biopsychosocial Assessment
Robert R. Perkinson, Ph.D.

DATE _____

PATIENT NAME _____

DEMOGRAPHIC DATA:

Age _____ Marital status _____ Race _____ Sex _____ Children _____

Residence _____

Others in residence _____

Length of residence _____

Education:

☐ Less than sixth grade	☐ High school graduate
☐ Sixth grade	☐ Some college
☐ Seventh grade	☐ College graduate
☐ Eighth grade	☐ Postgraduate work
☐ Some high school	☐ Postgraduate degree

Occupation _____

Characteristics of Informant:

☐ Reliable   ☐ Unreliable

CHIEF COMPLAINT

_____

_____

_____

BIOPSYCHOSOCIAL ASSESSMENT

HISTORY OF THE PRESENT ILLNESS (age of onset, duration, patterns and consequences of use, current use, last use, previous treatments, tolerance, blackouts, and symptoms of abuse or dependence)

PAST HISTORY:

Place of birth _____ Date of birth _____ 19 ____

Developmental Milestones:

☐ Normal	☐ Reading
☐ Walking	☐ Spelling
☐ Talking	☐ Arithmetic
☐ Toilet training	

Specific disabilities _____

Raised with:
- ☐ Mother   ☐ Brothers
- ☐ Father   ☐ Sisters

Birth order _____

Significant others _____

Ethnic/cultural heritage _____

Description of home life _____

_____

_____

Grade school _____

_____

_____

High school _____

_____

_____

College _____

_____

Military History:

Branch _____

Highest rank _____

Discharge status _____

Problems _____

Occupational History:

Longest job held _____

Length of time at current job _____

Employment satisfaction _____

Work problems _____

Financial History:
- ☐ Good   ☐ Fair   ☐ Poor

Current annual income _____

Gambling History:
- ☐ None   ☐ Gambling problems (Explain _____)

Sexual History:

Sexual orientation _____

Physical abuse _____

Sexual abuse _____

Current sexual history _____

Relationship history _____

Recovery Environment: Family _____ Friends _____

Spiritual History:

☐ Believes in God ☐ Agnostic

☐ Higher Power ☐ Atheist

☐ Religious activities

Church _____ Denomination _____

Attends:

☐ Weekly ☐ Rarely

☐ Occasionally ☐ Never

Legal History:

Arrests _____

Pending litigation _____

Self-identified strengths _____
_____
_____

Self-identified weaknesses _____
_____
_____

Leisure activities _____

Depression _____

Mania _____

Anxiety _____

Panic attacks _____

Agoraphobia _____

Phobias _____

Eating disorder _____

MEDICAL HISTORY

Illnesses:

☐ Measles ☐ Pneumonia

☐ Mumps ☐ Tonsillitis

☐ Chicken pox ☐ Appendicitis

☐ Whooping cough ☐ Others _____

Hospitalizations:

☐ Tonsillectomy and adenoidectomy ☐ Appendectomy

☐ Chemical dependency

Allergies _____ Environmental allergens _____

Medications at present _____

FAMILY HISTORY

Father: Age _____
Health:
　□ Good　　　　　□ Fair　　　　　□ Poor
　Description _____
　_____

Mother: Age _____
Health:
　□ Good　　　　　□ Fair　　　　　□ Poor
　Description _____
　_____

Other relatives with significant psychopathology _____
_____

MENTAL STATUS EXAMINATION

Description:
　□ Well developed and well nourished　　□ Thin
　□ Obese　　　　　　　　　　　　　　　　□ Underweight
　□ Age _____ Race _____ Sex _____
　　Hair _____ Eyes _____
　　Distinguishing marks or characteristics _____

Appearance:
　□ Same as stated age　　　　　□ Older than stated age
　□ Younger than stated age

Dress:
　□ Casual　　　　□ Meticulously neat
　□ Appropriate　　□ Seductive
　□ Disheveled　　□ Eccentric
　□ Other_____

Personal hygiene:
　□ Good　　　　　□ Fair　　　　　□ Poor

Sensorium:
　□ Clear　　　　　　　　　□ Lethargic
　□ Alert　　　　　　　　　□ Drowsy
　□ Vigilant
　□ Other_____
　Factors Affecting Sensorium:
　　□ Alcohol　　　　　　　□ Medications
　　□ Drugs　　　　　　　　□ Withdrawal symptoms
　　□ Other_____

Orientation:

Person _____

Place _____

Time _____

Situation _____

Attitude Toward the Examiner:

☐ Cooperative   ☐ Distant

☐ Friendly   ☐ Aloof

☐ Pleasant   ☐ Casual

☐ Suspicious   ☐ Overly intellectual

☐ Hostile   ☐ Neutral

☐ Passive   ☐ Apprehensive

☐ Dependent   ☐ Seductive

☐ Withdrawn

Motor Behavior:

☐ Normal   ☐ Physical agitation

☐ Continuous movements or restlessness ☐ Tremor

Unusual and Inappropriate Movements:

☐ Slow or retarded   ☐ Inappropriate

☐ Tics   ☐ Hand wringing

☐ Tearful   ☐ Pacing

☐ Rigid   ☐ Apprehensive

☐ Tense   ☐ Angry

☐ Slouched

Eye Contact:

☐ Appropriate   ☐ Poor

Gait:

☐ Normal   ☐ Wide based

☐ Shuffling   ☐ Unsteady

☐ Other_____

Primary Facial Expression During Interview:

☐ Normal and responsive   ☐ Hostile

☐ Sad   ☐ Worried

☐ Neutral

☐ Other_____

Speech Quantity:

☐ Normal   ☐ Unspontaneous

☐ Talkative   ☐ Spontaneous

☐ Garrulous   ☐ Minimally responsive

Speech Quality:

☐ Normal
☐ Slow
☐ Rapid
☐ Pressured
☐ Hesitant
☐ Emotional

☐ Monotonous
☐ Soft
☐ Loud
☐ Slurred
☐ Mumbled

Speech Impairment:

☐ None
☐ Stuttering
☐ Other _____

☐ Marked by accent
☐ Articulation problem

Mood:

☐ Calm
☐ Cheerful
☐ Anxious
☐ Depressed
☐ Fearful
☐ Tearful
☐ Pessimistic
☐ Other _____

☐ Neutral
☐ Optimistic
☐ Elated
☐ Euphoric
☐ Irritable
☐ Angry

Client Report of Depression:

☐ None
☐ Mild

☐ Moderate
☐ Severe

Episodes of Depression:

☐ None
☐ One or two episodes during past 6 months

☐ Frequently during past 6 months
☐ Continuously during past 6 months

Client Report of Symptoms of Depression:

☐ None
☐ Poor appetite
☐ Loss of interests
☐ Guilt
☐ Motor retardation
☐ Other _____

☐ Sleep disturbance
☐ Fatigue
☐ Weight loss
☐ Loss of interest in sex

Observed Signs of Anxiety During Interview:

☐ None
☐ Physical indications
☐ Other _____

☐ Apprehensive manner
☐ Problems in attention

Client Report of Anxiety:

☐ None
☐ Mild

☐ Moderate
☐ Severe

Episodes of Anxiety:

☐ None

☐ One or two episodes during past 6 months

☐ Frequently during past 6 months

☐ Continuously during past 6 months

Client Report of Symptoms of Anxiety:

☐ None

☐ Shortness of breath

☐ Palpitations

☐ Chest pain

☐ Dizziness

☐ Faintness

☐ Sweating

☐ Other _____

☐ Paresthesias

☐ Muscle aches

☐ Cold hands

☐ Gastrointestinal symptoms

☐ Muscle twitching

☐ Dry mouth

Range of Affect:

☐ Appropriate

☐ Blunted

☐ Restricted

☐ Contradictory

☐ Other _____

☐ Labile

☐ Dramatized

☐ Flat

Thought Processes:

☐ Logical and coherent

☐ Blocking

☐ Circumstantial

☐ Tangential

☐ Flight of ideas

☐ Incoherent

☐ Other _____

☐ Neologisms

☐ Preservation

☐ Evasive

☐ Distracted

☐ Loose associations

☐ Clang associations

Thought Content—Preoccupations:

☐ None

☐ Presenting problem

☐ Obsessions

☐ Compulsions

☐ Phobias

☐ Suicide

☐ Other _____

☐ Violent acts

☐ Somatic symptoms

☐ Guilt

☐ Worthlessness

☐ Religious issues

☐ Sex

Thought Content—Delusions:

☐ None

☐ Persecution

☐ Somatic

☐ Ideas of reference

☐ Thought broadcasting

☐ Other _____

☐ Jealousy

☐ Grandiosity

☐ Religious

☐ Influence by others

☐ Control

Description of delusional material _____
_____

Quality of Delusional Material:
   ☐ Systematized   ☐ Poorly organized

Disorders of Perception:
   ☐ None   ☐ Tactile hallucinations
   ☐ Auditory hallucinations   ☐ Gustatory hallucinations incorporated into delusions
   ☐ Visual hallucinations   ☐ Fragmented and not incorporated into delusions
   ☐ Olfactory hallucinations

Suicidal Ideation:
   ☐ None   ☐ Ideation   ☐ Plan
   Details of current plans _____
   History of suicidal acts _____
_____

Homicidal Ideation:
   ☐ None   ☐ Ideation   ☐ Plan
   Details of current plans _____
   History of violent acts _____
_____

Obsessions:
   ☐ None   ☐ Death
   ☐ Illness   ☐ Contamination
   ☐ Violence   ☐ Doubt
   ☐ Other_____

Compulsions:
   ☐ None   ☐ Checking
   ☐ Hand washing   ☐ Touching
   ☐ Counting
   ☐ Other _____

Phobias:
   ☐ None   ☐ Insects
   ☐ Public places   ☐ Dogs
   ☐ Closed spaces   ☐ Social security
   ☐ Heights   ☐ Rodents
   ☐ Snakes   ☐ Travel
   ☐ Flying
   ☐ Other _____

Estimated Range of Intellectual Ability:
   ☐ Normal   ☐ Below average
   ☐ Above average   ☐ Borderline retarded
   ☐ Superior   ☐ Retarded

Abstracting Ability:

☐ Normal ☐ Impaired

Disturbances in Consciousness:

☐ No recent disturbances ☐ Recent history of seizures

☐ Recent history of loss of consciousness ☐ Recent history of blackouts

Concentration:

☐ Normal ☐ Moderately impaired

☐ Mildly impaired ☐ Severely impaired

Memory Functions:

☐ Intact ☐ Recent memory deficit

☐ Immediate memory deficit ☐ Remote memory deficit

Confabulations:

☐ None ☐ Suspected ☐ Definite

Amnesia:

☐ None ☐ Less than 1 month

☐ Less than 1 day ☐ Several months

☐ Less than 1 week ☐ Years

Impulse Control:

☐ Good ☐ Fair ☐ Poor

Judgment:

☐ Good ☐ Fair ☐ Poor

Insight:

☐ Minimal: No understanding of problem or acceptance of personal responsibility

☐ Insightful: Accepts personal responsibility and desires professional assistance

Appendix 33

Anger Management
Robert R. Perkinson, Ph.D.

Anger is a feeling that helps you to adapt to your environment. It is designed to make stress stop. It helps you to establish and maintain boundaries around yourself. It gives you the energy and direction to defend yourself from a physical attack.

Chronic anger is painful. It results in broken relationships. It does not help; it hurts. Studies show that people who are chronically angry die years earlier than they should. They have more colds and bouts with the flu as well as more mental and physical illnesses. Chronic anger has many painful consequences.

The reason why you are reading this exercise is that your anger sometimes gets out of control. When you are angry, you do things that you feel guilty about later. Chronic anger is a shameful cycle of pain. You do not want to hurt others, but you find yourself doing it anyway—over and over again.

A lot of this exercise was taken from *When Anger Hurts* (McKay, Rogers, & McKay, 1989). When you get the opportunity, get that book and read it. This exercise will help you to manage your anger. This will not be easy, and you will have to work very hard. Learning new behaviors takes a lot of practice. You have had years of training in how to act angry. Now you need to learn new skills to deal with problems. Using the techniques described here, you will feel angry less often. When you feel angry, you will be able to solve problems rather then make them worse.

YOUR ANGER JOURNAL

Keep an anger journal every day. Write down every time that you feel angry. Write down exactly what happened in detail, and rate your angry feelings on a scale from 1 (*as little anger as possible*) to 100 (*as much anger as possible*). Rate your aggressiveness from 1 to 100. The more you look at each situation, the more you will learn about yourself and the more you will learn to control your behavior. Your journal might look something like this:

December 4: 8 a.m.—Kathy asked me to take out the garbage three times while I was watching TV. I felt like she was trying to drive me crazy. She knew I had had a hard day and needed some time alone. At the same time, the kids were fighting in the other room.
    Intensity of anger felt: 100
    Aggressiveness: 90. I told her to shut up and leave me alone. I threw a pillow against the wall.

December 4: The sales meeting ended before I got a chance to share my concerns with the boss. I needed to talk to him and reassure him about my work. I know my sales have been falling off a bit lately. I felt more hurt than anything else.
    Intensity of anger felt: 75
    Aggressiveness: 0. I didn't do anything, but boy was I fuming.

By monitoring your anger, you will be able to observe your progress. You will feel successful as you see yourself handling your anger better.

THE ANGER MYTH

There is a myth that anger has to be expressed or else you will explode into a violent rage. The anger will build up like water behind a dam. If you do not express it, then it will come bursting out all at once and destroy everything in the process. Research strongly disagrees with this myth. The research shows that anger does not help. The more you act angry or think angry thoughts, the more you feel angry. Anger feeds on itself. It never helps to hit walls or pillows or to yell. It just makes you act more angry.

WHAT DOES ANGER DO TO PEOPLE?

1. Anger stuns and frightens people.
2. Anger makes people feel bad about themselves.
3. The more anger you express, the less effective your anger becomes. People get used to your anger and shrug it off.
4. People distance themselves from you.
5. Anger cuts you off from genuine closeness.
6. The more you act aggressively, the more you want to continue the attack and really rub people's noses in it.
7. Anger causes continued aggression from both parties.
8. Anger does not stop. It goes on and on, fueling itself in the process.
9. You resort to anger over and over again. Each episode gets worse.
10. Anger leads to rigidity. Both parties become stuck and inflexible.
11. Anger breeds the desire for revenge.
12. Anger is trying to control the other person, but inevitably you lose control.
13. Anger causes the other person to act defensive and resistive.
14. People shield themselves from your anger by avoiding you.

Angry people feel like victims caught in a trap. They desire closeness but have a fear of abandonment. Their friends seem selfish and insensitive, their employers seem cheap and uncaring, and their lovers seem unappreciative and withholding. Life is no fun.

Anger leads to helplessness in four steps:

1. You think that something is wrong with you.
2. You think that the other person should fix you, but he or she will not.
3. You blow up at that person.
4. The other person withdraws even farther away.

ANGER IS A CHOICE

You do not have to act angry. You can solve your problems in other ways. Until now, anger has been automatic. It has been a decision made without thinking or a choice made out of habit. You spent years thinking that anger was saving you or helping you, while all the time it was hurting you. You want to be loved and accepted. Anger never will get you that. Believe it or not, you can feel angry and act in a way that is more productive. Remember that the function of anger is to stop stress. Your problem is stress, not anger.

Anger helps you to cope with stress in several ways:

1. Anger blocks the awareness of pain.
2. Anger discharges high levels of fear, hurt, guilt, and sadness.
3. Anger discharges the pain that develops when your needs are frustrated.
4. Anger erases guilt.
5. Anger places the blame on someone else.

There are many ways of discharging stress other than acting angry. You can cry, exercise, work, make a joke, write in your journal, go through a relaxation exercise, verbalize your feelings, ask for what you want, problem solve, listen to music, and many other things.

ANGER IS A TWO-STEP PROCESS

1. You become aware of stress.
2. You blame someone else.

What will not help you is blaming someone or thinking about what he or she should have done differently.

To *blame,* you have to believe, "The other person purposely did something wrong that hurt me." To *should,* you have to believe, "The other person should have known better than to do what he or she did."

The should and blame are inaccurate thinking. The truth is that if the person had known better, he or she would not have done it. The other person was not trying to hurt you. The other person was just trying to meet his or her own needs.

To rid yourself of anger, you must stop blaming others.

The only thing that always is true when you are angry is that you are in pain. The trigger thoughts that fuel your anger usually are false. Your anger may have no legitimate basis. If you use inaccurate thinking, then you will generate a storm of inaccurate feelings. Armed with the real facts, you might not get angry at all.

It is not that anger builds; it is stress that builds. You need coping skills to deal with stress.

WHAT IS STRESSING YOU?

Go back to your anger journal and look at each anger-producing situation.

1. Figure out what was stressing you before you got angry. What was the emotional pain, physical pain, frustration, or threat that preceded the anger? Prior to feeling angry, were you aware of any internal feeling of hurt, fear, sadness, or guilt? Did you feel uncomfortable physically or psychologically? Write down these things.
2. Try to figure out the trigger thoughts. What were you thinking between the situation and the anger? Did you use the blame or should. Write down exactly what you were thinking.

Bob came home from work to find several soda cans lying in the middle of the living room floor. He thought, "The kids know better than this. They only think about themselves. Nobody appreciates what I do around here. They don't care if I come home to a dirty house." Bob rated his anger at 100. He yelled at the kids and scored himself aggressively at 85. Later he felt guilty about yelling at the children and had to apologize.

Look at how Bob's inaccurate thinking inflamed his anger:

The kids should know better.
They only think about themselves.
They don't care about me.
Nobody appreciates what I do around here.
I live in a dirty house.

Thinking like that, it is no wonder Bob got angry. But he was not thinking accurately. His angry feelings came from inaccurate thinking. He ended up feeling angry because of how he interpreted the actions of others.

BLAMING

The impulse to assign blame lies at the root of all chronic anger. When you decide who is responsible for your pain, you feel justified in acting aggressively. You see yourself threatened, and you need to protect yourself. You are the helpless victim of another person's stupidity or selfishness.

There is pleasure in blaming. You can escape the responsibility for your own problems by blaming someone else. You can turn the focus off of your mistakes and concentrate on the other person's mistakes. The problem with blaming is that it is not true. The truth is that other people are not responsible for your life; you are.

1. You are the only one who understands what you need.
2. Other people need to focus on their own needs.
3. People's needs occasionally will come into conflict with yours.
4. Your satisfaction in life depends on how well *you* meet your needs.

STRATEGIES FOR GETTING YOUR NEEDS MET

You must develop new skills for meeting your needs better. With your counselor's help, develop the following coping skills and practice them often.

1. Learn to give people rewards when they do something that you want them to do. Reinforce each person often. The more reinforcing you act toward others, the more reinforcing they will act toward you.
2. Learn to take care of your needs yourself. Do not count on others to meet your needs.
3. Develop new sources for support, nourishment, and appreciation. Join that AA/NA group and go often. Take someone out for coffee. Call your sponsor.
4. Learn to say no.
5. Learn how to share how you feel and to ask for what you want.
6. Learn to let go and let God.

TAKING BACK THE RESPONSIBILITY

Go to your journal and examine your anger-generating situations.

1. What was stressing you at the time?
2. What were your trigger thoughts?
3. What could you have done differently?
4. How could you have met your own needs?
5. How could you have found other sources of support?
6. What limits did you fail to set? Were you unable to say no?
7. How could you have negotiated better for what you wanted?
8. How could you have let go and let God?

COMBATING TRIGGER THOUGHTS

Inaccurate thinking leads you to feel inaccurate pain. If you blame, then you judge people all day by your own rules. Someone cuts in front of you in traffic and you fume, "That idiot knows better than that!" But the fact is that many drivers think it is fine to cut in line. The problem with blaming is that people rarely agree with you. People all have their own sets of rules and judge themselves by their own standards. People often do not do what they think they should do; they do what works for them.

The Entitlement Fallacy

The entitlement fallacy is the belief that you deserve things because you want them very bad. Your need justifies the demand that someone give you what you want. The feeling of entitlement engulfs you. How can the other person say no? The truth is that people will give you what they want to give you and nothing more. They are trying to meet their own needs, not yours.

The Fallacy of Fairness

The idea here is that there is an absolute standard of conduct that everyone has to follow. Everyone should know these rules and follow them. If they do not, then they are bad and deserve to be punished. The problem with this thinking is that there is no absolute right and wrong standard of conduct. What is fair is totally subjective. The other person could be functioning from an entirely different set of values.

Blame

Assigning blame lets you escape the responsibility of handing your problems. Blaming triggers anger by making your pain other people's fault. Blaming labels people as bad when they are doing all that they can with the coping skills they have at their disposal. By blaming, you punish people for doing things that they could not help from doing.

Mind Reading

Sometimes you get angry when you try to read someone's mind. You think that you know a person did what he or she did. You think that you have the person all figured out. You assume that the person did something deliberately to harm you. This rarely is true. The other person almost always is trying to meet his or her own needs.

CHANGING YOUR TRIGGER THOUGHTS

Go back to your anger journal and determine what you were thinking between each situation and the anger. Pull out as many of these trigger thoughts as you can and write them down. This is uncovering your automatic thinking.

Once you have a list of the trigger thoughts, go back and develop thoughts that are accurate. What thinking would have been appropriate for each situation?

You will be amazed at how your inaccurate thinking fuels your anger. Keep a record of your thinking for at least 12 weeks. In time, you will be able to catch yourself in the old thinking. Once you are thinking accurately, you will act appropriately. Soon the old thinking will not sound so convincing and so right. You will not feel like a victim anymore.

STOPPING ESCALATION

Gerald Patterson of the Oregon Social Learning Center found that anger between people depends on *aversive chains* of behavior where people attempt to influence each other through a rapid exchange of punishing communications. These chains are more likely to occur when the people have relatively equal power such as like husband and wife, parents and children, and co-workers. Aversive chains usually begin with small events and develop along predictable lines. Early exchanges often are overlooked because they seem unimportant.

Aversive chains are the building blocks to violence.

Most aversive chains never pass beyond the first link. Someone in the family teases or insults another, and there is no response. Because no one reacts to the provocation, the problem stops after a few seconds. Three- or four-link chains usually last no longer than a half minute and exist even in healthy homes. If an aversive chain lasts longer than a half minute, then yelling, threatening, or hitting may occur. The longer a chain lasts, the more likely it is that things are going to get out of control.

Stop an aversive chain at the earliest possible moment.

The last link in an aversive chain is a trigger behavior. These behaviors usually precede violence. Triggers are verbal or nonverbal behaviors that bring up feelings of *abandonment* or *rejection.* These feelings are too painful to deal with, and the person feeling them needs them to stop right now.

A variety of statements can put the last link in an aversive chain. These are the responses that you need to eliminate, replacing them with your new coping skills.

Verbal Trigger Behaviors

1. Sarcastic advice: "Tell them to give you a raise. We need the money."
2. Global labeling: "All women are like that."
3. Criticism: "You didn't shovel the walk. You made a little path."
4. Blaming: "If you'd just do some work around here."
5. Abrupt limit setting: "That's it. I'm out of here."
6. Threatening: "If you don't like it, then get out."
7. Cursing: "Shut the hell up."

8. Complaining: "Ever since I married you, I've been unhappy."
9. Mind reading: "You're trying to drive me crazy."
10. Stonewalling: "There's nothing more to talk about."
11. Sarcastic observations: "Did you dump the trash in your room?"
12. Humiliating statements: "When we got married, you were better looking."
13. Dismissing statements: "Get out."
14. Put-downs: "Is this what you call clean?"
15. Accusations: "You did it again, didn't you?"
16. Laying on the guilt: "You know I can't stand that."
17. Ultimatums: "If you don't shape up, I'm leaving."

Nonverbal Trigger Sounds

1. Groaning: "I've had it with you."
2. Sighing: "You are such a burden."

Voice Quality Triggers

1. Whining (irritating tone)
2. Flatness in voice (as though you checked out a long time ago)
3. Cold tone (the other person will never reach you)
4. Throaty constriction (barely controlled rage)
5. Loud and harsh tone (threatening)
6. Mocking and contemptuous tone (shaming)
7. Mumbling under your breath (the other person has to guess what you said)
8. Snickering (laughing at the other person)
9. Snarling (you had better back off)

Trigger Gestures

1. Finger pointing
2. Shaking a fist
3. Flipping the bird
4. Folding arms
5. Waving away

Trigger Facial Expressions

1. Looking away
2. Rolling the eyes
3. Narrowing the eyes
4. Opening eyes wide
5. Grimacing
6. Sneering
7. Frowning
8. Tightening the lips
9. Raising an eyebrow
10. Scowling

Trigger Body Movements

1. Shaking the head
2. Shrugging the shoulders
3. Tapping a foot or finger
4. Leaning forward (intimidating)
5. Turning away

6. Putting hands on hips
7. Making quick and sudden movements
8. Kicking or throwing an object
9. Pushing or grabbing

Spend time each evening reviewing your anger journal. Write down your verbal and nonverbal trigger behaviors. In time, you will be able to recognize your patterns. Begin eliminating your trigger behaviors and using your new coping skills instead.

Example of an Aversive Chain

Bob comes home from the office and sees his spouse, Patty, sitting quietly on the couch. The boss got on his case again today, and Bob needs some support. Rather than asking Patty for what he needs, Bob says the following:

"I can see you had a hard day in front of the television."

"I've been working my tail off." Patty is instantly defensive.

"I know what you do. You lay around all day." Bob crosses his arms sarcastically.

"I work every bit as hard as you do." Patty looks at him angrily.

"Do I have to cook dinner too?" Bob walks into the kitchen.

"What's wrong with you today?" Patty gets up and follows him.

"Don't yell at me!" Bob screams.

"Nothing I do pleases you anymore." Patty begins to cry.

"If you don't like it, then get the hell out!" Bob is out of control, shaking in fury.

Bob will not get Patty's support now. He needed his wife to help him, but he got the exact opposite of what he wanted. Now his needs are more frustrated. He fumes and primes himself for the next battle.

At every point along this aversive chain, Bob and Patty could have deescalated the conflict. Remember that anger is a choice.

BREAKING AVERSIVE CHAINS

Time Out

The best thing you can do when you find yourself in an aversive chain is to call a "time out." The first party to recognize an aversive chain makes a time out sign (a "T" made with both hands in front of the body). This person says, "Time out." The other person only returns the gesture and says, "Okay, time out." The person who called time out then leaves the aversive situation for a predetermined amount of time, usually an hour. The person who leaves agrees to return and work on the problem after the time is up or to make an appointment to work on it later. Time out never should be used to avoid a problem. Time out is meant to avoid escalating stress. Time out says, "It's time to separate. I'll be right back."

Each person should know exactly what is going to happen after a time out has been called. They need to be certain that the other person is going to return. Abandonment and rejection issues are involved here, and they create a lot of fear. A time out contract needs to be written and signed by both parties. The couple needs to practice using the time out several times in a nonthreatening situation.

After a called time out, wait for your feelings to cool down and then try to get accurate in your thinking. Take out these coping statements and read them to yourself.

"Don't blame."

"Don't try to fix the other person."

"What can I do differently?"

"The other person is not trying to hurt me. The other person is meeting his or her own needs."

"The other person is doing the only thing that he or she knows how to do at the moment."

"If I want the situation to change, then I need to change my behavior."

Rechannel

If you see yourself in an aversive chain, rechannel the conversation to a subject that is nonthreatening. The earlier in the aversive chain this is done, the more effective it will be. Sometimes you can just keep quiet and that is enough. Do not fuel the anger with your old trigger behaviors. De-fuse it with your new coping statements.

"There is no absolutely right or wrong answer here."

"We both are partially right."

"It's time to rechannel this discussion."

"Let's go over this later."

"Can we talk about this in an hour?"

Inquiry

When you see yourself in an aversive chain, pull information from the other person. This makes the other person feel important and loved. Remember that anger is a response to pain. Ask the person about how he or she is feeling and thinking.

"What's hurting you?"

"I'm concerned about you."

"Tell me what is hurting you."

"What do you think we need to do to solve this problem?"

Mind Reading

Mind reading takes a road map from our past and places it unrealistically over the present. We expect people to respond to us in the same way as others have in the past. If our parents were not trustworthy, then we assume that other people are not trustworthy. If we got hurt by a past relationship, then we expect the same thing from the next relationship.

The key to preventing mind reading is to check it out with the other person. Do not assume that you know what the other person is thinking. Ask the other person.

Once you begin asking the other person how he or she feels and what he or she thinks, you will learn a lot about yourself. You will learn about your old maps and how inaccurate they are.

"How do you feel?"

"What do you want me to do?"

"Tell me more about what you are thinking."

"What do you suggest we do to resolve the problem?"

IMPROVING SELF-TALK

You need to develop many positive things to say to yourself. Make a list of positive self-statements and keep them with you. When you are feeling uncomfortable, take them out and read them over to yourself. Some work better than others. Memorize the ones that work for you.

"I'm a good person."

"I'm smart and capable."

"I am God's creation."

"No matter what happens, I'm going to be all right."

"I can take care of myself."

Reassure Yourself

You may have to reassure yourself that you are going to be able to get through an aversive chain.

"I can handle this."
"I can call a time out if I need to."
"If I find myself getting angry, I can deal with it."
"I can find the appropriate coping strategy."
"I believe in myself."

Stop Trigger Thoughts

Do not allow yourself to fall back into old thinking. You are not a victim. You always have a choice.

"I am responsible for what happens to me."
"I am never a victim. I have a choice."
"I can take care of my own needs."
"Don't blame."
"People never do what they should do."
"I am free to do anything I want."
"There is no right or wrong answer."
"The amount of support that I'm getting is all I can get at the moment."
"Anger never will get me what I want."
"Don't mind read."

Physiological Coping

Monitor your physiological functioning. If you feel uptight, then tell yourself to relax. This reduces your stress and makes you deal with the situation more accurately.

"Take a deep breath."
"Relax."
"Feel your arms and legs become loose and limp."
"Stay calm."
"Visualize one of your favorite places."

Problem Solving

When you have a problem, use these problem-solving skills. Continue to process through the options until everyone agrees to try a solution.

1. Write down the problem.
2. Communicate your feelings.
3. Ask for what you want.
4. Acknowledge the other person's point of view.
5. Develop a list of options.
6. Discuss the pros and cons of each option.
7. Keep working until you reach a consensus.

YOUR COPING SCRIPT

Prepare for an angry situation with a set of coping statements. Pick the coping statements that seem to work best for you. You might have to change them from time to time and from situation to situation. What are you going to say to yourself the next time you find yourself getting angry?

To reassure yourself: _____

To stop the trigger thoughts: _____

To cope physiologically: _____

To move to problem solving: _____

Memorize all four sentences. When you find yourself in an aversive chain, say them over to yourself.

MOTIVATING YOURSELF

Each morning, go over the costs of your anger. Explore its toll on you and on those you love. Review the consequences of your last anger episode. Make a contract with your significant other to work on practicing the new coping skills and practice them often. You can do it.

TIME OUT CONTRACT

When I realize that my (or my partner's) anger is rising, I will give a "T" time out sign and leave at once. I will not hit or kick anything, and I will not slam the door.

I will return in no more than 1 hour. I will take a walk to use up the energy, and I will not drink or use drugs while I am away. I will try not to focus on resentments.

When I return, I will start the conversation with, "I know that I was partly wrong and partly right." I will then admit to a mistake that I made.

If my partner gives a "T" sign and leaves, then I will return the sign and let my partner go without a hassle no matter what is going on. I will not drink or use drugs while my partner is away. I will try to avoid focusing on resentments. When my partner returns, I will start the conversation with, "I know that I was partly wrong and partly right." I will then admit to a mistake that I made.

Name _____ Date _____

Name _____ Date _____

Appendix 34

Narcissism
Robert R. Perkinson, Ph.D.

This might be a difficult exercise for you to read, so you need to be open-minded and willing to learn something new about yourself. You have some narcissistic traits that get you into trouble and lead you to chemical use. For example, you tend to be too sensitive to criticism. Whenever someone criticizes you even a little, you get hurt and sometimes retaliate. "How dare you criticize me!" Underneath the anger, you feel wounded. You think that to be loved, you have to be the best, the brightest, the most beautiful, or the most successful. You do not know how to be genuinely close to others, but you have a great need for people to love you. The real problem is that, underneath it all, you do not feel good about yourself.

You feel ashamed of who you are. You fear that other people are better than you are.

Narcissus was a beautiful person in Greek mythology who refused to love others. As punishment for his indifference, the gods made him fall in love with himself. He became so enamored with himself that he could not stop gazing at his reflection in a pool of water. Finally, he fell into the water and drowned. Narcissism is a term for people who have an exaggerated need to be admired. Because of this need, they develop an exaggerated sense of their own importance. They exaggerate their talents, accomplishments, and achievements so as to be respected. They stretch the truth to build their fragile self-images. Narcissistic individuals develop an overwhelming need to feel special, and they expect to be treated in special ways. They become excessively concerned with themselves and their needs, losing the capacity to be sensitive to the needs of others. Their relationships start out well but end up in disaster. At first, everything seems fine, and the love is wonderful. But when the other person begins to make demands, the anger gets going.

Alcoholics Anonymous (1976) says that this self-centeredness is at the root of our addiction:

> Each person is like an actor who wants to run the whole show [and] is forever trying to arrange the lights, the ballet, the scenery, and the rest of the players in his own way. If his arrangements would only stay put, if only people would do as he wished, the show would be great. Everybody, including himself, would be pleased. Life would be wonderful. In trying to make these arrangements, our actor may sometimes be quite virtuous. He may be kind, considerate, patient, generous, even modest and self-sacrificing. On the other hand, he may be mean, egotistical, selfish, and dishonest. But as with most humans, he is more likely to have varied traits.
>
> What usually happens? The show doesn't come off very well. He begins to think life doesn't treat him right. He decides to exert himself more. He becomes, on the next occasion, still more demanding or gracious, as the case may be. Still, the play does not suit him. Admitting he may be somewhat at fault, he is sure that other people are more to blame. He becomes angry, indignant, [and] self-pitying. What is his basic trouble? Is he not really a self-seeker even when trying to be kind? Is he not a victim of the delusion that he can wrest satisfaction and happiness of this world if he only managed well? (p. 61)

As you read this exercise, you might not think that you are self-centered. The very idea may make you feel angry. To have any flaw would dent that perfect image you have of yourself. And that is the problem. So long as you need to be perfect, criticism sends you tumbling into shame. If you need to be right all of the time, others never seem to respect you. This is what happens. You think that you need to be the best at everything, and then someone comes along who is as good as, or better than, you are. Then you feel humiliated. Critical comments by others send you off the edge of sanity. You fume, you rage, and you get even. You cannot stand the suggestion that you are not perfect in every way.

To understand the trap of narcissism, you need to understand the narcissistic traits. Let's look at a few and see whether any of them fit you.

1. Do you often desire to be the center of attention?
2. Do you want to be the life of the party?
3. Do you feel resentful when your friends achieve something?
4. Do you feel unappreciated?
5. Do you want a beautiful woman or man to hang all over you so that other people can see how wonderful you are?
6. Do you think that you are more intelligent than most?
7. Do you tend to brag about your accomplishments?
8. Do you make a good first impression but have difficulty following through?
9. Do you think people would be better off if they would follow your direction?
10. Do you tend to resent authority figures?
11. Do you try to control people close to you?
12. Do you have difficulty accepting criticism?
13. Do you tend to be unsatisfied in interpersonal relationships?
14. Are you obsessed with money and material things?
15. Are you good at charming others to get what you want?
16. Do you fantasize about big plans and schemes?
17. Do you relish being the big shot?
18. Do you feel that you do not get the respect you deserve?
19. Do you believe that the rules and laws are made for other people?
20. Do you want to be God?

These are the immature narcissistic needs, or the infantile needs, of an individual who wants to be in control. They are the needs of someone who is desperate for attention. But no amount of love would be enough for you. You always would need more and more love. Other people have tried to love you, and they always have fallen short, haven't they? Then you blame them without looking at yourself. It is always the other person's fault and never your own. If the other person would just recognize you for the great person that you are and do what you want him or her to do, then things would go fine.

Narcissistic traits are why you are spiritually bankrupt. This is why you have been feeling so empty. This is why you never fit in. Now let's look at the crux of the issue. When you look at these characteristics carefully, you can see that you have been trying to be God. But you are not God, and so long as you try be God, you will fail.

A FEELING OF WORTHLESSNESS

Underneath your need to be in control is the feeling of worthlessness. You seem to vacillate between being the greatest person and being the worst. There is no middle ground. You are either on the top or on the bottom—never in between, never normal. The reason why you need constant reassurance from others is that you do not feel good about yourself. You feel inadequate. To counteract this feeling, you exaggerate your talents and accomplishments. This is a vain attempt to get people to love you. But people cannot love you until they know you. You cannot lie and feel loved. That is impossible. Intimacy necessitates truth.

Give a few examples of when you lied about your accomplishments or talents to manipulate how someone felt about you.

1. _____
2. _____
3. _____
4. _____
5. _____

Because you feel worthless, you have a difficult time hearing the word *no*. When someone says no, you feel that you are bad. Either you are the best or the worst. When someone says no, you get angry and go into a rage. That makes everything worse.

Give a few examples of when someone told you no and you exploded.

1. _____
2. _____
3. _____
4. _____
5. _____

Because of your feelings of worthlessness, you need to feel special and other people need to recognize your unique abilities. You believe that only special people of high status can really understand you. Because you have a need to be perfect, you tend to routinely overestimate your capabilities. For example, you think that you are going to make all A's in your classes and get angry at the teacher when you get lower grades. It is always the teacher's fault, or the boss's fault, or the spouse's fault—never your own fault. You need to be admired and respected even when you have not worked for it. You expect to start at the top rather than work your way up like other people must do.

Give an example of when you expected to be respected and you did not deserve it.

_____
_____
_____

It is important for you to see how these unrealistic ideals set you up to fail. No one is perfect, so when you expect this of yourself, you ultimately fail. When you think that your work has to be perfect, you end up feeling humiliated when someone points out that you did something wrong.

Give a few examples of when someone criticized you and you got furious.

1. _____
2. _____
3. _____
4. _____
5. _____

Because of your feelings of worthlessness, you spend a lot of time fantasizing about success, power, brilliance, and/or ideal love. How wonderful this new job will be, or this new love, or this new ability. This immature need for unlimited success sets you up to fail. You end up feeling more miserable.

Discuss the last romance you had and what happened. Describe how perfect you thought it was going to be and how it actually turned out.

_____
_____
_____

Love and sex put you at high risk because you put unrealistic expectations on the relationship. You expect the other person to meet your needs to feel important, special, loved, powerful, brilliant, and beautiful. But there is no way in which a person can meet these needs, so the relationship fails and you sink into despair.

Give two examples of how relationship problems lead to chemical use.

1. _____
_____
_____

2. _____
_____
_____

A narcissistic person feels jealous of others and their accomplishments. By constantly comparing yourself to others, you end up feeling bad.

List a number of people who you are envious of, and write down exactly what they have that you want.

1. _____
2. _____
3. _____
4. _____
5. _____

It is important for you to recognize how you constantly compare yourself to others and how you end up feeling either superior or inferior to them. Either way, you have separated yourself from love. Intimacy necessitates equality. Both partners need to come into a relationship feeling good about themselves.

TO LOOSEN THE NARCISSISTIC BONDS

These narcissistic traits enslave you. You never will be perfect. You never will be the most brilliant, or the most beautiful, or the most powerful, or the most loved, or the most wonderful, or the most special. Not everyone will worship you. You believe that to be accepted, you have to be the greatest, but you do not. This is a lie.

You Must Get Honest

Honesty is a wonderful thing. You cannot solve problems without the facts. If you make up the facts, then the problems never will be solved and you will be back to the misery. You never will feel loved if you make up who you are. Even if you fool the other person, you know that the person does not love you. You never will feel known until you tell the truth. The first thing that you need to do is not tell the old lies—you know, as if you are someone special with special talents. If you never worked for the CIA, then do not tell people that you did. If you did not make a lot of money, then do not tell people that you did. If you did not save a person from drowning, then do not say that you did. You get what I mean. You have a million stories that are not true. You have to stop lying. If you do not stop lying, then you will be unhappy.

List a few of the lies you told to get people to like you.

1. _____
2. _____
3. _____
4. _____
5. _____

Promise yourself that you never will tell these lies again. Wake up every morning and be grateful that you have not lied that day. Then try to get through the next hour without lying. If you make it, then congratulate yourself. That is a victory. Check out how you feel. You will be feeling good about yourself. When you lie, check out how you feel. You will be feeling frightened and bad about yourself. Dishonesty is the main reason why you have been isolated. Only by being honest will you begin to feel accepted.

You Must Go to Meetings

To loosen the bonds of narcissism, you must go to meetings and trust someone. This is very difficult because the only person you trust is yourself. But in this illness, if you rely only on yourself, then you will be sick. You need to turn your will and your life over to someone who can manage your life. Start with anyone you can such as your counselor. Lay your trust in that person, and whatever you do, do not trust yourself. Your best judgment got you into this mess. You do not know the way out. Someone else is going to have to show you the way. Name the person(s) who you are going to try to trust.

_____

_____

_____

When you feel like taking the controls back again, do not do so. When someone makes a suggestion, try it.

You Must Seek a Higher Power

You need to seek a Higher Power of your own understanding. There is only one you, and you are special. But you are not better than everyone; you are equal to everyone. This makes life better, not worse. This alone gives you the opportunity to love rather than rule. Everyone has his or her unique place in God's plan. Whatever you do, God will be there for you, loving you. Take a risk and ask God to come into your life. Say something like this: "God, I don't know if you are out there or not, but if you are, I need you to help me." Then ask God a question: "God, what is the next step in my relationship with you?" Now be quiet. Do not be afraid. Wait. A word or phrase will come floating through your mind. It will be something like this: "Trust me" or "Pray." That is God speaking to you inside of your thinking.

Write down what happened.

_____

_____

_____

That is the next step. If you take that step, then you will feel the peace that AA calls serenity. God will tell you the next step, not the second or the third step. If you follow God's plan step by step, then you are free.

Appendix 35

Honesty for Gamblers

This is an exercise to help you get honest with yourself. In recovery, it is essential to tell the truth. As you will hear at every Gamblers Anonymous meeting, this is a program of rigorous honesty. Those who do not recover are people who cannot, or will not, completely give themselves to this simple program.

Dishonesty to self and others distorts reality. You never will solve problems if you lie. You need to live in the facts. You must commit yourself to reality. This means accepting everything that is real.

People who are pathological gamblers think that they cannot tell the truth. They believe that if they do, then they will be rejected. The facts, however, are exactly the opposite. Unless you tell the truth, no one can accept you. People have to know you to accept you. If you keep secrets, then you never will feel known or loved. You are only as sick as your secrets. If you keep secrets from people, then you never will be close to them.

You cannot be a practicing gambling addict without lying to yourself. You must lie, and believe the lies, or else the illness cannot operate. All of the lies are attempts to protect you from the truth. If you had known the truth, then you would have known that you were sick and needed treatment. This would have been frightening, so you kept the truth from yourself and from others. Let's face it. When we were gambling, we were not honest with ourselves.

There are many ways in which you lied to yourself. This exercise will teach you exactly how you distorted reality, and it will start you toward a program of honesty. Respond to each of the following as completely as you can.

1. *Denial:* This is telling yourself or others, "I don't have a problem." Write down a few examples of when you used this technique to avoid dealing with the truth.

    _____

    _____

    _____

2. *Minimizing:* This is making the problem smaller than it really is. You may have told yourself, or someone else, that your problem was not that bad. You may have told someone that you lost a little money when, in fact, you lost a lot. Write down a few examples of when you distorted reality by making the problem seem smaller than it actually was.

    _____

    _____

    _____

3. *Hostility:* This is getting angry or making threats when someone confronts you about your gambling. Give a few examples of when you expressed such hostility.

    _____

    _____

    _____

4. *Rationalization:* This is making an excuse. "I had a hard day. Things are bad. My relationship is bad. My financial situation is bad." Give a few examples of when you thought that you had a good reason to gamble.

    _____

    _____

    _____

5. *Blaming:* This is shifting the responsibility to someone else. "The police were out to get me. My wife is overreacting." Give an example of when you blamed someone else for a problem that you caused by gambling.

_____

_____

_____

6. *Intellectualizing:* This is overanalyzing and thinking to excess about a problem. This avoids doing something about it. "Sure I gamble some, but everyone I know gambles. I read this article that said this is a gambling culture." Give an example of how you use intellectual data and statistics to justify your use.

_____

_____

_____

7. *Diversion:* This is bringing up another topic of conversation to avoid the issue. Give an example.

_____

_____

_____

Make a list of five lies about your gambling problem that you told to someone close to you.

1. _____
2. _____
3. _____
4. _____
5. _____

Make a list of five lies about your gambling problem that you told to yourself.

1. _____
2. _____
3. _____
4. _____
5. _____

Make a list of 10 people to whom you have lied.

1. _____
2. _____
3. _____
4. _____
5. _____
6. _____
7. _____
8. _____
9. _____
10. _____

How do you feel about your lying? Describe how you feel about yourself when you lie.

_____

_____

_____

What do you think will change in your life if you begin to tell the truth?

_____

_____

_____

How do you use lies in other areas of your life?

_____

_____

_____

When are you the most likely to lie? Is it when you have been gambling?

_____

_____

_____

Why do you lie? What does it get you? Give five reasons.

1. _____

2. _____

3. _____

4. _____

5. _____

Common lies of gamblers are listed below. Give a personal example of each. Be honest with yourself.

1. Breaking promises: _____

_____

_____

2. Pretending you have not gambled when, if fact, you have: _____

_____

_____

3. Pretending that you remember how long you had been gambling when, in fact, you lost all track of time: _____

_____

_____

4. Telling someone that you gamble no more than others: _____

_____

_____

5. Telling yourself that you were in control of your gambling: _____

_____

_____

6. Telling someone that you rarely gamble: _____

_____

_____

7. Hiding your gambling: _____

_____

_____

8. Hiding money for gambling: _____

_____

_____

9. Substituting gambling for other activities and then telling someone that you were not interested in doing what that person wanted to do: _____

_____

_____

10. Saying that you were too sick to do something when, if fact, you really wanted to gamble: _____

_____

_____

11. Pretending not to care about your gambling problem: _____

_____

_____

People who are pathological gamblers lie to avoid facing the truth. Lying makes them feel more comfortable, but in the long run they end up feeling isolated and alone. Recovery demands living in the truth. "I am a pathological gambler. My life is unmanageable. I am powerless over gambling. I need help. I can't do this alone." All of these are honest statements from someone who is living in reality.

You can either get real and live in the real world or live in a fantasy world of your own creation. If you get honest, then you will begin to solve real problems. You will be accepted for who you are.

Wake up tomorrow morning and promise yourself that you are going to be honest all day. Write down in a diary when you are tempted to lie. Watch your emotions when you lie. How does it feel? How do you feel about yourself? Write it all down. Keep a diary for 5 days and then share it with your group. Tell the group members how it feels to be honest.

Write the word "TRUTH" on a piece of paper and hang it on your bathroom mirror. Commit yourself to rigorous honesty. You deserve to live a life filled with love and truth. You never need to lie again.

Appendix 36

Step One for Gamblers

We admitted we were powerless over gambling—that our lives had become unmanageable.
—Gamblers Anonymous (1989b, p. 38)

Before beginning this exercise, read Step One in *G.A.: A New Beginning* (Gamblers Anonymous, 1989b).

No one likes to admit defeat. Our minds rebel at the very thought that we have lost control. We are big, strong, intelligent, and capable. How can it be that we are powerless? How can our lives be unmanageable? This exercise will help you to sort through your life and to make some important decisions. Answer as completely as you can each question that applies to you. This is an opportunity for you to get accurate. You need to see the truth about yourself.

Let's pretend for a moment that you are the commander in a nuclear missile silo. You are in charge of a bomb. If you think about it, this is exactly the kind of control that you want over your life. You want to be in control of your thinking, feeling, and behavior. You want to be in control all of the time, not just some of the time. But if you do something by accident, or if you do something foolishly, then you might kill a lot of people.

What is the first thing a compulsive gambler ought to do in order to stop gambling? The compulsive gambler needs to accept the fact that he or she is in the grip of a progressive illness and has a desire to get well. (Gamblers Anonymous, 1989a, p. 8)

To accept powerlessness and unmanageability, a gambler must look at the truth. People who are powerless over gambling do things that are harmful to themselves and others. They do most anything to stay in action—to keep gambling. Gamblers do not consider the consequences of their behavior, and they keep gambling until they are on the verge of death.

Gamblers are *in action* when they plan a bet, make a bet, or wait for a bet to come in. Once the bet is in, they are out of action. Being in action is a primary goal of compulsive gamblers. By staying in action, gamblers feel how they want to feel. They escape reality. They live in a fantasy world of their own creation. Now it is time to get honest with yourself.

POWERLESSNESS

People who are powerless do things that they feel bad or guilty about later. To gamble, they may lie, cheat, steal, hurt their family members, or do poor work. Make a list of the things that made you feel the most uncomfortable in the past.

1. _____
2. _____
3. _____
4. _____
5. _____

People who are powerless will gradually lose respect for themselves. They will have difficulty in trusting themselves. In what ways have you lost respect for yourself due to gambling?

1. _____
2. _____
3. _____
4. _____
5. _____

People who are powerless will do things that they do not remember doing. When gamblers gamble, they can lose all track of time. They might think that they have been gambling for only a few minutes when, in fact, they have been gambling for many hours. If you gamble enough, you cannot remember things properly.

Describe several situations when you lost track of time while you were gambling.

1. _____
2. _____
3. _____
4. _____
5. _____

People who are powerless cannot keep promises they make to themselves or others. They promise that they will cut down on their gambling, and they do not. They promise that they will not gamble, and they do. They promise to be home, to be at work, to be at the Cub Scout meeting, or to go to school, but they do not make it. They cannot always do what they want to do. They disappoint themselves, and they lose trust in themselves. Other people lose trust in them. Gamblers can count on themselves some of the time, but they cannot count on themselves all of the time.

1. Did you ever promise yourself that you would cut down on your gambling?   Yes _____   No _____
2. What happened to these promises?

_____
_____
_____

3. Did you ever promise yourself that you would quit entirely?   Yes _____   No _____
4. What happened to your promise?

_____
_____
_____

5. Did you ever make a promise to someone that you did not keep because you were gambling? Give a few examples.

_____
_____
_____

6. Are you reliable when you are gambling?   Yes _____   No _____

People who are powerless lose control of their behavior. They do things that they would not normally do when not in action. They might get into fights. They might yell at people they love—their spouses, children, parents, or friends. They might say things that they do not mean.

Have you ever gotten into a fight when you were gambling? Describe each instance.

_____
_____
_____

The desire to gamble is very powerful. It makes a gambler feel irritable and impatient. People who are powerless say things that they do not mean. They say angry things that they feel bad about later. We might not remember everything we said, but the other person does remember.

Have you ever said something that you did not mean? What did you say? What did you do?

_____

_____

_____

People are powerless when they cannot deal with their feelings. They may gamble because they feel frightened, angry, or sad. They medicate their feelings with gambling.

1. Have you ever gambled to cover up your feelings? Give a few examples.

_____

_____

_____

2. List the feelings that you have difficulty dealing with.

_____

_____

_____

People are powerless when they are not safe. What convinces you that you no longer can gamble safely?

_____

_____

_____

People are powerless when they know that they should do something, but they cannot make themselves do it. They might make a great effort to do the right thing, but they keep doing the wrong thing.

1. Could you cut down on your gambling every time you wanted for as long as you wanted?
   Yes _____   No _____

2. Did gambling ever keep you from doing something at home you thought you should do? Give some examples.

_____

_____

_____

3. Did gambling ever keep you from going to work? Give some examples.

_____

_____

_____

4. Did you ever lose a job because of your gambling? Write down what happened.

_____

_____

_____

People are powerless when other people have to warn them that they are in trouble. You may have felt as though you were fine, but people close to you noticed that something was wrong. It probably was difficult for them to define just what was wrong, but they worried about you. It is difficult to confront people when they are wrong, so most people avoid the problem until they cannot stand the behavior anymore. When gamblers are confronted with their behavior, they feel annoyed and irritated. They want to be left alone with the lies that they are telling themselves.

Has anyone ever talked to you about your gambling? Who was this? How did you feel?

_____

_____

_____

People are powerless when they do not know the truth about themselves. Gamblers lie to themselves about how much they are gambling. They lie to themselves about how often they gamble. They lie to themselves about the amount of money they are losing, even when the losses are obvious. They blame others for their problems. Some common lies that they tell themselves include the following:

"I can quit anytime I want to."
"I only gamble a little."
"The police were out to get me."
"I only gamble when I want to."
"Everybody does it."
"I gamble, but I don't have a problem."
"Anybody can have financial problems."
"My friends won't like me if I don't gamble."
"I never have problems when I gamble."
"I can pay the money back later."
"From now on, I'll just gamble a little."
"When I win, I'm going to buy a present for my family."

Gamblers continue to lie to themselves to the very end. They hold on to their delusional thinking, and they believe that their lies are the truth. They deliberately lie to those close to them. They hide their gambling. They make their problems seem smaller than they actually are. They make excuses for why they are gambling. They refuse to see the truth.

1. Have you ever lied to yourself about your gambling? List some of the lies that you told yourself.

_____

_____

_____

2. List the ways in which you tried to convince yourself that you did not have a problem.

_____

_____

_____

3. List some of the ways in which you tried to convince others that you did not have a problem.

_____

_____

_____

"Therefore, it is not surprising that our gambling careers have been characterized by countless vain attempts to prove we could gamble like other people. The idea that somehow, some day, we will control our gambling is the great obsession of every compulsive gambler. The persistence of this illusion is astonishing. Many pursue it to the gates of prison, insanity, or death." (Gamblers Anonymous, 1989a, p. 2)

UNMANAGEABILITY

Imagine that you are the manager of a large corporation. You are responsible for how everything runs. If you are not a good manager, then the business will fail. You must carefully plan everything and carry out those plans well. You must be alert.

You must know exactly where you are and where you are going. These are the skills that you need to manage your life effectively.

Gamblers are not good managers. They keep losing control. Their plans fall through. They cannot devise and stick to things long enough to see a solution. They are lying to themselves, so they do not know where they are. They feel confused. Their feelings are being medicated, so they cannot use their feelings to give them energy and direction for problem solving.

You do not have to be a bad manager all of the time. It is worse to be a bad manager some of the time. It is totally confusing. Most chemically dependent persons have flurries of productive activity during which they work too much. They work themselves to the bone, and then they let things slide. It is like being on a roller-coaster. Sometimes things are in control, and sometimes things are out of control. Things are up and down, and chemically dependent persons never can predict which way things are going to be tomorrow.

People's lives are unmanageable when they have plans fall apart because they are gambling.

Make a list of the plans that you failed to complete because of your gambling.

1. _____
2. _____
3. _____
4. _____
5. _____

People's lives are unmanageable when they cannot manage their finances consistently.

1. List any money problems that you are having.

_____
_____
_____

2. Is any of this trouble the result of your gambling? Explain how gambling has contributed to the problems.

_____
_____
_____

People's lives are unmanageable when they cannot trust their own judgments.

1. Have you ever been so absorbed in your gambling that you did not know what was happening around you? Explain.

_____
_____
_____

2. Did you ever lie to yourself about your gambling? Explain how your lies contributed to your being unable to manage your life.

_____
_____
_____

3. Have you ever made a decision while gambling that you were sorry about later? Explain.

_____
_____
_____

People's lives are unmanageable when they cannot work or play normally. Gamblers miss work and recreational activities because of their gambling.

Have you ever missed work because you were gambling? List the times.

1. _____
2. _____
3. _____
4. _____
5. _____

Have you ever missed recreational or family activities because you were gambling? List the times.

1. _____
2. _____
3. _____
4. _____
5. _____

People's lives are unmanageable when they are in trouble with other people or society. Gamblers break the rules of society to get their own way. They have problems with authority.

1. Have you ever been in legal trouble when you were gambling? Explain the legal problems you have had.

_____
_____
_____

2. Have you ever had problems with your parents because of your gambling? Explain.

_____
_____
_____

3. Have you ever had problems in school because of your gambling? Explain.

_____
_____
_____

People's lives are unmanageable when they cannot consistently achieve goals. Gamblers reach out for what they want, but something keeps getting in the way. It does not seem fair. They keep falling short of their goals. Finally, they give up completely. They may have had the goals of going to school, getting a better job, working on family problems, getting in good physical condition, and/or going on a diet. No matter what the goals are, something keeps going wrong with the plans. Gamblers constantly try to blame someone else, but they cannot work long enough to reach their goals. Gamblers are good starters, but they are poor finishers.

List the goals that you had for yourself that you did not achieve.

1. _____
2. _____
3. _____
4. _____
5. _____

People's lives are unmanageable when they cannot use their feelings appropriately. Feelings give us energy and direction for problem solving. Gamblers medicate their feelings by staying in action. Gambling gives them a different feeling. Gamblers become very confused about how they feel.

1. What feelings have you tried to alter with gambling?

_____

_____

_____

2. How do you feel when you are gambling? Describe in detail.

_____

_____

_____

People's lives are unmanageable when they violate their own rules by violating their own morals and values. Gamblers compromise their values to continue gambling. They have the value not to lie, but they lie anyway. They have the value not to steal, but they steal anyway. They have the value to be loyal to spouses or friends, but when they are gambling they do not remain loyal. Their values and morals fall away, one by one. They end up doing things that they do not believe in. They know that they are doing the wrong things, but they do them anyway.

1. Did you ever lie to cover up your gambling? How did you feel about yourself?

_____

_____

_____

2. Were you ever disloyal when gambling? Explain.

_____

_____

_____

3. Did you ever steal or write bad checks to gamble? Explain what you did and how you felt about yourself later.

_____

_____

_____

4. Did you ever break the law when gambling? What did you do?

_____

_____

_____

5. Did you ever hurt someone you loved while gambling? Explain.

_____

_____

_____

6. Did you treat yourself poorly by refusing to stop gambling when you knew that it was bad for you? Explain how you were feeling about yourself.

_____

_____

_____

7. Did you stop going to church? How did this make you feel about yourself?

_____

_____

_____

People's lives are unmanageable when they continue to do something that gives them problems. Gambling creates severe financial problems. Even if gamblers are aware of the problems, they gamble anyway. They see gambling as the solution.

Gambling causes psychological problems. Compulsive gambling makes people feel depressed, fearful, anxious, and/or angry. Even when gamblers are aware of these symptoms, they continue to gamble.

Gambling creates relationship problems. It causes family problems in the form of family fights as well as verbal and physical abuse. It causes interpersonal conflict at work, with family, and with friends. Gamblers withdraw and become isolated and alone.

1. Did you have any persistent physical problems caused by, or exacerbated by, gambling? Describe the problems.

_____
_____
_____

2. Did you have any persistent psychological problems, such as depression, that were caused by your gambling? Describe the problems.

_____
_____
_____

3. Did you have persistent interpersonal conflicts exacerbated by gambling? Describe the problems.

_____
_____
_____

"We know that no real compulsive gambler ever regains control. All of us felt at times we were regaining control, but such intervals—usually brief—were inevitably followed by still less control, which led in time to pitiful and incomprehensible demoralization. We are convinced that gamblers of our type are in the grip of a progressive illness. Over any considerable period of time, we get worse, never better." (Gamblers Anonymous, 1989a, p. 3)

You must have good reasons to work toward a new life free from gambling. Look over this exercise and list 10 reasons why you want to stop gambling.

1. _____
2. _____
3. _____
4. _____
5. _____
6. _____
7. _____
8. _____
9. _____
10. _____

After completing this exercise, take a long look at yourself. What is the truth?

1. Have there been times when you were powerless over gambling?   Yes _____   No _____
2. Have there been times when your life was unmanageable?   Yes _____   No _____

Appendix 37

Step Two for Gamblers

[We] came to believe that a power greater than ourselves could restore us to a normal way of thinking and living.
—Gamblers Anonymous (1989b, p. 39)

Before beginning this exercise, read Step Two in *G.A.: A New Beginning* (Gamblers Anonymous, 1989b).

In Step One, you admitted that you were powerless over gambling and that your life was unmanageable. In Step Two, you need to see the insanity of your disease and seek a power greater than yourself. If you are powerless, then you need power. If your life is unmanageable, then you need a manager. Step Two will help you to decide who that manager can be.

Most gamblers revolt at the implications of the phrase "restore to a normal way of thinking and living." They think that they may have a gambling problem, but they do not feel as though they have been abnormal.

In Gamblers Anonymous (GA), the word *normal* means being of sound mind. Someone with a sound mind knows what is real and knows how to adapt to reality. A sound mind feels stable, safe, and secure. Someone who is abnormal cannot see reality and is unable to adapt. A person does not have to have all of reality distorted to be in trouble. If you miss some reality, then you ultimately will get lost. One wrong turn is all that it takes to end up in a ditch.

Going through life is like a long journey. You have a map given to you by your parents. The map shows the way in which to be happy. If you make some wrong turns along the way, then you will end up unhappy. This is what happens in gambling. Searching for happiness, we make wrong turns. We find out that our map is defective. Even if we followed our map to perfection, we still would be lost. What we need is a new map.

Gamblers Anonymous gives us this new map. It puts up 12 signposts to show us the way. If you follow this map as millions of people have, then you will find the joy and happiness that you have been seeking. You have reached and passed the first signpost, Step One. You have decided that your life is powerless and unmanageable. Now you need a new power source. You need to find someone else who can manage your life.

Gamblers Anonymous is a spiritual program, and it directs you toward a spiritual solution. It is not a religious program. Spirituality is defined as the relationship you have with yourself and all else. Religion is an organized system of faith and worship. Everyone has spirituality, but not everyone has religion.

You need to explore three relationships very carefully in Step Two: the relationships with yourself, with others, and with a Higher Power. This Higher Power can be any Higher Power of your choice. If you do not have a Higher Power right now, do not worry. Most of us started that way. Just be willing to consider that there is a power greater than you in the universe.

To explore these three relationships, you need to see the truth about yourself. If you see the truth, then you can find the way. First you must decide whether you were abnormal. Did you have a sound mind or not? Let's look at this issue carefully.

People are abnormal when they cannot remember what they did. They have memory problems. To be abnormal, they do not have to have memory problems all of the time; they just need to have them some of the time. People who gamble might not remember what happened to them when they were gambling. Long periods of time can pass during which gamblers are relatively unaware of their environment.

List any memory problems that you have had while gambling. Did you ever find that you had spent more time gambling that you remembered?

_____

_____

_____

People who are abnormal lose control over their behavior. They do things when they are gambling that they never would do otherwise.

List three times when you lost control over your behavior while gambling.

1. _____
2. _____
3. _____

List three times when you could not control your gambling—when you told yourself to stop but you could not.

1. _____
2. _____
3. _____

People who are abnormal consider self-destruction.

Did you ever consider hurting yourself when you were gambling or suffering from gambling losses?

Yes _____   No _____

Describe what happened.

_____
_____
_____

People who are abnormal feel emotionally unstable.

Have you ever thought that you were going crazy because of your gambling?   Yes _____   No _____

Describe this time.

_____
_____
_____

Have you recently felt emotionally unstable?   Yes _____   No _____

Describe how you have been feeling.

_____
_____
_____

People who are abnormal are so confused that they cannot get their lives in order. They frantically try to fix things, but problems remain out of control.

List some personal, family, work, or school problems that you have not been able to control.

_____
_____
_____

People who are abnormal cannot see the truth about what is happening to them. People who are gambling hide their gambling from themselves and from others. They minimize, rationalize, and deny that there are problems.

Do you feel that you have been completely honest with yourself?   Yes _____   No _____

List some of the lies that you told yourself.

_____

_____

_____

People who are abnormal cut themselves off from healthy relationships. You might find that you cannot communicate with your spouse as well as you used to. You might not see your friends as often. More and more of your life centers around gambling.

List three people you have cut yourself off from.

1. _____

2. _____

3. _____

As your gambling increased, did you go to church less often?   Yes _____   No _____

List any relationships that you have damaged in your gambling.

_____

_____

_____

People who are abnormal cannot deal with their feelings. Problem gamblers cannot deal with their feelings. They do not like how they feel, so they gamble to medicate their feelings. They may gamble to feel less afraid or sad. They may gamble to feel more powerful.

List the feelings that you wanted to change by gambling.

_____

_____

_____

Now look back over your responses. Get out your Step One exercise and read through it. Look at the truth about yourself. Look carefully at how you were thinking, feeling, and behaving when you were gambling. Make a decision. Do you think that you had a sound mind? If you were unsound at least some of the time, then you were abnormal. If you believe this to be true, then say this to yourself: "I am powerless. My life is unmanageable. My mind is unsound. I have been abnormal in thinking and living."

A POWER GREATER THAN OURSELVES

Consider a power greater than yourself. What exists in the world that has greater power than you do—a river, the wind, the universe, the sun?

List five things that have greater power than you do.

1. _____

2. _____

3. _____

4. _____

5. _____

The first Higher Power that you need to consider is the power of the GA group. The group is more powerful than you are. Ten hands are more powerful than two. Two heads are better than one. Gamblers Anonymous operates in groups. The group works like a family. The group process is founded in love and trust. Each member shares his or her experiences, strengths, and hopes in an attempt to help himself or herself and others. There is an atmosphere of anonymity. What you hear in group is confidential.

The group acts as a mirror reflecting you to yourself. The group members will help you to discover the truth about who and what you are. You have been deceiving yourself for a long time. The group will help you to uncover the lies. You will come to understand the old GA saying, "What we cannot do alone, we can do together." In group, you will have greater power over the disease because the group will see the whole truth better than you can.

You were not lying to hurt yourself; you were lying to protect yourself. In the process of building your lies, you cut yourself off from reality. This is how compulsive gambling works. You cannot recover from addiction by yourself. You need power coming from somewhere else. Begin by trusting your group. Keep an open mind.

You need to share in your group. The more you share, the closer you will get and the more trust you will develop. If you take risks, then you will reap the rewards. You do not have to tell the group everything, but you need to share as much as you can. The group can help you to straighten out your thinking and restore you to sanity.

Many gamblers are afraid of a Higher Power. They fear that a Higher Power will punish them or treat them in the same way that their fathers or mothers did. They might fear losing control.

List some of the fears that you have about a Higher Power.

_____

_____

_____

Some gamblers have difficulty in trusting anyone. They have been so hurt by others that they do not want to take the chance of being hurt again.

What has happened in your life that makes it difficult for you to trust?

_____

_____

_____

What are some of the things you will need to see from a Higher Power that will show you that the Higher Power can be trusted?

_____

_____

_____

Who was the most trustworthy person you ever knew?   Name _____

How did this person treat you?

_____

_____

_____

What do you hope to gain by accepting a Higher Power?

_____

_____

_____

Gamblers Anonymous wants you to come to believe in a power greater than yourself. You can accept any Higher Power that you feel can restore you to sanity. Your group, nature, your counselor, and your sponsor all can be used to give you this restoration. You must pick this Higher Power carefully. We suggest that you use GA as your Higher Power for now. Here is a group of people who are recovering. They have found the way. This program ultimately will direct you toward a God of your own understanding.

Millions of gamblers have recovered because they were willing to reach out for God. Gamblers Anonymous makes it clear that nothing else will remove the obsession to gamble. Some of us have so glorified our own lives that we have shut out God. Now is your opportunity. You are at a major turning point. You can begin to open your heart and let God in, or you can keep God out. God tells us that all who seek will find.

Remember that this is the beginning of a new life. To be new, you have to do things differently. All that the program is asking you to do is be open to the possibility that there is a power greater than yourself. Gamblers Anonymous does not demand that you believe in anything. The Twelve Steps are simply suggestions. You do not have to swallow all of this now, but you need to be open. Most recovering persons take the Second Step a piece at a time.

First you need to learn how to trust yourself. You must learn how to consistently treat yourself well.

> What do you need to see from yourself that will show you that you are trustworthy?

_____

_____

_____

Then you need to begin to trust your group. See whether the group members act consistently in your interest. They will not always tell you what you want to hear. No real friend would do that. They will give you the opportunity and encouragement to grow.

> What will you need to see from the group members that will show you that they are trustworthy?

_____

_____

_____

Every person has a unique spiritual journey. No one can start this journey with a closed mind.

> What is it going to take to show you that God exists?

_____

_____

_____

Step Two does not mean that we believe in God as God is presented in any religion. Remember that religion is an organized system of worship. It is human-made. Worship is just a means of assigning worth to something. Many people have been so turned off by religion that the idea of God is unacceptable. "We found that some of the obstacles preventing us from attempting to believe were pride, ego, fear, self-centeredness, defiance, and grandiosity" (Gamblers Anonymous, 1989b, p. 40).

> Describe the religious environment of your childhood. What was it like? What did you learn about God?

_____

_____

_____

> How did these early experiences influence the beliefs that you have today?

_____

_____

_____

What experiences have caused you to doubt God?

_____

_____

_____

Your willingness is essential to your recovery.

Give some examples of your willingness to trust in a Higher Power of your choice. What are you willing to do?

_____

_____

_____

Describe your current religious beliefs.

_____

_____

_____

Explain the God of your own understanding.

_____

_____

_____

List five reasons why a Higher Power will be good for you.

1. _____
2. _____
3. _____
4. _____
5. _____

If you asked the people in your GA group to describe God, you would get a variety of answers. Each person has his or her own understanding of God. It is this unique understanding that allows God to work individually for each of us. God comes to each of us differently.

Appendix 38

Step Three for Gamblers

[We] made a decision to turn our will and our lives over to the care of this power of our own understanding.

—Gamblers Anonymous (1989b, p. 40)

Before beginning this exercise, read Step Three in *G.A.: A New Beginning* (Gamblers Anonymous, 1989b).

You have come a long way in the program, and you can feel proud of yourself. You have decided that you are powerless over gambling and that your life is unmanageable. You have decided that a Higher Power of some sort can restore you to normal thinking and living.

In Step Three, you will reach toward a Higher Power of your own understanding. This is the miracle that you have been searching for. It is the major focus of the Gamblers Anonymous (GA) program. This is a spiritual program that directs you toward the ultimate in truth. It is important that you be open to the possibility that there is a God. It is vital that you give this concept room to blossom and grow.

> Many of us used our sponsor, other members, or the fellowship as this Higher Power, but eventually, as we proceeded with the work required in these steps, we came to believe this Higher Power to be a God of our own understanding. (Gamblers Anonymous, 1989b, p. 40)

Step Three should not confuse you. It calls for a decision to correct your character defects under spiritual supervision. You must make an honest effort to change your life.

The GA program is a spiritual one. Gamblers in recovery must have the honesty to look at their illness, the open-mindedness to apply the solution being told to themselves, and the willingness to apply this solution by proceeding on with the recovery process. If you are willing to seek God, then you will find God. That is GA's promise.

UNDERSTANDING THE MORAL LAW

All spirituality has, at its core, what is already inside of you. Your Higher Power lives inside of you. Inside of all of us, there is inherent goodness. In all cultures, and in all lands, this goodness is expressed in what we call the moral law. Morality demands love in action and in truth. It is simply stated as follows: Love God all you can, love others all you can, and love yourself all you can. This law is very powerful. If some stranger were drowning in a pool next to you, then this law would motivate you to help. Instinctively, you would feel driven to help, even if it put your own life at risk. The moral law is so important that it transcends our instinct for survival. You would try to save that drowning person at your own risk. This moral law is exactly the same everywhere—in every culture. It exists inside of everyone. It is written on our hearts. Even among thieves, honesty is valued.

When we survey religious thought, we come up with many different ideas about God and about how to worship God. But when we look at saints of the various religions, we see that they are living practically indistinguishable lives. They all are doing the same things. They do not lie, cheat, or steal. They believe in giving to others before they give to themselves. They try not to be envious of others. To believe in a Higher Power, you must believe that this good exists inside of you. You also must believe that there is more of this good outside of you. If you do not believe in a living, breathing God at this point, do not worry. Every one of us has started where you are.

All people have a basic problem: We break the moral law, even if we believe in it. This fact means that something is wrong with us. We are incapable of following the moral law. Even though we would deem it unfair for someone to lie to us, occasionally we lie to someone else. If we see someone dressed in clothes that look terrible, then we might tell the person that he or she looks good. This is a lie. We would not want other people lying to us like that. In this and other situations, we do not obey the very moral law that we know is good. We might even stand there and watch that other person drown.

You must ask yourself several questions. Where did we get this moral law? How did this law of behavior get started? Did it just evolve? The GA program believes that these good laws come from something good. People in the program believe that you can communicate with this goodness.

We do not know everything about the Higher Power. Much of God remains a mystery. If we look at science, we find the same thing; most of science is a mystery. We know very little about the primary elements of science such as gravity, but we make judgments about these elements using our experience. No one has ever seen an electron, but we are sure that it exists because we have some experience of it. It is the same with the Higher Power. We can know that there is a power greater than ourselves if we have some experience of this power. Both science and spirituality necessitate a faith based on experience.

Instinctively, people know that if they can get more goodness, they will have better lives. Spirituality must be practical. It must make your life better, or you will discard it. If you open yourself up to the spiritual part of the program, then you will feel better immediately.

By reading this exercise, you can begin to develop your relationship with a Higher Power. You will find true joy here if you try. Without some sort of a Higher Power, your recovery will be more difficult. A Higher Power can relieve your gambling problem as nothing else can. Many people achieve stable recovery without calling their Higher Power "God." That certainly is possible. There are many wonderful atheists and agnostics in our program. But the GA way is to reach for a God of your own understanding.

You can change things in your life. You really can. You do not have to drown in despair any longer.

THE KEY TO STEP THREE

The key to working Step Three is willingness. You must have the willingness to turn your life over to the care of God as you understand God. This is difficult for many of us because we think that we are still in control. We are completely fooled by this delusion. We feel as though we know the right thing to do. We feel that everything would be fine if others would just do things our way. This leads us to deep feelings of resentment and self-pity. People would not cooperate with our plan. No matter how hard we tried to control everything, things kept getting out of control. Sometimes the harder we worked, the worse things got.

HOW TO TURN IT OVER

To arrest gambling, you have to stop playing God and let your God take control. If you sincerely want this and you try, then it is easy. Go to a quiet place and talk to your Higher Power about your gambling. Say something like this: "God, I am lost. I can't do this anymore. I turn this situation over to you." Watch how you feel when you say this prayer. The next time you have a problem, stop and turn the problem over to your Higher Power. Say something like this: "God, I can't deal with this problem. You deal with it." See what happens.

Your Higher Power wants to show you the way. If you try to find the way yourself, you will be constantly lost.

Step Three offers no compromise. It calls for a decision. Exactly how we surrender and turn things over is not the point. The important thing is that you be willing to try. Can you see that it is necessary to give up your self-centeredness? Do you feel that it is time to turn things over to a power greater than yourself?

List the things you have to gain by turning your will and your life over to a Higher Power.

1. _____
2. _____
3. _____
4. _____
5. _____

Why do you need to turn things over to a Higher Power?

_____
_____
_____

We should not confuse organized religion with spirituality. In Step Two, you learned that spirituality deals with your relationships with yourself, with others, and with your Higher Power. Religion is an organized system of faith and worship. It is human-made, not God-made. It is humans' way of interpreting God's plan. Religion can be very confusing, and it can drive people away from God.

Are old religious ideas keeping you from God? If so, then how?

_____

_____

_____

A great barrier to finding your Higher Power may be impatience. You may want to find God right now. You must understand that your spiritual growth is not set by you. You will grow spiritually when God feels that you are ready. Remember that we are turning this whole thing over. Each person has his or her unique spiritual journey. Each individual must have his or her own walk. Spiritual growth, not perfection, is your goal. All that you can do is seek the God of your understanding. When God knows that you are ready, God will find you.

Total surrender is necessary. If you are holding back, then you need to let go absolutely. Faith, willingness, and prayer will overcome all of the obstacles. Do not worry about your doubt. Just keep seeking.

List 10 ways in which you can seek God. Ask someone in the program, a clergy person, or your counselor to help you.

1. _____
2. _____
3. _____
4. _____
5. _____
6. _____
7. _____
8. _____
9. _____
10. _____

What does the saying, "Let go and let God," mean to you?

_____

_____

_____

What are some ways in which you can put Step Three to work in your life?

_____

_____

_____

What things in your life do you still want to control?

_____

_____

_____

How can these things be handled better by turning them over to your Higher Power?

_____

_____

_____

List five ways in which you allowed gambling to be the God in your life.

1. _____
2. _____
3. _____
4. _____
5. _____

How did gambling separate you from God?

_____
_____
_____

What changes have you noticed in yourself since you entered the program?

_____
_____
_____

Of these changes, which of them occurred because you listened to someone other than yourself?

_____
_____
_____

Make a list of the things that are holding you back from turning things over.

1. _____
2. _____
3. _____
4. _____
5. _____

How do you see God caring for you?

_____
_____
_____

How do you understand God now?

_____
_____
_____

Write down your spiritual plan. What are you going to do on a daily basis to help your spiritual program grow?

_____
_____
_____
_____
_____

Appendix 39

Step Four for Gamblers

[We] made a searching and fearless moral and financial inventory of ourselves.
—Gamblers Anonymous (1989b, p. 68)

Before beginning this exercise, read Step Four in *G.A.: A New Beginning* (Gamblers Anonymous, 1989b).

You are doing well in the program. You have admitted your powerlessness over gambling, and you have found a Higher Power that can restore you to normal thinking and living. Now you must take an inventory of yourself. You must know exactly what resources you have available, and you must examine the exact nature of your wrongs. You need to be detailed about the good things about you as well as the bad things about you. Only by taking this inventory will you know exactly where you are. Then you can decide where you are going.

In taking this inventory, you must be detailed and specific. It is the only way of seeing the complete impact of your disease. A part of the truth might be, "I told lies to my children." The complete truth might be, "I told my children that I had cancer. They were terrified and cried for a long time." These two statements would be very different. Only the second statement tells the exact nature of the wrong, and the patient felt the full impact of the disclosure. You can see how important it is to put the whole truth before you at one time—the truth that will set you free.

The Fourth Step is a long autobiography. You can write it down carefully. Read this exercise before you start, and underline things that pertain to you. You will want to come back and cover each of these issues in detail as you write it down. If the problem does not relate to you, then leave it blank. Examine exactly what you did wrong. Look for your mistakes, even where the situations were not totally your fault. Try to disregard what the other person did, and concentrate on yourself instead. In time, you will realize that the person who hurt you was spiritually sick. You need to ask God to help you forgive that person and to show that person the same understanding that you would want for yourself. You can pray that this person finds out the truth about himself or herself.

Review your natural desires carefully, and think about how you acted on them. You will see that some of them became the God of your life. Sex, food, money, relaxation, relationships, sleep, power, and influence all can become the major focus of our lives. The pursuit of these desires can take total control and can become the center of our existence.

Review your sexuality as you move through the inventory. Did you ever use someone else selfishly? Did you ever lie to get what you wanted? Did you coerce or force someone into doing something that he or she did not want to do? Who did you hurt, and exactly what did you do?

In working through the inventory, you will experience some pain. You will feel angry, sad, afraid, ashamed, embarrassed, guilty, and lonely. The Fourth Step is a grieving process. As you see your wrongs clearly, you may feel that no one will ever love you again. But remember that God created you in perfection. You are God's masterpiece. There is nothing wrong with you. You just made some mistakes.

Now let's take a basic look at right and wrong.

1. *Pride:* Too great an admiration of yourself

Pride makes you your own law, your own moral judge, and your own Higher Power. Pride produces criticism, back-stabbing, slander, barbed words, and character assassinations that elevate your own ego. Pride makes you condemn as fools those who criticize you. Pride gives you excuses. It produces the following:

   a. Boasting or self-glorification
   b. Love of publicity
   c. Hypocrisy or pretending to be better than you are
   d. Hardheadedness or refusing to give up your will

e. Discord or resenting anyone who crosses you

f. Quarrelsomeness or quarreling whenever another person challenges your wishes

g. Disobedience or refusing to submit your will to the will of superiors or to a Higher Power

2. *Covetousness or avarice:* Perversion of humans' God-given right to own things

Do you desire wealth in the form of money or other things as an end in itself rather than as a means to an end such as taking care of the soul and body? In acquiring wealth in any form, do you disregard the rights of others? Are you dishonest? If so, then to what degree and in what fashion? Do you give an honest day's work for an honest day's pay? How do you use what you have? Are you stingy with your family? Do you love money and possessions for these things in themselves? How excessive is your love of luxury? How do you preserve your wealth or increase it? Do you stoop to devices such as fraud, perjury, dishonesty, and sharp practices in dealing with others? Do you try to fool yourself in these regards? Do you call stinginess "thrift"? Do you call questionable business "big business" or "drive"? Do you call unreasonable hoarding "security"? If you currently have no money and little other wealth, then how and by what practice will you go about getting it later? Will you do almost anything to attain these things and kid yourself by giving your methods innocent names?

3. *Lust:* Inordinate love and desires of the pleasures of the flesh

Are you guilty of lust in any of its forms? Do you tell yourself that improper or undue indulgence in sexual activities is required? Do you treat people as objects of your desire? Do you use pornography or think unhealthy sexual thoughts? Do you treat other people sexually the same way in which you want to be treated?

4. *Envy:* Sadness at another person's good

How envious are you? Do you dislike seeing others happy or successful, almost as though they have taken from you? Do you resent those who are smarter than you are? Do you ever criticize the good done by others because you secretly wish you had done it yourself for the honor or prestige to be gained? Are you ever envious enough to try to lower another person's reputation by starting, or engaging in, gossip about that person? Being envious includes calling religious people "hypocrites" because they go to church and try to be religiously good even though they are subject to human failings. Do you depreciate well-bred people by saying or feeling that they put on airs? Do you ever accuse educated, wise, or learned people of being highbrow because you envy their advantages? Do you genuinely love other people, or do you find them distasteful because you envy them?

5. *Anger:* A violent desire to punish others

Do you ever fly into rages of temper, become revengeful, entertain urges to "get even," or express an "I won't let him get away with it" attitude? Do you ever resort to violence, clench your fists, or stomp about in a temper flare-up? Are you touchy, unduly sensitive, or impatient at the smallest slight? Do you ever murmur or grumble, even regarding small matters? Do you ignore the fact that anger prevents development of personality and halts spiritual progress? Do you realize at all times that anger disrupts mental poise and often ruins good judgment? Do you permit anger to rule you when you know that it blinds you to the rights of others? How can you excuse even small tantrums of temper when anger destroys the spirit of recollection that you need for compliance with the inspirations of God? Do you permit yourself to become angry when others are weak and become angry with you? Can you hope to entertain the serene spirit of God within your soul when you often are beset by angry flare-ups of even minor importance?

6. *Gluttony:* Abuse of lawful pleasures that attach to eating and drinking of foods required for self-preservation

Do you weaken your moral and intellectual life by excessive use of food and drink? Do you generally eat to excess and, thus, enslave your soul and character to the pleasures of the body beyond its reasonable needs? Do you kid yourself that you can be a "hog" without affecting your moral life? When gambling, did you ever win big, only to return and immediately gamble to win more? Did you gamble so much that your intellect and personality deteriorated? So much that memory, judgment, and concentration were affected? So much that personal pride and social judgment vanished? So much that you developed a spirit of despair?

7. *Sloth:* Illness of the will that causes a neglect of duty

Are you lazy or given to idleness, procrastination, nonchalance, and indifference in material things? Are you lukewarm in prayer? Do you hold self-discipline in contempt? Would you rather read a novel than study something requiring brain work such as the Gamblers Anonymous (GA, 1989b) book? Are you fainthearted in performance of those things that are morally or spiritually difficult? Are you ever listless with aversion to effort in any form? Are you easily distracted from things spiritual, quickly turning to things temporal? Are you ever indolent to the extent where you perform work carelessly?

PERSONALITY DEFECTS

1. *Selfishness:* Taking care of your own needs without regard for others
   a. The family would like an outing. Dad would like gambling, golf, and fishing. Who wins?
   b. Your child needs a new pair of shoes. You put it off until pay day but then gamble away the paycheck.
   c. You are afraid to dance because you might appear awkward. You fear any new venture because it might injure the false front that you put on.

2. *Alibis:* The highly developed art of justifying gambling and behavior through mental gymnastics
   a. "A few dollars won't hurt anything."
   b. "Starting tomorrow, I'm going to change."
   c. "If I didn't have a wife and family."
   d. "If I could start all over again."
   e. "A little gambling will help me to relax."
   f. "Nobody cares anyway."
   g. "I had a hard day."

3. *Dishonest thinking:* Another way of lying

We may even take truths or facts and, through some phony hop-scotch, come up with exactly the conclusions that we had planned to arrive at. Boy, we are great at that business.

   a. "My secret love is going to raise the roof if I drop her. It is not fair to burden my wife with that sort of knowledge. There-fore, I will hang on to my girlfriend. This mess isn't her fault." (good solid con)
   b. "If I tell my family about the $500 bonus, then it will all go for bills, clothes, the dentist, and so on. I've got to have some gambling money. Why start a family argument? I'll leave well enough alone."
   c. "My husband dresses well, he eats well, and the kids are getting a good education. What more do they want from me?"

4. *Shame:* The feeling that something irreparable is wrong with you
   a. No matter how many people tell you it is okay, you continue to berate yourself.
   b. You keep going over and over your mistakes, wallowing in what a terrible person you are.

5. *Resentment:* Displeasure aroused by a real or imagined wrong or injury accompanied by irritation, exasperation, and/or hate
   a. You are fired from your job. Therefore, you hate the boss.
   b. Your sister warns you about excessive gambling. You get fighting mad at her.
   c. A co-worker is doing a good job and gets accolades. You have a legal record and suspect that he might have been promoted over you. You hate his guts.

    d. You may have a resentment toward a person or a group of people, or you may resent institutions, religions, and so on. Anger and resentment lead to bickering, friction, hatred, and unjust revenge. They bring out the worst of our immaturity and produce misery to ourselves and all concerned.

6. *Intolerance:* Refusal to put up with beliefs, practices, customs, or habits that differ from our own
    a. Do you hate other people because they are of another race, come from a different country, or have a different religion? What would you do if you were one of those other persons? Kill yourself?
    b. Did you have any choice in being born a particular color or nationality?
    c. Isn't our religion usually "inherited"?

7. *Impatience:* Unwillingness to calmly bear delay, opposition, pain, or bother
    a. A pathological gambler is someone who jumps on a horse and gallops off madly in all directions at the same time.
    b. Do you blow your stack when someone keeps you waiting over the "allotted time" that you gave that person?
    c. Did anyone ever have to wait for you?

8. *Phoniness:* A manifestation of our great false pride; a form of lying; rank and brash dishonesty; the old false front
    a. "I give to my love a present as evidence of my love. Just by pure coincidence, it helps to smooth over my last binge."
    b. "I buy new clothes because my business position demands it. Meanwhile, the family also could use food and clothes."
    c. A joker may enthrall a GA audience with profound wisdom but not give the time of day to his or her spouse or children.

9. *Procrastination:* Putting off or postponing things that need to be done; the familiar "I'll do it tomorrow"
    a. Did little jobs, when put off, become big and almost impossible later? Did problems piling up contribute to gambling?
    b. Do you pamper yourself by doing things "my way," or do you attempt to put order and discipline into your life?
    c. Can you handle little jobs that you are asked to take care of, or do you feel picked on? Or, are you just too lazy or proud?

10. *Self-pity:* An insidious personality defect and a danger signal to look for

Stop self-pity in a hurry. It is the buildup to trouble.

    a. "These people at the party are having fun with their gambling. Why can't I be like that?" This is the "woe is me" syndrome.
    b. "If I had that guy's money, I wouldn't have any problems." When you feel this way, visit an alcoholic ward, cancer ward, or children's hospital and then count your blessings.

11. *Feelings easily hurt:* Overly sensitive to the slightest criticism
    a. "I walk down the street and say 'Hello' to someone. They don't answer. I'm hurt and mad."
    b. "I am expecting my turn at the GA meeting, but the time runs out. I feel as though that's a dirty trick."
    c. "I feel as though they are talking about me at meetings when they're really not."

12. *Fear:* An inner foreboding, real or imagined, of doom ahead

We suspect that our use of gambling, behavior, negligence, and so on are catching up with us. We fear the worst.

    a. When we learn to accept our powerlessness, ask a Higher Power for help, and face ourselves with honesty, the nightmare will be over.

13. *Depression:* Feeling sad or down most of the day
    a. You keep going over all of the things that are going wrong.
    b. You tend to think that the worst is going to happen.

14. *Feelings of inadequacy:* Feeling as though you cannot do something
    a. You hold on to a negative self-image, even when you succeed.
    b. Feelings of failure will not go away.

15. *Perfectionism:* The need to do everything perfect all of the time
    a. Even when you have done a good job, you find something wrong with it.
    b. Someone compliments you on something. You feel terrible because it could have been better.
    c. You let your expectations get too high.

PHYSICAL LIABILITIES

1. Diseases, disabilities, and other physical limitations about how you look or how your body functions
2. Sexual problems or hang-ups
3. Negative feelings about your appearance
4. Negative feelings about your age
5. Negative feelings about your gender

TIME OUT

If you have gone through the exercise to this point without coming up for air—it figures. We did our gambling the same way. Whoa! Easy does it! Take this in reasonable stages. Assimilate each portion of the exercise thoughtfully. The reading of this is important, but the application of it is even more important. Take some time to think and rest, and let all of this settle in. Develop some sort of a workable daily plan. Include plenty of rest.

When compulsive gamblers stop gambling, a part of their lives is taken away from them. This is a terrible loss to sustain unless it is replaced by something else. We cannot just boot gambling out the window. It meant too much to us. It was how we faced life, the key to escape, and the tool for solving life's problems. In approaching a new way of life, a new set of tools is substituted. These are the Twelve Steps and the GA way of life.

The same principle applies when we eliminate our character defects. We replace them by substituting assets that are better adapted to a healthy lifestyle. As with substance use, you do not fight a defect; you replace it with something that works better. Use what follows for further character analysis and as a guide for character building. These are the new tools. The objective is not perfection; it is progress. You will be happy with the type of living that produces self-respect, respect and love for others, and security from the nightmare of gambling.

VIRTUES

1. *Faith:* The act of leaving the part of our lives that we cannot control (i.e., the future) to the care of a power greater than ourselves, with the assurance that it will work out for our well-being

This will be shaky at first, but with it comes a deep conviction.

   a. Faith is acquired through application—acceptance, daily prayer, and meditation.
   b. We depend on faith. We have faith that the lights will come on, the car will start, and our co-workers will handle their end of things. If we had no faith, then we would come apart at the seams.
   c. Spiritual faith is the acceptance of our gifts, limitations, problems, and trials with equal gratitude, knowing that a Higher Power has a plan for us. With "Thy will be done" as our daily guide, we will lose our fear and find ourselves.

2. *Hope:* The feeling that what is desired also is possible

Faith suggests reliance. We came to believe that a power greater than ourselves would restore us to sanity. We hope to stay free of gambling, regain our self-respect, and love our families. Hope resolves itself into a driving force. It gives purpose to our daily living.

    a. Faith gives us direction, hope, and stamina to take action.

    b. Hope reflects a positive attitude. Things are going to work out for us if we work the program.

3. *Love:* The active involvement in someone's individual growth

    a. Love must occur in action and in truth.

    b. In its deeper sense, love is the art of living realistically and fully, guided by spiritual awareness of our responsibilities and our debt of gratitude to God and to others.

Analysis. Have you used the qualities of faith, hope, and love in your past? How will they apply to your new way of life?

THE LITTLE VIRTUES

1. *Courtesy:* Some of us are actually afraid to be gentle persons. We would rather be boors or self-pampering types.
2. *Cheerfulness:* Circumstances do not determine our frames of mind. We do. "Today I will be cheerful. I will look for the beauty in life."
3. *Order:* Live today only. Organize one day at a time.
4. *Loyalty:* Be faithful to who you believe in.
5. *Use of time:* "I will use my time wisely."
6. *Punctuality:* This involves self-discipline, order, and consideration for others.
7. *Sincerity:* This is the mark of self-respect and genuineness. Sincerity carries conviction and generates enthusiasm. It is contagious.
8. *Caution in speech:* Watch your tongue. We can be vicious and thoughtless. Too often, the damage is irreparable.
9. *Kindness:* This is one of life's great satisfactions. We do not have real happiness until we have given of ourselves. Practice this daily.
10. *Patience:* This is the antidote to resentments, self-pity, and impulsiveness.
11. *Tolerance:* This requires common courtesy, courage, and a "live and let live" attitude.
12. *Integrity:* This involves the ultimate qualifications of a human—honesty, loyalty, sincerity.
13. *Balance:* Do not take yourself too seriously. You get a better perspective when you can laugh at yourself.
14. *Gratitude:* The person without gratitude is filled with false pride. Gratitude is the honest recognition of help received. Use it often.

Analysis. In considering the little virtues, ask where you failed and how that contributed to your accumulated problem. Ask what virtues you should pay attention to in this rebuilding program.

PHYSICAL ASSETS

1. *Physical health:* How healthy am I despite any ailments?
2. *Talents:* What am I good at?
3. *Age:* At my age, what can I offer to others?
4. *Sexuality:* How can I use my sexuality to express my love?
5. *Knowledge:* How can I use my knowledge and experience to help myself and others?

MENTAL ASSETS

1. Despite your problems, how healthy are you emotionally?
2. Do you care for others?
3. Are you kind?
4. Can you be patient?
5. Are you basically a good person?
6. Do you try to tell the truth?
7. Do you try to be forgiving?
8. Can you be enthusiastic?
9. Are you sensitive to the needs of others?

10. Can you be serene?
11. Are you going to try to be sincere?
12. Are you going to try to bring order and self-control into your life?
13. Are you going to accept the responsibility for your own behavior and stop blaming others for everything?
14. How are you going to use your intelligence?
15. Are you going to seek God?
16. How might you improve your mind furthering your education?
17. Are you going to be grateful for what you have?
18. How can you improve your honesty, reliability, and integrity?
19. In what areas of your life do you find joy and happiness?
20. Are you humble and working on your false pride?
21. Are you seeking the God of your own understanding?
22. In what ways can you better accept your own limitations and the limitations of others?
23. Are you willing to trust and follow The Higher Power of your own understanding?

THE AUTOBIOGRAPHY

Using this exercise, write your autobiography. Cover your life in 5-year intervals. Be brief, but try not to miss anything. Tell the whole truth. Write down exactly what you did. Consider all of the things you marked during the exercise. Read the exercise again if you need to do so. Make an exhaustive and honest consideration of your past and present. Make a complete financial inventory. Mark down all debts. Exactly who do you owe, and what amount do you owe? Do not leave out relatives or friends. List all persons or institutions that you harmed with your gambling, and detail exactly how you were unfair. Cover both assets and liabilities carefully. You will rebuild your life on the solid building blocks of your assets. These are the tools of recovery. Omit nothing because of shame, embarrassment, or fear. Determine the thoughts, feelings, and actions that plagued you. You want to meet these problems face-to-face and see them in writing. If you wish, you may destroy your inventory after completing the Fifth Step. Many people hold a ceremony in which they burn their Fourth Step inventories. This symbolizes that they are leaving the old life behind. They are starting a new life free of the past.

Appendix 40

Step Five for Gamblers

[We] admitted to ourselves and to another human being the exact nature of our wrongs.
—Gamblers Anonymous (1989b, p. 69)

Before beginning this exercise, read Step Five in *G.A.: A New Beginning* (Gamblers Anonymous, 1989b).

With Steps One to Four behind you, it is now time to clean house and start over. You must free yourself of all the guilt and shame and go forward in faith. The Fifth Step is meant to right the wrongs with others and your Higher Power. You will develop new attitudes and a new relationship with yourself, others, and the Higher Power of your own understanding. You have admitted your powerlessness, and you have identified your liabilities and assets in the personal inventory. Now it is time to get right with yourself.

You will do this by admitting to yourself, and to another person, the exact nature of your wrongs. In your Fifth Step, you are going to cover all of your assets and liabilities detailed in the Fourth Step. You are going to tell one person the whole truth at one time. This person is important because he or she is a symbol of the Higher Power and all humankind. You must watch this person's face. The illness has been telling you that if you tell anyone the whole truth about you, then that person will not like you. That is a lie, and you are going to prove that it is a lie. The truth is this: Unless you tell people the whole truth, they cannot like you. You must actually see yourself tell someone the whole truth at one time and watch that individual's reaction.

It is very difficult to discuss your faults with someone. It is hard enough just thinking about them yourself. But this is a necessary step. It will help to free you from the disease. You must tell this person everything, the whole story, all of the things that you are afraid to share. If you withhold anything, then you will not get the relief you need to start over. You will be carrying around excess baggage. You do not need to do this to yourself. Time after time, newcomers have tried to keep to themselves certain facts about their lives. Trying to avoid this humbling experience, they have turned to easier methods. Almost invariably, they wound up gambling again. Having persevered with the rest of the program, they wondered why they failed. The reason is that they never completed their housecleaning. They took inventory all right, but they hung on to some of the worst items in stock. They only *thought* that they had lost their egotism. They only *thought* that they had humbled themselves. But they had not learned enough of humility and honesty in the sense necessary until they told someone their whole life stories.

By finally telling someone the whole truth, you will rid yourself of that terrible sense of isolation and loneliness. You will feel a new sense of belonging, acceptance, and freedom. If you do not feel relief immediately, do not worry. If you have been completely honest, then the relief will come. The dammed-up emotions of years will break out of their confinement and, miraculously, will vanish as soon as they are exposed.

The Fifth Step will develop within you a new humbleness of character that is necessary for normal living. You will come to recognize clearly who and what you are. When you are honest with another person, it confirms that you can be honest with yourself, others, and your Higher Power.

The person who you will share your Fifth Step with should be chosen carefully. Many of us find a clergy person, experienced in hearing Fifth Steps, to be a good option. Someone further along in the Gamblers Anonymous program might also be a good choice. It is recommended that you meet with this person several times before you do the step. You need to decide whether you can trust this person. Do you feel that this person is confidential? Do you feel comfortable with this person? Do you feel that this person will be understanding and loving?

Once you have chosen the person, put your false pride aside and go for it. Tell the individual everything about yourself. Do not leave one rock unturned. Tell about all of the good things, and about all of the bad things, that you have done. Share the details, and do not leave anything out. If it troubles you even a little, then share it. Let it all hang out to be examined by that other person. Every good and bad part needs to be revealed. After you are done, you will be free of the slavery to lies. The truth will set you free.

Appendix 41

Relapse Prevention for Gamblers

There is some bad news about relapse, and there is some good news. The bad news is that many patients have problems with relapse in early recovery. About two thirds of patients coming out of addiction programs relapse within 3 months of leaving treatment (Hunt, Barnett, & Branch, 1971). The good news is that most people who go through treatment ultimately achieve a stable recovery (Frances, Bucky, & Alexopolos, 1984). Relapse does not have to happen to you, and even if it does, you can do something about it. Relapse prevention is a daily program that can prevent relapse. It also can stop a lapse from becoming a disaster. This relapse prevention exercise has been developed using a combination of the models of Gorski and Miller (1986) and Marlatt and Gordon (1985). This exercise also uses both the disease concept model and a behavioral approach.

RELAPSE IS A PROCESS

Relapse begins long before you gamble again. There are symptoms that precede gambling. This relapse prevention exercise teaches how to identify and control these symptoms before they lead to problems. If you allow these symptoms to go on without acting on them, then gambling will result.

The Relapse Warning Signs

All relapse begins with warning signs that will signal you or your loved ones that you are in trouble. If you do not recognize these signs, then you will decompensate and finally return to gambling again. All of the signs are reactions to stress, and they are a reemergence of the disease. They are a means by which your body and mind are telling you that you are having problems. Gorski and Miller (1982) recognized 37 warning signs in alcoholics who relapsed. You might not have all of these symptoms before you begin gambling again, but you will have some of them long before you gamble. You must determine which symptoms are the most characteristic of you, and you must come up with coping skills for dealing with each symptom.

Listed next are the 37 warning symptoms. Circle the ones that you have experienced before you gambled.

1. Apprehension about well-being
2. Denial
3. Adamant commitment to stop gambling
4. Compulsive attempts to impose abstinence on others
5. Defensiveness
6. Compulsive behavior
7. Impulsive behavior
8. Loneliness
9. Tunnel vision
10. Minor depression
11. Loss of constructive planning
12. Plans beginning to fail
13. Idle daydreaming and wishful thinking
14. Feeling that nothing can be solved
15. Immature wish to be happy
16. Periods of confusion
17. Irritation with friends
18. Easily angered

19. Irregular eating habits
20. Listlessness
21. Irregular sleeping habits
22. Progressive loss of daily structure
23. Periods of deep depression
24. Irregular attendance at meetings
25. Development of an "I don't care" attitude
26. Open rejection of help
27. Dissatisfaction with life
28. Feelings of powerlessness and helplessness
29. Self-pity
30. Thoughts of social gambling
31. Conscious lying
32. Complete loss of self-confidence
33. Unreasonable resentments
34. Discontinuing all treatment
35. Overwhelming loneliness, frustration, anger, and tension
36. Start of controlled gambling
37. Loss of control

What to Do When You Experience a Warning Sign

When you recognize any of these symptoms, you need to take action. Make a list of the coping skills you can use when you experience a symptom that is common for you. This will happen. You will have problems in recovery. Your task is to take affirmative action at the earliest possible moment. Remember, a symptom is a danger signal. You are in trouble. Make a list of what you are going to do. Are you going to call your sponsor, go to a meeting, call your counselor, call someone in Gamblers Anonymous (GA), tell someone, exercise, read the *Combo Book* (Gamblers Anonymous, 1989a), pray, become involved in an activity you enjoy, turn it over, or go into treatment? Detail several plans of action.

Plan 1. _____
Plan 2. _____
Plan 3. _____
Plan 4. _____
Plan 5. _____
Plan 6. _____
Plan 7. _____
Plan 8. _____
Plan 9. _____
Plan 10. _____

You need to check each warning symptom daily in your personal inventory. You also need to have other people check you daily. You will not always pick up the symptoms in yourself. You may be denying the problem again. Your spouse, your sponsor, or a fellow GA member can warn you when he or she believes that you may be in trouble. Listen to these people. If they tell you that they sense a problem, then take action. You may need professional help in working the problem through. Do not hesitate in calling and asking for help. Anything is better than relapsing. If you overreact to a warning sign, you are not going to be in trouble. But if you underreact, you might be headed for real problems. Pathological gambling is a deadly disease. Your life is at stake.

THE HIGH-RISK SITUATIONS

Marlatt and Gordon (1985) found that relapse is more likely to occur in certain situations. These situations can trigger relapse. They found that people relapsed when they could not cope with life situations except by returning to their addictive behaviors. Your job in treatment is to develop coping skills for dealing with each high-risk situation.

Negative Emotions

About 35% of people who relapse do so when they feel negative feelings that they cannot cope with. Most feel angry or frustrated, but some feel anxious, bored, lonely, or depressed. Almost any negative feeling can lead to relapse if you do not learn how to cope with the emotion. Feelings motivate you to take action. You must act to solve any problem.
Circle any of the following feelings that seem to lead you to gamble.

Loneliness	Aggravated
Anger	Expansive
Rejection	Miserable
Emptiness	Unloved
Annoyed	Worried
Sad	Scared
Exasperated	Spiteful
Betrayed	Tearful
Cheated	Helpless
Frustrated	Neglected
Envious	Grief
Exhausted	Confused
Bored	Crushed
Anxious	Discontented
Ashamed	Aggravated
Bitter	Irritated
Burdened	Overwhelmed
Foolish	Panicked
Jealous	Trapped
Left out	Unsure
Selfish	Intimidated
Testy	Distraught
Weak	Uneasy
Sorry	Guilty
Greedy	Threatened

Develop a Plan to Deal With Negative Emotions

These are just a few of the feeling words. Add more if you need to do so. Develop coping skills for dealing with each feeling that makes you vulnerable to relapse. Exactly what are you going to do when you have this feeling? Detail your specific plan of action. Some options include talking to your sponsor, calling a friend in the program, going to a meeting, calling your counselor, reading some recovery material, turning it over to your Higher Power, and getting some exercise. For each feeling, develop a specific plan of action.

Feeling

Plan 1. _____

Plan 2. _____

Plan 3. _____

Feeling

Plan 1. _____

Plan 2. _____

Plan 3. _____

Feeling

Plan 1. _____

Plan 2. _____

Plan 3. _____

Continue to fill out these feeling forms until you have all of the feelings that give you trouble and you have coping skills for dealing with each feeling.

Social Pressure

About 20% of people relapse in social situations. Social pressure can be direct (e.g., someone directly encourages you to gamble), or it can be indirect (e.g., a social situation where people are gambling). Both of these situations can trigger intense craving, and this can lead to relapse. For example, more than 60% of alcoholics relapse in bars.

Certain friends are more likely to encourage you to gamble. These people do not want to hurt you. They want you to relax and have a good time. They want their old friend back. They do not understand the nature of your disease. Perhaps they are pathological gamblers themselves and are in denial.

High-Risk Friends

Make a list of the friends who might encourage you to gamble.

1. _____

2. _____

3. _____

4. _____

5. _____

What are you going to do when they suggest that you gamble? What are you going to say? In group, set up a situation where the whole group encourages you to gamble. Consider carefully how you feel when they are encouraging you. Listen to what you say. Have them help you to develop appropriate ways in which to say no.

High-Risk Social Situations

Certain social situations will trigger craving. These are the situations where you have gambled in the past. Certain bars or restaurants, the race track, a particular part of town, certain music, athletic events, parties, weddings, and family get-togethers are some of the situations that can trigger intense cravings.

Make a list of five social situations where you will be vulnerable to relapse.

1. _____

2. _____

3. _____

4. _____

5. _____

In early recovery, you will need to avoid these situations and friends. To put yourself in a high-risk situation is asking for trouble. If you have to attend a function where there will be gambling, then take someone with you who is in the program. Go with someone who will support you in recovery. Make sure that you have a way home. You do not have to stay and torture yourself. You can leave if you feel uncomfortable. Avoid all situations where your recovery feels shaky.

Interpersonal Conflict

About 16% of people relapse when they are in a conflict with some other person. They have a problem with someone, and they have no idea how to cope with the problem. The stress of the problem builds and leads to gambling. This conflict usually happens with someone who they are closely involved with—spouse, children, parents, siblings, friends, boss, and so on.

You can have a serious problem with anyone, even strangers, so you must have a plan for dealing with interpersonal conflict. You will develop specific skills in treatment that will help you to communicate even when you are under stress.

You need to learn and repeatedly practice the following interpersonal skills.

1. Tell the truth all of the time.
2. Share how you feel.
3. Ask for what you want.
4. Find some truth in what the other person is saying.
5. Be willing to compromise.

If you can stay in the conflict and work it out, that is great. But if you cannot, you have to leave the situation and get help. You might have to go for a walk, a run, or a drive. You might need to cool down. You must stop the conflict. You cannot continue to try to deal with a situation that you believe is too much for you. Do not feel bad about this. Interpersonal relationships are the hardest challenges that we face. Carry a card with you that lists the people you can contact. You might want to call your sponsor, your minister, your counselor, a fellow GA member, a friend, a family member, your doctor, or anyone else who may support you.

In an interpersonal conflict, you will fear abandonment. You need to get accurate and reassure yourself that you have many people who still care about you. Remember that your Higher Power cares about you. Remember the other people in your life who love you. This is one of the main reasons for talking with someone else. When they listen to you, they give you the feeling that you are loved.

If you still feel afraid or angry, then get with someone you trust and stay with that person until you feel safe. Do not struggle out there all by yourself. Every member of GA will understand how you are feeling. We all have had these kinds of problems. We all have felt lost, helpless, hopeless, and angry.

Make an emergency card that includes all of the people who you can call if you are having difficulty. Write down their phone numbers, and carry this card with you at all times. Show this card to your counselor. Practice asking someone for help in treatment once each day. Write down the situation and show it to your counselor. Get into the habit of asking for help. When you get out of treatment, call someone every day just to stay in touch and keep open the lines of communication. Get used to it. Do not wait to ask for help at the last minute. This makes asking more difficult.

Positive Feelings

About 12% of people relapse when they are feeling positive emotions. Think of all the times you gambled to celebrate. That has gotten to be such a habit that when something good happens, you will immediately think about gambling. You need to be ready when you feel like a winner. This may be at a wedding, a birth, a promotion, or any event where you feel good. How are you going to celebrate without gambling? Make a celebration plan. You might have to take someone with you to a celebration, particularly in early recovery.

Positive feelings also can work when you are by yourself. A beautiful spring day can be enough to get you thinking about gambling. You need an action plan for when these thoughts pass through your mind. You must immediately get accurate and get real. In recovery, we are committed to reality. Do not sit there and imagine how wonderful you would feel if you gambled. Tell yourself the truth. Think about all of the pain that gambling has caused you. If you toy with positive feelings, then you ultimately will gamble.

Circle the positive feelings that may make you vulnerable to relapse.

Affection	Sexy
Bold	Wonderful
Brave	Cool
Calm	Relaxed
Capable	Reverent
Boisterous	Silly
Confident	Vivacious
Delightful	Adequate
Desire	Efficient
Enchanted	Successful
Joy	Accomplished
Free	Hopeful
Glad	Orgasmic
Glee	Elated
Happy	Merry
Honored	Ecstatic
Horny	Upbeat
Infatuated	Splendid
Inspired	Yearning
Kinky	Bliss
Lazy	Excited
Loving	Exhilarated
Peaceful	Proud
Pleasant	Aroused
Pleased	Festive

A Plan to Cope With Positive Feelings

These are the feelings that may make you vulnerable to relapse. You must be careful when you are feeling good. Make an action plan for dealing with each positive emotion that makes you vulnerable to gambling.

Feeling
    Plan 1. _____
    Plan 2. _____
    Plan 3. _____

Feeling
    Plan 1. _____
    Plan 2. _____
    Plan 3. _____

Feeling
    Plan 1. _____
    Plan 2. _____
    Plan 3. _____

Continue this planning until you develop an approach for each of the positive feelings that makes you vulnerable.

Test Personal Control

About 5% of people relapse to test whether they can gamble again. They fool themselves into thinking that they might be able to do so normally. This time they will gamble only a little. This time they will be able to control themselves. People who fool themselves this way are in for big trouble. From the first bet, most people are in full-blown relapse within 30 days.

Testing personal control begins with inaccurate thinking. It takes you back to Step One. You need to think accurately. You are powerless over gambling. If you use, then you will lose. It is as simple as that. You are physiologically, psychologically, and socially addicted to gambling. The cells in your body will not suddenly change no matter how long you are clean. You are gambling dependent in your cells. This never will change.

How to See Through the First Temptation

You need to look at how the illness part of yourself will try to convince you that you are not a problem gambler. The illness will flash on the screen of your consciousness all of the good things that gambling did for you. Make a list of these things. In the first column, marked "Early Gambling," write down some of the good things that you were getting out of gambling. Why were you gambling? What good came out of it? Did it make you feel social, smart, attractive, intelligent, brave, popular, desirable, relaxed, and/or sexy? Did it help you to sleep? Did it make you feel confident? Did it help you to forget your problems? Make a long list. These are the good things that you were getting when you first started gambling. This is why you were gambling.

Now go back and place in the second column, marked "Late Gambling," how you were doing in that area once you became dependent. How were you doing in that same area right before you came into treatment? Did you still feel social, or did you feel alone? Did you still feel intelligent, or did you feel stupid? You will find that a great change has taken place. The very things that you were gambling for in early gambling, you get the opposite of in late gambling. If you were gambling to be more popular, then you were feeling more isolated and alone. If you were gambling to feel brave, then you were feeling more afraid. If you were gambling to feel smart, the you were feeling stupid. This is a major characteristic of pathological gambling.

Early Gambling	*Late Gambling*
1. _____	1. _____
2. _____	2. _____
3. _____	3. _____
4. _____	4. _____
5. _____	5. _____
6. _____	6. _____
7. _____	7. _____
8. _____	8. _____
9. _____	9. _____
10. _____	10. _____

Take a long look at both of these lists and think about how the illness is going to try to work inside of your thinking. The addicted part of yourself will present to you all of the good things that you got in early gambling. This is how the disease will encourage you to gamble. You must see through the first use to the negative consequences that are dead ahead.

Look at the second list. You must be able to see the misery that is coming if you gamble. For most people who relapse, there are only a few days of controlled gambling before loss of control sets in. There usually are only a few hours or days before all of the bad stuff begins to click back into place. Relapse is terrible. It is the most intense misery that you can imagine.

Lapse and Relapse

A lapse is the first bet. A relapse is continuing to gamble until the full biological, psychological, and social disease is present. All of the complex biological, psychological, and social components of the disease become evident very quickly.

The Lapse Plan

You must have a plan in case you lapse. It is foolish to think that you never will have a problem again. You must plan what you are going to do if you have problems. Hunt et al. (1971), in a study of recovering addicts, found that 33% of patients lapsed within 2 weeks of leaving treatment. Fully 60% lapsed within 3 months. At the end of 8 months, 63% had used. At the end of 12 months, 67% had used.

The worst thing you can do when you lapse is to think that you have completely failed in recovery. This is inaccurate thinking. You are not a total failure. You have not lost everything. You have made a mistake, and you need to learn from it. You let some part of your program go, and you are paying for it. You need to examine exactly what happened and get back into recovery.

A lapse is an emergency. It is a matter of life or death. You must take immediate action to prevent the lapse from becoming a full relapse. You must call someone in the program, preferably your sponsor, and tell that person what happened. You need to carefully examine why you slipped. You cannot gamble and use the tools of recovery at the same time. Something went wrong. You did not use your new skills. You must make a plan of action to recover from your lapse. You cannot do this by yourself. You are in denial. You do not know the whole truth. If you did, then you would not have relapsed.

Call your sponsor or a professional counselor and have him or her develop a new treatment plan for you. You might need to attend more meetings. You might need to see a counselor. You might need outpatient treatment. You might need inpatient treatment. You have to get honest with yourself. You need to develop a plan and follow it. You need someone else to agree to keep an eye on you for a while. Do not try to do this alone. What we cannot do alone, we can do together.

THE BEHAVIOR CHAIN

All behavior occurs in a certain sequence. First there is the *trigger.* This is the external event that starts the behavioral sequence. After the trigger, there comes *thinking.* Much of this thinking is very fast, and you will not consciously pick it up unless you stop and focus on it. The thoughts trigger *feelings,* which give you energy and direction for action. Next comes the *behavior* or the action initiated by the trigger. Last, there always is a *consequence* for any action.

Diagrammed, the behavior chain looks like this:

Trigger → Thinking → Feeling → Behavior → Consequence.

Let's go through a behavioral sequence and see how it works. On the way home from work, Bob, a recovering gambler, passes the convenience store (this is the trigger). He thinks, "I've had a hard day. Maybe I'll do a couple of pull tabs to unwind" (the trigger initiates thinking). Bob craves gambling (the thinking initiates feeling). He turns into the convenience store and begins to gamble (the feeling initiates behavior). Bob relapses (the behavior has a consequence).

Let's work through another example. It is 11 p.m., and Bob is not asleep (trigger). He thinks, "I'll never get to sleep tonight unless I gamble" (thinking). He feels an increase in his anxiety about not sleeping (feeling). He gets up and gambles (behavior). He loses all of his money and is so depressed that he cannot work the next morning (consequence).

How to Cope With Triggers

At every point along the behavior chain, you can work on preventing relapse. First you need to examine your triggers carefully. What environmental events lead you to gamble? We went over some of these when we examined high-risk situations. Determine what people, places, and/or things make you vulnerable to relapse. Stay away from these triggers as much as possible. If a trigger occurs, then use your new coping skills.

Do not let the trigger initiate old behavior. Stop and think. Do not let your thinking get out of control. Challenge your thinking and get accurate about what is real. Let's look at some common inaccurate thoughts.

1. It is not going to hurt.
2. No one is going to know.
3. I need to relax.
4. I am just going to spend a couple of bucks.
5. I have had a hard day.
6. My friends want me to gamble.

7. I never had a problem with sports betting.
8. It is the only way I can sleep.
9. I can do anything I want to do.
10. I am lonely.

All of these inaccurate thoughts can be used to fuel the craving that leads to relapse. You must stop and challenge your thinking until you are thinking accurately. You must replace inaccurate thoughts with accurate ones. You are a pathological gambler. If you gamble, then you will die. That is the truth. Think through the first bet. Get honest with yourself.

How to Cope With the Craving to Gamble

If you think inaccurately, then you will begin craving. This is the powerful feeling that drives compulsive gambling. Craving is like an ocean wave. It will build and then wash over you. Craving does not last long if you move away from gambling. If you move closer to a gambling situation, then the craving will increase until you gamble. Immediately on feeling a desire to gamble, think this thought:

"Gambling is no longer an option for me."

Now what are your options? You are in trouble. You are craving. What are you going to do to prevent a relapse? You must move away from the gambling situation. Perhaps you need to call your sponsor, go to a meeting, turn it over, call the GA hotline, call the treatment center, call your counselor, go for a walk or run, or visit someone. You must do something besides thinking about gambling. Do not sit there and ponder gambling. You will lose that debate. This illness is called the great debater. If you leave it unchecked, then it will seduce you into gambling.

The illness must lie to work. You must uncover the lie as quickly as possible and get back to the truth. You must take the appropriate action necessary to maintain your recovery.

Develop a Daily Relapse Prevention Program

If you work a daily program of recovery, then your chances of success increase greatly. You need to evaluate your recovery daily and keep a log. This is your daily inventory.

1. Assess all relapse warning signs.
   a. What symptoms did I see in myself today?
   b. What am I going to do about them?

2. Assess love of self.
   a. What did I do to love myself today?
   b. What am I going to do tomorrow?

3. Assess love of others.
   a. What did I do to love others today?
   b. What am I going to do tomorrow?

4. Assess love of God.
   a. What did I do to love God today?
   b. What am I going to do tomorrow?

5. Assess sleep pattern.
   a. How am I sleeping?

6. Assess exercise.
   a. Am I getting enough exercise?

7. Assess nutrition.
   a. Am I eating right?

8. Review total recovery program.
   a. How am I doing in recovery?
   b. What is the next step in my recovery program?

9. Read the *Twenty-Four Hours a Day* book (Walker, 1992).

10. Make conscious contact with God.
    a. Pray and meditate for a few minutes.
    b. Relax completely.

Fill out this inventory every day following treatment, and keep a journal about how you are doing. You will be amazed as you read back over your journal from time to time. You will be surprised at how much you have grown.

Make a list of 10 reasons why you want to stay free from gambling.
   1. _____
   2. _____
   3. _____
   4. _____
   5. _____
   6. _____
   7. _____
   8. _____
   9. _____
  10. _____

Never forget these reasons. Read this list often, and carry a copy with you. If you are struggling in recovery, then take it out and read it to yourself. You are important. No one has to live a life of misery. You can recover and live happy, joyous, and free.

Appendix 42

Adolescent Unit Point System

Adolescents will carry a report card with them during the day for the staff to add and subtract points. Patients will count up their points each day and place the total on a chart that they keep in their room or in the hallway. The most important part of the program is that staff members need to catch the patients displaying appropriate behavior and reward them. Patients can be rewarded for any behavior that staff members want to see them increase such as being quiet in their room, making a positive recovery statement, being cooperative with the staff, and getting along with each other. The more points staff members hands out, the better and more quickly the maladaptive behavior will come under control. Patients will work for points if they can turn the points in for reinforcers that they want to earn. Points need to be taken away by the staff, or by the group, only if the behavior is bad enough to warrant a consequence. The best way in which to take away points is by the group process or a trial. For the first few days that patients are in treatment, all of the reinforcers need to be positive. Later, a staff member might need to tell a patient something like this: "I'm going to fine you occasionally. That doesn't mean I am mad at you, and you shouldn't get mad at me. After all, these are just points, and you can earn them back." Patients need to be taught how to receive criticism. After a consequence, the staff member might say, "That's good. You looked me in the eye, didn't mumble anything under your breath, and took the points off your card. Good job."

Points will be routinely given for the following behaviors:

Patients will get up in the morning.	100 points
Patients will shower.	100 points
Patients will dress.	100 points
Patients will clean their rooms.	100 points
Patients will be ready for breakfast on time.	100 points
Patients will remember to carry around the point system card.	100 points
Patients will complete chores by 10 a.m.	100 points
Patients will be on time for each group activity.	100 points
Patients will participate in each group.	100 points
Patients complete Feelings sheets.	Up to 1,000 points
Patients will complete all assignments given to them by the group manager.	100 points
Patients will complete each assignment given to them by their counselor.	100 points
Patients will cooperate with the teacher and will study during study time.	100 points
Patients will go to bed at 11 p.m. and be quiet after lights out.	100 points
The counselor or staff will grade patients on daily participation in recovery.	Up to 100 points
Patients will assist the staff with duties such as filling water tank and leading AA meetings.	Up to 1,000 points

Patients can turn in their points for the following rewards:

Sega	500 points per 15 minutes for each player
One 5-minute telephone call	1,000 points
One call to parents *or* from parents	No charge

Store items	As marked
A meal out with a staff member	20,000 points
Saturday sleep until 11 a.m. group (must get up for breakfast)	5,000 points
Sunday sleep until lunch (must get up for breakfast)	5,000 points
Cassettes/CDs	Charge or use as reward? (ability to check out being considered)
Special privileges—anything the patient wants that is appropriate	Points negotiable
Special trip to a store or shopping	Under consideration

Patients can lose points for the following misbehaviors:

All contraband such as cigarettes, lighters, tapes, and CDs	Contraband will be taken away (discharge also is possible)
Being disrespectful to the staff	–1,500 points
Physical aggression	–5,000 points
Verbal aggression	–1,500 points
Violation of unit rules (e.g., doors not open at all times in opposite-sex rooms, being out of room after staff advised to be in room)	–1,500 points
Violation of *group* rules	–1,500 points
Being late for groups and activities or leaving during groups	–2,000 points
Smell of smoke in room	–1,000 points
Caught with cigarette lit	–2,000 points

All large fines (more than 10,000 points), unless set, need to be adjudicated by the community group. The group will vote by secret ballot as to the guilt or innocence of the individual and set a consequence by a majority secret ballot. The person accused and the staff will not vote, but the staff will retain the right to veto any ruling.

ADDITIONAL GUIDELINES

Phone Calls

1. Phone calls will cost 1,000 points for 5 minutes.
2. All phone calls will be dialed by the on-duty staff.
3. All phone calls will be placed on the hallway phone.
4. Outgoing phone calls will be allowed from 8:00 p.m. to 9:30 p.m.
5. Incoming phone calls will be allowed from 4:30 p.m. to 9:30 p.m.

Radios

1. No radios will be allowed in the hallway.
2. If radios are left on in a patient's room and no one is in the room, then the radio will be taken away for 24 hours.
3. If a patient is asked to turn down the volume of the radio and he or she refuses, then the radio will be taken away for 24 hours.

Smoking

1. Patients on the adolescent unit who are 18 years old will be given two cigarettes at a time by the on-duty staff.
2. If lighters and cigarettes are found on the adolescent unit, then these will be taken away and destroyed.

Doors

1. Doors are to remain open at all times.

POINT CARD

Room Checks	Group	Activities of Daily Living	Behavior/Attitude
100	100	100	100
200	200	200	200

Name: _____

Date: _____

Morning

Room Checks	Group	Activities of Daily Living	Behavior/Attitude
100	100	100	100
200	200	200	200
300	300	300	300
400	400	400	400

Morning Total: _____

Afternoon

Room Checks	Group	Activities of Daily Living	Behavior/Attitude
100	100	100	100
200	200	200	200
300	300	300	300
400	400	400	400

Afternoon total: _____

Evening

Room Checks	Group	Activities of Daily Living	Behavior/Attitude
100	100	100	100
200	200	200	200
300	300	300	300
400	400	400	400

Evening total: _____

Extra points given (up to 1,500): _____

Total points given: _____

Points deducted: _____

Total points deducted: _____

Today's total: _____

Appendix 43

National Household Survey on Drug Abuse, 1999

ILLICIT DRUG USE

- In 1999, an estimated 14.8 million Americans were current illicit drug users, meaning that they had used an illicit drug during the month prior to the interview. This estimate represents 6.7% of the population age 12 years or over.
- Marijuana is the most commonly used illicit drug. It is used by 75% of current illicit drug users. Approximately 57% of current illicit drug users reported that they consumed only marijuana, 18% used marijuana and another illicit drug, and the remaining 25% used an illicit drug but not marijuana during the past month. Therefore, about 43% of current illicit drug users (an estimated 6.4 million Americans) were current users of illicit drugs other than marijuana and hashish, with or without the use of marijuana (Figure A43.1).

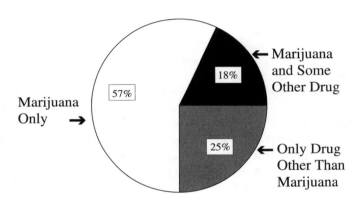

14.8 Million Illicit Drug Users

Figure A43.1
Types of Drugs Used During Past Month by Illicit Drug Users Age 12 Years or Over, 1999

- Of the 6.4 million users of illicit drugs other than marijuana, 4.0 million were using psychotherapeutics nonmedically. This represents 1.8% of the population age 12 years or over. Psychotherapeutics include pain relievers (2.6 million users), tranquilizers (1.1 million users), stimulants (900,000 users), and sedatives (200,000 users).
- An estimated 1.5 million Americans were current cocaine users. This represents 0.7% of the population age 12 years or over. The estimated number of current crack users was 413,000.
- An estimated 900,000 Americans were current hallucinogen users. This represents 0.4% of the population age 12 years or over.
- An estimated 200,000 Americans were current heroin users. This represents 0.1% of the population age 12 years or over.

Age

- Rates and patterns of drug use showed substantial variation by age. For example, 4.1% of 12-year-olds reported current illicit drug use. The primary drugs used by these 12-year-olds were inhalants and psychotherapeutics (2.2% and 1.4%, respectively). Only 0.6% of the 12-year-olds used marijuana. By age 14 years, however, marijuana was the dominant drug, with a prevalence of 5.9%. Overall, the rate of current illicit drug use among 14-year-olds was 9.2% (Figure A43.2).

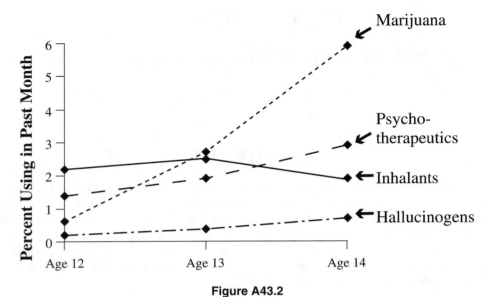

Figure A43.2
Illicit Drug Use Among Youths Ages 12 to 14 Years, 1999

- Among youths ages 12 to 17 years, 10.9% had used an illicit drug within the 30 days prior to the interview. Of this group, 7.7% had used marijuana and 5.3% had used some illicit drug other than marijuana.
- The highest rate of illicit drug use was found among persons ages 18 to 20 years, with rates of current use between 20% and 21%. For these older youths, use was dominated by marijuana, with 18% currently using marijuana. The rates of use generally decline in each successively older age group, with only 1.7% of persons ages 50 to 64 years and 0.6% of those age 65 years or over reporting current illicit use. An exception to this pattern of declining rates is the 40- to 44-year age group, which had a rate of 8.6%, somewhat higher than the rate for persons ages 30 to 39 years. Members of this cohort were teenagers during the 1970s, the period when drug use incidence and prevalence rates were rising dramatically (Figure A43.3).

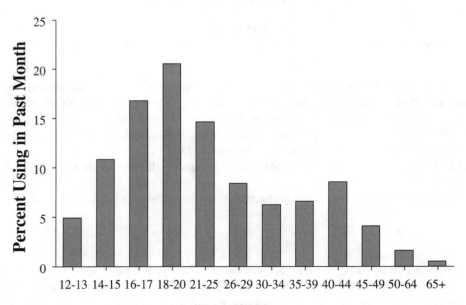

Figure A43.3
Illicit Drug Use by Age, 1999

- The rate of illicit drug use during the past month among youths was higher among those who currently were using cigarettes or alcohol than among youths not using cigarettes or alcohol. Only 5.6% of nonsmoking youths used illicit drugs; among youths who used cigarettes, the rate of past month illicit drug use was 41.1%. The rate of illicit drug use also was associated with the level of alcohol use. Among youths who were heavy drinkers, 66.7% also were current illicit drug users. Among nondrinkers, only 5.5% were current illicit drug users.
- The rates of nonmedical use of psychotherapeutics were higher among youths (2.9%) and young adults (3.7%) than among older adults (1.3%). Nevertheless, more than half of current users were age 26 years or over, and the rate for persons ages 35 to 44 years was above 2% to 3%.
- The rates of cocaine use were 0.5% for youths ages 12 to 17 years, 1.7% for young adults ages 18 to 25 years, and 0.5% for adults age 26 years or over. About half of all current cocaine users were age 26 or over.
- The rates of hallucinogen use were 1.1% among youths ages 12 to 17 years, 1.8% among young adults ages 18 to 25 years, and 0.1% among adults age 26 years or over. More than 80% of hallucinogen users were under age 26.

Gender

- As in prior years, men continued to have a higher rate of current illicit drug use than did women (8.7% vs. 4.9%). However, the rates of nonmedical psychotherapeutic use were similar for males (1.9%) and females (1.7%).
- Among youths ages 12 to 17 years, the rate of current illicit drug use was slightly higher for boys (11.3%) than for girls (10.5%). Whereas boys ages 12 to 17 had a slightly higher rate of marijuana use than did girls in this age group (8.4% vs. 7.1%), girls were somewhat more likely to use psychotherapeutics for nonmedical reasons than were boys (3.2% vs. 2.6%).
- Among pregnant women ages 15 to 44 years, 3.4% reported using illicit drugs during the month prior to the interview. This was significantly lower than the rate among nonpregnant women in this age group (8.1%). Among pregnant women ages 15 to 17 years and 18 to 25 years, the age groups with generally higher levels of use, the rates were 7.5% and 6.5%, respectively (Figure A43.4).

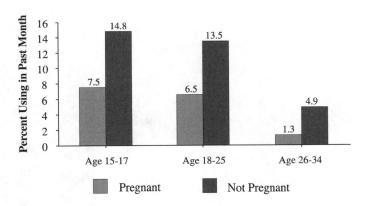

Figure A43.4
Illicit Drug Use Among Women by Pregnancy Status and Age, 1999

Race/Ethnicity

- The rates of current illicit drug use for major racial/ethnic groups were 6.6% for Whites, 6.8% for Hispanics, and 7.7% for Blacks. The rate was highest among the American Indian/Alaska Native population (10.6%) and among persons reporting multiple races (11.2%). Asians had the lowest rate (3.2%) (Figure A43.5).

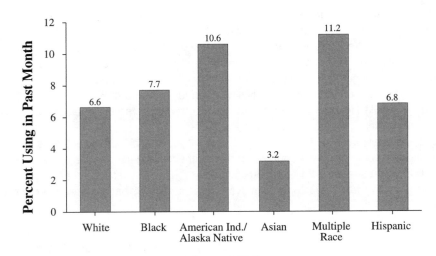

Figure A43.5
Illicit Drug Use by Race/Ethnicity, Age 12 Years or Over, 1999

- American Indians/Alaska Natives also had the highest rate among youths ages 12 to 17 years (19.6%). The rates of use were 8.4% for Asian youths, 10.7% for Black youths, 10.9% for White youths, 11.4% for Hispanic youths, and 11.6% for youths reporting multiple races (Figure A43.6).

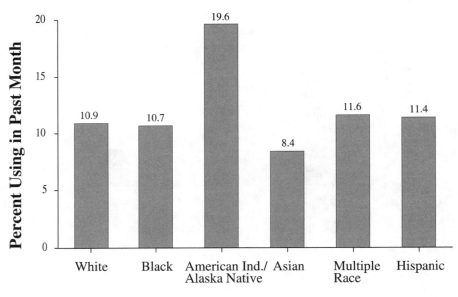

Figure A43.6
Illicit Drug Use by Race/Ethnicity, Ages 12 to 17 Years, 1999

- Although overall rates were similar for White, Black, and Hispanic youths ages 12 to 17 years, there were gender differences within these major racial/ethnic groups. Among Whites, boys and girls were about equally likely to be current illicit drug users (10.8% for males vs. 11.1% for females). However, among Blacks and Hispanics, rates were higher among boys than among girls (12.6% vs. 8.7% for Blacks and 12.3% vs. 10.5% for Hispanics, not a statistically significant difference).
- Among youths ages 12 to 17 years, the rate of current hallucinogen use was highest among American Indians/Alaska Natives (3.7%) and lowest among Blacks (0.2%). The overall rate for this age group was 1.1%.

Education

- Illicit drug use rates remained highly correlated with educational status. Among adults age 18 years or over, college graduates had the lowest rate of current use (4.8%). The rate was 7.1% among adults who had not completed high school. This is despite the fact that adults who had completed 4 years of college were more likely to have tried illicit drugs in their lifetimes than were adults who had not completed high school (45.6% vs. 30.0%).

College Students

- In the college-age population (ages 18-22 years), the rate of current illicit drug use was the same (19.4%) among full-time undergraduate college students as among other persons ages 18 to 22 years (including part-time students, students in other grades, and nonstudents).

Employment

- Current employment status also was highly correlated with rates of illicit drug use. An estimated 16.5% of unemployed adults (age 18 years or over) were current illicit drug users, compared to 6.5% of full-time employed adults and 8.6% of part-time employed adults.
- Although the rate of drug use was higher among the unemployed, most drug users were employed. Of the 12.3 million adult illicit drug users, 9.4 million (77%) were employed either full-time or part-time.

Geographic Area

- The rates of current illicit drug use were 7.9% in the West region, 7.4% in the Northeast, 6.7% in the Midwest, and 5.6% in the South.
- The rate of illicit drug use in metropolitan areas was higher than the rate in nonmetropolitan areas. Rates were 7.1% in large metropolitan areas, 7.0% in small metropolitan areas, and 5.2% in nonmetropolitan areas. Rural nonmetropolitan counties have lower rates of illicit drug use than do other counties. Rates were 4.2% in completely rural counties and 4.8% in less urbanized nonmetropolitan counties (Figure A43.7).

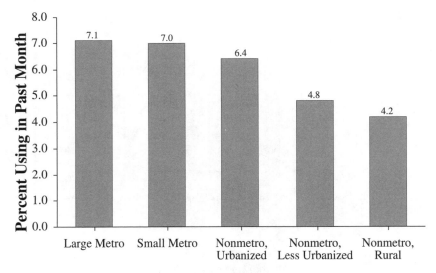

Figure A43.7
Illicit Drug Use by County Type, Age 12 Years or Over, 1999

- Among youths, rates of any illicit drug use were more similar across county types. Rates ranged from 9.7% in completely rural counties to 12.0% in counties in small metropolitan areas. The rate of use for youths in large metropolitan areas was 10.5%.

ALCOHOL USE

Estimates for the prevalence of alcohol use in 1999 are primarily at three levels defined for this report as follows:

Current use: At least one drink during the past 30 days (includes binge and heavy use)

Binge use: Five or more drinks on the same occasion at least once during the past 30 days (includes heavy use)

Heavy use: Five or more drinks on the same occasion at least five different days during the past 30 days

- Nearly half (47.3%) of Americans age 12 years or over reported being current drinkers of alcohol. This translates to an estimated 105 million people.
- Approximately one fifth (20.2%) of persons age 12 years or over (45 million people) participated in binge drinking at least once during the 30 days prior to the interview. This represents approximately 43% of all current drinkers.
- As observed during prior years, the level of alcohol use was strongly associated with illicit drug use. Among the 12.4 million heavy drinkers, 30.5% (3.8 million people) were current illicit drug users. For binge drinkers who were not heavy drinkers, 14.8% (4.8 million people) reported illicit drug use during the past month. Other drinkers (i.e., alcohol use but not binge drinking during the past month) had a rate of 5.1% (3.1 million people) for current illicit drug use. Persons who did not use alcohol during the past month were least likely to use illicit drugs (2.7% or 3.2 million people).

Age

- For current alcohol use, binge drinking, and heavy alcohol use, 21 years was the age of peak prevalence.
- The prevalence of current alcohol drinking increased with age, from 3.9% among 12-year-old youths to a peak of 66.6% for 21-year-olds. Unlike prevalence patterns observed for cigarettes and illicit drugs, current alcohol use remained steady among older age groups. More than 60% of persons ages 21 to 25 years and 59.5% of persons ages 26 to 29 years reported current alcohol drinking. The prevalence of alcohol use dropped slightly for persons in their 30s and 40s. By ages 50 to 64 years, drinking during the past month was reported by 47.2% of respondents. In addition, 32.7% of persons age 65 years or over reported current drinking (Figure A43.8).

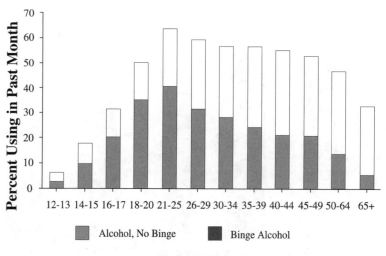

Figure A43.8
Alcohol Use by Age, 1999

- The highest prevalence of both binge and heavy drinking was observed for young adults (ages 18-25 years), with the peak rate occurring among 21-year-olds. The rate of binge drinking was 38.3% for young adults ages 18 to 25 years and 45.6% at age 21. Heavy alcohol use was reported by 13.3% of persons ages 18 to 25 years and by 17.4% of 21-year-olds.

- Among youths ages 12 to 17 years, 18.6% reported using alcohol during the month prior to the interview. Of these, 10.9% were binge drinkers and 2.5% were heavy drinkers.

Underage Alcohol Use

- About 10.4 million persons ages 12 to 20 years reported drinking alcohol during the month prior to the interview (29.4% of this age group). Of these, 6.8 million (20.2%) were binge drinkers and 2.1 million (6.0%) were heavy drinkers.
- Binge alcohol drinking rates were 1.7% for 12-year-olds, 3.7% for 13-year-olds, and 7.3% for 14-year-olds.
- Males ages 12 to 20 years were more likely than their female counterparts to report binge drinking (22.3% vs. 16.0%).
- Among people ages 12 to 20 years, prior month alcohol use rates ranged from 20.8% for Asians and 21.2% for Blacks to 32.1% for Whites. Binge drinking was reported by 21.9% of underage Whites and 22.6% of underage American Indians/Alaska Natives but was reported by only 6.8% of underage Asians and 11.6% of underage Blacks.
- Across geographic regions, underage current alcohol use rates ranged from 24.6% in the South Atlantic region and 24.8% in the East South Central region to 33.7% in the New England region and 34.4% in the West North Central region.
- Underage current alcohol use rates were similar in large metropolitan areas (28.3%), small metropolitan areas (31.4%), and nonmetropolitan areas (29.2%).

Gender

- With the exception of adolescents, males were more likely than females to report alcohol drinking during the past month. More than half (54.0%) of males (age 12 years or over) were current drinkers, compared to 41.1% of females.
- For the youngest age group (ages 12-17 years), males and females had comparable rates of current alcohol use (19.2% for males and 18.1% for females).
- Among pregnant women ages 15 to 44 years, 13.8% used alcohol and 3.4% were binge drinkers. These rates are substantially lower than the rates for nonpregnant women in this age group (49.3% and 19.4%, respectively).

Race/Ethnicity

- Whites were more likely than any other racial/ethnic group to report current use of alcohol. An estimated 51.0% of Whites reported use during the past month. The next highest rates were for persons of multiple races and Hispanics (41.8% and 39.9%, respectively). The lowest current drinking rate was observed for Asians (31.9%).
- Binge alcohol use was least likely to be reported by Asians (10.5%). Binge alcohol use among American Indians/ Alaska Natives, persons of multiple races, Whites, and Hispanics ranged from 20.0% to 21.0%, whereas the rate for Blacks was 16.5%.

Education

- Among persons ages 18 to 25 years, alcohol consumption during the past month was most prevalent among persons with a college education (74.0%), compared to 64.7% of persons with some college, 53.8% of persons with only a high school diploma, and 46.1% of persons in this age group who lacked a high school diploma. A similar pattern of increasing rates with increasing educational attainment was seen for binge drinking, ranging from 34.0% among persons who had not completed high school to 43.0% among persons with a college degree.
- As seen for young adults ages 18 to 25 years, college graduates age 26 years or over were most likely to report alcohol use during the past month (61.8%), compared to 32.6% of their peers with the least education.
- Binge drinking among persons age 26 years or over was equally likely for persons without a high school education and those with a college degree (16.7% and 16.1%, respectively).

College Students

- Young adults (ages 18-22 years) enrolled full-time in college were more likely than their peers not enrolled full-time (this category includes part-time college students and persons not enrolled in college) to report all three levels of drinking. Past month alcohol use was reported by 63.2% of full-time college students and by 52.1% of their counterparts who were not currently enrolled (Figure A43.9).

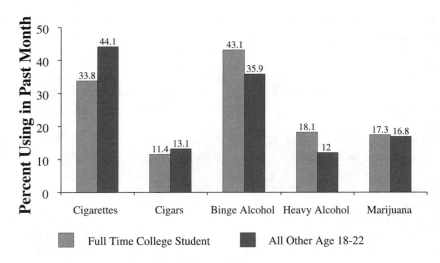

Figure A43.9
Substance Use by College Enrollment, Ages 18 to 22 Years, 1999

- Among full-time college students ages 18 to 22 years, males were more likely than females to report binge and heavy drinking. Among full-time male college students, 53.2% reported binge drinking and 26.6% reported heavy drinking. For males who were not full-time college students, 45.1% reported binge drinking and 17.6% reported heavy alcohol use. More than a third (34.2%) of female full-time college students were binge drinkers, and 10.7% reported heavy alcohol use. Among females who were not full-time college students, 26.3% reported binge drinking and 6.0% reported heavy alcohol use.

Employment

- Rates for current alcohol use were 62.5% for full-time employed persons ages 18 to 25 years, compared to 52.1% for their unemployed peers.
- Unemployed persons age 26 years or over were nearly twice as likely as full-time employed persons in that age group (12.6% vs. 6.2%) to be heavy alcohol drinkers.

Geographic Area

- Among young adults ages 18 to 25 years, the rate of alcohol use during the past month was lowest in the East South Central region (49.6%) and highest in the New England region (67.9%).
- Among all people age 12 years or over, the rate of alcohol use was highest in large metropolitan areas (50.4%) and lowest in completely rural areas (38.1%). However, there was less variation across county types in the rates of binge and heavy drinking. The rate of heavy alcohol use was 5.1% in large metropolitan areas and 5.8% in completely rural areas.

TOBACCO USE

- An estimated 66.8 million Americans reported current use of a tobacco product in 1999, a prevalence rate of 30.2% for the population age 12 years or over. Of the users, 57.0 million (25.8%) smoked cigarettes, 12.1 million (5.5%) smoked cigars, 7.6 million (3.4%) used smokeless tobacco, and 2.4 million (1.1%) smoked tobacco in pipes.
- Cigarette use during the past month was highly correlated with illicit drug use, and this association was strongest for adolescents. Among youths ages 12 to 17 years, 41.1% of past month smokers reported past month use of an illicit drug, compared to 5.6% of their adolescent nonsmoking peers. Among persons ages 18 to 25 years, cigarette smokers were about four times more likely to report the use of an illicit drug during the past month (31.0% vs. 8.0%). For past month cigarette smokers age 26 years or over, 10.1% reported current use of an illicit drug, compared to 2.5% for their nonsmoking peers.

Age

- Up to age 20 years, current cigarette smoking rates increase steadily with age, from 2.2% among 12-year-olds to 43.5% among 20-year-olds. Overall, 14.9% of youths ages 12 to 17 years were current cigarette smokers. Among young adults ages 18 to 25 years, the rate was 39.7%. Among adults age 26 years or over, the rate was 24.9%. After age 25 years, rates generally decline, reaching 22.5% for persons ages 50 to 64 years and 10.7% for persons age 65 years or over (Figures A43.10 and A43.11).

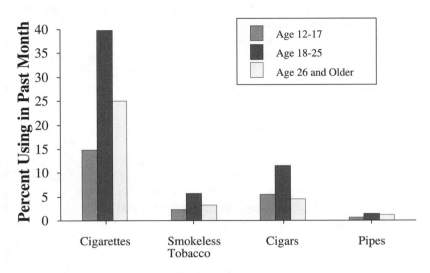

Figure A43.10
Current Tobacco Use by Age, 1999

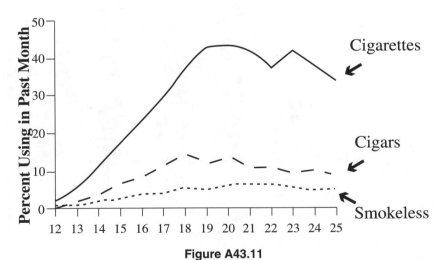

Figure A43.11
Current Tobacco Use by Single Year of Age, 1999

- Use of smokeless tobacco during the past month was reported by 5.7% of young adults ages 18 to 25 years, 2.3% of youths ages 12 to 17 years, and 3.2% of persons age 26 years or over.
- More than 1 in 10 young adults (11.5%) ages 18 to 25 years reported smoking cigars during the month prior to the interview. This rate is more than twice that found for any of the other age groups. The current rate of cigar use was 5.4% among youths ages 12 to 17 years and 4.5% among persons age 26 years or over.
- Nearly half (44.7%) of persons ages 18 to 25 years reported the use of some tobacco product during the past month.

Gender

- Males were more likely than females to report the use of any tobacco product during the past month. More than one third (36.5%) of males age 12 years or over were current users of any tobacco product, compared to 24.3% of females.
- For the youngest age group (ages 12-17 years), males and females generally were equally likely to report the use of cigarettes during the past month (about 15% for both). However, Black males in this age group were more likely to report current cigarette use than were their Black female counterparts (10.3% vs. 6.9%).
- Males were about 10 times more likely than their female counterparts to report current use of smokeless tobacco (6.5% of males age 12 years or over vs. 0.6% of females in this age group).
- As seen for smokeless tobacco, males also were more likely than females to report the use of cigars during the past month. Specifically, males were five times more likely than females to report the past month use of cigars (9.5% vs. 1.7%).
- Only 17.0% of pregnant women ages 15 to 44 years smoked cigarettes, compared to 30.5% of nonpregnant women in the same age group.

Race/Ethnicity

- American Indians/Alaska Natives were more likely than any other racial/ethnic group to report the use of tobacco products. For past month use (age 12 years or over), 43.1% of American Indians/Alaska Natives reported using at least one form of tobacco. The next highest rates were for non-Hispanic Whites and persons of multiple races (31.9% and 34.0%, respectively). The lowest current tobacco use rates were observed for Asians (18.6%) (Figure A43.12).

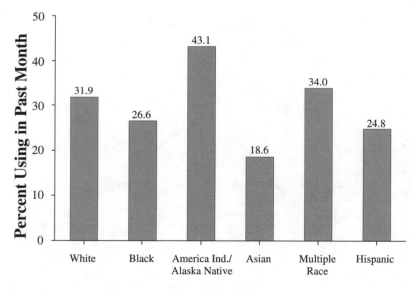

Figure A43.12
Tobacco Use by Race/Ethnicity, Age 12 Years or Over, 1999

- Current cigarette smoking rates among persons age 12 years or over were 36.0% for American Indians/Alaska Natives, 29.8% for persons of multiple races, 27.0% for Whites, 22.6% for Hispanics, 22.5% for Blacks, and 16.6% for Asians.

Education

- Among persons ages 18 to 25 years, the prevalence of cigarette smoking decreased with increasing levels of education. College graduates were the least likely to report smoking cigarettes (28.4%), compared to 36.4% of persons with some college, 41.9% of young adults ages 18 to 25 years with only a high school diploma, and 47.2% of persons lacking a high school diploma.
- As seen for the younger adult age group, college graduates age 26 years or over were the least likely to report past month cigarette use (13.3%), compared to 27% to 30% of persons with less education.

College Students

- Young adults (ages 18-22 years) enrolled full-time in college were less likely than their peers not enrolled full-time (this category includes part-time college students and persons not enrolled in college) to report current cigarette use. Past month cigarette use was reported by 33.8% of full-time college students, compared to 44.1% of their nonenrolled peers.

Employment

- Rates for current cigarette smoking were 42.2% for full-time employed persons ages 18 to 25 years and 45.7% for their unemployed peers.
- Unemployed persons age 26 years or over were nearly twice as likely as full-time employed persons (43.0% vs. 28.2%) to be current cigarette smokers.

Geographic Area

- Cigarette use rates varied by region of the country. Past month cigarette use ranged from a low of 21.9% for persons living in the Pacific portion of the West region to 30.5% for persons living in the East South Central region.
- Among adolescents and young adults, the prevalence of past month cigarette use was highest in completely rural counties, compared to small or large metropolitan areas. Among youths ages 12 to 17 years, past month cigarette use was reported by 19.2% of those living in completely rural counties, compared to 13.3% of adolescents living in large metropolitan areas. Among young adults ages 18 to 25 years, the rate of past month cigarette use was 43.1% in completely rural areas, compared to 37.5% in large metropolitan areas.

Usual Brand Used

- Three brands accounted for most of adolescent cigarette smoking. Among current smokers ages 12 to 17 years, 54.5% reported Marlboro as their usual brand. Newport was reported by 21.6% of youth smokers, and Camel was reported by 9.8%. No other individual cigarette brand was reported by even 2% of youths.
- There were notable racial/ethnic differences with regard to brand of cigarette smoked most often during the month prior to the interview. Nearly half of White smokers age 12 years or over (42.2%) and about two thirds of Hispanic smokers (61.2%) reported using Marlboro. Nearly half of Black smokers (43.9%) reported using Newport.
- Racial/ethnic differences in usual cigarette brand used also were evident among adolescent smokers (ages 12-17 years). More than half of White (58.4%) and Hispanic (59.7%) adolescent smokers reported Marlboro as their usual brand. About three quarters (73.9%) of Black adolescent smokers reported Newport as their usual brand (Figure A43.13).

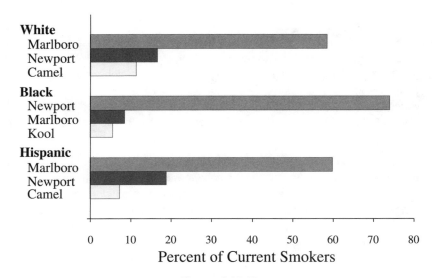

Figure A43.13
Cigarette Brand Used Most Often During Past Month by Race/Ethnicity, Ages 12 to 17 Years, 1999

- Racial/ethnic differences also were evident for brand of cigar smoked most often during the month prior to the interview. The single specific cigar brand most popular among both Whites and Hispanics age 12 years or over was Swisher Sweets (18.8% and 13.2%, respectively). For Blacks, the specific cigar brand cited most often was Black & Mild (58.5%).

TRENDS IN INITIATION OF SUBSTANCE USE

Estimates of drug use incidence, or initiation (i.e., number of new users during a given year), provide another measure of the nation's drug problem. They can suggest emerging patterns of use, particularly among young people. In the past, increases and decreases in incidence usually have been followed by corresponding changes in the prevalence of use. The incidence estimates are based on the National Household Survey on Drug Abuse (NHSDA) questions on age at first use, year and month of first use for recent initiates, the respondent's date of birth, and the interview date. Using this information along with editing and imputation when necessary, an exact date of first use is determined for each substance used by each respondent. For age-specific incidence rates, the period of exposure was defined for each respondent and age group for the time that the respondent was in the age group during the calendar year. Incidents of first use also were classified by year of occurrence and age at the date of first use. By applying sample weights to incidents of first use, estimates of the number of new users of each drug for each year were made. These estimates include new users at any age, including ages under 12 years, and also are shown for two specific age groups (12-17 and 18-25 years). In addition, the average age of new users in each year and age-specific rates of first use were estimated. These rates are presented in this report as the number of new users per 1,000 potential new users because they indicate the rate of new use among persons who have not yet used the drug (i.e., potential new users). More precisely, the rates are actually the numbers of new users per 1,000 person-years of exposure. The numerator of each rate is the number of persons in the age group who first used the drug during that year, whereas the denominator is the person-time exposure measured in thousands of years. Each person's exposure time ends on the date of first use. For age-specific estimates, exposure is limited to time during the year that the person was in the age group. Persons who first used the drug during a prior year have zero exposure to first use during the current year, and persons who still have never used the drug by the end of the current year had a full year of exposure to risk.

The incidence estimates are based on retrospective reports of age at first drug use by survey respondents interviewed during 1999 and, therefore, may be subject to several biases including bias due to differential mortality of users and nonusers of each drug, bias due to memory errors (recall decay and telescoping), and underreporting bias due to social acceptability and fear of disclosure. It is possible that some of these biases, particularly telescoping and underreporting because of fear of disclosure, may be affecting estimates for the most recent years more significantly. However, further analysis is needed to show the magnitude of these biases.

Marijuana

- An estimated 2.3 million Americans used marijuana for the first time in 1998. The number increased from approximately 1.4 million in 1990 to 2.6 million in 1996, remained level in 1997, then dropped between 1997 and 1998. The number of new marijuana users per year reached its highest level (3.4 million) in 1977. It is interesting to note that the decrease in prevalence of marijuana use that occurred during the 1980s did not begin to occur until several years after the peak in incidence.
- The rising incidence during the 1990s seemed to have been fueled primarily by the increasing rate of new use among youths ages 12 to 17 years (from 45.6 per 1,000 potential new users in 1991 to 90.8 in 1997). This is in contrast to the epidemic of the late 1960s and early 1970s, where there were similar increases among young adults as well as youths, but with the rates among young adults dominating until 1972. The rates of marijuana initiation for youths from 1995 to 1998 were at their highest levels since the peak levels of the late 1970s. However, the 1998 rate for youths (81.0 per 1,000 potential new users) was significantly lower than the 1997 rate (90.8) (Figure A43.14).

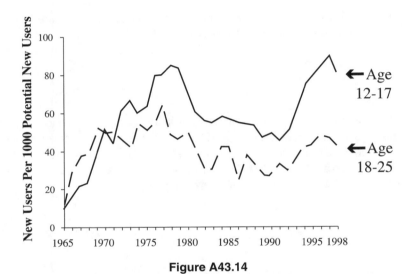

Figure A43.14
Age-Specific Rates of First-Time Use of Marijuana, 1965-1998

Heroin

- There were an estimated 149,000 new heroin users in 1998, not statistically different from the 189,000 new users in 1997 or the 132,000 new users in 1996. Estimates of heroin incidence are subject to wide variability and usually do not show any clear trend.
- The rate of heroin initiation for 12- to 17-year-olds increased from less than 1.0 per 1,000 potential new users during the 1980s to nearly 2.0 during the period 1996 through 1998.
- A large proportion of the recent heroin initiates are young and are smoking, sniffing, or snorting heroin. Among the estimated 471,000 persons who used heroin for the first time during 1996 through 1998, about one quarter (125,000) were under age 18 years and another 47% (222,000) were ages 18 to 25 years at the time that they first used. Only 37% reported having ever injected heroin by 1999. Most (89%) were living in metropolitan areas.

Cocaine and Crack Cocaine

- The annual number of new users of any form of cocaine rose from 514,000 in 1994 to 934,000 in 1998. However, this was a lower level than those during the early and mid-1980s. Recent initiation was at a lower rate than at its peak in 1983, when the number of new initiates was estimated to be 1.6 million.
- The rates of initiation among different age groups have been increasing during recent years. In particular, the rate among youths ages 12 to 17 years increased from 5.1 per 1,000 potential new users in 1992 to 13.1 in 1996 and has remained level since then. Historically, most initiation of cocaine use has taken place among young adults ages 18 to

25 years. The rate for that age group fell from a high of 30.5 per 1,000 potential new users in 1983 and 1984 to 9.1 in 1994. Initiation rates among this age group have increased to 20.8 per 1,000 potential new users in 1998.

- The number of new crack cocaine users was 371,000 in 1998. Although there has been little change in the overall number of new crack users per year since 1985, the age-specific rate of new use for ages 12 to 17 years increased from 1.4 per 1,000 potential new users in 1991 to 4.8 in 1997 and 3.6 in 1998.

Hallucinogens

- There were an estimated 1.2 million new hallucinogen users in 1998, nearly twice the average annual number during the 1980s. The rate of initiation among youths ages 12 to 17 years increased between 1991 and 1996, from 14.5 to 25.9 per 1,000 potential new users. Over the same period, the rate for ages 18 to 25 years rose from 14.5 to 21.1 per 1,000 potential new users. Both age groups had constant rates during the period 1996 through 1998.

Inhalants

- There were an estimated 991,000 new inhalant users in 1998, up from 390,000 in 1990. The rate of first use among youths ages 12 to 17 years rose significantly between 1990 and 1998, from 11.6 to 28.1 per 1,000 potential new users. In addition, for young adults ages 18 to 25 years, there was an increase in the rate of first use between 1990 and 1998, from 4.6 to 11.2 per 1,000 potential new users.

Psychotherapeutics

- An estimated 1.6 million Americans used prescription-type pain relievers for nonmedical reasons for the first time in 1998. This represents a significant increase since the 1980s, when there were generally fewer than 500,000 initiates per year. Among youths ages 12 to 17 years, the incidence rate increased from 6.3 per 1,000 potential new users in 1990 to 32.4 in 1998. For young adults ages 18 to 25 years, there also was an increase in the rate of first use between 1990 and 1998, from 7.7 to 20.3 per 1,000 potential new users (Figure A43.15).

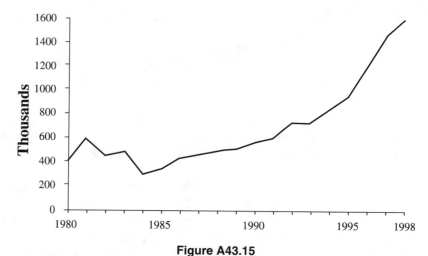

Figure A43.15
Annual Numbers of New Users of Pain Relievers for Nonmedical Reasons, 1980-1998

- There were an estimated 378,000 new methamphetamine users in 1998, up from 149,000 in 1990. The rate of first use among youths ages 12 to 17 years rose significantly between 1990 and 1998, from 2.2 to 7.4 per 1,000 potential new users. For young adults ages 18 to 25 years, there also was an increase in the rate of first use between 1990 and 1998, from 3.0 to 6.1 per 1,000 potential new users.

Alcohol

- In 1997, there were approximately 4.7 million new users of alcohol, compared to about 3.2 million new users in 1992. The rate of new use of alcohol among the 18- to 25-year age group has begun to rise during recent years (157.5 per 1,000 potential new users in 1989, compared to 219.3 in 1997). In addition, the rate of initiation of alcohol use among the 12- to 17-year age group increased from 117.6 per 1,000 potential new users to 216.8 over the same period.

Cigarettes

- An estimated 3.4 million people tried their first cigarette in 1997. The rate of initiation among youths ages 12 to 17 years between 1990 and 1997 increased from 100.9 to 159.2 per 1,000 potential new users (Figure A43.16).
- An estimated 1.6 million people began smoking on a daily basis in 1998. More than half of these new daily smokers were under age 18 years. This translates to more than 4,000 new regular smokers per day, of which more than 2,000 were youths.

Smokeless Tobacco

- An estimated 1.1 million people tried smokeless tobacco for the first time in 1998. Most new users were under age 18 years. The rate of initiation among youths ages 12 to 17 years has remained constant at approximately 30 per 1,000 potential new users since the 1970s (Figure A43.16).

Cigars

- An estimated 4.9 million people tried cigars for the first time in 1998. This translates to about 13,000 per day. This represents more than a threefold increase in cigar initiation since 1991, when there were only 1.5 million new cigar smokers. The average age of cigar initiates has changed little since the 1980s, and incidence rates have increased among both youths (from 21.4 per 1,000 potential new users in 1991 to 97.6 in 1998) and young adults (from 27.1 per 1,000 potential new users in 1991 to 89.0 in 1998) (Figure A43.16).

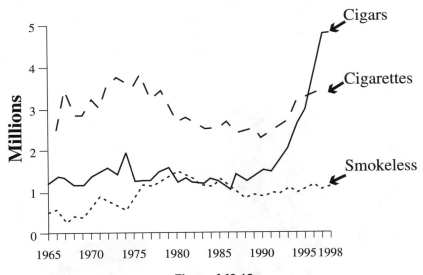

Figure A43.16
Annual Numbers of New Tobacco Users, 1965-1998

PREVENTION-RELATED MEASURES

The NHSDA questionnaire includes an extensive set of items concerned with substance abuse prevention issues. These include measures of risk and protective factors related to individual, peer, family, and community characteristics. Data on attitudes and beliefs about drug use, drug selling and crime in the neighborhood, drug availability, and participation in substance abuse education programs are obtained. Selected results from the 1999 sample of youths ages 12 to 17 years are given in what follows.

- More than one third (37.2%) of youths believed that there was a great risk of harm if they smoked marijuana once a month. Those reporting that they believed there was a moderate or great risk had a past month prevalence rate of marijuana use of only 3.1%. Those reporting that they believed there was no risk or only a slight risk had a rate of 18.5%.

- Overall, 42.0% of youths ages 12 to 17 years had at least a few friends who used marijuana. Most youths (62.2%) ages 16 to 17 years reported having at least a few friends who used marijuana. Only 0.7% of those who reported having no friends who used marijuana had used marijuana during the past 30 days. By contrast, 8.6% of those with a few marijuana-using friends had used the drug during the past 30 days. Of those youths who reported that most of their friends used marijuana (11.7% of all youths), 37.0% had used marijuana during the past 30 days. Of those youths who reported that all of their friends used marijuana (2.1% of all youths), 58.2% had used marijuana during the past 30 days.

- In 1999, 4.8% of the youths had stolen or tried to steal something worth more than $50 during the past year (one or more times), 3.8% had sold illegal drugs at least once during the past year, and 3.6% had carried a handgun during the past year. Of those youths who reported having stolen something once or twice during the past year, 28.6% had used marijuana during the past month. Only 6.2% of those who did not steal reported current use of marijuana.

- More than half (56.5%) of youths reported that obtaining marijuana was fairly or very easy. Among those who said that the drug was difficult to obtain, only 1.5% reported current use. But 12.9% of those who said that it was fairly or very easy to obtain reported current use.

- Among youths ages 12 to 17 years, 15.6% had been approached during the past 30 days by someone offering to sell them drugs. Of these youths, 28.1% reported current use of marijuana.

- Just 6.5% of youths reported that their parents would neither approve nor disapprove if they smoked one or more packs of cigarettes per day, whereas 87.4% thought their parents would strongly disapprove. Those youths who thought that their parents would neither approve nor disapprove of their cigarette use were more likely to have used marijuana during the past month (19.6%), compared to those who indicated that their parents would strongly disapprove (5.7%) (Figure A43.17).

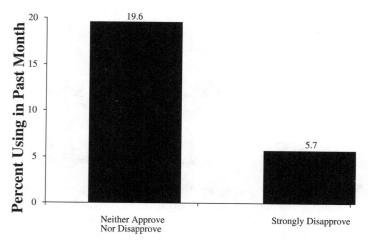

Response to Question: How do you think your parents would feel about you smoking one or more packs of cigarettes per day?

Figure A43.17
Marijuana Use by Perceived Parental Attitude About Cigarette Use, Ages 12 to 17 Years, 1999

- More than half (56.6%) of all youths had talked with a parent about the dangers of drugs and alcohol during the past year. However, there was little difference in rates of marijuana use between this group and those who had not discussed drugs with their parents.
- The majority (59.6%) of youths reported having an alcohol or drug education class or experience in school during the past year. The rate of current marijuana use among this group was 7.4%, compared to 8.3% for youths who had not had such a program.

SUBSTANCE DEPENDENCE AND TREATMENT

In 1999, the NHSDA included a series of questions to assess dependence on substances based on the seven criteria for dependence in the *DSM-IV* (American Psychiatric Association, 1994). These questions ask about health, emotional problems, attempts to cut down on use, tolerance, withdrawal, and other symptoms associated with substance use. This section presents estimates of the prevalence of alcohol and drug dependence based on these data as well as estimates of substance abuse treatment received during the 12 months prior to the interview.

- An estimated 3.6 million Americans (1.6% of the total population age 12 years or over) were dependent on illicit drugs in 1999. An estimated 8.2 million Americans (3.7%) were dependent on alcohol. Of these, 1.5 million people were dependent on both alcohol and illicit drugs. Overall, an estimated 10.3 million people (4.7%) were dependent on either alcohol or illicit drugs.
- Of the 3.6 million people dependent on illicit drugs, 2.3 million (65%) were dependent on marijuana and hashish. However, among users of a specific drug, the rate was highest for heroin. Among past year users of heroin, 35% were dependent on heroin. Among past year users of marijuana, 12% were dependent on marijuana. Among users of cocaine, 21% were dependent on cocaine.
- Adults who had first used drugs at a young age were more likely to be dependent on drugs than were adults who had initiated use at a later age. Among those who had first tried marijuana at age 14 years or under, 8.9% were dependent on an illicit drug during the past year, compared to only 1.7% of adults who had first tried marijuana at age 18 years or over (Figure A43.18).

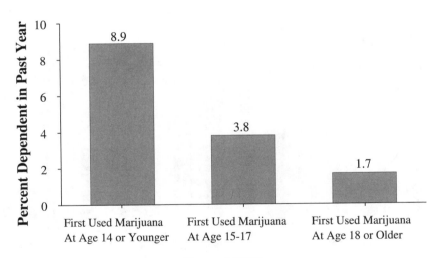

Figure A43.18

Dependence on Illicit Drugs by Age at First Use of Marijuana, Adults, 1999

Age

- Rates for substance dependence showed substantial variation by age. The rate for illicit drug dependence was 0.5% at age 12 years. Rates increased for each successive year of age until the highest rate (6.8%) was reached at age 18 years. The overall rate for youths ages 12 to 17 years was 3.3%. After age 18, the rates generally decline in each successively older age group. The rate for persons ages 18 to 25 years was 4.7%, and the rate for persons age 26 years or over was 0.9% (Figure A43.19).

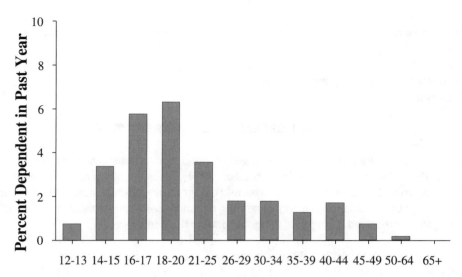

Figure A43.19
Dependence on Illicit Drugs by Age at First Use of Marijuana, Adults, 1999

- Rates for alcohol dependence by age show a similar pattern to rates for illicit drug dependence by age, reaching a peak at age 21 years with a rate of 11.7% and generally declining for successively older age groups. The rate for persons ages 12 to 17 years was 3.6%, the rate for persons ages 18 to 25 years was 9.2%, and the rate for persons age 26 years or over was 2.8% (Figure A43.20).

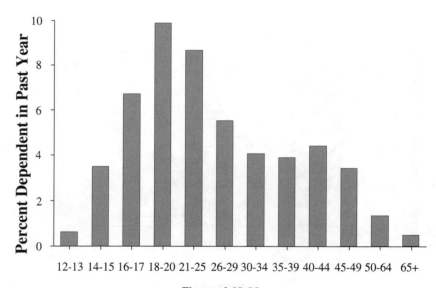

Figure A43.20
Illicit Drug Dependence by Age, 1999

Gender

- Males were more likely than females to be dependent on illicit drugs. In 1999, 2.0% of males (age 12 years or over) were dependent on illicit drugs, compared to 1.3% of females. Males also were more likely to be dependent on alcohol (4.9% vs. 2.6%) and more likely to be dependent on alcohol or illicit drugs (6.0% vs. 3.4%) (Figure A43.21).

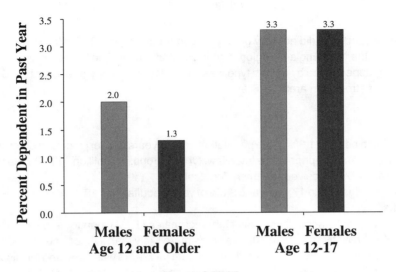

Figure A43.21
Illicit Drug Dependence by Age and Gender, 1999

- However, for the youngest age group (12-17 years), the percentage dependent on illicit drugs was the same for both males and females (3.3%). The rates for adolescent males and females also were essentially the same for alcohol (3.3% for males and 3.9% for females) and for alcohol or illicit drugs (5.6% for males and 5.8% for females).
- Among Whites ages 12 to 17 years, the percentage dependent on illicit drugs was significantly higher for females than for males (3.9% vs. 2.8%), whereas among Blacks ages 12 to 17 years, the rate was significantly higher for males than for females (3.2% vs. 1.7%). For Hispanics, the rate for males was higher than that for females (4.9% vs. 3.0%), but this difference was not statistically significant.

Race/Ethnicity

- Blacks age 12 years or over were more likely to be dependent on illicit drugs than were Whites, but they were not more likely to be dependent on alcohol than were Whites. In 1999, 2.3% of all Blacks were dependent on illicit drugs, compared to 1.5% of all Whites, and 3.8% of all Whites were dependent on alcohol, compared to 3.1% of all Blacks.
- Rates for illicit drug dependence varied by race/ethnicity. The rate was 4.7% among American Indians/Alaska Natives. Rates for other groups were 2.6% for persons reporting multiple races, 2.3% for Blacks, 1.9% for Hispanics, 1.5% for Whites, and 0.8% for Asians.
- The rates of alcohol dependence ranged from 7.7% among persons reporting multiple races to 2.2% among Asians.

Education

- As with the case for illicit drug use, the rate of illicit drug dependence was highly correlated with educational status. Among adults age 18 years or over, those who had not completed high school had the highest rate of illicit drug dependence (2.3%), whereas college graduates had the lowest rate of illicit drug dependence (0.6%).
- In contrast to illicit drug dependence, the rate of alcohol dependence was not highly correlated with education status. The rates of alcohol dependence ranged from 4.5% among adults who had not completed high school to 3.0% among college graduates.

Employment

- Rates of illicit drug dependence and alcohol dependence were associated with employment status. An estimated 6.7% of unemployed adults were dependent on illicit drugs, whereas only 1.3% of full-time employed adults were dependent on illicit drugs. An estimated 11.4% of unemployed adults were dependent on alcohol, whereas only 4.0% of full-time employed adults were dependent on alcohol.

Geographic Area

- Rates of illicit drug dependence did not vary greatly by geographic region. The rate was 1.2% in the South Atlantic region, it was 2.3% in the New England region, and it was 2.2% in the Pacific region.
- The rate of illicit drug dependence by county type was lowest for completely rural counties (0.9%) and was highest for counties in small metropolitan areas (1.8%).

Treatment for Substance Abuse

- An estimated 2.8 million people (1.3% of the population age 12 years or over) received some kind of drug or alcohol treatment during the 12 months prior to the interview. Of this group, 1.6 million (0.7%) received treatment for illicit drugs, and 2.3 million (1.0%) received treatment for alcohol.
- In 1999, 1.3% of youths ages 12 to 17 years and 2.0% of young adults ages 18 to 25 years received treatment during the past 12 months.
- The rate of treatment for substance abuse was higher for males (1.7%) than for females (0.9%).
- American Indians/Alaska Natives were nearly five times more likely than Whites to have received treatment during the 12 months prior to the interview (5.2% vs. 1.1%). The rate for Blacks was 1.8% and for Hispanics was 1.5%. Only 0.3% of Asians had received treatment for substance abuse during the past 12 months.

SOURCE: U.S. Department of Health and Human Services. (1999). *National Household Survey on Drug Abuse 1999.* Washington, DC: Department of Health and Human Services, Substance Abuse and Mental Health Services Administration.

Appendix 44

Drug Categories for Substances of Abuse

To assist you in locating substances in this appendix, the following cross-reference by category is provided.

Narcotics

Alfentanil

Cocaine[a]

Codeine

Crack cocaine[a]

Fentanyl

Heroin

Hydromorphone

Ice

Meperidine

Methadone

Morphine

Nalorphine

Opium

Oxycodone

Propoxyphene

Depressants

Amobarbital

Benzodiazepine

Chloral hydrate

Chlordiazepoxide

Diazepam

Glutethimide

Meprobamate

Methaqualone

Nitrous Oxide

Pentobarbital

Phenobarbital

Secobarbital

Stimulants

Amphetamine

Benzedrine

Benzphetamine

Butyl nitrite

Dextroamphetamine

Methamphetamine

Methylphenidate

Phenmetrazine

Hallucinogens

Bufotenine

LSD

MDA

MDEA

MDMA

Mescaline

MMDA

Phencyclidine

Psilocybin

Cannabis

Lorazepam

Marijuana

Tetrahydrocannabinol

Alcohol

Ethyl alcohol

Steroids

Dianabol

Nandrolone

---

a. Cocaine, although classified under the Controlled Substances Act as a narcotic, also is discussed as a stimulant.

DRUG CATEGORY PROFILES

Narcotics

Drug	Dependence: Physical/Psychological	How Used	Duration (hours)
Opium	High/High	Oral, smoked	3-6
Morphine	High/High	Oral, smoked, injected	3-6
Codeine	Moderate/Moderate	Oral, injected	3-6
Heroin	High/High	Smoked, injected, sniffed	3-6
Hydromorphone	High/High	Oral, injected	3-6
Meperidine	High/High	Oral, injected	3-6
Methadone	High/High	Oral, injected	12-24

What are narcotics?	Drugs used medicinally to relieve pain High potential for abuse Cause relaxation with an immediate "rush" Initial unpleasant effects—restlessness, nausea
Possible effects	Euphoria Drowsiness, respiratory depression Constricted (pinpoint) pupils
Symptoms of overdose	Slow and shallow breathing, clammy skin Convulsions, coma, possible death
Withdrawal syndrome	Watery eyes, runny nose, yawning, cramps Loss of appetite, irritability, nausea Tremors, panic, chills, sweating
Indications of possible misuse	Scars (tracks) caused by injections Constricted (pinpoint) pupils Loss of appetite Sniffles, watery eyes, cough, nausea Lethargy, drowsiness, nodding Syringes, bent spoons, needles

Depressants

Drug	Dependence: Physical/Psychological	How Used	Duration (hours)
Barbiturates	High/Moderate	Oral	1-16
Methaqualone	High/High	Oral	4-8
Tranquilizers	High/High	Oral	4-8
Chloral hydrate	Moderate/Moderate	Oral	5-8
Glutethimide	High/Moderate	Oral	4-8

What are depressants?	Drugs used medicinally to relieve anxiety, irritability, tension
	High potential for abuse, development of tolerance
	Produce state of intoxication similar to that of alcohol
	Combined with alcohol, increase effects and multiply risks
Possible effects	Sensory alteration, anxiety reduction, intoxication
	Small amounts cause calmness, relaxed muscles
	Larger amounts cause slurred speech, impaired judgment, loss of motor coordination
	Very large doses may cause respiratory depression, coma, death
	Newborn babies of abusers may show dependence, withdrawal symptoms, behavioral problems, birth defects
Symptoms of overdose	Shallow respiration, clammy skin, dilated pupils
	Weak and rapid pulse, coma, death
Withdrawal syndrome	Anxiety, insomnia, muscle tremors, loss of appetite
	Abrupt cessation or reduced high dose may cause convulsions, delirium, death
Indications of possible misuse	Behavior similar to alcohol intoxication (without odor of alcohol on breath)
	Staggering, stumbling, lack of coordination, slurred speech
	Falling asleep while at work, difficulty concentrating
	Dilated pupils

Stimulants

Drug	Dependence: Physical/Psychological	How Used	Duration (hours)
Cocaine[a]	Possible/High	Sniffed, smoked, injected	1-2
Amphetamines	Possible/High	Oral, injected	2-4
Methamphetamine	Possible/High	Oral, injected	2-4
Phenmetrazine	Possible/High	Oral, injected	2-4
Methylphenidate	Possible/Moderate	Oral, injected	2-4
Other stimulants	Possible/High	Oral, injected	2-4
Ice	High/High	Smoked, oral, injected, inhaled	4-14

a. Cocaine, although classified under the Controlled Substances Act as a narcotic, also is discussed as a stimulant.

What are stimulants?	Drugs used to increase alertness, relieve fatigue, feel stronger and more decisive
	Used for euphoric effects or to counteract the "down" feeling of tranquilizers or alcohol
Possible effects	Increased heart and respiratory rates, elevated blood pressure, dilated pupils, and decreased appetite
	High doses may cause rapid or irregular heartbeat, loss of coordination, collapse
	May cause perspiration, blurred vision, dizziness, a feeling of restlessness, anxiety, delusions
Symptoms of overdose	Agitation, increase in body temperature, hallucinations, convulsions, possible death

Withdrawal syndrome	Apathy, long periods of sleep, irritability, depression, disorientation
Indications of possible misuse	Excessive activity, talkativeness, irritability, argumentativeness or nervousness
	Increased blood pressure or pulse rate, dilated pupils
	Long periods without sleeping or eating
	Euphoria

SUBSTANCES OF ABUSE: BRIEF PROFILES

Cocaine

Also known as:

Coke, dust, snow, flake, blow, girl

You probably know why cocaine is abused:

- Carefree feeling
- Euphoria
- Relaxation
- In control

But did you know that:

- A cocaine "high" lasts only about 5 to 20 minutes.
- Cocaine use may cause severe "mood swings" and irritability.
- You need more and more cocaine each time you want a "high."
- Cocaine increases your blood pressure and heart rate, and this is particularly dangerous if you have a heart condition.
- One use can cause death.
- Possession and use are illegal and can result in fines and arrest.

Crack

Also known as:

Crack, crack cocaine, freebase rocks, rock

You probably know why crack is abused:

- Quick high
- Power
- Euphoria

But did you know that:

- Crack is almost instantly addictive.
- One use could cause a fatal heart attack.
- Repeated use may cause insomnia, hallucinations, seizures, and paranoia.
- The euphoric effects of crack last for only a few minutes.

- Possession and use are illegal in all 50 states.
- There are more hospitalizations per year resulting from crack and cocaine use than from the use of any other illicit substance.

Ice

Also known as:

Meth, crystal, crank, methamphetamine

You probably know why ice is abused:

- Temporary mood elevation
- Exhilaration (high)
- Increased mental alertness
- Upper—increase wakefulness

But did you know that:

- Ice is extremely addictive, sometimes with just one use.
- Ice can cause convulsions, heart irregularities, high blood pressure, depression, restlessness, tremors, and severe fatigue.
- An overdose can cause coma and death.
- When one stops using ice, one may experience a deep depression.
- Ice causes a very jittery high along with anxiety, insomnia, and sometimes paranoia.

Inhalants

Some of the substances that are abused:

- Butyl nitrite
- Amyl nitrite (gas in aerosol cans)
- Gasoline and toluene vapors (typewriter correction fluid, glue, marking pens)

You probably know why inhalants are abused:

- Cheap high
- Quick buzz
- Fun

But did you know that inhalants may cause:

- Loss of muscle control
- Slurred speech
- Drowsiness or loss of consciousness
- Excessive secretions from the nose and watery eyes
- Brain damage and damage to lung cells

DRUG CATEGORY PROFILE

Hallucinogens

Drug	Dependence: Physical/Psychological	How Used	Duration
PCP Angel dust Loveboat	Unknown/High	Smoked, oral, injected	Up to days
LSD Acid Green/Red dragon	None/Unknown	Oral	8-12 hours
Mescaline, peyote	None/Unknown	Oral, injected	8-12 hours
Psilocybin	None/Unknown	Oral, injected, smoked, sniffed	Variable
Designer drugs[a] Ecstacy, PCE	Unknown/Unknown	Oral, injected, smoked	Variable

a. Phencyclidine analogs, amphetamine variants

What are hallucinogens?	Drugs that produce behavioral changes that often are multiple and dramatic
	No known medical use, but some block sensation to pain and use may result in self-inflicted injuries
	"Designer drugs," made to imitate certain illegal drugs, often are many times stronger than drugs they imitate
Possible effects	Rapidly changing feelings, immediately and long after use
	Chronic use may cause persistent problems, depression, violent behavior, anxiety, distorted perception of time
	Large doses may cause convulsions, coma, heart/lung failure, ruptured blood vessels in the brain
	May cause hallucinations, illusions, dizziness, confusion, suspicion, anxiety, loss of control
	Delayed effects—"flashbacks" may occur long after use
	Designer drugs—one use may cause irreversible brain damage
Symptoms of overdose	Longer, more intense "trip" episodes, psychosis, coma, death
Withdrawal syndrome	No known withdrawal syndrome
Indications of possible misuse	Extreme changes in behavior and mood
	Person may sit or recline in a trance-like state
	Person may appear fearful
	Chills, irregular breathing, sweating, trembling hands
	Changes in sense of light, hearing, touch, smell, time
	Increase in blood pressure, heart rate, blood sugar

SUBSTANCES OF ABUSE: BRIEF PROFILE

Hallucinogens

Types:

- LSD (acid, red/green dragon)
- Ecstacy (designer drug)

- PCP (angel dust, loveboat)
- PCP and cocaine ("Beam me up, Scottie")
- Mescaline
- Psilocybin

You probably know why hallucinogens are abused:

- Fun
- Stimulation or depression
- Behavioral changes

But did you know that:

- One use of LSD or PCP may cause multiple and dramatic behavioral changes.
- Large doses of hallucinogens may cause convulsions, ruptured blood vessels in the brain, and irreversible brain damage.
- Many hallucinogens cause unpleasant and potentially dangerous "flashbacks" long after the drug was used.
- Most hallucinogens cause hallucinations—changes in perception of time, smell, touch, and so on.

DRUG CATEGORY PROFILE

Cannabis

Drug	Dependence: Physical/Psychological	How Used	Duration (hours)
Marijuana Pot Grass	Unknown/Moderate	Smoked, oral	2-4
Tetrahydrocannabinol	Unknown/Moderate	Smoked, oral	2-4
Hashish	Unknown/Moderate	Smoked, oral	2-4
Hashish oil	Unknown/Moderate	Smoked, oral	2-4

What is cannabis?	Hemp plant from which marijuana and hashish are produced Hashish consists of resinous secretions of the cannabis plant Marijuana is a tobacco-like substance
Possible effects	Euphoria followed by relaxation; loss of appetite; impaired memory, concentration, knowledge retention; loss of coordination; more vivid sense of taste, sight, smell, hearing Stronger doses cause fluctuating emotions, fragmentary thoughts, disoriented behavior, psychosis May cause irritation to lungs, respiratory system May cause cancer
Symptoms of overdose	Fatigue, lack of coordination, paranoia, psychosis
Withdrawal syndrome	Insomnia, hyperactivity, sometimes decreased appetite
Indications of possible misuse	Animated behavior and loud talking followed by sleepiness Dilated pupils, bloodshot eyes Distortions in perception, hallucinations Distortions in depth and time perception, loss of coordination

SUBSTANCES OF ABUSE: BRIEF PROFILE

Marijuana

Also known as:

Pot, grass, joints, roaches, reefer, weed, Mary Jane

You probably know why marijuana is abused:

- Relaxation
- Euphoria

But did you know that:

- Marijuana may cause impaired short-term memory, a shortened attention span, and delayed reflexes.
- During pregnancy, marijuana may cause birth defects.
- Marijuana may cause a fast heart rate and pulse.
- Repeated use of marijuana may cause breathing problems.
- Possession of marijuana is illegal in all 50 states.
- Marijuana may cause relaxed inhibitions and disoriented behavior.

DRUG CATEGORY PROFILE

Alcohol

Drug	Dependence: Physical/Psychological	How Used	Duration (hours)
Ethyl alcohol	Possible/Possible	Oral	1-4
Ethanol	Possible/Possible	Oral	1-4

What is alcohol?	Liquid distilled product of fermented fruits, grains, vegetables Used as solvent, antiseptic, sedative Moderate potential for abuse
Possible effects	Intoxication Sensory alteration Anxiety reduction
Symptoms of overdose	Staggering Odor of alcohol on breath Loss of coordination Slurred speech, dilated pupils Fetal alcohol syndrome (in babies) Nerve and liver damage
Withdrawal syndrome	Sweating Tremors Altered perception Psychosis, fear, auditory hallucinations

Indications of possible misuse   Confusion, disorientation, loss of motor nerve control
                                  Convulsions, shock, shallow respiration
                                  Involuntary defecation, drowsiness
                                  Respiratory depression, possible death

SUBSTANCES OF ABUSE: BRIEF PROFILE

Alcohol

Also known as:

Booze, juice, brew, vino, sauce

You probably know why alcohol is abused:

- Relaxation
- Sociability
- Cheap high

But did you know that:

- Alcohol is a depressant that decreases the responses of the central nervous system.
- Excessive drinking can cause liver damage and psychotic behavior.
- As little as two beers or drinks can impair coordination and thinking.
- Alcohol often is used by substance abusers to enhance the effects of other drugs.
- Alcohol continues to be the most frequently abused substance among young adults.

DRUG CATEGORY PROFILE

Steroids

Drug	Dependence: Physical/Psychological	How Used	Duration
Dianabol	Possible/Possible	Oral	Days to weeks
Nandrolone	Possible/Possible	Oral	Days to weeks

What are steroids?   Synthetic compounds available legally and illegally
                      Drugs that are closely related to the male sex hormone (testosterone)
                      Moderate potential for abuse, particularly among young males

Possible effects   Increase in body weight
                      Increase in muscle strength
                      Enhance athletic performance
                      Increase physical endurance

Symptoms of overdose Quick weight and muscle gains
                      Extremely aggressive behavior or "road rage"
                      Severe skin rashes
                      Impotence, withered testicles
                      In females, development of irreversible masculine
                        traits

Withdrawal syndrome	Significant weight loss
	Depression
	Behavioral changes
	Trembling
Indications of possible misuse	Increased combativeness and aggressiveness
	Jaundice
	Purple or red spots on body, unexplained darkness of skin
	Persistent unpleasant breath odor
	Swelling of feet or lower legs

SUBSTANCES OF ABUSE: BRIEF PROFILE

Steroids

Types:

Anabolic (male hormone, steroids most frequently abused), cortical, estrogenic (female hormone)

You probably know why steroids are abused:

- Increase strength
- Increase muscle size
- Help muscles to recover

But did you know that abuse of steroids may cause:

- Severe acne, rashes, stunted growth
- Sexual function problems
- Women to take on masculine traits, develop hairiness
- Behavioral changes, aggressiveness ("paranoid rages")
- Long-term effects such as cholesterol increases, heart disease, liver tumors, cancer, cataracts, death

---

SOURCE: U.S. Department of Labor. *America in jeopardy: The young employee and drugs in the workplace.* Washington, DC: U.S. Department of Labor, Office of the Assistant Secretary for Policy.

Appendix 45

Adult Inpatient Program Schedule

Time	Monday	Tuesday	Wednesday	Thursday	Friday
7:00 a.m.	Wake-up call	Wake-up call	Wake-up call	Wake-up call	Wake-up call
7:00-7:45	Medications and blood pressure at the nurses' station	Medications and blood pressure at the nurses' station	Medications and blood pressure at the nurses' station	Medications and blood pressure at the nurses' station	Medications and blood pressure at the nurses' station
7:45-8:05	Breakfast	Breakfast	Breakfast	Breakfast	Breakfast
9:00-9:45	Lecture	Lecture	Lecture	Lecture	Lecture
10:00-11:30	Interpersonal group	10:00-11:00 Spirituality group 11:00-11:45 Fifth Step review	Interpersonal group	Interpersonal group	Interpersonal group
11:45-12:05	Noon meal	Noon meal	Noon meal	Noon meal	Noon meal
12:30-2:00 p.m.	Individual counseling 12:30-1:30 Gambling group	Individual counseling	Individual counseling	Free time	Individual counseling
1:00-2:00	Young adult group	1:30-3:00 Interpersonal group	Young adult group	Free time	Young adult group
2:00-3:00	Contracts group	3:00-3:30 Family conjoints (if scheduled) Free time	Contracts group	Video	Contracts group
3:30-4:00	Lecture	Video	Topic group	Men's and women's groups	Lecture
4:30-5:00	Exercise time	Exercise time	Exercise time 4:30-5:15 Gambling group	Exercise time 4:30-5:15 Gambling group	Exercise time
5:15-5:35	Evening meal	Evening meal	Evening meal	Evening meal	Evening meal
5:45-7:00	Free time	Free time	Free time	Free time 6:45 Outside aftercare (if scheduled)	Free time
7:00-8:00	AA speaker	AA speaker 7:30 Outside AA meeting (if scheduled)	AA speaker	NA speaker	AA speaker 7:00 Outside GA meeting
Following the AA meeting	Personal inventory group	Personal inventory group	Personal inventory group	Personal inventory group	Personal inventory group
Following the personal inventory group	Relaxation group	Relaxation group	Relaxation group	Relaxation group	Relaxation group
9:00	Free time	Free time	Free time	Free time	8:30 Talking circle

Appendix 46

Adolescent Inpatient Program Schedule

Time	Monday	Tuesday	Wednesday	Thursday	Friday	Saturday	Sunday
7:00 a.m.	Wake up Showers	Wake up Showers	Wake up Showers	Wake up Showers	Wake up Showers	Wake up Showers	Sleep in
8:00	Room checks Goals	Room checks Goals	Room checks Goals	Room checks Goals	Room checks Goals	Room checks Goals	Sleep in
8:20	Breakfast	Breakfast	Breakfast	Breakfast	Breakfast	Breakfast	Wake up Showers
9:00	Lecture: Dr. Ron	Medical lecture	Daily meditation	Daily meditation	Community group	Daily meditation	9:15 Breakfast
9:30	Chores	Chores	Chores	Chores	Chores	Chores	Chores
10:00	Study time	Study time/ Inipi	Study time	Study time	Study time/ Group	Study time	Church
11:00	Exercise	Exercise	Exercise	Exercise	Exercise	Study time Interpersonal group	Church
12:20 p.m.	Lunch	Lunch	Lunch	Lunch	Lunch	Lunch	Lunch
1:00	Study time	Study time	Arts/Crafts	Study time	Group	Video	Free time
2:00	Interpersonal group	Recreation	Study time	Contracts group	Recreation	Recreation	Visitors
3:00	Red road	Contracts group Conjoints	Talking circle	Leisure Education	Recreation	Recreation	4:30 Visitors leave
4:30	Room checks Goals	Room checks Goals	Room checks Goals	Room checks Goals	Room checks Goals	Room checks Goals	Family process group
5:00	Red road	Group	Spirituality group	Video	Video	Group	Room checks Goals
5:45	Dinner	Dinner	Dinner	Dinner	Dinner	Dinner	Dinner
6:30	Study time	Study time	Study time	Study time	Study time	Study time	Study time
7:00	Topic group AA	Topic group AA	Topic group AA	Topic group AA	Corrective thinking	Topic group	Topic group
8:00	Recreation time Showers Phone	Recreation time Showers Phone	Recreation time Showers Phone	Recreation time Showers Phone	Recreation time Showers Phone	Recreation time Showers Phone	Recreation time Showers Phone
10:00	In rooms	In rooms	In rooms	In rooms	In rooms	In rooms	In rooms
10:30	Lights out	Lights out	Lights out	Lights out	Lights out	Lights out	Lights out

Appendix 47

Adult Outpatient Program Schedule

WEEK 1
Monday

6:00-6:30 p.m.	Open—Serenity Prayer
	Commitments
	Open discussion
	Group rules
6:30-7:15	Interpersonal relationship group
7:15-7:30	Break
7:30-9:00	Continue interpersonal group
9:00	Close—Lord's Prayer

Tuesday

6:00-6:30 p.m.	Open—Serenity Prayer
	Commitments
6:30-7:15	Spirituality group
7:15-7:30	Break
7:30-9:00	Continue spirituality group
	Family interpersonal group
9:00	Close—Lord's Prayer

Wednesday

6:00-6:30 p.m.	Open—Serenity Prayer
	Commitments
	Open discussion
	Beck Depression Inventories
6:30-7:15	Contracts group
7:15-7:30	Break
7:30-9:00	Continue contracts group
9:00	Close—Lord's Prayer

Each week, the schedule stays the same on Mondays and Wednesdays. The following schedules are rotating schedules on Tuesdays for each additional week.

WEEK 2
Tuesday

6:00-6:30 p.m.	Open—Serenity Prayer
	Commitments
6:30-7:15	Disease concept video and discussion
7:15-7:30	Break
7:30-9:00	Lecture and discussion on progression/Jellinek chart
	Family interpersonal group
9:00	Close—Lord's Prayer

WEEK 3
Tuesday

6:00-6:30 p.m.	Open—Serenity Prayer Commitments
6:30-7:15	*Recovery and the Family* video and discussion
7:15-7:30	Break
7:30-9:00	Lecture and discussion on family dynamics Family interpersonal group
9:00	Close—Lord's Prayer

WEEK 4
Tuesday

6:00-6:30 p.m.	Open—Serenity Prayer Commitments
6:30-7:15	*Chalk Talk* video and discussion
7:15-7:30	Break
7:30-9:00	Lecture and discussion on Steps One, Two, and Three Family interpersonal group
9:00	Close—Lord's Prayer

WEEK 5
Tuesday

6:00-6:30 p.m.	Open—Serenity Prayer Commitments
6:30-7:15	*Feelings* video and discussion
7:15-7:30	Break
7:30-9:00	Lecture and discussion on Steps Four, Five, Six, and Seven Family interpersonal group
9:00	Close—Lord's Prayer

WEEK 6
Tuesday

6:00-6:30 p.m.	Open—Serenity Prayer Commitments
6:30-7:15	*Medical Aspects* video and discussion
7:15-7:30	Break
7:30-9:00	Lecture and discussion on Steps Eight and Nine Family interpersonal group
9:00	Close—Lord's Prayer

WEEK 7
Tuesday

6:00-6:30 p.m.	Open—Serenity Prayer Commitments
6:30-7:15	*HIV* video and discussion
7:15-7:30	Break
7:30-9:00	Lecture and discussion on Steps Ten, Eleven, and Twelve Family interpersonal group
9:00	Close—Lord's Prayer

WEEK 8
Tuesday

6:00-6:30 p.m.	Open—Serenity Prayer Commitments
6:30-9:00	Social and recreational activities
9:00	Close—Lord's Prayer

Appendix 48

Adolescent Outpatient Program Schedule

WEEK 1
Monday

4:30 p.m.	Open—Serenity Prayer
	Highs and lows
	Open discussion
4:45	Interpersonal relationship group
5:20	Break
5:30	Continue interpersonal relationship group
6:30	Close—Lord's Prayer

Wednesday

4:30 p.m.	Open—Serenity Prayer
	Highs and lows
	Open discussion
4:45	Contracts group
5:20	Break
5:30	Continue contracts group
6:30	Close—Lord's Prayer

Thursday

4:30 p.m.	Open—Serenity Prayer
	Highs and lows
	Open discussion
4:45	*Pot* video
5:20	Break
5:30	Read, complete, and discuss *Pot* handout
6:30	Close—Lord's Prayer

Each week, the schedule stays the same on Mondays and Wednesdays. The following schedules are rotating schedules on Thursdays for each additional week.

WEEK 2
Thursday

4:30 p.m.	Open—Serenity Prayer
	Highs and lows
	Open discussion
4:45	*Three-Headed Dragon* video
5:20	Break
5:30	Discuss video and handout
6:30	Close—Lord's Prayer

WEEK 3
Thursday

4:30 p.m.	Open—Serenity Prayer
	Highs and lows
	Open discussion
4:45	*Step One* video
5:20	Break

5:30	Facts about alcohol test and discussion
6:30	Close—Lord's Prayer

WEEK 4
Thursday

4:30 p.m.	Open—Serenity Prayer
	Highs and lows
	Open discussion
4:45	*Teens and AA* video and discussion
5:20	Break
5:30	Sponsorship role-playing
6:30	Close—Lord's Prayer

WEEK 5
Thursday

4:30 p.m.	Open—Serenity Prayer
	Highs and lows
	Open discussion
4:45	*Soft Is the Heart of a Child* video
5:20	Break
5:30	Discuss systems dynamics roles
6:30	Close—Lord's Prayer

WEEK 6
Thursday

4:30 p.m.	Open—Serenity Prayer
	Highs and lows
	Open discussion
4:45	*What's Wrong With This Picture* video
5:20	Break
5:30	Values exercise and discussion
6:30	Close—Lord's Prayer

WEEK 7
Thursday

4:30 p.m.	Open—Serenity Prayer
	Highs and lows
	Open discussion
4:45	*Epitaph for a Drug User* video
5:20	Break
5:30	Lecture and discussion on HIV and AIDS
6:30	Close—Lord's Prayer

WEEK 8
Thursday

4:30 p.m.	Open—Serenity Prayer
	Highs and lows
	Open discussion
4:45	*Fetal Alcohol Syndrome* video
5:20	Break
5:30	Discussion regarding fetal alcohol syndrome and fetal alcohol effects
6:30	Close—Lord's Prayer

Appendix 49

Gambling Inpatient Program Schedule

WEEK 1

Day	Time	Activity
Monday	12:30-1:30 p.m.	Contracts
Tuesday	3:00-4:00 p.m.	Conjoint with family (family program)
	5:30-6:30 p.m.	Individual session
Wednesday	4:15-5:15 p.m.	Interpersonal group—journaling
Thursday	2:00-3:00 p.m.	Hooked video
	6:00-9:00 p.m.	Gambling group—outreach
Friday	4:15-5:15 p.m.	Group education (progression/characteristics)
	6:30-7:30 p.m.	Outside GA meeting
Saturday	3:00-5:00 p.m.	Individual sessions

WEEK 2

Day	Time	Activity
Monday	12:30-1:30 p.m.	Group—questions and contracts
Tuesday	3:00-4:00 p.m.	Conjoint with family (family program)
	5:30-6:30 p.m.	Individual session
Wednesday	4:15-5:15 p.m.	Interpersonal group—journaling
Thursday	2:00-3:00 p.m.	Compulsive Gambling (Part 1) video
	6:00-9:00 p.m.	Gambling group—outreach
Friday	4:15-5:15 p.m.	Group education (budgeting/financial)
	6:30-7:30 p.m.	Outside GA meeting
Saturday	3:00-5:00 p.m.	Individual sessions

WEEK 3

Day	Time	Activity
Monday	12:30-1:30 p.m.	Group—contracts and "Twenty Questions"
Tuesday	3:00-4:00 p.m.	Conjoint with family (family program)
	5:30-6:30 p.m.	Individual session
Wednesday	4:15-5:15 p.m.	Interpersonal group—journaling
Thursday	2:00-3:00 p.m.	Compulsive Gambling (Part 2) video
	6:00-9:00 p.m.	Gambling group—outreach
Friday	4:15-5:15 p.m.	Group (relapse prevention)
	6:30-7:30 p.m.	Outside GA meeting
Saturday	3:00-5:00 p.m.	Individual sessions

WEEK 4

Day	Time	Activity
Monday	12:30-1:30 p.m.	Group—contracts and "Twenty Questions"
Tuesday	3:00-4:00 p.m.	Conjoint with family (family program)
	5:30-6:30 p.m.	Individual session
Wednesday	4:15-5:15 p.m.	Interpersonal group—journaling
Thursday	2:00-3:00 p.m.	Broken Circle video
	6:00-9:00 p.m.	Gambling group—outreach
Friday	4:15-5:15 p.m.	Group (resentments/regrets)
	6:30-7:30 p.m.	Outside GA meeting
Saturday	3:00-5:00 p.m.	Individual sessions

NOTE: Individual sessions are to include assessments, evaluations, individual financial responsibility, and continuing care plans. Family conjoints are to be done during week of the family program, or more as needed, and are to be assessed on an individual basis.

Aspects of the gambling program are combined with all addiction-based disorders.

Family dynamics:	Family program scheduled for the first Monday and Tuesday following admission.
Problem solving:	Daily interpersonal groups
Relapse prevention:	Weekly in a 4-week cycle (triggers, thoughts, feelings, and slips)
Cross-addiction:	Lecture
Spirituality:	Weekly sessions with clergy

Appendix 50

Gambling Outpatient Program Schedule

WEEK 1

Monday	6:00-9:00 p.m.	Open Introductions Commitments Meetings attended Interpersonal group—share problems, feelings, and concerns and apply problem-solving skills
Wednesday	6:00-9:00 p.m.	Open Introductions Commitments Educational/Family group Family dynamics—identifying roles in the family
Thursday	6:00-9:00 p.m.	Open Introductions Commitments Contracts group—written exercises presented to the group

WEEK 2

Monday	6:00-9:00 p.m.	Open Introductions Commitments Meetings attended Interpersonal group—share problems, feelings, and concerns and apply problem-solving skills
Wednesday	6:00-9:00 p.m.	Open Introductions Commitments Educational/Family group Resolving conflicts—Communication Skills exercise (Appendix 14)
Thursday	6:00-9:00 p.m.	Open Introductions Commitments Contracts group—written exercises presented to the group

WEEK 3

Monday	6:00-9:00 p.m.	Open Introductions Commitments Meetings attended Interpersonal group—share problems, feelings, and concerns and apply problem-solving skills
Wednesday	6:00-9:00 p.m.	Open Introductions Commitments Educational/Family group Progression of gambling illness and characteristics of a compulsive gambler
Thursday	6:00-9:00 p.m.	Open Introductions Commitments Contracts group—written exercises presented to the group

WEEK 4
Monday	6:00-9:00 p.m.	Open
		Introductions
		Commitments
		Meetings attended
		Interpersonal group—share problems, feelings, and concerns and apply problem-solving skills
Wednesday	6:00-9:00 p.m.	Open
		Introductions
		Commitments
		Educational/Family group
		Lecture and discussion—relapse triggers
		Compulsive Gambling (Part 1) video
Thursday	6:00-9:00 p.m.	Open
		Introductions
		Commitments
		Contracts group—written exercises presented to the group

WEEK 5
Monday	6:00-9:00 p.m.	Open
		Introductions
		Commitments
		Meetings attended
		Interpersonal group—share problems, feelings, and concerns and apply problem-solving skills
Wednesday	6:00-9:00 p.m.	Open
		Introductions
		Commitments
		Educational/Family group
		Lecture—similarities of chemical addictions and compulsive gambling
		Compulsive Gambling (Part 2) video
Thursday	6:00-9:00 p.m.	Open
		Introductions
		Commitments
		Contracts group—written exercises presented to the group

WEEK 6
Monday	6:00-9:00 p.m.	Open
		Introductions
		Commitments
		Meetings attended
		Interpersonal group—share problems, feelings, and concerns and apply problem-solving skills
Wednesday	6:00-9:00 p.m.	Open
		Introductions
		Commitments
		Educational/Family group
		Lecture—transition from treatment to GA and aftercare
		Discharge planning group and referrals—develop a long-term personal recovery plan
Thursday	6:00-9:00 p.m.	Open
		Introductions
		Commitments
		Contracts group—written exercises presented to the group

Appendix 51

Intensive Outpatient/Partial Care/Day Treatment Program Schedule

WEEK 1
Monday

9:00 a.m.	Lecture—Jellinek chart
10:00	Interpersonal group
11:00	Gambling group—contracts
12:00 p.m.	Lunch
12:30	Topic group—relapse prevention
1:30	Medical aspects of alcoholism I and II—video and discussion
2:30	Reading group—NA
3:00	Close for the day

Tuesday

9:00 a.m.	Working a recovery program
10:00	Interpersonal group
11:00	Spiritual group—*Spiritual Aspects of Recovery* Father Martin video
12:00 p.m.	Lunch
12:30	Individual sessions and homework
1:30	Personal inventory group
2:30	Reading group—GA
3:00	Close for the day

Wednesday

9:00 a.m.	Lecture—Step One
10:00	Interpersonal group
11:00	Gambling group—budget
12:00 p.m.	Lunch
12:30	*Three-Headed Dragon* video and discussion
1:30	Topic group—sexuality
2:30	Reading group—AA
3:00	Close for the day

Thursday

9:00 a.m.	Community group
10:00	Interpersonal group
11:00	*Big Steve* video and discussion
12:00 p.m.	Lunch
12:30	Contracts group—all clients
1:30	Gambling group—journal
2:30	Treatment progress review
3:00	Close for the day

WEEK 2
Monday

9:00 a.m.	Lecture—Steps Two and Three
10:00	Interpersonal group
11:00	Gambling group—contracts
12:00 p.m.	Lunch
12:30	Topic group—spiritual assessment
1:30	HIV/AIDS video and discussion

2:30	Reading group—NA
3:00	Close for the day

Tuesday

9:00 a.m.	Lecture—stress management
10:00	Interpersonal group
11:00	Spiritual group—*Values* Father Martin video
12:00 p.m.	Lunch
12:30	Individual sessions and homework
1:30	Personal inventory group
2:30	Reading group—GA
3:00	Close for the day

Wednesday

9:00 a.m.	Lecture—Steps Four and Five
10:00	Interpersonal group
11:00	Gambling group—budget
12:00 p.m.	Lunch
12:30	*Everybody Wins* video and discussion
1:30	Topic group—addictive relationships
2:30	Reading group—AA
3:00	Close for the day

Thursday

9:00 a.m.	Community group
10:00	Interpersonal group
11:00	*Disease Concept* video and discussion
12:00 p.m.	Lunch
12:30	Contracts group—all clients
1:30	Gambling group—journal
2:30	Treatment progress review
3:00	Close for the day

WEEK 3

Monday

9:00 a.m.	Lecture—Steps Six and Seven
10:00	Interpersonal group
11:00	Gambling group—contracts
12:00 p.m.	Lunch
12:30	Topic group—guilt
1:30	*Back to Basics* Father Martin video and discussion
2:30	Reading group—NA
3:00	Close for the day

Tuesday

9:00 a.m.	Lecture—cross-addiction
10:00	Interpersonal group
11:00	Spiritual group—*I Am My Brother's Keeper* Father Martin video
12:00 p.m.	Lunch
12:30	Individual sessions and homework
1:30	Personal inventory group
2:30	Reading group—GA
3:00	Close for the day

Wednesday

9:00 a.m.	Lecture—Steps Eight and Nine
10:00	Interpersonal group
11:00	Gambling group—journal
12:00 p.m.	Lunch

12:30	*Even Up the Odds* video and discussion
1:30	Topic group—control
2:30	Reading group—AA
3:00	Close for the day

Thursday

9:00 a.m.	Community group
10:00	Interpersonal group
11:00	*Recovery and the Family* video and discussion
12:00 p.m.	Lunch
12:30	Contracts group—all clients
1:30	Gambling group—educational/interpersonal/budget
2:30	Treatment progress review
3:00	Close for the day

WEEK 4

Monday

9:00 a.m.	Lecture—Step Ten
10:00	Interpersonal group
11:00	Gambling group—contracts
12:00 p.m.	Lunch
12:30	Topic group—spiritual death
1:30	*Bill W. Story* video and discussion
2:30	Reading group—NA
3:00	Close for the day

Tuesday

9:00 a.m.	Lecture—denial
10:00	Interpersonal group
11:00	Spiritual group—*Feelings* Father Martin video
12:00 p.m.	Lunch
12:30	Individual sessions and homework
1:30	Personal inventory group
2:30	Reading group—GA
3:00	Close for the day

Wednesday

9:00 a.m.	Lecture—Step Eleven
10:00	Interpersonal group
11:00	Gambling group—journal
12:00 p.m.	Lunch
12:30	*Relapse Prevention: The Facts* video and discussion
1:30	Topic group—frozen feelings
2:30	Reading group—AA
3:00	Close for the day

Thursday

9:00 a.m.	Community group
10:00	Interpersonal group
11:00	*Medical Aspects of Mind-Altering Drugs* video and discussion
12:00 p.m.	Lunch
12:30	Contracts group—all clients
1:30	Gambling group—educational/interpersonal/budget
2:30	Treatment progress review
3:00	Close for the day

Appendix 52

Pressure Relief Group Meeting and Budget Forms

TO THE GAMBLERS ANONYMOUS GROUP

When a member attends his or her first meeting, it is important that a pressure relief meeting be explained to him or her and that a member will contact him or her within 30 days to arrange a pressure relief meeting.

The member should be told to contact all creditors and tell them that he or she will be back to them in 30 days. It should be emphasized that no payments should be made and also that no commitment of dollar amounts should be promised. Each member should be told to choose someone to take care of his or her money (spouse if married). It is suggested that the member's name be removed from all items of value (e.g., house, cars, stocks, bonds, bank books, credit cards, checking accounts). The member should be told not to carry more money than he or she needs for daily essentials.

The pressure relief meeting should be given only by a Gamblers Anonymous (GA) member experienced in pressure relief procedures. There should be at least one other GA member and a Gam-Anon member present. The pressure relief meeting should not take place at a member's home; there could be too many distractions. Do not plan a pressure relief meeting at a GA meeting room prior to a regularly scheduled meeting.

One week prior to the pressure relief meeting, the member should be given copies of the budget forms.

The pressure relief committee should schedule a reevaluation date approximately 6 months after the pressure relief meeting.

Dear Gamblers Anonymous Member:

According to the standards set forth by your local Gamblers Anonymous chapter, you are now eligible for a pressure group.

An integral part of your recovery is that of making financial restitution. Considering the fact that your debts usually are much greater than those of the average individual, it is vitally important that great care be taken when planning a manageable budget. The key word is manageable. It is very difficult for anyone to live a normal life while being overburdened with financial pressures, especially for a compulsive gambler.

The main concepts behind a compulsive gambler's pressure relief meeting are to allow the gambler and his or her family to be able to lead a normal life and, at the same time, make financial restitution to his or her creditors.

The first step in planning a budget requires total honesty. If you have withheld any information pertaining to your debts, now is the time to become totally honest. Hopefully, by now you have followed the advice of your fellow Gamblers Anonymous members and have done the following:

1. Contact all creditors and ask for a 30- to 45-day moratorium on payments. Be sure not to pay anyone, and do not make any financial commitments.
2. Choose someone to handle your money (spouse if married).
3. Turn all ownership of properties (e.g., home, car) over to someone else.
4. Remove your name from all bank books, checking accounts, and credit cards.
5. Turn over all paychecks uncashed with stubs attached to the individual who will manage your money.

THE CHOICE IS YOURS

The choice between paying over a long period of time, while functioning and living as a human being, or complete collapse due to immense financial pressures that cannot be met is, in reality, not a choice at all but rather the only avenue that will return you back to sanity and solvency. You have to be honest, forthright, and humble in regard to the debts that you owe and in your determination to repay them. Gamblers Anonymous's experience has shown that our creditors, in a very human and helpful way, will respond to sincerity, honesty, and courage but will rightfully reject arrogance and self-pity. Everyone is willing to help a person who is down (and who wants to get back up), but much more important is the willingness to help yourself. This is the key. This is the quest. This is the never-ending endeavor.

Have faith in the Gamblers Anonymous program and follow the budget that will be set up for you. If you adhere to the budget and refrain from gambling, your financial pressures will soon be relieved, and this will greatly improve your chances for recovery. Remember that you have a gambling problem, not a financial problem. Go slow; take it *one day at a time.*

DIRECTIONS

Please complete these pages with the most accurate and up-to-date information that you have available. Do not leave anything out.

TO THE CREDITOR

Dear Creditor:

The attached budget has been prepared for _____, who is a member of Gamblers Anonymous. He/she has admitted that he/she is a compulsive gambler and that his/her life has become unmanageable. An integral part of the compulsive gambler's recovery is to make restitution to all of his/her creditors. Due to the fact that the compulsive gambler has accumulated a large debt, it may be necessary to repay you over a long period of time. If a previous repayment schedule already exists, the compulsive gambler may have to give you smaller payments and, therefore, take longer to repay his/her debt.

As you can see by the prepared budget, the compulsive gambler must provide for all living expenses for himself/herself and his/her family before paying his/her debts. The repayment schedule has been prepared by experienced members of Gamblers Anonymous. The amount suggested for repayment of each debt was based on the amount originally borrowed, the balance due, and the original monthly payment.

The compulsive gambler is not claiming bankruptcy and is not running away. He/she wants to repay his/her debts.

Your cooperation is greatly appreciated.

Gamblers Anonymous is not responsible for the information listed on this form, nor does it guarantee the compliance of the proposed financial arrangement on this form.

Signed:

Pressure Relief Chairperson

Name _____ Spouse's Name _____ Date _____

GA Group _____

Budget Committee Chairperson _____ Others _____

Member's Phone _____ Chairperson's Phone _____

Reevaluation Date _____

BUDGET

Expenses	Per Month[a]	Per Week
Alimony		
Allowance (children)		
Allowance (member)		
Allowance (spouse)		
Auto insurance		
Auto license		
Auto payment		
Auto registration		
Auto repairs		
Auto taxes/Tolls		
Babysitter		
Cable TV		
Car fare		
Child support/Day care		
Children's activities		
Christmas/Hanukkah gifts		
Cigarettes		
Clothing		
Coal/Wood/Kerosene		
Dentist		
Doctor		
Donations (e.g., church, temple, GA, Gam-Anon)		
Drugs and toiletries		
Dry cleaning and laundry		
Electricity		
Emergencies (e.g., home repairs)		

Expenses	Per Month[a]	Per Week
Eyeglasses/Contacts		
Family entertainment		
Film and developing		
Food		
Gamblers Anonymous conferences		
Garbage removal		
Gas (home)		
Gasoline (auto)		
Gifts (e.g., birthdays, anniversaries)		
Haircuts/Beauty salon		
Homeowner's/Renter's insurance		
Life insurance (term)		
Life-liner contribution		
Lunches (work)		
Medical insurance		
Mortgage (first)		
Mortgage (second)		
Mortgage (third)		
Music lessons		
Newspapers/Magazines		
Oil heat		
Pet care		
Postage		
Rent		
Savings/Retirement funds		
School tuition		
Taxes (income)		
Taxes (property)		
Telephone		
Therapy/Counseling		
Union/Club dues		
Vacation		
Water		
ITEMS NOT LISTED:		
TOTAL EXPENSES		

a. 4.33 weeks per month.

LIST OF CREDITORS

Please list, in the following order, (1) bad checks or debts for which you may be prosecuted, (2) court-ordered judgments, (3) credit unions, (4) bank or finance company loans, (5) back taxes, (6) credit cards, (7) bookmakers and loan sharks, (8) family and friends, and (9) others.

Creditor's Name	Date of Debt	Original Amount	Present Balance	Monthly Payment	Months in Default	Co-Signer

REPAYMENT SCHEDULE

Creditor's Name	Original Balance	Balance	Monthly Payment	Weekly Payment	Date of First Payment	Estimated Date of Last Payment

FINANCIAL SUMMARY

Income	Per Month	Per Week
Primary job		
Secondary job		
Pensions		
Child support		
Alimony		
Property income		
Spouse's income available		
Other income		
TOTAL		

TOTAL INCOME: _____

SUBTRACT TOTAL EXPENSES: _____

AMOUNT AVAILABLE FOR REPAYMENT: _____

Gamblers Anonymous is not responsible for the information listed on this form, nor does it guarantee the compliance of the proposed financial arrangement on this form.

Appendix 53

Heroin: Abuse and Addiction
National Institute on Drug Abuse

TREATMENTS FOR HEROIN ADDICTION

A variety of effective treatments are available for heroin addiction. Treatment tends to be more effective when heroin abuse is identified early. The treatments that follow vary depending on the individual, but methadone, a synthetic opiate that blocks the effects of heroin and eliminates withdrawal symptoms, has a proven record of success for people addicted to heroin. Other pharmaceutical approaches (e.g., LAAM (levo-alpha-acetylmethadol), buprenorphine), as well as many behavioral therapies, also are used for treating heroin addiction.

Detoxification

The primary objective of detoxification is to relieve withdrawal symptoms while patients adjust to a drug-free state. Not in itself a treatment for addiction, detoxification is a useful step only when it leads to long-term treatment that either is drug free (residential or outpatient) or uses medications as part of the treatment. The best-documented drug-free treatments are the therapeutic community residential programs lasting at least 3 to 6 months.

Methadone Programs

Methadone treatment has been used effectively and safely to treat opioid addiction for more than 30 years. Properly prescribed methadone is not intoxicating or sedating, and its effects do not interfere with ordinary activities such as driving a car. The medication is taken orally, and it suppresses narcotic withdrawal for 24 to 36 hours. Patients are able to perceive pain and have emotional reactions. Most important, methadone relieves the craving associated with heroin addiction (craving is a major reason for relapse). Among methadone patients, it has been found that normal street doses of heroin are ineffective at producing euphoria, thereby making the use of heroin more easily extinguishable.

Methadone's effects last for about 24 hours—four to six times as long as those of heroin—so people in treatment need to take it only once a day. Also, methadone is medically safe even when used continuously for 10 years or more. Combined with behavioral therapies or counseling and other supportive services, methadone enables patients to stop using heroin (and other opiates) and return to more stable and productive lives.

Methadone doses must be monitored carefully in patients who are receiving antiviral therapy for HIV infection so as to avoid potential medication interactions.

LAAM and Other Medications

LAAM, like methadone, is a synthetic opiate that can be used to treat heroin addiction. LAAM can block the effects of heroin for up to 72 hours with minimal side effects when taken orally. In 1993, the Food and Drug Administration approved the use of LAAM for treating patients addicted to heroin. Its long duration of action permits dosing just three times per week, thereby eliminating the need for daily dosing and take-home doses for weekends. LAAM will be increasingly available in clinics that already dispense methadone. Naloxone and naltrexone are medications that also block the effects of morphine, heroin, and other opiates. As antagonists, they are especially useful as antidotes. Naltrexone has long-lasting effects, ranging from 1 to 3 days depending on the dose. Naltrexone blocks the pleasurable effects of heroin and is useful in treating some highly motivated individuals. Naltrexone also has been found to be successful in preventing relapse by former opiate addicts released from prison on probation.

Another medication to treat heroin addiction, buprenorphine, is a particularly attractive treatment because, compared to other medications such as methadone, it causes weaker opiate effects and is less likely to cause overdose problems. Buprenorphine also produces a lower level of physical dependence, so patients who discontinue the medication generally have fewer withdrawal symptoms than do those who stop taking methadone. Because of these advantages, buprenorphine may be appropriate for use in a wider variety of treatment settings than is the case with the currently available medications. Several other medications with potential for treating heroin overdose or addiction currently are under investigation by the National Institute on Drug Abuse.

Behavioral Therapies

Although behavioral and pharmacological treatments can be extremely useful when employed alone, science has taught us that integrating both types of treatments ultimately will be the most effective approach. There are many effective behavioral treatments available for heroin addiction. These can include residential and outpatient approaches. An important task is to match the best treatment approach to meet the particular needs of the patient. Moreover, several new behavioral therapies, such as contingency management therapy and cognitive-behavioral interventions, show particular promise as treatments for heroin addiction. Contingency management therapy uses a voucher-based system, where the patient earns points based on negative drug tests that the patient can exchange for items that encourage healthy living. Cognitive-behavioral interventions are designed to help modify the patient's thinking, expectancies, and behaviors and to increase skills in coping with various life stressors. Both behavioral and pharmacological treatments help to restore a degree of normalcy to brain function and behavior, with increased employment rates and lower risk of HIV and other diseases and criminal behavior.

OPIOID ANALOGS AND THEIR DANGERS

Drug analogs are chemical compounds that are similar to other drugs in their effects but differ slightly in their chemical structure. Some analogs are produced by pharmaceutical companies for legitimate medical reasons. Other analogs, sometimes referred to as "designer" drugs, can be produced in illegal laboratories and often are more dangerous and potent than the original drugs. Two of the most commonly known opioid analogs are fentanyl and meperidine (e.g., marketed under the brand name Demerol).

Fentanyl was introduced in 1968 by a Belgian pharmaceutical company as a synthetic narcotic to be used as an analgesic in surgical procedures because of its minimal effects on the heart. Fentanyl is particularly dangerous because it is 50 times more potent than heroin and can rapidly stop respiration. This is not a problem during surgical procedures because machines are used to help patients breathe. On the street, however, users have been found dead with the needles used to inject the drug still in their arms.

Methadone Programs

There are approximately 980,000 heroin addicts in the United States, and 20% receive methadone or LAAM. A patient who comes into a methadone clinic first receives a complete physical, biopsychosocial, and treatment plan. The patient is stabilized on liquid methadone (up to 100 milligrams per day). Then the counselor begins to talk to the patient about treatment. Does the patient want to be on methadone forever, or does the patient want to work toward abstinence? All patients need to be encouraged to move toward abstinence as the ultimate goal.

The patient needs to be stabilized on enough methadone to get his or her life back from abusing drugs on the street. Methadone levels are taken to verify compliance. When the time is right, methadone is tapered very slowly, as little as 2 milligrams per month or as much as the patient can comfortably tolerate. At any point, the patient may reach a level where he or she cannot decrease any further without going into uncomfortable withdrawal symptoms. The patient is maintained at the lowest level until another decrease can be attempted.

All patients have a monthly drug screen, and if their urine is found to be positive for substances of abuse, then they discuss this with their counselors and make plans for abstaining. Patients should not be discharged from treatment just because they use. Recovery is a program of progress, not perfection.

Patients can earn take-home doses of methadone by having clean urine samples for a required period, usually one take-home dose for each month clean. They can get guest doses from another clinic if they travel.

Patients should get individual, group, or family therapy each month as needed. The extent of this counseling is negotiated between the patients and their counselors. All methadone patients need to be examined for chronic pain syndromes to meet the needs of this population. A pain management team is used to help these patients manage the pain and the addiction simultaneously. Patients need to be educated about pregnancy, parenting, reproductive health, and HIV/AIDS as they go through treatment.

More information on methadone can be obtained from the National Association of Methadone Advocates (www.methadone.org) and the National Institute on Drug Abuse (nida.nih.gov).

Appendix 54

South Oaks Gambling Screen

1. Indicate which of the following types of gambling you have done in your lifetime. For each type, mark one answer: *not at all, less than once a week,* or *once a week or more.*

	Not at All	Less Than Once a Week	Once a Week or More
a. Played cards for money	_____	_____	_____
b. Bet on horses, dogs, or other animals (in off-track betting, at the track, or with a bookie)	_____	_____	_____
c. Bet on sports (parley cards, with a bookie, or at jai alai)	_____	_____	_____
d. Played dice games (including craps, over and under, or other dice games) for money	_____	_____	_____
e. Went to casino (legal or otherwise)	_____	_____	_____
f. Played the numbers or bet on lotteries	_____	_____	_____
g. Played Bingo	_____	_____	_____
h. Played the stock and/or commodities market	_____	_____	_____
i. Played slot machines, poker machines, or other gambling machines	_____	_____	_____
j. Bowled, shot pool, played golf, or played some other game of skill for money	_____	_____	_____

2. What is the largest amount of money you have ever gambled with on any one day?
   - _____ Never have gambled
   - _____ More than $100 up to $1,000
   - _____ $10 or less
   - _____ More than $1,000 up to $10,000
   - _____ More than $10 up to $100
   - _____ More than $10,000

3. Do (Did) your parents have a gambling problem?
   - _____ Both my father and mother gamble (gambled) too much.
   - _____ My father gambles (gambled) too much.
   - _____ My mother gambles (gambled) too much.
   - _____ Neither parent gambles (gambled) too much.

4. When you gamble, how often do you go back another day to win back money you lost?
   - _____ Never
   - _____ Some of the time (less than half of the time) I lost
   - _____ Most of the time I lost
   - _____ Every time I lost

5. Have you ever claimed to be winning money gambling but were not really winning? In fact, you lost?

_____ Never (or never gamble)

_____ Yes, less than half of the time I lost

_____ Yes, most of the time

6. Do you feel that you have ever had a problem with gambling?

_____ No

_____ Yes, in the past, but not now

_____ Yes

	Yes	No
7. Did you ever gamble more than you intended?	_____	_____
8. Have people criticized your gambling?	_____	_____
9. Have you ever felt guilty about the way in which you gamble or what happens when you gamble?	_____	_____
10. Have you ever felt as though you would like to stop gambling but did not think that you could?	_____	_____
11. Have you ever hidden betting slips, lottery tickets, gambling money, or other signs of gambling from your spouse, children, or other important people in your life?	_____	_____
12. Have you ever argued with people you like over how you handle money?	_____	_____
13. (If you answered yes to Question 12): Have money arguments ever centered on your gambling?	_____	_____
14. Have you ever borrowed from someone and not paid the person back as a result of your gambling?	_____	_____
15. Have you ever lost time from work (or school) due to gambling?	_____	_____
16. If you borrowed money to gamble or to pay gambling debts, where did you borrow from? (Check yes or no for each.)		
a. From household money	_____	_____
b. From your spouse	_____	_____
c. From other relatives or in-laws	_____	_____
d. From banks, loan companies, or credit unions	_____	_____
e. From credit cards	_____	_____
f. From loan sharks (shylocks)	_____	_____
g. You cashed in stocks, bonds or other securities	_____	_____
h. You sold personal or family property	_____	_____
i. You borrowed on your checking account (passed bad checks)	_____	_____
j. You have (had) a credit line with a bookie	_____	_____
k. You have (had) a credit line with a casino	_____	_____

Scores are determined by adding up the number of questions that show an "at risk" response, indicated as follows. If you answered the preceding questions with one of the following answers, then mark the space next to that question:

Questions 1 to 3 are not counted.

_____ Question 4: Most of the time I lost *or* Every time I lost

_____ Question 5: Yes, less than half of the time I lost *or* Yes, most of the time

_____ Question 6: Yes, in the past, but not now *or* Yes

_____ Question 7: Yes

_____ Question 8: Yes

_____ Question 9: Yes

_____ Question 10: Yes

_____ Question 11: Yes

Question 12 is not counted.

_____ Question 13: Yes

_____ Question 14: Yes

_____ Question 15: Yes

_____ Question 16a: Yes

_____ Question 16b: Yes

_____ Question 16c: Yes

_____ Question 16d: Yes

_____ Question 16e: Yes

_____ Question 16f: Yes

_____ Question 16g: Yes

_____ Question 16h: Yes

_____ Question 16i: Yes

Questions 16j and 16k are not counted.

TOTAL = _____ (20 questions are counted)

3 or 4 = Potential pathological gambler (problem gambler)

5 or more = Probable pathological gambler

Appendix 55

Barriers in Thinking

BLUEPRINT FOR CHANGE

● **Barriers in Thinking**	➤ **Appropriate Staff Responses**	❖ **Steps to Responsible Thinking**

1. Closed Thinking
• Non-receptive
• That's my business
• "He started it."
• Good at pointing out faults of others
• Little or no self-discipline
• Deceives by omitting facts
• Is not self-critical
• Disregards feedback from others.
	➤ Require complete honesty
	➤ Point out lies
	➤ Point out contradictions
	➤ Check to see if the individual has understood what has been said.
	➤ Avoid argument—stay focused by calmly repeating yourself
	  • "Can you and I have an agreement?"
	  • "What Thinking led you to choose . . ."
	  • "Let's look at what others who've succeeded have done."
	➤ Help the individual see their part in the situation.
		1. Open Channels
		❖ Receptive to positive change
		❖ Is doing things differently
		❖ Communicates openly and honestly
		❖ Evaluates self honestly and critically

2. Victim Role
• Sees self as victim (not victimizer)
• "She started it."
• "I couldn't help it"
• "He didn't give me a chance"
• Blames others or authorities to make them feel it is their fault
• Blames environment, poverty, race, etc.
• States that others can't be trusted.
	➤ Accept no excuses
	➤ Bring the focus back to the individual
	➤ Emphasize reasons the individual cannot be trusted or has betrayed trust.
	➤ Never let betrayal, rule-breaking, or crime go unnoticed/ without consequences
	➤ Insist on trust being earned
	  • "What led you to choose . . . ?"
	  • "What is your responsibility?"
	  • "What will you do differently?"
		3. Personal Accountability
		❖ Proves to be reliable, prompt, and prepared
		❖ Fulfills commitments and promises
		❖ Takes responsibility for choices and actions
		❖ Works at changing destructive patterns

● **Barriers in Thinking**	➤ **Appropriate Staff Responses**	❖ **Steps to Responsible Thinking**
3. Superior Self-Image • Focuses only on positive traits • "I'm a good guy" • "There's nothing wrong with me . . ." • "It's no big deal . . ." • Refuses to admit harm to others • Fails to acknowledge own destructive behavior	➤ Point out harm that's been done (use ripple chart) ➤ Do not allow minimizing, point to reality of their behavior ➤ Help the individual realize that good actions do not cancel out harmful actions • "Look inside yourself and decide." • "Ask yourself on the inside . . ." • "Only you can convince yourself." • "What effect have you had on others?"	**3. Self Respect** ❖ Shows gratitude ❖ Earns others' respect ❖ Explores alternatives before acting ❖ Controls feelings and works toward positive solutions
4. Reckless Attitude • Says, "I can't," when means "I won't" • No concept of obligation • Unwilling to do anything boring or disagreeable • Considers responsible living to be dull and unsatisfying • Complies only when immediate benefits exist • Exhibits self-pity • Psychosomatic aches and pains to avoid effort • Tries to prove inability when actually refusing to comply • Denies obligation by saying, "I forgot" • Lacks empathy for others • Fails to put self in others' place • Apathetic • Gets excited doing the forbidden • Does not look for alternatives • Short attention span • Gives up or quits early	➤ Do not accept "I can't," when it means "I won't" ➤ Give consequences for lack of effort ➤ Point out the energy the individuals have for activities they like ➤ Explain how to meet obligations ➤ Encourage individuals to stick with it until genuine interest develops ➤ Ask how they would feel if others did not meet obligations or "forgot," such as parents not feeding or providing for them. ➤ Use a "victim script" to get the individual to develop empathy for others ➤ Emphasize consequences of failing to meet obligations or being irresponsible ➤ Emphasize consequences of crime or breaking rules. ➤ Emphasize consequences of apathy and procrastination • "What do you want to accomplish?" • "What are your obligations to . . . ?" • "What can you do to improve your relationship with . . . ?"	**4. Daily Effort** ❖ Is considerate of others ❖ Has healthy relationships ❖ Works toward resolution ❖ Balances time, work, and fun to achieve what is expected ❖ Fulfills obligations to family, friends, teacher, employer, community ❖ Realizes that interest and motivation follow effort and change

● Barriers in Thinking	➤ Appropriate Staff Responses	❖ Steps to Responsible Thinking
5. Instant Gratification—"I want it now" • Does not learn from past mistakes • Demands an immediate response • Makes decisions on feelings • Fails to plan ahead except to accomplish the forbidden or to imagine getting away with it • Believes success comes overnight • Thinks failure is anything less than #1 • Easily slips into "0" State when tactics are interrupted • Blames someone or something immediately. Does not suspend judgment for more information	➤ Point out irresponsible decision-making based on feelings or assumptions ➤ Help individuals examine faulty assumptions and find facts ➤ Explain how some decisions cannot be made immediately or may not work out as planned ➤ Emphasize that time and effort are necessary to gain benefits or payoffs from being responsible ➤ Help individuals establish habits of thinking ahead at every step ➤ Help them view things in stages of accomplishment ➤ Aid them in building toward something important to them ➤ Assist them in the process of learning from mistakes 　• "What's important about . . .?" 　• "How will this affect your future?" 　• "Have you done the same thing before?" 　• "What are the facts?"	**5. Self Discipline** ❖ Exhibits patience with others ❖ Shows patience when facing problems ❖ Plans and builds toward the future ❖ Makes decisions on facts, not feelings ❖ Learns from the past and relies on guilt feelings to consider the effects upon others
6. Fear of "Losing Face" • Profound fear of personal insults • Has irrational fears but refuses to admit them • Feels put-down when things don't go his or her way • Experiences "0" State—powerless when held accountable	➤ Identify and challenge fears ➤ Teach that criticism is something everyone needs when it is accurate ➤ Address the individuals' need to trust responsible others ➤ Show where his or her expectations were unrealistic 　• "What would it take for you to respect yourself?" 　• "Who do you trust?" 　• "If you could get help with something, what would that be?"	**6. Courage Over Fear** ❖ Sees criticism as helpful feedback ❖ Acts on feedback from others ❖ Trusts others and asks for advice or help on what to do or how to do things ❖ Admits fears ❖ Meets challenges without dodging

References

Abelson, H. I., Fishburne, P., & Cisin, I. H. (1977). *National Survey on Drug Abuse, 1977: A nationwide study—Youth, young adults, and older adults, Vol. 1: Main findings* (Publ. No. [ADM] 78-618). Washington, DC: Government Printing Office.

Adams, E. H., Blanken, A. J., Ferguson, L. D., & Kopstein, A. (1990). *Overview of selected drug trends.* Rockville, MD: National Institute on Drug Abuse.

Adams, R. D., & Victor, M. (1981). *Principles of neurology.* New York: McGraw-Hill.

Adinoff, B., Bone, G. H. A., & Linnolila, M. (1988). Acute ethanol poisoning and the ethanol withdrawal syndrome. *Toxicology Management Review, 3,* 172-196.

AIDS and Chemical Dependency Committee. (1988). *Guidelines for facilities treating chemical dependency patients at risk for AIDS and HIV infection* (2nd ed.). New York: American Medical Society on Alcoholism and Other Drug Dependencies.

Aigner, T. G., & Balster, R. L. (1978). Choice of behavior in Rhesus monkeys: Cocaine versus food. *Science, 201,* 534-535.

Al-Anon Family Group Headquarters. (1973). *Alateen: A day at a time.* New York: Author.

Al-Anon Family Group Headquarters. (1995). *One day at a time in Al-Anon.* New York: Author.

Alberti, R. E., & Emmons, M. L. (1995). *Your perfect right: A guide to assertive living.* Atascadero, CA: Impact Publishers.

Alcoholics Anonymous. (1976). *Alcoholics Anonymous.* New York: Alcoholics Anonymous World Services.

Alcoholics Anonymous. (1981). *Twelve Steps and Twelve Traditions.* New York: Alcoholics Anonymous World Services.

Alexander, E. J. (1951). Withdrawal effects of sodium amytal. *Diseases of the Nervous System, 12,* 77-82.

Alexander, J. F. (1974). Behavior modification and delinquent youth. In J. C. Cull & R. E. Hardy (Eds.), *Behavior modification in rehabilitation settings.* Springfield, IL: Charles C Thomas.

Alexander, J. F., & Parsons, B. V. (1973). Short term behavioral intervention with delinquent families. *Journal of Abnormal Psychology, 81,* 219-255.

American Psychiatric Association. (1994). *Diagnostic and statistical manual of mental disorders* (4th ed.). Washington, DC: American Psychiatric Press.

Anderson, J. (1941, March). Alcoholics Anonymous. *The Saturday Evening Post.*

Anglin, M. D., & Hser, Y. (1990). Treatment of drug abuse. In M. Tonry & J. Q. Wilson (Eds.), *Drugs and crime* (pp. 339-460). Chicago: University of Chicago Press.

Anthenelli, R. M., & Schuckit, M. A. (1994). Genetic influences in addiction. In N. S. Miller & M. C. Doot (Eds.), *Principles of addiction medicine* (sec. 1, chap. 6, pp. 1-14). Chevy Chase, MD: American Society of Addiction Medicine.

Appenzeller, O., Standefer, J., Appenzeller, J., & Atkinson, R. (1980). Neurology of endurance training: V. Endorphins. *Neurology, 30,* 418-419.

Atkinson, R. M., & Kofed, L. L. (1984). Substance use and abuse in old age. *Substance Abuse, 5,* 30-42.

Balster, R. L., & Chait, L. D. (1978). The behavioral effects of phencyclidine in animals. In R. C. Petersen & R. C. Stillman (Eds.), *PCP phencyclidine abuse: An appraisal* (Publ. No. [ADM] 78-728, pp. 53-65). Washington, DC: Government Printing Office.

Baum, R., & Iber, F. L. (1980). Initial treatment of the alcoholic patient. In S. E. Gitlow & H. S. Peyser (Eds.), *Alcoholism: A practical treatment guide.* New York: Grune & Stratton.

Beattie, M. (1987). *Codependent no more: How to stop controlling others and start caring for yourself.* Center City, MN: Hazelden.

Beck, A. T. (1967). *Depression: Clinical, experimental, and theoretical aspects.* New York: Harper & Row.

Beck, A. T. (1972). *Depression: Causes and treatment.* Philadelphia: University of Pennsylvania Press.

Beck, A. T. (1976). *Cognitive therapy and the emotional disorders.* New York: International Universities Press.

Beck, A. T. (1978). *Depression Inventory.* Philadelphia: Center for Cognitive Therapy.

Beck, A. T., & Emery, G. (1979). *Coping with anxiety and panic: SCT method.* Philadelphia: Center for Cognitive Therapy.

Beck, A. T., & Greenberg, R. (1974). *Coping with depression.* Philadelphia: Center for Cognitive Therapy.

Beck, A. T., Rush, J. A., Shaw, B. F., & Emery, G. (1979). *Cognitive therapy of depression.* New York: Guilford.

Beck, A. T., Ward, C. H., Mandelson, M., Mock, J., & Erbaugh, J. (1961). An inventory for measuring depression. *Archives of General Psychiatry, 4,* 561-571.

Beitman, B. D., Carlin, A. S., & Chiles, J. C. (1984). Pharmacotherapy-psychotherapy triangle: A physician, a non-medical psychotherapist, and a patient. *Journal of Clinical Psychiatry, 45,* 458-459.

Benson, H. (1975). *The relaxation response.* New York: William Morrow.

Berne, E. (1964). *Games people play: The psychology of human relationships.* New York: Grove.

Bettet, P. S., & Maloney, M. J. (1991). The importance of empathy as an interviewing skill in medicine. *Journal of the American Medical Association, 266,* 1831-1832.

Block, J. (1971). *Lives through time.* Berkeley, CA: Bancroft Books.

Blumenthal, S. J. (1990). An overview and synopsis of risk factors, assessment, and treatment of suicidal patients over the life cycle. In S. J. Blumenthal & D. I. Kupfer (Eds.), *Suicide over the life cycle: Risk factors, assessment, and treatment of suicidal patients.* Washington, DC: American Psychiatric Press.

Bradshaw, J. (1988). *Healing the shame that binds you.* Deerfield Beach, FL: Health Communications.

Bradshaw, J. (1990). *Homecoming: Reclaiming and championing your inner child.* New York: Bantam Books.

Braunwald, E., Isselbacher, K. T., Petersdorf, R. G., Wilson, J. D., Martin, J. B., & Fauci, A. S. (1987). *Harrison's principles of internal medicine.* New York: McGraw-Hill.

Brostoff, W. S. (1994). Clinical diagnosis. In N. S. Miller & M. C. Doot (Eds.), *Principles of addiction medicine* (sec. 4, chap. 1, pp. 1-4). Chevy Chase, MD: American Society of Addiction Medicine.

Brown, B. W., Monck, E. M., Carstairs, G. M., & Wing, J. K. (1962). Influence of family life on the course of schizophrenic illness. *British Journal of Preventative Social Medicine, 16,* 55-68.

Burant, D. (1990). Management of withdrawal. In A. Geller (Ed.), *Syllabus for the review course in addiction medicine.* Washington, DC: American Society of Addiction Medicine.

Burns, D. D. (1980). *Feeling good: The new mood therapy.* New York: Signet.

Burns, D. D. (1990). *The feeling good handbook.* New York: Penguin.

Caracci, L., Megone, P., & Dornbush, R. (1983). Phencyclidine in an East Harlem psychiatric population. *Journal of the National Medical Association, 75,* 869-874.

Carroll, M., & Comer, S. (1994). The pharmacology of phencyclidine and the hallucinogens. In N. S. Miller & M. C. Doot (Eds.), *Principles of addiction medicine* (sec. 2, chap. 7, p. 153). Chevy Chase, MD: American Society of Addiction Medicine.

Carroll, M., & Comer, S. (1998). Phencyclidine and the hallucinogens. In A. W. Graham, T. K. Schultz, & B. B. Wilford (Eds.), *Principles of addiction medicine* (sec. 2, chap. 7, pp. 1-9). Chevy Chase, MD: American Society of Addiction Medicine.

Centers for Disease Control. (1990). *HIV/AIDS surveillance report.* Atlanta, GA: Author.

Centers for Disease Control. (2000). *Tobacco information and prevention source.* Atlanta, GA: Author.

Chatlos, J. C., & Jaffe, S. L. (1994). A developmental biopsychosocial model of adolescent addiction. In N. S. Miller & M. C. Doot (Eds.), *Principles of addiction medicine* (sec. 17, chap. 1, pp. 1-5). Chevy Chase, MD: American Society of Addiction Medicine.

Chopra, G. S., & Smith, J. W. (1974). Psychotic reactions following cannabis use in East Indians. *Archives of General Psychiatry, 30,* 24-27.

Cloptin, P. L., Janowsky, D. S., Cloptin, J. M., Judd, L. L., and Huey, L. (1979). Marihuana and the perception of affect. *Psychopharmacology, 61,* 203-206.

Cohen, H. L., Filipczak, J. A., & Bis, J. S. (1965). *Case project: Contingencies application for special education* (progress report). Washington, DC: U.S. Department of Health, Education, and Welfare.

Cohen, H. L., & Filipczak, J. A. (1971). *A new learning environment.* San Francisco: Jossey-Bass.

Cohen, S. (1979). Inhalants. In R. I. DuPont, A. Goldstein, and J. O'Donnell (Eds.), *Handbook on drug abuse* (pp. 213-220). Washington, DC: Government Printing Office.

Committee for the Study and Treatment and Rehabilitation Services for Alcoholism and Alcohol Abuse. (1990). *Broadening the base of treatment for alcohol problems.* Washington, DC: National Academy of Science.

Conte, H. R., Plutchik, R., Wild, K. V., & Karasu, T. B. (1986). Combined psychotherapy and pharmacotherapy for depression: A systematic analysis of the evidence. *Archives of General Psychiatry, 43,* 471-479.

Cook, R. F., Hostetter, R. S., & Ramsay, D. A. (1975). Patterns of illicit drug use in the army. *American Journal of Psychiatry, 132,* 1013-1017.

Creager, C. (1989, July-August). SASSI test breaks through denial. *The Professional Counselor,* p. 65.

Csikszentmihalyi, M., & Larson, R. (1984). *Being adolescent.* New York: Basic Books.

Custer, R. L. (1984a). *Forward in sharing recovery through Gamblers Anonymous.* Los Angeles: Gamblers Anonymous Publishing.

Custer, R. L. (1984b). Profile of a pathological gambler. *Journal of Clinical Psychiatry, 45,* 35-38.

Davidson, W. S., II, & Seidman, E. (1974). Studies of behavior modification and juvenile delinquency: A review, methodological critique, and social perspective. *Psychological Bulletin, 81,* 998-1011.

Davis, B. C. (1982). The PCP epidemic: A critical review. *International Journal of Addiction, 17,* 1137-1155.

Dietch, J. (1983). The nature and extent of benzodiazepine abuse: An overview of recent literature. *Hospital and Community Psychiatry, 34,* 1139-1145.

Domino, E. F. (1978). Neurobiology of phencyclidine: An update. In R. C. Peterson & R. C. Stillman (Eds.), *PCP phencyclidine abuse: An appraisal* (Publ. No. [ADM] 17-728, pp. 18-43). Washington, DC: Government Printing Office.

Dorland's illustrated medical dictionary. (1965). Philadelphia: W. B. Saunders.

Dorus, W., Kennedy, J., Gibbons R. D., & Raci, S. D. (1987). Symptoms and diagnosis of depression in alcoholics. *Alcoholism, 11,* 150-154.

Douvan, E., & Adelson, J. (1966). *The adolescent experience.* New York: John Wiley.

DuPont, R. L. (1994). Laboratory diagnosis. In N. S. Miller & M. C. Doot (Eds.), *Principles of addiction medicine* (sec. 4, chap. 2, pp. 1-8). Chevy Chase, MD: American Society of Addiction Medicine.

Ellis, A. (1962). *Reason and emotion in psychotherapy.* New York: Lyle-Stuart.

Emrick, C. D. (1987). Alcoholics Anonymous: Affiliation process and effectiveness as treatment. *Alcoholism, 11,* 416-423.

Evans, M. A., Marty, R., Brown, D. J., Rodda, B. E., Kippinger, G. F., Lemberger, L., & Forney, R. B. (1973). Impairment of performance with low doses of marijuana. *Clinical Pharmacological Therapy, 14,* 936-940.

Ewing, J. A. (1984). Detecting alcoholism: The CAGE Questionnaire. *Journal of the American Medical Association, 252,* 1905-1907.

Eysenck, H. J., & Eysenck, S. B. J. (1976). *Personality structure and measurement.* London: Routledge & Kegan Paul.

Featherly, J. W., & Hill, E. B. (1989). *Crack cocaine overview, 1989.* Washington, DC: U.S. Department of Justice.

Fischman, M. W., Schuster, C. R., Rosnekov, L., Shick, J. F. E., Krasnegor, N. A., Fennell, W., & Freedman, D. X. (1976). Cardiovascular and subjective effects of intravenous cocaine administration in humans. *Archives of General Psychiatry, 33,* 983-989.

Folkins, C. H., & Sime, W. E. (1981). Physical fitness training and mental health. *American Psychologist, 36,* 373-389.

Folstein, M. F., Folstein, S. W., & McHugh, P. R. (1975). Mini-Mental State: A practical method of grading the cognitive state of patients for the clinician. *Journal of Psychiatric Research, 12,* 189-198.

Frances, R. J., Bucky, S., & Alexopolos, G. S. (1984). Outcome study of familial and nonfamilial alcoholism. *American Journal of Psychiatry, 141,* 11.

Frances, R. J., & Franklin, J. E., Jr. (1988). Alcohol and other psychoactive substance use disorders. In J. A. Talbott, R. E. Hales, & S. C. Yudofsky (Eds.), *The American Psychiatric Press textbook of psychiatry.* Washington, DC: American Psychiatric Press.

Freedman, D. X. (1968). The use and abuse of LSD. *Archives of General Psychiatry, 18,* 300-347.

Freud, S. (2000). *The standard edition of the complete psychological works of Sigmund Freud.* New York: Norton.

Fudala, P. J., Yu, E., Macfadden, W., Boardman, C., & Chiang, C. N. (1998). Effects of buprenorphine and naloxone in morphine-stabilized opioid addicts. *Drug and Alcohol Dependence, 50,* 1-8.

Fultz, J. M., & Senay, E. C. (1975). Guidelines for the management of hospitalized narcotics addicts. *Annals of Internal Medicine, 82,* 815-818.

Gabel, R. H., Barnard, N., Norko, M., & O'Connell, R. A. (1986). AIDS presenting as mania. *Comparative Psychiatry, 27,* 251-254.

Gambert, S. R. (1992). Substance abuse in the elderly. In J. H. Lowinson, P. Ruiz, R. B. Millman, & J. G. Langrod (Eds.), *Substance abuse: A comprehensive textbook* (2d ed.). Baltimore, MD: Williams & Wilkins.

Gamblers Anonymous. (1989a). *The combo book.* Los Angeles: G.A. Publishing.

Gamblers Anonymous. (1989b). *G.A.: A new beginning.* Los Angeles: G.A. Publishing.

Gary, V., & Guthrie, D. (1972). The effect of jogging on physical fitness and self-concept in hospitalized alcoholics. *Quarterly Journal of Studies on Alcohol, 33,* 1073-1078.

Gawin, F. H., & Ellinwood, E. H. (1988). Cocaine and other stimulants: Actions, abuse, and treatments. *New England Journal of Medicine, 318,* 1173-1182.

Gawin, F. H., & Kleber, H. S. (1986a). Abstinence symptomatology and psychiatric diagnosis in cocaine abusers. *Archives of General Psychiatry, 43,* 107-113.

Gawin, F. H., & Kleber, H. S. (1986b). Pharmacologic treatments of cocaine abuse and substance abuse. *Psychiatry in Clinics of North America, 9,* 573-583.

Geller, A. (1990). Protracted abstinence. In A. Geller (Ed.), *Syllabus of the review course in addiction medicine.* Washington, DC: American Society of Addiction Medicine.

Geller, A. (1994). Management of protracted withdrawal. In N. S. Miller & M. C. Doot (Eds.), *Principles of addiction medicine* (sec. 11, chap. 2, pp. 1-6). Chevy Chase, MD: American Society of Addiction Medicine.

Gerstein, D. R., & Harwood, H. J. (Eds.). (1990). *Treating drug problems.* Washington, DC: National Academy Press.

Gessner, P. K. (1979). Drug withdrawal therapy of the alcohol withdrawal syndrome. In E. Majchowicz & E. Moble (Eds.), *Biochemistry and pharmacology of ethanol* (Vol. 2). New York: Plenum.

Gilman, A. G., Goodman, L. S., & Gilman, A. (1980). *Goodman and Gilman's The pharmacological basis of therapeutics.* New York: Macmillan.

Glynn, T. J. (1990). Methods of smoking cessation: Finally some answers. *Journal of the American Medical Association, 263,* 2795-2796.

Gold, M. S. (1994a). Marijuana. In N. S. Miller & M. C. Doot (Eds.), *Principles of addiction medicine* (sec. 2, chap. 8, pp. 1-6). Chevy Chase, MD: American Society of Addiction Medicine.

Gold, M. S. (1994b). Opioids. In N. S. Miller & M. C. Doot (Eds.), *Principles of addiction medicine* (sec. 2, chap. 4, pp. 1-6). Chevy Chase, MD: American Society of Addiction Medicine.

Goldman, A. R. (1989). *Accreditation and certification: For providers of psychiatric, alcoholism, and drug abuse services.* Bala Cynwyd, PA: Practical Communications.

Goodwin, D. W. (1971). Blackouts and alcohol induced memory dysfunction. In N. K. Mello & J. H. Mendelson (Eds.), *Recent advances in studies in alcohol.* Rockville, MD: National Institute on Mental Health.

Goodwin, D. W. (1985). Alcoholism and genetics. *Archives of General Psychiatry, 42,* 171-174.

Goodwin, D. W., Crane, J. B., & Guze, S. B. (1969). Alcoholic blackouts: A review and clinical study of 100 alcoholics. *American Journal of Psychiatry, 126,* 174-177.

Gorski, T. T. (1989). *Passages through recovery.* Center City, MN: Hazelden.

Gorski, T., & Miller, M. (1982). *Counseling for relapse prevention.* Independence, MO: Independence Press.

Gorski, T. T., & Miller, M. (1986). *Staying sober: A guide for relapse prevention.* Independence, MO: Herald House/Independence Press.

Gottchalk, L., McGuire, F., Haser, F., et al. (1979). *Drug abuse deaths in nine cities: A survey report* (Research Monograph No. 29). Rockville, MD: National Institute on Drug Abuse.

Gould, L. C., & Keeber, H. D. (1974). Changing patterns of multiple drug use among applicants to a multimodality drug treatment program. *Archives of General Psychiatry, 31,* 408-413.

Graham, A. W., Schultz, T. K., & Wilford, B. B. (Eds.). (1998). *Principles of addiction medicine* (2nd ed.). Chevy Chase, MD: American Society of Addiction Medicine.

Graziano, A. M., & Mooney, K. C. (1984). *Children and behavior therapy.* New York: Aldine.

Greenberg, R. L., & Beck, A. T. (1987). *Panic attacks: How to cope, how to recover.* Philadelphia: Center for Cognitive Therapy.

Greist, J. H., Klein, M. H., Eischins, R. R., Faris, J., Gurman, A. S., & Morgan, W. P. (1979). Running as treatment for depression. *Comprehensive Psychiatry, 20,* 41-54.

Griffith, J. D., Cavanaugh, J., Held, J., & Oates, J. A. (1972). Dextroamphetamine. *Archives of General Psychiatry, 26,* 97-100.

Group for the Advancement of Psychiatry Committee on Alcoholism and the Addictions. (1991). Substance abuse disorders: A psychiatric priority. *American Journal of Psychiatry, 148,* 1291-1300.

Gunderson, J. G., & Zanarine, M. C. (1987). Current overview of the borderline diagnosis. *Journal of Clinical Psychiatry, 48*(Suppl. 8), 5-11.

Hamilton, M. (1959). The assessment of anxiety states by rating. *British Journal of Medical Psychology, 32,* 50-55.

Hardman, J., Limbird, L. E., Molinoff, P. B., Ruddon, R. W., & Gilman, A. G. (1996). *Goodman and Gilman's The pharmacological basis of therapeutics* (9th ed.). New York: McGraw-Hill.

Harris, M. J., Jeste, D. V., Gleghorn, A., & Sewell, D. D. (1991). New-onset psychosis in HIV-infected patients. *Journal of Clinical Psychiatry, 52,* 369-376.

Havens, L. (1978). Explorations in the use of language in psychotherapy: Simple empathetic statements. *Psychiatry, 41,* 336-345.

Henningfield, J. E. (1984). Pharmacologic basis and treatment of cigarette smoking. *Journal of Clinical Psychiatry, 45,* 24-34.

Herbert, M. (1982). Conduct disorder. In A. E. Kazdin & B. B. Lahey (Eds.), *Advances in clinical and child psychology* (Vol. 5). New York: Plenum.

Hesselbrock, M. N., Meyer, R. E., & Kenner, J. J. (1985). Psychopathology in hospitalized alcoholics. *Archives of General Psychiatry, 46,* 3-5.

Hirschfeld, R. M. A., & Goodwin, F. K. (1988). Mood disorders. In J. A. Talbott, R. E. Hales, & S. C. Yudofsky (Eds.), *The American Psychiatric Press textbook of psychiatry.* Washington, DC: American Psychiatric Press.

Hoffmann, N. G. (1991, June). *Treatment outcomes from abstinence based programs.* Paper presented at the meeting of the International Institute on the Prevention and Treatment of Alcoholism, Stockholm, Sweden.

Hoffmann, N. G. (1994). Assessing treatment effectiveness. In N. S. Miller & M. C. Doot (Eds.), *Principles of addiction medicine* (sec. 9, chap. 5, pp. 1-9). Chevy Chase, MD: American Society of Addiction Medicine.

Hoffmann, N., & Harrison, P. (1987). *A 2-year follow-up of inpatient treatment.* St. Paul, MN: Chemical Abuse Treatment Outcome Registry.

Hollister, L. E. (1974). Interactions in man of delta-9-tetrahydrocannabinol. I: Alphamethylparatyrosine. *Clinical Pharmacological Therapy, 15,* 18-21.

Hollister, L. E. (1986). Health aspects of cannabis. *Pharmacology Review, 38,* 1-20.

Hubbard, R. L. (1992). Evaluation and treatment outcome. In J. H. Lorvinson, P. Ruiz, R. B. Millman, & J. G. Langrod (Eds.), *Substance abuse: A comprehensive textbook.* Baltimore, MD: Williams & Wilkins.

Hubbard, R. L., & Anderson, J. A. (1988). *Follow-up study of individuals receiving alcoholism treatment.* Research Triangle Park, NC: Research Triangle Institute.

Hubbard, R. L., & DesJarlais, D. C. (1991). Alcohol and drug abuse. In E. E. Holland, R. Petels, & G. Knox (Eds.), *Oxford textbook of public health* (2nd ed., Vol. 3). London: Oxford University Press.

Hubbard, R. L., Marsden, M. E., Rachel, J. V., Harwood, H. J., Cavanaugh, E. R., & Ginzburg, H. M. (1989). *Drug abuse treatment: A national study of effectiveness.* Chapel Hill: University of North Carolina Press.

Hughes, J. R., & Hatsukami, D. (1986). Signs and symptoms of tobacco withdrawal. *Archives of General Psychiatry, 43,* 289-294.

Hunt, W. A., Barnett. L. W., & Branch, L. G. (1971). Relapse rates in addiction programs. *Journal of Clinical Psychology, 27,* 455-456.

Institute of Medicine. (1989). *Research effectiveness in the prevention and treatment of alcohol related problems.* Washington, DC: National Academy Press.

Institute of Medicine. (1995). *Federal regulation of methadone treatment.* Washington, DC: National Academy Press.

Jacobs, J. W., Bernhard, M. R., Delgado, A., & Strain, J. J. (1977). Screening for organic mental syndromes in the medically ill. *Annals of Internal Medicine, 86,* 40-46.

Jaffe, J. H. (1980). Drug addiction and drug abuse. In A. G. Gilman, L. S. Goodman, & A. Gilman (Eds.), *Goodman and Gilman's The pharmacological basis of therapeutics.* New York: Macmillan.

Joint Commission on Accreditation of Healthcare Organizations. (1988). *Consolidated standards manual.* Chicago: Author.

Joint Commission on Accreditation of Healthcare Organizations. (1992). *Patient records in addiction treatment: Documenting the quality of care.* Oakbrook Terrace, IL: Author.

Jones, R. T. (1971). Marijuana-induced "high": Influence of expectation, setting, and previous drug experience. *Pharmacological Review, 23,* 359-369.

Jones, R. T., Bennowitz, N., & Bachman, J. (1976). Clinical studies of cannabis tolerance and dependence. *Annals of the New York Academy of Science, 282,* 221-239.

Juergens, S. M. (1994). Sedative-hypnotics. In N. S. Miller & M. C. Doot (Eds.), *Principles of addiction medicine* (sec. 2, chap. 3, pp. 1-10). Chevy Chase, MD: American Society of Addiction Medicine.

Kagan, J. (1989). Temperament contribution to social behavior. *American Journal of Psychology, 44,* 668-674.

Kagan, J., Reznick, J. S., & Gibbons, J. (1989). Inhibited and uninhibited types of children. *Child Development, 60,* 838-845.

Kagan, J., Reznick, J. S., & Snidman, N. (1987). The physiology and psychology of behavioral inhibition in children. *Child Development, 58,* 1459-1473.

Kalant, H., Engel, J. A., Goldberg, L., Griffiths, R. R., Jaffe, J. H., Krasnegor, N. A., Mello, N. K., Mendelson, J. H., Thompson, T., & Van Ree, J. M. (1978). Behavioral aspects of addiction: Group report. In J. Fishman (Ed.), *The basis of addiction: Report of the Dahlem workshop on the basis of addiction* (pp. 463-495). Berlin: Abakon Verlagsgesellschaft.

Kandel, D. (1978). Antecedents of adolescent initiation into stages of drug use. In D. Kandel (Ed.), *Longitudinal research on drug use.* Washington, DC: Hemisphere.

Karasu, T. B. (Chair). (1989). *Treatments of psychiatric disorders.* Washington, DC: American Psychiatric Press.

Kasser, C. L., Geller, A., Howell, E., & Wartenberg, A. (1998). Principles of detoxification. In A. W. Graham, T. K. Schultz, & B. B. Wilford (Eds.), *Principles of addiction medicine* (2nd ed., sec. 6, chap. 7, p. 423). Chevy Chase, MD: American Society of Addiction Medicine.

Khantzian, E. J., & Treece, C. (1985). DSM-III psychiatric diagnosis of narcotics addicts: Recent findings. *Archives of General Psychiatry, 42,* 1067-1071.

King, G. S., Smialick, J. E., & Troutman, W. G. (1985). Sudden death in adolescents resulting from the inhalation of typewriter correction fluid. *Journal of the American Medical Association, 253,* 1604-1609.

Kinney, J., & Leaton, G. (1987). *Loosening the grip: A handbook of alcohol information.* St. Louis, MO: Time Mirror/Mosby.

Klein, D. F., Gittelman, R., Quitkin, F., & Rifkin, A. (1980). *Diagnosis and drug treatment of psychiatric disorders: Adults and children.* Baltimore, MD: Williams & Wilkins.

Klerman, G. L., Weissman, M. M., Rounsaville, B. J., & Chevron, E. S. (1984). *Interpersonal psychotherapy of depression.* New York: Basic Books.

Kosten, T. R., Rounsaville, B. J., & Kleber, H. D. (1985). Comparison of clinical ratings to self-reports of withdrawal during clonidine detoxification of opiate addicts. *American Journal of Drug and Alcohol Abuse, 11,* 1-10.

Ledwidge, B. (1980). Run for your mind: Aerobic exercise as a means of alleviating anxiety and depression. *Canadian Journal of Behavioral Science, 12,* 127-140.

Leshner, A. I. (1998, May-June). Research advances in treating heroin addiction. *The Counselor,* p. 8.

Lesieur, H. R., & Blume, S. D. (1987). The South Oaks Gambling Screen (SOGS): A new instrument for the identification of pathological gamblers.

Lewinsohn, P. M., Munoz, R. F., Youngren, M. A., & Zeiss, A. M. (1978). *Control your depression.* Englewood Cliffs, NJ: Prentice Hall.

Littleton, J. (1995). Acamprosate in alcohol dependence: How does it work? *Addiction, 90,* 1179-1188.

Littleton, J. (1996). The neurobiology of craving: Potential mechanisms for acamprosate. In M. Soyka (Ed.), *Acamprosate in relapse prevention of alcoholism* (pp. 27-46). Berlin: Springer-Verlag.

Lowinson, J. H., Marion, I. J., Herman, J., & Dole, V. P. (1992). Methadone maintenance. In J. Lowinson, P. Ruiz, R. B. Millman, & J. G. Langrod (Eds.), *Substance abuse: A comprehensive textbook.* Baltimore, MD: Williams & Wilkins.

Lynch, K. R., & Ollendick, T. H. (1977). Juvenile corrections: A model program. *American Journal of Corrections, 39,* 6-7.

Manthey, M. (1991). Commitment to my co-workers. In S. Cox & D. Miller (Eds.), *Leaders empower staff.* Minneapolis, MN: Creative Management.

Marlatt, A. G., & Gordon, J. R. (1985). *Relapse prevention.* New York: Guilford.

Masterson, J. F., Jr., & Costello, J. (1980). *From borderline adolescent to functioning adult: The test of time.* New York: Brunner/Mazel.

Mayo-Smith, M. (1998). Management of alcohol intoxication and withdrawal. In A. W. Graham, T. K. Schultz, & B. B. Wilford (Eds.), *Principles of addiction medicine* (2nd ed., sec. 6, chap. 2, pp. 431-440). Chevy Chase, MD: American Society of Addiction Medicine.

McKay, M., Rogers, P. D., & McKay, J. (1989). *When anger hurts: Quieting the storm within.* Oakland, CA: New Harbinger.

McLellan, A. T., Luborsky, L., & Woody, G. E. (1980). An improved diagnostic evaluation instrument for substance abuse patients: The Addiction Severity Index. *Journal of Nervous and Mental Disease, 168,* 26-33.

Mee-Lee, D. (1985). The Recovery Attitude and Treatment Evaluator (RAATE): An instrument for patient progress and treatment assignment. In *Proceedings of the 34th International Congress on Alcoholism and Drug Dependence* (pp. 424-426).

Mee-Lee, D. (1988). An instrument for treatment progress and matching: The Recovery Attitude and Treatment Evaluator (RAATE). *Journal of Substance Abuse Treatment, 5,* 183-186.

Mee-Lee, D., Gartner, L., Miller, M. M., Shulman, G., & Wilford, B. (1998). *Patient placement criteria for the treatment of substance-related disorders* (2nd ed.). Chevy Chase, MD: American Society of Addiction Medicine.

Melges, F. T., Tinklenberg, J. R., Hollister, L. E., & Gillespie, H. K. (1970). Temporal disintegration and depersonalization during marijuana intoxication. *Archives of General Psychiatry, 23,* 204-210.

Miller, G. A. (1985). *The Substance Abuse Subtle Screening Inventory Manual.* Bloomington, IN: SASSI Institute.

Miller, J. D. (1983). *National Survey on Drug Abuse: Main findings, 1982.* Rockville, MD: National Institute on Drug Abuse.

Millon, T. (1981). *Disorders of personality: DSM-III Axis II.* New York: John Wiley.

Morrison, M. A., & Smith, Q. T. (1990). Psychiatric issues of adolescent chemical dependence. In A. Geller (Ed.), *Syllabus for the review course in addiction medicine.* Washington, DC: American Society of Addiction Medicine.

Morse, R. M. (1994). Elderly patients. In N. S. Miller & M. C. Doot (Eds.), *Principles of addiction medicine* (sec. 18, chap. 2, pp. 1-6). Chevy Chase, MD: American Society of Addiction Medicine.

Naditch, M. P., & Fenwick, S. (1977). LSD flashbacks and ego functioning. *Journal of Abnormal Psychiatry, 86,* 352-359.

Nahas, G. G. (1973). *Marihuana: Deceptive weed.* New York: Raven.

Narcotics Anonymous. (1988). *Narcotics Anonymous.* Van Nuys, CA: Narcotics Anonymous World Service Office.

National Institute on Alcohol Abuse and Alcoholism. (1993). *Eighth special report to the U.S. Congress on alcohol and health* (Publ. No. 94-3699). Bethesda, MD: National Institutes of Health.

National Institute on Alcohol Abuse and Alcoholism. (1997). *Ninth special report to the U.S. Congress on alcohol and health* (Publ. No. 97-4017). Bethesda, MD: National Institutes of Health.

National Institute on Drug Abuse. (1986). *Drug use among American high school students and other young adults: National trends through 1985.* Washington, DC: U.S. Department of Health and Human Services.

Nestler, E. J. (1998). Neuroadaptation in addiction. In A. W. Graham, T. K. Schultz, & B. B. Wilford (Eds.), *Principles of addiction medicine* (2nd ed., sec. 1, chap. 5, pp. 57-71). Chevy Chase, MD: American Society of Addiction Medicine.

Offer, D. (1986). Adolescent development: A normative perspective. In *American Psychiatric Association annual review* (Vol. 5). Washington, DC: American Psychiatric Press.

Offer, D., & Offer, J. B. (1975). *From teenage to young manhood: A psychological study.* New York: Basic Books.

Offer, D., Ostrov, E., & Howard, K. I. (1981). *The adolescent: A psychological self-portrait.* New York: Basic Books.

Ollendick, T. H., & Cerny, J. A. (1981). *Clinical behavior therapy with children.* New York: Plenum.

O'Malley, S. S., Jaffe, A. J., Chang, G., Schottenfeld, R. S., Meyer, R. E., & Rounsaville, B. (1992). Naltrexone and coping skills therapy for alcohol dependence: A controlled study. *Archives of General Psychiatry, 49,* 881-887.

Patterson, G. R. (1977). *Families: Applications of social learning to family life* (rev. ed.). Champaign, IL: Research Press.

Patterson, G. R., & Gullion, M. E. (1976). *Living with children: New methods for parents and teachers* (rev. ed.). Champaign, IL: Research Press.

Perkinson, R. R. (2000). *God talks to you.* Bloomington, IN: 1st Books Library.

Perkinson, R. R., & Jongsma, A. E. (1998a). *The chemical dependence treatment planner.* New York: John Wiley.

Perkinson, R. R., & Jongsma, A. E. (1998b). *The chemical dependence treatment planner with disk.* New York: John Wiley.

Perkinson, R. R., & Jongsma, A. (2001). *The addiction treatment planner.* New York: John Wiley.

Perry, S. W., & Jacobsen, P. (1986). Neuropsychiatric manifestations of AIDS-spectrum disorders. *Hospital and Community Psychiatry, 37,* 135-142.

Phillips, E. L. (1968). Achievement place: Token reinforcement procedures in a home-style rehabilitation setting for "pre-delinquent" boys. *Journal of Applied Behavior Analysis, 1,* 213-223.

Pierce, J. P., Fiore, M. C., Novotny, T. E., Hatziandreu, E. J., & Davis, T. (1989). Trends in cigarette smoking in the United States: Projections to the year 2000. *Journal of the American Medical Association, 261,* 61-65.

Plutchik, R. (1980). *Emotion: A psychoevolutionary synthesis.* New York: Harper & Row.

Post, R. M., Kotin, J., & Goodwin, F. K. (1974). The effects of cocaine in depressed patients. *American Journal of Psychiatry, 131,* 511-517.

Prochaska, J. O., & DiClemente, C. C. (1983). Stages and processes of self-change of smoking: Toward an integrative model of change. *Journal of Consulting and Clinical Psychology, 51,* 390-395.

Prochaska, J. O., DiClemente, C. C., & Norcross, J. C. (1992). In search of how people change: Applications to the addictive behaviors. *American Psychologist, 47,* 1102-1114.

Prochaska, J. O., Norcross, J. C., & DiClemente, C. C. (1994). *Changing for good.* New York: William Morrow.

Reifler, B., Raskind, M., & Kethley, A. (1982). Psychiatric diagnosis among geriatric patients seen in an outreach program. *Journal of the American Geriatrics Society, 30,* 530-533.

Richels, K., Case, W. G., Downing, R. W., & Winokur, A. (1983). Long-term diazepam therapy and clinical outcome. *Journal of the American Medical Association, 12,* 767-771.

Rosenbaum, J. F., Biederman, J., Hirshfeld, D. R., Bolduc, E. A., & Chaloff, J. (1991). Behavioral inhibition in children: A possible precursor to panic disorder or social phobia. *Journal of Clinical Psychiatry, 52*(11, Suppl.), 5-9.

Sanders, M. R., & Glynn, T. (1981). Training parents in behavioral self-management: An analysis of generalization and maintenance. *Journal of Applied Behavior Analysis, 14,* 223-237.

Schuckit, M. A. (1984). *Drug and alcohol abuse: A clinical guide to diagnosis and treatment.* New York: Plenum.

Schuckit, M. A. (1994). Dual diagnosis: Psychiatric pictures among substance abusers. In N. S. Miller & M. C. Doot (Eds.), *Principles of addiction medicine* (sec. 6, chap. 1, pp. 1-4). Chevy Chase, MD: American Society of Addiction Medicine.

Secretary of Health, Education, and Welfare. (1977). *Marihuana and health: Seventh annual report to the U.S. Congress.* Washington, DC: Government Printing Office.

Selye, H. (1956). *The stress of life.* New York: McGraw-Hill.

Selzer, M., Winokur, A., & van Rooijen, C. (1975). A self-administered Short Michigan Alcoholism Screening Test. *Journal of Studies on Alcohol, 36,* 117-126.

Sharp, C. W., & Brehm, M. L. (Eds.). (1977). *Review of inhalants: Euphoria to dysfunction* (Publ. No. [ADM] 77-553). Washington, DC: Government Printing Office.

Sharp, C. W., & Carroll, L. T. (Eds.). (1978). *Voluntary inhalation of industrial solvents* (Publ. No. [ADM] 79-779). Washington, DC: Government Printing Office.

Siever, L. J., & Davis, K. L. (1991). A psychobiological perspective on the personality disorders. *American Journal of Psychiatry, 148,* 1647-1658.

Siever, L. J., Llar, H., & Coccaro, E. (1985). Psychobiology substrates of personality. In *Biological response styles: Clinical implications*. Washington, DC: American Psychiatric Press.

Smith, C. M. (1977). The pharmacology of sedative/hypnotics, alcohol, and anesthetics: Sites and mechanisms of action. In W. R. Martin (Ed.), *Drug addiction: I. Morphine, sedative/hypnotics, and alcohol dependence*. Berlin: Springer-Verlag.

Soujanen, W. W. (1983). Addiction and the minds of adolescents. In R. C. Bersinger & W. W. Suojanen (Eds.), *Management and the brain: An integrative approach to organization behavior* (pp. 77-92). Atlanta: Georgia State University Press.

Spalt, L. (1979). Evidence of an X-linked recessive genetic characteristic in alcoholism. *Journal of the American Medical Association, 241,* 2543-2544.

Spelberger, C. D. (1983). *Manual for the State-Trait Anxiety Inventory*. Palo Alto, CA: Consulting Psychologists Press.

Spitzer, R. L. (1987). *Diagnostic and statistical manual of mental disorders* (3rd ed., rev.). Washington, DC: American Psychiatric Press.

Stern, M. J., & Cleary, P. (1981). National Exercise and Heart Disease Project: Psychosocial changes observed during a low-level exercise program. *Archives of Internal Medicine, 141,* 1463-1467.

Stimmel, B., Goldberg, J., Rotkopf, E., et al. (1977). Ability to remain abstinent after methadone detoxification: A six year study. *Journal of the American Medical Association, 237,* 1216-1220.

Stuart, R. B. (1971). Behavioral contracting within the families of delinquents. *Journal of Behavior Therapy and Experimental Psychology, 2,* 1-11.

Sue, D. W., & Sue, D. (1999). *Counseling the culturally different: Theory and practice* (3rd ed.). New York: John Wiley.

Talbott, J. A., Hales, R. E., & Yudofsky, S. C. (Eds.). (1988). *American Psychiatric Press textbook of psychiatry*. Washington, DC: American Psychiatric Press.

Tarasoff v. Regents of the University of California, 551 P.2d, 334 at 340 (1976).

Tennant, F. S., Jr., & Grossbeck, C. J. (1972). Psychiatric effects of hashish. *Archives of General Psychiatry, 27,* 133-136.

Thacore, V. R., & Shukla, R. S. P. (1976). Cannabis psychosis and paranoid schizophrenia. *Archives of General Psychiatry, 33,* 383-386.

Thompson, T., & Pickens, R. (1970). Stimulant self-administration by animals: Some comparisons with opiate self-administration. *Federal Processes, 29,* 6-12.

Turner, C. E. (1980). Chemistry and metabolism. In R. L. Peterson (Ed.), *Marijuana research findings* (Research Monograph No. 13, Publ. No. [ADM] AD-1001). Rockville, MD: National Institute on Drug Abuse.

U.S. Department of Health and Human Services. (1999). *National Household Survey on Drug Abuse 1999*. Washington, DC: Department of Health and Human Services, Substance Abuse and Mental Health Services Administration.

U.S. Department of Justice. (1983). *Let's all work to fight drug abuse*. Washington, DC: Author.

U.S. Department of Labor. *America in jeopardy: The young employee and drugs in the workplace*. Washington, DC: U.S. Department of Labor, Office of the Assistant Secretary for Policy.

U.S. Surgeon General. (1979). *Smoking and health* (Publ. No. [PHS] 79-50066). Washington, DC: Government Printing Office.

Vaillant, G. E. (1984). Alcohol abuse and dependence. In L. Grinspoon (Ed.), *American Psychiatric Association annual review* (Vol. 3). Washington, DC: American Psychiatric Press.

Vaillant, G. E. (1977). *Adaptation to life*. Boston: Little, Brown.

Vardy, M. M., & Kay, F. R. (1983). LSD psychosis or LSD induced schizophrenia? *Archives of General Psychiatry, 40,* 877-883.

Volpicelli, J. R., Alterman, A. L., Hayashida, M., & O'Brian, C. P. (1992). Naltrexone in the treatment of alcohol dependence. *Archives of General Psychiatry, 49,* 876-880.

Walker, R. (1992). *Twenty-four hours a day.* Center City, MN: Hazelden.

Wallach, J. (1992). *Interpretation of diagnostic tests: A synopsis of laboratory medicine* (5th ed.). Boston: Little, Brown.

Washton, A. M., Gold, M. S., & Pottash, A. C. (1984). Adolescent cocaine abusers. *Lancet, 2,* 746.

Weedman, R. (1992). *Dancing the tightrope.* Naples, FL: Healthcare Network.

Weinhold, B. K., & Weinhold, J. B. (1989). *Breaking free of the co-dependency trap.* Walpole, NH: Stillpoint.

Weiss, R. D., Mirin, S. N., Griffin, M. L., & Michaels, J. K. (1988). Psychopathology in cocaine abusers: Changing trends. *Journal of Nervous and Mental Disorders, 176,* 719-725.

Wells, K. C., & Forehand, R. (1981). Childhood behavior problems in the home. In S. M. Turner, K. S. Calhoun, & H. E. Adams (Eds.), *Handbook of clinical behavior therapy.* New York: John Wiley.

Wells, K. C., & Forehand, R. (1984). Conduct and oppositional disorders. In P. H. Bornstein & A. E. Kaydin (Eds.), *Handbook of clinical behavior therapy with children.* New York: Dorsey.

Wesson, D. R., & Smith, D. E. (1977). Cocaine: Its use for central nervous system stimulation including recreational and medical uses. In R. C. Peterson & R. C. Stillman (Eds.), *Cocaine: 1977* (Research Monograph No. 13, pp. 137-150). Washington, DC: Government Printing Office.

Westley, W. A., & Epstein, N. B. (1969). *The silent majority.* San Francisco: Jossey-Bass.

Widiger, T., & Frances, A. (1989). Epidemiology, diagnosis, and comorbidity of borderline personality disorders. In *American Psychiatric Association annual review* (Vol. 8). Washington, DC: American Psychiatric Press.

Wikler, A. (1976). Aspects of tolerance to and dependence on cannabis. *Annals of the New York Academy of Science, 282,* 126-147.

Wilcox, R. E., Gonzales, R. A., & Erickson, C. K. (1994). In N. S. Miller & M. C. Doot (Eds.), *Principles of addiction medicine* (sec. 1, chap. 3, p. 4). Chevy Chase, MD: American Society of Addiction Medicine.

Wise, R. A., & Kelsey, J. E. (1998). Behavioral models of addiction. In A. W. Graham, T. K. Schultz, & B. B. Wilford (Eds.), *Principles of addiction medicine* (2nd ed., sec. 1, chap. 3, pp. 37-49). Chevy Chase, MD: American Society of Addiction Medicine.

Wolf, M. M., Philips, E. L., & Fixsen, D. L. (1975). *Achievement place phase II: Final report.* Lawrence, KS: Department of Human Development.

Woods, J. H., & Carney, J. (1977). Narcotic tolerance and operant behavior. In N. A. Krasnegor (Ed.), *Behavioral tolerance: Research and treatment implications* (Publ. No. [ADM] 78-551, pp. 54-66). Washington, DC: Government Printing Office.

Woodward, J. J. (1994). Alcohol. In N. S. Miller & M. C. Doot (Eds.), *Principles of addiction medicine* (sec. 2, chap. 2, pp. 1-12). Chevy Chase, MD: American Society of Addiction Medicine.

Woody, G. G., Lubrorsky, L., McLellan, T., O'Brien, C. P., Beck, A. T., Blaine, J., Herman, I., & Hole, A. (1984). Psychotherapy for opiate addicts: Does it help? *Archives of General Psychiatry, 40,* 639-643.

Zegans, L. S. (1982). Stress and the development of somatic disorders. In L. Goldberger & S. Brenznitz (Eds.), *Handbook of stress: Theoretical and clinical aspects.* New York: Free Press.

Zung, W. W. K. (1971). A rating instrument for anxiety disorders. *Psychosomatics, 12,* 371-379.

Index

About the Author

Robert R. Perkinson, Ph.D., is Clinical Director of Keystone Treatment Center in Canton, South Dakota. He is a licensed psychologist, South Dakota certified chemical dependency counselor, Level III; an internationally certified alcohol and drug counselor; a licensed marriage and family therapist; and a nationally certified gambling counselor. He is an internationally known motivational speaker and the author of numerous articles in the field of addictions. He is the author of two other books: *The Chemical Dependence Treatment Planner* and *God Talks to You.* He has Web pages (www.robertperkinson.com and www.godtalkstoyou.com) where he answers questions for free and provides useful information. He has been practicing in the field of addictions for more than 27 years.